A Profane Wit

John Wilmot, Second Earl of Rochester. Portrait by Sir Peter Lely. Collection of Sir Harry Malet, Somerset County Council, Dillington House. Reproduced by permission.

A Profane Wit

The Life of John Wilmot, Earl of Rochester

James William Johnson

®R The University of Rochester Press

First published 2004

University of Rochester Press
668 Mt. Hope Avenue, Rochester, NY 14620, USA
www.urpress.com
and of Boydell & Brewer Limited
PO Box 9, Woodbridge, Suffolk IP12 3DF, UK
www.boydellandbrewer.com

ISBN: 1–58046–170–0

Library of Congress Cataloging-in-Publication Data

Johnson, James William, 1927–
  A profane wit : the life of John Wilmot, Earl of Rochester / James William
Johnson.
    p. cm.
  Includes bibliographical references and index.
  ISBN 1–58046–170–0 (hardcover : alk. paper)
  1. Rochester, John Wilmot, Earl of, 1647–1680. 2. Poets, English–Early
modern, 1500–1700–Biography. 3. Great Britain–History–Restoration,
1660–1688–Biography. 4. Great Britain–Court and courtiers–Biography. I. Title.
  PR3669.R2J65 2004
  821′.4–dc22

                                                                    2004019052

A catalogue record for this title is available from the British Library.

This publication is printed on acid-free paper.
Printed in Canada.

CONTENTS

Contents

ILLUSTRATIONS

ACKNOWLEDGMENTS

Many libraries and collections provided help in researching this book. I thank the staffs of them all: University of Rochester Library, Folger Shakespeare Library, William Andrews Clark Library, Huntington Library, Houghton and Widener Libraries at Harvard, Beinecke Library at Yale, Princeton University Library, Joint University Libraries at Vanderbilt University, British Library, Library of Shakespeare's Birthplace, Nottingham University Library, Bodleian Library. I am also endebted to the Vicars of Spelsbury Church and Adderbury Church for use of the church records.

Emma Butterfield of the National Portrait Gallery, Barbara Thompson of the Courtauld Institute, and Martin Durrant of the Victoria and Albert Museum were most helpful in securing illustrations and permissions. Ellie Ferguson of Boydell and Brewer also provided much-needed, on-the-scene assistance.

Research grants from the American Council of Learned Societies, Fulbright Commission, Folger Shakespeare Library, and Guggenheim Foundation allowed me the time and funds to travel to those libraries. The University of Rochester also assisted me steadily with sabbaticals and grants.

Many friends and colleagues gave me help with research, advice, and support: Kathrine Koller, William E. Diez, Bernard N. Schilling, George H. Ford, Rowland L. Collins, Lewis Beck, Willson Coates, H. T. Swedenberg, James Osborn, Cyrus H. Hoy, Frances Mayhew Rippy, David Vieth, J. Paul Hunter, Ken Robinson, Jeremy Treglown, Paul Hammond, Claude Rawson, Mrs. Sylvia Free of the Burford School, Dean T. Binyon of Wadham College, James R. Sutherland. I am especially grateful to Larry D. Carver, whose parallel interest in Rochester helped sustain my own over the years and whose insights and research provided valuable aid.

The staff of the University of Rochester Press encouraged my labors and devoted much thought and energy to bringing this book into print. Tim Madigan, Mark Klemens, Susan Dykstra-Poel, and Sue Smith have my lasting gratitude. I also thank Steve Huff and Louise Goldberg for their contributions.

Dr. Miranda Johnson-Haddad gave her expert, scholarly help with reading proof; Reed Johnson led the cheerleading team; and without Nan Johnson's patience with recalcitrant computers and printers and her unceasing

encouragement, this book literally would never have come into print. I thank
and love them all.

James William Johnson
July 2004

INTRODUCTION

THE ROCHESTER LEGENDS

The very name of Rochester is offensive to modest ears. . . .
—David Hume, *History of Great Britain* (1757)

Early in the morning of July 26, 1680, John Wilmot, Baron of Adderbury, Viscount Athlone, and Earl of Rochester, died at the age of thirty-three, ravaged by the effects of syphilis and gonorrhea. After lying on his deathbed for nine weeks of bodily torment and even worse "agonies of his Mind [that] sometimes swallowed up the sense of what he felt in his Body," he died, according to Bishop Gilbert Burnet's avidly read account of the final days, without a shudder or sound.[1]

The death of the brilliant but infamous peer immediately produced a sheaf of elegies that hailed his Christian demise. Samuel Woodford devoted fourteen stanzas to describing the departed's life and deathbed repentance, concluding, "Rochester in the LAMB'S fresh blood new dy'd / All robed in white sings Lauds to him whom he deny'd." An anonymous elegy hailed him as "*Seraphic* Lord! whom Heav'n for wonders meant. . . ." Samuel Holland likewise proclaimed: "The Mighty *Rochester* a *Convert* Dies,/ He fell a Poet, but a Saint shall Rise." And there were others.[2]

The poetic efforts at sanctifying John Wilmot were soon followed by two highly influential prose treatises by notably pious men of the cloth. In *A Sermon Preached at the Funeral of the Honorable John Earl of Rochester*, Robert Parsons concluded with an exhortation to family and friends to "turn their sorrows into joys, by the comfortable consideration of his being a Penitent upon earth, and a Saint in heaven." Subsequently, Burnet's *Some Passages in the Life and Death of John Earl of Rochester, Written by His Own Direction on His Death-bed* appeared (1680), furthering the canonizing process.

Burnet went into detail about Wilmot's last agonizing days of suffering, repentance, and joyous conversion, evoking the pattern of saints and martyrs set up by earlier *vitae* or saints' legends, and declaring, "Now he is at rest, and I am very confident enjoys the Fruits of his late, but sincere Repentance."[3] These two prose works, authorized by Rochester and his family, were a clear attempt to recast the events of his life in such a way as to make him a moral exemplum for the ages. His family went about destroying such evidence as might diminish his evolving legendary status as penitent and saint; they made valiant attempts as late as 1749 to suppress material that sustained his earlier, ungodly reputation.

But in their zeal to stress the miracle of his Christian conversion, they permitted him to be described as "the greatest of sinners" and subverted their own purpose. His mother and wife looked on approvingly as Robert Parsons spoke, then printed, provocative statements like these:

> For this was the heightening and amazing circumstance of his sins, that he was so diligent and industrious to recommend and propagate them; not like those of old that *hated the light*, but those the Prophet mentions, *Is. 3.9 who declare their sin as Sodom, and hide it not, that take it upon their shoulders, and bind it to them, framing Arguments for Sin.* . . .[4]

Parsons's hyperbolic language peaked in a comparison of Rochester to a Miltonic Lucifer:

> And truly none but one so great in parts could be so; as the chiefest of the Angels for knowledge and power became most degenerate.

Instead of assisting a saintly legend, such statements encouraged a diabolic counter-legend. What, exactly, did the dead Earl do to cause his own chaplain to call him an example of wickedness "as remarkable as any place or age can produce"?

Unfortunately for his hagiographers, Rochester's life had been recorded by numerous diarists, letter-writers, and journal-keepers. Surreptitious copies of his "Panegyricks upon Vice" existed in numbers too great to destroy. And tales about him repeated by word of mouth persisted. From these grew the counter-legendary Earl described a century later by Dr. Samuel Johnson:

> Thus in a course of drunken gaiety and gross sensuality, with intervals of study perhaps yet more criminal, with an avowed contempt for all decency and order, a total disregard to every moral, and a resolute denial of every religious obligation, he lived worthless and useless, and blazed out his youth and his health in lavish voluptuousness, till, at the age of one and thirty, he had exhausted the fund of life, and reduc'd himself to a state of weakness and decay.[5]

Concerning details in support of this colorful depiction, Johnson said, "[I]t is not for his honour that we should remember [them], and which are not now distinctly known."

In the nineteenth century, shocked by their explicit sexuality, moralists destroyed some of the branded Earl's printed works, and his poetry, if printed at all, was severely bowdlerized. His deathbed repentance, however, was perpetuated by Sunday School tracts that reprinted some of the more titillating rhetoric from Parsons and Burnet, thereby sustaining curiosity about what sins caused so passionate a conversion. A few literary historians made bold to suggest that Rochester's poetry had merit; but the condemnation of the moralists found a voice in Sir Sidney Lee's essay on John Wilmot in the *Dictionary of National Biography*. Condemning the "dissolute" life of the "profligate" nobleman, Lee said of his poetry:

> The sentiment in his love songs is transparently artificial whenever it is not offensively obscene. Numerous verses of gross indelicacy which have been put to his credit . . . may be from other pens. But there is enough foulness in his fully authenticated poems to give him a title to be remembered as the writer of the filthiest verse in the language.

Lee's quasi-official version of Rochester's life and work was challenged in due course, but it shows how an interpretation of a writer's character based on the opinions of selected contemporaries can persist, appealing to the biases of successive times and critics and affecting literary judgments. For three centuries, the man and his writings were widely castigated in ways often more revealing of his critics than of Rochester himself. Unluckily for his personal reputation, Rochester's reported actions ranged from the merely foolish to the genuinely criminal, all of them shocking to his devout contemporaries. Some of his actions were violently destructive. For these excesses, he was labeled "the Mad Earl."

Any attempt to reconstruct the life and thought of a seventeenth-century English poet-nobleman will inevitably reflect the presuppositions of the biographer and his own age. This work is as grounded in the twentieth century, as Gilbert Burnet's was in the seventeenth, and Samuel Johnson's in the eighteenth. Where they saw Rochester from theologically oriented points of view, condemning his personal sexuality as well as his sexually explicit writings, the post-Freudian biographer is expected not only to deal with the sexual aspects of Rochester's life and works but also to search for their causes in his psyche.

Only in the past few decades have scholars been free to discuss openly the previously tabooed, sexual dimensions of English life in the seventeenth and eighteenth centuries. But if such studies have done much to reveal what men and women did sexually in those centuries, they have not always identified the bio-psychological origins of sexual behavior. Some reflect the traditional assumption defined by Michel Foucault: "Sexuality was conceived of as a constant. The hypothesis was that where it was manifested in historically singular forms, this was through various mechanisms of repression to which it was bound to be subjected in every society." Foucault's own hypothesis held that sexuality is an idiosyncratic way of fashioning the self "in the experience of the flesh" constituted from and around certain forms of behavior that exist in relation to historically specifiable systems of knowledge (i.e., rules of what is or is not "natural.")[6]

In *Making Sex: Body and Gender from the Greeks to Freud*, Thomas Laqueur goes even farther, asserting that the very concept of the "natural" is erroneous:

> The comfortable notion is shaken that man is man and woman is woman and the historian's task is to find out what they did, what they thought, and what was thought about them. That "thing," sex, about which people had beliefs seems to crumble. . . . The record on which I have relied bears witness to the fundamental incoherence of stable, fixed categories of sexual dimorphism, of male and/or female. The notion, so powerful after the eighteenth century that there has to be something . . . which defines male as opposite to female and which provides the foundation for an attraction of opposites is entirely absent from classical or Renaissance medicine.[7]

In *Epistemology of the Closet*, Eve K. Sedgwick asserts that the very term "homosexual" gained acceptance only as recently as the last third of the nineteenth century and that the binary thinking it embodied has led to "a chronic, now endemic crisis of homo/heterosexual definition, indicatively male."[8] Sedgewick's "Introduction: Axiomatic" and Laqueur's chapter on Renaissance representations of sexuality and the medical theories of William Harvey (1578–1657) provide a broader context for the literary commentators and sexual historians who have tried to account for the polymorphous sexuality observable in seventeenth-century England.

Rochester's biographer inevitably confronts the problem of how much, if any, of his "creative" writing evidences his private, psycho-sexual, or biographical "reality." To some extent the same question may be asked of his presumably factual writings—letters, journals, and the like. In Rochester's case, the problem is greater because recent critical studies have tended to accentuate his shifting "personae," and the masks he often wore, poetically as well as socially.

Without trying "bladders of philosophy" to navigate such ontological and epistemological seas, I assume that whatever a man writes is *some* version of his thought, however fanciful or artificial. In instances where Rochester's candid, private utterances—to his wife, Henry Savile, or Gilbert Burnet, for example—correspond closely to ideas expressed in his poems, one may reasonably assume these reflect genuinely held beliefs. Where testimony of Rochester's interest in Lucretius is given by four separate people who knew him, it may be given creditability. Thanks to many scholars' research, there is now sufficient historical documentation of Rochester's life and times to attempt a synthesis between the many facets of his complex mind and actions and his works.

All this research derives, of course, from twentieth-century perspectives. Can such investigations as these be used to illuminate the bio-psychic dimensions of John Wilmot, Earl of Rochester? Since Rochester was preoccupied with his own and human sexuality in general, it is sometimes possible to correlate his views on a given sexual practice (e.g., masturbation) with those of his contemporaries (Aubrey, Pepys). Often, however, Rochester's inability to understand his own feelings and behavior caused him to fall back on the fixed ideas of his day and explain his actions by the temporary influence of devils or angels, or to wave away any effort to "know thyself" by simply labeling himself "the oddest, most fantastical man alive."[9]

This leaves his biographer the choice either of simply reporting and not accounting for his behavior or relying on sexual historical theorists like Laqueur, Sedgwick, and Stone on the one hand or R. D. Laing, Melanie Klein, D. W. Winnicott, and Robert Stoller, modern psychiatric theorists, on the other. In this version of his life, I have included within the text itself such psychosexual explanations as I think are justified by Rochester's own testimony or by the reconstructions of scholars; and I have put into the Notes references to modern psychiatric theories that may be helpful in making this highly complex man comprehensible. I do not pretend to psychiatric expertise; indeed, I am suspicious of efforts to "psychoanalyze" a man of a distant time and place. Yet in my hope to make the man Rochester more accessible to twenty-first-century readers, I feel justified in using certain twentieth-century terminology. Furthermore, the striking contemporaneity of Rochester's character and thought—he often appears to be a twentieth-century man displaced anachronistically into the seventeenth century—may warrant the occasional use of cultural assumptions that were only beginning to develop in his lifetime.

A CHRISTIAN UPBRINGING (1647–1655)

> But now Methinks some formal Band and Beard
> Takes me to Task. . . .
>
> —Rochester, *"Satyr" against Man*

John Wilmot was born at 11:00 a.m. on April 1, 1647. The astrologer and almanac-maker John Gadbury, who later recorded that information, used it to cast a horoscope, which declared that the conjunction of Venus and Mercury gave the infant an inclination to poetry, while the position of the sun "bestowed a large stock of generous and active spirits, which constantly attended this excellent native's mind, insomuch that no subject came amiss to him."[1]

Whatever the stars told about his talent as a poet, his birth on All Fools' Day was more portentous. The future Earl of Rochester was a life-long trickster and wearer of disguises. The capricious April weather that characterizes its fools was reflected in his intellectual and emotional shifts: his wild swings from gaiety to despair, from insouciant skepticism to terrified faith. His birth date also symbolized the vicissitudes of the England he was born into.

John Wilmot's parents were hardy survivors in the turbulent life of the seventeenth century. His mother, born Anne St. John on November 5, 1614, was one of the ten children of Sir John St. John of Lydiard Tregoze, in Wiltshire. As the second child and oldest daughter, Anne received as much, but no more, education than most daughters of the gentry, who were expected to marry young and begin producing male heirs. Nevertheless, she had great inborn intelligence that turned into shrewdness and iron determination during the years that ended the reign of Charles I and took the lives of three of her brothers, who died in the Royalist cause. Samuel Cooper's watercolor portrait on vellum of her was made in the year of John Wilmot's birth, when she was thirty-three. It shows a pretty woman, fashionably dressed in brocade and pearls with a hairdo of curls. Her full-lipped mouth and slightly overlong nose keep something of a girlish mien, but her clear, intelligent eyes are knowing and sad. She had long since experienced life's bitterness.[2]

As a girl, Anne St. John had disliked Lydiard Tregoze ("that dull place") and her father's tendency to stay there for long stretches of time. She preferred the family estates at Battersea and Wandsworth owned by her father's uncle, Oliver St. John, the Viscount Grandison. These were within reach of the amusements of London as well as the royal courts at St. James, Hampton, and Windsor, and the eligible young noblemen who gathered there. The extensive St. John estates lay in Battersea across the Thames from the stretch of north bank where the Danvers family held land in Chelsea that once belonged to Sir Thomas More, and where their neighbors from Oxfordshire, the Lees of Ditchley, also owned riverside properties.[3]

In October 1632 at Battersea, Anne St. John married her first husband, Sir Francis Henry (Harry) Lee, a dashingly handsome young cavalier. She was not quite eighteen, and he was sixteen, when they became wife and husband. The Dowager Lady Lee (born Eleonore Montagu) was a troublesome mother-in-law. She did not care for the St. John family and criticized them openly. She probably felt that her son was marrying at too early an age into a family whose political sympathies were distasteful to her. In any case, not long after the young couple was wed, the elder Lady Lee remarried, taking a substantial portion of the Lee property with her in the form of a jointure (joint holding of property by husband and wife with the wife as sole heir), and so creating bad blood between herself and son that lasted until his death in 1639.[4]

Harry and Anne Lee apparently had a happy enough marriage, short though it was; in later life she always showed a preference for her children by her first husband to John Wilmot, the son by her second. Three children of the St. John–Lee union survived infancy: a daughter, Eleonora, who was her mother's darling; a son, Henry ("Harry"); and another son, Francis ("Frank"), born after his father's death. During the seven-year span of their marriage, the widening rift between Charles I and Parliament created tensions among the Lees. Harry Lee was a passionate Royalist, as was his wife. His mother, however, was sympathetic to the Puritans, and her second husband, Lord Sussex, was one of the leaders of the Parliamentary rebels. When the King, in a show of strength, led troops against the insurgent Scots in 1639, the twenty-three-year-old Harry Lee followed him in a burst of Royalist loyalty. It was a fatal decision. Lee caught the smallpox; and soon after his return to Chelsea he died, refusing to let his wife near him for fear she might be infected.[5] At the age of twenty-four, Anne Lee found herself widowed, pregnant, and custodian of a toddler baronet. Despite the birth of another male child, her grief at the loss of her beloved husband was deepened when "her darling," their only daughter, died just thirteen months later. To compound her troubles, she was entangled in the legal process of sequestration, by which the Lee estates were placed in custody while titles were cleared and lines of inheritance were established.[6]

By terms of the sequestration, Anne Lee lost all claim to the estates of her husband and sons if she married again. She did not lack for suitors. In January 1641 her father, Sir John St. John, wrote to Edward Hyde, his long-time friend and relative by marriage, that a "gentleman of ffortune" had proposed to "my daughter Lee" with promises of a jointure and a settlement for any future children. Lady Lee refused him, however, and Sir John archly suggested that were Hyde single, she might have preferred him to all others. She had proposed many toasts to Hyde's health during the recent Christmas holidays, Sir John reported.[7]

Whatever her secret preferences, the widowed Anne Lee stayed unmarried for five years. They were fearful ones for a young woman with small children in the very part of Oxfordshire where the first major battles of the Civil Wars were fought after the King raised his standard at Nottingham in 1642. In October of that year, Anne Lee supplied arms for the King's forces at the Battle of Edgehill; and when Edward Hyde, the future Lord Clarendon and Lord Chancellor of England, fled from Oxford, she hid him at Ditchley and supplied him with horses for his escape. Censured by her neighbors, she tried unsuccessfully to defend her actions to Lord Saye and the Parliamentarians, but her plea of her "mony fears" won the pity of at least one neighbor and long-time friend.[8]

Anne Lee was learning the hard lessons of surviving in a hostile, changeable world. In a letter to Hyde, she portrayed herself as filled with fear at her "ignorance . . . in worldly affaires" and a "deptter" to the kindness of a "few frinds," Hyde being "the cheefest." She then demonstrated her womanly wiles. In a postscript, she wrote: "I have ventured too prove my self a clowne too let you tast a country veneson pye if you like it command more when you please."[9]

Young Lady Lee's supportive "frinds" included men of various classes. There was a family retainer, "Geo. Pickering, Gent.," who served the Lees for thirty years and conspired with the young widow to outsmart the ploys of Lady Sussex to regain control of her grandsons' estates. After she became the Countess of Rochester, Anne Lee rewarded him by honoring his request to be buried near the Lee vault in the parish church at Spelsbury.[10] John Cary, Esq., of Oxford— always referred to as "Honest Cary"—was a trustworthy and long-serving agent for the Lees; and Cary's wife was another friend to Harry's "relict." A still stronger ally was Sir Ralph Verney of Claydon, Buckinghamshire, an old friend of Harry's father and the future godfather and official guardian of John Wilmot. And there was Edward Hyde himself, whose rise to greatness after 1660 was accompanied by his increasing services to Lady Lee and her various relatives.

Hyde's generosity lay in the future, however. During the 1640s he was in exile on the continent following Prince Charles, the young king-to-be; and

Lady Lee was forced to rely for help on the men near her in Oxfordshire. One of these was Henry Wilmot of Adderbury, who had been a companion-in-arms of Harry Lee, and who was, like him, a passionate Royalist.

The Wilmots (also Willmots and Wylmutes) had settled in Adderbury before Henry Wilmot gained fame as an aide-de-camp to the Stuarts. Their fortune had begun to improve when Henry's father, Charles Wilmot, was one of a band of adventurers and fortune hunters in Ireland during the reign of Elizabeth I. His part in putting down Tyrone's Rebellion in 1600–1602 gained him the gratitude of the Crown; and with the demonstration of his continued loyalty, he was rewarded with a series of offices and titles, culminating with his being made the Lord-President of Connaught and, in 1621, Viscount Athlone. Having made his fortune, Charles Wilmot came to England to augment his respectability. He purchased the manor house at Adderbury in 1629, and began what promised to be a worthy and dignified retirement.[11]

Charles Wilmot was twice married, and he fathered two sons by his first wife, Sarah Anderson: Arthur, who died unexpectedly in Dublin in 1632, and Henry, who succeeded his older brother as heir to their father's title and estates. Living as he had in a world ruled by primogeniture (preeminent legal rights of the first-born son), Henry had prepared himself for a career as a professional soldier, like his father before him.[12] Baptized on October 26, 1613, Henry Wilmot spent his boyhood, as did his own sons in time, with a continually absent father. There were assertions after his death that he attended Oxford. No official university records support these claims, although Charles, his father, was listed as entering Oxford in July 1587. Henry's surviving letters give no evidence of a superior literacy: the much-admired Latin documents attributed to him during his service as Charles II's envoy to the German princes at Ratisbon were the work of official scribes. Letters in his own hand, hastily written battlefield dispatches, are literate but little more.[13]

In any case, Henry Wilmot's life was one of professional military activity. Between 1635 and 1637, he served Charles I in the Dutch service as a Lieutenant of the Horse, being wounded at Breda. In 1640 he was made Commissioner General of the Horse and a member of the Council of War. In the same year, he went on the Scottish Expedition in the Second Bishop's War under the command of the Earl of Arundel; he was wounded and captured at the Battle of Newcastle, then released at York on September 30. As the M.P. from Tamworth, he always argued for reconciliation between opposing factions in Parliament, but in June 1641, he was accused of participating in the "Army Plot" against Parliament and sent to the Tower.

He surfaced again in Oxfordshire when fighting broke out there in 1642. In August, when the men of Adderbury, sympathizers with the Parliamentarians,

HENRY·WILMOT, *FIRST EARL of ROCHESTER*, *from a Drawing in the Possession of Hendras Sutherland Esq.*

Publish'd 7 Dec 1816 by T. RODD. 2. Great Newport Street.

Figure 1. Henry Wilmot, First Earl of Rochester. Artist unknown. National Portrait Gallery, London. Reproduced by permission.

tried to go to the help of Banbury under Royalist siege, Henry Wilmot "threatened he would hang up the men and send the soudiers to their wives and children." At the Battle of Edgehill in October 1642, he led the left wing of the cavalry beside the King. In July 1643, he distinguished himself for courage at Roundway Down.[14] He had a reputation for good luck, perhaps because he was often wounded without being killed and often captured only to escape.

Figure 2. Anne St. John Wilmot, Countess of Rochester. Watercolor on vellum by Samuel Cooper. From the Collection at Althorp. Reproduced by permission.

Edward Hyde wrote to him on one occasion: "y^e truth is, you have soe good luck in all things, y^t I would fayne learne of you."[15]

The period 1643–44 was crucial for Henry Wilmot. His father Charles had died, leaving the family estates to him along with the Athlone title; his first wife, Frances Norton, died about the same time or earlier, leaving him with a young son, Charles. During these losses, Wilmot continued serving his monarch with steady determination. On June 29, 1644, he was created Baron Wilmot of Adderbury. The next day, he fought in the Battle of Cropredy Bridge, north of Banbury. Wounded twice and captured twice, he was rescued once by Lord Cornwallis, and then again by young Sir Robert Howard and his men. Despite his luck, he was arrested by Parliamentary forces on August 8, deprived of his command, and sent out of the country to France, where he joined Henrietta Maria the Queen Mother and was much celebrated for his bravery and loyalty.[16]

In April or May 1644, Henry Wilmot married the widow of Harry Lee.[17] The Lee property had recently emerged from sequestration with a penalty of

£2,000 attached, but allowing Anne Lee to remarry while remaining guardian to her sons' property. Whether the marriage was one of love, convenience, or common cause is difficult to determine. Wilmot's son Charles was heir to the family property when the marriage took place, so Anne Lee could not expect to gain anything from the Adderbury or Athlone holdings. Wilmot's future in 1644 was neither secure nor promising with the Royalists losing ground before the Parliamentary forces; on the other hand, Anne Wilmot had provoked the hostility of Oxfordshire Parliamentarians in general, and the particular animosity of Lord Saye and Lady Sussex.[18] Both Wilmots brought young children by former marriages to their union. There must have been love on both sides since each was giving additional hostages to fortune. An equally strong bond was their dedication to the Royal Cause: Henry Wilmot's military career kept the pair apart for most of their married life until he died in 1658. Their continual separations over fourteen years caused some malicious speculation about the paternity of John Wilmot.[19] However, Henry Wilmot loved cloak and dagger work; at times, he came to England in disguise. He was secretly at Ditchley in July 1646, when John Wilmot was conceived, as a letter in the Clarendon archives proves.[20]

He was back in 1651 to raise troops of loyalists for the coming Battle of Worcester in September. Following the disastrous rout of Charles II's forces at Worcester, the King was compelled to disguise himself by cutting his hair and dressing as a servant, to hide in an oak tree at Boscobel, and to dodge circuitously from place to place, traveling by night until he made his way to the coast. During these royal travails, Henry Wilmot proved his utter loyalty by accompanying his master, forging ahead to arrange for safe lodgings, raising funds, and finally arranging for a ship to carry the King into a continental exile that lasted until 1660. Charles Stuart displayed his gratitude by conferring the title Earl of Rochester on Henry Wilmot in 1652.[21]

In 1654 Lady Rochester went to France, joining her husband at Brussels in July after he finished some diplomatic duties at Ratisbon.[22] Wilmot made what seems to have been a final trip to England in 1655, trying to stir up the abortive Yorkshire uprising. After 1656 he remained on the continent working for the King's restoration to the throne of England. He impoverished himself on Charles's behalf to the point of pawning his man-servant Rose to pay off his huge debts. In October 1657, he was reported to be very ill. By February 1658, Henry Wilmot was dead.[23] Thus, when he was only ten years old, John Wilmot lost the father he probably saw no more than a dozen or so times in his life.

How the early death of his father affected him is difficult to assess. Rochester's writings mention his father only once—for the "daring loyalty" to the King the son took as a model and tried to emulate. He spoke of all he "owed" to his parents; but the "duty" he always expressed to his mother applied to his duty to "Love and Honour" an absentee father as well. Rochester could hardly have loved a father he scarcely knew, although he could have loved an idealized image of that father. Like John Wilmot, many boys lost their fathers but managed to survive in an era when the average adult male was dead at 32.[24] Some, however, like Anthony Wood, suffered life-long anxiety and depression—as did Rochester himself—probably as a result of the early loss of a father. Gilbert Burnet's threat of an eternity separated from a loving Father/God affected Rochester considerably, and it is obvious that fear of a Father/God determined many actions in his life as well as his deathbed repentance. It is equally obvious that Rochester looked for substitute fathers for many years, finding them in tutors, older male friends, and most strikingly in King Charles II, for whom Rochester's own father had served as a surrogate parent. The depth and extent of the psychic wounds he suffered from the premature loss of his father, though unknowable, also appear to have been a strong element in his continual, and ultimately unsuccessful, struggle to free himself from his imperious mother.

In April 1658, Charles II requested permission from the Governor of Nieufort for Rose to carry the late Earl's Will to his widow in England. Sometime later, the countess planned to have his body brought back to Ditchley and buried in Spelsbury Church beside the body of her first husband. Prudently, and characteristically, she postponed having a funeral tablet made until after the Restoration of Charles II in 1660, when Henry Wilmot's famous loyalty could be properly acknowledged with a Latin epitaph.[25]

During their many years of separation, Lady Rochester learned to manage without her husband, as army wives must do. The challenges she faced left little time for her to nurture her children; that she left to wet nurses and tutors. Less than two years after John Wilmot was born, Charles I was executed on January 30, 1649. The shock waves that followed were all the more severe on the household at Ditchley for the family of a Royalist soldier, chief adviser to the court in exile, spy, and furtive insurrectionist.

In 1650 the Committee for Compounding declared that all property belonging to Henry Wilmot since May 1642 must go into sequestration. Calling upon the advice of Sir Ralph Verney and her other friends, his wife engaged in a series of legal maneuvers at which she would become an expert. Some properties were not Wilmot but Lee estates in trust, she claimed. Others had been mortgaged by old Charles Wilmot before his death. Even Adderbury Manor, which had served as headquarters for Prince Rupert and his Royalist troops in 1645, had been "sold" to Edward Ashe, Esq. Since the word of aristocrats was still held sacred, and official record-keeping was casual, to say the least, no

papers of transfer needed to be produced. The Countess had the cooperative
"word" of Ashe and other allies that all she claimed was true.[26]

She was also helped by the fact that her close friend and agent, Honest John
Cary, was the Commissioner of Sequestrations for Oxfordshire from 1652 until
1656. Like his lady, Cary was a master of red tape: not receiving letters from
his superiors in London, needing additional instructions before he could take
action, misreading instructions when they finally arrived. Hard-pressed by her
husband's known seditious activities, Lady Rochester was forced to rely on
Puritan relatives who had influence in Parliament. Fortunately, her brother, Sir
Walter St. John, was married to a cousin, the Lady Joanna, whose father,
Oliver St. John, was the second most powerful man in the government after
Oliver Cromwell. Lady Rochester wrote directly to Cromwell in 1656, asking
his aid. All the properties in question were Lee estates, she told him, and the
Lees were known Parliamentarians. Cromwell passed her request on to the
Committee for Compounding. His death in 1658 terminated the effectiveness
of that Committee; thus the Countess managed to keep the Lee and Wilmot
properties intact. When Dr. Robert Parsons preached John Wilmot's funeral
sermon, his strongest praise for his mother's maternal qualities was the shrewd
management of his entitlements.[27]

After his birth in the low, Elizabethan half-timbered manor house at
Ditchley in 1647, John Wilmot spent his infancy and boyhood there in carefully supervised seclusion. He was far from isolated, however: the "family"
included many servants, as well as tenants living on the estate. The large,
extended St. John, Lee, and Wilmot families followed the custom of the day in
making frequent, prolonged visits to each other. Little John was very fond of
his Uncle Walter and Aunt Joanna, who rode up often from Chelsea to visit.
The estimable John Cary was on hand regularly to see to sales, purchases, and
accountings. Cary's sizeable family was also on hand; several of the Cary children were married in the Ditchley chapel. The numerous interrelated Verneys,
Dentons, and Gardiners, longtime friends of the Lees, were regular visitors
as well.

As the *Verney Papers* show, much was going on around Ditchley in the 1650s.
Lady Joanna exchanged "receipts" and homemade remedies (dried, powdered
mistletoe) for the "falling sickness" (epilepsy) with old Aunt Isham. Lady
Rochester and Sir Ralph Verney, John's guardian, exchanged their troubles
with Parliament and the Puritans and made plans for settling the futures of
"Mun" (Edmund Verney) and "Harry" (Henry Lee) to their parental satisfaction. Lady Sussex, reconciled with her former daughter-in-law in the cause of
matrimony, sent eligible young ladies on visits to Ditchley to see and be seen.
At one point, the Verney squire and Wilmot lady attempted matches for their

sons in turn with Miss Margaret Eure. Frank Lee actually proposed to her, but no marriage took place after all the fuss. There was endless discussion and correspondence about politics, money, property, and legal matters, and constant talk about human concerns: births, marriages, sicknesses, and deaths.[28]

Although he had three half-brothers, John Wilmot grew up as an only child. His paternal half-brother, Charles Wilmot, may have lived briefly at Ditchley after Henry Wilmot married Anne Lee, but, when Henry went into exile in France, young Charles soon followed him there and entered school in Paris. Edward Hyde described Charles, in 1653, as "a fyne youth," dutiful and promising. The boy appears to have died soon after.[29] John Wilmot's Lee half-brothers, Frank in particular, seem to have been fond of him; but they were separated from him by age, being eight or more years older than he. In 1653, when John was six and a half, Harry and Frank set off late in the year with their tutor, Mr. Godfrey, to enter De Veau's Academy in Paris. Once there, Harry and the tutor became seriously ill in January 1654, and the hapless Mr. Godfrey died on January 17 or thereabout, as Hyde informed Henry Wilmot.[30] When word came to Ditchley, Lady Rochester left hurriedly for France to see to her sons' welfare, arriving there about February 13. Harry recovered, but then Lady Rochester and Frank fell ill and were unable to travel. Not until early summer, after she had seen her husband in Brussels, did his mother return to young John after an absence of five months.[31]

After the ill-fated expedition to Paris when he was sixteen, Harry Lee had no more schooling, probably to his relief. His mother needed him to strengthen her position with the Parliamentarians while she maintained her secret ties with Hyde and the Stuarts. She arranged an ideal marriage for Harry with Ann Danvers, the daughter of her neighbor at Cornbury, Sir John Danvers, a prominent Puritan and Parliamentarian whose Oxfordshire property was adjacent to the Ditchley estate. The Danverses' riverside estate in Chelsea was also happily contiguous to Lee and St. John holdings across the Thames in Battersea. Harry and his bride were married in Spelsbury Church in May 1655.[32]

The young couple thrived in the role of Baron of Ditchley and his lady. As the Ranger of Wychwood Forest, Harry rode to hounds, hunted boars and stags, and sat in Parliament as an M.P. As newlyweds, often accompanied by Lady Rochester, Harry and Ann Lee rode about the county making wedding calls, planning parties, talking politics, and advising Penelope and John Denton to kick a "vilin" man-servant out of doors.[33] Their first surviving child, a daughter Eleonora, was born at Ditchley on June 3, 1658.[34]

Frank Lee left for the continent and the Grand Tour after Mistress Eure rejected him. A studious sort, he lacked Harry's robustness; after his return from the Tour, he had a long illness. He studied at Oxford, taking the M.A. degree belatedly in 1663. He, too, made a suitable marriage to Lady Eleonore Pope, daughter of the Earl of Downe. His new sister-in-law was fond of young John Wilmot and kind to him, as he remembered for years to come, although eventually they engaged in a vehement quarrel over property rights.[35]

Growing up in this family flux during a troubled era, his father constantly absent and his mother often inattentive or away for extended periods, little John Wilmot followed the prescribed routines for a young male of his class. Once he passed from the care of nurses, he began schooling at the hands of a series of tutors and schoolmasters.[36] His first teacher may have been Mr. Godfrey. At the time of Godfrey's departure for Paris in 1653, Lady Rochester enlisted the services of Francis Giffard—like Godfrey, a Cambridge M.A.—who arrived at Ditchley early in 1654 shortly before the Countess departed abruptly for five months, leaving John in the care of a virtual stranger. Not quite seven, he was given into the total control of his first governor, a young clergyman in his early twenties.[37]

The roles of the "governor" and the governed child were set forth by John Wilmot in his adulthood when he wrote a letter to his own seven-year-old son in long-established parental formulas:

> I hope Charles when you receive this, and know that I have sent this gen-tleman to bee y^r tutour, you will bee very gladd to see I take such care of you, and bee very gratefull, wch is best showne in being obedient & dilli-gent, you are now growne bigg enough to bee a man if you can bee wise enough; & the way to bee truly wise is to serve god, learne y^r booke & observe the instructions of y^r Parents first and next y^r Tutour, to whom I have intirely resign'd you for this seven yeare, and according as you imploy that time you are to bee happy or unhappy for ever. . . .[38]

His clerical training at Cambridge had equipped Francis Giffard expertly to instruct his young charge at Ditchley in the ways to be happy or unhappy "for ever." This allusion to Christian eternity—and salvation or damnation in it—was an essential part of schooling in seventeenth-century England.[39] The role of Christian faith, and the implanting of it in children of tender age, was dis-cussed in many educational tracts of the time; and the importance of that faith being Protestant was not only an historical legacy, but also a burning issue in an era when succession to the throne of England depended upon the future monarch's religious beliefs.[40]

The English fear and distrust of Roman Catholicism, or "Popery," rooted in a longstanding dislike of things Italian or Spanish, had intensified in the early 1640s, and it was widely believed that Catholics were somehow responsible for the outbreak of the Civil War. A flurry of localized anti-Catholic panics took place in 1640 and 1641 amid rumors that Catholics were storing arms in London and Oxford, among other places. Crudely written and argued pamphlets fed fears that papists, especially English Recusants, were gathering forces to disrupt the nation. Under Charles I, most Catholics were members of the gentry; it has been estimated that as many as one-fifth of the peerage in the early seventeenth century were papists. When the civil wars began, as Robin Clifton has pointed out, the Royalist cause was feared by many to be pro-Catholic.[41]

> The horrors that Popery held for non-Catholic Englishmen were great: Protestants were not taught to regard Catholicism simply as an alternative, or even as an aberrant, form of Christianity. In pamphlet and sermon popery was presented as essentially the *debasement* of Christ's teaching, a total and blasphemous perversion of Apostolic practice. As such it was far more repugnant and damnable than any form of paganism. It was debased and perverted because successive generations of believers had slightly modified the uncompromising message of Christ in order first to permit, and then to license, their worldly pursuits and pleasures.[42]

After Cromwell and his followers succeeded in doing away with Charles I, members of the Stuart camp saw plainly that a Stuart Restoration could be accomplished only if it was identified with the Protestant religion. As the King's supporters well knew,

> seventeenth century Protestants were educated from birth to make certain assumptions about the nature of the Catholic religion and to expect certain specific patterns of behaviour from papists, and it was within the framework of these beliefs that accusations of popish responsibility for the war were heard and believed. . . .[43]

Young Prince Charles accordingly surrounded himself with such stalwart opponents of Popery as Edward Hyde and Henry Wilmot. John Wilmot's parental legacy was ostentatiously and unwaveringly Protestant. Henry Wilmot was seen in his Paris exile serving at the Protestant altar in the presence of Charles II and the Duke of York. Rough trooper that he was, he never swore, "not so much as a single dam-me," one Protestant biographer wrote. The pious Edward Hyde was unable to fault Wilmot's Protestantism; indeed, he attested to it.[44] As for Anne Wilmot, her Christian piety was proved by the testimony of the clergymen she sponsored (Robert Parsons, most notably), the approbation of neighbors who called her "the good lady at Ditchley," and the numerous references in her letters to "God's will," "devils," and "God's mercy." She was a parishioner of several churches in Oxfordshire—at Spelsbury, Woodstock, and Adderbury—where her regular attendance was recorded by gratified vicars.[45]

Although the Countess of Rochester was a staunch Anglican, her Christian charity (or possibly her instinct for survival, or her inordinate ambition) caused her to tolerate the Puritanism of her brother's and her son's wives. She even managed to endure a Pope's picture on the walls of Ditchley along with a painting of Jesus. But the library at Ditchley contained such testimony of pious Protestantism as Bishop Ussher's *The Principles of the Christian Religion*, a pioneering effort to establish orthodox Anglican beliefs.[46] As a child, John Wilmot was dominated by that mother in those surroundings with a clergyman for a tutor. There were always household chaplains, sometimes more than one, present at Ditchley. Surrounded by praying clergymen during an adult illness, Rochester remarked that "it was but a piece of his breeding."[47]

If the religious atmosphere at Ditchley was not unusual, the oppressiveness of certain Protestant principles imparted by the Reverend Mr. Giffard to his seven-year-old pupil stayed with John Wilmot all his life. The terrible wrath of a vengeful God the Father, the burning eternity of a Protestant Hell, the sinfulness of thoughts, the temptations of the weak flesh—these and other tenets were dutifully drilled into little John's head. They later emerged as references in his correspondence, ironic metaphors, images in his erotic poetry, and, two years before his death, as an intense desire to disprove the immortality of the soul.[48]

The procession of clergymen who visited Rochester in 1679–80, before his death, included Francis Giffard, who recounted the visit to Thomas Hearne:

> The occasion was this. Says his Lordship, "Mr. Giffard, I wonder you will not come and visit me oftener. I have a great respect for you, and I should be extremely glad of your frequent conversation." Says Mr. Giffard (who could say anything to him), "My Lord, I am a clergyman. Your Lordship has a very ill character of being a debauched man and an Atheist, and 'twill not look well in me to keep company with your Lordship as long as this character lasts, and as long as you continue this course of life." "Mr. Giffard," says my Lord, "I have been guilty of extravagances, but I assure you I am no atheist," with other words to that effect.[49]

Assuming that, in his old age, Giffard reported the interview accurately, it reveals much about Rochester's relationship with him. Giffard's pietistic reprimand was usual for the time, however lacking in Christian charity it may seem; but that Giffard could say anything to a man whose wit was widely feared shows that the mature Rochester remained in awe of his first mentor, eager to placate him, still professing belief in the awful God that mentor had described to him. Rochester's dependency on Giffard was intensified by his mother's departure soon after the governor's arrival. The boy's anxieties and fears at the separation naturally caused him to want to win his tutor's approval. Giffard found his ward "very hopeful and ready to do anything that he proposed to him and very well inclined to laudable undertakings." Little John was eager to please; Giffard lauded him for being "very virtuous and good natured . . . willing and ready to follow good advice." The intelligent child quickly learned to act the role of model pupil. Giffard revealed other significant nuances in the early tutor-student relationship. "Mr. Giffard used to lie with him in the family, on purpose that he might prevent any ill accidents."[50] Later on, when John Wilmot left Ditchley to attend grammar school, Giffard shared lodgings with him in the town of Burford. Thus for a period of about six formative years, a young man in his twenties lived in physical intimacy with Wilmot when he was, first, a fatherless, impressionable child and then a pubescent boy.

This was a common practice in the late seventeenth century, approved by aristocratic parents. Lawrence Stone remarks on parental "indifference to the dangers of adolescent homosexual contact," citing the testimony of John Marston, the homophile poet, and others, that such tutor-student sleeping arrangements often led to sexual activity.[51] There is no evidence that Francis Giffard engaged in overt sexual behavior with John Wilmot, but Wilmot's adult homosexual interests may have begun in emotions he experienced as a child. Rochester's sexual orientation is significant because of the obsession with varieties of sexuality in his writings and his own psychosexuality as a vital part of his creativity.[52] His directly sexual (or erotic) works—as distinguished from his moral and/or satiric uses of sexuality—imply a complex gender identity that enabled him to write feminist and misogynistic poetry with equal conviction. His absorption with varieties of sexual feelings and experiences, which made the name of Rochester offensive to modest ears for generations of pious readers, makes him all the more interesting to readers of a post-Freudian age.[53]

Francis Giffard's combination of hellfire doctrines with subliminal sexuality produced constrictive terrors in his pupil. Thomas Hearne quoted Giffard. "He says my Lord had a natural distemper upon him which was extraordinary and he thinks might be one occasion of shortening his days, which was that he sometimes could not have a stool for three weeks or a month together." Rochester's constipation was explained by the contemporary theory that "fumes" ascended to the brain while warming the body and causing both physical and emotional "warmth" or feverishness. If medical theories of the seventeenth century were limited in accounting for chronic constipation, Freud's postulates about bowel retention and parsimony might be invoked since Rochester was preoccupied with money all of his life and was notably unwilling to pay his debts.[54]

Probably as the result of religious terrors, John Wilmot's fear of the dark, beginning in childhood, continued all his life in the form of "general and Dark Horrours that Nature [Mortality] raised in him, especially in some Sicknesses," as Burnet put it.[55] As an adult, Rochester's fear of death made him turn to alcohol and sexual promiscuity for temporary escape. Death was ubiquitous in seventeenth-century England; John Wilmot's childhood was as marked by it as by other kinds of absence and separation. In addition to unrecorded deaths of relatives, stillbirths, and infant deaths, four of his close male relatives died before he reached the age of twelve, including two half-brothers and, most importantly, his father. By the time he was twenty, Rochester was the only surviving male heir of his generation of Wilmots and Lees. His uncertainties and ambivalences about sexuality and money were caught up in his apprehensions about death. Death so filled his mind that, as Dr. Samuel Johnson said, "the whole of life [was] keeping away the thoughts of it."

These morbid obsessions lay in the future, however. Certainly the sense of fun and play shown in his adult "frolics" (so-called) and the keen imagination and wild fantasizing visible in his writings first appeared in childhood.[56] His Lee brothers, in turn, were Rangers of Wychwood forest and Woodstock; there the boy learned the proper pursuits of country-bred aristocrats: breeding dogs, horses, and hawks; deer and boar hunting; horse racing at Woodstock. His interest in these was an important part of his own breeding that stayed with him. Despite its subterranean terrors, Rochester's life as a boy was privileged and superficially pleasant.

Apparently, as his letter to his own son showed, it never occurred to John Wilmot to doubt the principles or methods by which he was brought up, however great his other doubts or unhappy his life might be at times.[57] His explanation for the extravagances and passionate outbursts that plagued his life was always that a devil possessed him and destroyed his repose. He seems not to have suspected that his repose may have been destroyed in childhood—first by his parents and next by his tutor.

A CLASSICAL EDUCATION (1656–1659)

> Mr. Collins of Magdalen's tells me (as Mr. Giffard has done)
> that the mad Earl of Rochester understood little or nothing of
> Greek.
>
> —Thomas Hearne, *Collections*

Just as Rochester's other attributes were disputed after his death, his ability as a scholar of the classics provoked disagreement. In the sermon preached at his funeral, Robert Parsons, household chaplain to the Earl's family, asserted that John Wilmot was a man of "most rare parts, and his natural talent was excellent, much improved by learning and industry." He was "thoroughly acquainted with all classical authors, both Greek and Latin, a thing very rare (if not peculiar to him) among those of quality."[1] Anthony Wood later appropriated Parsons's evaluation, word for word, in the life of Rochester composed for the *Athenae Oxoniensis*.[2]

Gilbert Burnet, spiritual counselor to him in his last months, likewise extolled Rochester's "shining parts," his perfect mastery of Latin and the masterworks composed in it, and his "peculiar delight which the greatest Wits have ever found in those Studies." He had relished the beauty of the Latin language "to his dying-day."[3] On the other hand, Francis Giffard, Wilmot's governor in childhood, told Thomas Hearne that Wood and Burnet had been mistaken in saying the Earl was "so great a master of classical learning," that in fact "My Lord understood very little or no Greek, and that he had but little Latin. . . ."[4]

This sharp difference of opinion shows how reports of Rochester's life and talents were biased by those with personal concerns. Robert Parsons exaggerated the Earl's accomplishments ("all classical authors") to flatter as well as console his wife and mother, who sponsored the publication of the sermon, and then assured Parsons's ecclesiastical livelihood.[5] Burnet emphasized the Earl's superior intellect and classical (read "pagan") expertise to underscore the importance of his conversion into a model of Christian piety and hope.[6] Giffard, who was "supplanted" (his word) as Wilmot's educational supervisor, naturally felt resentment. Furthermore, his doubt that Wilmot received the same supervised training at Oxford that Giffard had provided at Ditchley and Burford was well grounded.[7]

Nevertheless, Parsons, Burnet, and Giffard—as well as Anthony Wood and those Oxonians (Hearne, Collins) who later disparaged Rochester's scholarship—all agreed that mastery of ancient languages and literature, Latin in particular, was a transcendent accomplishment, and that the aristocracy in general were deficient in attaining it. Increasingly after 1660, scholarly and professional writers used linguistic proficiency and knowledge of the classics as accolades in their dedications of published works to aristocratic patrons. Some aristocrats, notably the Earl of Roscommon, together with several members of Rochester's own circle of wits (e.g., Sir Charles Sedley, Sir Henry Savile, Sir Francis Fane), actually deserved them.[8]

In an age when comparatively few aristocrats bothered to master the ancient tongues, Rochester's reputation as a Latinist was significant, and the reasons for it are revealing. He was probably motivated by a combination of parental and pedagogical expectations as well as the classical enthusiasms of several friends and peers. His father's reputation as a skilled and eloquent writer of Latin prose, deserved or not, was one factor. John Wilmot held the accomplishments of his father as a constant standard for himself in his youth.[9] Despite her own lack of classical education, his mother also esteemed her husband's reputation as diplomat, enshrining him in a Latin epitaph befitting the aristocracy—lesser "gentlemen" were remembered in English.[10] Clearly, Wilmot men were expected to be proficient in Latin, the language of diplomacy.

With her Lee sons, for political and financial reasons the Countess had encouraged Harry Lee to assume his baronial duties with minimal schooling; but after sending her younger Lee son on the Grand Tour, she oversaw his subsequent study for an Oxford M.A. In fact, Frank Lee studied there *after* his Wilmot half-brother had already gotten a Master's degree. Lady Rochester understood well the status conferred by classical learning.

In his years of schooling, Rochester had talented and determined teachers to goad and stimulate him: first the Reverend Mr. Giffard, then John Martin, and finally Dr. Andrew Balfour, who supervised his Grand Tour. Dr. Balfour's classical expertise, so clearly apparent in his account of their Tour, was particularly important, coming after the learning gap at Oxford and lasting for three full years. Rochester himself acknowledged Balfour's significant role in his education. His later associations, both social and literary, with scholars of various achievements also helped to sustain his classical interests. Such associates as Thomas Hobbes, John Dryden, John Oldham, Nathaniel Lee, and Charles Blount were able Latinists whose interests affected Rochester and stimulated him. Equally importantly, Rochester's intelligence and lively curiosity were motivations to learning in themselves.

Accordingly, he began to study Latin at the age of seven under the watchful eye of Francis Giffard, and in time he read the authors who would influence his own thought and writing. Rochester's various works—letters, lyric and satiric poetry, prose pamphlets, and plays—show directly his knowledge of Greek writers including Homer, Longinus, Pindar, Anacreon, and Plutarch. His acquaintance with Latin authors included Cicero, Livy, Seneca, Ovid, Horace, Catullus, Lucretius, Martial, Juvenal, Tibullus, Petronius, Lucan, and Augustine. Many of these were identified as important to Rochester by Robert Wolseley, a friend, admirer, and early editor of his, and by Thomas Rymer, the classicist-turned-moralist who censured the obscenity in Wycherley and Dryden but admired Rochester's translation/paraphrase of Anacreon, even with its hint of pederasty.[11] On the whole, the evidence for John Wilmot's ability as an enthusiastic classicist is convincing.

Modern commentators claim to have found the possible influence of other authors in various poems: Epicurus, Pliny, and Sextus Empiricus among them.[12] Of course, Rochester may not have read all of the ancient writers, nor did he necessarily consult the Latin or Greek originals.[13] Translations of some were available in English during his lifetime, and in several instances he may have been more dependent on a French translation than a Latin original.[14] Nevertheless, through association with classical scholars such as Dr. John Fell and Robert Whitehall in repeated visits to Oxford, Rochester could have absorbed some knowledge through conversation.

He may have been a more accomplished reader of the classics than even his admirers claimed.[15] His revision of Fletcher's historical drama, *Valentinian*, for instance, makes changes in details about the reign of the Emperor of Rome recorded only by such recondite sources as Procopius and Evagrius.[16] In any case, Rochester's reading in the classics, the ancient historians in particular, led him to adopt some political and philosophical principles in adulthood that left their mark on his writings as well as his Parliamentary career.

In Rochester's era, most seven-year-old boys set out to learn the language by reading some elementary work in Latin, generally Roman history in an abridgment of Livy or Dionysus of Halicarnassus. The three most frequently used texts in the seventeenth century were Trogus Pompeius, whose condensation of Livy had been used as a school text by the Romans themselves; Justin, whose *History of the World* placed Roman events into the contexts (often fanciful or erroneous) of Jewish and Greek historiography; and Lucius Annaeus Florus, the most widely used of the three texts, which turned Livy into a biography of the Roman body politic. Mr. Giffard had a close knowledge of all these authors; he probably introduced little John Wilmot to classical study by means of those standard works.[17]

Thus, along with the religious precepts given him by Mr. Giffard, Rochester absorbed ideas about the secular culture from which Christianity emerged. Roman civilization was the highest manifestation of human attainment possible without the revealed religion of the New Testament. Mighty Rome had lost its sustaining strength and *virtus*, and been overrun by barbarian invasions. The cyclic paradigm of Roman history provided instruction for the wise, containing as it did similarities to the life-cycle of a man. Pagans such as Achilles, Aeneas, Damocles, Cincinnatus, Diogenes, Timon of Athens, and Timon of Phlius, and the subjects of Plutarch's *Lives* (Anthony and Cleopatra) were exemplary of right and wrong conduct. Rochester's works cite all of these. Above all, history was "useful," teaching by examples. It was certainly no accident that playwrights hoping to get patronage from the adult Rochester dedicated plays about Nero, or Titus and Berenice to him.[18]

In 1656, after two years of Giffard's tutoring, the Countess decided that it was time for her promising son to enroll in a suitable grammar school. Sending her boys off for schooling away from home at a tender age was an item of conviction with Lady Wilmot, as with other English aristocrats, then and now; but the disastrous experience of the Lees at De Veau's Academy in Paris had dampened her enthusiasm for continental education.

Of the prestigious public schools, Dr. Richard Busby's Westminster in London was the most famous. Busby had reigned supreme at Westminster since 1636, enduring through political upheavals because Parliamentarians as well as Royalists revered his abilities as scholar and teacher.[19] Busby's pupils revered him too for his kindly attentions—or else they stood in awe of his birch rod, famed for flogging Latin and Greek into dullards. His pupils included John Dryden, Robert South, John Locke, Robert Whitehall, and a host of other future poets, divines, and politicians. Westminster might appear the best place for young Rochester, who himself acknowledged Busby's preeminence in a lampoon composed in 1675. Rochester pointed out the historical inaccuracies in Nathaniel Lee's *Sophonisba*, an historical drama about Hannibal and Rome's Punic Wars with Carthage: "I laugh, and wish the hot-brain'd, Fustian Foole,/ In Busbys hands, to be well lasht at Schoole."[20]

But Rochester's mother had reason to question whether London in 1656 was a sensible place to locate a boy whose father had tried to start an uprising against the forces of Parliament in Yorkshire a year earlier. The Countess herself, in 1656, was writing false claims about Wilmot properties to Oliver Cromwell, the Lord Protector, whose London presence potentially threatened the safety of her son.[21] Dr. Busby, it is true, was a firm Royalist, like the

Wilmots. He had led his pupils in prayers for the King in 1649 when Charles I was beheaded little more than a stone's throw away at Whitehall. But Busby was directly answerable to the agents of Parliament; his power of defiance was limited, after all. If Cromwell decided to seize Henry Wilmot's son as a "pawn," could Busby prevent it?[22]

The risk of schooling in London was too great. The Countess decided to send John Wilmot to the Burford Grammar School, where John Martin, "a noted master," had recently become head.[23] Burford was a short distance away from Ditchley; it was a Royalist town, and the local gentry need have no fears for the safety of sons in the town-sponsored Grammar School. So off little Wilmot went to Burford, accompanied by Mr. Giffard, to find lodgings. As a "petty," (i.e., "petit" or younger boy), Wilmot was permitted to attend the school only by taking separate lodgings in town.[24]

One of the Cotswold villages thriving on the wool trade, Burford was a pretty little town, sloping downhill in a row of stone buildings to the meandering Windrush River. The Free School stood at the bottom of the hill next to the Church of Saint John Baptist and its graveyard. Despite its picturesque appearance, the school building was low and dark inside with small windows. Mists from the stream chilled the rooms in winter and left cold drafts in the open stretches of the Church. The physical atmosphere was sometimes as oppressive as the memories of recent events were depressing to Royalists. Only seven years earlier, Oliver Cromwell had stood in the pulpit of Saint John Baptist, sermonizing the captive survivors of his bloody destruction of the Levellers, the last of the anti-Parliamentary parties.[25]

Simon Wysdome, founder of the Grammar School in 1571, had painstakingly spelled out in the twelve items of its *Constitucions*, the school's administrative and financial arrangements with the town, the duties of its masters and wardens, the number of students (forty "men children having noe infirmite or sickness"), the daily routine to be followed, and other matters.[26] Some of these provisions had been allowed to lapse by subsequent masters, whose haphazard record-keeping frustrated Christopher Wase in 1673, when he compiled his *Survey of Grammar Schools*. John Martin told Wase no warden's book for the Grammar School had been located after a long search; and the names of previous masters had to be collected from the memories of the oldest Burfordites.[27]

By Wysdome's provisions, the "peties" were to be instructed by "gramarian schollers of the said free scole" until such a time as finances permitted hiring "some other usher or mete Scholler." In other words, the younger boys were often taught by the older. There was no limit to the number of younger boys attached to the school; but those coming from the country—boys whose fathers did not live in Burford—had to pay twelve pence at the time of entry, and six pence for each quarter. It is safe to assume that, as a young nobleman from a distinguished Oxfordshire family, accompanied by his own tutor, John Wilmot was not treated as any ordinary petty. It is even possible that he lived in the house of John Martin, the head master; the *Constitucions* provided for such an arrangement.[28]

Nevertheless, he had to follow the strict daily routine. Master and students assembled at six o'clock in the morning in summer (at seven in winter), had lessons until eleven, then ate dinner, resumed study from one until six o'clock in summer (four in winter), and concluded the day with prayers, psalm-singing, and a selection read from the Old or New Testament. Before the school day started, if there was a morning service, the students marched two by two in a column to church, summer and winter, where they were "TO SERVE god devoutlie in singing or sayinge of Salmes." In the event of no church service, the scholars were led in religious worship in the classrooms.

On Sundays, unless there was "some Reasonable cause to the contrary," the boys had to assemble by the second peal of the bell ringing Matins, when the master led them to church, "there to serve god devoutly." There were also special religious observations at Christmas, Whitsuntide, Allhallowtide, and the end of the school year.

Unfortunately, no record of the curriculum at Burford Grammar School now exists. Burnet said of Rochester's time at Burford, "When he was at School he was an extraordinary Proficient at his Book: and those shining parts which have since appeared with so much lustre; began to shew themselves: He acquired the *Latin* . . . and was exactly versed in the incomparable Authors that write about Augustus's time. . . ."[29] Apparently, unlike Westminster School, Burford did not teach Greek. The emphasis was entirely Roman with students applying themselves to perfecting their Latin, probably by the common practice of translating Latin texts into English and then back into Latin.[30] The Augustan authors studied would have included Virgil, Livy, Horace, Ovid, Tibullus, and Propertius. Rochester's schoolboy exercises introduced him to ways of translating, paraphrasing, metaphrasing, and parody that he later used as a poet. Some of his extant writings are English versions of the Augustans he might have studied at Burford.

Ovid was the first to contribute models for translation, adaptation, and loose imitation when Wilmot began his poetic career as Courtier to Charles II in 1665. A favorite with Restoration courtiers, Ovid was much admired for his *Epistles* or *Heroides*, which Wilmot could have read under John Martin, and for his erotic *Amores* and *Ars Amatoria*, which Wilmot certainly did not—at least not then.[31] Horace's *Satires* also became a significant source for Rochester later in works discovered under Martin. Rochester's adaptations of Ovid and Horace began literary forms that became hallmarks of English literature in the hands of John Dryden and Alexander Pope: epistolary satires, mock dialogues, and the ironic critical survey of contemporary writers. These genres or modes may well have had their genesis when the schoolboy Wilmot labored over Latin texts in a cold Burford schoolroom, committing to memory passages and meters that in time would transmute into the mock-Ovidian "An Heroical Epistle," or the Horatian "Timon" and "An Allusion to Horace."[32]

Rochester's experiences at Burford as a schoolboy left him, as most boys, with a jumble of feelings about himself, his school, and what he was taught there. Twenty years later, he "lay his thoughts open without any Disguise" to Gilbert Burnet, promising to reveal his "Principles" and tell plainly "what stuck with him." Knowing his fear of death, Burnet asked him why "ill men" felt such terror at the prospect of dying whereas good men felt joy. Rochester "was willing to ascribe it to the Impressions they had from their Education."[33]

If his education at Burford introduced him to pagans whose works suggested possible alternatives to Christian salvation or damnation, the Burford ritual also reinforced the somber Protestant beliefs he learned as an impressionable child at Ditchley. When he left Burford at the age of twelve or so, he took with him strictures and fears built into his mind by his schooling. This conversation with Burnet, in his last year of life, showed that John Wilmot never shook off some religious principles and their attendant emotions which, like his love of the Latin language, stuck with him until his dying day.

GROWING DEBAUCHED AT OXFORD
(1660–1661)

When my Lord came to Oxford he soon grew debauched. . . .
—Thomas Hearne, *Collections*

There he first suck'd from the breasts of his Mother the
University those perfections of Wit, and Eloquence, and
Poetry, which afterwards by his own corrupt stomach, or ill
juices after, were turn'd into poison to himself or others.
—Robert Parsons, *Sermon*

How long Rochester stayed at Burford is uncertain, but it could not have been more than three years. As early as February 1659, the countess determined to send him to Oxford. John Cary paid "Caution Money" (a fee deposit) for him to Wadham College on March 1, 1659.[1] But family problems may have delayed his entering for a time. Frank Lee was sick and convalescing after returning from his Grand Tour, and at the end of March, another blow fell on the Ditchley household. One of his correspondents told Edward Hyde on March 25:

> Sir Harry Lee is much bewailed, who, having obtained leave [from Parliament] to hunt for three or four days, overheated his blood and died on Monday last at Ditchley of the smallpox.

Hyde requested further information about his "friends at Ditchley," asking "whether the brother succeeds or some other heir." Broderick wrote back that the Countess of Rochester "presents her service to you" and "the widow is with child."[2]

Since the dead Harry's only child was a ten-month-old girl, Eleonora, and laws of primogeniture pertained, the succession of the Lee estate had to await the birth and determine the sex of the posthumous infant. The determination came on July 24, 1659, when Anne, another girl, was born. A week later, Harry's widow, Ann Danvers, was dead. Thus Frank Lee succeeded his brother as Baron of Ditchley, and the Countess of Rochester became guardian to two more infant heiresses.

Political uncertainties also may have kept John Wilmot at home longer than was intended. In early 1659 Wadham College had as its Warden John Wilkins, who was married to Oliver Cromwell's sister and who was, according to Anthony Wood, "a notorious complyer with the Presbyterians (from whom he obtained the Wardenship. . .)." After the death of the Lord Protector in 1658, Wilkins's fortunes became increasingly unstable. At last, in September 1659, he was replaced by Walter Blandford, who had shown the ability to combine political adaptability with strict academic discipline. Although Blandford had prudently acceded to the pressures of the Parliamentary Visitors when they came to Wadham, where he was then a Fellow, he nevertheless would be made a Commissioner to Charles II in 1660, and thereafter go on to greater glories as Vice-Chancellor of the University, Bishop of Oxford, and Bishop of Worcester.[3] Blandford was a man on the rise: firmly Anglican, a devout author-itarian, but politically flexible after Lady Wilmot's own ways.[4]

In January 1660, John Wilmot was admitted to Wadham as a Fellow Commoner, or nobleman, together with several other young men of notably Royalist persuasion.[5] The Countess had planned for Mr. Giffard to attend her son to Oxford, but then she decided it would not be necessary. Giffard accompanied the young Earl to Oxford in January; but soon after, on February 10, he was ordained a deacon at Lincoln. The Countess, however, had no intention of releasing her son from stringent supervision: she entrusted him to Warden Blandford, who turned him over to Phineas Berry (or Bury) as tutor.

Berry had his duties spelled out for him in official Latin: his main task was *Exercidis & Actibus Scholasticis interesse.* Unfortunately, he was too easy-going or unambitious to compel his scholars to hard study. Called "a great coffey-drinker," he was reluctant to confront or discipline students even as an elected Proctor. On one occasion he took no notice when unruly students kicked a kid-derkin (small barrel) along Catte Street during a formal procession. He some-times neglected to appear at official academic functions. What energy he had went into meeting crises: young William Foulconer died at college; Francis Pyle was always missing examinations and running off to London.[6] In contrast with them, young Rochester *Dominus*, that docile and obedient lad, was easy to over-look. Berry let the boy follow his own ways without much supervision. Though he may have succeeded Mr. Giffard, Berry did not truly replace him as Rochester's mentor. With Giffard "supplanted," it came as no surprise to him that the Earl "grew debauched," as Giffard told Thomas Hearne.

When Rochester entered Wadham, it was a new and comparatively poor college. Founded in 1613, it had attracted a few bequests of books and several outstanding scholars, but in 1660 it was a lesser-known college, seemingly out of the academic mainstream. W. Fulman's *Academiae Oxoniensis Notitia* (1665) could muster up little to say in praise of it. Wadham consisted of a Warden or *Custos*; fifteen Fellows (*Socii*); fifteen pupils (*Discipuli*); and assorted menials. It had two famous alumni (*Viri Clari*): Humphrey Sydenham the doctor and John Gauden.[7]

But these bare facts were not the complete story about Wadham. One of the former Fellows was Christopher Wren, still in Oxford in 1660 lecturing in astronomy. Under John Wilkins, a group of men interested in the New Science had begun to meet informally at lodgings and coffee houses, to discuss the so-called Natural Philosophy. In 1660 the group would become the Royal Society, the future locus of gentlemanly scientific investigation for Samuel Pepys, John Evelyn, John Dryden, and many others, who mingled with Sir Isaac Newton, Robert Boyle, and other serious pioneers in biology, physics, and astronomy. In 1667 Thomas Sprat, a Wadham graduate, would publish the *History of the Royal Society*.[8] Young Rochester entered Wadham at a time of burgeoning ideas and experimentation.

For a while, custom may have kept John Wilmot at his books. As a Fellow Commoner or nobleman, he had access to the Fellows' Common Room and Library, where he had the opportunity to gain considerable knowledge about the Greco-Roman world on his own through English translations of many classics. In addition to such standard authors as Horace, Ovid, Polybius, Seneca, Lucan, and Plutarch, there was Chapman's Homer, the *Epistles* of Phalaris, and the romances of Heliodorus.[9] To professional classicists, Oxford dons, or displaced tutors, translations and adaptations were things to sniff at; but they became increasingly acceptable after the Restoration as a way to get classical knowledge for those denied a university education. In 1660–61 they could provide at least a nodding acquaintance with "all classick Authors, both Greek and Latine" for a youth like Rochester. The Wadham Library also contained the works of the major Elizabethan and Jacobean playwrights, along with Shakespeare; the youth's theatrical interests also may have developed there.[10]

By March 1660, however, political disruptions in London shook the Oxonian cloisters. The Free Elections for Parliament clearly indicated that the Cromwell Era was ending, and Royalist Oxford began to rumble with the approaching events of April and May. When Charles Stuart returned to England from Holland on May 25 and made a triumphant entry into London on May 29, the eruption came.[11] Books were tossed aside and glasses raised. A sheep's rump, symbol of the vanquished Rump Parliament, was tossed through the window of Dr. Greenwood, the Vice-Chancellor who earlier had brought

Figure 3. King Charles II. Unknown artist, 1665. National Portrait Gallery, London. Reproduced by permission.

Parliamentary troops into Oxford to awe Royalist scholars. Lectures gave way to drunken, bawdy songs, while dialogues about Caesar, Cicero, and Pompey were replaced with talk of the King, Clarendon, and General Monck, who restored Charles II to the throne. In the weeks following, the academic order was lost in anarchy as carousing, rioting, and whoring students grew increasingly wild and licentious.

Caught up in the abandonment of the times, barely thirteen and innocent for his years, John Wilmot found himself changing as rapidly as the world around him.[12] He was leaving a childhood of dutiful submission to lessons and schoolmasters in Puritan England. He was now the youth, Lord Rochester the son of Lord Wilmot, with great expectations of rewards from the restored Stuart monarch. No one was there to keep watch on him. His mother was busy at Ditchley with her duties and schemes.[13] Mr. Giffard's ties with the Wilmots were ended, and he was bent on his ecclesiastical career. Warden Blandford was trying to control the boiling mobs of undergraduates, and Phineas Berry, Rochester's "good-natured" tutor, could not keep up with all that needed to be done. Left on his own, sharing the excitement of the day, John Wilmot fell under the tutelage of Robert Whitehall, a man not at all like Mr. Giffard and certainly not the kind of governor the countess would have chosen for her son.

Like Anthony Wood, John Fell, and Robert South, Robert Whitehall was a constant fixture at Oxford. Before entering Christ Church as a student in 1643, Whitehall had been a pupil of Dr. Busby's at Westminster. In 1648, when the Parliamentary Visitors asked him about his political sympathies, as a Royalist he committed a foolhardy act that Wood reported as follows:

> "My name's Whitehall, God bless the poet,
> "If I submit the king shall know it:
> quoth Robert Whitehall to the Visitors, *anno* 1648. The said Whitehall was turned out of his place; but, by cringing to the committee at London, became soon after fellow of Merton Coll. where, following the trade of drinking as he was wont, procured to himself a red face.[14]

Temporarily chastened by his experience with the Visitors, Whitehall extended himself to win the patronage of the most prominent Puritan in his home shire, "*Rich: Ingoldesbie* the Regicide," Wood called him. Whitehall "acted the part of a Mimick and Buffoon purposely to make him merry." The ploy was so successful that Whitehall adopted it as a *modus vivendi*. Once established in Merton, he steadily played the role of Merry Andrew, scoring off on both political sides with impunity. In 1651, however, he committed another versified blunder. Whitehall wrote a hudibrastic poem, *Technepolaimogama; or, The Marriage of Armes and the Arts, July 12, 1651*, in which he mocked the way that "Sable Gownes so large and wide/ Demonstrate they can Sayle 'gainst winde and Tide." Whitehall obliquely confirmed his Royalist sympathies in the lurching meters of the verse, which guyed the submission of Oxford's timorous dons to Parliament. Whitehall was vain and imprudent enough to have the piece published in London, concealing his identity slightly by using only his initials on the title page.[15]

With the establishment of the Protectorate, however, Parliament and its leaders became too formidable to beard openly; Whitehall then decided to ingratiate himself with the Cromwells through eulogies in Latin. But Oxford itself and its denizens continued to be objects of his heavy wit. In 1655 he became a member of the *Terrae Filii* (Sons of the Earth), the official University satirists who lampooned themselves together with their fellows on academic occasions. Whitehall also devoted himself to drinking and furthering his career. His impromptu Latinate wit on one occasion was set down by Wood. A group of medical students were on their way to Aylesbury to dissect a woman who had been hanged. The weather was cold and rainy, the roads were horribly muddy, and when his miserable companions began to grouse, Whitehall remarked cheerfully, "Omnis commoditas sua fert incommoda secum." (In free translation, "Every pleasure trip has its little inconveniences.")[16]

Anthony Wood never doubted that such advancement as Whitehall got was less the result of merit than fawning sycophancy. He remarked acidly:

> by vertue of the Letters of *Rich; Cromwell* Chancellour of this Univ. of *Oxon*, he was actually created Bach. of Phys. in 1657. Since which time he made divers sallies into the practice of Physick, but thereby obtained but little reputation, and lesser by his Poetry, to which he much pretended, having been esteemed no better than a meer Poetaster and time-serving Poet. . . .[17]

In August 1657, Whitehall went to Dublin University at the request of Henry Cromwell. There he stayed until the reversal of Cromwell fortunes set him loose to seek his fortune. Once again, he managed to get his place at Merton, where he returned sometime before 1660. Indefatigable, eternally optimistic, he turned coat, confident that he would succeed under Stuart patronage.

He began composing a series of verse tributes to every potential sponsor: Charles II, Lord Clarendon, Catherine of Braganza, the Duke of Monmouth, and James II. (Poor Queen Catherine fled London in 1665 to escape the Plague, only to face Robert Whitehall in Oxford. She had to endure sixteen recited stanzas of doggerel from him as he kneeled before her.)[18] In 1660 he was, as a raffish punster noted, "loyned with sack and faced with claret"—a bibulous, bumptuous, redfaced, rhyming Falstaff on the lookout for a Prince Hal to help make his fortune. In young Lord Rochester, he thought he had found one.

There can be no doubt that Robert Whitehall contributed substantially to the debauching of John Wilmot. Anthony Wood, whose cynical gaze took in all aspects of life at Oxford, said flatly that the older man "absolutely doted" on the youth. (A few years later, Wood candidly said that the Electors to a Fellowship at All Souls chose a handsome young man with a view to "kissing and slobbering him.")[19] The possible result of a tutor absolutely doting on a thirteen-year-old boy was frankly stated by John Marston:

> Had I some snout-fair brats, they should endure
> The new-found Castilian calenture
> Before some pedant tutor in his bed
> Should use my fry like Phrygian Ganymede.[20]

Growing awareness of pederastic activity led eventually to a report by Dudley Ryder (1762–1847) that "among the chief men in some of the colleges sodomy is very usual. It is dangerous sending a young man who is beautiful to Oxford." A major scandal in the early eighteenth century caused Wadham, Rochester's own college, to be dubbed "Sodom," which wags call it to this day. A Warden, accused with abundant proof of his forcible rape of a student, hurridly left for France while less substantial rumors of homosexual activity between other dons and students continued to circulate.[21]

Whitehall himself left evidence of homophile tendencies in a highly misogynistic tract titled *The Woman's Right Proved False* (1674). In the Preface he wrote:

> be pleased to know ye Author as yet lives in Batchelours Row at the Sign of hope in ye land of Love [slang for Oxford]. And now I am certain I shall conjure up a thousand conjectures as well as Interrogatories in your minds about it. . . . May be he is overwhelmed in Love he dares not reveal and was minded to obviate & remove all suspicion by palliating it with a contrary guise. . . .[22]

Given young Rochester's known good looks and his sleeping arrangements with Francis Giffard, it is small wonder that he should become the object of Robert Whitehall's doting or that he would accept such attentions as natural. It is quite possible that Rochester became actively homosexual during his time at Oxford. In his later writings, he described homosexual acts between men and boys.[23] If he learned about such acts during his Oxford days, he was far from unique. He had certainly discovered the practice of self-masturbation as a part of awakening sexuality, later assuming it impossible that schoolboys would forget to "frig."[24]

In the turbulent, sexually charged atmosphere of Oxford following the Restoration, thirteen-year-old Rochester also may have begun his heterosexual career. In 1661, when Lord Clarendon came to Oxford for the Convocation at which Rochester graduated, he reproved the Principal of Magdalen, Dr. Henry Wilkinson: "I heare your hall entertaineth not only factious but debauched scholars." Clarendon said proctors had told him that more Magdalene scholars were taken at "innes, alehouses, and whorehouses than any other house in Oxford hath; to which the Doctor replied but little. . . ."[25]

If Robert Whitehall did not directly arrange Rochester's entry into sexual sophistication, he certainly assisted it by providing the youth with the license of disguise. By lending his academic gown for night-time explorations at inns, taverns, and brothels, Whitehall encouraged John Wilmot to engage in the sensual and emotional "disorders" which "he came to love too much." Disguised in Whitehall's gown, Rochester found "good-fellows," presumably the sort of companions that Whitehall himself employed in the trade of drinking; but he doubtless found much, much more, given the nature of his surroundings in 1660–61.[26]

By assuming disguises as he sexually matured, Rochester grew accustomed to separating the elements of selfhood: boy and youth, innocent and experienced, open and secret. His burgeoning sexuality, which probably began with solitary masturbation, initiated habits of concealment that were encouraged by his wearing the clothing of an older, more experienced man. Concealing his "true" identity from others forced John Wilmot to contrive personae and play roles that would inevitably become part of a larger, highly complex self-image.[27] When the adolescent youth began his sexual experimentation, the moral strictures and fears of his childhood were still very strong. For years at Burford School, he had gone daily to services at Saint John Baptist and seen these words in Elizabethan lettering beneath the east window:

1 THE NYGHT IS PASSED AND THE DAY IS COME NYE. LET US THEREFORE
2 CAST AWAIE THE DEDES OF DARCNNESS. AND LET USPUT [*sic*] ON THE ARMOURE OF LYGHTE. LET US WAL
3 KE HONESTLY AS IT WERE IN THE DAYELYGHT: NOT IN EATYNGE AND DRYNCKNGE. NETHER IN
4 CHAMBURYNGE AND WA[N]TONESS: NETHER IN STRYFE AND ENVYINGE: BUT PUT YE ON THE LORDE
5 JESUS CHRISTE + AND MAKE NOT PROVYSYON FOR THE FLESH. TO FULFYLL THE LUSTES OF IT.
6 ALL TRANSYTORY THYNGES SHALL FAYLE AT THE LAST AND THE WORCKER THEREOF SHALL GO WITHALL
7 OF ERROUR & FEARE GOD[28]

Emerging from his nights of fleshly experimentation into the Oxford daylight, casting off Robert Whitehall's clothing, could John Wilmot fail to remember, however reluctantly, frightening injunctions of this kind? But the deeds of darkness proved too enticing to resist.

During his debauching at Oxford, along with learning to disguise himself and feign to be or feel what he was not (or feign not to feel what he did), Rochester developed some creative predispositions.[29] The tensions between his impulses toward moral anarchy and his unyielding self-judgment, fomented in his adolescence, would conjoin in strange ways in his adult compositions, as critics have pointed out. Indeed, Wilmot's equilibrist consciousness became identical with his creative imagination.[30]

If Rochester learned much from him that did no good, Robert Whitehall actually helped the young student as a classicist and poet. Whitehall knew Latin of the scholastic variety, and he used it with an easy, Goliardic familiarity. He could throw out ripostes in Latin, quote scraps of Greek, and extemporize in distiches.[31] Rochester learned from him by osmosis; almost surely, his ability to make the rhymed impromptus that delighted the court of Charles II derived from Robert Whitehall's example.[32] He also began to write "occasional," or situational poetry with Whitehall's encouragement, if not assistance.

As a long-time Oxonian and academic survivor, Whitehall well knew that state occasions always elicited Latin poems from scholarly petitioners. When the Restoration came about, the Oxford establishment was anxious to assure King Charles of its loyalty. Royalist though it had been in the 1640s, the University had made numerous concessions to the Parliamentarians during their supremacy. Naturally, those who had accommodated themselves to the Cromwells did not want that fact to prejudice the restored monarch against Oxford. As a token of their renewed dedication to the Stuarts—and reminder of their august learning—Oxonians planned a volume of poetic tributes to Charles, hoping to win his friendship with an assortment of encomiums in Latin, Greek, Hebrew, Arabic, and English.

The *Britannia Rediviva* (Oxford 1660) began with a Dedication in Latin by John Conant, the new Vice-Chancellor, urging the King to "Accept the tribute of the Muse" and rejoicing that Christ once again ruled in England now that a Stuart was enthroned. Some of Oxford's most eminent scholars then offered their tributes, imitations of Virgil and other Augustan poets. Pococke contributed stanzas in Arabic and Hebrew. Dr. Robert South's Latin lines displayed ecclesiastical dignity and sonority. And Warden Walter Blandford's hyperbolic paean began with a paraphrase of Virgil's *Aeneid*: "Arma virumque cano, Qualem nec Troi Heros / Aequat. . . ."[33] The "very learned" Phineas Berry, Rochester's indolent tutor, contributed nothing to the volume, interestingly enough.

As for Robert Whitehall, his part in compiling the anthology is suggested by the facts that his Latin poem is longer than anybody else's and that he also contributed a poem in English as the final verse in the second section of *Britannia Rediviva*.[34] With all their effort to appeal to the King by comparing him to Aeneas, the epic founder of Rome, Whitehall and his colleagues could hardly overlook the opportunity to spotlight John Wilmot, the son of Henry

Wilmot, a *fidus Achates* to Charles Stuart in exile. After the opening classical section came another section in English with verses by various nobles, Fellows, and graduates (including John Locke). The first poem in this section, "To His Sacred Majesty," presented the name of its author with aristocratic simplicity in boldfaced type at least three times larger than other authorial names:

ROCHESTER

The King did not need his spectacles to see young Lord Rochester's signature or the institutional hopes pinned on him.

The eighteen-line poem concluded with a pointed reference to Rochester's father, the "faithful Achates":

> And though my youth, not patient yet to bear
> The weight of Armes, denies me to appear
> In Steel before You, yet, Great Sir, approve
> My manly wishes, and more vigorous love;
> In whom a cold respect were treason to
> A Fathers ashes, greater than to you;
> Whose one ambition 'tis for to be known
> By daring Loyalty Your WILMOT's Son.[35]

Certainly, the concluding statement of ambition to inherit the Royalist legacy of Henry Wilmot genuinely expressed the hope of John Wilmot—and his mother.

The following year (1661), two more poems appeared under Rochester's name: the Latin "In Obitum Serenissimae Mariae Principis Arausionensis," on the death by smallpox of Charles II's sister, the Princess of Orange; and "To Her Sacred Majesty, the Queen Mother, on the Death of Mary Princess of Orange," its English accompaniment. Anthony Wood later wrote:

> [T]hese three copies were made, as 'twas then well known, by Robert Whitehall a physician of Merton college, who pretended to instruct the count . . . in the art of poetry.[36]

If Rochester's English poem in the *Britannia Rediviva* is compared with the clearly inferior one by Whitehall, however, it is difficult to suppose that Whitehall's customary limitations as a poetaster could have produced "To His Sacred Majesty." Wood may have been quite literal in saying Whitehall pretended to teach Rochester how to write poetry.

The Merton physician may have had a hand in writing the ten line Latin poem, though it is of the straightforward, simple variety that an ingenious boy with shining parts might well have prepared for through written exercises at

Burford. "In Obitum," like Dryden's verses on the death of Lord Hastings, shows a preoccupation with the symptoms of smallpox; but Rochester's *pustula vulnus* cannot compare with Dryden's rosebud sores filled with tears. Rochester's line of poetic reasoning is based on simple premises: smallpox is incurable; and if a lady erupts with it, she may as well be dead since her beauty is destroyed.

> Vultu foemineo quaevis vel pustula vulnus
> Lethale est, pulchras certior ense necat.[37]
> (The pustulent sore is deadly to the female face:
> It kills beauty as surely as the cutting sword.)

The Latin lines display an awareness of syntactic balance and contrast of the sort characteristic of later neo-classical English verse:

> Evadat forsan femina, Diva nequat.
> (Escapes perhaps the woman, the Goddess cannot ever.)

And the concluding couplet evokes a Platonic contrast between the transient beauty of the body and the complete, formal beauty (*tota venustas*) of the mind. As a specimen of Anglo-Latin poetry of the day, "In Obitum" is far from contemptible; it is discernibly better than the Latin poem in 1661 known to be Robert Whitehall's.[38]

Of the three poems that could have been influenced by Whitehall, "To Her Sacred Majesty, the Queen Mother" is most like Whitehall's own compositions. Its forty-eight lines display the verbal padding, irregular meters, and awkward syntax typical of Whitehall. There are the same tactless, even gauche, sentiments:

> You that in mighty wrongs an Age have spent,
> And seem to have out-liv'd even bannishment:
> Whom traiterous mischeif sought its earliest prey,
> When unto sacred blood it made its way;
> And thereby did its black designe impart,
> To take his head, that wounded first his heart:
> You that unmov'd great Charles his ruine stood
> When that three Nations sunk beneath the load. . . .

To be sure, the boy Rochester might have written such a piece without Whitehall's cooperation. Even the greatest poetic genius needs to practice its craft, leaving behind *juvenelia* that the poet's admirers would like to ignore. Rochester has left samples of adult poetry even cruder than "To Her Sacred Majesty."[39] Nevertheless, we may tentatively conclude that young Wilmot was the author of "To His Sacred Majesty" and "In Obitum." If he also wrote "To Her Sacred Majesty," he at least went on to write far better works, whereas Whitehall did not.

Rochester's poetic tributes to the King, his sister, and mother were meant to call attention to the son of Henry Wilmot, who had served the Stuart cause so long and with such ultimate sacrifice. The poems alone did not attain this end. The King had a retentive memory for his friends and Rochester's mother; and her brother-in-law, Sir Allen Apsley, Keeper of the Purse for the Duke of York, stood ready to jog it or appeal to Lord Clarendon if it lapsed. Charles II was well aware of Lord Wilmot's son. In February 1661, young Rochester was granted an annual pension of £1500, retroactive to the previous year.[40] In September 1661 Edward Hyde, Lord Clarendon—the King's representative as well as an old friend of Rochester's grandfather, mother, and father—bestowed an honorary Master's degree on the fourteen-year-old boy, who was wearing a scarlet doctor's gown, and kissed him affectionately on the left cheek.[41]

Although his time at Oxford as a student was ending, Rochester continued to return there in future years, keeping up ties with Robert Whitehall, Dr. John Fell, Dr. Thomas Pierce, and other University officials. He also took on protégés, notably John Oldham, and established friendships with William Wycherley, Francis Fane, and other Oxford alumni. His affection for his alma mater had been firmly established during his reckless student days. Characteristically, the new graduate ordered four handsome silver pint pots as a gift to Wadham and departed from Oxford, leaving unpaid debts among the tradesmen.[42]

4

THE GRAND TOUR (1662–1664)

The Knowledge of these Secrets, I gathered in my Travels
abroad (where I have spent my Time ever since I was Fifteen
Years old . . . in France and Italy. . . .)
—Rochester, *Dr. Bendo's Advertisement*

In keeping with family practice, the young Earl was to make the Grand Tour to complete his education; but Robert Whitehall was not to accompany the Tourist, for all his poetic effusions.[1] The King appointed Dr. Andrew Balfour, a graduate in medicine at the University of Caen, as Wilmot's *Gubernator* (governor); and a pass was issued on November 21, 1661, permitting him to travel beyond seas without restriction. Both the choice of tutor and the unrestricted pass allowing him to go into Italy had significant effects on John Wilmot.[2]

Dr. Balfour, a Scot, had lived abroad for fifteen years and had absorbed sophisticated tolerance with his continental education. As a classicist specializing in physic (i.e., medicine), he was like Robert Whitehall, but the similarity stopped there. Balfour was a genuine scholar and intellectual who went on to eminence as a botanist and physician. He collected ancient coins with expertise; he spoke excellent Latin; and he was a natural-born teacher.[3] In 1668, four years after returning from his tour with Rochester, Dr. Balfour wrote a travel guide to France and Italy for a Scottish nobleman, Lord Murray. Published in 1700, the *Letters Write* [*sic*] *to a Friend* provides useful information about the probable Grand Tour he supervised for John Wilmot. The section on Italy clearly reflects their experiences.[4]

Assuming his role as Wilmot's governor in 1661, Balfour soon realized what damage the lacuna in his charge's education at Oxford had done. Balfour did not have a high opinion of Wadham in the first place; he omitted it from his list of the best Oxford colleges.[5] Consequently, he began a strategy that his pupil long remembered. Gilbert Burnet wrote:

[Rochester] often acknowledged to me, in particular three days before his Death, how much he was obliged to Love and Honour this his

Governour . . . for his great Fidelity and Care of him, when he was under
his trust. But no part of it affected him more sensibly, than that he engaged
him by many tricks (so he expressed it) to delight in Books and reading. . . .[6]

The books Balfour used to trick Rochester were the classical works, even the
French romances, referred to in his *Letters*. As a student, Rochester learned
some French and Italian during his stay abroad, and he grew acquainted with
plays, satires, and *libertin* works in those languages.

The travelers and their entourage set out for France in late 1661, or early
1662, when John Wilmot was in his fifteenth year. They left from London,
stopping south of the Thames in Southwark to get horses from the Rye carrier
and give him their baggage. After a two-day ride, they stayed in Rye until they
could get passage across the Channel. After landing at Dieppe, they lodged *À la
Bastile* ("they are all verie civil people") and shopped for tortoise shell combs
and ivory boxes before going on to Rouen. In Rouen, they took in the sights
and climbed to the top of the great Church to see "the biggest bell in the
world." They took a side trip to Santeville to taste the famous cream and, insofar as the season allowed, to permit Balfour to start his practice of collecting
plants or "Herbalize by the way." They then took the messenger to Paris for
13 or 14 francs each (horse, lodging, and diet included). Once there, they stayed
with M. Haes and his family ("very honest people") in Faubourg St. Germain
until they could find more suitable, permanent quarters.[7]

Balfour felt that in winter there was little to be seen or learned outside Paris,
so he and Rochester remained in the city from January until June 1662.[8] There
was, of course, a great deal to see and do in Paris and its vicinity. Balfour's
botanical interests led him—and his charge—to many gardens: the Luxembourg,
King's, Tuilleries, and some private ones. Balfour's interest in "herbalizing"
and the role of plants in medicine stimulated John Wilmot's own interest in
such matters, begun possibly as the boy listened to his Aunt Joanna exchange
"receipts" with old Aunt Isham back at Ditchley. Balfour may even have seen
to it that Rochester enrolled in M. Barlet's course in "chymie" at the College
de Camray for three weeks ("ten Crowns for the Course, and two Crownes for
his Book"). In later life, Rochester showed his interest by reading medical
books, concocting home remedies and swapping them with friends, posing as a
physician, and keeping a home collection of "chimists" (chemicals).[9]

The many libraries and booksellers in Paris helped Balfour begin his campaign to seduce his pupil back to books and reading. The King's Library and
bookstalls on the Rue St. Jacques and the new bridge behind Notre Dame
were places to browse and purchase. New books were to be found at the Palace
Gate, "*French* Books, as *Romances*, &c" at the Place de Sorbonne, and old books
of all sorts at Mont. St. Hiller.[10]

Balfour had a number of contacts in Paris, many of them Catholic. M. Marchant, for example, not only had an admirable garden; he also could direct one to Barlet's course at Cambray, show where to get mathematical instruments and microscopes, or have a portrait painted. In the Jesuits College, "a Scots Father" showed visitors around the Bibliothek and Mathematical House, where the hypotheses of Copernicus, Tycho Brahe, and Ptolomeus were represented in motion.[11]

Outside Paris, many other fascinating sights could be seen. At the Abbey of St. Denys, the travelers saw one of the nails "that fixed our *Saviour's* Bodie to the Cross," a pot from the wedding at Cana, the "Lantern that was carried before *Judas*, when He betrayed our Saviour; and a thousand other things of great Value." Dr. Balfour's interest in the relics of Catholic France was genuine and constant throughout the tour with Rochester. His predilections may have been one reason King Charles chose him as Rochester's guide to France and Italy.[12]

Other trips to Paris outskirts included visits to Malmaison and Versailles ("A House begun by the late King, but finished by the present, a most delicat fine place").[13] A trip to St. Cloud, "A House belonging to the present Duke of *Orleans*," permitted Rochester to present himself formally and kiss the hand of Madame the Duchess. As a matter of course, King Charles provided a letter to Madame, his favorite sister, Henrietta—or "Minette," as he called her.[14] She had been escorted to France by the Duke of Buckingham in 1661 to make a royal marriage intended to strengthen diplomatic ties between Charles and his cousin, the French monarch. Her husband, Monsieur the Duke of Orleans, a bisexual transvestite, was the brother of Louis XIV. Madame could provide entry into royal circles for the young English lord.

One can only conjecture about the acquaintances Rochester made during his first visit to France. In later years, he had an intimate knowledge of gossip in the circles around the Sun King. He could have met Philibert Comte de Gramont (or Grammont) as early as 1662. Their acquaintance was documented by both men, and they knew each other before 1665, as Gramont's own gossipy *Memoirs* of the Court of St. James makes clear.[15] Gramont was a practitioner of the philosophical and sexual *libertinage* that began in France in the early seventeenth century in the skeptical tradition of Montaigne, and that found expression in the writings of such wits as Théophile de Viau, Maturin Regnier, Jean DeHenault, Antoine Baraby de La Luzerne, and Jacques Valée Des Barreaux.[16]

At the time Rochester visited France on his Grand Tour, the last three were still alive, as were Nicolas Boileau-Despréaux (1636–1711), witty poet and critic, and François the Duc de La Rochefoucauld (1613–1680) whose satires and *maximes* were being circulated and talked about in the early 1660. Rochester's later writings imply knowledge of these French *littérateurs* but explicit evidence of his reading their published works is no stronger than evidence that he met the men themselves in 1661–1664, although one critic has suggested that Rochester actually met Des Barreaux.

The English youth may have been introduced by Madame to the dramas of Pierre Corneille or even to the eminent author himself. Corneille's *La Toison d'or* (The Golden Fleece) was staged late in 1661, and *Sertorius* early in 1662.[17] It is even more likely that Rochester met Molière through Madame. The rising playwright had attracted the attention and sponsorship of Monsieur in 1658 with a *divertissement* after a play of Corneille's. Early in 1662, Molière was working on his *succès de scandale*, *L'École des femmes* (The School for Wives), which ran for nine months with time out for revisions. It is amusing to conjecture that Rochester's interest in sexually risqué drama was stimulated early on, in part by Molière.[18]

Rochester delighted in music, and he retained his fondness for French *aires* all of his life, taking pleasure in them when other sources of pleasure failed him. Jean-Baptiste Lully, the Master of Court Music, had attained great prominence in 1661, and in 1662 he began his collaboration with Molière. Lully became a particular favorite of Rochester's, whose own "Song" compositions possibly owed to his early delight in the sung music of Lully. Some of Rochester's "Songs" were set to music during the Earl's lifetime; and one scholar has suggested that they were actually sung at Court. Other Songs, set to music after his death, influenced lyric traditions.[19]

Whatever the effects of his exposure to the arts and libertine practices of the French Court may have been, Rochester's education remained firmly under the control of Andrew Balfour. After residing in Paris until May to see the King's garden in full bloom, they left in June 1662 for a summer tour through "the Garden of *France*," along the Loire from Orleans to Nantes. After Orleans, they went to Blois, noted for its watch-making, excellent claret, and pure French, according to Balfour. The castle garden was supervised by a friend of Balfour's, and they spent time there. They took day trips to Chambord to the palace of François I, and probably to Vendome to view "the Holy Teare, which is preserved in the Cathedrall Church with much veneration."[20]

From Blois to Amboise to Tours, they visited caves, noted rare lizards and birds, and saw the largest pair of hart's horns in existence. Tours was the site of the convent where St. Francis was buried, "which People visit with great Veneration."[21] Saumaise was "famous for it's [sic] Protestant University" but Balfour thought it worth taking pains to see the Notre Dame d'Ardeliers, "a Place of great devotion." They took horses for a three-day trip to Doué with its Roman amphitheater; Loudon, where they saw an old woman formerly possessed by demons but miraculously cured when the rubric JESUSMARIAJOSEPH appeared on her hand; Chinon, where Rabelais had his first breeding in a convent; and a monastery where the Lady Abbess was sister to Henrietta Maria, the Queen Mother of England.[22]

The tutor and pupil went through La Flèche (the Jesuits College, "by far the best they have in *France*"), Angiers (another wine pot from Cana), and by water to Nantes. They were at the farthest point of their route and ready to return to Paris. At Le Mans Balfour discovered a new variety of citrus—he carried a carpetbag to stow the results of his herbalizing—and they stopped at Chartres to gaze at "the great Church thereof (which is a most stately Fabrick)." It was then early August, and time to stay in Paris during the "Dog Days" to plan the next trip to Provence and Languedoc.[23]

When the hot weather ended, they started out again for southern France by messenger; Lyons had many worthwhile sights, especially the Church of St. John with figures of "the blessed Virgine" and an angel in the pose of the Annunciation.[24] From Lyons, they took a boat down the Rhone to Avignon, stopping at Vienne to look at "*Le Maisone de Pillate* [*sic*], . . . the retreat of *Pontius Pilate*, driven here, by, God knows, what accident." Avignon and the surrounding country were the property of the Pope, governed by a Papal Legate. Balfour felt it important to stay several days to see everything: the Churches and Religious Houses, the Legate's Palace, and the Jewry, "where the Jewes dwell." It was worth staying through Saturday "to see their *Synagogue* and manner of Worship . . . and possibly see a *Circumcision*."

Near Avignon was Orange, held by the Dutch king, the site of a Roman triumphal arch and theater, "both of which shows something of the *Roman* Greatness in Respect of Modern Times."[25] The waterfall at Vaucluse was a great sight to witness; and so were the ruins of two castles, "whereof did sometimes live that noble Philosopher and Poet *Franciscus Petrarcha* and . . . *Donna Laura* his Mistress." Balfour admired the Sonnets vastly, "in which her Memorie is like to live as long as Wit and Learning continues in reputation." Rochester's governor was a man of polymathic interests, from Roman history to herbs, Roman Catholicism to love lyrics of the Italian Renaissance. He imparted many of these to his pupil.[26]

It appears that in the autumn of 1662, they went a circuitous route from Avignon back to Paris.[27] They marveled at the Roman aqueduct. Nîmes itself had a "brave Amphitheater built by the *Romans*, in greater integritie yet than any that ever I saw in *Italy*." In Montpellier they lingered, getting acquainted with faculty at the University. Rochester retained only happy memories of Montpellier, carrying a doctor's gown as a souvenir and, years later, donning it in nostalgic disguise. He hoped always to return there someday.[28] At Pesenas, they saw the gardens of Prince Condé, the libertine founder of the Order of Sodomites; at Narbonne, they visited the church with its painting showing Lazarus being raised from the dead. Toulouse had much to visit, including the Cordelier, where hundreds of dried corpses stood about the walls, one being a king's former mistress. The water journey to Bordeaux enabled them to visit Julius Caesar Scaliger's birthplace; and in Bordeaux they feasted on truffles and ortolans.[29] The remainder of the trip was equally instructive.

Back in Paris for the winter of 1662–63, they planned their future expedition to Italy. Since Dr. Balfour believed that one ought to go from France to Italy in the late autumn rather than the spring, they had ample time to see the parts of Provence they had missed before.[30] So in the summer of 1663, they set out once again for the Provence, this time heading east to Marseilles and Monaco.

Balfour's points of interest in Marseilles included the Cathedral Church in the architectural style of a temple to Diana, and the market filled with Levantine treasures including trees of red coral.[31] On their journey to Fravole, they stopped at St. Beaume, where "in the midle [sic] of a vast and terrible Rock, there is a great cave where *St. Maria Magdalen* did penance for many years before her death"; once a day the angels had carried the saints there to console the penitent. It had been made into a chapel, "a Place of much Devotion." In a small town nearby was the relic of Mary Magdalen's uncle, a former Bishop of Marseilles.[32]

They continued on to Cannes and Nice; after a trip to Monaco to see the palace and the Prince's wardrobe, they returned to Cannes to hire a felucca to take them into Italy. Balfour wrote:

> A Felluck will serve to carrie half a dozen of persons with ease, besides the Rowers. . . . You may provide every morning to take along with you, Wine and what Victuals you please, the rather because sometimes it will happen that you will have no conveniency of any Town about Mid-day, and therefore must Dine aboard Your Fellucke.[33]

Sailing along the Riviera, they made stops to see the sights or stay overnight and get provisions.

Once into Liguria, they had to send a boatman ashore with their papers before landing. There was a great dread of the Plague in Liguria; foreign travelers needed certificates of freedom from infection before they could enter. Balfour and Rochester had taken care to get their certificates at Cannes before embarking.[34] But if Rochester's body was free from bubonic infection, he had entered a country that many Englishmen believed would infect his mind most fatally.

Arriving in Italy, Rochester and his guide encountered customs men. Firearms had to be left at town gates, though dagger-wearing was permitted in Naples, Venice, and Milan. They were also searched for any "Prohibited Book," but the worldly bibliophile, Dr. Balfour, soon discovered bribes: "yet there are wayes enough to convey Books, or any other thing of whatsoever Nature . . . which you will easily understand, after your being a while in the Country."[35] Balfour decided that the water was not safe to drink anywhere in Italy. The travelers would have to make do with wine.

After a final disembarkation from the *felluca*, Rochester and Balfour resumed their land journey with a retinue of servants and dogs. Their first major stop was "*Genoua la Superba*, so called from the sumptuousness of its buildings . . . it is said they account usury no great Sin."[36] In Livorno (Leghorn), a free-trade city, they were hosted by the resident colony of English merchants in the Levant trade. Here they easily shipped to England the cargo of souvenirs they had acquired in France; Dr. Balfour quickly mastered the art of writing lading-bills. He also relished the "delicat" oysters available in Livorno.[37]

In Pisa the tourists saw "the crooked Steeple, which leanes to one side very far from the perpendicular." Balfour explained that "the ground hath misgiven on the one side by little and little, or rather, insensibly, which may be some part of the Reason why it hath hung together so long without falling. . . ." After a brief trip to the republic of Lucca they took horses to Florence, "a new Town, but one of the most beautifull in all *Italy*."[38] The beauties of Florence commanded their attention for some days. They saw the ducal palaces, the treasures of the Uffizi, the statue of Perseus with the head of Medusa, the Duomo with its multicolored marbles and brass doors, Sante Croce and Michelangelo's tomb, the Medici Chapel (unfinished but "the most Glorious thing extant in the world"), and many other wonders. An English compatriot, Dr. Kirton, a physician, helpfully directed them to the best booksellers and places worth visiting.[39]

When they finally left for Rome, they chose the *Viturin* way of travel, hiring horses and paying for their own "entertainment" at each stop. As Balfour thought, "it is best to be Master of your own Purse, and not live at the discretion of Your Conductor." This method exposed them to "some Incommoditie," however. The sheets at Italian inns were "very nasty" and if money or "fair words" could not procure clean ones, they had to sleep in their clothes, covering their heads and taking care not to "touch any unclean thing."[40] Of the hill towns along the way, Siena claimed their notice because of the relic in the Church of St. Dominic—St. Catherine's head—and the library of Aeneas Sylvius, once a Papal legate to Scotland and afterward himself Pope Pius II. Montesiascone had a famous muscatel wine worth stopping for. (A German once drank himself to death there in muscatelic frenzy!) And Viterbo, the last stop before the Campagna di Roma, had interesting flora to inspect.[41]

Had they been going through the Campagna in the summer, they would have traveled by night to avoid sleeping there (and possibly getting malarial fever); but, since they were on the road in late October or early November, they rode horseback by day. Arriving at last at the walls of Rome, they declared their destination, went through Customs, and received their official billet. They then proceeded to the English *pensione* in la strada del Populo, the alla villa di Londra, until they could learn of "a convenient *Camera locanda*." Young Lord Rochester had arrived in the citadel of Popery.[42]

Dr. Balfour had confidential friends in the highest levels of the Vatican. One was an Englishman, William Lesly, of whom Balfour spoke in the language of nuance:

> *Signior don Gulielmo Lesly* . . . is Chaplain to Cardinal *Carlo Barberino* and lives *nella Cancellaria*. I dare be confident to give you this man for one of the most faithfull Friends in the World, and one in whose goodness, prudence, Kindness, and good Conduct you may trust ten Thousand Lives: to be short you will find I am not mistaken, when I call him *deliciae Lumani generis*, [*sic*] for in all my lifetime I never knew another like him. . . .[43]

The prudent and trustworthy Fr. Lesly saw to it that John Wilmot and his tutor were extended a most cordial reception by the Holy Mother Church. Lesly introduced them to his patron, Cardinal Barberino, one of the most powerful men of the most powerful families in the Vatican aristocracy. The Cardinal received them graciously, saw that they were permitted to scrutinize rare manuscripts belonging to his brother, Cardinal Francesco Barberino, the Cardinal-Protector of England; and when they left Rome, he provided letters of entry to other Catholic plenipotentiaries.[44] Throughout their residence of approximately four months in Rome, Rochester and his guide were given royal treatment by Church officials. They were conducted personally through the Vatican Library by the Papal Librarian, the distinguished Leo Allatius.[45] They toured the art gallery, admiring the Laocoön and other classic works of art. They strolled through the private Vatican gardens laid out by Tobias Aldinus. And, through the kind agency of Fr. Lesly, they attended "The Court; that is, the Pope [Alexander VII], Cardinals, Prelates, Monsigniore &c" and were present on "great Holy days, when the Pope Celebrats Mass in person" to see "the Grandeur of the Court and the forme of a Cavalcata, together with the Pope's ordinary Guards."[46]

All this attention was calculated. After all, the young English Lord had been given special permission to travel into Italy by King Charles II, whose private inclination toward Catholicism was probably conjectured if not positively known by persons *nella Cancellaria*. The Vatican potentates surely knew about the leanings of the Duke of York. What a triumph for Holy Mother Church if the son of the famous Henry Wilmot, and a favorite of the English King and the Heir Apparent, should become a Catholic convert, or Recusant![47]

The lure of Catholicism must have been strong for John Wilmot. Before leaving England, he had seen such prominent Catholics as Henrietta Maria the Queen Mother, Henry Jermyn the Baron of Dover, Lord Bellasis, Baron Arundell of Wardour, and many others established at court. His own second cousin, Barbara Palmer, had converted to become one of a series of Catholic royal mistresses. And he knew of Charles II's marriage in 1662 to the Catholic Princess of Portugal, Catherine of Braganza, on terms providing for Catholic chapels to be established at Whitehall.[48]

Moreover, his travels had shown him that wealth and power were attached to alliance with the Vatican. At the Catholic French Court, King Charles's own sister, Madame, was a Roman Catholic. Paris was home to many Irish Catholic supporters of Charles, who were unable to return to England after the Restoration because of the First Act of Settlement. In 1662 they had reason to hope that the King and his ministers would soon persuade Parliament to ease its strictures on Catholic Royalists.[49] In Rome, the Italian and Vatican aristocracies openly flaunted power and riches appealing to a young English Lord with little real property but great expectations and a sense of aristocratic superiority.

Most of all, the terrible prospect of eternal damnation in a flaming hell that Rochester had been taught in Protestant England could be lessened by the Catholic rites of Confession, Penitence, and the granting of Indulgences: the opportunity to escape divine punishment by donating to the Church treasury. Any guilty fears that John Wilmot had taken upon himself through his "disorders" at Oxford could be obliterated by buying a Pardon. English Puritans deplored the moral loopholes of Roman Catholicism: "Of all religions, to the carnal man none is so pleasant as Popery is, in which be so many kinds of satisfaction to be obtained." These satisfactions could exert great appeal for apprehensive sinners, however. In a poem attributed to Rochester, the attraction of Popery was explicated sardonically:

> If *Rome* can pardon Sins, as *Romans* hold . . .
> If they can purchase *Pardons* with a Sum,
> For Sins they may commit in time to come,
> And for Sins past, 'tis very well for *Rome*.

Whether Rochester succumbed to that attraction during his Grand Tour under the broadminded supervision of Dr. Balfour has not yet been discovered.

Possibly, he did. If so, he obviously would have to take scrupulous care to keep his conversion a secret for many reasons, not the least being that, whatever their hopes, Catholics in England were still subject to forfeiting their rights, wealth, and property.

While Rochester contemplated the attractions of Catholicism, Dr. Balfour was bringing to life Roman history and literature. The Farnese Palace had "the noblest piece of Art extant in *Rome*": a *tauro* mentioned by Pliny. The Bernini fountain in the Piazza Navona with its Egyptian obelisk was sometimes permitted to overflow so that in the evenings, while taking the air, the gentry could ride their carriages through the water, "which is one of the greatest *Gusto's* in *Rome*."[50] The Medici palace had the statue of Venus "of *Grecian Antiquitie*" and ruins restored by Michelangelo. They also went to Hadrian's tomb, the Capitoline with its many Roman artifacts and the equestrian statue of Marcus Aurelius, the Temple of Minerva, the Pantheon, the Colosseum, the Baths of Caracalla and Diocletian, the aqueducts, the forum of Trajan, and the arches of Titus and Septimius Severus.[51]

Rochester was getting a thorough indoctrination into Roman history with his classical tour. They even went into the catacombs:

> They are *Caverns* digg'd under ground in the forme of a Town and all along as you go upon the one Hand and the other, as thick as they can stand one by another, are holes or nests wherein were placed the bodies of the Dead, one by one, upright upon their feet, and so the nests Plastered over. The Bodies and reliques of many Saints and Martyrs have been found here . . . with the Inscription *Pro CHRISTO*. You must take good lights and a good guide to conduct You, for some have mistaken their Way and never found an outgate.[52]

We can only speculate about Rochester's response to his trip into the labyrinthine, claustrophobic House of Death. With his fear of the dark and his apprehension of dying, he could not have gone without fear that he might lose the way and perish in prolonged agony, surrounded by corpses. He may have been impelled toward a more indulgent Roman Catholic form of Christianity. Or he may have escaped into the emotional release of erotic carnality, as he would do habitually later on.

There were many sexual temptations in Rome. The English generally expected that young men on the Grand Tour would acquire some sexual experience before returning home, and Italy was viewed as offering maximum opportunities.[53] Rochester may have first discovered such sexual artifacts as dildos and pictorial erotica in unsupervised rambles about the Eternal City. In his writings, he specifically associated the dildo, or artificial phallos, and the *Postures* of Pietro Aretino with his sojourn in Italy.[54]

He assuredly discovered Aretino's writings and saw the famous headless statue just off the Piazza Navona to which scrawled personal insults were attached. Indeed, he may have been introduced to Aretino's wit by Dr. Balfour. On a visit to the Pantheon, a pagan temple to all the gods, Balfour noted that the brass doors had been stripped by Pope Urban VIII, a Barberino pontiff, to adorn the altar of St. Peter's. The doors were then replaced with lead, and Urban VIII ordered an inscription celebrating himself for preserving them. Balfour observed, "Upon this occasion was that *Pasquinad; Quod non fecerent Barbari, fecere Barberini.*" ("What the Barbarians did not do, the Barberini did.")[55]

Pietro Aretino, the "Scourge of Princes," (1492–1556) had transformed such insults into a distinctive literary style or mode, the *pasquinate* or *pasquinade*. John Wilmot's own future *pasquinades*—or lampoons, as they came to be called in England—resembled those of Aretino, making Rochester something of a Scourge of Princes himself at the Court of St. James. Aretino's *sonetti lussuriosi*, attached to the erotic drawings of Giulio Romano, the *pozitione* or *Postures* were replete with demotic references to *cazzi, potta, cul,* and *genti fottenti e fottuti,* despite Aretino's disingenuous claim of writing "chaste" language. Rochester in time penned the English equivalents of Aretino's Italian. Moreover, Aretino's *ragionamenti* or dialogues between sexually-experienced women were echoed in Rochester's verse satires.[56]

Italy also acquainted John Wilmot with puppet shows, the *commedia dell'arte* and characters from other farcical plays: the irascible, devil-defying Punchinello; Harlequin the motley wit and romantic clown; and especially Scaramuchio, the braggart-poltroon who sometimes appeared as a Spanish grandee. His boyish delight in these Italian stereotypes remained with him. When traveling companies made the comic figures widely known in England in the 1670s, Rochester was satirically linked with "Scaramouch" even as he lampooned John Sheffield the Earl of Mulgrave by terming him Punchinello and Harlequin.[57]

Before leaving the Eternal City, Balfour made sure Rochester visited the holy sites of Christianity and Catholicism as well as the pagan monuments.[58] It was then late February of 1664 and, according to Dr. Balfour, time for an expedition to Naples. Accordingly, they set out on the Appian Way, where Balfour continued his lectures: quoting Juvenal on the wine of Setia and citing Strabo on the geography of Terracina. Cicero had his villa at Mola; and nearby was a huge rock, rent from top to bottom, "which they say, happened when the Saviour of the World Suffered upon the Cross."[59] There were potential hazards on the way through the Campagnia: the Turks occasionally landed along the shore, and brigands swooped down from the hills to terrorize travelers. The customs men of Naples could be demanding, but "a little Money" accomplished wonders. And the marvelous sights were worth the trouble.

As Balfour pragmatically remarked, "But he that will gather Roses, must not be affraid [*sic*] to prick his Fingers"[60]

Naples provided sites that enabled Balfour to quote the classical writers Rochester had studied at Burford. There were many Catholic sites and relics to visit as well: the churches were the most numerous of any European city. There were Norman forts and Spanish castles to see, tombs to visit, and the markets filled with exotica from Aleppo and Constantinople to inspect, to say nothing of the wonderful book stalls.[61] Side trips took them to Virgil's tomb, the black, dismal Lake Avernus, the Elysian Fields (blooming with anemones in March), and other sites made immortal by the *Aeneid*.[62]

When they visited the Grotto de I Cani, they practiced the inadvertent cruelty to animals typical of the times. There, when dogs were overcome by the fumes, they were revived by being thrown into the lake.

> I remember one of our Dogs did recover without being thrown into the Lake. . . . It is very True that, That [dog] which was thrown in the Lake recovered much sooner and better; whereas the other remained paralytick and impotent to move his hinder quarters (tho' he could Sit upon his foremost Leggs and bark). . . .[63]

Rochester's tutor was a mixture of religious credulity and scientific skepticism, like many of his peers.

Visiting Cumae, they saw the very cave where Aeneas had encountered the Sybil. Balfour quoted Virgil at length.[64] Near Baia they came to a ruin that apparently captured Rochester's imagination: "The House of *Agrippina, Nero's* Mother, who was put to Death here by her Sons [*sic*] Command." His fascination with Nero and the Neronian Court was to haunt John Wilmot later.[65] Before leaving Naples, the two travelers went to Mount Vesuvius, "the burning Hill, about 8 miles distant from the Town." When they stood at the top, surveying the "Field of Ashes of uncertain deepthness [*sic*]," the smoke and flame left Balfour—and Rochester—with a mental image of hellish devastation and a ruined city.[66]

Their itinerary demanded that they return to Rome in April: if one did not leave Rome before May 20, opined Balfour, the weather became too hot to journey on, at least until September. So Rochester and his mentor once again went to Rome. They left Rome in early May, bound for Venice.[67] In Loretto, the Governor provided a guide to show them the sights. These included "the House in which the blessed Virgin is said to have been born": it was "brought hither from *Judea* Miraculously by *Angels*, as is beleeved" and contained "a little Dish, out of which our Saviour is said to have Eat his Meat whilst he was yet a Babe."[68] For once, Dr. Balfour's pious credulity was severely tested, as his rhetorical qualifications indicate.

At Rimini, they visited the Malatesta palace and Roman monuments. Soon after, they crossed the Rubicon, pausing at the historic river to record the Latin inscription on a pillar to Caesar and Innocent X.[69] They went on to Bologna, visiting the Church of Corpus Christi to see:

> the intire Body of St. Katharine ... that Died at *Bolognia*, in the Year 1463. She sits in a Chair, with a Religious Habit. ... In one Hand She holds a Crucifix, the other is placed upon a Pillow. They use in the presence of a great deal of Companie to paire her Nails every Month, and to cut her Hair once a Year, after they are grown.[70]

They also saw the library of Ulysses Aldrovandus, the great botanist, in the palace of the Papal Legate. Balfour venerated Aldrovandus but neglected to purchase his works.

In Ferrara, they paid homage at the sepulcher of "the famous Poet *Ariosto*" before going to Venice. By this time, it was July. They arrived at the Queen of the Adriatic and gazed upon it with wonder: "Nothing in Nature can appear more prodigious than to see a Vast big Town seated in the middle of the Sea. . . ." The English Consul, Giles Jacob, welcomed them and gave them lodging in his own house, where they stayed for nine or ten weeks, reveling in Venetian delights.[71]

Everything about Venice was dazzling: the Rialto, St. Marks with its four Byzantine horses, the Doge's palace, the grand new Palladian church of San Giorgio Maggiore erected when Venice was spared the plague in 1576, Murano glass, and of course the fleet of gondolas, reminiscent of the water boats on the Thames at home but "much cleaner and finer."[72] Most impressive of all was Venetian music:

> it were to be wished that a Man might happen to be at *Venice* in the time of the Carnaval, because of the *Opera's* and fine shows that are to be seen, and the Extraordinarie Musick at that time. In the *Summer* time the great Divertisement is to go in Gondole upon the great Canale, where towards the Evening, one may see Five, or six hundred Gondols touring up and down, full of Ladies and Gentlemen, &c severalls of them with Musick, both Vocal and Instrumental; which is one of the greatest *Gusto's* imaginable.[73]

As Balfour indicated, opera was flourishing in Venice; but Claudio Monteverdi's *The Coronation of Poppaea* (1642) had fallen into silence by the 1660s. The frankly sexual, amoral libretto by Gian Francesco Busenello was published in the 1650s, however, and had become a popular text for Venetian libertines. Rochester could have discovered Busenello's text and been stimulated in his own burgeoning libertinism, together with his interest in Nero and Poppea Sabina, piqued earlier in Baia and apparent in his involvement with Lee's *Nero* ten years later.[74] *Poppea* told the story of the seduction of the bi-sexual Emperor Nero by Poppea, the wife of the future Emperor Otho. Roman decadence found modern forms in Venetian practices of the seventeenth century.

At the time of his visit, various sexual activities were flourishing so openly that Rochester could hardly avoid observing them. The famous Venetian courtesans, whose specialized techniques were pictured in Romano's illustrations in the *Postures*, were much on the scene. Some of them dressed as men to cater to the male taste for sodomy.[75] And homosexual friendships had grown increasingly popular among Venetian men from 1620 to 1650, with some leading citizens openly living with male lovers. Newly turned seventeen, Rochester was sufficiently adult to elude Dr. Balfour's supervision; he may even have donned a mask and domino to join in the Venetian refinements of love.

The Venetian visit ended all too soon, but the travelers had to cross the Alps before the winter snows fell. They began the last lap of their tour, going to Padua in early October. Padua supplied not only more antique relics but the University as well. Rochester signed the Visitor's book on October 26, 1664.[76] After Padua, they went on to Vicenza and Verona, sightseeing as they went. They paused on the shores of Lago di Garda, where Balfour was delighted by French cuisine at low prices.[77] Refreshed, they proceeded to Brescia and Bergamo (where there was a rare library at the Dominican retreat).

Milano lay ahead. They viewed its glories with somewhat jaded eyes. The Duomo was "one of the greatest and most Glorious in *Italy* . . . but that which is to be pitied is, that the design is *Gothick*."[78] Moreover, it was unfinished after two hundred years of work and too dark inside. The Exchange, castle and fortress of the Sforzas, and other sites received dutiful regard. They visited the Lazaretto, unused between 1658 and 1663 but ready to shelter victims if the Plague struck again. Ironically, at the time Rochester and Balfour were there, the Plague had already been introduced into Holland by a Turkish ship and was finding its way into England.[79]

En route from Milan to Pavia, they spent the night at a Carthusian monastery. Once in Turin, they went to see the famous Shroud, "upon which the *Visage* of our Saviour & the greatest part of his Body is impressed."[80] They were to cross the Alps from Turin to Lyons; so they left Turin at ten o'clock in the morning one November day, and proceeded into the hill village of Monte Cene, where they hired muleteers to take them through the Alps. Balfour had heard some horrifying tales from other travelers about the perils of the steep ascent on the Italian side in the winter. The French side was equally perilous:

> So that verie often you will chance to pass under horrible Rocks that hang over the high way, and when the Snow is new fallen and they loaden with it, the least noise in the World would bring down a whole Mountain of

Snow. So that if a Passinger were so caught, you might look upon him as
buried till the following Spring.[81]

Aware of these dangers, Balfour saw to it that his charge crossed the Alps
before the heavy snows. They were carried by porters in wooden seats or "bar-
rows" part of the way until they reached a plain above the cloud line, where
they rode horseback until the descent.[82] On the French side, they rode down
in guided sleighs; and after a few days' travel, they arrived safely outside
Grenoble, where the Carthusian monks at the Charter House (the Grande
Chartreuse) made them welcome. They stayed for a couple of days in the
rooms formerly reserved for English Catholics before "their defection from the
Faith." Leaving "a little Drink-Money to the Servants," they departed for
Grenoble and Lyons.[83]

And so they came to Paris. Now a clever, handsome young man in his eighteenth year, manners polished by his continental experiences, Rochester paid
his compliments to Madame and renewed his French acquaintance. Corneille's
Othon, a neo-Roman drama about one of Nero's successors to the throne, was
acted late in 1664; and so was the early version of Molière's *Tartuffe*, the exposé
of clerical hypocrisy.[84] The English youth may have had a last continental
insight into the complexities of paganism and Catholicism through the Parisian
theatre.

When Rochester left Paris, Madame made him the bearer of a letter to her
brother. It is likely that she wittingly inaugurated Rochester as a courier
between them in their hidden counterpart to public negotiations between
France and England.[85] Rochester would willingly act in this role in the future.
Thus John Wilmot's continental Grand Tour came to a close. He had seen a
rich array of cultures, been exposed to beliefs that utterly contradicted those of
his boyhood, and been taught in steady company by a man at once knowl-
edgeable, skeptical, and credulous. Andrew Balfour was venerated by his grateful pupil; his role in creating Wilmot's emotional and intellectual dilemmas can
not be underestimated. He even stayed with the Wilmots for a time, once the
travelers were back in England.[86]

After three years of studying abroad and living privately, Rochester returned
to Restoration court life. On Christmas Eve in 1664, he presented Madame's
letter to the King at Whitehall, making a ceremonial reentry into public life. It
was the beginning of a meteoric career that made him the symbol of his age.
Suitably enough, his return was accompanied by a comet streaking across the
wintry skies of London, to the fascination of those who saw it.[87]

5

CAMPAIGNS AND ENGAGEMENTS (1665)

> When my young Masters Worship comes to Towne
> From Pedagogue, and Mother just sett free,
> The Heyre, and Hopes of a great Family. . . .
> —Rochester, "A Letter from Artemiza"

A lthough much had altered in England during his tour abroad, Rochester had seen enough contrivances and changes of fortune in 1660–61 to alert him that he must make his own way with the Stuarts and their ministers when he returned home. In the two years before his departure, his mother had become a mistress of manipulation, setting an example for him. While her unlucky brother, Sir Walter St. John, dallied in 1660 between his old Puritan alliances and the incoming Royalists, affecting delight at "Joyous May Day" and belatedly panicked and sending a "present" of money to Lord Clarendon, the Countess of Rochester was swiftly using every resource to assure the political and financial future of the Lees and Wilmots.[1]

She saw to it that her son, Frank Lee, sent £500 to the King before his return in May; only a month later, in June 1660, the Lees were granted all of their former rights in Cornbury and Wychwood despite their interim associations with Cromwell and the Parliamentarians. At his mother's bidding, Frank stood for Parliament in 1661, and he was returned by the borough of Malmesbury to sit in the Cavalier Parliament where expectations were great that Loyalists would be rewarded through the Act of Indemnity and Oblivion.[2]

Under this Act, such traitors as Lord Saye, Oliver St. John, and Sir John Danvers (deceased) lost all of their rights and possessions. Undaunted at her close ties with Danvers, who was branded a "regicide," Lady Rochester claimed her late son Harry and his wife had lent money to Danvers that he never repaid and their heirs were thus entitled to his estates. On October 21, 1661, the King gave Danvers's Chelsea estate in trust to Sir Ralph Verney to be held for Eleonora and Anne Lee, "the remainder of the property to be for their use, under direction of the Countess of Rochester, their grandmother and guardian."

The Countess's family thereby controlled a vast tract of land west of London on both sides of the Thames, reaching south from Chelsea to Battersea to Wandsworth.[3]

The Countess had forwarded her son Rochester's claims also; he was granted a retroactive pension in February 1661. Payments on May 20 and June 19, 1661, and in March 1662, brought it up to date.[4] The young Earl had been introduced at Court; he probably had participated in the Coronation ceremonies on April 23, 1661, riding among his fellow peers in the processional on the previous day, sitting in Westminster Abbey during the ceremony, and dining at Whitehall with the colorful company afterward.[5]

Lord Clarendon's affectionate kiss at the Oxford Convocation in September 1661 was a token of the fondness for the young noble at Whitehall, as was the monarch's personal selection of the governor for his travels. Even at fourteen, Rochester had begun to learn the ways of the Stuart Court and the methods of achieving one's ends there. While he was away on the continent, his crafty mother kept their obligation to the Wilmots before the eyes of the King and Lord Chancellor. Soon after Rochester's departure, the Countess wrote a postscript in a letter to Clarendon:

> I must in my nex thank you for your good favors too my sonne Rochester
> I hope hee will inherit his mothers hart and then I am sure hee will bee
> your Lo:s faithfull sarvant.[6]

In April 1662, she had occasion to write twice to the Lord Chancellor about John Wilmot's affairs. In a letter dated "Dichly this 23: of Apr;" she wrote:

> My lord I had the honer of a letter from your Lo:sp this day, in which you
> are pleased too command the yearly value of my sonne Rochesters estate in
> Oxfordshere; it is soe small a thing that I can in very short tell it you.
> All that hee is at present intitled too there is not above forty pounds a yeare,
> which decended from my lord his father; the rest of the estate at athurbury
> which is taken too bee his is the Bishops of Winchester: now made to myself
> in lease for three Lives, for which estate I have made my apearance of horse
> too the Malitia of this county, my sonne having noe titell too it at all, at
> present nor hearafter, but as I shall please, I am My lord
> Your very humbell sarvant A Rochester[7]

Then she penned a second, covering letter:

> My lord, I have writ you rather more then less the value of what my sonne
> Rochester has in Oxfordshere; the truth is, though it bee but Little yet if my
> lords creditors could find it out from the bishops, they would lease upon it
> for dept and therefore I shall entreat you my lord to concider before you send
> this leter how prejuditiall it may bee too my sonne too have the commitioners

to see it (under my hand), my lord owing monys in oxford. I have obeyed
your commands, and shall leave it too your Lo:sp discretion too doe what
you please in it, I am my lord your humbell sarvant A Rochester[8]

The Countess's mixture of formality and familiarity, deference and independence, shows the nice distinctions in personal and financial relationships
that she had mastered since her days as Harry Lee's young widow. Her candid statement about her son's lack of income and abundance of debts
was an obvious reminder of Henry Wilmot's self-impoverishment to serve the
Stuarts. At the same time, Wilmot's widow clearly was not to be expected to
repair the damages out of her own income or money from the Lee estates.[9]

The Countess neglected to mention that, as John Wilmot's guardian, she
had sold a house in Scotland Yard left to him by his father, and had used the
money to secure the lease on the house at Adderbury. Nor did she mention that
she had just spent £2,000 in refurbishing and richly furnishing Adderbury
Manor to make it "fit for a family who at that time were not possessed of any
other save only a house near Scotland Yard."[10] She asserted blandly that the
young Earl had no title to the Wilmot family manor but as she might please,
then asked—and was no doubt given—the Lord Chancellor's cooperation in concealing her son's supposedly meager income from his creditors. The Countess's
business morality was typical of the Restoration period; she differed from her
contemporaries in nothing but her managerial acumen. Gilbert Burnet's evaluation of her role in young Rochester's fortunes was accurate as far as it went:

> [Henry Wilmot] left his Son little other Inheritance, but the Honor and
> Title derived to him, with the pretensions such eminent Services gave him
> to the King's favor: These were carefully managed by the great prudence
> and discretion of his Mother. . . .[11]

However, even before Rochester left on the Grand Tour, his mother was
scheming to insinuate herself into the inner circles of power, where she could
advance her own fortunes as well as her family's.

On April 11, 1661, she asked Clarendon to mention her to the King as a
replacement for Lady Derby, a recently deceased attendant to the Royal
Bedchamber. She failed to get this post; but Clarendon did help her become
Groom of the Stole to his daughter, Anne Hyde, the Duchess of York, a post
she retained until the Duchess's death in 1671.[12] Indeed, her closeness to the
Duchess was such that when Lady Denham, one of the Duke of York's reputed
mistresses, died suddenly, Lady Rochester was suspected by some of having
poisoned her.[13] And the knowledge she gained about the Duke of York enabled
her to give an insider's advice years later to her grandson when the Duke had
become James II.[14]

If the Countess had the ear of the Duchess of York, her brother-in-law, Allen Apsley ("Ned"), Master of the Duke of York's household, was a favorite of both the Duke and the King. Clarendon, also her relative by marriage, had the King's ear as Lord Chancellor. And yet another relative of Lady Rochester's, the infamous Barbara Palmer, Lady Castlemain, had more than the King's ear.[15] The nineteen-year-old Barbara—auburn-haired, beautiful by standards of the day, and totally amoral—had discovered soon after Charles II was restored to the throne that the way to the royal purse, if not the royal heart, lay through the King's bed. She had begun her sexual career as the willing playfellow of the Earl of Chesterfield. Married in 1659 to Roger Palmer, who went to the continent as soon as possible after his wife became the King's whore, she enthralled Charles with "all the tricks of Aretin."[16]

When the King married the Portuguese princess, Catherine of Braganza in 1662, Barbara, pregnant with Stuart issue, proposed that she have her lying-in (delivery) at Hampton Court, where the royal couple were honeymooning. Thwarted in that, Barbara had her way in almost everything else, resorting to her strident larynx when her other parts temporarily lost their effect.[17] By 1663 she was the subject of much gossip outside of Whitehall as well as in it, where her apartments had been relocated more conveniently to the King's.[18] In Cousin Barbara, Lady Rochester had a powerful ally as she contrived an advantageous match for her son Rochester in 1664 on the eve of his return from France.

In the London seasons of 1663 and 1664, one of the most sought-after young heiresses was thirteen-year-old Elizabeth Mallet of Enmore, Somerset. Her maternal grandfather, Sir Frances Hawley of Buckland House, was an enormously wealthy—and endlessly greedy—entrepreneur, whose expertise at getting estates from the King was unrivalled. Hawley's dutiful daughter Untia [or Unton] had married John Mallet III of an ancient Somerset family; when he died young in March 1656, leaving his holdings to their only child, Elizabeth, Untia married again.

Sir John Warre, her second husband, was the sort of vigorous Somerset squire that Fielding wrote about later. He was always bustling about in his various roles: land developer, farmer, recruiter for the colonies, and Peace Justice. He remained an indulgent step-father even after his own son Francis was born in 1659. The Warres allowed Elizabeth all the incomes from her properties, which amounted to £2,000 a year—with rumors of £2,500 in the future. Many of these scattered estates (Curry Mallet, Shepton Mallet) were held in trust by her grandfather, who had no intention of letting her marry anybody with little or no fortune.[19]

The first candidate for Mrs. Mallet's hand (and money) was the blackguard Charles Berkeley, Viscount Fitzhardinge. Fitzhardinge had tried to ingratiate

Figure 4. Barbara Palmer, Duchess of Cleveland. Portrait by Sir Peter Lely. National Portrait Gallery, Collection of H.M. the Queen. Reproduced by permission.

himself with the Duke of York, who made a morganatic marriage with the pregnant Anne Hyde, by saying that he, himself, had had previous carnal knowledge of her.[20] When the Duke then reaffirmed his marriage vows, Fitzhardinge had the embarrassment of apologizing to both the Duchess and her father, the Lord Chancellor Clarendon, who, naturally, detested him.

Figure 5. Catherine of Braganza. Unknown artist. National Portrait Gallery, London. Reproduced by permission.

Fitzhardinge's pursuit of Elizabeth Mallet in 1663 and October 1664 was recorded in family letters.[21] But he dropped out of the competition, wedding Mary Bagot on December 18, 1664, only days before Lord Rochester came on the scene.

The removal of Fitzhardinge from consideration was hardly noticeable, so numerous were other contenders for the "fortune of the North." Lord John Butler, a younger son of James Butler, the Duke of Ormonde, had been proposed as her husband by Ormonde himself in the summer of 1664. William Fielding, the son of Lord Desmond and heir to an earldom, had the support of the Queen

Figure 6. Elizabeth Mallet. Portrait by Sir Peter Lely. Sotheby's, London. Reproduced by permission.

Mother in his suit. Another high-born contender was William Herbert, heir to the Earl of Pembroke.

Then in a letter on December 5, 1664, the Earl of Sandwich, Edward Montagu, the King's Admiral and patron of Samuel Pepys, proposed to make his son, Lord Hinchingbrooke, a prospect for Lord Hawley's granddaughter, having attempted unsuccessfully to pair him off earlier in 1662 with Anne Scott, the heiress whom the King decided to bestow on his own bastard son, James Crofts the Duke of Monmouth. Like Rochester, Hinchingbrooke was away on the Grand Tour but was expected back in England by the summer of 1665.[22]

Lady Rochester's cabal of relatives, however, was working for the candidacy of John Wilmot to notable effect, as Henry Bennet, Lord Arlington and Secretary of State, informed Sandwich in mid-December of 1664. On December 18, he wrote:

> my Lady Castlemain hath rigged the King, who is also seconded in it by my Lord Chancellor, to recommende my Lord of Rochester. Now these personages being with soe much advantage and preference upon the stage, I feare noe other can with any probability of succeeding enter; what I further heare of the Lady is that Shee declares shee will choose for herselfe. If shee hold to it, the game is upon equal terms at least.[23]

Sandwich had been prepared for this answer by two letters sent to him by Sir John Warre and Sir Francis Hawley on December 17 in response to Sandwich's previous inquiries to them. Sir John told Sandwich:

> we are at present able to make no return without disobliging my Lord Duke of Ormond, for my Lord being in our county this summer, made some proposals himself on behalf of his son my Lord John, which have been ever since, and are still in treaty, and what conclusion they have will be speedily known. . . .[24]

Sandwich discreetly told the Secretary of State he thanked him for his return to early inquiries about the lady: hearing that others were also candidates with the King's recommendation, he would suppress any thought that might deviate from his Majesty's pleasure. Lord Fitzhardinge also probably dropped his suit because he learned of the King's pleasure. With Charles II favoring his cause, Rochester seemingly enjoyed a preferred standing with the rich Elizabeth Mallet. His mother and her friends had set up the prize for him; it was now up to him to win her.

Whatever her elders thought to the contrary, Mrs. Mallet was serious about making her own choice. Lord Hawley and her parents viewed Lord John Butler as the most suitable candidate for her hand, although they kept him from making his suit in person.[25] Lord Hinchingbrooke's courtship was also being carried on by surrogates, a common practice of the day. Lord Rochester, however, was very much on the scene and he was encouraged by the King himself to address the heiress.[26]

Neither Lord Hawley nor the Warres looked upon him with favor—he was said to have no fortune—nevertheless, he was handsome: tall, graceful, well-shaped. His complexion was fair, of a rosy hue; and his good breeding and wit

Figure 7. John Wilmot, Second Earl of Rochester. Portrait by Sir Peter Lely, ca. 1666–67. Victoria and Albert Museum, London. Reproduced by permission.

were striking.[27] He charmed the Court circle with his clever ripostes and deft imagination. He was far too attractive for a flirtatious fifteen-year-old to reject out of hand. Moreover, he could write the sort of fashionable, amorous, pastoral poetry that delighted Elizabeth Mallet's girlish heart.

Rochester's schoolboy translations of the Latin poets, his undergraduate poetizing under the supervision of Robert Whitehall at Oxford, and his constant exposure to Dr. Balfour's raptures about Petrarch and Ariosto as well as Ovid and Virgil equipped him well to join the Courtiers at Whitehall who still cherished the tradition of *sprezzatura* embodied by Sir Philip Sidney (1554–1586) and the so-called "Cavalier poets."[28] Accomplished young aristocrats were supposed to talk, dance, fight, make love, and toss off poems with casual expertise while professing themselves mere amateurs. Two poets of that tradition were still alive and considerable presences at Court among "the mob of gentlemen who wrote with ease," when Rochester arrived there.

Sir John Denham was fifty years old in 1665, married to a young wife and recovering from a fit of madness. His writing career was largely over, though he was still respected for a tragedy, *The Sophy* (1641), a nature poem, *Cooper's Hill* (1642), and a collection of pieces including a translation of Virgil in 1656. His fortunes had suffered under the Parliamentarians but he flourished after the Restoration. Denham, noted for his piercing, "goose-grey" eyes, may have been a "Sweet Swan," as John Aubrey called him, but "He was satyricall when he had a mind to it." His debut as a poet in the 1640s was sensational; as Edmund Waller put it, "he broke-out like the Irish Rebellion."[29]

Waller himself was one of the writers in the assemblage around the glamorous Duke of Buckingham, who possibly introduced Rochester to him. Waller had ties with the Sidneys and had written poems to the Lady Dorothy Sidney as "Sacharissa." A collection of his poetry published in 1664 was much admired at the time young Rochester came to Court. The youth was vastly impressed by the venerable Waller, fifty-nine years old in 1665, and by his "smooth" pastorals, eulogies, and elegies. Such Wallerian efforts as this were the models for Rochester's verse between 1665 and 1670 in versification, tropes, and often sentiments:

> Chloris! farewell. I now must go;
> For if with thee I longer stay,
> Thy eyes prevail upon me so,
> I shall prove blind, and lose my way.

However, after 1669, as Rochester's own eye became more jaundiced, his tone more ironic, and his literary purview more satiric, he would discard Waller as his poetic model. The "something magisteriall" Waller would disapprove of Rochester's new style, declaring "that Satyricall writing was downe-hill, most easie and naturall; that at Billingsgate one might hear great heights of such witt. . . ." Waller prided himself that all *his* writings were "free from Offence." Although Rochester wrote a savage parody of him in 1673, he retained his respect for Waller's poetic talent. In 1675 he asserted that Waller was best suited to be the Poet Laureate; and his habit of quoting Waller's lines, as shown in a letter to Lady Rochester as late as 1678–79, was remarked by both Sir George Etherege and John Dennis.[30] In 1665 Rochester imitated Waller sufficiently well to please both him and his admirers.

Despite his poetic addresses to "Celia" and "Chloris" in the Wallerian modes, however, two years elapsed between Elizabeth Mallet's first meeting with Rochester and their marriage. The long delay was certainly due in part to the mercenary stalling of Lord Hawley and Sir John Warre. Even so, the King was repeatedly urging her to accept Rochester as her husband early in 1665, and resisting the royal pleasure took more than boundless greed in her guardians and mere whim or stubbornness on her part.[31] As for Rochester, he claimed to be moved to desperate action by his passion. If she was to elope with him eventually, what prevented her initially?

In a century when romantic love was less important than money in arranging a marriage, we may wonder whether an impecunious John Wilmot indeed felt so passionately as he professed about a young woman he had known for only a few weeks but who was "an heiress, vastly rich." Rochester himself admitted he often used artifice to prevail over reluctant women.[32] Some of his earliest adult poetry, composed in the late 1660s and including a poetic exchange with his future wife, provides insight into his attitudes toward love and marriage at that time. Ostensibly Ovidian exercises in amorous playfulness or Petrarchan love metaphors, Rochester's pastoral dialogues and companion-pieces disclose real contradictions in his feelings.[33]

"A Pastoral Dialogue between Alexis and Strephon" superficially contrasts the attitudes of two swains toward the nymph Corinna. Alexis speaks in Petrarchan oxymorons and paradoxes. He sighs that he is lost: scorched and frozen by a "killing Sweetness" in one he does not name. If she should then become enflamed toward him, he will feel the pleasure of a triumphant scorn. "To see my Tyrant at my Feet/ Whils't taught by her, unmov'd/ I sit A Tyrant in my turn."[34] Clearly, for Alexis love is a contest for dominance, but he is determined not to submit himself to female tyranny by feeling too passionately. Male conquest seems to be the ideal for him but he typically fears rejection by a woman.

In professed contrast, Strephon, "dazled" and bewitched by the beauty of a specified "Corinna," laments that he is "frighted, and alone." Where Alexis feels "lost," Strephon has "lost" something (his heart, his freedom). He does not blame Corinna, who is "nice" and "fair" and who has been taught that "Honor" must make her remain "insensible" (inexperienced and unfeeling) to love (i.e., sexual consummation). Unlike Alexis, however, Strephon is willing to admit his love and his enslavement, he says, because life is mean—and meaningless—without Corinna's love:

> My rifled Love would soon retire,
> Dissolving into Aire,
> Should I that Nymph cease to admire,
> Blest in whose Arms I will expire,
> Or at her Feet despair.

Stripped of love, his soul would evaporate.

Strephon's determination ("I will") to attain sexual bliss ("expire," i.e., "die" or experience orgasm) or else to attach himself ostentatiously to Corinna's feet suggests that for him the strategy of courtship is to try different approaches until one works. While disguised as unselfish adoration, Strephon's changeability has male conquest as its *goal*—not a theoretical *ideal*—despite the risk of temporary rejection. The conflict between male and female wills remains the same as Alexis envisions it, however.[35]

Viewed closely, the "Dialogue" contains a good deal of masculine egotism along with a youthful cynicism toward courtship and love. Unlike Alexis, Strephon will play by the artificial rules of courtship; but seduction is still the name of the game.[36] The choice of "Corinna" as the nymph's name hints at misogyny. Rochester eventually used "Corinna" as a name for sluttish women and prostitutes. Indeed, all of the names in his pastorals have allusive dimensions beyond their conventional surfaces.[37]

"Strephon" reappears in a dialogue with "Daphne," whose name signifies laurel or the triumphant prize won by the determined runner. Apollo's Daphne was virtuous: she fled when pursued by the patron-god of poets. But in Rochester's dialogue, Strephon is the one in flight ("Love Commands another way") and Daphne initially urges him to dissemble love for her out of pity. He callously answers that women feign with pleasure but men are pained to dissemble. Strephon declares that Cupid is like all boys, wanting a plaything to toy with, then "wantonly" throwing it away. Daphne's reply rings some ironic variations on the Petrarchan paradox:

> Still on Wing, or on his Knees,
> Love does nothing by degrees:
> Basely flying when most priz'd,
> Meanly fawning when despis'd.
> Flattering or insulting ever,
> Generous and grateful never. . . .

Strephon insists that sexual fidelity is not natural; Daphne's answer shows plainly that their relationship has been a sexual one that pleased her. When she laments her ruin and seeks to know who her rival is, Strephon replies that the chief charm a woman can have is an "aversion" to "Tedious, trading, Constancy." This telling phrase sums up Strephon's attitude toward marriage and monogamy. Daphne then reveals her own infidelity to him and scornfully declares:

> Woman-kind more Joy discovers
> Making Fools, than keeping Lovers.

Like his male contemporaries, young Rochester held to a sexual double standard. It was man's nature to crave variety.[38] Virtuous young women who refused his advances were cruel and unkind. If a woman succumbed, however, she was a broken toy, fit only to be tossed aside; she had lost her virtue. A woman who played the man's game of inconstancy was a slut and a whore, deserving his contempt. To marry such a woman was unthinkable—unless a man wanted to risk leaving his property to another man's bastard. A husband was not expected to be faithful; his wife, of course, was.[39]

These were the beliefs of the men Rochester chose to imitate when he entered manhood in the Court of Charles II. With no father present to instruct him during his boyhood, and supervised by clergymen-tutors through most of his adolescence, Rochester's indoctrination as a male had been his undergraduate experiences at Oxford. With Charles II as a substitute father—he was, after all, the *pater patriae*, the patriarchal father of his country—Rochester inevitably adopted libertine attitudes toward male-female relationships.[40] These were confirmed by the circle of rakes Rochester entered, all of whom were senior to him by four to twenty years and thus considerably more experienced in the ways of the world.

Given the assumptions of his society and class, the male attitudes in the pastorals and his stated views about constancy, the sincerity of his "love" in Rochester's first poems presumably addressed to Mrs. Mallet is dubious. One of his two "Celia" poems, "The Discovery," indicates this. (The reference to "blazing Comets in a Winters Sky" suggests a composition date early in 1665.) The lover's appeal to "Celia" follows the rhetorical strategy outlined by Strephon in his discourse with Alexis; his sentiments therefore appear to be more a conventional exercise in versified persuasion than genuine passion. Mrs. Mallet may have suspected this to be so. Her poem to "Thyrsis" ("Nothing adds to your fond fire,/ More than Scorne, and cold disdaine") suggests reasons for her hesitation to marry him. Its placement in the Nottingham Ms. PwV 31, a collection of Rochester's manuscript poems, suggests that it was composed about this time. She had felt his "Pow'rfull Charmes" and used

"Kindnesse" to "cherish" his desire, but had been abused and insulted by his liaisons with other women:

> You that cou'd my Heart subdue;
> To new Conquests, ne'er pretend,
> Let your example make me true. . . .

She had also recognized a certain perversity in her suitor that was manifested in his later behavior as husband to her and as lover to other women; her insight gave her pause:

> You insulted on your Slave,
> Humble Love you soone refus'd . . .
> You grow Constant through despair,
> Love return'd, you wou'd abuse.[41]

It is evident that in 1665–66 Rochester not only patronized the brothels in a section of London called Little Sodom but he also followed the fashionable practice of taking an actress for a mistress.[42] She was Sarah Cooke, a novice with the King's Company. Rochester's talent at disguising himself and acting out roles naturally led him to take an interest in the London theaters; and he apparently coached Sarah, the first of such tutees, in acting. Not until late 1666, when he finally persuaded Mrs. Mallet to marry him, did Rochester get rid of his mistress by arranging with Tom Killegrew, director of the King's Theatre and father of "Lying Harry" Killegrew, Rochester's rakehell friend, for her to go off in the provinces with Thomas Coysh's troop of traveling players.[43] Mrs. Mallet could hardly avoid knowing about Miss Sarah.

And there was another problem. Encouraged by his rakish companions to drink freely, thereby inciting him to displays of his spontaneous wit, Rochester found that "Intemperance . . . was growing on him."[44] At least one woman who was the object of his amorous intentions ("Chloris") resented his paying more attention to his male friends and the bottle than he did to her. Rochester addressed "Chloris" in several versions of "Song," also titled "To A Lady, in A Letter," justifying his conduct with winning impudence:

> Lett us (since witt has taught us how)
>   Raise pleasure to the topp,
> If Rivall bottle you'l allow
>   I'le suffer rivall fop. . . .
>
> Upbraide mee not that I designe
>   Tricks to delude your charmes
> When running after mirth and wine
>   I leave your Longing Armes.

> For wine (whose power alone can raise
>   Our thoughts soe farr above)
> Affords Idea's fitt to praise
>   What wee thinke fitt to Love.[45]

Elizabeth Mallet certainly was not ready to accept without question Lord Rochester, who had no fortune, drank too much, chased other women, and displayed a measure of arrogance toward her when she showed kindness to his cause. Particularly at a time when she had other suitors, including the absent Lord Hinchingbrooke, who might surpass them all in appeal. A manuscript poem in Rochester's hand, preserved together with their poetic exchange, seems to reflect his emotional frustrations at this impasse. Reproving the "Hard hearted saint . . . Soe unrelenting pittiless to mee," he says:

> My hopes your selfe contriv'd with cruell care
> Through gentle smiles to leade mee to despaire. . . .

His beloved has rejected him while she permits a "Blundring blockhead . . . rivall" to make love to her. This boorish rival (Lord John Butler?) "would have a passion, for 'twas fine," but thinks only of his clothes and what to say next to her. In contrast, her martyred true love, long torn between hopes and fears, cannot dissemble a contentment he does not feel. His wishes,

> like mee bashfull and humble growne
> Hover att distance about Beautyes throne
>   There worship and admire and then they dye
> Daring noe more Lay Hold of her than I.[46]

On May 4, 1665, Rochester's plump friend and fellow-rake, Henry Savile, told his brother, "My lord of Rochester is encouraged by the king to make his [addresses] to Mrs. Mallet."[47] Misreading the extent of the King's encouragement, John Wilmot unwisely decided to lay hold of his reluctant mistress. He may have thought such a move would romantically sweep away all her resistance to him and conquer where poetry had not.

Accordingly, he made elaborate plans; and on the night of May 26, 1665, when she was going home after dining with her new friend Frances Stuart at Whitehall, Mrs. Mallet found her coach abruptly halted by a group of armed men who seized and spirited her away. For succinctness and color, nothing can match the account of the abduction given by Samuel Pepys to Lady Sandwich, the mother of Lord Hinchingbrooke.

> Here, upon my telling her a story of my Lord Rochester's running away
> on Friday night last with Mrs. Mallet, the great beauty and fortune of the

> North, who had supped at White Hall with Mrs. Stewart, and was going
> home to her lodgings with her grandfather, my Lord Haly, by coach; and
> was at Charing Cross seized on by both horse and foot men and forcibly
> taken from him, and put in a coach with six horses and two women pro-
> vided to receive her, and carried away. Upon immediate pursuit, my Lord
> of Rochester (for whom the King had spoken to the lady often, but with
> no success) was taken at Uxbridge; but the lady is not yet heard of, and
> the King mighty angry, and the Lord sent to the Tower. . . .[48]

His arrest at Uxbridge shows that Rochester chose this route out of
London with deliberation, deciding to carry his maiden captive to Adderbury,
just off the Banbury road. His strategy was to no avail.[49] Rochester had
badly underestimated the influence of Sir Francis Hawley on the King. Not
only had Hawley supported Charles' father with money and a horse troop;
he had given money to Charles himself and made additional large loans,
which the King sometimes was unable to repay.[50] Charles was used to
appeasing Lord Hawley; now the King was chagrined and angry. The morning after the kidnapping, he issued warrants to convey Rochester to the
Tower of London for his "high misdemeanours" and to Sir John Robinson,
Keeper of the Tower, to receive the Earl as a prisoner. He also issued a warrant
requiring

> assistance in the search after divers armed men who aided the Earl of
> Rochester in taking by force of arms Mrs. Elizabeth Mallet, without her
> consent, and carrying her from the city into the country; also aid for Sir
> John Warre in searching for the said Mrs. Mallet and restoring her to her
> friends.[51]

The search was successful. Mrs. Mallet was soon restored to her friends (i.e.,
family) but her abductor-lover was not restored to his. John Aubrey saw him
taking exercise in the Tower, where he remained for three weeks.[52]

This was ample time for him to realize with fright the consequences of his
folly. He sent a "Humble Peticon" to the King, declaring that no misfortune
on earth would be worse than losing His Majesty's favor. If he had reflected
on the fatal consequences of incurring the royal displeasure, he would have
chosen death ten thousand times rather than done it. He cast himself in all
humility and sense of his fault at the King's feet, beseeching that a first error
be pardoned and that one offense not be his ruin. He prayed humbly to be
restored to favor, that he might kiss the King's hand. "Inadvertency, Ignorance
in ye Law, and Passion were ye occasions of his Offence."[53]

The King could not forgive the young rascal right away; however, he moved
steadily to mend the situation. The mass outbreak of the Plague in London

soon after the kidnapping expedited matters. On June 9, the King found occasion to send Lord Hawley off on a mission; Mrs. Mallet's grandfather was dispatched with a letter to Lord Sandwich, congratulating him for his recent naval victory over the Dutch.[54] With Lord Hawley out of the way and the gentry fleeing London, the King released Rochester from the Tower on June 19. On June 29, 1665, the Court itself left London for an extended stay in Hampton Court, Salisbury, and finally Oxford, not returning to the capital until February 1666 after the Plague abated.[55]

Her abduction in no way diminished Elizabeth Mallet's desirability as a match to those with eligible sons in want of a fortune. Soon after she reappeared, the heiress was the center of a new round of negotiations. On June 6, Lady Sandwich told Pepys in confidence that "my Lord Rochester is now decidedly out of hopes of Mrs. Mallet"; Lord Hinchingbrooke was the leading contender for her hand, needing only approval from the King.[56] When the Warres fled London for Somerset, an agent of the Duke of Ormonde followed in July, intent upon sealing the marriage agreement for Lord John Butler. The King saw to it that Mrs. Mallet's male relatives were kept busy on royal errands during the summer and fall; with all the bustle, the Rochester Affair appeared on its way to being forgotten.[57]

Rochester, however, was far from forgetting how the King's anger jeopardized his future and fortunes. He soon hit upon the way to redeem himself. Five years earlier as a schoolboy, he had told His Sacred Majesty that his one ambition was to be known as "your Wilmot's son" by daring loyalty. The very conditions needed to show such loyalty had been developing while Rochester was concentrating on gaining Mrs. Mallet for a wife.

Anglo-Dutch relations grew highly charged over sea rights during the 1650s and 1660s, with an expanding Dutch fleet operating in waters claimed by the English.[58] Dutch fishermen and Dutch trade routes between Scandanavia and the Mediterranean used the North Sea and English Channel, both the asserted territory of England. The Dutch East India fleet had also clashed with the English at Amboyna in Indonesia and staked a virtual monopoly on merchant shipping in Asia. Disputes over sea rights had led to the First Anglo-Dutch War (June 1652–April 1654). The Treaty of Westminster in 1654 did not satisfy the ambitions of English merchants; the various Navigation Acts had not worked; and with the arrogant, unimaginative Sir George Downing as English envoy to the Hague in 1661–62 and 1663–65, tensions continued to mount.

In 1664 the escalation reached a peak when English and Dutch ships fought off the coast of West Africa and Barbados and Nieuw Amsterdam (New York) was captured by the English. Thereafter, English raiders systematically hit Dutch merchant ships and won more than one hundred prizes. In March 1665 the Second Anglo-Dutch War was declared; and in June, the English fleet won a signal victory in a sea battle off Lowestoft under the Duke of York. This victory enabled King Charles to send Lord Hawley off with a congratulatory message to Lord Sandwich.[59]

The moment was ripe for John Wilmot to prove himself Henry Wilmot's son by fighting for the King. Burnet, who glossed over the circumstances of Rochester joining the fleet in the summer of 1665, wrote:

> He thought it necessary to begin his life with these Demonstrations of his Courage in an Element and way of fighting, which is acknowledged to be the greatest trial of clear and undaunted Valour.[60]

Rochester's decision was recorded by Henry Savile, who told his sister-in-law, "The only volonteers that are gone lately are, my Lord of Rochester, George Hamilton, and Sir Thomas Clifford.[61] On July 17 the volunteer joined the fleet at Flamborough Head just as Sandwich was preparing to go to sea again. He carried a letter from the King, asking Sandwich to accommodate the young Earl, and the Lord Admiral wrote that he had settled the youth into naval life as well as he could on his own ship.[62]

If he wanted to undergo the greatest trial of courage, Rochester soon got his wish. On August 2, 1665, he was under full fire. For ten days after he joined the fleet the English had failed to locate the Dutch. Then on July 26, they learned that ships of the Dutch East India fleet were hiding in the port of Bergen, Norway, then a possession of the King of Denmark.[63] Knowing the port was too small for his large ships, Sandwich ordered twenty of his "fourth and fifth-rate friggots" to go and take the Dutch. Well aware of his need to prove himself to Sandwich (father to one of his rivals for Elizabeth Mallet), Rochester volunteered to go in the *Revenge*, the flagship of Sir Thomas Teddiman. He later wrote to his mother,

> it was not fitt for me to see any occasion of service to the King without offering my self, soe I desired & obtained leave of my Ld Sandwich to goe with them & accordingly the thirtieth of this month we sett saile at six o'clock at night. . . .[64]

The next day, July 31, they docked at Cruchfort, fifteen leagues south of Bergen, where the towering rocks of the fjords frightened the English sailors. When the twenty ships tried to dock in a space too small, they nearly met with disaster:

> in a moment wee were all together upon one another ready to dash in peeces having nothing but bare Rocks to save ourselves, in case wee had

binn lost; but it was Gods great mercy wee gott cleere & only that, for wee
had no humane probability of safety. . . .

The distressing experience reminded Rochester, only lately turned eighteen,
that the next day would bring battle. Suddenly the prospect of dying became
immediate, and he began to agonize over questions of the soul and immortality, as men do at such times. Childhood fears surged up again, and he
began to question the teachings of his governors. Did he really have a soul,
as they said? Could it return to earth and testify to a life after death? He
voiced his fears to two young companions, Edward Montagu and George
Windham. The brother of one of Rochester's classmates at Oxford, Windham
had come with the fleet certain he would never return to England. Anxiously,
he entered into a pact with Rochester that if one was killed, he would reap-
pear to the other. The youths followed "Ceremonies of Religion," taking an
oath forbidden by religious authorities, but Rochester was in doubt and
wanted proof. Ned Montagu, however, was too terrified to join the other two;
he had "such a strong Presage in his Mind of his approaching death."[65]
Somehow, the frightened boys got through the night by talking about the
gold, spices, and other plunder they might share when the East India fleet was
captured.

On August 1, the expeditionary fleet arrived at Bergen, in high hopes of
booty to be gotten from the laden Dutch ships waiting for an escort convoy.
The English "came bravely into the Harbour in the midst of the towne and
Castles and there Anchored close by the Dutch men," in Rochester's words.
For twenty-four hours, the Governor of Bergen tried to stall for time with Sir
Thomas Clifford, the representative of King Charles. An exchange of empty
messages was carried by young Ned Montagu, who was cousin to Lord
Sandwich and Gentleman-Groom to Queen Catherine. Clifford had reluctantly
decided to risk the youth as his emissary and a possible hostage.[66]

When they realized the Dutch were using the delay to strengthen the
town's fortifications, the English hoisted their fighting colors and opened fire,
which the town cannon and Dutch ships instantly returned. In the hellish
exchange, the wind acted against the English, covering them with smoke and
preventing their fireships from reaching the Dutch ships. In the barrage, 100
Dutch and 118 English died, including six captains.[67] On the *Revenge*, in spite
of his terrors, Montagu placed himself in a position of danger. Inexperienced
as they were, all three youths behaved bravely until Windham faltered and
began to tremble violently. Montagu ran to hold him up in his arms just as a
cannon ball exploded beside them, killing Windham instantly and ripping out
Montagu's stomach. Rochester, horrified, saw it all. Montagu died soon after.

In spite of their pact, no spirit returned to tell Rochester what awaited him after death; the confusion and doubt that resulted haunted him for the rest of his life.[68]

On August 3, the day after the disastrous battle, Rochester wrote a long, deferential letter to his mother. She could not have discerned any mental anguish in the boyish, swaggering report.

> Madam I hope it will not bee hard for your La^{sp} to believe that it hath binn want of opportunity & noe neglect in mee the not writing to your La^{sp} all this while, I know noe body hath more reason to express theire duty to you, than I have, & certainly I will never bee soe imprudent as to omitt the occasions of doing it.

A bravado account of the battle followed, concluding:

> Mr Mountegue and Thom: Windhams brother were both killed with one shott just by mee, but God Almyghty was pleased to preserve mee from any kind of hurt, Madam, I have bin tedious but begg your la^{sps} pardon who am I
>
> Your most obedient son
Rochester

A not-very-subtle postscript dispelled any hint of spiritual distress: "I have binn as good a husband as I could, but in spight of my teeth have binn faine to borrow mony."

John Wilmot had long since learned to conceal his true feelings from everyone including his mother: to dissemble and act a suitable, self-serving role. The letter itself was an act of self-dramatization with its heavy parchment paper, ornate script, and elaborate phrasing. Wilmot obviously intended that it be shown to the King and serve as an ex officio account of the Battle of Bergen. Sir Thomas Clifford, the King's official representative on the scene and the future Lord Treasurer, witnessed Wilmot's behavior under fire and praised his courage highly, as did Sandwich the Lord Admiral.[69] To all appearances, the young Earl emerged from his fiery baptism seasoned but unscarred.

After Bergen, Rochester returned to the main fleet under Sandwich at Flamborough Head on August 18, in what state of mind he did not reveal for years. For three weeks, they cruised, looking for more of the Dutch fleet. On September 9, they found it. In the first encounter with eighteen Dutch vessels, they burned two, captured most of the rest, and took 1,000 prisoners. Soon after, they sighted forty sail of ships commanded by the wily Dutch Admiral Bancker; but a rising storm prevented them from attacking. Again, Rochester's courage was unquestionable.

On September 12, Lord Sandwich wrote an account of these events to the King, mentioning that Rochester had showed himself brave, industrious, and of useful parts. Rochester himself carried this letter, together with another from Sandwich to Arlington, the Secretary of State, telling him that Rochester could provide further details by word of mouth.[70] The youth who had left England in disgrace returned in triumph as a war hero and trusted courier after two months at sea.

The Plague was raging in London the week in September that Rochester returned home; mortality bills showed that nearly 1,500 people were buried in a seven-day period, September 12–19.[71] Avoiding the city, Rochester traveled directly from the port at Southwold Bay to Oxford. There, about September 15, he presented himself with his reports to the King. Delighted with the news and Rochester's conduct, Charles was ready to forgive fully the escapade of May. As a sign of his renewed favor, he ordered the Privy Seal to pay John Wilmot the sum of £750 without account as a royal free gift, which Rochester received on October 31.[72]

In the weeks following, the youthful veteran found himself back in familiar surroundings among familiar faces. He probably spent some time at Ditchley and Adderbury with his mother, Frank and Eleonore Lee, their infant son Edward Henry, and his nieces Ellen and Nan (who adored their heroic uncle). He may well have posed for his dashing portrait in armor at this time.

But he also had to resume his part in the King's amusements, hunting and horse racing at Woodstock among them. The trivial activities and sexual contrivances of the Court were much the same despite war and the Plague; but though he rejoined them, the young Earl was changed. His experiences with death and sea battle had left deep if invisible scars. Subliminal images of war and combat were scored on his mind; and for a long while after, they became metaphors for his poetic visions of friendship, politics, and love.[73]

PURSUITS AND CONQUESTS (1666)

As Shipps, just when the Harbour they attaine,
Are snatch'd by sudden Blasts, to Sea againe.
Soe Loves fantastick-Stormes reduce my heart,
Half Rescu'd, and the God resumes his Dart.
—Rochester, "To Love"

Returning to the Court of Charles II, Rochester was reunited with the coterie of rakehells who came to be called "the Merry Gang." The foremost of these were three of his special friends: Charles Sackville Lord Buckhurst, the future Earl of Middlesex and Dorset; Sir Charles Sedley; and Sir Henry Savile. Born in 1643, Sackville Lord Buckhurst was just four years older than Rochester. Son of Richard Sackville the Fifth Earl of Dorset, the genial but rather grossly featured Charles would become the generous patron of many a Restoration author and no mean poet and satirist himself. He went briefly to Westminster School in 1657, then was tutored and taken on a Grand Tour that ended in 1660 soon after the Restoration of Charles II. Grateful to the Royalist Sackvilles—Buckhurst's grandmother had been his governess—the King showered titles and holdings on the father and son. In March 1661, Charles Sackville returned to Parliament as the Member for East Grinstead; it is reasonable to assume that he and John Wilmot met about that time, possibly during the festivities of the Coronation in April 1661.[1]

While Rochester was abroad, Buckhurst was getting into trouble. In February 1662, he and his brother were arrested and accused of killing and robbing a tanner. The two young noblemen claimed they were chasing a robber and killed the tanner by mistake, but they were put into Newgate Prison; gossip abounded, and not until June, when they pled the King's pardon, were they acquitted. On June 16, 1663, Buckhurst and Sedley got drunk at the disreputable Cock Tavern in London. They moved out on a balcony, where their noisy carousing attracted a crowd. When Sedley stripped and began a rowdy parody of a sermon—some reports said he pissed on the spectators—the

The Right Honble Charles Earl of Dorset and Middlesex, Baron Buckhurst,
Lord Chamberlain of the Houshold, One of their Maj^ties most Honble Privy Council; Lord
Lieutenant of the County of Sussex, and Knight of the most Noble Order of the Garter etc.

Figure 8. Charles Sackville, Sixth Earl of Dorset. John Simon after Sir Godfrey
Kneller. National Portrait Gallery, London. Reproduced by permission.

scandalized crowd drove them indoors with a barrage of bottles. They were
subsequently brought before the King's Bench and Sedley was fined 2,000
marks, but Buckhurst got off scot free. Such luck caused Rochester once to tell
the King, tongue in cheek, "he did not know how it was, but [Buckhurst]
might do anything, yet was never to blame."[2]

Meanwhile, Buckhurst started his literary career. In August 1662, he began translating Corneille's *Pompey* in collaboration with Sedley and Edmund Waller; supposedly, he was responsible for Act IV. Early in 1663 he joined Sedley and George Etherege in writing satires against Lord Chesterfield, whose own amorous caterwauling deafened him to rumors that his wife was being pursued by the Duke of York. In the same year, Etherege dedicated his first play, *The Comical Revenge, or Love in a Tub*, to Buckhurst.[3] The two became great friends, joining to convey one Mrs. Cuffley, a "bedraggled nymph," across the Thames for some sexual antics in a tree. Thereafter, they never tired of referring to their arboreal cavorting.[4]

Late in 1664, before the Second Anglo-Dutch War was officially declared, a threatened confrontation between English ships and the Dutch fleet led Buckhurst to volunteer for sea duty. Sometime between November 30 and December 3, he conceived (and possibly wrote) his most famous poem, "To all you Ladies now at Land." After returning to Court in late December, he and Rochester would have had contact with each other for the next five months. Apparently, he returned to duty at sea in June 1665, about the time Rochester did.[5] Unlike Rochester, however, Buckhurst suffered no moral crisis, religion being a matter of indifference to him. When the two reunited in 1666, the twenty-two-year-old rake continued his enthusiasm for women, wine, wit, and camaraderie and encouraged the nineteen-year-old Rochester to do the same.

Buckhurst's sometime partner in debauchery, Sir Charles Sedley, at twenty-seven was senior to both Sackville and Rochester. Born in 1639, he was seventeen when he entered Wadham College, Oxford in March 1656, preceding Rochester there by four years, but he left without a degree. In that year he inherited the baronetcy from his brother. In 1657 he married the daughter of Earl Rivers, Katherine Savage, who eventually went insane. He was a favorite of King Charles; but he rejected his rakish life about 1672 and consequently spent less time at Court and more in writing lyric poetry, translations, and plays. His daughter, the clever but homely Katherine Sedley, became the mistress of James II.[6]

Sedley's literary output was greater than that of the other rakes. He had the classical expertise to metaphrase Horace, Virgil, Ovid, and seventeen epigrams of Martial. In addition to his part in *Pompey the Great*, he wrote an original comedy, *The Mulberry Garden* (1668), as well as *Anthony and Cleopatra* (1677) and an adaptation of Terence's *The Eunuch: Bellamira* (1687).[7] In the mid-60s, his main productions were some of his ninety lyrics, but he was already acting as a combination seducer and on-the-spot dramatic critic, to the annoyed admiration of Samuel Pepys:

> to the King's [Theatre] to *The Mayds Tragedy*; but vexed all the while with two talking ladies and Sir Ch. Sidley, yet pleased to hear their discourse,

Figure 9. Sir Charles Sedley. Unknown artist. Private Collection. Reproduced by permission.

he being a stranger; and one of the ladies would, and did, sit with her mask on all the play. . . . He would fain know who she was, but she would not tell. . . . He was mighty witty. . . .[8]

Of the three friends to Rochester, Henry Savile became the most cherished and intimate. Although he wrote a few satires, his major literary talent was expressed in letters, including a number to Wilmot. Savile was about six years older than his friend—he was born in either 1641 or 1642—but they had a true marriage of minds despite the difference in ages. Savile's older brother, George, was heir to the title of Earl of Halifax; as a younger son, Henry therefore had to get his own fortune.[9]

In 1665, he was given a post as one of his Gentlemen of the Bedchamber by the Duke of York, who wanted to oblige the Saviles. In the course of his duties, Henry naturally came into frequent contact with Rochester's mother, Uncle Apsley, and Rochester himself. According to Pepys, the Duchess of York was smitten by the young Gentleman, who was ruddy-faced and plump even at twenty-four. Her father, the Lord Chancellor, however, said of Henry Savile that he was "a young Man of Wit, and incredible Confidence and Presumption [who] omitted no Occasion to vent his Malice against the Chancellor." In time, Savile also showed his malice against his sponsor York in a squib or lampoon, "Advice to a Painter to draw the Duke by."[10]

As attendant to York, Commander of the Fleet, Savile inevitably had to be at sea much of the time in 1665–67. After he and Rochester reunited in the autumn of 1665, they were both off to the fleet again in the summer of 1666. But they had time to deepen their friendship and possibly to share their woes as lovers. Savile cherished a hopeless infatuation for his sister-in-law, the

Figure 10. Sir Henry Savile. Portrait by Sir Godfrey Kneller. Reproduced courtesy of Abbot Hall Art Gallery, Kendal, Cumbria.

Lady Dorothy Savile. When he left for sea duty, he wrote a dramatic farewell letter to her, saying he might be fortunate enough never to see England again but so long as he was servant to anyone, he was perfectly hers. Possibly Savile was overly affected by Ovid's *Heroides*, verse-letters from lost and tragic lovers and a great favorite of the Court in that period.[11]

As for Rochester, Cupid's dart drove him on in pursuit of Elizabeth Mallet. On July 30, 1665, just a few days before Rochester was caught up in the Battle of Bergen, the Duke of Ormonde's agent, Nicholls, had gone to Somerset, armed with a letter from Lord John Butler and instructions from Lord John's father, the Duke, to consummate the marriage agreement. Sir John Warre, however, refused to permit Mrs. Mallet to see the letter and became angry with Nicholls. The distressed Elizabeth could only show her feelings by toasting Lord Ormonde and Lord John with a "pretty big glass half full of claret."[12]

When Nicholls tried to converse secretly with Elizabeth, Lady Warre intervened. Nicholls wrote:

> I told the young lady this morning that . . . Lord John would come to see her. It was before her mother, for she watched me so close that I had not an opportunity otherwise. The mother said she would not see him. I asked her, Madam, I hope you will see him and she made no reply. Why, Betty, says her mother, you have promised your grandfather at which she answered that without her grandfather's leave she would not, but spoke it in the manner of trouble and disconsolancy that I never saw. . . .[13]

We may be sure, the art of gossip being what it was, that Lord Rochester learned about this state of affairs soon after his return from the fleet in September 1665. His suit suffered another severe blow when, in late February 1666, Betty Mallet sent an emissary to the Earl of Sandwich, proposing that she marry his son Hinchingbrooke without the consent of her guardians. She was distressed that all her marital prospects were thwarted by her grandfather's greed. He had recently ceased negotiations with Sandwich, as he did earlier with Ormonde, and after seven months of frustration, Mrs. Mallet was ready to renounce her promise not to entertain any suitors without his permission. Sandwich told Pepys:

> that for the match propounded of Mrs. Mallet for my Lord Hinchingbrooke, it hath been lately off, and now her friends bring it on again, and an overture hath been made to him by a servant of hers to compass the thing without consent of friends, she herself having a respect to my Lord's family, but my Lord will not listen to it but in a way of honour.

If she felt she was being treated as a Smithfield bargain by her suitors as well as her guardians, Mrs. Mallet had good cause. It was small wonder that Gramont described her at this period as "the melancholy heiress" (*la triste héritière*)![14]

Meanwhile John Wilmot, her would-be husband, received further marks of the monarch's approval and support. After the return of the Court to London on February 1, 1666, Rochester was sworn Gentleman of the Bedchamber on March 21. For an annual salary of £1,000, he joined eleven other noblemen in periodic attendance to the King: helping to dress and undress him, serving his private meals, seeing him into bed at night, and sometimes sleeping on a pallet at his feet.[15] Inevitably, given the King's sexual proclivities, the young Gentleman of the Bedchamber became intimately aware of bed partners brought to his master through secret passages by a trusted Page, possibly Thomas Chiffinch or, later, by his notorious brother William.[16] These ladies included, of course, Rochester's own cousin Barbara, Lady Castlemain.

Such experiences were hardly incentives to a stricter sense of sexual morality on Rochester's part. Neither was his increased contact with George Villiers, the "Great Duke" of Buckingham, also a Gentleman of the Bedchamber. Villiers's illicit passion for Anna Maria, the "predatory and destructive" if beautiful Countess of Shrewsbury, had been mounting for several years.[17] Early in 1668, it would explode in public scandal. Prior to that, in early 1667, he would lose his place in the Bedchamber and be banished for plotting against the King himself. Nevertheless, Rochester was irresistibly drawn to Buckingham, who was almost twenty years his senior.

The extent of Buckingham's influence on John Wilmot would be difficult to estimate, in matters moral, philosophical, political, and literary. Rochester's first session in Parliament in 1667 found him acting in concert with Villiers and his allies (notably Bennet Lord Arlington).[18] Many subsequent sessions saw them engaged in complex interactions that reflected Buckingham's personal relationship with the King and which affected young Rochester's own relations with his substitute father.

The Duke had been reared as a virtual son by James I at the death of the Duke's father, a great favorite of the King, who was said to have cherished a homosexual passion for the elder Villiers. Almost as brothers, young Villiers and Charles Stuart had been in exile, often in company with Rochester's father. Villiers had been with Royalist troops at the Battle of Worcester, together with Henry Wilmot, although he had been more nuisance than help.[19] In 1657, he returned from continental exile to England and made a fortunate if opportunistic match with Mary Fairfax, daughter of Sir Thomas Fairfax, the great Parliamentary General. Upon the Restoration, however, he resumed his place near the King, with whom he had a brother-like rivalry at times. Rochester could learn much about his royal master from a man so intimate with him—or so Rochester thought.

Buckingham's literary influence also was substantial. He wrote verse, erotic and satiric; he had even tried his hand at a play in 1662, an adaptation of Ben Jonson's *Volpone*, set in Venice, where he had traveled in his youth. As a literary patron, Buckingham was the center of a cluster that included Samuel Butler (his sometime secretary and dramatic collaborator), Abraham Cowley, Sir John Denham, Matthew Clifford, Thomas Sprat (Wadham graduate and historian of the Royal Society) and Edmund Waller. Several of them, notably Denham and Waller, strongly influenced Rochester's early attempts at writing poetry.[20] Buckingham reportedly brought Nathaniel Lee from Cambridge to London, where he became a protégé of Rochester's. And Villiers and Rochester conjoined in some writing projects, ranging from parodies of Dryden's *The Conquest of Granada* (1670) to lampoons on

Sir Carr Scroop, the Julian satires (mid-1670s) to the attributed *A Session of the Poets* (1676).

There were other connections between the two friends. They were related by marriage, for example; both were kin to Lady Castlemain, whom they slyly called "Cousin Barbara." Rochester's contacts with Madame in France were another mutual link. Before his entanglement with Lady Shrewsbury, Villiers had been enamored of the Princess Henrietta and had passionately followed her to France in 1661, when she became the Duchess of Orleans by marriage to Monsieur (who soon grew jealous of his bride's gallant and packed him back home to England).[21]

In addition to ties of kinship and circumstance, George Villiers and John Wilmot shared a number of interests, the most basic being money, wenching, witty company, music, and literature. Rochester's acquaintance with botany and chemistry, begun on the Grand Tour with Balfour, was stimulated by Buckingham's fascination with chemistry.[22] In his mansion at Whitehall, Wallingford House, the Duke had an elaborate and expensive laboratory, where he conducted experiments including glass-making.[23] The older man also was very fond of music, French in particular; he kept a resident quartet of musicians and he himself played the violin with considerable finesse.[24] He and Rochester were drawn together by their concern with dog and horse breeding and horse racing as well.

A letter from Buckingham to Rochester when they were on Chamber duty together suggests the degree of their intimacy:

> My Lorde
> Being to goe a hunting tomorrow and not knowing whither I shall returne time enoughf to doe my duty to his Majesty, I hope your Lordship will not refuse mee the fauour to wayte for mee that day and ly in the bed-chamber at night. I am very perticular in this matter that your Lordship may see I am a man of businesse, and take the liberty of troubling you upon this occasion becawse I had rather bee oblidged to you then any body else. I am
>
> > My Lorde
> > Your lordships
> > Most humble seruant
> > Buckingham
> > Sunday at night[25]

In sum, Rochester had much to learn in courtly—i.e., worldly—matters; and the versatile Buckingham appeared to be a fitting tutor in such knowledge. John Dryden and Samuel Butler might deride Buckingham's whimsical interests and capricious actions and Samuel Pepys might wonder at the Duke's popularity, but to an impressionable young nobleman, the Duke was the glass of fashion and a model to emulate.[26] He was not a wise choice.

In the company of Buckingham, Savile, Buckhurst, and Sedley, Rochester took on their attitudes toward fellow courtiers.[27] He did not join in their disparagement of the Howard family, Sir Robert Howard in particular, probably because Sir Robert had rescued Rochester's father years earlier at the Battle of Cropredy Bridge in 1644. Indeed, Rochester remained consistently friendly with Sir Robert for many years. But he began to absorb the rakes' mimicking behavior toward the pietistic, rather pompous Lord Chancellor, Lord Clarendon, who was blamed for arranging a bad royal marriage between Charles II and the infertile Catherine of Braganza.[28] Urged to find a rhyme for "Lisbon," Rochester mocked his erstwhile benefactor in a drinking impromptu and bogus "toast":

> A health to Kate
> Our Soveraigns Mate
> Of the Royal House of Lisbone:
> But the Devil take Hyde,
> And the Bishop beside,
> Who made her bone his bone.

As for lesser courtiers, Rochester cheerfully joined his companions in deriding them, including their earlier favorite target, Lord Chesterfield. Chesterfield continued his compulsive amours with various ladies, notably Henrietta Maria Price, a Maid in Waiting to Queen Catherine. Miss Price's gift of a pair of Italian gloves to Chesterfield occasioned Rochester's mock epistle with its sexual double entendres and suggestion that Miss Price was too aggressive and Chesterfield was "troubled with love against [his] will."[29] Such bagatelle amused Rochester's friends until serious reverses in the Anglo-Dutch war dispersed them all again to sea duty.

On June 1, 1666, the Four Days Battle, an encounter began between the English and Dutch fleets off Ostend. The English, under the command of George Monck the Duke of Albermarle, engaged with a large enemy force that repeatedly drove them aground and scattered them widely. During the charges, retreats, and counter-charges, ten English captains were killed and eight wounded, nine English ships were lost or sunk, and 1,500 men were wounded. Rumors and reports began filtering into the Office of the Navy and to Bennet Lord Arlington, the Secretary of State, by June 3. On June 6, Sir Thomas Clifford, aboard the *Royal Charles* off Saxham, provided more dismal details: in addition to the wounded, 1800 men were killed and, Clifford said, "Some of the English captains deserve hanging." His letter was forwarded to the King as the official account.

During the battle, both the *Royal Charles* and the *Royal Catherine* had run aground but managed to free themselves. Among the English captains accused of rank cowardice was Sir Thomas Teddiman, Rochester's commander at Bergen. There were frightened attempts to transfer blame. Accusations were angrily exchanged, and the Duke of York, as Commander of the King's Navy, came in for serious castigation. Newly turned nineteen, Rochester went to sea again for reasons easily conjectured. Sir Edward Spragge, commander of the *Royal Charles*, wrote to the King on June 20 that Rochester had come on board just as the ship was entering the Middle Grounds. The ships, Sir Edward was pleased to say, were in excellent fighting condition. The news was meant to be reassuring.[30]

Rochester's second experience with sea warfare was as bloody and horrendous as his first, but, whatever his private fears, the young Earl again behaved valorously. In the St. James's Fight on July 25, all the volunteers who accompanied him on board were killed: one, the brother of Sir Hugh Middleton, was shot, and he died in Rochester's arms. His commander, Sir Edward Spragge, was dissatisfied with the way one captain was conducting his ship in the battle. He asked for a volunteer to undertake the vastly dangerous mission of going in a small boat through the barrage of fire to carry a message but "could not easily find a Person that would chearfully venture through so much danger."

> This Lord [Rochester] offered himself to the Service; and went in a little boat, through all the shot, and delivered his Message, and returned back to Sir *Edward*: which was much commended by all that saw it.[31]

Rochester had demonstrated his loyalty to the King and once more proved himself Henry Wilmot's son. His bravery may have sprung from a desire to confront—and perhaps expunge—the fear of death and the spiritual chaos that followed his earlier battle experiences.

In July and August 1666, Lord Hawley was in the retinue of Queen Catherine when she went to Tunbridge Wells to take the waters. Lady Warre and Elizabeth Mallet were also there, as was the dilatory Lord Hinchingbrooke. While Hawley wrote bubbling letters expressing his pleasure at being attendant upon the Queen, Elizabeth was giving Lord Hinchingbrooke his walking papers—with a discernible measure of satisfaction. His utter lack of romantic abandon in February when she offered herself as his wife had dampened any girlish dreams she might have spun about him; and the tedious off-and-on negotiations between her guardians and the Montagues had reduced the appeal of marriage with him. Hinchingbrooke's father, Lord Sandwich, told Pepys:

> The business between my Lord Hinchingbrooke and Mrs. Mallet is quite broke off, he attending her at Tunbridge, and she declaring her affections to be settled—and he not being fully pleased with the vanity and liberty of her carriage.

Hinchingbrooke had already surmised that she had affection for someone else.[32]

When the Great Fire of London broke out in a bakery in Pudding Lane on September 2, 1666, Rochester was apparently still on naval duty; no evidence places him in London during the destruction that followed. Feeding on wooden houses, large stores of combustibles in warehouses beside the Thames, and everything else in its path, the holocaust ravaged the city. Caught in a hell on earth, people scurried frantically, screaming, cursing, and praying while trying to save their goods.[33] Pepys bustled about through the chaos while John Evelyn stood on the south bank of the Thames and felt as though he was witnessing the destruction of Sodom or Judgment Day.[34] The courtiers evacuated Whitehall, but the King and the Duke joined the fire-fighters, standing in mire, passing buckets of water and tossing out guineas to encourage their efforts.[35]

Evidence of the disaster soon reached Oxford, where the sound of the fire was audible "like the rage of a great sea, while smoke darkened the sun." Rumors that the French were responsible caused a near panic, and a swine-herd at Oxford calling his pigs was mistaken for a fire alarm and induced mass hysteria.[36] Even with a distant experience of the Great Fire, at his return to the city Rochester was imprinted with images of fire and desolation like those he had seen at Vesuvius. Together with the Biblical Sodom and hellfire, such classical versions of the burning city as Seneca's *Troas* (*Troy*), and the remembered blaze of sea battles became vivid fire-tropes in his poems, plays, and letters.[37]

Elizabeth Mallet was back in London soon after the Fire ended. Rochester was there too but their courtship appeared to be a stalemate. Despite his pension and salary from Bedchamber duties, Rochester was still said to have no fortune. Mrs. Mallet's guardians remained determined that some advantageous financial settlement between themselves and a future bridegroom be made. Sir George Carteret smugly told Lord Sandwich on September 10 that "the Lady of the West is at Court without any suitors, nor is like to have any." However, the Warres' neighbor in Somerset, Sir Francis Popham, seemed to win their favor in the autumn of 1666 to the extent that he was thought by some to be the most likely to gain Mrs. Mallet.[38]

During the autumn and early winter months of 1666, Rochester was engaged in a flurry of busy pranks, perhaps in an effort to forget the horrors of war and to postpone confronting his religious doubts. The merry gang were ready to assist him. Etherege's 1664 play, *Love in a Tub*, was revived in October.[39] It may have stimulated Rochester to try his hand at a comedy. A fragment in his early script survives in a scene showing Mr. Dainty, a Frenchified fop, at his toilette with his valet and then with a peddler wench.[40] Short though it is, the fragment displays an ear for badinage and a taste for the sort of wit written by Etherege and, later, Wycherley. Gramont included in his *Memoirs* of Rochester at this time a conversation between the young rake and his actress-mistress, Sarah Cooke, that echoed Horner's strategic pretence of impotence to aid his seduction of Mrs. Dainty Fidget (among others) in Wycherley's *The Country Wife* (1675).[41] Rochester's role in the Restoration theater was being scripted in the mid-1660s.

In the fall season of 1666, the current toast was Miss Anne Temple, who had a pretty shape, fine teeth, languishing eyes, and ingenious looks but who, Gramont said, was a credulous coquet: simple, vain, suspicious, and very silly.[42] Rochester decided to amuse himself with this poor butterfly and began the process of seduction. His efforts included the poetic, it appears. "The Submission," written in anapestic meter unusual among Rochester's early poetry, contains an oblique reference to Temple. This playful, light-hearted verse jauntily celebrates love at first sight of a beautiful, innocent "Olinda" and concludes:

> Too bright is my *Goddess*; her Temple too weak
> Retire Divine Image I feel my heart break
> Help Love I dissolve in a Rapture of Charms
> At the thought of those Joyes I should meet in her Arms.

Olinda's qualities, as well as the onomastic "Temple," suggest she was in fact Miss Anne.[43]

The silly Temple, however, had a protector, the Lady Dorothy Howard, erroneously designated "Miss Hobart" by tradition. The intelligent and virtuous Howard, a Maid in Waiting to the Duchess of York, was admired by both Pepys and Evelyn.[44] She distrusted rakish Rochester and tried to warn Temple of his wiles. In turn, Rochester spread the malicious story that Howard's interest in Temple was lesbian. He recruited his fellow-reprobate, Henry Killegrew ("Lying" Harry), in a scheme that involved wearing masks, pretending to mistake the masked Temple for Howard, and "disclosing" Howard's sexual designs. The credulous Temple swallowed the story; and when Howard afterward entered Temple's bedroom, the foolish girl awoke the Duchess of York's household with her screams. Or so said Gramont years later.[45] Temple did manage to escape his seductive web, however, and Rochester continued to hold a grudge against Dorothy Howard, whom he slandered as Doll Howard in the lampoon, "Signior Dildo," as late as 1673.

In the aftermath of these events, Rochester cast off his mistress Sarah Cooke, thereby opening the way for a serious campaign to convince Elizabeth Mallet to marry him. His long pursuit of her had strengthened his chances and her desirability, thus his love and determination to make her his wife.

On November 15, 1666, the Queen's Birthday Ball at Whitehall was a glittering affair attended by the observant Samuel Pepys. The King wore a rich silk vest trimmed with silver; the Duke of York and other nobles were dressed in cloth of silver; and the lovely Frances Stuart was stunning in white and black lace, her hair and shoulders dressed with diamonds. Only the honoree, plain Queen Catherine, was not bejeweled.

The merrymakers included Lord Rochester, his friend the Duke of Buckingham, Prince Rupert, the Duke and Duchess of Monmouth, Lady Castlemain, Lord and Lady Arlington, and many others—including Miss Anne Temple. The French dances, courantes, and branles went on too long for Pepys' taste (Lady Castlemain was not among the dancers) but Pepys doubted he would ever again see so much gallantry. Pepys did not mention Elizabeth Mallet but she was assuredly there with her dear friend, the stunning Mrs. Stuart, who had so far successfully evaded Buckingham's plot to procure her for the King and thus strengthen his influence in political matters.[46] As usual at Whitehall, a sparkling surface concealed murky eddies of intrigue. Rochester was quickly learning how to peer into the seamy depths of the Court and to take a gleefully ironic delight in what was revealed there.[47]

Meanwhile, Mrs. Mallet was trying to release herself from her own set of intrigues and sort out her options. The "Lady of the West" gave a reckoning of her "servants" to William Ashburnham, Cofferer of the King's household, possibly at the Birthday Ball or soon after. Ashburnham passed her views on to Pepys at dinner on November 25:

> that my Lord Herbert would have had her—my Lord Hinchingbrooke was indifferent to have had her—my Lord Jo. Butler might not have her—my Lord of Rochester would have forced her; and Sir [Francis] Popham (who nevertheless is likely to have her) would kiss her breach to have her.[48]

Her blunt, somewhat ribald summary with its ostensible dismissal of Rochester showed that Mrs. Mallet had regained whatever self-confidence she lost in earlier months. She was misleading Ashburnham, however, perhaps deliberately so.

It is clear that she was carrying on a secret correspondence with Rochester in the latter months of 1666. Several of Rochester's poems datable before 1671 suggest they may have been a part of his renewed, secret courtship. With the help of trustworthy agents and bribe-taking maids, cajoling verses might be passed by a lover to a young woman newly defiant of parental authority. Her approach to Lord Sandwich in February had showed she was not averse to a clandestine marriage. This time, she might be persuaded to run away with Rochester voluntarily.

The early "Song" in Rochester's hand ("Att last you'l force mee to confess") in the collection with the lovers' poetic exchange implies his unsuccessful attempt to feign indifference. One of the "Celia" poems, "The Advice," evokes the image of a raging, passionate love that is ready to surge out of bounds and reproaches Celia for living upon modesty and foregoing love's sensation. The "Prayer-Book" verse pleads for mercy, which will lead to pity, then love and heavenly joy.[49] Artifices though they are, such verse depicts states of emotion that we can imagine Rochester feeling—or simulating—in 1666. Such verse clearly evoked a response in Mrs. Mallet. On the other hand, the terms they are couched in are quite appropriate to *billets doux* sent secretly to a mistress as well as a prospective wife.

Mrs. Mallet's poetic exchange with Rochester intimated that the wrong to her of his old infidelities would be compounded by a refusal to mend his ways. She may have dismissed him to Ashburnham because she was piqued at his open attentions to Anne Temple. Then again, he did get rid of the obstructive Sarah Cooke.[50] The byplay with Temple could have been a strategy intended to deceive Mrs. Mallet's family while Rochester continued his romantic, secret courtship. Whatever the hidden motivations, in the heady atmosphere of the Queen's Birthday Ball with her secret suitor now a dashing war hero—he had even given up his drinking—how was Betty Mallet to deny him any longer?[51] His continuous and ardent courtship had convinced her that he genuinely loved her. He was certainly "in love" with her and she with him. The King continued to urge the match. She had written off her other suitors. She had declared her affections settled. Her resistance was at an end. At the close of 1666, Mrs. Mallet was ready to become Rochester's bride—without her friends' consent.

MAN'S ESTATE (1667)

They have not lost their Loyalty by fire;
Nor is their courage or their wealth so low,
That from his Wars they poorly would retire,
Or beg the pity of a vanquished foe.
—John Dryden, "Annus Mirabilis,
The Year of Wonders 1666"

Though I am justly proude of being y^{rs}, yett give mee leave
to tell you, there cannott bee more glory in y^r service than
there is pleasure & true Pride in freedome. . . .
—Rochester, *Letters*

Despite English conquest of the Dutch fleet in the St. James's Fight in the summer of 1666, a certain nervousness about the Second Anglo-Dutch War prevailed at the start of 1667.[1] When the war began in 1665, although France had a treaty of alliance with Holland, Louis XIV tried to effect a compromise settlement between the antagonists, not being eager to risk French assets. When his efforts failed, Louis declared war against England on January 16, 1666. After a year of little involvement, France began dispersing men and ships to many widely scattered places, and anxious conjectures increased at Whitehall. To add to the tension, money to pay English seamen was lacking; battle ships were useless so long as they were unmanned.[2]

Even so, a measure of lingering Christmas cheer was evident before and after Twelfth Night. Flagons of ale with apples were drunk, card-playing went on, and Robert Whitehall sent Lord Rochester a miniature of himself in academic regalia (somewhat the worse for wear) as a Christmas present.[3] Play-going continued at the King's and Duke's Theaters, newly reopened in October 1666 after the Great Fire. The popular Mary Knepp appeared in a series of roles at the King's House, including a revival of Dryden's *The Indian Emperor* on January 15. On January 23, when Knepp acted in a revival of Fletcher's *The Humorous Lieutenant*, the Pepyses went backstage and she brought to them "a most pretty woman," Nell Gwyn, who was catching the eye of the public—and some predatory noblemen—in the role of Celia. Pepys thought her "a mighty pretty soul" and both the Pepyses kissed her.[4]

Events at Court in January had tongues busy. The death of Margaret, Lady Denham, reportedly by poisoning, set rumors soaring, as did the autopsy, which suggested that neither Sir John Denham nor the Duke of York, her putative lover, had taken her virginity. The trepanning of Prince Rupert's skull, infected by a head wound, also fed the gossips.[5] Then, on January 29, to the astonishment of practically everyone, Elizabeth Mallet eloped with John Wilmot.[6]

The lovers evidently were married secretly outside London; their reappearance at the Duke's Theater on February 4 at a performance of *Heraclius* caused a stir. Samuel Pepys and his wife were part of a full house there; and Pepys had just been admiring Francis Stuart with her hair done up in stylish puffes when he spotted the newlyweds.

> Here I saw my Lord Rochester and his lady, Mrs. Mallett, who hath after all this ado married him; and, as I hear some say in the pit, it is a great act of charity, for he hath no estate. But it was pleasant to see how everybody rose up when my Lord Jo. Butler, the Duke of Ormonds son, came into the pit toward the end of the play, who was a servant to Mrs. Mallett, and now smiled upon her and she on him.[7]

A few days later, Lord John, the gallant loser, was back on his way to Dublin. Mrs. Mallet's other disappointed suitors went their several ways.[8]

Although their marriage proved, throughout its thirteen-year-long duration, to be one of growing and finally great mutual love, the young husband and wife soon discovered that romantic passion did not eliminate the trials of accommodation involved in every marriage. John and Elizabeth Rochester were strong-willed people whose first wedded years set them in frequent conflicts over money, in-laws, religion, sex, and children. Once their honeymoon was over, they began a series of clashes that made their first years of marriage often unhappy for them both, though much more for Elizabeth than John.

At the start, the bride's wealth caused problems, both expected and otherwise, for the new groom. He had to wrest her fortune from his wife's tenacious relatives, who were both stunned and angry at their elopement. They resisted making a marriage settlement; but Lord Hawley met his match in Rochester's mother. From Ditchley, on February 15, the Countess wrote to John Wilmot's legal guardian, Sir Ralph Verney:

> about my sonne Rochester's suden marage with Mis Mallet, contrary too all her frinds' exspectation. The King I thank god is very well satisfyed with it, & they had his consent when they did it—but we are in some care

how too get the estate, they [the bride's family] are come to desire too
parties with frinds, but I want a knowing frind in business, such a won as
Sr Ralph Verney—Mas: Coole the lawer & Cary I have heare, but I want
one more of quality to help mee.[9]

In time, Rochester received all of his bride's entitlements, including river
patents granted to her dead father.[10] When that happened, he had to contend
with her cavils about his management of her business affairs and her tendency
to be imperious toward a husband with lesser means than she.

Even as the tense negotiations of the marriage settlement dragged on, yet
another source of irritation began. Young Lady Rochester was compelled to stay
at Ditchley under the stern eye of her mother-in-law. The Dowager Countess had
forgotten her own troubles as a bride; her dictatorial ways with her daughter-in-
law, who became pregnant soon after the wedding, led to some querulous letters
between the young wife and her husband, who was obliged to be away on Bed
Chamber duty in the spring and summer of 1667. Their separation, the first of
many, displeased the abandoned bride. The new husband tried to assure her of
his love while showing some unease at the confines of marriage:

> Madam
> If itt were worth anything to bee belov'd by mee you were the richest
> woman in ye world; but since my Love is of soe little value, chide y^r owne
> eyes for making such poore conquests. . . . I write to assure y^r La^{sp} 'tis
> nott through vanity that I affect the title of y^r servant, but that I feele a
> truth wth in my heart. . . . That there is Left for mee, noe pleasure but in
> y^r smiles, noe life but in y^r favour, noe Heaven but in y^r Love. . . .[11]

Lady Rochester continued to chafe, however. The Countess, it seems, was
suspicious of her son's wife, perhaps because of her capricious behavior before
marriage, and she insisted that the younger woman accompany her on various
rounds to supervise family properties and make visits. Rochester tried to ease
the tensions by letter:

> I will only desire you not to bee too much amaz'd at the thoughts my
> mother has of you, since being meer imaginations they will easily vanish as
> they were groundlessly created, for my own part I will make it my endeavor
> they may . . . you must I think obey my mother in her commands to waite
> on her at Alesbury as I told you in my last letter. . . .[12]

Just when it appeared that Sir John Warre was about to agree to a financial
settlement and receive his erring stepdaughter back into the arms of her friends,
she had a miscarriage.[13] Rochester, who had been on his best behavior, wrote
a hasty apology to his father-in-law. He had been "forc't by the news of my

wives not being well" to leave town without waiting on Sir John but, admitting his fault, proposed to wait on him in a week:

> to receive y^r pardon, & put you in minde of performing y^r promise, & shew you the way hither, where (upon my word) is one very much transported wth the thoughts of being soe happy as to see you & for my owne part I begg you to beleive that noe man does more heartily desire any good in this world, than I doe the honour of your freindshipp & kindnes nor can any one have a greter value & service for you than has
>
>   Your humble servant
>   Rochester[14]

Meanwhile, the Anglo-Dutch War was renewing in intensity. Hopes for a peace settlement favoring England were encouraged at a conference in Breda on May 4, when the French again urged a genuine compromise; but the Dutch, who wanted major concessions from the English, secretly resolved to strike a telling blow against their fleet.[15] On May 27, a Dutch force of sixty-four warships set out for the English coast. Under Admiral De Ruyter, on June 10 the Dutch bombarded the unfinished fortress at Sheerness, which surrendered. The Dutch followed their reconnaissance force up the Medway River, a branch of the Thames, where the English had placed a heavy chain across the waters for security. An unseasonably high tide on June 12 enabled the Dutch to break the chain and fall upon the English ships anchored at Chatham. They burned three and towed away the *Royal Charles* in a final gesture of triumphant arrogance. It was an unmitigated disaster for the English and a disgrace for the King, who was rumored to have been dallying with his mistress even as the Dutch worked their destruction. A bawdy verse-lampoon began circulating:

> As Nero once wth Harp in hand surveyhed
> His flaming Rome, and as i^t burnt he play'd:
> Soe our great Prince when ye Dutch fleet arrived,
> Saw his ships burnt, & as they burnt hee sw[ived].[16]

The Kent militia was alerted along the river banks to prevent a land invasion; and Prince Rupert, recovered from his surgery, marshaled a horse troop. Both Rochester and Sir John Warre were given commissions in the troop retroactive for the previous year, whereupon it was dispatched under Rupert's leadership to Woolwich to build batteries and, later, to refortify the Medway.[17] As sporadic warfare continued, new negotiations for a peace agreement began. On July 21, the Treaty of Breda ended the Second Anglo-Dutch War. When the horse troops were disbanded, Rochester resumed his role as husband and manager of his wife's estates in Somerset.[18]

Since the Wilmot house at Scotland Yard in London had been sold and the Dowager Countess legally owned the rights to Adderbury Manor in Oxfordshire, the young Rochesters were more or less forced to make their residence on Mallet estates in Somerset. The manor at Enmore near Cannington became their chief home in the West in 1667 and thereafter.[19] Doubtless the move was a relief of sorts to Lady Rochester—it separated her from her mother-in-law—but it also was far from the delights of London.

Before departing from Adderbury in the summer of 1667, however, Rochester undertook the seemingly perverse task of persuading his bride to convert to Catholicism. Under his command in Prince Rupert's Horse Troop had been Stephen College, a former joiner (i.e., carpenter) at the Court of St. James. Although College professed to be a life-long Protestant, he had worked for several members of the Roman Catholic clergy, including a Jesuit priest Thomson, who trusted him. Fr. Thomson, S.J., known to John Evelyn as a connoisseur of the newly stylish *chinoiserie*, was clearly a very fashionable spiritual adviser to the highest royalty.[20] Rochester (it was reported) approached College and "employed him to bring Thomson, a priest, to his lady to pervert her." College himself testified only that Rochester had summoned him from his work for the Catholic Brooke family to Adderbury and, with his lady standing beside him, had asked College to carry a letter to Thomson, which he did. Subsequently, College worked on the Rochester estate at Enmore.[21]

Rochester's reasons for urging his wife to become a Recusant remain unclear. The simplest explanation would be that he himself had converted earlier and wanted her to share that faith. He had expressed religious doubts at the Battle of Bergen seventeen months before their marriage, however, and the strength of his Christian faith in general at the time of his marriage is questionable. He had been exposed to the skeptical thought of Thomas Hobbes by 1667, and although evidence suggests Rochester did not become a full-fledged skeptic and "Hobbist" until later, Hobbes's sardonic views toward Catholic relics and icons were enough to shake the faith of a young man attracted to Catholicism.[22] Rochester may have wanted to shore up his weakening faith by making his wife a spiritual ally.

We may more reasonably suppose, however, that his motives were more worldly. He could have been moved simply by the belief that advancement at Court would be helped by his lady's conversion to Rome. Rochester's closest relatives were in a position to know that James the Duke of York, the legal heir to the throne, was of strong Catholic persuasion; in 1669 he would be received secretly but formally into the Church by Fr. Joseph Simons, S.J., the superior of all English Jesuits after 1667. York's Protestant Duchess, Anne Hyde, was also leaning toward Catholicism and in 1670, after hearing the fervent arguments of leading Anglican clergymen, she too converted, a fact made known after her death to the consternation of Parliament and the English public.[23]

Whatever her husband's reasons, Lady Rochester followed his wishes. Raised in a home with resident chaplains, Elizabeth Wilmot was inclined to religion and piety.[24] Rochester once playfully described her pictured face as a "severity of the Count'nance, somwhat inclin'd to prayer & prophesy" and Gilbert Burnet stopped just short of calling her a saint.[25] If she had qualms about becoming a Catholic, she also wanted to please her new husband; she gave in to his urgings, setting the pattern for their future differences. After studying with Fr. Thomson, Lady Rochester became a Catholic Recusant. Long after Rochester began denouncing the Jesuits as buggers and Romanism as a fraud, she remained true to her faith, even during the anti-Catholic persecutions beginning with the Test Act in 1673 and throughout the Popish Plot witch hunts of 1678–79. She returned to the Anglican Church only in 1680, again at the urgent request of her husband, who was then dying.

While the Rochesters were beginning their marital adjustments, other events were combining in a way that affected the Earl's future politically as well as personally. Encouraged, perhaps, by the example of the Wilmots' elopement a few weeks before, the beauteous Frances Stuart also eloped and secretly married Charles Stuart, the widowed Duke of Richmond. The King, long an adoring but thwarted contender for her favors, was furious.[26] From the time of her first appearance at Court, the King had lusted for the stunning beauty—as had York—and Buckingham had tried to manipulate her into the monarch's bed but with no success.[27] However, Lady Castlemain, whom rumor said Frances was to displace as chief mistress, had cagily persuaded "la belle Stuart" to enact a mock wedding in February 1663 with Castlemain dressed as the groom and Stuart as the bride.[28] Thereafter, when the King visited Castlemain's chambers in the morning, he found the two ladies temptingly in bed and ready to breakfast with their admirer.

Despite such suggestive charades, Stuart presumably had remained chaste. Tired of his Queen, tiring of the strident (and promiscuous) Castlemain and wanting novelty, the King was pressuring Stuart to become his mistress in March of 1667, when the Duke of Richmond bore her away in marriage.[29] Enraged, the King blamed his woes on Clarendon, who had played a role in making Kate of Lisbon his bone and bane.[30]

After the naval fiasco on the Medway, the outraged English populace also looked for someone to blame. Clarendon's palatial new house in London caught their eye as a symbol of corruption in high places. Unwisely, when the fire-damaged St. Paul's was pulled down, Clarendon bought its ancient, venerable stones for his own house. Irate Londoners began breaking the windows,

cutting down trees in the garden, and writing scurrilities on the walls.[31] His
critics called it "Dunkirk House," because Clarendon had supposedly "sold"
English Dunkirk to the French for private gain, and Andrew Marvell penned
a satire, "Clarendon's Housewarming."[32] Dissatisfied Dissenters and thwarted
Catholics joined in the clamor; and disgruntled Royalists, who blamed
Clarendon for the Act of Indemnity that denied them their anticipated rewards,
added to the general criticism:

> Old fatguts himself,
> With his tripe and his pelf,
> With a purse as full as his paunch is. . . .[33]

Clarendon's woes increased. Lady Castlemain and Buckingham intensified
their continuous attacks on him, together with Bennet Lord Arlington, long the
Chancellor's enemy. Clarendon managed to get Buckingham thrown in the
Tower for authorizing a horoscope on the King, a treasonable action.[34] His coun-
terattacks against Castlemain and Arlington were largely ineffectual, however.

Harkening back to the Great Fire, clergymen began comparing London
(and Whitehall) to Sodom; and when Charles II was virtually compelled to
summon Parliament, shortly before he entered the opening session on July 29,
1667, a Quaker

> came naked through the hall, only very civilly tied about the loins to avoid
> scandal, and with a chafing- dish of fire and brimstone burning on his
> head, did pass through the Hall, crying "Repent! Repent!"[35]

Unable to justify his policies or explain the mismanagement of military
affairs, the King hastily prorogued (dismissed without dissolving) Parliament the
same day, ordering Clarendon to declare for re-assembly on October 10. When
Parliament reconvened on that date, Clarendon was absent, stripped of his
office, forced into exile, and threatened with impeachment for treason. Many
of his critical contemporaries blamed the character of the Lord Chancellor for
his downfall:

> Pride, lust, ambition, and the people's hate,
> The kingdom's broker, ruin of the state,
> Dunkirk's sad loss, divider of the fleet,
> Tangier's compounder for a barren sheet,
> This shrub of gentry married to the crown
> (His daughter to the heir) is tumbled down.[36]

Clarendon himself later blamed his disgrace on the malicious contrivances of
Buckingham, Arlington, and "the lady" (Castlemain) Some historians have also

GEORGE VILLERS DUKE OF BUCKINGHAM.

Figure 11. George Villiers, Second Duke of Buckingham. Portrait by Sir Peter Lely. National Portrait Gallery, London. Reproduced by permission.

seen a plot-scenario at work in the events of 1667.[37] Recent, more disinterested commentators have seen Clarendon's ouster as the inevitable consequence of historical circumstances that enhanced personal conflicts.[38] However, Rochester's part in Clarendon's downfall, previously unexamined, suggests that the "conspiracy" theory may be more true than is generally believed.

On July 29, 1667, the Lord Chancellor Clarendon was instructed by the King to issue a summons to the Earl of Rochester to take his seat for the first time in the upcoming October session of the House of Lords even though he was underage (*infra aetatem*). The summons was sent to Rochester on September 8; and when the Lords convened on October 10, John Wilmot was duly present, although he was seven months short of his majority.[39] It would appear that the King was trying to reconstitute the Lords by adding peers who would follow his wishes. The King also had to strengthen his ministry, particularly as it soon became apparent that shedding Clarendon threatened to create as many problems as it solved. The Earl, far from retiring into private life as Charles had expected, became invigorated by his dismissal. He made it clear that he hoped for restitution and intended to participate in the next Parliamentary session, and the fear grew that he and his friends would put pressure on the government as Buckingham had done.

In these circumstances, Charles II bowed to the inevitable and came to terms with Buckingham. On September 4, the Duke was given a long private conversation with him, and eleven days later he was restored to all his offices. On the 23rd, Buckingham reappeared in the Privy Council, now as a respected adviser of the King, a position emphasized by his waiting upon him that night in the capacity of Gentleman of the Bed Chamber.[40]

With Buckingham and Rochester literally and figuratively at his side, the King opened Parliament on October 10. Buckingham's allies proposed thanks to the King for dismissing Clarendon from the Privy Council, thereby stirring up suspicions on all sides, although at last the Lords concurred.[41] The Committee on Privileges, alerted, questioned the right of young Lord Rochester to be seated, since he was underage. While they debated his case, the Earl disappeared for a few days, returning in time to hear the reading of an Act for punishing and suppressing atheism and profaneness and profane cursing and swearing. The next day, he was present to concur in the Chancellor's dismissal, the first step in the ritual of banishment.

When the King had a summons sent to John Sheffield the Earl of Mulgrave, also underage, presumably to strengthen the royal hand, the Lords petitioned that he be "sparing of Writs of this Nature for the future." Unlike Rochester, who was clearly eager to remain a part of the impeachment proceedings, Mulgrave declined to answer the summons. He did not take his seat in the Lords until well after Clarendon's business had been settled. If Mulgrave, who owed little to the Lord Chancellor, avoided involvement without suffering any consequences, why did Rochester persevere in conspiring with Buckingham and Arlington to follow the King's bidding?

Rochester saw plainly that whatever favors Clarendon had in his power to do, the King was the final dispenser of benefits. And the benefits did not go to the godly and moral but to those who pleased Charles II. Rochester's own relatives had proved that. Ned Apsley, who showed up drunk in the House of Commons during the impeachment, pandered to both the King and the Duke. Buckingham had armed his servants, plotted against the king, and been involved in illegal dueling. The King overlooked it all so long as Buckingham followed the royal bidding.[42] Lady Castlemain had grown rich and powerful ministering to Charles's sexual pleasures. If an ambitious young lord wanted gold—and Rochester did—he saw the quickest way to get it.

Clarendon appealed his dismissal, and Rochester attended the sessions assiduously all through October. Faced with the imminent vote on Clarendon's impeachment, the Lords did not seat Mulgrave and, on November 9, raised again the question of Rochester's right to be seated. The Commons passed a motion to arrest Clarendon for treason, but the Lords hesitated, concerned for their rights and fearful that a dangerous precedent was involved: accusing a man of a capital crime and arresting him without specific grounds. As the issue was debated, Rochester was steadily present, disappearing for a few days to attend the festivities of the Queen's Birthday.[43]

Then, on November 20, the Lords requested a conference with the Commons; but a group of twenty-eight peers signed a Demurrer, stating their conviction that Clarendon should be arrested immediately without specific charges. The Demurrer, engineered by Bennet Lord Arlington, the Secretary of State, had as its three top signers the Duke of Buckingham, George Monck the Duke of Albemarle, and the Earl of Rochester. Thus John Wilmot conspired to destroy Edward Hyde, the Earl of Clarendon, the man who befriended his grandfather and father, who was sheltered by his mother during the Civil Wars and who protected her in France, who enriched the estates of his family, and secured sinecures and promotions—possibly even a rich wife—for Rochester himself in his first years at Court.[44]

Although the Demurrer proved that Rochester and his co-signers were the King's men, willing to do his bidding even when the rights of the peers themselves were at risk, the Clarendon problem was not yet solved. During the last weeks of November, the Lords and Commons shunted the issue back and forth, the former refusing to indict without specific charges, the latter refusing to confer. From November 21 to 27, Rochester appeared faithfully; then abruptly on November 28 he was absent, called home by a family crisis.

In his absence the Clarendon affair went on to its destined end. On December 12 Hyde was declared a traitor and banished perpetually. Although he was not present at the vote, Rochester had proved himself an ingrate, if nothing worse, to the benefactor to whom his mother had once declared her hope that her son would inherit her heart and thus forever be Hyde's loyal servant.[45] Neither maternal rhetoric nor maternal hope has ever proved binding on a

Figure 12. Edward Hyde, First Earl of Clarendon. David Loggan after portrait by Sir Peter Lely. National Portrait Gallery, London. Reproduced by permission.

son's behavior; nonetheless, the Dowager Countess could not have been pleased at the part her son Rochester played in Clarendon's disgrace. She had worked too long to build a strong alliance with her kinsman and had benefited too often from her ties with him. But another, more immediate and personal calamity at Ditchley kept Rochester and his mother working together temporarily.

Frank Lee, Rochester's kind half-brother and the sole adult Lee male and head of the family, had fallen ill with the scourge of the Lees, smallpox. On December 4, he died, leaving his widow, Eleonore Pope, and two infant sons: Edward Henry, not yet two, and Francis, a baby.[46] At a stroke, the Countess found herself once again in the situation of the 1640s: matriarch of a proud family, the Lees of Ditchley, whose future depended upon an infant baron and some girl children.

With the Lee-Hyde alliance gone, the Countess would try to use her son Rochester, as she once used Frank Lee, to rebuild political and financial ties and maintain the family estates. Rochester assumed the hereditary posts of the male Lees as Ranger of Wychwood Forest and Game-Keeper of Oxfordshire.[47] The Countess had been thinking of moving permanently from Ditchley to Adderbury, but Frank Lee's death changed her mind; she had better stay where she could supervise the interests of her only grandson, Edward Henry Lee. Rochester could take on the responsibilities of Adderbury. The stage was thereby set for family contentions in the future when Wilmot interests differed from those of the Lees, as they were bound to do.

Not yet legally of age but firmly set in his role as a man, politically and domestically, Rochester wrote to his wife at Enmore to inform her of changes: directly about the external, indirectly about changes in himself and his feelings:

> The alteration of my mothers former resolutions (who is now resolv'd against ever moving from hence) puts mee upon some thoughts wch were allmost quite out of my head; but you may bee sure I shall determine nothing that does not tend as much to your reall happiness as lies in my power. I have therefore sent you this letter to prepare you for a remove first hither, & afterwards as fate shall direct, which is (I find) the true disposer of things whatever we attribute to wisdome or providence; bee therefore in a readiness upon the first notice from mee to put that in execution wch I shall first informe you particularly of . . . God bless you.
>
> yours
> Rochester[48]

Bemused at the changes in his life, the twenty-year-old Earl was feeling the perplexity of making decisions when neither human experience (wisdom) nor divine will (providence) seemed to prevail, when only chance or accidents (fate) controlled what happens. Although he clung by habit to Christian truisms, Rochester's doubts about God's providence and the worth of human reason were increasing. Despite such doubts, he realized the need to plan for himself and his dependents in the hopes of attaining "real happiness"; this was part of a man's responsibilities. Although his mother and his bride had not proved compatible, he hoped that by locating them some twenty miles apart, at

Ditchley and Adderbury respectively, peace could be maintained and, on occasion, he could act both roles: the dutiful son and the loving husband. He could also attend more easily to his various duties—and pleasures—in London and Oxfordshire. Or so he hoped.

By the close of 1667, at the age of twenty, Rochester had taken irrevocable steps into manhood. He had made decisions that committed him to a course of life he had been taught as a boy to consider immoral, even sinful. By joining Buckingham in the political overthrow of old-fashioned, moralistic Clarendon, he had committed a symbolic action. By aligning himself with such amoral caterers to the King's desires as Buckingham, Castlemain, and Arlington, he had appropriated their values together with their methods. By the end of the year, his transition was complete: from an ambitious, ingenious student to a rewarded minion whose fate depended upon serving the pleasures of his royal master, King Charles II.

THE KING'S PIMP (1668–1669)

> But to confess the truth, my advice to the lady you wot of has
> ever been this: . . . cherish [the King's] love wherever it
> inclines, and . . . with hand, body, head, heart and all the fac-
> ulties you have, contribute to his pleasure all you can and
> comply with his desires throughout . . . you may judge
> whether I was a good pimp or no.
> —Rochester to Savile (June 1678)

When Rochester told Gilbert Burnet that he once had been continually drunk for five years, he must have been referring to the period from 1668 to 1672.[1] During those years, his literary output was slight, his attendance in Parliament was sporadic, and scandalized stories about his drinking, wenching, and brawling proliferated. Burnet blamed the drinking for most of Rochester's postwar problems: risk-taking searches for diversion and unleashed sensuality that destroyed his health. But like other young men who fight in wars and survive but lose their ideals, John Wilmot seems rather to have used alcohol to fend off a sense of nothingness, to anesthetize his fear of death and suppress a growing rage at life and the world.

Rochester's inclination for the bottle was a bequest of temperament from his soldier-father, along with other characteristics: "a haughty and ambitious nature" and "a pleasant wit." Clarendon, who had ample opportunity to observe both the Wilmots, described the father in terms that also applied to the son. "Wilmot loved debauchery" and was "inspired" in its "very exercise":

> He had, by his excessive good fellowship, (in every part whereof he
> excelled, and was grateful to all the company,) made himself so popu-
> lar . . . that he had, in truth, a very great interest; which he desired might
> appear to the King, that [the King] might have the more interest in him.[2]

In combat, however, Henry Wilmot shunned all drink or "Dutch courage."[3] His son, who also grew abstemious in combat, had no restraints to check him once his military duties were over and his disapproving bride was off in the country. On the contrary, his interest with Charles II required that he amuse the monarch and his roistering companions and be a constant source of witty entertainment.

> And the natural heat of his fancy, being inflamed by Wine, made him so extravagantly pleasant that many to be more diverted by the humor, studied to engage him deeper in Intemperance. . . .[4]

In the company of Buckhurst, Savile, Sedley, Buckingham, and other Court wits, it was tempting for Rochester to drown his memories of war, religious doubts, and mortal fears in the "cup that banishes care," as Horace called it. Drink was a way to deaden doubt while he was following his plan to gain riches by pleasing the King; but it also removed the mask of inhibitions that Rochester had donned to hide his deep-seated feelings. By postponing his confrontation with the roiling emotions that moved him to poetic creativity, wine also delayed his development as a poet.

The exile of old Lord Clarendon removed whatever restraints his presence had imposed on the son of Henry Wilmot. Clarendon's disapproval of the King's "ministers" had been obvious. He blamed them when the King "indulged to his youth and appetite that license and satisfaction that it desired, and for which he had opportunity enough. . . ."[5] It was one thing to mock the old gentleman behind his back. It was much easier to have him absent. With Clarendon gone, the two most influential men at Court were Buckingham and Arlington, neither of whom provided much of a moral example.[6]

Henry Bennet, Lord Arlington, had a long relationship with the Wilmots.[7] A Royalist in the Civil Wars, he acquired a distinctive saber cut on his nose, which he emphasized with a plaster as a black badge of courage. In 1645 he had followed the Stuarts to France; after 1651 he gravitated into the circle around Charles Stuart, where he became friends with Henry Wilmot and a perpetual contender with Edward Hyde for influence over the heir to the throne. A diplomatic mission kept him in Spain until 1661 and gave him a sobriquet: "the stiff-necked Spaniard." He apparently met John Wilmot before the young lord left for the Grand Tour in 1661; and he kept watch over Rochester's career before his return in 1664.[8]

From 1661 to 1665, Bennet steadily rose in power. Siding with Lady Castlemain and those Courtiers who subsequently formed the CABAL (Clifford, Ashley, Buckingham, Arlington, Lauderdale) after Clarendon's fall, he had become Secretary of State despite Clarendon's opposition. Bennet wrote the pro-Catholic Declaration of Indulgence in 1663 that raised a storm of Protestant protests and intensified the mutual antagonism between him and Clarendon.[9]

Bennet's good offices toward John Wilmot during his courtship of Elizabeth Mallet and naval service drew the young man closer into the Secretary's orbit. When Arlington masterminded strategy of the King's supporters during the Clarendon trial and drew up the Demurrer of the Twenty-Eight Peers in November of 1667, Rochester followed Buckingham into alliance with him. Rochester wanted to gain royal favor and riches; and Arlington's methods of doing this were obviously successful. Arlington provided a model of pimping as a means to money and power. He began by procuring Barbara Villiers, progressing to La Belle Stuart, and at last arranging for Louise de Kéroualle, for whose conduct he gave advice in a letter of 1671 to Colbert de Croissy, the French Ambassador, that foreshadowed Rochester's advice to Nell Gwyn by way of Savile in 1678:

> The young lady must be counseled to manage well the good graces of the King, not to speak to him of [political] affairs, and not to show any aversion to those who are near him, and, in short, to let him find only pleasure and joy in her company.

Bennet's procuring, his advantageous marriage to a wealthy heiress in May 1666, his connection with such French savants as St. Evremond, his lavish style of life at Goring House, and his wedding a beloved child-daughter to a bastard-son of the King and Lady Castlemain: all served as examples to John Wilmot in his own rise at Court.

Arlington was not the only member of the royal circle to use petticoat strategy to gain the King's favor. Buckingham, of course, had tried it with limited success. Anthony Ashley Cooper, Lord Shaftesbury, attempted it; and even Charles Sackville, Lord Buckhurst, prepared for the King's sexual pleasures when he paid £100 a year to lie with the pretty, witty actress Nell Gwyn.[10] Buckhurst seduced Nelly from the stage (and the arms of her current lover, the handsome actor Charles Hart) in July of 1667. Thereafter, the two of them joined with Sedley in a *ménage à trois* at Epsom Wells. Nelly returned to the stage at the end of August; and after a possible liaison with Buckingham, who together with Sir Robert Howard was searching out new favorites for the King, she passed on to the bed of Charles II, who she playfully insisted was *her* Charles III.[11]

1668 was a time of unprecedented debauchery for all the rakes in Rochester's circle. In January, Buckhurst got into a violent quarrel with Aubrey de Vere, the Earl of Oxford, and a duel was narrowly averted.[12] In the same month, the tempestuous affair between Buckingham and the Countess of Shrewsbury climaxed with a furious duel between the Duke and the Earl of Shrewsbury, who was severely injured. The affair lead to horrified (but baseless) gossip that the lady, disguised as a boy, had held the Duke's horse as her husband was wounded and then had engaged sexually with her bloody lover.[13] Unabashed at their infamy, Buckingham, Buckhurst, and Sedley sat in the pit with the author at the première of Etherege's suggestive comedy, *She Would if She Could*, at Lincoln's Inn Fields on February 6.[14]

Into this riotous atmosphere, Rochester returned in February 1668, after seeing to family matters, while his wife stayed at Adderbury to settle their new household. He was ready for diversion from the somber business following Frank Lee's death. For the next three months, he joined in the amusements of the Court wits and attended sessions of Parliament in a desultory fashion, following up on the King's business after the displacement of Clarendon. On February 17, he first came to the Lords, where the King's money bills were pending.

Charles needed funds for his public projects and private pleasures, but Parliament was loath to be further manipulated and the rate of absenteeism among the Lords was high. After attending sessions twice in February and once in March, Rochester was present at both morning and afternoon sessions on April 24, when Sir William Penn, another intended scapegoat, was charged with plundering the Dutch East India fleet and cheating the King.[15]

The bloody duel between Buckingham and Shrewsbury in January led to further scandal when, after both received royal pardons, Shrewsbury died several weeks later. With the case involving murder, the King felt obliged to institute laws against dueling. On April 24, Rochester was named to a Committee to draft legislation to outlaw duels and see to its passage. At last in early May, after Parliament tarried over bills for rebuilding the burned City, the King was voted his monies and he promptly prorogued it until October 1669.[16]

During the spring, Rochester was on Bedchamber duty, sporadically if not regularly.[17] Even so, he had plenty of time to return to his old drinking habits and to engage in the "great sensuality" that alcohol stimulated.[18] About this time, Wilmot and his crew formed a sexual society, the "Ballers," dedicated to such pastimes as drinking, sexual exhibitions, and dancing naked with the young women in a brothel kept by "Lady" Bennett, the enterprising widow of a baker. One of Henry Savile's letters to Rochester makes it clear the Earl was a mastermind among the Ballers.[19]

Their group activities provided the model for the conclusion of Act II of the bawdy playlet, *Sodom*:

> *A Dance*
> *Six naked men and six naked women appear and dance. In their dancing the men do obeisance to the women's cunts, kissing and tonguing them often. The women in like manner do ceremony to the men's pricks, kissing the glans, quidling and dandling their cods, and so fall to copulation, after which the women sigh, the men look simply and so sneak off.*

Such drolleries were sustained by the illegal importation of French wines and dildos (artificial penises made of leather) by one or another of the Ballers, who at intervals found it prudent to steal off to France. Harry Killegrew had recently come from France when he and Dick Newport met up with Pepys in a tavern on May 30, 1668, and acquainted him with the Ballers' doing "all the roguish things in the world." Sober-citizen Pepys, scandalized as he was that Killegrew and Newport tried to grab every woman who walked by them, sounded a bit wistful when he recorded the meeting:

> But Lord, what loose cursed company was this that I was in tonight; though full of wit and worth a man's being in for once, to know the nature of it and their manner of talk and lives.[20]

Among Rochester's other claims to preeminence among the Ballers was his ability to charm and seduce any virgin he put his mind to. Not only Gramont but Savile admired his talent at harvesting maidenheads. Since the King preferred sexually experienced women for mistresses, it became the agreeable duty of the seductive Earl to initiate young women into the techniques of love detailed in Ovid's *Ars Amatoria* and depicted in the sixteen *Postures* of Aretino in preparation for their role as Charles II's *houri*.[21]

Burnet's *History* implied strongly that Jane Roberts, the daughter of a clergyman, followed Moll Davis and Nell Gwyn in sequence as the King's mistresses; we may surmise that Rochester's lessons to her were given in 1668.[22] Unhappy Jane, like Rochester himself, had been thoroughly indoctrinated with Christian prohibitions which, though strong, nevertheless failed to keep her from a life of promiscuity. She became the King's mistress for a time and survived a first discarding by a piteous plea, hair flowing loosely as she knelt in nightdress at Charles's feet—or so the story went.[23] After she was discarded a second time, she sank to new lows, becoming infected with diseases that led her to death within a dozen years. Her eleventh-hour repentance prepared the way for Rochester's own deathbed conversion a year later.[24]

Burnet said of the period following Clarendon's exile:

> At this time the court fell into much extravagance in masquerading; both king and queen, and all the court, went about masked, and came into houses unknown, and danced. People were so disguised, that without being on the secret none could distinguish them.[25]

Traveling incognito, aristocrats cast off the responsibilities of their public roles, such as they were, and indulged their fantasies. Oddly enough, they could find a justification of sorts for masking in the philosophy of Thomas Hobbes.[26] On one occasion, however, Queen Catherine, in disguise, found herself confused

and stranded in a strange part of the city, having lost her sense of place and
thus her identity.

For Rochester, since it was habitual, masquerading came easily. Burnet
wrote that Rochester was so clever at disguising himself and acting as a porter,
beggar or carman (chair-bearer) that even those in on the secret could "per-
ceive nothing by which he might be discovered." Burnet did not suspect that
Rochester might be disclosing some of his deepest feelings through his por-
trayals of the low born. What Rochester viewed as his basic or "base" nature
could be enacted by assuming the guise of the *villein* or villain.[27] Certainly,
Rochester's life was an incessant attempt both to succeed by the aristocratic
conventions of his era and to break free of, even destroy them. Since dress
"reinscribes a person's sex, rank, age, occupation—all the distinctive features of
the self," his disguises may have been something of "a meditation on [his] cultural classification" as an aristocrat.[28]

Discussing the mysterious ambiguities of Pierrot in the *commedia dell arte*, a
critic has observed:

> To don the mask is an old instinct in man who longs at some time or other
> (if only in childhood) to assume a secondary personality, or to appear as
> the personality he mostly conceals. The freeing of the conventional
> self . . . when he dons the mask, is an illustration of his need for expression
> of the other self who may indeed be the basic truer self.[29]

Burnet conjectured Rochester's motives for disguise as "sometimes to follow
some mean Amours, which, for the variety of them, he affected," and at "other
times, meerly for diversion, he would go about in odd shapes. . . ."[30] Back in
Adderbury, as lord of the manor, he diverted himself by dressing as a tinker and
knocking out the bottoms of clients' pots and pans or acting as a tramp and
decoying other vagabonds into criticizing Lord Rochester for stinginess and then
having them dunked in a barrel of beer.[31]

On his return to London, the devil between the thighs took command at
Brentford and he resumed disguise for sexual purposes.

> Disguise has its own eroticism and its own metaphysics. Eroticism is the
> easiest to represent. It has frequently been attested to in literature and
> manners. In Aretino's *Dialogues of Courtesans*, teachers of the profession on
> numerous occasions advised their adepts to disguise themselves and pre-
> tend to be boys, as the most effective means to rouse passion.[32]

Nell Gwyn demonstrated that she could rouse emotions in male spectators by
appearing as a boy, Florimel in Dryden's *Secret Love* in March 1667. And
Edward Kynaston was equally provocative when he appeared in women's

dress.³³ The "disguises" of actors, crossed-dressed and otherwise, were manifestations of what Jan Kott has further explicated:

> not only was it an attempt at eroticism free from the limitations of the body. It was also a dream of love free from the limitations of sex; of love pervading the bodies of boys and girls, men and women, in the way that light penetrates through glass.

Rochester's "The Fall," a quasi-Wallerian lyric written ca. 1667–68, suggests such a poly-sexual longing.³⁴ Moreover, if in his first years of pimping for Charles II his amours were heterosexual and intensely phallic, some of his poems were dreams of love pervading the bodies of boys as well as women. His academic reading in the Roman poets had given him sufficient knowledge of Latin to go on into the arcane reaches of their poly-erotic compositions: Petronius's "*Foeda est in coitu et brevis voluptas*," for instance. In such pan-sexual writings, the literary precedents for Aretino's empathetic depiction of a woman's feelings in the *Dialogues* could be found. Rochester's similar adaptations of Petronius, Ovid, or Anacreon suggest a thinly disguised homosexuality. "The Platonick Lady" declares:

> I love a youth, will give mee leave
> His Body in my arms to wreath;
> To presse him Gently and to kisse,
> To sigh and looke with Eyes that wish. . . .³⁵

As a pimp to Charles, who was no pederast, Rochester's orientation was heterosexual. However, he apparently was also a lover of youths in the style of fellow rakes who, craving variety, turned to sexual experimentation with boys.

> In 1670 a reckless sexual practice like sodomy (reckless because it could have grave legal consequences) was the province of the abandoned rake, who was also likely to be a libertine in religion and a republican in politics. The rake always took the active (or penetrator's) role in sodomy; his passive partner was a younger, late adolescent male. But the rake was also quite sexually interested in women and was in no way effeminate in behavior or dress.³⁶

In several of Rochester's works, *The Tragedy of Valentinian* among them, an adult male speaker describes the pleasure of sexual activities with boys; e.g., a "Song" ("Love a Woman! y'are an Ass") and "The Disabled Debauchee." For the first years of his marriage, Rochester's genuine ardor for his wife appears to have confirmed his heterosexuality. But after 1670 there is strong evidence for his interest in man-boy love, perhaps in part as a renewal of his desire for variety but possibly also because of his venereal woes and growing misogyny.³⁷

Not that the Rochesters' marriage was idyllic in its early years. From Adderbury, Lady Rochester sent peremptory directions to her husband about purchases and other matters. She also demanded accounts from her estates in Somerset, which she had once accused her guardians of cutting timber from. Rochester tried teasing her by playing the hen-pecked husband in "To his more than Meritorious Wife," *bagatelle* verse of a different sort than that used in their courtship:

> I am by Fate Slave to your Will,
> And I will be Obedient Still,
> To Shew my Love I will compose ye,
> For your fair fingers ring a Posie,
> In which shall be express'd my Duty,
> And how I'le be for ever true t'ye,
> With Low made Legs and Sugard Speeches,
> Yielding to your fair Bum the Breeches,
> And shew my Self in all I can,
> Your very Humble Servant Jan.

Of course, Rochester was *not* being forever true to his wife, although it may have been true that he was "endeavouring every day to get away from this place [Whitehall] which I am soe weary of, that I may be said rather to languish than live in it," as he wrote to her in May 1668.[38] Lady Warre made a visit to Lady Rochester in the country at this time and informed her daughter that Rochester was not languishing so totally as he said. Letters from an exchange between husband and wife show the problems of newlyweds at odds about money and in-laws and who is to obey whom.

> The stile of y^r La^{sps} last though kinder than I deserve, is nott without some alloy from y^r late conversations wth those whom I should extreamly honor if they would doe mee the right and you the justice never to come neare you when I am really as well wth you as I wish & you pretend . . . in the meane time I will exercise my usuall tallent of patience and submission. . . . Blancourt is going in to the West, att whose returne you may expect an Account of y^r intire revenue, wch I will bee bould to say, has hitherto, & shall (as long as I can gett bread without itt) bee wholly imploy'd for the use of y^r self & those who depend on you; if I prouve an ill steward, att least you never had a better. . . .[39]

> Madam
> It was the height of Complyance forc't mee to agree y^r La^{sp} shoult [*sic*] come into Oxfordshire. If it does not please you 'tis not my fault, though much my expectation . . . if y^r La^{sp} had return'd moneys out of Somerts for the Buying those things you sent for they myght have bin had by this time, But the little I gett here will very hardly serve my owne turne; however

I must tell you that 'twas Blancourt's fault you had nott the Holland &
other things sent you a fortnight agoe. Next weeke I goe into the West &
att my returne shall have the Happiness of waiting on y^r La^{s}p.[40]

Having finished some end-of-season business in London, including petitioning for further Royal concessions and receiving a warrant for £1,000 for
Bedchamber duties, Rochester went to Somerset in June to oversee the estate
at Enmore. He then went to Adderbury, where he successfully appeased his
wife for the time being. Domestic harmony restored, Lady Rochester became
pregnant in July 1668. This time, she would carry the child successfully to
full term.

Back beside the King in September, Rochester made some influential literary contacts through his rakish friends. Buckhurst had been browsing at a
bookseller's and casually picked up a copy of *Paradise Lost*. A fast perusal
pleased him and he bought a remaindered copy for a pittance, being told it
was so much waste paper by the seller, who urged Buckhurst to recommend it
to his friends.[41] One of these was John Dryden. Another was probably
Rochester, who under the spell of Milton's erotic descriptions of Adam's and
Eve's love-making reflected and composed his own version of "The Fall":

> How blest was the Created State
>   Of Man and Woman, e'er they fell,
> Compar'd to our unhappy ffate!
>   We need not fear another hell:
>
> Naked beneath cool shades they lay,
>   Enjoyment waited on desire;
> Each member did their wills obey
>   Nor could a wish set pleasure higher. . . .[42]

This wistful description shows not only Rochester's knowledge that carnal
pleasure has limits but also Thomas Hobbes's impact on his thought. In the
Leviathan, Hobbes speculated about the Adam and Eve story as an example of
the judicature of good and evil, "nakedness" as experienced by them, and the
epistemology of thought as reality. Like the first parents, Rochester's fallen
man and woman, "poor Slaves to hope and fear," risk the shame of judging
their nakedness to be uncomely.[43] His depiction of Hell as a state of mind,
while echoing the view of Milton's Lucifer, also followed the precedent of
Hobbes.[44]

Rochester knew Hobbes through many agents, including the King, who had
been tutored by him and who delighted in the "Evil Genius of Malmesbury";
but Hobbes was also the long-time librarian of the Cavendishes, and young

William Lord Cavendish was a member of the rakes' circle at Court.[45] A handsome, charming womanizer like Rochester, he had gone on the Grand Tour with a tutor-clergyman whose influence left little imprint. In September 1668, a Cavendish protégé, Thomas Shadwell, published his first play, acted earlier in May: *The Sullen Lovers, or The Impertinents.*[46] Rochester delighted in the play, became friends with its author, and alluded to it in his own later satires.[47]

Literary interests, however, were overshadowed by the growing debauchery of Court rakes in the late months of 1668. In September, Buckingham was restored to his place as Gentleman of the Bedchamber, and Buckhurst became Groom of the Chamber. They, with the King and Sedley, staged a riotous progress. In Thetford they forced a group of fiddlers to play all the obscene songs they knew. The King was too drunk at Saxham to see Arlington, who traveled over from London to confer. And after their return to London, Sedley and Buckhurst ran through the streets "with their arses bare," beating the watchman, and making noise all night.[48] Rochester also provided the King with amusement.

On December 2, Pepys heard Charles's "silly discourse" about Rochester having his clothes and gold stolen by one wench while he was abed with another. The Earl's clothes turned up later, stuffed in a feather bed, but the gold was "all gone." Rochester turned the tables, according to another story, by accompanying the King in disguise to a brothel and sneaking off his clothes and money while Charles made sport. Trapped, the embarrassed monarch offered to pay for his pleasure with a ring, which was recognized—as was its royal owner. Such farcical doings were widely talked about.[49]

In the first months of 1669, Rochester made a series of blunders that sent him to France. Throughout 1668, Secretary of State Arlington had been secretly carrying on negotiations to form a Triple Alliance with Sweden and Holland while extracting funds from France for England's "friendship," all the while pretending to be open in order to deceive a suspicious Parliament. On December 27, 1668, Rochester was present at a state dinner that Arlington gave for the French Ambassador Colbert as preparation for the Treaty of Dover. Charles's sister, Madame, was acting as doppelgänger to Colbert in the secret negotiations.[50]

On January 25, 1669, Charles disclosed his plans to York, Arlington, Clifford, and Lord Arundel of Wardour, declaring his willingness to proclaim himself a Catholic publicly. Matters were at this stage when, on February 17, Conrad Van Beuningen, the Dutch Ambassador—Arlington called him "a prying, talking, pressing man"—gave a banquet for the King. Van Beuningen correspondingly suspected that Arlington was "desirous to transfer his affections" to the French. Just when it was vital to maintain the delicate balance of diplomatic courtesy, Rochester committed a technical act of treason at the ambassadorial dinner. He boxed old Tom Killegrew (or Killigrew), manager of the King's Theater, on the ear in the King's presence.[51]

Killegrew could be maliciously clever and he was not slow to direct his barbs at the mighty. When the handsome but dense Duke of Monmouth asked Killegrew what he would give to be as young as Monmouth, Tom replied that he would be content to have as little wit. He told Charles II that he governed as if he had a mind to go travel again. And with reference to the royal mistresses, he told the King that "one prick in our day costs more maintenance than a thousand concubines in Solomon's." At the dinner, Killegrew directed his "mirth and raillery" at Rochester, reportedly with some jest about Rochester's marriage. Probably drunk, Rochester lashed out in sudden anger.[52]

The King reacted by downplaying the matter: Pepys said he "passed by the thing" and pardoned the miscreant. Charles went even farther and made a public appearance with the Earl the following day. Courtiers said the King had cheapened himself by his actions and Pepys declared it was "to the King's shame to have so idle a rogue his companion."[53] Tom Killegrew's reaction went unreported; but his son Harry took offense to the extent that Rochester felt it necessary to apologize to his fellow Baller "for the affront he offered his father."[54] Possibly Rochester thought it best to avoid a duel of honor when he had been charged with drawing up legislation against it. He was not so lucky the next time.

The worst consequence was that the episode had seriously antagonized Lord Arlington. As Secretary of State he was displeased that the King of England had been lowered in the eyes of diplomats he wanted to impress with national power and prestige. It was a personal embarrassment as well. His wife was connected to the Dutch royal family; William of Orange (the future William III of England) always called her "ma cousine." And Arlington not only admired Tom Killegrew as a dramatist—as a young Oxonian, he had written some effusive prefatory verses to Killegrew's *The Prisoners and Claracilla, Two Tragedies* (London 1641); Killegrew was Arlington's uncle by marriage to the beautiful Cecilia Crofts.[55] Rochester offended a powerful man.

Nevertheless, flushed with the King's support (and wine too, no doubt), the twenty-two-year-old rake soon got into another scrape coming from complex interactions between Buckingham, Tom Killegrew, Henry Savile, and Sir Robert Howard. Howard had been made the butt of several literary jokes in recent months. Shadwell had lampooned him as Sir Positive At-All in *The Sullen Lovers* (possibly at the suggestion of Dryden, Howard's brother-in-law).[56] An attempt by Howard at sylvan allegory, *The Duel of the Stags*, a tribute to his new friend and ally Buckingham, had evoked a scabrous parody, *The Duel of the Crabs* (i.e, crab lice) by Buckhurst.[57] At Tom Killegrew's request, Howard wrote a comedy, *The Country Gentleman*, into which Buckingham inserted a scene parodying Sir William Coventry and his pride in a round desk.[58] Coventry threatened to slit the nose of any actor who played "Sir Cautious Trouble-all," his avatar, and sent his great-nephew, Henry Savile, with a dueling challenge to Buckingham, a legal offense by the Lords' new legislation.[59]

Savile was arrested and put into Westminster Gate House, where "rogues" (a legalism for vagrants or vagabonds) were confined. Incensed at this treatment of his Gentleman of the Bedchamber, the Duke of York had Savile transferred to the Tower. Subsequently, the Duke dimissed him from service; and Savile's friends rallied round him. One night after a dinner with Savile in the Tower that included too much wine, a fight broke out between the Duke of Richmond and James Hamilton. Rochester was involved in the fracas; and when word got about that another duel challenge was involved, Rochester's critics, including Arlington, renewed their pressure against him.[60]

Once more, the King acted as an indulgent father; Rochester accompanied him to the races at Newmarket in early March. Lady Rochester's pregnancy was nearing its close and the father-to-be resisted notions of leaving the country in the standard way until he was given some "sober advice" to follow a face-saving tactic. A new diplomat, Ralph Montagu, was departing for Paris, with a company of English noblemen; Rochester would be one of them. At Newmarket, he wrote a reassuring love-note to his wife:

> I'le hould you six to fower I love you wth all my heart, if I would bett wth other people I'me sure I could gett two to one, but . . . I am not in paine to satisfye many, it will content mee if you beleive mee & love mee.
>
>   R[61]

Pocketing a letter from the King to Madame, he set off for France in late March or early April.[62]

Rochester stayed in France from April through July 1669, where he managed—as always—to get involved in situations that gained wide attention. On April 15, he was one of the company when Ralph Montagu was formally installed as the English Ambassador to Louis XIV; but the Sun King refused to permit Rochester to kiss his hand when Madame tried to present him to the royal presence. Those that struck in Kings' presences should have no countenance from him. (Colbert had dutifully reported events at the Dutch Ambassador's dinner.) As a gratuitous reproof, the monarch added that no one frowned on by "the King his good brother of England" should find favor with him.[63]

Rochester managed to repay the slur on both himself and, by implication, King Charles, whose letter to Madame plainly showed he did not frown on John Wilmot. The Sun King, it was reported, had inscribed on a marble pillar at the completed Versailles a Latin distich celebrating his supposed military conquests, which was translated into English as:

> *Lorain* a Day, a Week *Burgundy* won,
> *Flanders* a Month; what would a Year have done?

Rochester was said by a creditable source to have written beneath it:

> Lorrain he Stole, by Fraud he got Burgundy
> Flanders he bought 'ods you Shall pay for't one day.

Four years later, in 1673, he still nursed his resentment. He poetically dubbed Louis "the Hector of France;" and in 1676, the French King became Tarsehole the King of Gomorrah in the final version of *Sodom*.[64]

On April 19, as he was crossing the Pont Rouge in a sedan chair, six armed men set upon him, robbed him of cloak and watch, twenty pistoles, and a very fine periwig.[65] He managed to get through May without further scrapes; but on June 21, a more serious incident got international attention and presented the opportunity for Louis XIV's snub to be more than revenged. Lord Cavendish was also in Paris and Rochester went with him to the theater at the Palace of Orléans to see his old comic favorite, *Scaramuchio*. Seven or eight of Louis's personal guardsmen were seated on the stage alongside the English visitors and one of them insulted Cavendish, who struck him in the face.[66] (Perhaps the cowardly actions of the braggart Scaramouche gave rise to unflattering comparisons.) The group of Frenchmen attacked en masse: Cavendish suffered seven or more wounds from their swords and would have been killed if his Swiss servant had not picked him up and thrown him into the orchestra pit. Rochester prudently retreated and saved himself.[67]

When he learned of the event, Ralph Montagu took immediate diplomatic advantage of it. He proceeded to St. Germain to demand justice from the French King, who was outraged at his guardsmen—he threatened to hang them all—and chagrined that "such a thing should happen to be done by his officers to any strangers, much more to the English and to people of that quality." The guardsmen were punished; Cavendish recovered from his wounds; and Rochester was free to pursue the other amusements Paris offered.[68]

These were, of course, numerous; some were arcane and exotic. Rochester probably grew acquainted with such French sexual variations as transvestism, pedophilia, and male homosexual societies. All existed in the France of Louis

XIV and all were accessible to an English aristocrat who was interested in experimentation and acquainted with such French *libertins* as Gramont, Jean-Baptiste Lully, and the Duc d'Orléans, all of whom were involved with the secret Order of Sodomites that flourished at the time.

Certainly the transvestism of Philippe the Duc d'Orléans was no secret. Raised in as effeminate a way as possible to prevent him from rivaling his brother the King, Monsieur was given to fussing with his hair and complexion, wearing elaborate gowns, jewelry, and ribbons, and engaging in the pastimes of ladies of the Court. His taste was greatly admired by them and he suggested ways they might improve their dress and appearance. He had a lover, the handsome Chevalier de Lorraine, who was envious of Monsieur's wife, Madame. Monsieur himself was jealous of other men's attentions to her, probably desiring them to be attentive to him.[69]

Another outstanding transvestite of the day was François Timoléon the Abbé de Choisy, who dressed as a girl for Monsieur's frequent visits, and who in time masqueraded as a woman although he was heterosexual. Choisy spent some time on the stage at Bordeaux as an "actress" in comedy much admired for "her" beauty; he had "lovers to whom I granted small favors, but was very discrete as to great favors, and had a reputation for prudence and virtue." Choisy prevailed on several women in his life to dress as men. He even went through a marriage ceremony with one young woman, she dressed as the groom and he as the bride. Later in this tradition, the most famous of transvestites, the Chevalier D'Éon, excelled.[70]

Rochester was of course familiar with cross-dressing by actors, on and off the English stage. In female dress, Thomas Kynaston in *The Silent Woman* was described by Pepys as the prettiest woman in the house; and great ladies like Castlemain took him carriage-riding in St. James's Park wearing his finery. Although Kynaston's transvestism may have been connected with homosexuality, much cross-dressing was not. Even the redoubtable Sam Pepys amused himself at times by donning his wife's gowns; and Clarendon's youngest son, Henry Hyde, Lord Cornbury—a distant cousin of Rochester's—not only dressed as a woman but had his portrait painted as such when he served as the governor of New York under Queen Anne.[71] Rochester also masqueraded as a woman on several occasions, if an authentic source and a somewhat dubious one are accurate. His masquerades were heterosexual in intent, according to the sources; but if seduction was his goal, his highly successful impersonation of women was also proof of his ability to identify with a female self.[72]

The Paris visit in 1669 also could have revealed sexual activity between men and boys. A poem that purportedly described Rochester's daily routine (and was attributed to him), the "Regime d'viver" (ca. 1673) contains these lines:

> I send for my *Whore*, when for fear of a *Clap*,
> I Spend in her hand, and I spew in her *Lap* . . .
> If by chance then I wake, hot-headed, and drunk,
> What a coyle do I make for the loss of my *Punck*?
> I storm and I roar, and I fall in a rage,
> And missing my *Whore*, I bugger my *Page*. . . .[73]

Rochester's *Sodom* also made the practice of buggery a response to the fear of getting the clap (gonorrhea) or the pox (syphilis) from women. However he contracted it, Rochester himself began to be treated for venereal complaints soon after his return from Paris in 1669; his intensified interest in sodomy began soon afterwards.

In Paris, as Gramont made plain, courtiers were far more sophisticated about homosexuality than those at Whitehall, who in 1666 "were simple enough there never to have heard tell of such Grecian refinements in the art of love."[74] Buckingham, however, knew first hand about those refinements by the mid-70s when he reputedly had a sexual relationship with Kynaston the actor.[75] When the Ballers got crab lice and worse from Lady Bennett's seraglio, some of them felt tempted, like Henry Savile, to "turn Turk" and try pederasty as a substitute. But Francis Fane was skeptical:

> The pox gotten from boys cannot ever be cured
> the boy at parris.

The French Order of Sodomites went even further and extolled sexual relations between men. Founded as a secret society by Gramont, the Marquis de Béran, and Prince Condé (or Conti), the members pledged to forego women in order to engage in sex with each other.[76] They elected a "King" who regulated the code of homosexual conduct and presided over the sexual rites; Jean-Baptiste Lully, Italian by birth as was Prince Conti, was one of the Kings. The Sodomites wore under their cloaks a golden cross showing a man trampling a naked woman underfoot.[77] Even the Dauphin was said to belong to the Order, which was abolished by Louis XIV when he discovered it.

Rochester made implicit allusion to the Order of Sodomites in his mock tragedy, *Sodom*, which showed buggery between adult males. Although he called himself "un bougré" to Savile, in only one quasi-autobiographical work did he suggest a taste for such activity.[78] The dividing line between "boys" and sexually mature men is sometimes blurred in Rochester's writing, however, and the sexual ambiguities in his revision of Fletcher's *Valentinian*, are pronounced. In

Rochester's version, where the sexual relationship between the Emperor and Lycias the eunuch (a Rochester innovation) counterpoints the rape of Lucina, Lycias is called a "boy" but his age is indeterminate. We must conclude that John Wilmot was not particularly concerned with distinctions of age, homosexually speaking.[79]

In the months of his Paris exile, as Rochester looked beyond the conventional limits of carnal "love," events at Adderbury defined him ever more firmly in traditional roles. When he left Paris to return home, he entered into a new stage of life that polarized his obligations, raised him to new extremes of love, and renewed his interest in poetry but hastened his abandonment of Edmund Waller's premise that true wit must be "free of offense."

LOVE RAISED TO EXTREMES (1669–1670)

> Eager desires confound my first intent,
> Succeeding shame does more success prevent,
> And *Rage*, at last, confirms me impotent.
> —Rochester, "The Imperfect Enjoyment"

Just as the anticipated birth of his first child had made him reluctant to go to France, his wish to see his growing family made Rochester eager to return to England. Soon after arriving in Paris, he had sent an anxious note to his wife, who was on the verge of giving birth:

> I should be infinitely pleased (Madam) with the newes of your health; hitherto I have not bin soe fortunate to heare any of you but assure y^r selfe my wishes are of your side as much as is possible; pray only that they may bee effectuall, and you will not want for happiness.
>
> Paris the 22 of Aprill
> French Stile[1]

Lady Rochester's prayers were evidently successful: she was delivered of a daughter soon after Rochester arrived in Paris. Named Anne for Rochester's mother, the Wilmot heiress was christened on April 30, 1669, by the Vicar of Adderbury Church, William Beau the Bishop of Llandaff. A notation was made in the parish register of the baptism into the Protestant faith of "The Lady Ann daughter of the Right Honourable John Earl of Rochester."[2]

Beginning with his first daughter, Rochester delighted in his children. Referring to the newborn infant as "our sole daughter & heir issue female, the Lady ann" he bade his wife to "assure [her] of our best respects." His solitary boyhood seems to have made John Wilmot aware of children's needs. When he became a father, Rochester experienced a new kind of love from those he had known before. He treated each of his own children in turn with the loving, playful deference he showed toward his eldest. When his wife was displeased with him, he pretended to ask the three-year-old "my Lady Anne willmot" to "intercede" for him. He sent her costly presents and in outbursts of paternal feeling called her "the little girl whom my soul loveth."[3]

His flight at the performance of *Scaramouche* may have owed in part to new fatherhood, a realization of his paternal responsibilities and unwillingness to die before seeing his only child. In any case, Rochester's wish to go home was the reason for Ralph Montagu's mediating letter to Arlington on his behalf in mid-July.

> The reasons of my Lord Rochester's coming into France, I suppose, are not unknown to your Lordship; upon his return into England I believe there is nothing that he is more desirous of than Y[r] L[Ps] favour and countenance; and if hereafter he continues to live as discreetly as he has done ever since he was here, he has other good qualities enough to deserve it, and to make himself acceptable wherever he comes.[4]

Since the French assault on Rochester at the opera had strengthened England's diplomatic hand with Louis XIV, Arlington had no excuse to oppose his return. Consequently, Rochester was happily reunited with his wife and new daughter and enabled to resume his round of visits to their estates and the Woodstock horse races in September before going to London in October for the opening of Parliament.

Charles II summoned Parliament in dire need of money. It convened on October 19, 1669, but Rochester was absent, although the King certainly was counting on him to support the royal cause as before. The Earl had found himself suffering from a malady sometimes called the "straungery," or blockage of urine. Believing kidney stones to be the problem, he placed himself in the hands of a French physician, Monsieur Florence Fourcade (or Forcade), one of the King's surgeons. Fourcade ran a medical establishment where hot tubs, abstinence, and a diet of almonds, raisins, and "spoon meats" followed the "griping of the gut" (squeezing the urinary tract between thumb and forefinger).[5] Hopeful about his treatment, Rochester sent a packet of letters to his wife with a cheerful, covering note:

> From our Tubb at M[ns] Fourcards this 18[nt] of Octob:
> Wife; Our gutt has allready binn griped, & wee are now in bed soe that wee are not in a condition of writing either according to thy merritt or our desert. . . .[6]

She should hand out the letters "in what way soever by us inscribed or directed," see to the erection of the furnaces at home, and pay his respects to "the Lady ann."

By October 29, he felt well enough to appear in Parliament, where "several Papers by the Commissioners for taking Accompts of several Monies" were presented. On November 9, he was placed on a committee to consider these reports; and the next day he was present to vote on a bill outlining and defining "the Privileges and Procedures of Parliament." Thereafter, he failed to come to the Lords' sessions for several weeks, presumably plagued by his ills. When he returned, he was in the custody of the Gentleman Usher of the Black Rod, under arrest for illicit dueling. (So much for living discreetly after his return!) Ironically enough, Rochester found himself being judged by the dueling statute he had helped to draft and pass.[7]

On Wednesday, November 24, Sir Ralph Verney noted that Rochester and John Sheffield, the young Earl of Mulgrave, had gone off to fight on the previous Monday and there had been no word of them since.[8] Thus entered into John Wilmot's life the man who stayed an envious antagonist as long as he lived, who unsuccessfully tried to emulate Wilmot's social graces and poetic wit, who patronized writers dismissed by Wilmot and got them to defame him, and who did everything he could to blacken his name after Wilmot's death.

Although John Sheffield eventually gained great wealth and social position, winning the favor of Princess Anne, the future Queen, acquiring the title "Duke of Buckingham" when George Villiers died without heirs and buying Goring House, Lord Arlington's mansion, and renaming it Buckingham House (now Palace), he became a laughing stock to Rochester's circle. Vain, hyperthyroid Mulgrave was termed "goggle-eyed," "splay-footed" and a "looby" by Rochester himself, who also scorned him as "My Lord All-Pride" and "Bajazet" (a bombastic tyrant), names that stuck, to Mulgrave's irritation.[9]

Sir Carr Scroop (or Scrope), something of a buffoon himself to the Rochester circle, also launched a versified attack on Mulgrave's person and character:

> *Grandio* thinks himself a *Beau-Garcon*,
> *Goggles* his *Eyes*, writes *Letters* up and down;
> And with his sawcy *Love* plagues all the *Town*. . . .[10]

An anonymous lampoon summed up a widespread opinion of Mulgrave:

> Let Mulgrave like a Dog Kick'd out of doors
> For his Aspiring Projects & Amours
> Unman himself to Sneake, Fawn, Cringe, & Whine,
> And play ye Spaniel till they let him in.[11]

Born in 1648, one year almost to the day after Rochester's birth, Mulgrave's life was synchronized with Wilmot's in a delayed parallelism. Before 1669, where Rochester had excelled, Mulgrave had fallen short. In 1666 when

Figure 13. John Sheffield, Earl of Mulgrave, First Duke of Buckingham and Normanby. Unknown artist. National Portrait Gallery, London. Reproduced by permission.

Rochester distinguished himself for bravery at sea, Mulgrave volunteered for the Navy and went aboard a ship that never sailed. In 1667 when Rochester was given a commission in the horse troops, Mulgrave applied for one and was opposed by the Duke of Monmouth, who took an intense dislike to the swaggering youth. Mulgrave, however, won his commission—together with the lasting hostility of Monmouth. When Rochester, underage, entered Parliament in 1667

Figure 14. James Scott, Duke of Monmouth. Unknown artist. National Portrait Gallery, London. Reproduced by permission.

to serve his royal master, Mulgrave, also *infra aetatem*, never showed up although twice summoned. Throughout 1668, John Sheffield busied himself with the horse troops and bitter lawsuits against his mother and former guardian. Finally, he attained his majority in 1669 and celebrated it by challenging Rochester to a duel in November.[12]

The cause of the challenge, Mulgrave said in his *Memoirs* fifty years later, was that he was informed "Rochester had said something of me, which, according to his custom, was very malicious." His vanity threatened, Mulgrave had Colonel Edmund Ashton, "a very mettled friend of mine," deliver a challenge to Rochester, who denied he had ever made such remarks. Although convinced he never said them, Mulgrave insisted the duel be fought anyway:

> the meer report, tho' I found it to be false, obliged me (as I then foolishly thought) to go on with the quarrel; and the next day was appointed for us to fight on horseback, a way in England a little unusual, but it was his part to chuse.[13]

The events of the duel were the stuff of a farce-comedy—Sheridan's *The Rivals*, perhaps. Mulgrave and Ashton went to Knightsbridge to avoid being stopped in their plans. There they spent the night nervously in an inn, knowing that robbers and highwaymen used Knightsbridge as a gathering spot. Meanwhile, the King learned of the proposed encounter and sent one of his guards to prevent it. Failing to locate Mulgrave, the guard arrested Rochester in his chamber. The Earl gave his word of honor not to escape, then "pretending to have some Occasion to go into a little Back Room," slipped out a rear door. Frustrated in his effort to control the situation, the King dispatched additional searchers and reluctantly notified the House of Lords about the duel, which they were empowered to deal with.

> His Majesty says, as the Earl of *Rochester* is His Servant [Gentleman of the Bedchamber], He knows what course to take with him; but, in regard they are both Peers . . . desires their Lordships to take some Course with them.

Rising to the occasion, the Lords instructed the Usher of the Black Rod to find the errant nobles and haul them back in safe custody.

When Ashton and Mulgrave appeared at the rendezvous on November 23, they were disconcerted to see that Rochester's second was "an arrant Life-guard-man whom nobody knew" but who was armed and "extremely well mounted" whereas they "had only a couple of pads." The mettled Ashton blustered about his opponent's superior equipment. Finally, they all agreed to fight on foot; but Rochester told Mulgrave that "he was so weak with a certain distemper, that he found himself unfit to fight at all any way, much less a-foot."

Mulgrave was agreeably surprised that a man with such a reputation for courage would admit "weakness." He cannily decided to press his advantage and told Rochester they would be ridiculed at Whitehall if they backed down, even though there had been no reason for a duel in the first place. Seeing through Mulgrave's ploy and amused by it, Rochester said he would take the full onus. They then returned to London, where Ashton, no doubt anxious for his bully reputation,

> thought himself obliged to write down every word and circumstance . . . in order to spread every where the true reason of our returning without having fought.

Realizing the sort of fools he was dealing with, Rochester did not bother to contradict or resent Ashton's report.

When on November 24 Mulgrave made his maiden appearance in the House of Lords in custody of the Black Rod, he readily promised the Lord Keeper not to engage in any duel with Rochester and declared on his honor he would observe the pleasure of the House. The next day, to a similar charge, Rochester responded, tongue in cheek,

> I have never been angry with the Earl of *Mulgrave,* and I have no Reason to believe that he was so with me; for his lordship hath always carried himself so gently and civilly toward me.

Thereafter, for the remainder of the session, the two men duly showed up in the Lords, alternating their appearances, with Rochester present more often.[14]

When he left London for the country in early December 1669, Rochester was beginning a five-month period of seclusion; no records show him in the city before May 1670. Undoubtedly, this was a time of recuperation; the weakness caused by his "distemper" was genuine. The nature of the disease, it seems clear, was venereal; Rochester may even have been infected with syphilis for the second or third time without knowing it.[15] Medical diagnoses were random; and syphilitic symptoms were often taken for kidney stones, scurvy, scrofula, and other diseases. Since the treatment for most of these was the same—except for mercury draughts and viper peptic specified for *lues venerea*—and since all were virtually ineffective, a husband might persuade himself, "out of civility to his lady," that he suffered from something other than the pox.[16]

His reference to the tub at M. Fourcade's indicates that Rochester had suffered through hot baths to induce sweating, being wrapped in flannel, and subjected to clysters and vomiting.[17] An extended regimen of that sort was enough alone to weaken him but the progressive symptoms he showed in later years and recorded—weakness, dizziness, "pissing of blood," failing sight, crippled limbs, swollen lymph glands, and skin eruptions—suggest very strongly that by 1669 he was passing from the primary stage of syphilis into a remission of perhaps a year and so to secondary and tertiary stages with intermittent remissions.[18]

For someone with Rochester's priapic obsessions, the first symptoms of sexual malfunctioning indicated a distressing diminishment of sexual activity.

This could take the form of premature ejaculation, inability to climax more than once, or impotence. His anxieties (and imagination) stimulated, he explored those conditions and their psychological impact in several poems for which evidence exists of composition as early as 1670–71. "The Imperfect Enjoyment," one of Rochester's most discussed lyric poems, is the most revealing.[19] Various commentators have found in "The Imperfect Enjoyment" contradictions between rebelliousness and moral conventions; kingship and waging war seen in terms of whoring and debauching; an attack on pride in the flesh; public incompetence reflected in private impotence; a reversal of dominant roles between males and females; even a reflection of Rochester's bisexuality.[20]

Certainly in 1670–71 Rochester was revolving in his mind such concerns, which became thematic issues in his mature works. Emotionally and poetically, however, "The Imperfect Enjoyment" shows Rochester's transition from a youthful, erotic perspective to the ironic and satiric purview of his maturity; from egocentric to social questions; and from a conventional poetic diction to a realistic, even argotic, style. Indeed, the poem itself embodies the shift, juxtaposing idealized ecstasy with brutal disillusionment.

When he was in the country, Rochester was given to study, the classics in particular, as Gilbert Burnet testified. During his five-month rustication in early 1670 while reading Ovid, he found a personal experience paralleled in *Amores* III.vii:

> tacta tamen veluti gelida mea membra circuta
>   segnia propositum destituere meum;
> truncus iners iacui, species et inutile pondus,
>   et non exactum, corpus an umbra forem.[21]

Recognizing the ironic disparity between man's fancied ideal of sexuality and its embodied reality, Rochester converted the ordinary phenomenon of temporary impotence into an ingenious fusion of fantasy and reality which was romantic, ludicrous, and bitterly impassioned. He had found his poetic voice and he began forging a distinctive lyric mode.

The poem begins with lyrical eroticism:

> Naked she lay, claspt in my longing Arms,
> I fill'd with Love, and she all over charms,
> Both equally inspir'd with eager fire,
> Melting through kindness, flaming in desire. . . .
>
> My flutt'ring *Soul*, sprung with the pointed kiss,
> Hangs hov'ring o'er her *Balmy Brinks* of Bliss.
> But whilst her busie Hand, woul'd guide that part,

> Which shou'd convey my *Soul* up to her *Heart*,
> In liquid *Raptures*, I dissolve all o'er,
> Melt into Sperme, and spend at ev'ry Pore. . . .

The lady provides both loving encouragement and manual stimulation;

> But I the most forlorn, lost *Man* alive
> To shew my wisht Obedience vainly strive,
> I sigh, alas! and Kiss, but cannot Swive.

The rueful triplet concludes with a single line, reversing in diction from the opening poetic interjection, "alas" to the blunt "swive" ("fuck"). The rude disjunction of language, like the alliterative and euphemistic "Balmy Brinks of Bliss," which is reduced to the jarring monosyllabic "Cunt" and repeated twice, anticipates the male psychopathology in the rhetorical question addressed to his penis (soul):

> Through what mistaken *Magick* dost thou prove,
> So true to lewdness, so untrue to Love?

The erotic connection between a man's penis and his "soul" or spirit is lost when he sees sexual desire as "lewdness" opposed to spiritual "Love" and the "common *Whore*" as the reverse of a truly beloved woman or "great *Love*." Carnal ecstasy and spiritual ecstasy made antithetical, both a man's erection and spirit must fall. All women become either whores, a "tingling Cunt," or angels, spiritual creatures not to be polluted with the "clammy joys" of sperm.[22]

One critic has suggested that Rochester's conversion of Ovidian impotence into premature ejaculation in this poem is indicative of gnawing doubts about his own sexuality. But the diatribe against the penis, damning it to Shankers (cancre sores), Weepings (discharges), Straungery, and Stone contains the essence of Rochester's later sardonic satire. Here the degree of passion arises from newly aroused fears. Whatever the date of its composition, "The Imperfect Enjoyment" was almost certainly written after Rochester had manifested some of the very symptoms he lists.

Threatened by his awareness of being tied to a dying animal, Rochester attempted to objectify the penis as distinct from himself. He used the same technique with dark humor in 1673 when he personified the penis as "Count Cazzo"; but the overt seriousness of the self-contempt implicit in the penile curse here ("Rakehell Villain," "Base Recreant") would take the form of an intensely personal self-condemnation in "To the Post Boy" (1676) and the ultimate outburst of self-deprecation on his death bed in 1680. While damning his penis, Rochester also denied any consolation he might draw from a resulting "female" self by concluding in effect that to be female was to be a whore. With "The Imperfect Enjoyment," Rochester thus began a tortuous, introspective probing into his own psyche that made him unique among the Restoration wits.

The ambiguities of the penis/soul image receive an interesting treatment in "The Mistress, A Song," a poem of unknown date. Here, the question of whether man's immortal "soul" exists or does not exist is framed in terms of an emotional paradox: the presence or existence of sexual "love" (desire or lust) in the absence of its object. An age seems short as a winter's day in the embrace of the mistress.

> But, oh how slowly Minutes rowl,
>   When absent from her Eyes
> That feed my Love, which is my Soul,
>   It languishes and dyes. . . .
>
> Alas! 'tis Sacred Jealousie,
>   Love rais'd to an Extream;
> The only Proof 'twixt her and me,
>   We love, and do not dream
>
> Fantastick Fancies Fondly move;
>   And in frail Joys believe:
> Taking false Pleasure for true Love;
>   But Pain can ne're deceive.

These lines suggest a solution of sorts for the dilemma shown in "The Imperfect Enjoyment." If "false" sexual pleasure is not compatible with true "spiritual" or "soulful" love, the emotionally intense pain of "Sacred Jealousy" is nevertheless proof that the love is real. Rochester accepts the conventional moral disjunction between sacred and profane love. Implicitly, of course, such an assumption confirms the oppositions of body/spirit, lewdness/love, and whore/angel with yet another: pleasure/pain. Rochester's divided conscious-ness always looked for antitheses.

Alterations in health and attitudes that Wilmot was experiencing in 1670 came with changes in his role and obligations as a family man. Early in the year, Sir John Warre died, suddenly and without warning. As usual, he had been bustling about Somerset, always scheming to make money. On February 3, he wrote to Sir Francis Hawley detailing his desire to get the post of Customs Comptroller, which was worth only £60–70 a year, but Sir John was sure he could sell it for £300–400. Soon after, he was dead.[23]

In consequence, Rochester became more involved in the financial affairs of his wife's mother and step-brother and more closely concerned with managing Mallet-Wilmot holdings in the West. Mallet patents to dredge the Parrott and

Thone Rivers held promise for great profit; Rochester and Sir Francis Hawley began planning ways to carry out the dredging project and secure rights that would give them access to the port city of Bridgewater with no costs for shipping their own goods from there to Bradford Bridge.[24] Rochester also filed a joint suit to strip Sir Baynham Throckmorton, Kt., of the rangership at Kingswood, where his hell-for-leather riding disturbed the neighborhood.[25] In time, Rochester himself became an alderman for the town of Taunton and the Deputy Lieutenant of Somerset.[26]

His increasing responsibilities in the West created more divided interests and separated roles for Rochester: Somerset versus Oxfordshire, Enmore versus Adderbury. In Oxfordshire, Rochester's mother still exerted the power, holding the lease on Adderbury Manor as she did. She was also increasingly active in controlling the lives of Harry Lee's two daughters, Ellen (age 13) and Nan (11), and vying with his mother, Lady Lindsey, over the fortunes of young Edward Henry Lee, the older of the two last male descendents of her first husband. Edward Henry was five years old in 1670; his mother had remarried and was now the Countess of Lindsey, wife to Robert Bertie the Third Earl.[27] The Dowager Countess of Rochester and Lady Lindsey did not always see eye to eye on what was best for the Lee heir, and they both resorted to Sir Ralph Verney when a clash of wills occurred.

Rochester was fond of young Edward Henry Lee and he played a complicated part as uncle to the future Earl of Lichfield.[28] But with Sir John Warre dead, Rochester also found himself in something of a paternal role to his wife's ten-year-old step-brother, Francis Warre. The boy was the age John Wilmot had been at the death of his own father. Rochester began referring to "my brother" with the same courtly playfulness he used toward his own children. Francis had to be placed at Oxford, choose a profession, enter Parliament and find his niche at Court. Rochester apparently helped in all these matters; and later on, Francis Warre and his family were frequent visitors to the Rochesters. He was present at Woodstock when Rochester died.[29]

Rochester's role as *paterfamilias* was further confirmed when his wife became pregnant with a second child in late February or early March 1670. Given his sexual anxieties, it was probably reassuring to him to impregnate his Lady. That he did so suggests that he managed to convince himself that his recent troubles really were due to kidney stones and that he was cured. Later, when evidence that his problem was venereal became clear to him, he stayed away from her for some months with no explanation, much to Lady Rochester's bewilderment. If he was "barbarous" to Elizabeth Wilmot and "injured" her— and their only son—by impregnating, and thus infecting, her when his syphilis was latent, it was not intentional. Even if he had been totally indifferent to her welfare (and he was not), he certainly did not want to sire a child congenitally afflicted, as in fact he did.[30]

As Rochester tended to domestic duties, the flurry of trans-Channel visits that were a prelude to the secret Treaty of Dover in May 1670 was taking place. Buckhurst and Savile had gone to France in July 1669 just as Rochester was leaving it. In contrast to his treatment of Rochester, the Sun King presented each with his own portrait circled with diamonds, a £600 gift. Buckingham, who wrongly thought his was the key role in later negotiations with the French, would be given a jeweled sword by Louis in the aftermath of Dover in July 1670, when he went over to Paris to see to signing ceremonies, accompanied by Buckhurst and Sedley.[31] In May 1670, Buckhurst was back in France to request that Madame's proposed three-day visit to Dover be extended. Jealous of her influence with Louis XIV, Monsieur did not want her to come to Dover at all.

Various theories have been advanced about the reasons for Charles II signing a secret treaty with Louis XIV so soon after Arlington had concluded the Triple Alliance with Holland and Sweden against France.[32] The truth seems to be that, desperate for money and determined to be free of both ministerial and Parliamentary restraints, Charles bargained for French (and possibly hoped for Spanish and Papal) gold. He promised to declare himself a Catholic, launch a joint attack with France against Holland, and allow French troops to enter England to support him in case of trouble.[33] The treaty was to be signed in secret during what was supposedly a round of festivities for the amusement of the King and Madame at their first reunion since her marriage in 1661.

Of course, Lord Rochester's presence was required. He left his family at Enmore and went to London to resume his chores as Gentleman of the Bedchamber to the monarch. On May 16, Madame's ship arrived at Dover, escorted by the English fleet, and the celebrations began. The King adored his sister and she, him—some thought them unnatural in their intensity—and the celebration was joyous. Madame particularly enjoyed performances of Shadwell's *The Sullen Lovers* and John Caryll's *Sir Salomon Single*, in which the comedian James Nokes, playing Sir Arthur Addle, appeared in an exaggeratedly French costume, wearing the Duke of Monmouth's sword. The French were chagrined to see themselves aped by the buffoon Addle while the English roared with laughter.[34]

Amid the frolics, on May 27 the secret treaty was signed for England by the Catholic members of the Cabal (Arlington, Clifford) and Arundel of Wardour, also a Catholic, and for France by Colbert de Choisy. The Protestant members of the Cabal, Buckingham and Ashley Lord Shaftesbury, were kept ignorant of the Catholic clause. The secret business done, public merriment continued until Madame's tearful departure to France and a vengeful husband. On June 29, two weeks after her arrival home, Madame died after several agonized hours as Louis XIV wept by her bedside and her husband coldly suggested an emetic. Ralph Montagu sent the sad news by messenger to Charles, who was devastated.[35] It was rumored that she had been poisoned and the Kings of France and England were distraught at the implications. Charles required the steady presence of Rochester, who wrote a sympathetic but somewhat wry account of events to his wife.

She had returned to Adderbury and she sent him cheeses, sugar of roses, and other "good things" but no letter, although she had enclosed one to her mother, Lady Warre, in London for the summer. Communications between the Rochesters had become "very tedious," as he remarked, with some breakdowns apparent; and Rochester's shift of tones between his public and private messages reveals changes in the Wilmots' marriage after three years.[36]

> Pray doe not take itt ill that I have writt to you soe seldome since my comming to towne, my being in waiting; upon the sad accident of madam's death, (for wch the King endures the highest affliction immaginable) would not allow me time, or power to write letters. You have heard the thing, but the barberousness of the manner you may guess att by my relation:— Mounsieur since the bannishment of the Chevallier de Lorrain . . . has ever behav'd himselfe very ill to her in all things, threatning her upon all occasion that if shee did not gett Lorrain recall'd . . . the worst that could befall her . . . soe that shee returning to Paris, hee immediately carries her away to S^nt Cloud where having remain'd fifteen dayes, in good health she having bin bathing one morning [in the Seine], and finding herself very [thirsty] call'd for some succory water [a cordiall julep] . . . and being then very merry discoursing wth some of the Ladyes, . . . shee had noe sooner swallow'd this succory water but immediately, . . . she cryed she was dead, and sending for her confessour after 8 howers infinite torment in her stomack and bowells shee died, the most lamented (both in france & England) since dying has bin in fashion, but I will not keepe you too long upon this doleful relation: it is enough to make most wives in the world very melancholy, but I thanke you for . . . all my good things. Pray lett it not bee necessary for mee to put you too often in mind of what you ought not to bee less forward in doing than I in advising; I hope you will give mee noe occasion to explaine myselfe, for if I am putt upon that you will find mee very troublesomee . . . pray send mee some ale and re[mem]ber mee to nan. Shee has a present for her godaughter but I doe not know w^ht it is, send mee word and if it bee not what it should bee, Ile send another—
>
> tarara[37]

The letter shows shifting moods, from the stern admonition to do as he tells her without questioning him to the breezy farewell. (Probably he had instructed her to remain at Enmore during his absence.) Asserting his mastery, he reverts to his obliging manner: some agent (Cary or perhaps Blancourt) has made a purchase, a christening present for Rochester's niece, Nan Lee, to give to her goddaughter at Adderbury. Rochester himself will replace it with a more suitable gift if it is inappropriate in his wife's judgment.[38]

The offhand remark about Monsieur's alleged murder of his wife making most wives melancholy suggests a veiled threat. Rochester made such threats much more explicit in messages to both his wife and mistress at later times. Although "The Imperfect Enjoyment" absolves the woman of responsibility for male rage at himself, the note of misogyny in this letter, also found in Rochester's early pastorals, sounded strident after only a few more months as the bantering attitude toward death in this letter darkened into gloom. Misogynistic themes and attitudes then came to dominate his poems.

In the summer of 1670, however, despite the mourning for Madame, he found amusements. The Ballers carried on their diversions, and Rochester acquired lodgings of his own in London: he took a house on Portugal Row in Lincoln's Inn Fields, next door to the Duke's Theatre.[39] The move was indicative of his growing involvement with the London stage. Formerly a tennis court, the theater had been built by Sir William Davenant in 1660, when it rang innovations in sets and decorations. Upon Davenant's death in April 1668, his wife and son Charles became the nominal proprietors while the actors Thomas Betterton and Henry Harris acted as co-managers.[40]

Rochester knew all of them well. Twelve years old in 1670, Elizabeth Barry had come under the protection of Sir William Davenant before his death and she remained the ward of Lady Davenant until she became a neophyte actress and Rochester's mistress in 1673 at the age of fifteen.[41] Betterton, who co-starred with her in major plays of the 70s, 80s, and 90s, was so familiar with the Earl that he mimicked him to perfection in Etherege's *The Man of Mode* in 1676; and the Rochester circle of wits conferred Apollo's laurels on Betterton as the best of contemporary playwrights in the same year. Rochester even favored Charles Davenant with an Epilogue to *Circe*, when the young man first assayed writing a theatrical spectacle in May 1677. Although the Duke's Players moved to their grand new theater in Dorset Garden in November 1671, and Rochester himself moved to new lodgings in Whitehall, the ties between the Earl and the Duke's company, formed in 1670, stayed close.

At the end of August, Rochester left the city for Oxfordshire, where he thought to stop off for a brief visit with his wife before going on to the Woodstock Races and then back to London. But she had returned to Enmore. The Dowager Countess and Lady Rochester had had one of their tiffs and the younger woman decamped for Somerset. The old Countess exerted her authority on occasion, sweeping into Adderbury Manor and majestically clearing out her son's possessions as she pleased, to his frustrated annoyance. He could retaliate only by keeping away from her.[42]

As Rochester's responsibilities placed him increasingly in opposition to his mother's priorities, the wedge opened by his participation in the Clarendon impeachment widened, causing strains in their relationship, although he refused ever to permit an open or lasting rupture. He remained bound to the strong-willed woman who had dominated his childhood, even when she sided with the Lees against him in financial and family matters.[43] Relieved at not finding himself caught between mother and wife at Adderbury, Rochester wrote a charming, playful letter to his absent lady.

On Lady Rochester's behalf, he had brought a gift to Adderbury for Nan's god-child, probably a daughter of their neighbor, Sir Thomas Cobb. Sir Thomas and Lady Rochester were kindred, hospitable spirits, planning merriment for the county. As gentry, the Cobbs held an ornate, carved-oak pew next to the Rochesters' in Adderbury Church.[44] Rochester cheerfully reported the domestic news to his wife:

> Madam, I am at last come to Adderbury, where I find none but the housekeeper, the butler and rats who squeak mightily and are all in good health. Your daughter our next-door neighbour is well; I gave her your present which she received handsomely . . . I am glad to hear your ladyship is [in Somersetshire], I hope in good health, at this present writing. . . . Tomorrow I intend for Woodstock and from thence to London, where I hope to receive your commands. Present my humble duty to my Lady Warre, whose favours will ever be in my grateful memory, . . . to cousin Betty, sweet honey, Mrs. Windham, the sprite, and the little girl whom my soul loveth. I hope my brother [Francis Warre] is well, but it is not usual to present our service to men in ladies' letters, so like a well-bred gentleman I rest,
>
> > Madam
> > Your humble servant,
> > Rochester
>
> If you are pleased, I am pleased; were my mother pleased, all were pleased, which God be pleased to grant.[45]

The letter sent off, he went to the Woodstock races and then back to London. There he rejoined his latest mistress, one (Elizabeth?) Foster. She had passed herself off as an innocent girl from the north, but she was the low-born niece of a tavern-keeper in Knightsbridge; she had lost her virginity to one Butler, presumably a highwayman.[46] Pretending faithfulness to Rochester, this "Corinna," as he called her, had sexual relations with others and reinfected John Wilmot with a more virulent form of the pox without his knowledge.[47] Experiencing another attack of "kidney stones," to his distress, Rochester also found himself in other miserable extremes.

The first was financial. With Parliament reluctant to grant him funds and French money stipulated by the Treaty of Dover slow in coming, the impoverished King had fallen behind in meeting his obligations. For six years, therefore, Rochester had received no payments at all on his pension. Ill though he was, he attended Parliament, driven by financial necessity. On October 24, he came to the opening session. In November, he attended meetings nine times, once to see to a land matter of his Uncle Allen Apsley under the Lords' jurisdiction, the others to further the King's money bills.[48] But the money was not forthcoming.

At the same time, his marriage faced a crisis. Lady Rochester had been reunited with her mother when she returned to Somerset. Lady Warre's summer in London had provided her with some information about her son-in-law that she saw fit to pass on to her daughter. Impetuously, although she was eight months pregnant, Lady Rochester informed her husband that she was coming back to Adderbury. He sent her a note, terse with sarcastic innuendoes:

> You have order'd the matter soe well that you must of necessity bee att the place you intend before I can give you an answer to y^r letter, yett meethinks you ought rather to have resolv'd in the negative since it was w^{ht} I desir'd of you before, but the happy conjunction of my mother and you can produce nothing but extreme good carriage to mee as it has formerly done; you shew y^{r}selfe very discreet and kind in this and in other matters, I wish you very well, & my mother, but assure you, I will bee very backward in giving you the trouble of
>
> > Your humble servant
> > Rochester[49]

Lady Rochester reacted to this letter vehemently. She was advanced in pregnancy; she had not seen her husband for almost seven months; and Lady Warre's tales about his behavior in London had distressed her greatly. When he stated his intention not to return to Adderbury to see her, her anguish poured out. Vexed by her outburst, he wrote a *poseur* letter to her on November 20.

> My most neglected Wife, till you are a much respected Widdow, I find you will scarce bee a contented woman, and to say noe more than the plaine truth, I doe endeavour soe fairly to doe you that last good service [make her a widow], that none but the most impatient would refuse to rest satisfy'd; what evill Angell Enimy to my repose does inspire my Lady Warr to visitt you once a yeare & leave you bewitch'd for elev'n months after? I thanke my god that I have the Torments of the stone upon mee (wch are noe small ones) rather than that unspeakable one of being an eye wittness to y^r uneasinesses; Doe but propose to mee any reasonable thing upon Earth I can doe to sett you at quiett, but it is like a madd woman to lye roaring out of paine and never confess what part it is in; these three yeares

have I heard you continually complain nor has itt ever bin in my power to ob[tain] the knowledge of any considerable cause [to be] confident I shall nott have the like affliction three yeares hence, but that repose I owe to a surer freind than you [i.e., God]; when [that] time comes you will grow wiser, though I feare nott much Happyer.[50]

Miserable though he may have been, Rochester had to exert himself to keep the King's favor. Four days after writing this letter, he was present at the Lord Treasurer's dinner. Having made his own Procrustean bed three years before, he had no choice but to lie in it. By pleasing Charles II, he had betrayed his benefactors, associated with bawds and panderers, fallen into alcoholism, contracted a fatal disease, been exposed to violence that threatened his life, made bitter, powerful enemies, alienated his mother, and driven his wife to despair.

Still craving the wealth that led him into this course of life, he could not break away from it or imagine an alternate way of living. At the age of twenty-three, as he told Burnet, "he had broke the firm Constitution of his Health that seemed so strong that nothing was too hard for it, and he had suffered so much in his Reputation, that he almost despaired to recover it."[51] On November 24, 1670, John Evelyn saw Rochester at the Treasurer's dinner and summed up the widespread opinion about him in a succinct phrase: "a very prophane Wit."[52]

THE QUINTESSENCE OF DEBAUCHERY (1671)

My heart is glutted, yet I still desire
And turn my freezing atoms into fire.
Sodom, Act III

The miasmal conditions that depressed Rochester so much in late November were effectively dispelled in early December 1670, when he was exhilarated by the birth of a son. Little Lord Wilmot seemed to assure the continuation of the family line and earldom; his jubilant father planned a christening suitable for the "heir and hopes of a great family" in Adderbury Church between Christmas and New Year's Day. Rochester notified King Charles of the birth, soliciting Royal sponsorship; and he asked his closest friends, Savile and Sedley, to act as godfathers. The king completed the quartet by appointing Charles Sackville, Lord Buckhurst, as his representative at the christening.

A violent episode in London postponed the happy event, however. On December 21, a proposal before Parliament to tax the playhouses was opposed by the pleasure of the King, whereupon Sir John Coventry, the M.P. from Weymouth and a Knight of the Bath, rose and tartly asked "whether the king's pleasures lie among the men or women that acted." This snide comment on Charles's amours with Nell Gwyn, Moll Davis, Mary Knight, and other players angered the King's supporters, and Sir Thomas Sandys, possibly at the instigation of the Duke of Monmouth, recruited a gang to punish the upstart.[1]

On a night following, as Coventry and a servant were returning home from an eating place, "near Twenty Persons, armed, Horse and on Foot" waylaid him, "some of them wrapping him up in his Cloak, and holding him fast; and others cutting and mangling his Face, with a Knife, in a barbarous manner, when he could make no Defence of himself; robbing him of his Periwig and his Servant of his Sword and Belt." The House of Commons made such an uproar that Charles hastily instructed Royalist supporters to be ready for an emergency session.[2]

On Christmas Eve, Buckhurst sent Rochester the witty and affectionate message of one man-of-the-world to another, mingling Anglican liturgy with misquoted Latin in a sly allusion to Satanism and mocking himself as Heaven's general and Charles II as godhead.

> his majesty is graciously pleased to make mee his Leiuetenant generall against the world the flesh and the devil; a thursday I shall begin my march, and in the mean time am resolued to behaue myself so discreetly, that the Enemy [i.e., the Devil] as vigilant as hee is shall haue no suspition of the quarrell. I must confess tis with some unwillingness I begin a war against a prince I haue so long serv'd under; but since "pax queritur bello" and this short dispute is like to purchase a firmer peace hereafter, I will obey my king and my deare deare L. Rochester
>
> Your most humble and faithfull servant,
> C. Buckhurst[3]

Buckhurst wrote another note to Rochester on December 28.

> Wensday
>
> My Dear Lord
> I am just now comanded not to stir till after thursday for wee are like to haue warm doings in the house about Couentryes nose; I look upon myselfe as a greater sufferer then hee in this busines since it takes from [me] the greatest satisfaction I can euer haue in this world, my dear Lord Rochesters company, but my conscience will not giue me leaue to defer my Journey any longer than Saturday. Pray let your coach meet us at Alesbury, I hope both you and my L Wilmott will pardon my leauing him thus long in a danger you are niether of you as yet sensible of....[4]

On December 31, Buckhurst and Sedley arrived at Adderbury, bringing Henry Savile's "deplorable excuse" for not coming; and on January 2, 1671, Rochester's son and heir was baptized into the Protestant faith in the presence of the three temporarily reverent rakehells and members of the family. An entry was made in the Adderbury Parish Register in suitably ornate script.

> The Lord Charles, sonn of the Right Honourable John Lord Willmott Earle of Rochester Baptised January the 2th in the yeare of our Lord 1670.[5]

Perhaps the most interesting feature of the christening was that Lady Rochester did not attend it. As a future peer of the realm, Charles Wilmot necessarily had to be a Protestant; and his mother, who persisted as a Catholic, would have found it awkward either to attend or stay away from the Anglican ceremony. She solved the problem by going off to London before the new year. About the time of the christening, she was seeing Part I of John Dryden's flamboyant epic drama, *The Conquest of Granada*.[6]

Buried in the country for almost a year, she was ready for the delights of the city. Wet nurses were attending to her infant son, of course. Rochester's mother was on hand to begin her duties as the supervisor of Charles's Protestant upbringing, the role her son cast her in for whatever reasons.[7] With her maternal duties limited, Lady Rochester was free to accompany her Lee nieces, Ellen and Nan, into town while her husband and the dowager countess stayed behind to see to affairs at Adderbury and Woodstock. She was acting as chaperone to Ellen Lee, then of a marriageable age and being courted by the virile young James Bertie, Lord Norris the Baron of Rycott.

Bertie was a most acceptable suitor.[8] He had ties with the Lees through the marriage of his older brother Robert, the Third Earl of Lindsey, to Frank Lee's widow Eleonore, Edward Henry Lee's mother. As the Countess of Lindsey, she linked the Lees' interests at Ditchley, Cornbury, and Adderbury to those of the Berties at Abingdon, Wytham, and Rycott. What with mutual visits, hunting parties, house parties, dances, and card games, James Bertie's interest in pretty, sweet-tempered Ellen Lee had grown to matrimonial proportions.[9] He continued his suit in the early months of 1671 in London, while his gossipy younger sister, Lady Mary Bertie, reported the festivities in letters to her niece.

On January 2, 1671, Lady Mary wrote:

> I have noe news to send you but that my brother Norreyss Act is passed both Houses . . . There is letely come out a new play writ by Mr. Dreyden who made the *Indian Emperor*. It is caled the *Conquest of Grenada*. My brother Norreys took a box and carryed my Lady Rochester and his mistress [Ellen Lee] and all us to, and on Tuesday wee are to goe see the second part of it which is then the first tim acted . . . Here was the Duke of Buckingham and a greate deal of company dind here to-day.[10]

Lady Rochester, who loved the theater, must have been very pleased to see the two-part epic drama by Dryden, lately appointed Historiographer Royal and awarded the bays of the Poet Laureate in August 1670.[11] She had missed his earlier favorite, *Tyrannic Love*, acted in June 1669; she had just had her first child and her husband was off in France, wearing out his disgrace in exile. Dryden's tribute to Catherine of Braganza, Charles II's neglected Queen, who was believed to be pregnant at last, was vastly popular. Shortly before the play was acted, however, the Queen miscarried when her pet fox leaped upon her bed.[12]

The legendary St. Catharine, martyred by the lust of the Roman Emperor Maximin, was the most popular saint of the seventeenth century and a particular favorite with the Queen and Catholic members of the Court.[13] When Huysman painted the Queen as the Virgin-Martyr, it became the fad during the late 1660s for court beauties—and even City women like Elizabeth Pepys—to be painted as St. Catharine with nimbus and upraised eyes. Since many of them had suffered the new species of martyrdom later defined by Gibbon, it was an ironically suitable pose for Charles II's fair victims to take. Lady Castlemain, who had posed with the King's bastard son as the Virgin and Infant Jesus, also posed as the virginal St. Catharine.[14]

Tyrannic Love was kaleidoscopic in its moral ambiguities. Nell Gwyn, who had already given birth to a royal bastard by Charles II, returned to the stage to play the martyred virgin-saint.[15] Clearly the depiction of a Catholic apotheosis, the play stressed the broad opposition between paganism and Christianity to downplay "Popery"; and Dryden further shifted the emphasis by dedicating the printed work to the Protestant Duke of Monmouth.

The Emperor Maximin was a compendium of bombastic theatrics, and the homiletic play ended in an orgy of slaughter and blood, after which Nell Gwyn cast off her guise as the virgin martyr and told the Roman guard about to carry off her body:

> Hold, are you mad? you damn'd confounded dog,
> I am to rise, and speak the Epilogue.

The viewer of *Tyrannic Love* had to willingly suspend many types of disbelief, religious and moral as well as political and aesthetic. Its author, however, was quite positive that his Saint Catherine was a pattern of true piety.[16] Dryden was equally sure that in Almanzor, the vaunting, veering protagonist of *The Conquest of Granada*, he had created a "perfect pattern of Heroick vertue."[17] Intended as a compliment to the less-than-heroic Duke of York, Almanzor was a version of Corneille's Le Cid, the pivotal figure in a set of interlocking oppositions between Castilians, Aragonians, and Moors as well as subsets of tribesmen; and the military contests were paralleled by several love duels, in which Almahide, a chaste queen (played by the unchaste Gwyn) was caught between love for Almanzor (played by Nelly's former lover, Charles Hart) and duty to her jealous husband, Boabdelin (played by Kynaston). In a reprise of her comic epilogue to *Tyrannic Love*, Mrs. Nelly began this opus by reciting a comic prologue while wearing an absurdly wide-brimmed hat.

John Evelyn's wife thrilled at the "refined romance" of 'pure love' and 'nice valour' in *Granada*, but others more critical—Buckingham, Shadwell, Joseph Arrowsmith, and, yes, Rochester—thought the Spanish *comédie héroïque* more than a little ridiculous in its combination of high moralizing with blatant sexuality.[18] Buckingham began reviving the idea of a burlesque on the lines of his abandoned spoof of Sir Robert Howard. The result, *The Rehearsal*, was acted

on December 7, 1671, with John Lacy imitating Dryden in the person of
Mr. Bayes the foolish author and the character Drawcansir reducing Almanzor's
heroic stance,

> Spite of myself I'll stay, fight, love, despair:
> And I can do all this because I dare

into

> I drink, I huff, I strut, look big and stare;
> And all this I can do, because I dare.[19]

Later, Rochester opened his own heroic-parody, *Sodom*, with lines that reduced
Dryden's opening, regal speech by Boabdelin,

> Thus, in the Triumph of soft Peace I reign,
> And, from my Walls defy the Pow'rs of Spain;

into Bolloximian's salacious,

> Here in the Zenith of my Lust I reign;
> I swive to eat and eat to swive again.

Rochester evidently missed the first performances of *Granada*. In a letter
dated January 1671, Henry Savile in London wrote to him, apologizing for
missing young Charles's christening:

> it is a ceremony I was sorry to misse but y^r LP staying much with y^r Lady
> will I presume once a yeare furnish us with such solemnityes. . . .

Customs officials in the City had

> seized a box of those leather instruments [dildoes] y^r LP carryed downe
> one of . . . Y^r LP is chosen Generall in this warr betwixt the Ballers & y^e
> [customs men] . . . I know not how you can stay a moment where you are
> [blowing coales in the countrey] without breach of justice to your profes-
> sion and of kindnesse to y^r friends who linger in your absence. . . .[20]

Rochester probably returned to London in time to see a repeat performance
of *Granada* Part I on January 26 and Part II on January 31.[21] The Treasury
Book for 1671 records a payment of £1,000 arrears for Bed Chamber duties
on January 27; these payments had to be collected in person. Rumors of the
Earl's return to town may have raised false hopes in his London tailor, who
billed him for £232–18–4½ on January 25; this amount due on Rochester's

personal wardrobe and livery for his servants went back as far as August 14, 1667. Like many aristocrats, John Wilmot maintained his style of life at the expense of servants and working-class creditors.[22] Whether the hapless tailor got any part of Rochester's Bed Chamber money is unknown.[23] In any case, Rochester's friends had him in their midst by the first of February, 1671.

The interchangeability of reality and fantasy reached a high pitch of intensity during the first months of 1671. Lady Mary Bertie's letters captured the ambiguities of attitude and ambivalences of value at the time. They provide a unique insight into the world of Rochester and his wife.[24] On January 17, she wrote from Westminster:

> The Queen is preparing a ball to bee danced in the greate Hall by herselfe and the Dutchesse of Buckingham, Richmond, Monmouth, Mrs. Berkeley, and Madame Kerwell the French made of honor. There are no men of quality but the Duke of Monmouth, all the rest are gentlemen.

The Queen's proposed gala featuring herself with various of her husband's mistresses (past and future) was rehearsed through late January into February, absorbing ever more time, money, and attention while real events turned into intrusions of harsh fantasy:

> We are all sorry to hear of cousin Harry Bertie's death. . . . There are two very fine plays lately acted. I was at them both with my Lady Rochester and Mrs. Lee. They say the greate ball is to be danced on Munday night, and that day my brother Peregrine and all the troopes are to show in Hide Park beefore the Prince of Orange.

The ball was postponed but a Valentine Day party at Lady Rochester's forestalled disappointment. On February 16 Lady Mary wrote: "Wee was on Munday night to draw valentine with my brother Norreys' mistress who drew him." Bertie's courtship of Ellen Lee was proceeding steadily toward its climax.

On February 23, Lady Mary provided a fuller account of events at Westminster. She told her niece,

> I received yours and am glad you had so good diversion in drawing valentine, but I take it very ill that none of my nephews would draw mee. I was that night at my Lady Rochester where I drew one Mr. Thynne, a gentleman who useth to come thither. I was on Munday at Court to see the grane ballett danced. It was so hard to get room that wee were forced to goe by four a clocke, though it did not begin till nine or ten. The[y] were very richly [dressed] and danced very finely, and shifted [changed] their clothes three times. There was also fine musickes and excellent sing[ing]; some new songs [were] made purposely for it. After the ballet was over, several others danced, as the King, and Duke of Yorke, and Duke of

Somerset, and Duke of Buckingham. And the Dutchesse of Cleveland was very fine in a riche petticoat and halfe shirte, and a short man's coat very richly laced, a periwigg cravatt and a hat: her hat and maske was very rich.

Early in March, aristocratic games of pretence led to a violent and shocking episode. On March 4 Lady Mary reported it in some detail.

> I was with my Lady Rochester and my Lady Bettey Howard and Mrs. Lee at a play, and afterwards I suped at my Lady Rochester's and cam not home till almost 12 a clock. I doubt not but you have heard of the watch-man that was killed. They say that the gentlemen who were in it fled, and 'tis believed the two Dukes will also be tryed by their Peeres. They say the King hath put out a Proclamation to forbid maskerades and to command those who were concerned in killing the mane [man] to com to their trall [trial].

When a group of drunken aristocrats in costume, including the Duke of Monmouth and Robert Constable, Viscount Dunbar, began brawling outside a whorehouse in Whetstone Park, their rowdiness drew the notice of several men on watch. When the watchmen halted the troublemakers, the noblemen became angry at the supposed infraction of their superior rights. They drew their swords and chased off the watchmen, taking hold of one, a Peter Vernell. As Vernell screamed for help and his fellows cowered at a distance, several of the noble masqueraders held him down while Lord Dunbar stabbed him repeatedly in the head. The aristocratic gang then broke and ran off, leaving Vernell to bleed to death in the street.

Public anger at the grisly event grew when it was known that one of the King's bastard sons was involved, and the common people demanded justice. The widespread version of the crime had Vernell kneeling before his tormen-tors, pleading for his life before they stabbed him to death. As usual, Charles II waited until the atmosphere had cooled somewhat and then on March 23, and again on April 11, issued pardons for all involved. But indignation was such that Dunbar, a Scottish peer, was actually arrested and brought to trial at the Old Bailey on May 3, where he pleaded guilty to the charge of stabbing Vernell.[25]

Rochester was rumored to have been one of the cowardly assassins. An Italian diplomat, Giovanni Silvetti Antelminelli, named him with other nobles in a report to officials in Florence.[26] His account accepted the most lurid of the rumors, however. No mention of Rochester appears anywhere in the extant official documents related to the Vernell Affair, being notably absent from the King's official pardons. Ostensibly, he was innocent and the despair about his reputation later voiced to Burnet was occasioned by this earliest of several widespread slanders.[27]

But if his conduct in the first months of 1671 was not criminal, it was unde-niably negligent. Parliament was in continuous session from October 24, 1670, until April 22, 1671, but Rochester failed to attend almost every session.[28] He was present at the opening session in October, one of few peers who were. Attendance was so sparse, the king had to stress the need for full attendance and the surety of the lords' love for him. But Rochester's love had become suffi-ciently slack that he came only nine times, November 7–28; and after returning to London in late January, he stayed absent from the lords until Game Bills of interest to him as Ranger of Wychwood Forest and Game Keeper of Oxfordshire brought him back to attend four sessions between April 7 and 17.

During this Parliamentary sitting, strong anti-Catholic feeling was growing. Charles had retreated from his professed firm attraction to Rome at the time of the Dover Treaty but the Duke of York's attachment was stronger than ever.[29] Both he and his Duchess secretly converted, raising the specter of a Catholic king after Charles's death.[30] The House of Commons set up a committee in February 1671 to look into causes for the growth of Popery. Their report to the Lords was a preview of the Popish Plot uproar to come seven years later.

The report told of servants testifying that priests had "much endeavored to pervert [them] in the Principles of Religion," of Benedictines operating out of "the Convent built near Her Majesty's Chapel," and of "several Young Persons . . . sent beyond Seas . . . under Tutors and Guardians, who are not put to take the Oaths of Allegiance and Supremacy, and usually corrupt the Youths under their Tuition into Popery." On March 13, the king issued a proclamation against priests and ordered his judges to enforce the laws and penalties of the renewed Conventicle Act (1670) but also to distinguish between "those who had newly changed their Religion, and those who were bred up in it."[31] At the same time, Buckingham and Shaftesbury, the Protestant Cabalists, were seeing through the Lords the passage of a bill permitting Lord Roos to divorce his wife, a trial balloon that might be used to enable Charles II to set aside his barren Catholic Queen and sire a legitimate Protestant heir.[32]

In spite of his wife's persistent Catholicism, Rochester seemingly failed to realize the implications of such activities for him and his dependents. Before 1673 he was surprisingly impervious—or indifferent—to the possible personal impact of political shifts of power. He still seemed to think that the King's favor was all important and that Parliament and ministers were insignificant royal props. As late as 1676, he could tell Henry Savile:

> They who would be great in our little government seem as ridiculous to me
> as schoolboys who with much endeavour and some danger climb a crab[apple]
> tree, venturing their necks for fruit which solid pigs would disdain if they
> were not starving. These reflections . . . if taken into consideration would

save you many a weary step in the day and help [Henry Guy] to many an
hour's sleep which he wants in the night; but G—y would be rich, and by
my troth there is some sense in that.[33]

Certainly, this was Rochester's policy in 1671. The Lords sessions were talka-
tive and boring; he left at noon recess on April 11 and failed to return. There
were other pastimes in London much more amusing than watching Buckingham
maneuver in the Lords—parties, prostitutes, and plays, for example.

The ladies of Rochester's household continued their pursuit of happiness in
a series of gay contrivances through March, but the strain of the season began
to show. Rochester's mother had come to town and re-established authority
over her Lee grand-daughters. On March 16, Lady Mary Bertie wrote that she
had been out so late with Ellen Lee that she missed the post:

> Mrs. Lee was here on Munday, and wee were very merry dancing coun-
> try dances, but she was so ill with wearing a pair of perfumed bodyes
> [laced bodices] that she was forced to goe to bed in my bed, and she
> would fane have lane with mee all night, but her grandmother sent a
> chaire for her and would have her home, but she hath not beene very well
> never since.[34]

Despite her fatigue, James Bertie at last won the consent of Ellen and her
guardians to marriage, and his courtship became a formal engagement, though
no date for the marriage was set as yet.[35]

Sometime in March, the first work of a new playwright was acted. William
Wycherley—"brawny Wycherley," Rochester called him—was six years older than
the Earl and turning to the stage somewhat belatedly. During the Protectorate,
his Royalist father had sent him to France in 1655 to study. In his five years
there, Wycherley converted to Catholicism and acquired a taste for French misses,
wine, and other pleasures.[36] He was a student at Queen's, Oxford for some
months in 1660 while Rochester was at Wadham. Wycherley then went on to
Lincoln's Inn to study law. After that, he may have spent some time in Spain in
1664–65 as a member of Sir Richard Fanshawe's diplomatic party; he seems to
have known Spanish and been familiar with such Iberian writers as Calderon.[37]

Like Rochester, Wycherley had served in the fleet in the naval battles of
1665–66, after which he spent the years between 1667 and 1670 desultorily
practicing the law, writing rather feeble love poems, and frequenting the alehouses and theaters. He was well acquainted with works by his contemporaries:
Sir George Etherege ("Gentle George"), Sir Charles Sedley and Tom Shadwell
of the Rochester Circle, and James Howard, one of the writing Howard clan.
His first play showed some influences by all of them but marked a distinct new
talent in comedy.

Sharing many interests as they did, Rochester apparently became friends with Wycherley some time before *Love in a Wood* was staged in March 1671. An anecdote about the two, Lady Castlemain, and the Duke of Buckingham clearly implies he had. He was present at one of the opening performances and so was "Cousin Barbara," who, after presenting the king with several bastards had begun a sequence of amours with lovers of diverse skills and social class: Henry Jermyn, Baron of Dover; Charles Hart the actor; and Jacob Hall, an acrobatic rope-dancer reportedly able to perform even the impossible contortions in Aretino's *Postures*. Various other lovers were also mentioned by the gossips.

The risqué dialogue and bawdy action of *Love in a Wood* (the "wood" was St. James's Park) entertained the audience vastly. In one scene, three gallants were pursuing nocturnal amours with Ranger, the wittiest, declaring his intention to make "a Ramble to St. James's Park tonight, upon some probable hopes of some fresh Game I have in chase, I have appointed [my mistress] to stay at home, with a promise to come to her within this hour, that she might not foil the scent and prevent my sport." When Ranger remarks that women are poor credulous creatures, easily deceived, one companion answers, "We are poor credulous Creatures, when we think 'em so."[38] The scene apparently left a lasting impression on Rochester.

Lady Castlemain, on the other hand, was impressed by the manly physique of the playwright. A few days later as he was strolling in Hyde Park, Wycherley saw Castlemain's carriage roll by and the lady herself leaning provocatively out of the window, laughing, and shouting (according to one version): "You, Wycherley, you are a son of a Whore."[39] Realizing the invitation for what it was, Wycherley called on the lady a few days afterward and in short order became her lover. At a later performance he was seen sitting at Castlemain's feet, engaged in playful discourse. The published *Love in a Wood* was dedicated to her.

Buckingham had undergone great joy and great grief since he danced at the Queen's ballet in late February. Shortly after that event, his four-year-long liaison with Lady Shrewsbury produced a son. Delighted at what he considered an heir, Villiers gave the love-child his own name, persuaded the King to act as godfather, and even claimed his own birth-title, Earl of Coventry, for the infant. In all these actions, he was flouting convention in his usual offhanded way, perhaps in imitation of the King. His elation soon ended, however, when the third George Villiers died after a few weeks. Buckingham buried the small body in the family vault in Westminster Abbey—another blow at the very roots of the peerage—and went into deep mourning. In his commonplace book, he wrote, "My happiness is like a winter's sun, that rises late and sets, alas, betimes."[40]

He emerged from mourning with renewed interest in the elaborate new mansion he was having built at Cliveden and with renewed determination to wreck permanently Lady Castlemain's remaining influence over the King. His method was to set spies upon her and find out her infidelities; then, according to the story Wycherley told his friend John Dennis,

> after [Buckingham] knew them, he never fail'd to name them aloud, in order to expose the Lady . . . and among others he us'd to name Mr. Wycherley. As soon as it came to the knowledge of the latter, who had all his expectations from the Court, he apprehended the Consequence of such a Report, if it should reach the King. He applied himself to *Wilmot* Lord Rochester and Sir *Charles Sedley*, and entreated them to remonstrate to the Duke of *Buckingham*. . . . Upon their opening the Matter to the Duke, he cry'd out immediately, *that he did not blame* Wycherley, *he only accus'd his Cousin* . . . *Ay, but*, they reply'd . . . *you are about to ruine a Man with whose Conversation you would be pleas'd above all things.* Upon this Occasion they said so much of the shining Qualities of Mr. Wycherley, and of the charms of his Conversation, that the Duke . . . was impatient till he was brought to sup with him, which was in two or three Nights. After supper, Mr. Wycherley . . . thought himself oblig'd to exert himself, and the Duke was charm'd to that degree, that he cry'd out in a Transport, *By God my Cousin is in the right of it*; and from that very Moment made a Friend of him.[41]

Wycherley stayed a friend to Rochester and his circle, and he even joined the Ballers. The last of his four plays, *The Plain-Dealer*, was dedicated to Lady Bennett, and it acknowledged that after 1675 Wycherley suffered like his fellow roués from their common occupational hazard. He certainly affected Rochester's growing concern with theatrical matters in the 1670s.

In late March or early April 1671, John Wilmot left London briefly to accompany the ladies as far as Ditchley. He was eager to get back to the pleasures of the town, however, and soon departed without warning, leaving a saucy little note for his wife. In his characteristic style, it combined liturgical imagery, playful deference to his two-year-old daughter and four-month-old son, and sexual frankness.

> Runn away like a rascall without taking leave, deare wife . . . I have left you a prey to your owne immaginations, amongst my Relations, the worst of damnations; but there will come an hower of deliverance, till when, may my mother bee mercifull unto you, soe I committ you to what shall ensue, woman to woman, wife to mother, in hopes of a future appearance in glory . . . pray write as often as you have leisure to
>
> Yr
Rochester
>
> remember me to Nan, & my Ld Wilmot you must present my service to my Cosins, I intend to bee att the deflowring of my Neice Ellen if I heare

of it. Excuse my ill paper & my ill manners to my mother they are both the best the place & age will afford.[42]

This message suggests Rochester's relief at evading once again the no-man's-land between his wife and mother as well as a certain satisfaction at their confrontation as women. The belief that he could leave to them the external working out of hostilities that were, in truth, internally his as well, made him feel the clever rascal who needed no permissive females to allow him to do what he chose. For the moment, he felt released to pursue his own interests as a man of business, of pleasure, and of letters.

His business was taken care of by attending four meetings of Parliament in April before it was prorogued on April 22, 1671. Thereafter, Rochester was spared the tedium of attending the Lords. Instead, he could attend to his duties of pleasing the King and getting money, as well as his own sensual and literary interests. He was on Chamber duty at Windsor, it appears, during parts of the summer though he may have been in London for a while in July and seen *Juliana, or The Princess of Poland,* John Crowne's first play. Crowne, a young author born in America and a Harvard graduate, recorded the presence of "some great and noble persons" who "sat in a hot bath, rather than a theatre" during the ascent of the Dog Star.[43] He dedicated his next play to Rochester.

Early in the summer, however, the newly Catholic Duchess of York died; other members of the royal family were sick; and the King escaped to the country. Charles II spent time at Windsor from May 27 to July 13, and there Rochester became involved with John Dryden's latest dramatic effort, *Marriage A-la-Mode.* Rochester knew Dryden before that—through Sir Robert Howard, among others; but not until he became Poet Laureate and the acclaimed author of *Granada* did Dryden mingle with the court wits on something like an equal basis. *Granada* had consolidated his fame and made him a public figure, as well as a target for satirists, who sharpened their verbal darts and aimed at his vulnerable points.[44]

Learned and creative though he was, Dryden lacked physical grace and spontaneous wit. He was rather short, somewhat plump, and he covered a basic shyness with a self-confidence that at times approached arrogance. Thrown with really clever wits, he sometimes made an embarrassingly blunt *faux pas.* One such wit, Sir George Etherege, was present at Windsor when Dryden made the most foolish of his blunders. Etherege had gone on a diplomatic mission to Turkey in August, 1668, and upon his return to England in the summer of 1671, he was gladly welcomed by Rochester, Sackville, the King, and his other friends.[45] Reportedly, they all were present when the matter of how to spend the afternoon at Windsor arose and Dryden supposedly burst out with, "Let's Bugger one another now, by G—d."[46]

Dryden's malicious antagonist, Tom Shadwell, spread this story in 1682. Shadwell had a long history of baiting Dryden. In January 1671, at the time *Granada* was staged, Shadwell's *The Humorists* was acted. In it was a character, Drybob, a foolish coxcomb meant to lampoon Dryden. (A dry-bob was a harmless, glancing blow in combat or, in sexual terms, coitus without ejaculation.)[47] Rochester realized Dryden's social limitations while appreciating his literary genius; he also may have found in the older man a literary father-figure.[48] Dryden was sixteen years older than Rochester.

When Dryden showed him the manuscript of *Marriage A-la-Mode*, a combination of heroic drama and comedy of manners, Rochester "embellished" it—most probably, the comic secondary plot—and showed the result to the king. The extent of Rochester's contribution to the quartet entanglements of Palamede/ Doralice/ Rhodophil/ Melantha, who criss-cross in perpetually frustrated efforts to couple, is not documented. However, the comic sub-plot is a fugue of imperfect enjoyment, a subject of interest to Rochester. Dryden had not been very successful previously in writing comic dialogue or clever repartee, and the popular success of *Marriage A-la-Mode* may well have been due in large part to Rochester's rewritten dialogue, which remains witty today.

Dryden's published Dedication to Rochester is rhetorically opulent in the playwright's usual vein, but a private letter of thanks to him (written after it became clear that Rochester's patronage did not involve money) is stinting in gratitude.[49] Dryden may even have suggested slily that he had spoken better of him than Rochester deserved:

> [I] shou'd either have chosen some other Patron, whom it was in my power to have oblig'd by speaking better of him than he deserved or have made your Lordship onely a hearty Dedication of the respect and Honour I have for you, without giving you the occasion to conquer me, as you have done, at my own Weapon.[50]

Rochester's relationship with Dryden underwent interesting changes during the 1670s. The dynamics of their association reflected differences in age, background, and temperament as well as their separate involvements with people ranging from Charles II and Buckingham to Thomas Shadwell and John Crowne. One critic has observed:

> Dryden and Rochester form one of those pairs of English writers which seem to recur at intervals . . . the industrious professional on the one hand and the brilliant, dynamic, aristocratic amateur on the other. . . . In all these instances there seems to have been . . . a curious and ambiguous relationship which is partly attraction and partly antagonism . . . Much of the strength of English literature [is] due to this tension and interplay

between . . . the audacious rebel and the patient craftsman, or to use Nietzsche's famous distinction, the Dionysian and the Apollonian poet.[51]

In 1671, if "Apollonian" was not yet the most precise epithet for Dryden, Rochester was a veritable embodiment of the "Dionysian." The dissipations, Bacchic and otherwise, of the summer of 1671 proved Rochester's undoing. His pleasure at fathering a son, his delight at being reunited with Etherege and his other friends, and his compulsion to contribute to the hedonistic excesses of the King's amusement raised him to a manic fit of sorts.

In July, Charles was in great, high spirits. Colbert de Croissy reported that he occupied himself daily with "sport, sometimes partridge-shooting, sometimes stag-hunting; and occasionally even on his way he stops at a house where he finds other diversions."[52] Rochester was on hand for these activities. Meanwhile, he discovered that his mistress, Foster, had been betraying him with other lovers and that she had passed on more deadly forms of the pox to him. Infuriated, he threw the false Corinna out, subjecting her to a "treatment" that included castigating her to his friends and then making her the subject of one of his most vituperative and scurrilous verses, "A Ramble in Saint James's Parke," where he vowed:

> To plague this woman and undoe her . . .
> Loath'd, and dispis'd, Kick'd out of Town
> Into some dirty Hole alone
> To chew the Cudd of Misery
> And know she owes it all to Mee.[53]

His vengeance seems to have been successful but that did not relieve his anger—or distress—at learning that his malady was not kidney stones this time but a recurrence of the dreaded pox.[54]

Rochester could have made his annual trip to Somerset and Oxfordshire in August, but he was back in the city early in September, always subject to command performance. Colbert reported the feverish pinnacle of the summer to Louis XIV.

> The King of England was very pleased with the messages I gave him from the King [of France], and to give me further proof of his gratification he then . . . gave orders to Monsieur Clifford to have supper prepared at the Treasury. He made me sup there with him, the Duke of York, the Duke of Monmouth, my Lords Arlington, Ossory, Buckhurst, Rochester, Carlingford, Roscommon, and the Treasurer, where, after we had drunk the health of His Majesty and several others demanding respect, we passed on to the English toasts and much freer conversation. . . . And at length everyone got so uproarious that I think reason would have taken leave of

the company if the King had not retired. I thought I ought to give you an account of this debauch, since it marks the King of England's satisfaction with what I told him. . . .[55]

The debauch proved too much for Rochester in his weakened state. A day or so afterward, when he was preparing to dine at Garraway's Coffee House with Harry Killegrew, John Muddyman, and others, he abruptly left the company, complaining about his eyesight.[56] Sick, half-blind, he rode off to the country into a self-imposed exile to contemplate the damage he had done to his body and spirit.

11

SALLIES IN THE COUNTRY (1671–1672)

> Your friends in town, are ready to envy the leisure you have
> given your self in the Country: though they know, you are
> only their Steward, and that you treasure up but so much
> health as you intend to spend on them in winter. In the
> meane time you have withdrawn your selfe from attendance,
> the curse of Courts.
>
> —John Dryden to Rochester (1673)

Two somewhat cryptic letters from Lady Rochester suggest that when he fled from London in September 1671, Rochester avoided both Ditchley and Adderbury and went to Woodstock, where the half-timbered hunting lodge of the royal hunting preserve was located. Woodstock had been the king's property since the days of Henry II, who had established a libidinous precedent by keeping his mistress Rosamund there. Confronted by Henry's wife, Eleanor of Aquitaine, Rosamund drowned herself in a well or fountain still there in Rochester's time. As Game Keeper of Oxfordshire and Ranger of Wychwood, Rochester had the privileges of Woodstock Lodge, which he had visited ever since his boyhood.[1]

After September 1671, he apparently secluded himself there, resisting his wife's efforts to see him, although he was only a few miles away from Cornbury and Ditchley. The obvious explanation for his behavior is that he was taking the cure for *lues venerea*, probably under the supervision of a royal physician or nearby doctors at Oxford, and he wanted to conceal this from his wife. Baffled and distressed by his remote behavior, Lady Rochester sent an undated note to Woodstock:

> Though I cannot flater my selfe soe much as to expect it yett giue me leaue
> to wish that you would dine tomorrow att Cornbury where nesecity forces
> Your faithfull humble Wife
> E. Rochester
> If you send to command mee to woodstock when I am soe near as cornbury
> I shall not be alitle rejoyced.[2]

John Muddyman's letter to him in September 1671 expressed concern that the usual remedies for bad eyes—bathing them with water or wine—were not effective for Rochester. Muddyman had learned the facts about the false Foster and he told Rochester the latter part of his "treatment" of her was fully justified. The rest of the letter was filled with gossip: Etherege and Ashton had gotten into a fight at Covent Garden. Henry Savile had invaded the bedroom of the widowed Countess of Northumberland and been rewarded for his attempt at seduction by being chased out of the country. A "jury" of "mid-wives" including Lady Rochester's grandfather, Lord Hawley, had inspected a group of trollops, certifying some as safe and turning the others out to grass—like so many cattle—in the harsh season after Bartholomew Fair ended.[3]

We may wonder whether Rochester was too ill or too angry to be much amused. He was not too angry to write, however; and "A Ramble in Saint James's Parke" became one of his first important exercises in the kind of personal satire originated by Catullus, Martial, Juvenal, and Petronius, then adapted by Aretino. It was variously called the pasquinade, libel, lampoon, squib, burlesque, or travesty.[4] While it parodied Edmund Waller's poem, "On St. James's Park, As Lately Improved by His Majesty," it was stimulated in part by Wycherley's comedy, *Love in a Wood*, and it showed similarities to Catullus's *Carmina* XXXVII ("Salax taberna vosque contubernales. . . ."). Whatever its stimuli, "A Ramble in St. James's Parke" was distinctly Rochester's own.[5] Burnet said of Rochester's practices in this mode:

> he laid out his Wit very freely in *Libels* and *Satyrs*, in which he had a Talent of mixing his Wit with his Malice, and fitting both with such apt words, that Men were tempted to be pleased with them: from thence his composures came to be easily known. . . .[6]

When Burnet reproved him for this practice, Rochester gave his rationale for satire:

> He would often go into the Country, and be for some months wholly imployed in Study, or the Sallies of his Wit: Which he came to direct chiefly to *Satyre*. And this he often defended to me; by saying there were some people that could not be kept in Order, or admonished in any but this way. I replied, That it might be granted that a grave way of *Satyre* was sometimes no improfitable way of Reproof. Yet they who used it only out of spite, and mixed Lyes with Truth, sparing nothing that might adorn their *Poems*, or gratifie their Revenge, could not excuse that way of Reproach, by which the Innocent often suffer: since the most malicious things, if wittily expressed, might stick to and blemish the best men in the World. . . . To this he answered, A man could not write with life, unless he were heated by Revenge: For to make a *Satyre* without Resentments, upon

the cold Notions of *Phylosophy*, was as if a man would in cold blood, cut mens throats who had never offended him: And he said, The lyes in these Libels came often in as Ornaments that could not be spared without spoiling the beauty of the *Poem.*[7]

Rochester's reformational satire was based in the Hobbesian view of man as "an aggressive animal, perpetually in combat with his fellow creatures whose competitive and violent instincts were restrained only by the fear of violent death." His defense of lies as ornaments reflected the contemporary idea of "wit" as "a just mixture of Reason and Extravagance."[8] The result of wit, presumably, was a smile or laughter stemming from a feeling of relief or play. In his treatise *On Human Nature* (1650), Hobbes defined laughter as "nothing else but sudden glory arising from a sudden conception of some eminency in ourselves, by comparison with the infirmity of others, or with our own formerly."[9]

Any laughter that Rochester wanted to raise from "A Ramble" was clearly the derisive kind. Its targets were multiple. They included language, Waller, Foster/Corinna, her three lusting followers, the entire spectrum of London society, British history, classical mythology, human and animal copulation, the Devil of Christianity, cowards, school-boys, whores, Jesuits, doctors, atheists—and himself.[10]

The satire begins with a carnal parody of Waller's aesthetic paradise in "On St. James's Park" with all "feeling" reduced to sexual sensation. The "I" narrator, after "Much wine had past with grave discourse / Of who Fucks who," departs from his companions at the Bear Tavern and goes to St. James's to "relieve" his drunkenness with lechery. A mock history of the park follows:

> But tho' Saint James has the Honor on't
> 'Tis Consecrate to Prick and Cunt. . . .
> When auncient Pict began to whore
> Deluded of his Assignation
> (Jylting it seems was then in fashion)
> Poor pensive Lover in this place
> Wou'd frigg upon his Mothers face
> Whence Rowes of Mandrakes tall did rise
> Whose lewd Topps fuckt the very Skies
> Each imitative branch does twine
> In some lov'd fold of Aretine
> And nightly now beneath their shade
> Are Buggeries, Rapes, and Incests made.

An all-encompassing catalogue of fornicators follows: "Great Ladies, Chamber Mayds, and Drudges . . . Divines, Great Lords, and Taylors, Prentices, Poets, Pimps . . . doe here arrive, And here promiscuously swive." "I" sees his mistress, the "divine" Corinna, who proves "infinitely vile" when three wriggling-tailed "Knights" make up to her. The Whitehall Blade, Gray's Inn Wit, and Lady's Eldest Son are scornfully characterized before they go off in pursuit of Corinna, the "prowd Bitch." "I" asserts the right of women to be sexual beings but not as a "passive Pott for Fools to spend in." He then castigates himself as a fool deceived by Corinna, and after a deprecating oath, vows his vengeance upon her.

His shockingly frank, Anglo-Saxon language gives emotional force to Rochester's techniques of satiric reduction, as does his depiction of naked Londoners copulating in various ways and Corinna as a "dog-drawn bitch," locked in intercourse and dragged about. In his historical survey of satire, Matthew Hodgart notes:

> the naked man is caught with his trousers down, caught in the act of guilt or shame. Our first parents, Adam and Eve . . . became aware [after eating the apple] that they were simply naked, and in their embarrassment tried to conceal their parts with fig-leaves—the first victims of divine satire. . . . The animal world is continually drawn on by the satirist: he reminds us that homo sapiens despite his vast spiritual aspirations is only a mammal that feeds, defecates, menstruates, ruts, gives birth and catches unpleasant diseases.[11]

Corinna is pictured as the beloved woman formerly worshipped as divine but revealed to be a wanton whore; this revelation provides him with a purpose the "I" speaker clearly states:

> I'le make her feel my scorn and hate
> Pelt her with scandalls, Truth or lies. . . .

This threat, so close to Rochester's expressed theory of satire, indicates the biographical significance of "A Ramble" and suggests insights into the poet through his acknowledged feelings of "resentment," and desire for "revenge," as well as the significant comparison of dispassionate satire to cutting the throats of inoffensive men in cold blood.

Freud said of "aggressive" wit, whether obscene or satirical, that it allows one "to infer the presence of a concealed inclination to exhibitionism in [its] inventors." On at least two occasions, Rochester ran about naked in company with other men, once on Sunday in view of church-going villagers.[12] Freud noted also that aggressive wit operates best when it is made by "people in whose sexuality a powerful sadistic component is demonstrable, which is more or less inhibited in real life." "A Ramble" marks the poetic emergence of a streak in Rochester apparent in the physical kidnapping of his wife-to-be and one of his children, as well as verbal attacks on his wife and mistress.[13]

Yet no emotion or idea was ever simple to Rochester. He treated himself every bit as sardonically as he did Corinna:

> Why this Treachery
> To humble fond believing mee. . . .
> Did ever I refuse to bear
> The meanest part your Lust could spare
> When your lewd Cunt came spewing home
> Drench'd with the seed of halfe the Town
> My dram of sperm was sup't up after
> For the digestive surfeit water. . . .
> I was content to serve you up. . . .
> You that cou'd make my heart away
> For noise and Colour and betray
> The secretts of my tender houres
> To such knight errant Paramours. . . .[14]

It is difficult to imagine a more scathing portrait of a fool gulled by his own sexual needs and wishes: a willing, self-deluded dupe oblivious to the obvious. Yet, this very "fool" has the self-assurance and sophistication necessary to objectify and satirize himself![15]

Critics have observed that Rochester's imagery in "A Ramble" shows the same sort of theologically based moral referents he had been taught in his youth.[16] Often concealed, Platonic idealism in its Christian version, complete with the dualism of soul and body, provides the standard against which Rochester's ironic disparities operate, as it does in "A Ramble." The satire also displays Rochester's ability to transpose classical obscene satire for moral purposes. This talent was described by an early editor, Robert Wolseley. In rebuttal to the Earl of Mulgrave, who accused Rochester of "Bawdry barefac'd" and declared his "obscene Words, too grosse to move Desire," Wolseley said:

> Does he not know that obscene Satyre (of which nature are most of my *Lord Rochester's* obscene Writings . . .) has a quite different end, and is so far from being intended to raise, that the whole force of it is generally turn'd to restrain *Appetite*, and keep it within due Bounds, to reprove the unjust Designs, and check the Excesses of that lawlesse Tyrant?[17]

This justification of obscenity probably went over the heads of many readers, who made copies of "A Ramble" to send to patrons or friends; and it certainly did not appease women, who winced or gasped at its four-letter words and called them "lewd."[18]

Away from his wife during the last months of 1671, the recuperating Earl avoided being with her in the first months of 1672 as well. He recovered from his ailments sufficiently to return to London in quest of money from the

Treasury. On January 9, 1672, a letter writer related the latest gossip involving him. Sitting in a box at the Theatre Royal, Rochester was eating an orange and he flipped a peel into the pit below. It struck Dick Newport, who vaulted over the box rail and demanded to know who threw it. He angrily questioned Rochester "without satisfactory reply" and struck him a blow. Rochester struck back and, drawing their swords, the two made several passes at each other. Rochester was wounded in the stomach and Newport in the shoulders; "neither was in danger of death." The Duke of Monmouth, who was in the audience, arrested them, placed them under guard, and extracted their word of honor they would "engage themselves no further in this quarrel."[19]

Rochester petitioned the King for land on January 17 and the Treasury Committee for his back pension on January 25, but he left town soon after, perhaps to attend the wedding of Ellen Lee to James Bertie in Adderbury Church on February 1. Ellen's honeymoon set the pattern for her married life. She became pregnant in March and thereafter spent her tumescent days at Rycott and Adderbury, surrounded by Lees, Berties, and Wilmots, whose comings and goings were chronicled by Lady Mary Bertie. In time, she became the mother of six sons and three daughters. Rochester is not mentioned in Lady Mary's reports. If he attended the wedding, he presumably departed soon after, saying he was going to Bath but returning to Woodstock to continue his recovery from physical wounds and compose satirical balms for his emotional wounds. He was not in London. On March 1, the Treasury Committee agreed to hear his petition, but on March 16 a hearing was cancelled because Rochester was absent.[20]

Rochester's friend, Sir Robert Howard, had become Secretary of the Treasury in October 1671, however, and he was looking after Rochester's welfare.[21] He worked to pay arrears that amounted to £3,375 for six and 3/4 years as of Christmas 1670. Treasury records for the period are garbled, but Rochester appears to have received three payments amounting to £2,500 between November 17, 1671, and May 21, 1672. Parliament was due to convene on April 2; Lady Rochester's undated but pleading appeal to her husband appears to have been made in March 1672:

> If I could haue bin troubled att anything when I had the happyness of res-
> ceiuing a letter from you I should be soe because you did not name a time
> when I might hope to see you: the uncertainty of which very much aflicts
> me . . . I doe not think you design staying att bath now that it is like to be
> soe full and God knows when you will find in your hart to leaue the place
> you are in: . . . thear being soe short a time betwixt this and the sitting of
> Parlemant I am confident you will find soe much bussine[ss in London] as
> will not allow you to come into the country; thearfore pray lay your com-
> mands upon me what I am to doe and though it be to forgett my children

and the long hopes I haue liued in of seeing you, yett I will endeauour
to obey you or in the memory only torment my selfe with out giuing you
the trouble of puting you in the mind thear liues such a creature as your
faithfull humble.[22]

When she wrote this touching submission, Lady Rochester had clearly resigned
herself to the fact her husband had ways, sometimes cruel, of dealing with the
pertness and willfulness she had once shown as Betty Mallet. It was in effect a
surrender, however temporary, in the battle of the sexes.

The peripatetic lives of the Rochesters produced a number of undated messages that show repeated patterns of arrivals, reunions, and departures; a few
of them can be plausibly arranged to suggest the developments in their marriage at the start of its sixth year in the spring of 1672. The pair was reunited
by June 1, and Lady Rochester certainly knew the nature of her husband's
venereal malady by March 1673, when she was being treated for it herself.
Events between March and April 1672 may be conjectured through some
undated messages. If Rochester received the promise of patience and obedience
given in the letter above, it might have touched his heart and made him write
the following note. On the other hand, the note seems to imply that he had
simply had second thoughts.

The reference to his mother and cousins suggests that he wrote it at
Woodstock and sent it to her at Ditchley, or possibly Adderbury.

> I could scarce guess what measures you would take upon the Letter I sent
> you, & therfore have sent this second epistle together wth my Coach,
> humbly requesting you to doe therin as in your wisdome shall seeme meete,
> I being wth great advisedness most excellently your humble servant
>   Rochester
> My humble duty to mother, & my service to My Cozens[23]

Finally summoned to Woodstock, Lady Rochester hurried there, and husband and wife were reconciled, to the happiness of them both. Rochester possibly explained the cause of his staying away, even if he thought himself not
entirely cured. He could hardly keep the nature of his sickness a secret forever,
especially when his wife knew about his connections with other women. In her
joy at seeing him, she probably "forgave" him: with one obvious exception,
their marriage after 1672 appears free of the sorts of contention and mounting
frustrations seen in their letters between 1667 and 1671.

But their reunion was brief at best. Expecting Parliament to convene and
needing to pursue his case with the Treasury commissioners, Rochester was
compelled to return to London for a time. It appears that his wife went back

to rejoin her mother-in-law at Ditchley, where he sent her an affectionate, reassuring message:

> I will be with you shortly, & if my mother pleases, I will take the trouble of
> you & yours upon mee & thinke my selfe a very happy man; in the meane
> time, have but soe much discretion to dissemble a little & I will deliver you
> immediately; money you shall have as soone as ever I come to you.[24]

While the Wilmots engaged in their domestic vicissitudes in the first months of 1672, public events were combining to erupt into the Third Anglo-Dutch War. In the aftermath of the secret Treaty of Dover, England and France joined in war against Holland in the spring of 1672, France by land and England by water. On January 2, 1672, Sir Thomas Clifford had engineered the Stop of the Exchequer in order to get funds to strengthen the fleet. Louis XIV invaded the Dutch Republic, and on March 15, Charles II issued another Declaration for Tender Consciences intended to satisfy the pro-Catholic aspects of the Treaty of Dover. Jingoistic pamphlets tried to rally a wartime spirit with tales of Dutch refusal to honor the English flag in "English" waters; and on March 17, the Third Anglo-Dutch War was officially declared.[25] When Parliament convened on April 2, however, Protestant fury at the Declaration and general anger at England's violating the Triple Alliance to join Catholic France, its enemy, compelled the King to prorogue it on the same day for a period of six months.

England and Holland began a reprise of the Second Dutch War with the same rounds of naval encounters by the same ships, putative victories, and actual defeats. The English cause was lethally damaged in the Battle of Solebay (Southwold Bay) on May 28, when the Lord Admiral Sandwich was killed. His body washed ashore afterward wearing the sash of the Order of the Garter. A widespread account of the Battle was thought to have been written by Henry Savile, who was there to see it. Again, as in 1666, English morale was weakened by a Dutch victory and a London fire.[26]

Rochester avoided the sound and fury as much as possible. He had been through it all before—twice. In April–May 1672, he wanted only to get his Treasury money and go back to the country. On May 21, he received £500 and his petition for additional funds was sent to the king. Soon after that, he responded to the distressing news from his wife that his son was ill.

> Madam
> I am extreamly troubled for the sickness of yr son as well in consideration
> of the affliction it gives you, as the dearness I have for him myself; you have
> I heare done mee the favour to expect me long in the Country where I
> intended to have bin long agoe, but Court affaires are more hardly sollicited

now then ever, and having follow'd them till I had spent all my owne money & y^{rs} too, I was forc't to stay somthing longer here till I had con- triv'd a supply, wch being now dispatch'd I have nothing to hinder mee from what I heartily desire wch is to waite on y^{r} La^{sp} at Adderbury

I am y^{r} humble servant
Rochester[27]

When John Wilmot returned to his family in Oxfordshire, young Charles's and his own states of health caused the family to stay at Adderbury for the first few weeks of June. Some prudent estate-planning was done. On June 1 Lord and Lady Rochester co-signed an Indenture accounting for their property in Somerset and consigning it to future uses. The handsome, multicolored parch- ment, written in Latin, was a financial arrangement between the Rochesters and their trustees: Sir Allen Apsley, Sir William Windham, and Captain Edward Cooke. It was witnessed by their agents from Enmore, Richard Blancourt and Thomas Alcock.[28] The Wilmots may have been perennially in need of cash but they were very wealthy in property, as the assets listed in the Indenture showed. Even as dependents of sorts, they occupied sumptuous quar- ters at Adderbury Manor. In 1665, after the Dowager Countess had it rebuilt and refurbished, the manor was taxed for fourteen hearths. In 1676 Dr. Plot was calling it one of "our most stately buildings." An inventory taken in 1678 mentions Great and Little Halls, a Drawing Room, Great Room above stairs, Great Square Chamber, Lesser Dining Parlour, and eleven other rooms, not including offices.[29]

On June 17, 1672, Lady Rochester gave an elaborate party at Adderbury Manor to celebrate James Bertie's birthday. All was done "with great solem- nity," according to Bertie's sister. The bell was rung, the guests had "a great dinner," and they celebrated afterward by dancing sixteen dances. The weather was hot, so they danced first in the forecourt, then the garden, and finally in the Great Hall.[30] Soon afterward, the guests scattered and the Rochesters, their children and servants left for Enmore, where they stayed for at least three months.

Between September 1671 and September 1672, Rochester was in the coun- try for a total of nine months. Some of that time was spent in recovering from sickness and in study, but Rochester had work to do and duties to perform. Contrary to legend, he was not a mere drunken dilettante who spent all of his time copulating and penning clever verse. As Ranger of Wychwood, he had game, timber, and a crew of woodsmen to oversee. His own estates had to be supervised: breeding and racing horses; planting and harvesting crops; examin- ing accounts; talking with agents and tenants; buying and selling livestock. In Somerset, in the summer of 1672, he and Lord Hawley developed their plans for dredging the Parrot and Thone Rivers, a project that would need approval in the House of Lords. Rochester had to draft and introduce the necessary legislation. His duties increased in October, when he was made Deputy Lieutenant of Somerset.[31]

Even as he led his life of business, his imaginative life was preparing him to write the major works of 1674–76. In the country in 1671–72, he read Thomas Hobbes. He also read Roman authors, most significantly Lucretius, whom he admired above all others, as Dryden, Aphra Behn, Elizabeth Barry, and Robert Wolseley all attested.[32] It appears that he was also reading the erotic and satiric writings of Pietro Aretino. Certainly Aretino was on his mind. As he wrote the description of the trees in St. James's Park in "A Ramble," the engraved "Postures" may have been before his eyes on the walls of Woodstock Lodge:

> Each imitative branch does twine
> In some lov'd fold of Aretine.[33]

Aretino's *Ragionamenti*, or dialogues between prostitutes, probably gave Rochester the idea of combining a pasquinade against two of the King's more flagrant whores—Castlemain and Mary Knight—and two of Castlemain's gallants in a parody of Aretinian eroticism. The satiric "Advice" (or "Song") may have tapped "the comic spirit at its source in the sex relationship"; but it also showed Rochester's growing distrust of female sexuality.[34] The romping meter travestied the amoral nonchalance of the royal concubines.

> Quoth the Dutchess of Cleavland to Councillor Knight
> I'de faine have a Prick knew I how to Come by't
> But you must be secret and give your advice
> Though Cunt be not Coy, reputation is Nice.
> Knight
> To Some Celler in Sodom your Grace must retire
> Where Porters with Black Potts sett round the Cole Fire
> There open your Case, and your Grace cannot faile
> Of a dozen of Pricks for a dozen of Ale
> Dutchess Say you soe quoth the Dutchess
>
> Knight Ay by God quoth the whore
>
> Dutchess Then give me the Key that unlocks the back doore
> Ide raythr be Fuct by Porters and Carmen
> Then thus be abus'd by Churchill and German.[35]

Rochester's criticism of Cousin Barbara for repairing to Little Sodom to satisfy her sexual needs had an ironic twist. Rochester himself frequented London's red-light district in disguise—as she did—to carry on "low amours."

One of his disguises was that of a porter. It takes no stretch of imagination to suppose that Rochester had witnessed something like the sodomitic scene he envisions, just as he had witnessed Castlemain in the royal bed. His satiric view of her, however, implicitly indicts himself for the same sort of sexual hypocrisy. His verse exercises of 1672 included a saturnine self-awareness.

Among his other compositions in the summer of 1672 were letters to the Treasury, which elicited replies from Sir Robert Howard late in August and Sir Thomas Clifford early in September, urging Rochester's return to town. Howard's financial aid had an ulterior motive; the great success of his brother-in-law's *Marriage-A-la-Mode* in November (?) 1671 after it was "embellished" by Rochester made Howard think his own lagging literary career might be likewise assisted.[36] Howard wrote to the earl at Enmore on August 29, 1672:

> I will not dispute with you whither you or I shall receiue the most aduantage to our freindship but . . . I will [with] as much speed as I can endeauer to serue you in the particulars of your wages and pension. I cannot promise soe derectly as I wish . . . but I will doe all that is possible to assure you of the truth of what I professe to be soe really. Yo[r] most faithfull freind and humble seruant.[37]

From Whitehall on September 7, Clifford provided added incentive for Rochester to speed back to London.

> I thanke y[r] L[d]ship for your [o]blidging letter to me, I will ever to my power doe you service, this resolution is not newly taken vp but I have had it ever since I had the honor first to know you, we did this day set in our weekely bill 500£ for y[r] L[d]ship you must direct some body to follow it and empower him to receiue the money, the season of the year is such that I know you will not be long from vs noe one shall be gladder to see you than My Lord
>
> > Y[r] Lordships
> > Most Affectionate and
> > most Obedient Srvt[38]

Rochester's departure from Enmore raised again the specter of a rupture with his wife. The health of their twenty-month-old son had continued to worry them both during the summer: the Somerset air had done nothing to better his condition. Rochester decided to send him back to Adderbury, where the Dowager Countess would see that the Oxford physicians diagnosed him properly. The Earl himself was probably going to London by the usual route of the Woodstock Races and could accompany the child and his nurse into Anne Rochester's custody. Despite her earlier vow to forget her children if he commanded, Lady Rochester opposed his plan, telling him that she doubted he loved her, but to no avail. Off to Oxford and Adderbury little Charles went. Once in London, the unrepentant husband wrote a reassuring letter, in late September or early October.

> It were very unreasonable should I not love you whilst I beleive you a deserving good Creature, I am allready soe weary of this place [Whitehall] That upon my word I could bee Content To Pass my winter att Cannington, Though I apprehend the toediousness of itt for you, pray send mee word What lyes in my power to doe for y^r service and ease here. . . . Twas very well for y^r son as ill as you tooke it that I sent him to adderbury, for it proues att last to bee the kings evill that troubles him & hee comes up to London this weeke to bee touch't; my humble service to my Aunt Rogers, & Nanne. I write in bed & am affraid you can't reade it.[39]

The disease that little Charles Wilmot was supposed to have, the King's Evil or scrofula, was tuberculosis of the bones or lymph glands in the neck. It was thought from the time of Edward the Confessor in England that the king's touch could cure the Evil; and after the Restoration, Charles II cultivated belief in the touch as a way of enhancing the image of "His Sacred Majesty." The Royal physicians spread the idea, rooted in the belief of the Divine Right of Kings, that only those who truly believed in the monarch's Christ-like power to heal would be cured by his touch. In the case of infants, the parents had to have this faith in the healing monarch. In 1676 Robert Wiseman, serjeant-surgeon to Charles II, declared that he had witnessed hundreds of people cured without surgery; and in 1684 John Browne said that some 91,107 adults and infants had been touched by Charles Stuart in a monthly ritual that involved tickets and long lines of the credulous.[40] On one terrible occasion, the crowd of supplicants was so large and uncontrolled that John Evelyn saw several people trampled to death.

As John Browne carefully explicated in his *Adenochoiradelogia*, a father with the pox could produce a child with the Evil. There were many hereditary causes for the disease; and its symptoms were often confused with and identical to those of the pox.[41] Since John Wilmot's son manifested these symptoms in infancy and lived for only ten years, it is highly probable that his "scrofula" was in truth paresis, or congenital syphilis. Initially, the willingness of John Wilmot to believe in the divine touch of Charles Stuart seems incredible. As one who had seen the king drunk, silly, *in coitu* with a series of whores, was it possible that Lord Rochester could really believe his baby son would be cured by the touch of "the cully of Britain," as he subsequently called the king?

The question cannot be answered for sure; but given his fatherly "dearness," his deep-seated religious superstition, and the alternate surgical treatment for the Evil, Rochester's determination to try the King's Touch first is understandable.

In the 1676 *Treatises*, Robert Wiseman described how he "treated" in 1674 the four-year-old son of an unidentified "nobleman from the North." One hopes it was not little Charles Wilmot in 1674. Wiseman used a hot knife to cut into lesions on his young patient's neck; and when that did not work, while the child was held down screaming, Wiseman seared away the scrofulous swellings with a poker heated in the fire.[42]

Even as Rochester worried about his son's health and his own, other emotional clouds gathered. The warrant for £500 that Clifford told him in September was awaiting him was cancelled.[43] When Parliament convened on October 30, anti-Catholic feeling was still so strong that Charles prorogued it at the first session. By this time, Rochester was becoming aware that the legal consequences for Catholics, including his wife, might be serious. His wife had returned to Adderbury, doubtless in anxiety about her son; she and the old Countess clashed again. Although he made sport of it, Rochester could not have been as cheerful as he affected to be, resuming his pose as the submissive husband in a letter sent shortly before he left London in the late fall or early winter of 1672:

> The last letter I received from y^r honour was something scandalous, soe that I knew not well how to answer it; 'twas my designe to have writ to my Lady Anne willmot [his three-year-old daughter] to intercede for mee, but now wth joy I find my selfe again in y^r favour. It shall bee my endeavours to continue soe; In order to wch very shortly I will be wth you; in the meane time my Mother may bee pleas'd to dispose of my children, & my chimists, and my little doggs and whatever is myne as shee will, only if I may have nothing about mee that I like; it will bee the cause of making the felicity of waiting on her, befall mee very seldome, thus I remaine wth my duty to her, my service to you and all those things ____.[44]

Evidently, Rochester was with his wife shortly after sending this letter. The last weeks of 1672 left no record of his actions—unless, as seems very likely, that was the time when the first, most experimental of his social and literary satires was flowing out of his pent-up rage onto its scandalizing pages.

SODOM (1673)

Tell me, adandon'd *Miscreant*, prithee tell,
What damned Pow'r invok'd and sent from *Hell*
(If *Hell* were bad enough) did thee inspire,
To write, what *Fiends* asham'd wou'd blushing hear?
   —John Oldham, "Upon the Author of a Play call'd *Sodom*"

Although much remains unknown about the scandalous farce known as *Sodom*, which is preserved in eight manuscripts in English and one in French, there is considerable evidence that Rochester was author of the earliest version of the play in three acts and titled *Sodom and Gomorah*.[1] This evidence allows it to be dated not earlier than July 1672; a fuller five-act version titled *Sodom* can be dated ca. 1676–77. A printed version of 1689, attributed to the "E of R"—and subtitled *The Quintessence of Debauchery*, was destroyed, but the text was preserved in a manuscript copy made for Robert Harley, a long-time observer of Rochester and collector of his works. The 1689 version includes a Prologue, two acts, an Epilogue, and "Madam Swivia's Speech," all of which may have been added by other hands even after Rochester's death.[2] The later version differs substantially from the shorter one, and it may have been a group composition. Nonetheless, both internal and external evidence indicates that the early version, *Sodom and Gomorah* was primarily the work of Rochester and that he composed it in 1672–73.[3]

In his years of intimacy with the Court of Charles II from 1665 to 1672, John Wilmot had grown increasingly disgusted with the King and his amoral entourage. His spying on the secret lives of courtiers at St. James and Whitehall had unearthed every variety of what clergymen-tutors taught him was Devil-inspired sin. He had seen Dukes pandering; Countesses disguising themselves as common prostitutes in the seamier sections of London; fools promoted to eminence because of their sexual talents. He had seen his Cousin Barbara turn overt nymphomaniac, betraying the King with actors, jugglers, and (it was whispered) porters and chair-bearers as well as army officers and Earls. He had seen Charles II, his quasi-father, ignoring official responsibilities to squander public monies on the tribe of concubines who satisfied his lusts. His own participation in such activities led to the wry disgust he showed toward himself in "A Ramble."

Bad as the venal and venereal peccadilloes of the Court were, to Rochester the effort of mercenary artists to glorify such rapacious carnality was as ludicrous as it was hypocritical. Several satirists, some anonymous, had mocked the Court painters who represented fleet disasters as sea triumphs and the King and Duke of York as sea-gods and heroes.[4] Rochester's personal lampoons were, in effect, attacks on Court portraitists who crowned whores with saintly coronas, covered the half-naked bosoms of titled prostitutes with revealing satin drapery, or clothed cowards in armor. His pasquinades against Castlemain, Churchill, and their fellows stripped away such trappings of nobility to reveal the itching, ignoble, often diseased flesh beneath.

Rochester's scorn was equally strong for writers like Orrery, the Howards, and Dryden, who composed "Heroic Dramas" that rewarded real acts of selfishness, cowardice, and corruption with theatrical heroics of manqué supermen spouting rodomontade nonsense.[5] The disparity between Charles's hedonistic carnality and the poetic glorifications of "His Sacred Majesty," between the narrow stubbornness of York and the effusions of Dryden's Dedication to *The Conquest of Granada* provoked Rochester's contempt. Where Buckingham and his coterie were content to belittle the literary gaucheries of Dryden's opus in *The Rehearsal*, Rochester chose to reveal its psychological and moral hypocrisy. The Biblical city of Sodom, likened to London at the time of the Great Fire in 1666 and again in the fire of 1672, provided a suitable satiric device.

There were precedents for Sodomitic dramas going back to the Middle Ages, when the Catholic Church encouraged laymen guild members to stage Biblical episodes in ways that confirmed the teachings of Thomas Aquinas. The Manichaean heresy transmitted through Bulgaria had led the Church Fathers to denounce "buggery" or "sodomy" as "unnatural" (i.e., non-reproductive) sex. The story of Lot in Sodom was seen as proof of Divine condemnation of homosexuality; and such sexuality was made legally punishable by death in 1548.[6] Plays about Sodom, however, were acted in academic settings in England and elsewhere in the sixteenth and seventeenth centuries. Even Puritan restrictions under Cromwell allowed puppet plays about Sodom's destruction to be staged for their moral benefits. It is quite possible that Rochester saw such plays as a student at Oxford or later.[7]

The treatment of the Sodom story in *Sodom and Gomorrah*, however, was very different from the pietism of other playwrights—although in its way it is no less moralistic.[8] The farce simply transposes the sexual conduct and language of

London's Little Sodom and Whitehall into a low argot that jeers at the lofty, pretentious speech (and morality) of *The Conquest of Granada* and its like. Aside from their Biblical connotations of "unnatural" sexuality in Wilmot's short play, Sodom and Gomorah are pseudonyms for England and France, not locations in the ancient Middle East; and the destruction of the Cities of the Plain by fire and brimstone from heaven has no parallel in the first version of 1672–73. The only burning in the early version of *Sodom* is that of diseased flesh and tortured minds.

Likewise, the *dramatis personae* of *Sodom* are onomastic parodies of some of Dryden's heroic figures; the Biblical Lot, his wife, and Abraham do not appear.[9] The ranting Emperor Maximin of *Tyrannic Love* becomes *ballocks* or *bollox* (testicles) + *maximus* (large) or Bolloximian. (Its variant, Bolloxinian, is a composite of *bollox* and *ninny*.) Queen Catherine is transformed into Cuntagratia, martyred because she is deprived of sex: instead of being apotheosized, she becomes psychotically deranged. Lesser characters are obscenely labeled as sexual organs or processes: Clitoris, Fuckadilla, Borastus. And others, like Bolloximian, are composite names that characterize thinly veiled members of Charles II's circle; e.g., Pockanello or Pockinello, the poxed or "pocky" Punchinello. The play simply conflates Dryden's "heroic" characters with the notoriously sexual actors who portrayed them and the sexually notorious courtiers they were meant to compliment.

The "plot" of the three-act *Sodom* depends on a dramatic *ficelle* similar to that in Aristophanes's sex farce, *Lysistrata*, but reverses it. Where the women in *Lysistrata* deny intercourse to men to end a war, the men in *Sodom* wage the Battle of the Sexes by refusing to cohabit with women, who have infected them with venereal diseases. Bolloximian the King of Sodom issues an edict—which parodies Charles II's Declaration of Indulgence for Tender Consciences in March 1672—that the men of Sodom have "liberty" to indulge themselves with each other. Bolloximian himself is surrounded with courtiers whom he buggers with their grateful compliance. Like Charles's dependents, who were turned in their principles by his "pleasure," Bolloximian's catamites are "swived in their fundaments" for his needs and gratification. This political satire is fully, if covertly, developed, as some critics have noted.[10]

The "heroes" and "heroines" of *Sodom* are the same targets who people Rochester's verse satires: Charles II (Bolloximian); his queen, Catherine of Braganza (Cuntagratia); Lady Castlemain (the nymphomaniac Fuckadilla); John Sheffield the Earl of Mulgrave (Pockinello); Churchill (Pine); the Duke of York (Buggeranthus the impotent General); Henry Jermyn (Tewly or "tooly"); and in the 1676 version, the Duke of Monmouth (Pricket) and Louis XIV (Tarsehole the King of Gomorah).[11] There are specific references to Charles's dismissal of

Churchill as Castlemain's kept man, the birth of their daughter in July 1672, and other topical matters.[12] One of the most interesting features of the early *Sodom*, however, is its portrait of Louise de Kéroualle, or Madam Carwell (Kerwell) as the English called her, the King's new French mistress.

When Madame, the King's sister, came to Dover in May 1670, Kéroualle was in her retinue, and she caught Charles's eye.[13] After Madame died, Charles asked that Louise come to England and reminisce about her. Louis XIV, who had been trying for a long time to insinuate French spies into Whitehall, at once perceived the possibilities in a liaison between the English king and a French mistress-agent. Negotiations were carried on between Colbert and Arlington, who gave explicit instructions about how Louise was to conduct herself.[14]

As Castlemain faded in the King's favor, his interest in La Kéroualle flourished while she, using all her arts and wiles, kept away from his bed even as she danced in the Queen's Ballet in March, 1671, with other of his amorous targets. At last on October 10, 1671, Louise and the King were joined in a mock wedding staged at Euston, the country home of Lord and Lady Arlington. John Evelyn, scandalized, recorded events surrounding the bedding and impregnation of Louise, who just nine months later gave birth to a son the King acknowledged as his.[15]

Initially, the English dismissed "La Belle Bretonne" as innocuous, although Castlemain hated her with a passion. Evelyn said on first seeing her: "I now also saw that famed beauty (but in my opinion of a childish simple & baby face) . . . lately maide of honour to *Madame* & now to be so to the *Queene*."[16] If others were deceived by her baby face, Rochester was not. La Kéroualle was anything but simple and Rochester was well aware of her temperament. He probably knew her as early as the Dover visit—they obviously had contacts through 1670–71—but his country seclusion in October 1671 kept him from attending the King at Euston at the time of the mock wedding. Nevertheless, he knew Louise well enough to draw a scathing portrait of her as Clitoris in the early *Sodom*.

Clitoris (or Clytoris) is sexually experienced, somewhat contemptuous of the King's comparative prowess, and an adroit saluter of *derrières*. She describes her oral administrations to the Queen (perhaps a reference to her duties as Maid of Honor) in a complaining and derisive manner; and after the power of her tongue is extolled, she uses it to spread rumors of the King's infidelity and to raise the Queen's dissatisfaction. She gives Cuntagratia malicious advice, urging her to sexual *hubris*:

> [The King's] boundless pleasure buggers all he meets
> As linkboys, fiddlers, frigs in open streets,
> Forgets your joy; one cunt alone doth cloy.
> A man, a maid should uncontrolled enjoy.

Figure 15. Louise de Kéroualle, Duchess of Portsmouth. Portrait by Philippe Mignard. National Portrait Gallery, London. Reproduced by permission.

> Like him, run on with pleasure, build your throne,
> Fuck, frig, spend, riot, and the world's your own.[17]

Later in Act III, Clitoris similarly tells the King about the Queen's sexual displays in public, which Clitoris assisted (a possible glance at the Queen's Ballet), and expresses her fawning desire to take the Queen's place in his bed. The King denounces her in no uncertain terms.

Bollox. But of ambition, Clitoris, you sue,
Speak ill of her that I may fuck with you . . .
Pine, drag Clitoris to the bugg'ring hole;
There on a couch lay the base traitress down.
Fetch all the dogs and monkeys in the town,
Force 'em to act each with vig'rous fire;
Let 'em her cunt, her arse, her eyes quite tire.
Then drown'd in sperm, let the wild wretch expire.[18]

A lampoon so obviously an attack on Charles II and his mistress could be called treason. Rochester drew another satiric portrait of Charles and "Carwell" in 1673 in the notorious "Scepter-Prick" satire that got him exiled from Whitehall; but it was mild in comparison with the sodomitic travesty that preceded it.[19] The first version of *Sodom* may have been cathartic for its author; but it had to be scrupulously concealed from all but a few equally bawdy and cynical eyes. Later, in the 1676 version of the play, at a time when Rochester was in the bad graces of Kéroualle, the virulent attack on Clitoris was prudently expunged.

As the Clitoris section indicates, *Sodom* is grounded in a fierce misogyny. Women are condemned for their hypocrisy, their wanton sexual desires, their biological filth, their capacity to drain and exhaust men, and the venereal diseases they pass on to unsuspecting lovers. These, of course, are attitudes to be found also in "A Ramble in St. James's Parke"; but in *Sodom*, as in Rochester's later anti-feminist writings, they take on the dimensions of a furious jeremiad by an Old Testament prophet or the denouncing passion of a woman-hating Church father. From its early seeds in the pastorals, fed by malodorous experiences with promiscuous females, distrust of womankind grew into the vast, rank luxuriance of *Sodom*:

Their ulcered cunts, by being so abused
And having so much fuck therein infused,
And then not cleansed till they begin to stink,
May well be styled love's nasty common sink.[20]

Such tropes validate Robert Wolseley's contention that Rochester's intent in his obscene satire was not to raise desire but to repress that lawless tyrant. Any erotic dimensions of *Sodom* exist to make their emetic purgation more forceful emotionally.

The disgust with the lack of female hygiene, though extreme, is explainable: evidence from the period indicates widespread indifference to personal cleanliness and sanitation.[21] Stone reports that people in the seventeenth century washed no more than their faces, necks, hands, and feet; bathing in hot water was rare. Women neglected to wash their genitals even during menstruation.[22] Rochester's short poems, "On Mistress Willis" and "Song" contain pungent examples of male repugnance at female secretions and excretions.[23] He was not alone in his aversions.[24]

The crudity of subject matter and language in *Sodom* is paralleled by the crudity of its meter and syntax. In part, the awkwardly unheroic "Heroic Couplets" are a comment on Dryden's own stylistic lapses. But Rochester himself had not tried writing iambic pentameter verses before *Sodom* and his tries at the new form in the three-act farce provided the practice he needed when he came to write his own brilliantly polished satiric dialogues in 1674–76.[25] The final version of *Sodom* during Rochester's lifetime, revised in 1676 after the major satires were written, shows a command of form and tone lacking in the earlier, tentative version. Present from first to last, however, is a tension between sexual attraction and repulsion, idealism and disgust. Despite its bursts of hilarity and parodic wit, *Sodom* is a disturbing work, because it reveals a mind trapped and torn between equally powerful and frightening beliefs: pagan abandonment leading to hedonistic chaos as opposed to terrified submission to the punitive threats of Biblical laws. Its mocking laughter cannot conceal a nihilistic vision of terror.

David Farley-Hills remarks Rochester's "triumph over the threatening chaos by means of laughter," in his major works, laughter being "a transient defeat of nothingness which momentarily stems the reduction of everything to futility." The laughter provoked by the farcical *Sodom*, however, is less triumphant than transient.[26] A critic's comments on a *farceur* of the present century may be applied to the fears revealed in *Sodom*:

> [His] comedy personified this instinct for anarchy and . . . even invoked the traditional jester's symbol for it: the penis. Farce plays on a common recognition of insecurity and creates the illusion of mastery. [His] obsession with the penis, on and off stage, tried to turn his fears of inadequacy into a spectacle of potency and control.[27]

Throughout his life, as he wrote his obscenely revealing compositions, Rochester continued his day-to-day domestic and public lives. Both provided him with serious problems in 1673. Sometime in January, he returned to London, where Parliament convened on February 4. Its long months of inactivity had produced a monetary crisis for the King, who needed funds to continue the Third Anglo-Dutch War, and the time lapse had strengthened the anti-Catholic resolution of Protestant Parliamentarians to have the Declaration of Indulgence cancelled. In the Lords, the growingly ambitious Mulgrave became a steady attendant; Buckingham and the King were usually present, and so was the Fifth Earl of Dorset, Buckhurst's father, with whom Rochester was to share some joint financial schemes.

Rochester came to the Lords for the first time on February 10; but he then was absent with no excuse given until Feb. 18. A letter to his wife suggests that he probably went to Adderbury, or Enmore, to fetch her to London for medical care:

> I am sorry, Madam to heare that you are not well & as much troubled that you should believe I have not writt to you all this while . . . nothing is soe much my business now as to make hast to wait on you, I thinke in that I comply wth your commands as I doe with the hearty inclinations of
>
> > Your humble servant
> > Rochester[28]

Once she came to town, Lady Rochester's health—and the state of the Rochesters' marriage—drew the notice of letter-writing gossips. On March 20, 1673, Godfrey Thacker, a scandal-mongering, distant relation of the Earl of Huntingdon, penned some innuendoes about them:

> his pore lady is now not onely under the doctors hands; but under the sus-pition, of all that know them; to have been injured by him. I was never in Hatton garden since my comeing to towne; and so can give you no account of the coffin.[29]

Despite the implication that Rochester beat his wife, the "injury" was the pox. Those who knew the Earl well said later that his death was due to his deal-ings with women, remarking on the nastiness of one of his Woodstock partners and noting within the venereal context that he had treated his wife "bar-barously," though she was "so fine a woman." In a similar manner, Rochester's mother characterized the husband of Anne Lee, her grand-daughter, "whom hee used soe Barbarous . . . for hee gave her the pox. . . ."[30] Though the con-nection between Hatton Garden and Lady Rochester is not clear in Thacker's letter, the association of his ideas is. The Garden was the site of many estab-lishments that treated the pox; Rochester himself had been to one there. It is all too clear that Elizabeth Rochester's bad health was caused by syphilis.

If his wife's pains distressed him, so did his son's—perhaps even more. Young Charles probably was undergoing some treatment or other at the same time as Lady Rochester, possibly Wiseman's barbarous one with hot pokers. Unsurprisingly, the miraculous touch of His Sacred Majesty had failed to bring any improvement. Rochester's cynicism about the *pater patriae*, the Father of his Country, returned stronger than ever; and his doubts about a benevolent God the Father also were not lessened by seeing suffering innocence.[31] By 1673

Rochester had accepted Lucretius's disinterested gods and Hobbes's skepticism about revealed religion to the extent that he openly rejected Christian theology. As he told Robert Parsons, he "had form'd an odd Scheme of Religion to [him] self."[32] His dispute against "God and Piety" at "an Atheistical Meeting, at a person of Qualitie's" (Buckingham's?) probably took place in this year.[33]

During February and March of 1673, Rochester had cause to attend Parliamentary sessions with greater frequency and sense of urgency: he sat in the Lords twenty-two times.[34] Legislation to recompense him for dredging the Parrott and Thone Rivers on his land and allow him to transport goods free of charge to Bradford Bridge was first read on March 1. It was read a second time on March 14, and on the afternoon of March 22, following a morning session at which Rochester was charged once again with illegal dueling, the Parrott and Thone Rivers Bill was presented with committee approval by the Earl of Bridgwater. It was passed by the Lords on March 25 but with an amendment costly to John Wilmot. Andrew Marvell tersely told his constituents, "Rochester has lost his Bridge," and thus free conveyance of goods.[35]

The causes of the alleged duel between Rochester and the fiery-tempered Scotsman, Robert Constable, Viscount Dunbar, are not clear. Rochester's name had been linked with Dunbar's in the Vernell Affair in 1671 without apparent reason. Allegations of their intended duel in 1673 were made by the Catholic peer, Lord Bellasis (or Belasyse), Dunbar's father-in-law.[36] On March 21, the Earl Marshall Howard notified the Lords he had heard the report of a duel and "thought it his Duty (in the Concern of a Peer of this House) to give their Lordships notice." The concerned peer was Rochester; as a Scottish noble, Dunbar did not come under the English Lords' statutes.

On Saturday morning, March 22, 1673, with the King present, Rochester was brought into the Lords in the custody of the Earl Marshall, Henry Howard the Earl of Norwich. Commanded to give an account of the intended duel, Rochester replied that nobody had accused him of any such thing and until he was, he hoped the Lords would not expect him to accuse himself. Howard and Bellasis gave their accounts. Dunbar was brought in and stated that he had sent no challenge to his very good friend Rochester, and he was prepared to submit to the Lords' commands in the matter. After Dunbar withdrew, the Lords debated and resolved that the two peers should promise the House not to proceed any further in "this Business." Dunbar, recalled, agreed and Rochester said simply, "My Lords, I will obey your commands." Both were discharged from custody.[37]

Two subsequent developments suggest that the duel had been initiated by the drunken bully Dunbar and that Henry Howard had done Rochester a favor by bringing the proposed fight to the Lords' attention and having it stopped.

In May 1673, Dryden told Rochester in a letter that Etherege, who declared his friendship for Dunbar, had gotten into trouble over a lampoon that he wrote beginning, "I call a spade a spade; Eaton a bully." One of Etherege's "friends" [Buckhurst?] thinking the names "not heroique enough for the dignity of a Satyre," changed the line to read, "I call a Spade a Spade; Dunbar a Bully."[38] Dryden implied that Dunbar, ever the hothead, heard about the satire and confronted Etherege angrily.

Sometime before July 3, when the Duke's Players staged it, Henry Howard's protégé, Elkanah Settle, had his spectacular *The Empress of Morocco* performed at Court in the King's presence.[39] Howard had been on a diplomatic mission to Morocco in 1669–70 and the play was a compliment dedicated to him. Rochester provided the Second Prologue, spoken by gay, beautiful Lady Elizabeth Howard, Lady Rochester's frequent companion.[40] Rochester's Prologue would appear to be a repayment of sorts to Howard for sparing him the bother, and danger, of fighting Dunbar.

The Prologue showed that Rochester's practice with *Sodom* was helping him to write competent if not superior iambic pentameter couplets. The otherwise undistinguished verse is interesting, however, for its feminist views, written at the same period as Rochester's most splenetic woman-hating attacks. The Second Prologue to *The Empress of Morocco* is proof of Rochester's astonishing ability to impersonate, even empathize with, a female perspective. Other playwrights of the time had something of the same ability to write speeches for women, to be sure, but none showed the same capacity to express the extremes of gender-derived feelings successfully.

Certainly, the "feminist" views spoken by the Lady Betty Howard are comparatively mild:

> You Men would think it an ilnatur'd Jest,
> Should we laugh at you when you did your best . . .
> Few so ill bred will venture to a Play,
> To spy out Faults in what we Women say.
> For us no matter what we speak, but how:
> How kindly can we say—I hate you now.
> As for the men, if you'l laugh at 'em, do;
> They mind themselves so much, they'l ne'er mind you.[41]

Mild though they are, this defense of women and joke on men are previews of such later, full-fledged feminist credos by Rochester as the Empress's speeches in his scene for Sir Robert Howard's *The Conquest of China by the Tartars*, Lucina's speeches in *Valentinian*, the fragment (apparently another play prologue) beginning "What vaine unnecessary things are men," and Artemiza's "Letter" to Chloe.

The innuendo-filled apostrophe to Charles II concluding the Second Prologue also shows Rochester's multifaceted talent for writing clever compliments to and wicked satires about someone at the same time. The monarch is gently twitted for being enslaved to his amorous urges and the "soft sex." This badinage foreshadows the honed use of the same theme in the "Scepter-Prick" satire later in the year. The King was not the only object of double-edged wit. So was the speaker of the Prologue, Lady Elizabeth Howard, a kinswoman to Henry Howard and to John Dryden's wife and Lady Rochester's frequent companion.

Hypocritical, brilliantly versatile, or an emotional chameleon, Rochester had the genius to imagine himself in the person of the Lady Elizabeth. A flirtatious, temperamental, and willful beauty who got her way with crying fits, she eloped in July 1675 with Thomas Felton, a Groom of the King's Bed Chamber, acquired a reputation for promiscuity, and died in a fit of self-induced apoplexy in 1681. Rochester put into her mouth thoughts that she doubtless had but was unable to express. Then five or six months later, he put her among the secret masturbators in "Senior Dildo," pointing up the sensuality she demonstrated later. Ironically, in January of 1680, Lady Betty Felton sent Rochester a flirtatious copy of verses from a new translation of Ovid's *Heroides*, to which he replied with delicate, cavalier irony.[42] Rochester was a devastating satirist because his laser eye pierced through opaque facades as though they were transparent. To him they were.

His divertissements in the spring of 1673 flowered among great concerns for John Wilmot: worry about his wife and son, anxiety about money, fears about his own health, concealed angers and—to cap them all—a Parliamentary crisis about Catholic Recusants and a bitter family quarrel about the marital fate of Rochester's niece, Anne Lee.

The determination of Parliament to have the King's Declaration of Indulgence withdrawn persisted in spite of Charles's defense of its beneficial effects at the opening session on February 4. Refusing to vote funds, the Commons elected a critic of the Royalists, Sir Edward Seymour, as Speaker on February 18. On March 1, the Commons presented its response to the King's defense, Charles rejoined sharply, and Buckingham drafted an "Address of Thanks" to the Commons to defuse the situation and open the way to negotiations.[43] With Buckingham, Lauderdale, and Shaftesbury pressing him to dissolve Parliament and call for elections and Arlington urging him to acquiesce for the sake of getting money, Charles needed only Louis XIV's word and it came. The Declaration was cancelled on March 10.[44]

Triumphant, Protestants in Parliament began planning new legislative restrictions on Catholics.[45] On March 15 the Lords were considering such a bill, and the Earl of Bridgwater on March 17 gave a committee report on its progress. Rochester could have been involved with this committee—its members are not named in the Lords' *Journal*—or he may have been working behind the scenes to ensure that Recusants, like Lady Rochester, would have an escape clause if the legislation passed and got royal assent, as the Test Act did on March 29. In any case, he became aware of the consequences his stance on Catholic issues could take.[46] His embroilment with his mother over the question of Anne Lee's engagement was a case in point.

Delightful, clever little Nan Lee was a favorite of Rochester's and she adored him. After his death, she assumed the duties of his literary executrix, calling him her heart's pride and its guide in one of several elegiac poems:

> Weep drops of blood, my heart, thou'st lost thy pride,
> The cause of all thy hopes and fears, thy guide!
> He would have led thee right in Wisdom's way,
> And 'twas thy fault whene'er thou wen'st astray:
> And since thou stray'd'st when guided and led on,
> Thou wilt be surely lost now left alone.[47]

She had reason to regret not following Uncle Rochester's guidance in the choice of her husband, although in fact she had little say in the matter.

Nan was approaching her thirteenth birthday in July 1673 and was thus the age at which marriage was her destiny. The King declared it his pleasure that she marry John Arundell, who was reported to love her and she, him. The Arundells were Catholic supporters of the King, as Arundell of Wardour's services showed; and another Arundell, Lord Trerice, the father of John Arundell, would display his loyalty in the Danby crisis of 1678.[48] Charles II had his reasons for a marriage between the Lees and Arundells. Rochester, balancing perilously between the King's interests, his family's, Nan's, and his own, argued the Royal cause with his niece. Cary Gardiner implied in a September letter that some understanding between Arundells and Lees was made before the families left London in May.

Nan's legal guardian, Sir Ralph Verney, however, strongly favored another suitor: Thomas Wharton, the son of the fourth Baron Wharton, who was allied with Sir Ralph in the growing interests of the "Country party," a group of Whigs-to-be.[49] Sir Ralph's political concerns—or his reluctance to see her married to a Catholic—blinded him to the best interests of his young ward, whom he loved and treated as a daughter. He urged her marriage to Tom Wharton, a promising young Whig.[50] As for Nan's other legal guardian, the Dowager Countess of Rochester, her interest as always was money. The Wharton fortune was reason enough to marry her granddaughter to Tom, despite his reputation as a rakehell, gambler, and womanizer.

The Whartons in turn were eager to get their hands on Nan's dowry of £10,000 and her annual income of £2,500. Although Tom, then twenty-five, had no love for the girlish Nan—his biographer euphemistically wrote, "he had otherwise dispos'd of his heart"—he professed obedience to his father's wishes. After a prolonged card game, he rode at breakneck speed by calash and six horses from London to the Verney estate at Claydon, Bucks, just in time for the marriage articles to be drawn up.[51] The agreement was followed abruptly by the marriage at Adderbury Church on September 16, 1673. Even close members of Nan's family were taken by surprise. Unaware the wedding had already taken place, Lady Mary Bertie wrote on October 10: "My sister Anne Lee will be married very sudding for all things is conclud."[52] In gratitude to Sir Ralph for his role in the affair, Tom Wharton offered him as a gift the choice between £500 worth of plate and a Lely portrait of Anne Lee. Sir Ralph chose the portrait.

As time proved, Nan Lee would have been far better off if she had been guided by her Uncle Rochester's wisdom rather than the preference of her guardians. Wharton had been forced into the marriage "to enlarge his Fortune." Although his biographer wrote he "liv'd with her as became a Man of sense of good breeding," and she came to love the handsome cad to distraction, Nan's misery in their union finally drove her to think the unthinkable: divorce. Infected by him with syphilis, but compelled to remain his wife in name only, she died childless just twelve years after the wedding. The Dowager Countess never admitted her part in Nan's fate, but the embittered Nan got a revenge of sorts through her last Will and Testament.[53]

The disastrous marriage followed a summer of violent family quarrels and tempestuous confrontations among Wilmots, Lees, and Verneys. The King was furious at his will being thwarted, and Lord Rochester was again forcibly brought to acknowledge how much his own fortune depended on Charles II's favor. Sir Ralph Verney's sister, Cary Gardiner, reported to him the summer's traumatic events and her anxiety that Verney, a non-Courtier, had stirred the hornets' nest. On September 8, she told him that

> Mr. Arundell has the favour of the King and the othar [Wharton] looked on of no good reputation, so tis said tis done in oposistion to the King, who looks on my lady rochister as an ungratfull woman he having given her a good part of what this lady [Anne Lee] Injoys w[ch] was forfeted by treson, and his sevarall favours to my lord rochister, who they report cursis her and the young lady and all that has maid this match, beleveing it will slaken the King's kindness to him of the Court . . . tis said the King rit to Mistress Lee with his one [own] hand.[54]

Apprehensive that he had lost royal favor, Rochester returned to London in plenty of time for the first session of Parliament in October. There, he found a general state of uncertainty and anxiety. Before the Test Act passed on March 29, Rochester's friend and financial ally, Sir Thomas Clifford, attacked the bill violently in the Lords, claiming later he was speaking under divine inspiration. Following passage of the Act, Clifford publicly declared himself a Catholic, resigned from his Treasury post amid a blizzard of petitions from frantic Courtiers and withdrew to depressed seclusion at his country estate. When he died in mid-October, some claimed it was by suicide.[55]

The rest of the CABAL fell into disunity. In the final months of 1673, Arlington lost much of his power, Buckingham and Ashley began aligning themselves with the Country (Whig) party, and Lauderdale withdrew to Scotland, where he remained a veritable dictator.[56] When Parliament convened on October 20, the political disarray was apparent. Rochester was one of very few peers present in the Lords and Parliament was prorogued until October 27. A week later, the King presented his pressing need for more money to finance the Dutch War and assured the Lords of his efforts on behalf of "Established Religion and Laws" (i.e Protestantism). Rochester was put on the Committee for Privileges and the Committee on Petitions. Both committees were gaining increasing powers, but attendance remained small and after two meetings and two adjournments, Parliament was recessed until January 7, 1674.[57]

Anxious, with too much time on his hands, Rochester fell back into his habits of wine, women, and song writing. One of his lyrics, "Upon his Drinking a Bowl," mentions military events of the past summer, declaring "With *War* I've nought to do," envisions an artistic creation with Keatsian beauty and sensuality, then restates the cynical credo of a pagan hedonist—or English debauchee:

> *Vulcan* contrive me such a Cup,
>   As *Nestor* us'd of old;
> Shew all thy skill to trim it up,
>   Damask it round with *Gold* . . .
> But carve thereon a spreading Vine,
>   Then add Two lovely *Boys*;
> Their Limbs in Amorous folds intwine,
>   The *Type* of future joys.
> *Cupid*, and *Bacchus*, my Saints are,
>   May drink, and Love, still reign,
> With *Wine*, I wash away my cares,
>   And then to *Cunt* again.[58]

The image of the "amorous folds" amid the spreading vine recalls the description of the branch twining in some loved fold of Aretine in "A Ramble," with its similar, jolting demotic anti-climax. Whether romanticizing the erotic or denouncing the lewd, the polarities of Rochester's thought are ever apparent.

Some of the erotic elegance of this lyric may have owed to a new mistress. Sometime during 1673, the Earl acquired the novitiate actress to the Duke's Theatre, Elizabeth Barry.[59] Just fifteen, pretty but inexperienced, Mistress Barry left the protection of Lady Davenant for that of Lord Rochester. The gauche and seemingly untalented girl became a Galatea to his Pygmalion; during their first months of cohabiting, he coached her in the tricks of acting, imparting to her the secrets of feminine charm and coquetry he instinctively knew and had shown through Lady Betty Howard. By his own playful seductiveness, he showed her how to win over future audiences. His letters to her survive, undated but immediate.

> Madam,
> Nothing can ever be so dear to me as you are, and I am so convinced of this that I dare undertake to love you whilst I live. . . .

> Madam,
> There is now no minute of my life that does not afford me some new argument how much I love you. The little joy I take in everything wherein you are not concerned, the pleasing perplexity of endless thought which I fall into wherever you are brought to my remembrance; and lastly, the continual disquiet I am in during your absence, convince me sufficiently that I do you justice in loving you so as woman was never loved before.

> Madam,
> Believe me, dearest of all pleasures, that those I can receive from anything but you are so extremely dull they hardly deserve the name . . . You may be sure I cannot choose but love you above the world, whatever becomes of the King, Court, or mankind and all their impertinent business. I will come to you this afternoon.[60]

Rochester's amorous persiflage was a striking contrast to his attitudes toward women expressed in "Signior Dildo," a satire composed in late 1673.[61] In November, the Duke of York's second wife, Mary Beatrice D'Este (Mary of Modena) arrived in England with her attendants, having married York by proxy. The bride had been about to enter a convent when she was pressured by the Curia, the French Ambassador to Rome, and her relative, Cardinal Francesco Barberino, the Cardinal Protector of England, to marry James in hopes of securing a Catholic heir to the throne.[62] Naturally, the marriage and Mary's arrival caused great agitation among English Protestants determined to prevent such a succession.

Rochester amused himself at the flurry among Court ladies by attributing their excitement to the introduction of Italian dildos into Albion. He personified Signior Dildo and Count Cazzo (Italian for "penis"); and his account of Signior Dildo's progress into London and Count Cazzo's angry retreat is no less a spoof of male fears of impotence (or castration) than solitary female sexuality or specific ladies of the Court. The satire also makes use of specific events: the burning of the Ballers' dildos in 1670 and Henry Savile's spying a dildo when he stole into Lady Northumberland's bedroom in 1671. The frolicking, irregular anapestic meter recalls the Duchess of Cleveland's discourse with Mary Knight.

> You Ladyes all of Merry England
> Who have been to kisse the Dutchesse's hand,
> Pray did you lately observe in the Show
> A Noble Italian call'd Signior Dildo?
> The Signior was one of her Highness's Train
> And helpt to Conduct her over the Main,
> But now she Crys out to the Duke I will go,
> I have no more need for Signior Dildo. . . .

Several Court ladies who choose Signior Dildo as an escort had appeared in earlier satires (Cleveland, Knight, Dorothy Howard); others are new, sometimes surprising additions (Lady Elizabeth Howard, Tom Killegrew's wife). The poem follows in a tradition of earlier satires on woman, e.g., one in 1663 that began, "Cary's face is not the best."[63] But, given the time of its composition, its rowdy humor, and its good-natured if obscene depiction of female sexuality are rather surprising.

"Signior Dildo" shows women as carnal but human, not grotesques of the male imagination or even as castrating females. Its topical references ally it with darker Rochester poems, but "Dildo" is a *jeu d'ésprit* possibly because Rochester was emotionally disengaged from its events—more probably because the events never happened. Only when he described Cleveland and "Doll" Howard did his tone turn nasty for personal reasons or "revenge." Since these were "lies" in Howard's case, "Signior Dildo" provides a useful test for the success of Rochester's various theories and techniques of satire. So does the so-called "Scepter-Prick" satire, also written at the end of 1673. This satire on Charles II, Louise de Kéroualle and Nell Gwyn is a medley of perspectives, visual and mental, and a farrago of the satirist's conflicting emotions toward the King.

The poem begins with an initial statement of seeming admiration for "The easiest King and best bred man alive," whose peaceful aims and gentleness are contrasted with "the french Foole who wanders up and downe / Starving his

People, hazarding his Crowne." The focus then shifts from the King's character to a mixed "admiration" for the royal sexual equipment and a distrust of the "high Desires" that make Charles the "plaything" (in two senses) of his mistresses and therefore "little wiser than his brother" (i.e., something of a narrow-minded, obsessive fool).

The King may not be wrongly "ambitious" for "renown," but his sexual needs make him a "Poor Prince," governed by buffoons. He is "A merry Monarch, scandalous and poor." And the "proudest preemtoriest Prick alive," *is* both ambitious and wanton, willing to break through Safety, Law, Religion, even Life to reach its goal. Like the "Hector of France," Charles's prick is a lawless, destructive tyrant, as well as a "buffoon" that governs him. Like the proud Count Cazzo, it has a separate identity, a preemptive existence that subordinates its owner, now in his "declining years." *He* is an appendage to *It*, a once-mighty conqueror now flagging, which must be played with to be aroused. The two women who manage the arousal are "Carwell the most Deare of all his deares" and "poor laborious Nelly," who "imployes, hands, fingers, mouth, and thighs/ E'er shee can raise the Member she enjoys [gives joy to]."[64]

This contemptuous portrayal of weakness and decline explains and undercuts the "virtues" that were "admired" in the opening section of the satire. The easiness and lack of ambition are really laziness, increasing age, and a weakening of both will and sexual prowess in the forty-three-year-old Charles. The way is thus prepared for the explosive and revealing final couplet:

> I hate all Monarchs, and the Thrones they sit on
> From the Hector of France to the Culley of Britain.

The blustering bully in public and the privately gulled dupe or simpleton become reversed mirror-images. The latter was once the former; the former will become the latter. Both are fools and therefore contemptible and hateful.[65]

Although by modern standards Charles was not superannuated at the age of forty-three, the scorn of a twenty-five-year-old man for the sexual decline of a man that age, if naive, is understandable, even more so in a period when the average male was dead at thirty-two. Charles was past his prime and somewhat ridiculous in his sexual obsessions to Rochester, who already saw the limitations and consequences of bodily pleasure. The quasi-son witnessed the continuing preoccupations of his surrogate father and judged them foolish. Like Noah's son Ham, he had seen his "father" drunk and naked and he mocked him.

At twenty-five, Rochester was himself father or acting father to a sizeable family. His fatherly affection for his own son had led to a last act of trust in and test of the King's superior paternal powers; but despite Charles's touch, little Charles Wilmot remained a victim of the King's-Evil. Rochester was thoroughly disillusioned. Weary of his dependence on the grace and favor of the Father-King, he was frustrated by his continual need to court it. His growing desire to rebel had to stay hidden. By the end of 1673, however, the restraints were more than Rochester could maintain. He made an Oedipal break.

Amusement at "Signior Dildo" grew in December until a report of it reached the King's ears. Charles wanted to see the satire on the Court ladies; and on one of the wine-soaked evenings preceding Christmas, he asked Rochester for a copy. In a drunken fit of carelessness—or possibly urged subconsciously into reckless bravado—John Wilmot reached in his pocket and handed a "libel" to his Father-King to peruse.[66] It was the "Scepter-Prick" verses.

Charles's eye roved down the page and his fury grew as the satire sharpened:

> There reigns and oh long may hee reign and thrive The easiest King . . . Peace is his aime . . . And Love, he loves, for he loves fucking much . . . His Sceppter and his Prick are of a Length . . . Restlesse he rolls about from Whore to Whore . . . Poor Prince thy Prick will govern thee because it makes thee sportt . . . To Carwell . . . Offt he bewayles his fortune and her fate . . . For though in her he setles well his Tarse Yett his dull graceless Ballacks hang an [on his] arse . . . The Paynes itt cost the poor laborious Nelly . . . to raise the Member . . . I hate all Monarchs . . . Culley of Britaine.

The explosion came. Fire and brimstone of majestic wrath fell on Rochester's head; and like Lot, he fled from Sodom into the wilderness in search of refuge, a Little Zoar.[67]

NEW SCENES OF FOPPERY
(JANUARY–JUNE 1674)

And *Wit*, was his vain frivolous pretence
Of pleasing others, at his own expence.
For *Witts* are treated just like common *Whores*,
First they're enjoy'd, and then kickt out of *Doores*,
The pleasure past, a threatening doubt remains,
That frights th'enjoyer, with succeeding pains. . . .
      —Rochester, "Satyr," on Man

Rochester's "mistake" in handing Charles II his contemptuous lampoon had the immediate effect of getting the Earl expelled from Whitehall, but it also had the long-term effect of ending their relationship as indulgent but demanding father to capricious but charming son. The King's anger had exiled the younger man before, but it was tempered by a measure of tolerant amusement and Wilmot had been restored to full favor.[1] In December 1673, Charles was not amused. He had had a trying year all around, and the very people who should have honored his generosity had taxed his patience to the limit. Henry Wilmot had been Charles Stuart's benefactor; and as King, Charles became a benefactor in turn to Wilmot's widow, only to have her defy his pleasure in the Lee-Wharton marriage. He had given many favors to Wilmot's son only to be told, "I hate you" by the ingrate. This was the final straw. In the future, John Wilmot would have to earn the Royal good will by more than a flashing wit that proved to be double-edged and much too cutting.

In the winter of 1673–74 Rochester was banished under a darker cloud than ever before. Although he returned to Parliament in mid-February 1674 and soon after to somewhat better grace with the King, their relationship was that of two adult men, one subordinate to the other, with a constant degree of distrust, however disguised.[2] Instead of continuing to mimic Arlington's sycophantic ways to royal favor, Rochester began to adopt the more dangerous tactics of Buckingham: testing, bargaining, defying, and manipulating by pleasing. He did use one final trick of Arlington's, however.

Rochester's exile lasted for six or seven weeks. Parliament reconvened on January 7, with the Earl absent and no excuse given. Charles made another plea for funds, but the Lords defiantly turned to papist-hunting the next day, and in the days following they drew up a petition for a national fast to atone for "the calamitous Condition of the Kingdom," due to the Papists.[3] The Oath established by the Test Act was administered on January 13 and 14, Rochester of course still in absentia. On January 26, his name was placed on a list of peers who had not sworn their Protestant loyalty by declaring their disbelief in the Catholic doctrine of transubstantiation.[4] No money bills were passed, and the King saw clearly that he needed all the support in the Lords he could muster. This realization was an incentive to an earlier reconciliation with the Earl of Rochester than the King—and Rochester's enemies at Court—might have wished.

At the start of his banishment in December, Rochester probably went to Adderbury as usual, but he was too anxious about his status at Court and the religious mischief-making in Parliament to stay buried in the country. According to Gramont, he returned to the City of London, which traditionally was off limits to royal intrusion without permission of the Citizens or "Cits."[5] There, taking a house and masquerading as one among the set of merchants and bankers, he was able to keep abreast of news from Whitehall while amusing himself at the Cits' lavish feasts and parties. In company with the men at these entertainments, he "exclaim'd against the *Miscarriages* and *Blunders* of the *Government*," and he "rail'd with their *Wives*, against the *Vices* of a *licentious Court*, and inveigh'd against the King's Mistresses. . . . After which, to compleat their *Murmurings*, he added, He *wondered Whitehall was not yet destroy'd by Fire and Brimstone from Heaven, like Sodom and Gommorrah of old. . . .*"[6] Rochester acted his role so adroitly that he became much in demand at the Citizens' gatherings but he soon grew bored with "the heaviness of their entertainments."

Not all his time was spent play-acting the Cit. With the Lees and Wilmots out of royal favor, it was to Rochester's benefit to find some way to get them restored by nullifying the King's anger at Nan Lee's marriage into a family of the dissident Country Party. In July 1673, after Clifford's resignation, Charles had appointed Sir Thomas Osborne, the future Earl of Danby, as the Lord Treasurer. The break-up of the CABAL made clear that Danby was going to be the King's right arm and a powerful man.[7] It happened that Danby was married to Brigit Bertie, the sister of James Bertie (who was married to Ellen Lee) and Robert Bertie the Earl of Lindsey (who was married to the widow of Frank Lee). If these intricate ties could be strengthened by another alliance, one involving the King, the Lees and the Wilmots might appease Charles and regain their place in the sun.

The disintegration of the CABAL had cost Arlington much power, but he remained Lord Chamberlain and the King's censor, largely because he had been clever enough earlier, in August 1672, to marry his darling child-daughter, Isabella ("Tata"), to Henry Fitzroy, a bastard-son of the King and the Duchess of Cleveland. Although Fitzroy, the Duke of Grafton, was only nine years old and Tata was five, the King used such token marriages to bind chief officials to his cause. The child-bride would remain with her parents until she reached puberty, when another, official wedding would take place. If the Bennets could cement their fortunes with the King in this way, so could the Lees and Wilmots.[8]

In 1674 circumstances were perfect for such a match. The King's favorite bastard-daughter, the Lady Charlotte Fitzroy, was ten years old; Edward Henry Lee, the grandson of the Dowager Countess of Rochester and the half-nephew of John Wilmot, was eleven. Lady Charlotte's mother, Barbara the Duchess of Cleveland, was the Dowager Countess's cousin. Edward Henry's mother, the Countess of Lindsey, had been her daughter-in-law and she was also the sister-in-law of Danby the Treasurer. After a bad beginning, Rochester's Uncle Walter St. John (related to both children) had become an intimate at Court and Aunt Johanna (also related to them) was a great favorite of both Edward Henry and Charlotte.[9] No maze of such family, political, and financial implications could be more happily extended than by wedding the two pretty children. Negotiations proceeded in the early months of 1674 with Uncle Rochester playing a significant part.

Rochester returned to the House of Lords on February 16. The Oath was administered, but he did not take it. On the next day, however, he swore to his disbelief in the pernicious dogma of Roman Catholicism. There is no reason to doubt his sincerity. If as a youth he had succumbed to the lure of Vatican panoply and the promise of Papal Indulgence, he had long since discarded popery along with other religious artifacts. Thomas Hobbes had worked his ways, as had the sophisticated skepticism of Buckhurst, Buckingham, and even the King. Rochester left a literary record of his growing doubts. He had begun by questioning the nature and existence of the soul, mocked the simplicity of country parsons, toyed with pagan theology, accused the Jesuits of buggery, used sacred rituals and imagery to describe sexual obscenities, and defended the cause of atheism before people of quality. In spite of momentary misgivings, he had convinced himself to abandon the sacred for the profane. If forced to take an Oath renouncing *all* religion in 1674, he might have hesitated only briefly before taking it.[10]

Rochester was present at all of the final seven meetings of the Lords. On February 20, he was placed on a timber and wood committee, of interest to him because of posts he already held and even greater interest when he gained a far more important post several days later. On February 24, the King reported on the Peace Treaty ending the Third Anglo-Dutch War, and then he recessed Parliament until November 10. On February 27, Rochester was given the important post of Ranger of Woodstock Park, the royal preserve.[11]

Although his old schoolmate at Wadham, John Lovelace the third Baron of Hurley, was due to become the next Keeper of Woodstock, Rochester was given that post as well on May 2, clearly by preference because of his part in arranging the wedding between Edward Henry Lee and Charlotte Fitzroy.[12] Lovelace, a fellow reprobate and drinking companion, appeared unoffended, probably because of some under-the-table agreement with Rochester about cutting timber and killing deer.[13] But Lady Lindsey, Edward Henry's mother, viewed the arrangement as a temporary one with Uncle Rochester serving as a *pro tem* substitute until Edward Henry became a royal son-in-law. The stage was set in 1674 for one of the worst Wilmot-Lee family embroilments in 1675–76.

In the spring of 1674, however, Rochester had cause to congratulate himself for many reasons other than surviving his *faux pas* with the "Scepter-Prick" lampoon. His wife was nearing delivery of a third child, having become pregnant in October 1673 after a seemingly successful cure. If Clifford was dead, the new Treasurer Danby was behaving in a most friendly and encouraging manner; and Rochester's ally, Sir Robert Howard, remained in his advantageous Treasury post. The Earl's romance with Elizabeth Barry kept its charms; with his coaching, she had developed her skills as a mistress and was even showing some promise as a stage-actress. The theater season was invigorating, with new plays and friendships developing and some diverting quarrels to watch and urge on. Rochester was in excellent spirits. This state of mind stimulated his creativity, and he began the period of his finest, most brilliant and innovative writing.

Over the next three years, his compositions ranged from rococo love letters and lyrics to social satires in verse to set pieces for the theater; many reflected his close involvement with the London stage and its personnel. This undated poem, possibly addressed to Mrs. Barry, shows the shift from earlier war, mythological, and pastoral imagery to theatrical tropes:

> Leave this gawdy guilded Stage
> From custome more than use frequented
> Where fooles of either sex and age
> Crowd to see themselves presented.
> To loves Theatre the Bed
> Youth and beauty fly together
> And Act soe well it may be said

The Lawrell there was due to either.
Twixt strifes of Love and war the difference Lies in this
When neither overcomes Loves triumph greater is.[14]

Rochester's notation that contemporary plays reflected the playwrights' practice of mirroring the persons, actions, and concerns of their audiences and
themselves suggests the self-referential nature of the London stage in 1674.

In April, Dryden and Shadwell, not yet cleft apart by political interests, saw
the production of a musical version of *The Tempest*, to which both, along with
Davenant, had contributed. This "hybrid vehicle for stage display" followed an
Italian "Opera in musique" in January, a French "Ballet et Musique" in
February, and a dual-language "Vocal Representation," *Ariadne* by Pierre
Perrin, in March.[15] The musical *Tempest* was a spectacle in every sense of the
word: horrid spirits flying through the air, showers of fire, thunder claps—all the
stage effects. A popular success, it provoked a travesty by Thomas Duffett and
Rochester's scornful amusement, later expressed as a put-down in the Epilogue
to Francis Fane's *Love in the Dark* (1675):

As Charms are Nonsence, Nonsence seems a Charm,
Which hearers of all Judgment does disarm; . . .
Players turn Puppets now at your desire,
In their Mouth's Nonsence, in their Tails a Wire,
They fly through Clouds of Clouts, and Showers of Fire.[16]

Rochester consistently derided the earliest musicals as "tuneful nonsense."

His taste in traditional genres such as tragedy and comedy was somewhat
more indulgent, if Nathaniel Lee's *The Tragedy of Nero* is indicative. *Nero*, acted
on May 16, 1674, was a limited success; critics objected to Lee's conception of
Nero and some may have found the "Civil Tyrant" a simulacrum of Charles
II.[17] When Lee published the play, he dedicated it to Rochester and implied
that the Earl had some part in the writing.

Nathaniel ("Nat") Lee was the handsome, unstable son of a clergyman, who
was Chaplain in Ordinary to Charles II. (Sons of clergymen seemed to be
drawn magnetically to Rochester, John Crowne and John Oldham being other
cases in point.)[18] Nat Lee inherited from his father a zeal for the classics, a fero-
cious anti-Catholic bias, and a violent temper. Educated at Charterhouse and
Trinty, Cambridge, where he took his B.A. degree in 1669, he was in
Cambridge when the Duke of Buckingham came there in 1671 as the new
Chancellor. Joseph Spence recorded the story that "The Duke brought [Lee]
up to town where he never did anything for him."[19] Lee joined the Duke's
Company as an actor in the 1671–72 season; and although he had a genuine

talent for reading lines in a "pathetic" fashion, a severe case of stage fright as Duncan in *Macbeth* ended his acting career in February 1673.[20]

When Rochester first met Nat Lee is unknown; but given the Earl's ties with Buckingham and the Duke's Company, it is not unlikely that they had contact as early as 1671. In 1672 a version of Suetonius attributed to Andrew Marvell appeared: *The History of the Twelve Caesars . . . Newly Translated into English*, with its graphic portrait of Nero, who had interested Rochester ever since his tour in Italy. When Lee decided to abandon greasepaint for the writer's lamp, his classical training naturally suggested a Roman subject for a play dedicated to Rochester. He chose Nero, either oblivious to or dismissive of any thought that his choice might be a poor one for several reasons. Marvell had compared Charles II to Nero indirectly in the earlier *Advice to a Painter* ("Next, let the flaming *London* come in view, / Like Nero's Rome, burnt to rebuild it new"), and surreptitious broadside ballads had made more overt comparisons.[21]

The Tragedy of Nero has been described as "heroic, being a non-comic play mostly in couplets, but basically it is a blood-bath . . . we simply wallow in gross brutality."[22] To be sure, the reign of the historical Nero might be described in the same terms, as Suetonius and other historians made clear. The list of his atrocities was endless. Lee unwisely tried to include them all. Although it seems to have been somewhat successful with its audiences, *Nero* was savaged by self-appointed critics, and the author appealed to Lord Rochester for vindication.

> Your protection & favour is implor'd by this Humble-Supplicant in the behalf of a Civil Tyrant . . . and for which I have been sufficiently censur'd. . . . From the Criticks, whose fury I dread those Killmen and more then Jews; I appeal to your Lordship . . . To you whose Judgment vies with your Grandeur, who are as absolutely Lord of Wit as those prevaricators are its slaves. To you who by excellent Reading . . . have justly limited the mighty Sallies of an overflowing Fancy . . . and whose Writings are so exactly ingenious. . . .

Lee's baroque prose makes it difficult to see why he appealed to Rochester to justify his depiction of Nero. What Rochester might have done to vindicate the historical accuracy of Lee's *Nero* is not clear. Yet, it is clear that Rochester was associated with Nero in the minds of John Dryden and Thomas Lessey, among others.[23] It is also true that he called Lee a "hot-brained, fustian fool" for the historical inaccuracies of *Sophonisba*, his next "Roman" play, written without Rochester's help. Obviously, Rochester regarded himself as something of an authority on ancient history and was so regarded by others including Lee. These hints indicate that Rochester was closely associated with *Nero* and that its stinging critical reception reflected on him in some way.

Other clues may be found. *The Tragedy of Nero* contains some key passages for which parallels exist in Rochester's canon, including fragments in his own hand-writing among the Nottingham manuscripts. Act III of *Nero*, for example, contains a passage based on Lucretius, *De rerum natura*, I.1–5:

> Mother of Aeneas and his race, delight of men and gods, life-giving Venus. . . .

Compare with this, Lee's speech beginning:

> Model of Heav'n thou Ornament of Earth,
> Propitious Star that smiles on humane birth! . . .

and Rochester's:

> Great Mother of Aeneas, and of Love;
> Delight of mankind, and the powers above; . . .

The speech of Britannicus in Act IV.3 of *Nero* concludes:

> Some full-gorg'd Priest, nodding beneath a shade
> Tales of Elizium, and the dull pool, made,
> Whither, O whither, go we, when we dye?
> Why, there where babes not yet conceiv'd do lie?
> Death's nothing; nothing after death will fall;
> Time, and dark Chaos, will devour us all.

The paraphrase of Seneca's *Troas* by Rochester beginning "After Death, nothing is, and nothing Death," concludes:

> Dead, wee become the Lumber of the World,
> And to that Masse of matter shall be swept,
> Where things destroy'd, with things unborne are kept . . .
> For Hell, and the foule Fiend that Rules
> Gods everlasting fiery Jayles
> (Devis'd by Rogues, dreaded by Fooles)
> With his grim griezly Dogg, that keepes the Doore,
> Are senselesse Storyes, idle Tales
> Dreames, Whimseys, and noe more.[24]

Other similarities between Lee's *Nero* and the Rochester fragments may be found; but most striking is the speech by Petronius Arbiter as he observes Nero's seduction of Poppaea Sabina:

> She yields, she yields! her looks her thoughts betray!
> Greatness is entred, and her soul gives way. . . .

Rochester's enigmatic fragment titled "Sab: Lost" seems to be another version of a speech about Sabina's loss to Nero by Piso, her husband:

> She yields, she yields! Pale envy said amen:
> The first of women to the last of men. . . .

The fragmentary evidence about Rochester and Nat Lee fits to form a partial mosaic of a collaboration between them on *The Tragedy of Nero*, but many gaps remain and the issue cannot be resolved until those are closed. Overall evidence, however, demonstrates Lee's passionate and contradictory but lifelong emotional attachment to Rochester.[25]

Lee was not the only aspiring young playwright to meet critical discouragement in the spring of 1674. Elkanah Settle's *The Empress of Morocco*, published in October 1673, had drawn the spiteful attention of John Crowne, another dramaturgical contender, who proceeded to enlist the aid of John Dryden and probably Thomas Shadwell in writing a lengthy and contemptuous *Notes and Observations on The Empress of Morocco*.[26] The *Notes* were published anonymously in early 1674; they elicited several responses, including one from Settle himself, and the critical practice of close textual analysis was established along lines that owed much to the literary techniques of the lampoon.

Rochester's "Satyr," given the title "Timon" in 1704, was written in April or May of 1674.[27] In its treatment of the contemporary theater and its portraits of buffoon-critics, it has obvious ties to the controversy over the *Notes* at that period. Loosely based on Boileau's Third Satire and classical sources, "Timon" begins with a query by "A" (for Auditeur, Boileau's "Listener") to Timon: is he getting so old that he is drooping from a debauch of the night before? Timon's answer relating the events of the previous night makes up the rest of the poem. Rochester's practice in writing dramatic dialogue is apparent in this satiric "speaking" monologue.[28]

The "I" narrative voice and tone of "Timon" are similar to the "I" libertine-rake in "A Ramble," to which in some ways "Timon" appears to be an extension. Timon's night begins when he is strolling in St. James's Park and is seized by "a dull dining *Sot*," who forces Timon to dine with him by promising the company of "some *Wits*, of thy acquaintance," naming Sedley, Buckhurst, and Savile. He shows Timon a "Libel," wanting to know whether they are his. Timon replies that he might make a "Song to Phillis" (as Rochester had) "for my *Pintle's* sake" ("pintle" was slang for penis). Timon calls the libel insipid as the praise of virtuous Queens (a hit at Dryden's tributes to Queen Catherine) or Shadwell's lines before Sedley helped him with *Epsom Wells*. These details and his libertine sentiments equate the Timon-persona with Rochester and suggest ties with the *Notes* controversy.[29]

Whether he had in mind the misanthropic Timon of Athens (5th c. B.C.) embodied in Shakespeare's play or the skeptic Timon the Philosopher of Phlius (fl. ca. 250 B.C.) matters very little. The two were easily combined: the former cynically embittered by mankind's ingratitude and the latter the author of some *Silloi*, or "squint-eyed pieces," in mock-Homeric meter ridiculing his fellow "lovers of wisdom."[30] Rochester's choice of "Timon" as a satiric alter-ego discloses some of the darker aspects of his complex selves. In a survey of Rochester's satiric predecessors, from Juvenal to Aretino, Alvin Kernan remarks:

> [A]s the satirist continues to look into one sewer after another, turning always to the nasty, the rotten, and the obscene for his imagery . . . it begins to appear that he has a fixation or obsession . . . although he is the inveterate foe of vice, he himself has dark twists in his character: he is sadistic and enjoys his rough work; he is filled with envy of those same fools he despises and castigates; he has a taste for the sensational and delights in exposing those sins of which he himself is guilty. . . .[31]

Certainly, some passages in "Timon" suggest the applicability of this characterization to Rochester: the grotesque host and his wife, the bluntly obscene sexual allusions, the narrator's verbal slips into the first-person plural, the coarsely gluttonous meal, the tropes of disease, and the sadistic battle of the bullies that ends the poem.[32] Even so, other passages show Rochester at his most rational and playfully witty as he reduces ignorance and violence to nonsense. As Treglown says, "This kind of co-existence of positive and destructive attitudes in Rochester's work has often been noticed. What is so effective in *Timon* is the deftness with which they are worked together."[33]

The mention of Savile prepares the way for raillery about the "Visiters" who espied a "Tool" under the "small *Pillow*" of the "fair *Countess* [of Northumberland]." The hostess's castigation of coarse love and "our *Poetry*, Unfit for modest Eares" shows Rochester detached and laughing at himself. And the four critic-bullies, Shadwellian in name—Halfwit, Dingboy, Huffe, and Kickum—are reminders of Thomas Shadwell and a subtle way of implicating him in the subsequent dramatic nit-picking by brainless critics that parodies *Notes and Observations on The Empress of Morocco*.

Since "Timon" operates through satiric reversal, Halfwit and his companions stand antithetically to true wits such as Buckhurst and Sedley, whom Rochester praised as men of good taste and judgment in a later satire.[34] Clues about the real identities of these false wits are few, though they may have been immediately recognizable to Rochester's circle. Some of his targets in other satires or the boorish hectors linked with him by gossip may have been intended. It is especially tempting to see Dingboy as Robert Dunbar, or D—b— with the spaces filled in, partly because the name is unusual and Dingboy's negative comments about Etherege contrast with the others' positive attitudes toward Settle, Crowne, and Dryden. Rochester may have been alluding with ironic archness to the Dunbar-Etherege *contretemps* in the spring of 1673.

The selection of particularly vacuous lines for praise works to ridicule both the author of those lines and their admirer. Half-wit's encomium on the *Mustapha* of Roger Boyle, Lord Orrery, establishes the standard of bad taste and faulty judgment. The Rochester set did not admire Orrery.[35] Making him the icon of the Halfwits, the satire explodes the pretensions of "heroic" plays as Rochester had already done with *Sodom*. Dingboy's oath-filled preference for Etherege's "*Airy Songs*, and soft *Lampoons*," anticipates his cloddish cavils that Etherege is ignorant of "your *Nowns*, *Grammar*, and Rules of Art . . . Yet writ Two talking *Plays*, without one *Plot*." Dingboy's disparagement of Etherege acts in the same way as Halfwit's praise of Orrery: to reveal the critic as a fool.

Huffe's admiration for the very lines in Settle's *The Empress of Morocco* that Crowne damned so vigorously ties the literary satire in "Timon" to the *Notes* by Crowne openly. Huffe (and Rochester) make the lines even more ludicrous by exaggerating their alliteration to reveal Huffe's poor taste and Settle's gaucheries: "Their lofty Bulks the foaming Billows Bear" becomes "Whose broad-built-bulks, the boyst'rous Billows bear." "Was ever braver Language writ by Man?" Huffe asks rhetorically. Kickum declares himself for Crowne because of his romances that had outdone the French. Kickum particularly relishes cliché-ridden lines from Crowne's *The History of Charles the Eighth of France*, which Crowne had published in 1672 with a brash Dedication to Rochester.[36] At this point, the ironic convolutions of "Timon" become most complex: Rochester is ridiculing as a fool a man who praises a drama written by a foolish man who meant it to praise Rochester.

The host then damns Dryden with faint praise, singling out two lines from *The Indian Emperor* that contain a ludicrous birth simile and remarking, "What a brave *Midwife* is a Laureats head!" Having tried the chief participants in the "Morocco" controversy—Settle, Crowne, Dryden, and by implication Shadwell—and found them wanting, the "critics'" inane conversation concludes with the host's (and Rochester's) summarizing estimate: "But pox on all these *Scriblers*. . . ." Talk about military affairs leads to quarrels and fisticuffs among the four bullies, which end with a drinking reconciliation and Timon's retreat:

> I ran down Stairs, with a Vow never more
> To drink Bear Glass, and hear the *Hectors* roar.

The reference to Bear Tavern is a final link to "A Ramble."

Rochester turned from amusing theatrical diversions to more serious matrimonial duties in late May of 1674. Assuming his role as Keeper of Woodstock, he hurried there to prepare for the Royal party's arrival in early June, when Edward Henry Lee and the Lady Charlotte Fitzroy were to be married. With Rochester hosting the events, young Lee was made Baron of Spelsbury, Viscount Quarendon, and Earl of Lichfield on June 5, and the child wedding was solemnized. The celebration was spoiled temporarily when the bride accidentally broke a window in the Royal carriage and burst into tears, terrified that she would get the customary scolding and beating from her shrewish mother; but the King saw her crying, intervened, and restored peace.[37]

When the festivities ended, Lady Rochester returned to Adderbury for the birth of her third child. Still in manic spirits, Rochester went west, first to Enmore and then to Bath, for more roistering and writing. His sexual high jinks in "bawdy Bath" reputedly inspired some unknown lampooner (Captain Alexander Radcliffe?) to compose an obscene mock-heroic "The Argument," or "Bath Intrigues."[38] In it, the "Spiney *Lord*" R—— engages in a sexual marathon with three beldames, who accuse him of dry-bobs. Vowing revenge, he visits an old bawd, who provides him with a dildo, which he uses, as Paris did the golden apple with the three goddesses, to provoke a quarrel among the three ravenous contenders. Their pitched battle is stopped by a priest, who services them repeatedly with the device until he is exhausted.

The central idea of "The Argument," Rochester's revenge on a betraying prostitute, may allude to his actions toward Foster in 1671. The paraphernalia—crab lice, dildoes, whores, anti-Catholic sentiments—are staples of obscene Restoration satire, but a reference to a Knight of the Garter and his "monstrous parts" introduces a new satiric target, the Earl of Mulgrave. Mulgrave was awarded the Garter on April 23, 1674. Arrogant as ever, he became increasingly irritating to Rochester when John Dryden disengaged himself from Wilmot's parsimonious patronage at this time to seek Mulgrave's favor.[39]

Rochester's pastoral dialogue between Alexis and Strephon was said to have been written at Bath in 1674, but its style and content argue strongly for an earlier date.[40] A mock-pastoral "Song" ("In the Fields of Lincoln's Inn"), was printed in the 1680 edition of the *Poems on Several Occasions*. Like "An Argument" it is apparently a sexual spoof of Rochester ("Strephon"), who with "Corydon" engages in a duel of copulation with "Phyllis" as the dueling ground. The date of the "Song" is not known; but the two pairs of contesting shepherds (Alexis / Strephon and Strephon / Corydon), the identification of Rochester with Strephon, the similarity of the "Song" to "An Argument," and the date of 1674 suggest some connection.[41] Although it was attributed to Rochester, the spoof may have dated from 1674 and been by Sedley.

More appropriate to Rochester's mood than pallid pastorals was the sister-satire to "Timon": "Tunbridge Wells." Based on evidence in a passage that may be spurious, the composition date seems to be 1674, but another date postulated, 1673, conflicts somewhat with Rochester's known whereabouts, state of mind, and the personal quality of the satiric pieces he wrote in that year. The more social, generalized concerns of "Tunbridge Wells," the range of its *dramatis personae*, and its philosophical musings indicate its placement between the more limited and specific "Timon" and the broader philosophic speculations of the later "Satyr" on Man, and suggest a composition date in the summer of 1674.[42] Lines spoken by R——— in "The Argument" to describe Bath are a satiric microcosm of Rochester's treatment of Tunbridge Wells, another stylish watering-place or spa:

> *There is a place, a down a gloomy* Vale,   The Bath
> *Where burthen'd Nature lays her nasty* Tail;
> *Ten thousand* Pilgrims, *thither do resort,*
> *For ease, disease, for letchery, and sport*:

Although Lady Rochester is known to have been at Tunbridge Wells in 1666, no visit by Rochester is documented. In any case his observations of Bath equipped him to write knowingly about other watering places becoming newly fashionable in the Restoration era. Gramont described the scene at Tunbridge:

> The company there is always numerous . . . and, since those whose motive in visiting it is the quest of amusement always outnumber those who have been brought there by motives of necessity, the whole atmosphere is redolent of distraction and delight; intimacy ripens at the first acquaintance. . . . You may live at Tunbridge as highly as you please; large sums are staked at play; and the tender commerce flourishes.[43]

Rochester's perception of "the tender commerce" in the "Scene of Foppery" was considerably more jaundiced. Indeed, as a damning indictment of sex and society, "Tunbridge Wells" expands upon "A Ramble" while it conflates and condenses two types of comic drama: the social satire (e.g., Shadwell's *Epsom Wells*) and the sexual-intrigue farce (e.g., Wycherley's *Love in a Wood*).[44]

Rochester's narrator/persona as observer/participant gives the satire biographical dimensions along with dramatic immediacy. The diachronic and spatial movement of the narrator through Tunbridge Wells has been called "a list or catalogue of satirical epigrams linked by the peregrinations of an observer who vents his dyspeptic responses." With mock-Homeric references to Phoebus and Thetis, the narrator tells of waking at five and his horseback ride to "the Waters,"

> The Rendevouz of Fooles, Buffoones, and Praters.
> Cuckolds, Whores, Cittizens, their Wives and Daughters.

Redolent of the catalogue of London types in "A Ramble," this list of stereotypes prepares for later, extended descriptions of each.

Lines 11–50 show two sorts of Fooles, the "Bawling Fopp," compared to the comic actor James Nokes as Sir Nicholas Cully in Etherege's *Love in a Tub*, and the "Tall, stiffe Fool . . . in Spanish guise" who speaks in nonsensical proverbs and adages. Of these, the narrator says in an encompassing triplet:

> Noe Spleene, or Malice, need on them be throwne,
> Nature has done the Bus'nesse of Lampoone,
> And in their lookes, their Characters has showne.

Rochester obviously is referring to his own theory of satire here, to deflate those who are self-lampoons. Early mss. notations suggest the real identities of these caricatures as Sir Nicholas Crisp and Sir Francis Dorrell; but Rochester seldom wasted his wit on nobodies. The details about the Fopp as overgrown boy, his Knighthood, and "unlucky Starrs" evokes Mulgrave—a star-burst was the symbol of the Order of the Garter—while the stiff puppet-Spaniard Fool and reference to Cabal intrigues and the Master of Ceremonies reflect Arlington.[45]

Lines 51–82 display "Praters": "A Tribe of Curates, Priests, Canonicall Elves" and "Pert Bayes," "rais'd to an Arch-Deaconry, / By trampling on Religion, Liberty." Rochester's scorn for the clergy is overt here, anticipating the "Satyr" on Man soon after and recalling the anti-clerical sentiments he expressed to Burnet. The ecclesiastics' complaints about their diseases—stone, scurvy, straungery, even the spleen—have sexual connotations with their metaphoric relationship to "Their want of Learning, Honesty, and Braine, / The generall Diseases of that Traine." The indolent Arch-Deacon of Canterbury, Samuel Parker, satirized previously in Marvell's two-part *The Rehearsal Transprosed* (1672, 1673), epitomizes as "Bayes" Rochester's image of the complacent, self-serving prelate.[46]

Following a Lockean pattern of religious association, the buffoons make an initial appearance (lines 82–87) as "a fulsome Irish Crew of silly Macs." One critic has reproached Rochester for satirizing victims for qualities they cannot help—being born Irish and, one might add, Roman Catholic. Satirists have seldom felt compelled to be "fair" or "just," however, and Rochester's typical English disdain for the Irish, manifested earlier in his satire on Irish cattle and Irish whores, was a comic source of satire for Anglo-Irishmen from Swift to Sheridan. (We recall that the Wilmots had Irish origins and Rochester was

Viscount Athlone.) Moreover, the concluding and detailed treatment of another bunch of buffoons, the English cadets, in lines 160–77, is far more contemptuous than that about the Irish.

The madding crowd (lines 88–97) includes the squire, his wife, and daughters, among a medley of other social types. The foppish fool and his foolish inamorata (98–142) are the crowning jewel of "Tunbridge Wells," with brilliantly satiric dialogue and appearance. Posturing and prattling in the dance of seduction, they are left with the Scotch Fiddle (sexual itch); that leads to equally brilliant satire on colloquial talk between two wives, the first concerned with a husband who wants a son, her inability to conceive, and a sixteen-year-old daughter as yet without menses. The second wife has a remedy for the latter problem:

> Get her a Husband Madam,
> I Marry'd at that Age, and ne'er had had 'em:
> Was just like her; Steele-Waters, let alone
> A Back of Steele, will bring 'em better downe.

Speculating that the demanding husband—a "Poor foolish Fribble"—will be cuckolded by his wife's efforts to have a son, the observer remarks on the treachery of women in general and procurer midwives in particular; and Rochester regains some of the phallic robustness of his earlier verse.

> For here walke Cuffe, and Kick,
> With Brawney Back, and Leggs, and potent Prick.
> Who more substantially will cure thy Wife,
> And on her half-dead Womb, bestowe new life.
> From these, the Waters got the Reputation,
> Of good Assistants unto Generation.[47]

These lines rip off the genteel facade of Tunbridge Wells, Bath, and the other spas, revealing the "waters" as a pretense for reveling in promiscuous sensuality with strangers who become instant intimates. Rochester has expanded the sexual hedonism of Londoners at nighttime in St. James's Park to flagrant, wholesale pairings-off in broad daylight at country spas.

After a description of the "dreadfull Crew" of Cadets, younger sons in the military strutting about town in their red coats and singing bawdy songs while aspiring to "the Name of Young Gentlemen," the dyspeptic Observer reflects:

> Blesse me thought I, what thing is Man that thus
> In all his shapes, he is rediculous?
> Our selves, with noyse of Reason wee doe please
> In vaine: Humanity is our worst Disease.

Beasts void of reason, thus of foppery or pretense, are three times happier than vain men with their loud talk about being reasonable. This realization shames the narrator, who feels inferior to the horse he mounts to ride from Tunbridge Wells:

> For he doeing only things fit for his Nature,
> Did seem to me by much the wiser Creature.

Leaving off with this proto-Gulliverian sentiment, Rochester laid the groundwork for his next major satire.[48]

"Tunbridge Wells" also contains clues about another biographically interesting poem. The juxtaposition of Cuff and Kick, symbols of virility, with poor "Fribble" suggests some ambivalence in Rochester's thought in the summer of 1674. Himself an expectant father, he still retained his long-standing fascination with males of the lower classes as somehow more potent. This belief had appeared in several poems, and his previous disguises as porter or chairman had served him as an aphrodisiac. By the 1670s, the term "fribble" denoted "male sexual inadequacy, and may already have implied the homosexuality that became a standard meaning in the eighteenth century."[49] Rochester's physical inadequacies, the result of syphilis, caused him to brood on heterosexual impotence, and in his search for new stimuli, he showed a different attitude toward potent laborers.

The undated "Song" ("Love a *Woman*! y'are an *Ass*") renounces "The [female] idlest part of *Gods Creation*" in no uncertain terms: "Farewel *Woman*." The speaker will henceforth sit and drink with his "lewd well natur'd *Friend*" [Savile?] for the sake of gaining health, wealth, and mirth. If "busie *Love*," encroaches, his soft sweet Page will do the trick better than forty wenches. As for women:

> Let the *Porter*, and the *Groome*,
>   Things design'd for dirty *Slaves*,
> Drudge in fair *Aurelias*, Womb
>   To get supplies for Age, and Graves.

Familiar though the attitude toward women is here, the idea that copulation is not a pleasure but a burdensome obligation to beget is striking for Rochester. The "Song" relegates virile impregnators to the rank of slaves, makes heterosexual activity a duty, and replaces it with dexterous homosexual relief. These ideas appear in the 1673 *Sodom*, but not with such trenchant clarity; Dr. Flux's concluding homily in the play is a heterosexual manifesto.[50] Moreover, in the "Song," the substitution of wit, health, wealth, mirth, and friendship for the joys of fucking moves Rochester away from the hedonistic stance in earlier works toward the more moderate Epicureanism of the "Satyr" on Man and his later correspondence.[51] The "Song" may well have been composed sometime between 1673 and 1675, perhaps as part of Rochester's burst of creativity in 1674.

During his stay in Bath, Rochester wrote two exuberant letters to Henry Savile, the second of them with some leitmotifs of the "Song." The friendship between the two rakes was entering a new stage of intimacy after long periods of separation. After the Battle of Solebay in May–June 1672, Savile had unsuccessfully tried for the post of Secretary to the Duke of York, whose regular amanuensis was wounded in the Battle. (Samuel Pepys was another unsuccessful candidate.) He was given permission to dispense with attending the Duke as Groom; and after being appointed Envoy Extraordinary, he went to Paris in October 1672 with the Earl of Sunderland, his brother-in-law. He was discouraged about his prospects at Whitehall, writing gloomily to his brother Halifax and staying abroad until February 1673. He had a stroke of good luck in June 1673, when James Hamilton died and Savile succeeded him as Groom of the Bedchamber to the King. The fortunes of the Catholic York declined after the Test Act; Savile took revenge for what he saw as York's neglect of him by writing the libel, "Advice to a Painter to Draw the Duke By." In the summer of 1673 he bought the Parliamentary seat for Newark but in October he was kept from sitting in the Commons by a technicality.[52] He and Rochester could have been together often in the spring and fall of 1673. Rochester tweaked him afterward about his simultaneous wooing about that time of "the Black & faire Countesses" Clanbrassil and Fox.

In mid-June 1674, Savile rode to Portsmouth to attend the King on a yachting trip. Charles was very fond of sailing and he berthed the royal yachts there.[53] Two letters to Savile by Rochester from Bath in June indicate that the friends had been together often during the spring. The first, an elaborate parody of a letter requesting charity and blessing the alms-giver, asked Savile to scour London cellars for a quantity of good wine:

> Dear Savile,
> Do a charity becoming one of your pious principles, in preserving your humble servant Rochester from the imminent peril of sobriety, which, for want of good wine more than company (for I drink like a hermit betwixt God and my own conscience) is very like to befall me. Remember what pains I have formerly taken to wean you from your pernicious resolutions of discretion and wisdom. . . . So may thy wearied soul at last find rest, no longer hovering 'twixt th'unequal choice of politics and lewdness! May'st thou be admired and loved for thy domestic wit; beloved and cherished for thy foreign interest and intelligence.

There is a reference to Rochester's successful part in bringing off the union between his nephew and Charles II's bar-sinister daughter:

> Dear Savile, as ever thou dost hope to out-do
> Machiavel or equal me, send some good wine![54]

Savile performed his charitable act, it seems, sending a supply of wine to Bath by his servant Godfrey as he went on to Portsmouth. On June 22, Rochester wrote to him, perhaps inspired by draughts of Savile's Hippocrene, a gloriously fanciful letter in praise of the bottle with successive examples piling on top of each other in the style of such incremental poems as "Upon Nothing." The tone of the letter is notable for its intimacy, containing as it does the first hints of sexually ambiguous badinage:

> to bee from you, & forgotten by you att once, is a misfortune I never was Criminall enough to merritt, since to the Black & faire Countesses, I villainously betray'd the dayly addresses of y^r divided Heart; you forgave that upon the first Bottle & upon the second on my Conscience would have renounc'd them and the whole sex; oh that second bottle Harry is the sincerest, wisest, & most impartial downwright freind we have, tells us the truth of ourselves & forces us to speake truth of others, banishes flattery from our tongues and distrust from us above the meane Pollicy of Court prudence. . . . I have seriously considered one thinge, that of the three Buisnisses of this Age, Woemen, Polliticks & drinking, the last is the only exercise att wch you & I have nott prouv'd our selves Errant fumblers; if you have the vanity to thinke otherwise, when we meete next lett us appeale to freinds of both sexes & as they shall determine, live & dye sheere drunkards or intire Lovers; for as wee mingle the matter, it is hard to say wch is the most tiresome creature, the loving drunkard or the drunken Lover. . . .
>
> Bathe the 22 of June[55]

His Bath Intrigues at an end for the moment, it was time for Rochester to return to the sobriety of Adderbury and his duties as husband, father, son, uncle, and—most portentously—Keeper of Woodstock.

14

DOG DAYS AND MASQUES
(JULY–DECEMBER 1674)

But thoughts are giv'n, for Actions government,
Where Action ceases, thoughts impertinent:
Our *Sphere* of Action, is lifes happiness,
And he who thinks Beyond, thinks like an Ass.
                                    —Rochester, "Satyr" on Man

Rochester left Bath at the end of June 1674 in time to be present at the birth of his second daughter in early July. The Lady Elizabeth Wilmot was christened in Adderbury Church on July 13, 1674.[1] Named for her mother, Betty Wilmot seems to have been Rochester's favorite child. She was certainly the most devoted to him. He spoke of her lovingly as his surrogate: "Pray bidd my daughter Betty present my duty to my daughter Mallet."[2] Orphaned at seven, Betty eventually dazzled the world as the Third Countess of Sandwich.[3] She perpetually defended her father's name, openly berating Mulgrave when his *Memoirs* slurred Rochester's courage;[4] and she dedicated herself to the cause of the Stuart Pretenders. She was the longest-lived of the Wilmots, some-how avoiding the venereal legacy of her father. When she died at the age of eighty-three, she left a genetic facsimile of John Wilmot in the form of a prof-ligate grandson.[5]

The birth of his third child stirred a mixture of emotions in the twenty-seven-year-old father. Love for his wife resurged powerfully and the pair began a new phase of marriage, relatively free of major emotional battles. As always, Rochester was proud of his children and delighted by them. Yet he felt oddly alone, as he wrote reflectively to Henry Savile on August 8, probably from Woodstock. Back from Plymouth, Savile was on duty at Whitehall and soon to leave for Windsor.[6]

> if there bee a reall good upon Earth 'tis in the Name of freind, without
> wch all others are merely fantasticall; how few of us are fitt stuff to make
> that thing, wee have dayly the melancholy experience; However, Deare
> Harry let us not give out nor despaire . . . this thought has soe intirely

possest mee since I came into the Country (where only one can think, for you att Court thinke not att all . . .) y^t I have made many serious reflections upon it and amongst others, gather'd one Maxim . . . but while I grow into Proverbs, I forgett that you may impute my philosophy to the Doggdayes & living alone; to prevent the inconveniencyes of Sollitude and many others, I intend to goe to the Bath on sunday next in visitation of my Ld Treasurer. . . .

Urging Savile to "bee soe Pollitick or bee soe kind, (or a little of both wch is better) as to stepp down," to Bath, Rochester professed himself "Your hearty faithfull affectionate humble servant." Then in a postscript he added:

If you see the Dutch: of P. very often take some opportunity to talke to her about what I spoake to you att London.

Louise de Kéroualle had been created the Duchess of Portsmouth in July 1673; her influence over the King was now obvious, and Danby the Treasurer had shrewdly allied himself with her.[7]

Although Charles II lavished palaces, money, and jewels on her, Lady Portsmouth was pregnant, peevish, and lonely in 1674. Lady Castlemain hated her. The cheerfully vulgar Nell Gwyn found her French ways incomprehensible. And the English people pelted her carriage with mud and rocks whenever she appeared. On one occasion, mistaken for Kéroualle, Nelly had leaned from her carriage and shouted, "Nay, good people, I am the Protestant whore."[8] When Nell asked the King for money and he told her he had none, she said she would tell him how he could be free of want: "Send the French to France again, set me on the stage again, and lock up your own cod-piece."[9] That, Charles could never do. When Louise cajoled him early in 1674 to send for her sister, Henriette Mauricette, so she might have a friend with her, he sent a yacht to Brest and a gentleman to escort the lady, of whom the Marquis de Ruvigny flatly remarked, "Henriette de Kéroualle is nothing to look at." Granted an income of £600, the plain French sister was in need of an English husband with wealth. Searching about, Louise and the King settled on a real prize: drunken, blasphemous, murderous Philip Herbert, the Earl of Pembroke.

The pair were wed in December 1674. After lingering at Court for several weeks, they began a scandalous life together in the Herbert mansion at Wilton. Pembroke's brutal treatment forced Henriette to stay much at Whitehall under the reluctant protection of her sister and eventually to flee home to France. No love was wasted between Lady Portsmouth and her new brother-in-law, who called her "the grievance of the nation," and threatened to stand her on her head so the people of England could see what had intrigued the King to their cost.[10]

Rochester's business with Danby, the Lord Treasurer, in August 1674, and his request that Savile solicit Lady Portsmouth may have been connected with properties of Pembroke's mother, Anne the Dowager Countess of Pembroke and Montgomery, whose heirs also included the Sackvilles.[11] Rochester and Richard Sackville, the Earl of Dorset and Buckhurst's father, had their joint eye on manors at Byfleet and Weybridge held by the Dowager Countess. Rochester could have been sounding Danby on the matter in the late summer of 1674, and hoping to get Lady Portsmouth's aid in persuading the King to grant him and Dorset the manors in reversion. Since Portsmouth's sister had a potential interest in those properties, however, Louise could not be expected to take Rochester's side. A later petition to the King made jointly by Dorset and Rochester in 1675 naturally aroused her anger, as it did that of Philip Herbert, who bodily assaulted Buckhurst over Pembroke holdings as late as 1678 and then initiated a lawsuit in 1679.[12]

Whatever the result of his visit to Danby in Bath, Rochester had to be patient while Danby straightened out diplomatic matters and tried to replenish the Treasury.[13] Parliament was not due to meet until November 10; consequently, Rochester had plenty of time to think, first in the country and then in the city. One of the products of his contemplation was the best known of his works, a "Satyr" on mankind, which under various titles and in various stages of composition was widely circulated before its publication in June 1679.[14]

Rochester's "Satyr" was a congeries of ideas to be found in earlier writers including Juvenal, Lucretius, Montaigne, Boileau, and Hobbes most prominently but many others as well.[15] To twentieth-century readers, the "Satyr" against Man contains little or nothing that approaches the shocking elements in his other works. The storm that Rochester's verse-philosophy provoked among his contemporaries seems surprising, especially since it contains no sexual references or obscene language. If it made some of his readers curse and ban it, they feared, as Dr. Johnson remarked, that Rochester's personal reputation might have a greater impact on his audience than the same ideas would have if spoken by someone else.[16]

As an attack on all mankind rather than specific people known to be objects of Rochester's contempt, the "Satyr" has caused modern critics to question the extent to which its "I" speaker is the historical Rochester or its opinions his.[17] One commentator assumes the "I" to be an "unpleasant" satiric persona not to be confused with the author of the poem.[18] Another sees Rochester's "speaker" as a satiric device to target the reader; a third examines the "split vision" of a "speaker" both inside and outside the poem; and a fourth discounts a biographical interpretation, seeing the "Satyr" as a playful example of Rochester's interest not merely in disguise but the put-on.[19]

Other modern critics, however, regard the materialistic, hedonistic, or anti-rationalist views in the "Satyr" as reflecting Rochester's true beliefs.[20] And some see the "Satyr" as extra-ordinarily revelatory: "a sincere and bitter diatribe on the futility of the human reason," or "the desperate efforts of a moralist who doubts the validity of his own ideas to assert absolute values."[21] Significantly, none of Rochester's contemporaries appeared to doubt that the "Satyr" was Rochester's personal credo. And given his statements in the letter of August 8 about his "serious reflections" in country solitude, his "maxims" and "philosophy," the "Satyr" on man, like the other major satires, is biographically relevant.[22]

To be sure, Rochester's moods and tones in the letter change in dazzling succession from direct and honest expression of friendship to quasi-melancholy meditation on genuine friendships, mock-serious characterization of himself as a philosopher, then playful objectivity. But Rochester and Savile were developing a language of their own, whereby they told each other their most genuine concerns in arch terms.[23] The "Satyr" may not represent the author's state of mind with total consistency but it reveals John Wilmot at a crucial point of intellectual transition.

The "Satyr" on man, which critics designate "a formal classical satire," splits into two distinct sections, the first containing the materialistic principles of Lucretius and Hobbes, and the last a version of nominalism or social pragmatism.[24] Different commentators see these contradictory sections through a variety of interpretations, but all of them tacitly acknowledge the accurate insight of David Vieth: the two halves of the "Satyr" cannot be logically reconciled because of a lack of consistency in its conceptual terms.[25]

This lack is not surprising; Rochester was not a systematically trained thinker, despite exposure to Oxford scholasticism and the logic of Thomas Hobbes. But Rochester was a man of keen wit and innate good sense, and he questioned the holophrastic dogmatism of "moralists" who said one thing and did another, who eulogized absolutes such as "reason," "faith," and "good," but equivocated these verbal concepts by their actions. In 1679 Rochester denounced such verbal hypocrites to Bishop Burnet, who reluctantly agreed; but the "Satyr" of 1674 already contained a repudiation of false dogmatists:

> Is there a *Church-Man* who on *God* relyes?
> Whose Life, his Faith and Doctrine Justifies? . . .
> Whose envious heart makes preaching a pretence
> With his obstrep'rous sawcy Eloquence . . .
> Who hunt *good* Livings, but abhor *good* Lives. . . .[26] (my emphasis)

His equivocation of "good" in the last line shows Rochester's belief that inconsistency in conceptual terms was the practice of dogmatic moralists. His emphasis on the meanings of "nature," "sense," and "reason" throughout the "Satyr" are an effort to relate "thought" (cause) to "action" (effect)—thoughts are given for action's government—without the mediation of words whose meanings had been distorted by self-serving clerics and politicians:

> All this with indignation have I hurl'd,
> At the pretending part of the proud World,
> Who swolne with selfish vanity devise,
> False freedomes, holy Cheats, and formal Lyes
> Over their fellow *Slaves* to tyrannize. (ll. 174–78)[27]

There is sufficient evidence to show that by 1674, Rochester's disillusionment with clergymen, politicians, and society-at-large had turned to bitter amusement. His lampoons on specific Courtiers for greed and sexual cavorting had turned into satiric attacks on kings for hedonistic self-indulgence, their disdain for public good, and economic and military waste. Mockery of illiterate country parsons had become castigation of the clergy in general for their lack of learning, honesty, and brains and the Archbishop of Canterbury in particular for trampling on religion and liberty of conscience. In addition to being rutters and buggers, the English people at large were fools, the dupes of Court and Church. Humanity was a disease rather than a post-lapsarian consequence of Original Sin.[28]

What, then, was he to believe and where could he turn for reassurance when he experienced doubts at Woodstock in the late summer of 1674? Possibly to trust in friendship as "a reall good," he told Savile, "the most difficult & rare accident of life . . . allsoe the Best, nay perhaps the only good one."[29] This was one of the Principles of Epicurus that Rochester knew firsthand or through Lucretius:

> XXVII. Of the things that wisdom prepares for insuring lifelong happiness, by far the greatest is the possession of friends.[30]

He had already accepted and poetically adapted other Epicurean principles:

> I. That which is blessed and immortal is not troubled itself, nor does it cause trouble to another. As a result, it is not affected by anger or favor, for these belong to weakness. (Epicurus)

> > The *Gods*, by right of Nature, must possess
> > An Everlasting Age, of perfect Peace:
> > Far off, remov'd from us, and our Affairs:
> > Neither approach'd by *Dangers*, or by *Cares*. . . . (Rochester)

II. Death is nothing to us; for what has been dissolved has no sensation, and what has no sensation is nothing to us. (Epicurus)

> After Death, nothing is, and nothing Death. . . . (Rochester)[31]

After rejecting hedonistic sensationism (sexual bliss) as the greatest good ("Farewell, Woman") and replacing it with friendship, Rochester entertained other Epicurean principles. Growing into "maxims," they became axioms of a "Dog-Days" philosophy incorporated in the "Satyr" on mankind. Rochester's skill at compacting abstract principles into practical experience through colloquial language is nowhere more striking:

XXIII. If you struggle against all your sensations, you will have no standard of comparison by which to measure even the sensations you judge false. (Epicurus)

> Hunger call's out, my Reason bids me eat,
> Perversly yours, your Appetite does mock,
> This asks for Food, that answers what's a clock? (Rochester)

XXV. If you do not at all times refer each of your actions to the natural end [i.e. pleasure], but fall short of this and turn aside to something else . . . your deeds will not agree with your words. (Epicurus)

> That lust of *Pow'r*, to which he's such a *Slave*,
> And for the which alone he dares be brave . . .
> And screws his actions, in a forc'd disguise:
> Leading a tedious life in Misery,
> Under laborious, mean *Hypocrisie*. (Rochester)

XXXII. There is no such thing as justice or injustice among those beasts that cannot make agreements not to injure or be injured. (Epicurus)

> *Birds*, feed on *Birds*, *Beasts*, on each other prey . . .
> Prest by necessity, they Kill for Food, . . .
> With Teeth, and Claws, by Nature arm'd they hunt,
> Natures allowance, to supply their want. (Rochester)[32]

Exploring his changing attitudes by writing a "Satyr" on false beliefs and practices, Rochester used the rhetorical techniques of the classical orational argument: stating a proposition, giving supporting evidence, presenting the opposing viewpoint, refuting it, and concluding by reaffirming the truth of the original proposition. His conflicted selves lent force to the *disputatio*. His "I" (ego) argued for experiential or sensate reason against a clerical *adversarius*, who condemned wit and eulogized mankind. The *adversarius* need not be identified as an actual clergyman; it was a moralizing superego formed as part of his breeding.[33] "I's" views refuting the *adversarius* appear piecemeal in other of Rochester's works as ideas he held singly at one time or another. If they do not form a systematic "philosophy," that is because Rochester did not have one when writing the "Satyr" but was in the process of searching for one.[34] The contradictions and "open-ended" elements of the "Satyr" are due to its exploratory nature. Rochester was, after all, a poet—not an academic logician.

A theriophilic eulogy of beasts begins and ends the "Satyr":

> Were I (who to my cost already am
> One of those strange prodigious Creatures *Man*)
> A Spirit free, to choose for my own share,
> What Case of Flesh, and Blood, I pleas'd to weare,
> I'd be a *Dog*, a *Monkey*, or a *Bear*. . . .
> If upon *Earth* there dwell such *God-like Men* . . .
> If such there are, yet grant me this at least,
> *Man* differs more from *Man*, than *Man* from *Beast*.

Its animal references link the "Satyr" to the concluding praise of the horse in "Tunbridge Wells." The beast theme, a popular one in libertine writings and sermons of the day, hints also at "le mythe animal" popularized by several early translations of Aesop's *Fables*. Rochester could have come across Aesop in his Oxford days.[35] The animal references prepare the way in the "Satyr" for the parodic search of the "reasoning" pilgrim for the truth about humankind. The reference to Ingelo and *Patrick's Pilgrim* by "I" underscores the reasoner's laborious climb over mountains of "whimseys" heaped in his own brain and his fall into doubt's boundless sea.[36] We may wonder to what extent Rochester satirizes himself in the hapless searcher after truth, drowning in a sea of doubt, bourn up by books for a while and trying to swim while held up by "bladders of philosophy." (The "Satyr" itself ironically served him as just such an air-filled, quasi-philosophical bladder.) Certainly the next section describing the "Man of Wit" sounds a strongly self-rueful note.

Other passages, echoing sentiments Rochester expressed in confidence to Savile or his wife or Burnet, indicate his growing disgust with politicians as well as clergymen.

> But if in *Court*, so just a Man there be, (In
> *Court* a just Man, yet unknown to me)
> Who does his needful flattery direct,
> Not to oppress, and ruin . . .
> Whose passions bend to his unbyass'd Mind;
> Who does his Arts, and *Pollicies* apply,
> To raise his *Country*, not his *Family*;

> Nor while his Pride own'd Avarice withstands,
> Receives close Bribes, from Friends corrupted hands.

This indictment of Courtiers and Ministers revealed John Wilmot's true feelings in 1674. Having seen "Statesmen" from Clarendon to Danby grow wealthy through self-advancing policies and bribe-taking, Rochester had no illusions about their obsessive schemes to enrich their families and themselves. But like all his satires, this one included Rochester as well, who had abandoned every principle to gain "competent riches," most recently securing Lee-Wilmot fortunes through union with a royal bastard. The satirist admitted the innate nature of avarice and acknowledged, with a silent sigh, the unavoidable duty of paying court:

> Since flattery, which way so ever laid,
> Is still a Tax on that unhappy Trade.

Rochester might solace himself that he flattered the High and Venal with his tongue in his cheek and privately savaged them in lampoons. Nevertheless, he had to confront his own inability to act the honest, uncorruptible patriot he envisioned in the "Satyr" on man and whom, two years later in 1676, he would attempt to depict dramatically as Maximus in his revision of John Fletcher's *Valentinian*. Perhaps such civic-minded heroes might be found during the final days of a decadent and collapsing Rome—but could such a one survive in the corruptions of Restoration England? It appeared not.

"Is there a *Church-Man* who on *God* Relyes?" "I" answers his rhetorical question three times: not the Prideful Prelate, not the sensual tribe, not the doting Bishop. Then, after the three denials (by a Doubting Thomas or would-be Disciple Peter?), he draws a portrait of a meek humble Man, of honest sense,

> Who Preaching peace, does practice continence;
> Whose pious life's a proof he does believe,
> Mysterious truths, which no *Man* can conceive . . .
> If such God-like men live on earth,
> I'le here recant my *Paradox* to them,
> Adore those *Shrines of Virtue*, *Homage* pay,
> And with the *Rabble World*, their *Laws* obey.

The wistful quality of this description of the meek, humble man of God recalls Rochester's reply in 1679 to Burnet's urgings that he accept "mysterious truths which no man can conceive": "He said, They were happy that believed: for it was not in every mans power."[37] Rochester's doubting search for a Shrine of Virtue led him in turn to regard Robert Parsons, Gilbert Burnet, and Thomas Pierce; but the search ended only with his deathbed discovery of the Man of Sorrows, Jesus Christ.

The "Satyr" began to circulate in the autumn of 1674 when Rochester returned to London. Court attention was then focusing on the next entertainment at Whitehall. Musicals and masques of the spring created a hunger for elaborate spectacles. The Duke of Monmouth was an enthusiastic dancer, as was his Duchess before she dislocated her hip; and the Duke of York's daughters, the Princesses Mary (then 12) and Anne (9) had already danced in Court theatricals. Mary's dancing, which "almost ravished" Samuel Pepys as early as 1669, was particularly accomplished.[38] The nobility were ready to display their talents to each other once again—but through what theatrical piece?

John Dryden and Thomas Shadwell were logical choices to write a new masque, the musical *Tempest* having scored success in April; but Dryden had an unperformed opera on his hands, *The State of Innocence*, a musical version of Milton's *Paradise Lost*; his interest had turned to the epic, and the Laureate seemed to have no interest in another masque.[39] As for Shadwell, he was engrossed in other projects, including *Psyche* and, with his patron the Duke of Newcastle, *The Triumphant Widow*, a "proto-ballad-opera" acted in November 1674, which carried on the harassment of Settle.[40] The third member of the anti-Settle triumvirate, John Crowne, was at liberty in the late summer of 1674, however, having spent the earlier part revising a rhymed draft of *Andromache* by someone else.[41] Crowne later told John Dennis that he had been selected to write a new masque because Rochester recommended him.

> Yet it was neither to the Favour of the Court, nor of *Wilmot* Lord *Rochester*, one of the shining Ornaments of it, that he was indebted for the Nomination which the King made of him for the writing the Mask of *Calypso* [sic], but to the Malice of that noble Lord, who design'd by that Preference to mortify Mr. *Dryden*.[42]

When Crowne published *Calisto*, he displayed an unaccustomed modesty: he had been "unexpectedly called out of my Obscurity" and "invaded on the sudden by a powerful command, to prepare an entertainment for the court, which was to be written, learnt, practised, and performed in less time than was necessary for the writing alone." He had finished writing it in scarcely a month. Since rehearsals began on September 22, Crowne probably started his labors of composition in late August.[43] Crowne's preface brushed aside objections to his choice to write "a play & an opera in which ye splendour of ye English monarchy will be seen" in order "to divert their Maties and Court." Ignoring Rochester for suggesting him to the King, Crowne felt obliged to bend the knee to John Dryden, his Laureate collaborator on the *Notes and Observations*:

> I must confess it was great pity, that in an entertainment where the sense
> was so deliciously feasted, the understanding should be so slenderly treated;
> and had it been written by him to whom, by the double right of place and
> merit, the honour of the employment belonged, the pleasure had been in
> all kinds complete. However, this appeared not so contemptible but it
> attained the felicity for which it was made, to afford some delight to his
> [Charles II] Royal mind. . . .[44]

Given his mockery of Crowne's talents in "Timon," the question arises of why Rochester suggested him to write the script for play-acting nobles. As John Dennis claimed, he may have felt a sly delight at seeing Crowne preferred to the pompous Poet Laureate, now firmly attached to Mulgrave. Yet it seems more likely that once Dryden or Shadwell was eliminated from royal consideration, Rochester offhandedly suggested Crowne, thinking him as capable as anybody of writing "tuneful nonsense." Aware of Rochester's dismissal of his dramatic abilities, Crowne convinced himself that the Earl acted out of "malice" toward Dryden—or envy of Crowne's superior genius. These views he passed on to Dennis and "St. Evremond."[45] His social inferiors were unable to accept, in their self-importance, that Rochester usually regarded them with disdain or aloof amusement.

Hastily choosing a subject for the young princesses to act out ("I had but some few hours . . ."), Crowne blundered upon the myth of the nymph Calisto. Like many entertainments relished by Courtiers, this was a story of seduction and rape. Calisto, a virgin follower of Diana, was sighted by Jove, who lusted for her and, assuming the guise of Diana, raped her. After the pregnant Calisto was banished by the real Diana, the goddess of chastity, she gave birth to a son, Arcas. The jealous Juno changed Calisto into a bear, and Arcas was on the verge of killing her when Jove whirled them into the skies as constellations. Juno then extracted a promise from the Oceans that Arcas and Ursa Major would never dip down and bathe in their waters.[46] Rochester, who subsequently revised Fletcher's *Valentinian* as *Lucina's Rape*, may have relished the thought of seeing the Court nymphs acting *Calisto*, but Crowne eliminated the rape, inventing other characters and making Mercury the *deus ex machina* who solves all problems. He was also ordered to bring on a group of Africans at the finale, which he managed to do with some finesse.

Scripts in hand, the aristocratic cast began rehearsals that went on through December and January, 1674–75. Sir Christopher Wren turned his attention from rebuilding St. Paul's to planning alterations of the New Hall Theatre at

Whitehall. The acclaimed Robert Streeter created some elaborate scenery. Nicholas Staggins, newly sworn Master of the King's Music, wrote the songs and dance music, and a troop of French dancers headed by the celebrated M. St. André began practicing. As the Lord Chamberlain, Arlington began approving a flood of bills that eventually totaled more than £3500. The Treasury might be in perilous straits but the King and Court had to be amused.[47]

The autumn theatrical season, inaugurated by rehearsals of *Calisto* in late September, produced the annual Lord Mayor's pageant, *The Goldsmiths Jubilee; or London's Triumph* by Thomas Jordan on October 29, attended by the Royal Family and the "Chief Nobility." Newcastle's *The Triumphant Widow*, acted on November 26 with Shadwell's scene parodying Elkanah Settle, added new coals to the playwrights' bonfire of vanities. Again in December, *Calisto* occupied the attention of everyone at Court. Moll Davis came out of retirement to be the River; Mary Knight was to sing the role of Peace; and, at the summoning of the King, the virtuous Margaret Blagge reluctantly left her life of religious contemplation to be the goddess Diana. Provided with a book of religious instruction by John Evelyn, Mrs. Blagge avoided moral contamination offstage by withdrawing to one side and immersing herself in her orisons.[48]

During the autumn, Rochester lived quietly as the antics of his friends and enemies engaged the public eye. After ridding herself of Mulgrave as a lover in April, the Duchess of Cleveland took on Henry Savile, who continued as her gallant in the fall.[49] In September, Mulgrave's officious efforts to woo Moll Kirke away from her lover, the Duke of Monmouth, led to a public clash. Monmouth waylaid him on his way from Moll's house and locked him up.[50] In October "Lying" Harry Killegrew was promoted to Groom of the King's Bed-Chamber. Forced by Parliament early in 1674 to give up Lady Shrewsbury as well as his role of Councilor, Buckingham sold his various posts and went off in the autumn to his Yorkshire estates for what he declared was a permanent disengagement from politics.[51]

The political scene was full of polarizations. Deposed as Lord Chancellor in the wake of the CABAL breakup, Shaftesbury got more involved with the Country Party. When Parliament convened on November 10, Thomas Osborne was introduced officially as Lord Treasurer and Earl of Danby but the threat of efforts to remove Lauderdale, Danby's strong ally and the only remaining member of the CABAL still in power, compelled the King to prorogue until April 13, 1675.[52] Meanwhile, Rochester was reaping benefits from his new friendship with Danby. After receiving payments from the Treasury in January, April, and July (twice), he was given further grants on August 5, November 9, and November 20.[53]

In the final months of 1674, Buckhurst became the Earl of Middlesex and informed his horrified father Dorset that he meant to marry Lady Falmouth, whose reputation was somewhat rancid. Lady Portsmouth continued to recuperate from a bad case of pox that the King gave her and to amass more riches. In December, she collected more than £146,000 for living expenses. Portsmouth's alliance with Danby was also paying off.[54] And Mulgrave began insinuating himself with the Duke of York, thereby antagonizing Henry Savile. Their growing mutual anger would drag Rochester back into the limelight with a revival of the traditional Christmas brawl.

In anticipation of further moneys, on December 9, 1674, Rochester signed a letter of attorney appointing Richard Blancourt to receive £1,000 from the Exchequer.[55] He may have been planning to be out of London for a while. A letter to his wife at Enmore, presumably written in the early winter of 1674–75, states his intention to "come down" to her. He may have planned to bring her to town for the rest of the "season." She had sent him some portraits, perhaps as a Christmas present. His playful, loving (and synaesthetic) response shows their renewed intimacy.

> Deare Wife I receiv'd y^r three pictures & am in a greate fright least they should bee like you; by the biggnes of y^r heade I should apprehend you farr gone in ye Ricketts, by the severity of the Count'nance, somewhat inclin'd to prayer & prophesy, yett there is an alacrity in the plump cheeke, that seems to signify sack & sugar, & the sharp sighted nose has borrow'd a quickness from the sweet-smelling eye. I never saw a chin smile before, a mouth frowne, & a forehead mump; truly ye Artist has done his part, (god keep him humble) & a fine man hee is if his excellencyes doe not puff him up like his pictures; the next impertinence I have to tell you is that I am coming down to you. I have gott horses but want a coach; when that defect is supply'd you shall quickly have the trouble of
>
> Yr. humble servant
>
> Present my duty to my Lady & my humble service to my Sister, my brother, & all the Babyes not forgetting Madam Iane.[56]

If Lady Rochester joined her husband in London for Christmas, she was exposed to mixed events. The pitch of excitement over *Calisto* heightened with open dress rehearsals witnessed by noble guests. Mounting tensions between Savile and Mulgrave exploded into an open clash recorded by William Harbard in a letter to the Earl of Essex dated December 22, 1674. Danby gave a dinner at the Treasury on a Sunday night, and Savile "very drunck fel so fowly" on Mulgrave that the King commanded him to leave the royal presence. The next day Mulgrave sent a challenge to Savile by Lord Middleton, and Rochester agreed to serve his friend as second. Through royal intervention,

"There was noe harm done but D. [Duke of York] hath interested himself & prevailed wth Kg: to forbid Savel his presence."[57]

Rochester may have regretted momentarily his success at winning Savile away from "pernicious resolutions of discretion and wisdom," by exalting drink earlier in the year to "the highest point of sacred friendship." Savile's drunken fall from grace could have carried Rochester with him in another Christmas exile. Unlike earlier scrapes, however, Rochester faced no punishment. On December 22, he was given the privilege of reviewing all notices concerning Wychwood Forest, of which he was Ranger and Keeper.[58]

Despite his involvement in yet another duel, Rochester managed to conclude a year of literary and political success without self-destructive errors in judgment. If 1674 was something of a triumphant year, however, the next would reverse his fortunes and confront him severely with the consequences of his follies.

REVERSALS AND RECOGNITIONS (1675)

Ld Rochester Lord Middlesex Lord Sussex Harry Savill had
been deboysinge [debauching] all night wth ye K[ing]: as
they went to there lodgings they came to ye great diall in
ye privy garden sade [said] Kings & Kingdoms are overturned & soe shalt thou & took it in there Armes & flung it
downe.

—Fane Ms., f. 358

S ometime after 1671, Rochester moved from Portugal Row in Lincoln's Inn
Fields to the royal complex at Whitehall. Like Louis XIV at Versailles,
Charles II gathered his nobles about him. As time passed, the palace at
Whitehall was expanded by quarters for various favorites, including Lady
Portsmouth, who was difficult to please and had her apartment demolished and
rebuilt three times before moving into it in 1675.[1]

Ralphe Gastorex's survey of Whitehall showed the Privy Garden bordered
on the north by a row of apartments, Inigo Jones's banqueting hall and the
Court. East of the Garden lay the Stone Gallery with another row of apartments, backed by various buildings to the edge of the Thames River.[2] Whitehall
also had a sprawling maze of public rooms and service areas. These were situ-
ated between Whitehall Street and the Thames.[3] The king's laboratory stood
between the Stone Gallery and the river. Like an elaborate sundial in the Privy
Garden, the laboratory was evidence of the King's interest in science and
scientific experimentation.[4]

On January 4, 1675, Rochester's status at Court was shown by the King's
approval of a contract to erect "a small building in his Maj^ts Privie garden,
according to a designe signed by Mr. Surveyor," a structure consisting of two
stories and a garret "to correspond in hight and uniformitie of his Maties
Elaboratory." In a matter of days a work order was issued that

a building be erected for ye Earle of Rochester in his Ma^ts Privy Garden
at Whitehall betweene the Lord Keepers Lodgings & ye Lodgings his Lor^sp

now possesseth, with a Cellar & other conveniences as his Lor^{sp} shall desire, but soe that a light may be preserved into ye stone Gallery.[5]

Rochester's lodgings, next to those of Heneage Finch the Lord-Keeper, were near the Duchess of Portsmouth's "splendid," "glorious" new apartment. Construction on both was proceeding in the first months of 1675 and the ill-tempered Duchess may well have found cause for displeasure when Rochester's reconstruction commenced just as her third project was nearing completion. Both structures were destroyed by fire sixteen years later.[6]

Wren's remodeling of the New Hall Theatre was coming to an end; and excitement at Court over *Calisto* was stimulated by dress rehearsals in January. Wycherley's masterpiece, *The Country Wife*, on January 12 and 15 with the King's Players at Drury Lane, also caused a stir. For two years, Wycherley had worked at a snail's pace; perhaps he dallied overly long at Lady Bennett's bordello. Rochester was mightily pleased by the bawdy sex comedy featuring a Dionysiac rake pretending impotence to seduce very cooperative ladies. In his opinion, only Shadwell rivaled Wycherley in comic craft. A few months after *The Country Wife* appeared, Rochester compared the two:

> Of all our Moderne Witts, none seemes to me,
> Once to have toucht upon true Comedy,
> But hasty Shadwell, and slow Witcherley.
> Shadwell's unfinisht workes doe yet impart,
> Great proofes of force of Nature, none of Art . . .
> But Witcherley earnes hard, whate'er he gaines,
> He wants noe Judgment, nor he spares noe paines;
> He frequently excells, and at the least,
> Makes fewer faults, than any of the best.[7]

Anyone not prejudiced by Dryden's lampoon of Shadwell as the King of the Dunces, Macfleckno, can see the justice of this comparison. Rochester removed his friend, "refin'd" Etherege, from the "comic" competition by declaring him unique, a "Sheere Originall."

At last, the eagerly awaited *Calisto* was acted at Whitehall on February 15–16 (?) after many rehearsals and rewritings by Crowne.[8] Amid the kaleidoscopic scenery, costumes and music, spectators could identify Princess Mary as Calisto. The virtuous Margaret Blagge was a twenty-three-year-old Diana, swathed in £20,000 worth of borrowed jewels, some of which turned up missing, to her great distress. Henrietta Maria Wentworth (who started a love affair with the Duke of Monmouth during rehearsals) was Jove. Juno was Anne Fitzroy, a bastard daughter of the King who had married the Earl of Sussex the previous year in a double wedding at Woodstock with her sister Charlotte and Edward Henry Lee. Princess Anne appeared in an invented role, Nyphe [*sic*]. The lively Sarah Jennings, Princess Anne's closest confidante and the future Duchess of Marlborough, wife of Jack Churchill, acted a mischievous Mercury. The Duke of Monmouth led the gentlemen dancers while the homely Henriette Kéroualle, the newly-wed Countess of Pembroke, was among the female dancers, together with her sister-in-law, the Lady Katherine Herbert.[9]

Given the occasion and his part in its genesis, Rochester was among the packed crowd of spectators. He recorded his opinion of the lavish spectacle, author, and admirers. His judgments on Shadwell's *Psyche* (also staged in February 1675) signaled his response to the theatrical species that *Calisto* exemplified:

> For Songs and Scenes, a double Audience bring . . .
> Now to Machines, and a dull Mask you run . . .
> Where the worst Writer has the greatest Fame . . .
> 'Tis all damn'd stuff.

Calisto was acted for the populace at Drury Lane on March 22 or 30, 1675, a fact Rochester alluded to when he damned Crowne openly and with faint praise:

> I might as well admit,
> Crownes tedious Scenes, for Poetry, and Witt.
> 'Tis therefore not enough, when your false Sense
> Hits the false Judgment of an Audience
> Of Clapping-Foole . . .
> Tho' ev'n that Tallent, merritts in some sort,
> That can divert the Rabble and the Court. . . .

In resisting the popularity of masques, operas, and dance interludes, Rochester was not alone. Shadwell denigrated "Plays of this kind" in his Preface to *Psyche*: they were written "to entertain the Town with variety of Musick, curious Dancing, splendid Scenes and Machines." Nonetheless, popular taste compelled Wycherley to end *The Country Wife* with a dance, as the new practice demanded comedies must.[10]

Rochester's fondness for music may have caused him to take some pleasure in *Calisto*. An eighteen-year-old French musician newly come to England, James Paisable, played the recorder in the group performing Staggins's compositions.[11] Rochester treated him as a protégé. Paisable was one of few artists known to have stayed at one of Rochester's country retreats. He accompanied Rochester to Woodstock in 1677, and when he returned to London in October, he carried a letter from Rochester to Savile:

> The best present I can make at this time is the bearer, whom I beg you to take care of that the King may hear his tunes when he is easy and private,

because I am sure they will divert him extremely. And may he ever have harmony in his mind, as this fellow will pour it into his ears.

That Paisable stayed at Woodstock, noted for debauchery, as well as Rochester's reminder in the letter of a nude romp with Savile there, an allusion to the "refined pleasures" of the Prince of Orange (suspected to be homosexual), and a reference to himself as *un bougré* suggests that Rochester's interest in the French musician had homoerotic as well as melodic strains. Savile passed the young recorder-player on to the King, who "heard with very great delight Paisable's new compositions."[12]

Rochester also may have found amusement in *Calisto* from seeing "Mr. ffranshaw" dance.[13] Will Fanshaw (or Fanshawe) became something of a mascot or official fool to Rochester's circle after 1675, attaching himself to its leader as an admiring sycophant. Fanshaw, "a meager person of small attainments and unpleasant habits," was a Master of Requests.[14] He married the half-sister of the Duke of Monmouth, Mary Walters, after the death of her first husband, William Sarsfield, in 1675. The new couple were ridiculed thereafter for their aristocratic affectations. Mary, satirically called "the Princess," claimed Stuart blood through Monmouth, her half-brother, and she even "touched" for the King's Evil. Mary Fanshaw was born to the same mother, Lucy Walters, after the King acknowledged Monmouth (James Crofts) to be his bastard-son; Charles denied the paternity of Mary but allowed her a pension.

Will Fanshaw took foolish pride in his wife's pretensions but, like many contemporaries, no pride in bathing.[15] Nell Gwyn found him too odorous, on one occasion telling him to buy a new periwig so she would not smell him stink when he stood outside her front door.[16] Although Savile enjoyed making sport of him, Rochester felt pitying fondness for Fanshaw, agreeing in 1678 to oversee the Fanshaws' finances. The odd pair had five children and they were always short of money. Rochester's mother referred to Fanshaw with wry disapproval as "his great friend" but Rochester's summation of him—"poor wretch"—spoke volumes.[17]

If his friendships did not always match the Epicurean principles that he avowed, neither did he practice Epicurean moderation, reverting to sensual hedonism. Rochester's liaison with Elizabeth Barry provided him with amusement in 1675, as he coached her for a stage debut, which she made finally in September. He also diverted himself by framing head-turning compliments to her and arranging rendezvous:

> Madam,
> Your letter so transports me that I know not how to answer it. The expressions are so soft and seem to be so sincere, that I were the unreasonablest

creature on earth could I but seem to distrust my being the happier; and
the best contrivance I can think of for conveying a letter to me is making
a porter bring it [to] my footman wherever I am, whether at St. James's,
Whitehall or home. They are at present pulling down some part of my
lodging, which will not permit me to see you there, but I will wait on you
at any other place, what time you please.[18]

Madam,
So much wit and beauty as you have should think of nothing less than
doing miracles, and there cannot be a greater than to continue to love
me . . . to pick out the wildest and most fantastical odd man alive, and to
place your kindness there . . ., Here's a damned impertinent fool bolted in
that hinders me from ending my letter. The plague of [pox? hell?] take him
and any man or woman alive that take my thoughts off you. But in the
evening I will see you and be happy, in spite of all the fools in the world.[19]

If it seems strange that Rochester was sexually involved with Elizabeth Barry
and James Paisable at the same time, a rake's sometimes homosexual ventures
did not diminish his obsessive womanizing. Rochester poeticized such a ménage
with lines in "The Disabled Debauchee," dated 1675 by one manuscript
source. The debauchee, disabled by excesses, recounts and thus "renews . . . his
past delight":

> Nor shall our *Love-fits Cloris* be forgot,
> When each the well-looked *Link-boy*, strove t'enjoy,
> And the best Kiss, was the deciding *Lot*,
> Whether the *Boy* fuck'd you, or I the *Boy*.

The rake's tales would encourage "any *Youth* (worth being drunk)" to "fear no
lewdness he's called to by *Wine*." Such pagan morality can be found in
Catullus, Juvenal, Ovid, and Petronius, but not Epicurus. In Rochester, it
could be called polymorphous sexuality or rakish license.[20]

Accompanying his wife, who became pregnant in late March or early April,
Rochester went to the country to perform his spring duties, but returned to the
Lords on April 20, a week after Parliament convened.[21] At the opening session
on April 13, the King had declared it his desire that the Houses pass a Disaffected
Persons Bill, aimed at "the pernicious designs of ill men." Behind the scenes, the
Country Party was scheming to pass a law that all business before Parliament
must be dealt with before it was prorogued. This would seriously affect the
King's powers to control it and even compel him to declare new elections.
The Disaffected Persons Bill, on the other hand, would enormously strengthen
the powers of Danby and the King. Introduced on April 15 by the Earl of
Lindsey, Danby's brother-in-law, it required all M.P.s and office-holders to
swear they would never try to alter the government of the Church and State.[22]

Rochester came in time for the second reading of the bill and the vehement debate that followed. The Lord Keeper Finch urged passage with a lurid tirade against religious fanatics; but the peers were divided about whether their privileges were diminished by taking the required oath.[23] As a member of the Committee on Privileges, Rochester denied they would be; his new family ties and Danby's payments had assured his initial support. The Country Opposition made successive, unsuccessful moves to have the bill thrown out, contending that the Oath deprived peers of their rightful privileges.

With some of Rochester's friends opposing the Disaffected Persons Bill (especially George Savile the Earl of Halifax and Buckingham, back in the fray despite previous vows in exile), the debate dragged on. Rochester's committee attempted a compromise on April 30, adding a clause that the Lords would not have to take an oath of losing liberty and/or place through dissent. Finch persisted in his original proposal, however, and in May a stalemate resulted. All the while, Rochester balanced delicately between dependence on the royal bounty, new family allegiances, ties of friendship, and his new ideal of a disinterested public servant.

Rochester had some new disciples. Francis Fane, grandson of the Earl of Westmorland, had been created a Knight of the Bath at the Coronation of Charles II but was not a presence at Court, preferring to follow the ways of the law: he had attended Gray's Inn in 1655 after two years at Cambridge.[24] Despite friendships with Rochester and Dorset, he was not in the inner circle of wits. He joined in lampooning Mulgrave, translated and Christianized poems by Horace, wrote two plays, and after early retirement into the country kept the Commonplace Book begun by his gossip-loving father, Francis Fane the Elder. Fane the Younger may have met Rochester through the very respectable Verney family. He was an unusual friend for a man who embraced the likes of Will Fanshaw. Fane dutifully went through the gestures of a rake—he even got the pox, for which Rochester prescribed a cure in 1678—but he told Rochester without embarrassment that his hopes for eternal salvation were attached to his lordship's brilliant mind, a proof of immortality. In his private misgivings, Rochester may have found these professions reassuring. He accepted Fane into considerable intimacy and even invited him to write a masque for his revision of *Valentinian* in 1676. Fane is the only known instance of John Wilmot inviting, rather than being invited by, someone to a literary collaboration.[25]

Fane's admiration of Wilmot, stated in the dedication of his first play, is also obvious in his choice of subject for *Love in the Dark*, a comedy of intrigue on the order of *Love in a Tub* and *Love in a Wood*. Fane's mentor may have suggested the setting himself, thinking of his Grand Tour in 1664. First acted on May 10, 1675, the standard *dramatis personae* romped about Venice in Carnival time, carrying on romantic plots and masquerades, but the comedy came nowhere near those of Etherege and Wycherley.[26] Nevertheless, Rochester graced this routine fare with a clever Epilogue spoofing Dryden, Shadwell, and Crowne and thus continued the counter-sniping begun in 1674.

Another of the Earl's would-be protégés courted him at this time. Thomas Otway, a clergyman's son, had gone to Winchester, where he was friends with Anthony Cary, the Fifth Viscount Falkland, who may have introduced Otway to Rochester.[27] (Falkland did not have the means to be Otway's patron himself; he wrote to Rochester in November 1675 beseeching his aid in getting funds from the King.)[28] After Christ Church, Oxford, Otway took the road to London, hoping to win fortune and fame as an actor. However, he broke into a sweat of stage fright at his debut in Aphra Behn's *The Forc'd Marriage* on September 20, 1670, and after other futile efforts at acting, he turned playwright.[29]

According to an autobiographical poem of 1680, Otway drank and talked away the next two years before falling in love with "a deceitful Muse," perhaps Melpomene the Muse of Tragedy but probably Elizabeth Barry. Otway was besotted with love for Barry in 1673, but she chose Rochester, a more promising suitor than "the Scum of a Play-House."[30] The disappointed suitor did more talking and drinking and began a series of love lamentations to her in counterpoint to Rochester's triumphant ones. (Barry saved them all and published them together.) After two years Otway realized he could never win the young actress from "a Rival's Possession" and began to cultivate the taste-making Rochester for a patron.[31] Knowing Rochester's classical interests, Otway chose as his dramatic hero Alcibiades, the Greek darling of Socrates and betrayer of Athens. In the late spring of 1675, the would-be protégé was scribbling away.

The crisis in Parliament reached its peak on June 5. Angry at the continuing stalemate, the King denounced the apparent collusion between Lords and Commons to thwart his will and deny his royal prerogatives. On June 7, with Rochester present, the Lords replied:

> This House doth *unanimously* declare, That they are of Opinion, That no Member of this House hath done any Thing Contrary to his duty. . . . [my emphasis][32]

Danby had missed his best chance of gaining the powers he wanted; the Lords realized the strengths of their stand on religion and withholding funds; and the King had seen growing unwillingness in his nobles to obey his will.[33] On June 9, he tongue-lashed the Parliament and prorogued it to October 13.

None of this was lost on Rochester, who realized the import of the Lords' increased bargaining powers. To Savile, he wrote just a year later: "I would be glad to know if the parliament be like to sit any time, for the peers of England being grown of late years very considerable in the Government, I would make one at the session."[34] He also recognized the benefits to himself of extracting the greatest rewards for his support. On April 30, during the Lords' deliberations when his vote might yet be bought, Rochester was given another sinecure, succeeding his uncle, Allen Apsley, as Life Keeper of the Hawks. On June 23, a Royal Warrant was issued him for a grant for the manors of Twickenham and Edmonton, the manor of East and West Deeping, Lincs., and the manor of Chertsey, for forty-one years.[35]

Emboldened to an imprudent extent, Rochester joined with Lord Dorset in petitioning for reversion rights to Pembroke properties held by the dowager countess.[36] This move was bound to antagonize Lady Portsmouth on behalf of her sister, the Countess of Pembroke. Increased by his imperfectly concealed dislike of "Madam Carwell" (a.k.a. Clitoris), his unflattering portrayal of her in the bawdy Scepter-Prick satire, his irritating construction project in the Privy Garden, and heaven knows how many other offenses, Lady Portsmouth's annoyance with Rochester also peaked at the very time he risked the good will of the Lord Treasurer and his royal master.

Rochester was one of the peers whose support the King needed, however, so Charles attempted his old tolerant mien. He assumed a friendly guise after Parliament dissolved, engaging in drinking matches with Wilmot and other young hellions, including his own mentally unstable son-in-law, the Earl of Sussex.[37] Then may have been the "occasion of his majestie's saying, he would leave every one to his liberty in talking, when himself was in company, and would not take what was said at all amiss."[38] With hubristic recklessness, Rochester composed some impromptus in Martial-like, epigrammatic form:

> God bless our good and gracious King
>   Whose promise none relyes on
> Who never said A foolish thing
>   Nor ever did A wise one.[39]

Rochester was sufficiently aware of Charles II's double-dealings to assert his unreliability. As for the latter charges, legend says the King laughed them off, saying his words were his own but his actions were his ministers'.[40]

The barely veiled hostility in his impromptus indicated Rochester's increasing contempt for Charles II and his cohorts. His willingness to join the Lords finally in rejecting the King's Disaffected Persons Bill was evidence of his antagonism; but the true extent of his hostility, both political and personal, burst into the open on June 25 after one of the "convivial" debauches in the King's apartments. Making his drunken way from the royal quarters to his new lodgings by the

Stone Gallery, together with Buckhurst (now Earl of Middlesex) and two or three others, Rochester took the path through the Privy Garden, where they came upon the King's Sun Dial.[41] This elaborate apparatus designed to measure celestial motions was the monarch's pride, a symbol of his fascination with astronomy. Only days before, he had been conferring with Sir Christopher Wren about a new observatory at Greenwich; but the sundial erected in 1669 was special.[42]

It was the work of a Jesuit priest, Father Francis Hall (or Franciscus Linus), who had built an early version at Lièges, and who published a book in 1673 explaining how the Privy Garden version operated.[43] Pictured in Hall's *Explication of the Diall*, the Sun Dial resembled a fountain of glass spheres, or a giant candelabrum with tiered, branching arms ending in crystal globes.[44] Although a watchman was assigned to guard it, the revelers smashed it to pieces. Speeches attributed to Rochester in contemporary accounts range from the relatively innocuous words of Aubrey, "What, doest thou stand heer to marke time?" to Francis Fane's "Kings & Kingdoms are overturned & soe shalt thou," revised to read "Kings & Kingdoms tumble downe & soe shalt thou."[45] The revolutionary sentiments of Fane's initial version reflect the political conditions attending the dial-smashing. Fane may have realized the treasonous implications of the original speech—even in a private commonplace book—and decided to tone it down.

Both Fane and Aubrey indicated the deliberate violence of the destruction. Fane said the noble vandals took the "great diall" in their arms and "flung it down"; Aubrey, that the dial was "broken all to pieces" by Rochester, after whose speech, "Dash they fell to work." The political significance of the attack is made clear by the illustration in Hall's book. The King's Sun Dial featured glass portraits of King Charles, Queen Catherine, the Duke of York, the Queen Mother, and Prince Rupert. In smashing the images of the Stuarts physically, Rochester was translating into action on one occasion the iconoclasm he had verbally expressed on others.

Word of Rochester's latest folly swept through London. The King learned about his ruined plaything soon after the dial was wrecked. In a fury he left London for Plymouth and, on June 26, began a cruise on his yacht, the *Greyhound*, accompanied by Harry Savile.[46] The whereabouts of the yacht were unknown for ten days; reports said it had been blown off course by gales. Samuel Pepys at the Admiralty feared the King was dead; and the French Lady Portsmouth, terrified at her future if he should be so, grew distraught before the King landed on the Isle of Wight ten days after setting sail and allayed the fears of everyone—with the likely exception of John Wilmot.[47]

Sober again, Rochester rode off to the country to await the King's reaction to his latest, most outrageous challenge to royal patience. He did not have a long wait. Charles returned to London about July 9; on July 16, Rochester received an ominous official inquiry from Danby as Lord Treasurer, demanding that Rochester and his henchman Lovelace explain the illegal cutting of timber at Woodstock Park.[48] To make matters worse, in late July one John Crockson killed a Woodstock bailiff and Rochester filed a hasty request that Crockson receive no pardon without notice to himself as Ranger and Keeper.[49] If he suspected a pardon might be forthcoming for the killer of one of his rangers, Rochester feared the implications for himself as a judgment of his administration of royal grants.

To increase his apprehensions and anxiety were his doubts of Elizabeth Barry's fidelity during his exile. His usual declarations of floreate love were somewhat amended with other feelings in a letter he sent to her soon after leaving the city.

> Madam,
> To convince you how just I must ever be to you, I have sent this on purpose that you may know you are not a moment out of my thoughts. . . . I conjure you by all the assurances of kindness you have ever made me proud and happy with, that not two days can pass without some letter from you. . . . And, till the blessed hour wherein I shall see you again, may happiness of all kinds be as far from me as I do, both in love and jealousy, pray mankind be from you.[50]

The letter shows that Mrs. Barry was having doubts about her lover's constancy, as he was about hers. Tom Otway was not the only one of mankind drawn to the blossoming actress, made all the more desirable by being mistress to a nobleman who enjoyed success with many women. The dramatic protestations made by the lovers to each other, however, were hardly convincing to a pair fully aware that they were play-acting. Rochester's ploy of keeping Barry from other men by having her perpetually writing letters to him must have been obvious to her. She ignored his plea/command.

A letter from Savile in the late summer informed him that his standing at Court was even worse than Rochester feared. Knocked unconscious in a fall from his horse, having narrowly escaped a broken neck (he said), Rochester was bruised and bedridden when he read the news that the Duchess of Portsmouth had "more than ordinary indignation" against him. Rochester carefully composed a letter in reply. With many protestations ("By that God that made me, I have no more offended her in thought, word, or deed, no more imagined or uttered the least thought to her contempt or prejudice, than I have plotted treason . . ."), some hyperbolic declarations of admiration ("I thought the Duchess of P. more an angel than I find her a woman . . ."), and dramatic lamentations ("What ill star reigns over me, that I'm marked out for ingratitude, and only used barbarously by those I am obildged to?"), Rochester urged Savile to remain his trusting friend, try the Duchess once more, and put in a good word for him with Danby and the King.[51]

Savile knew all this humility and innocence was an act to impress Lady Portsmouth: Rochester's malicious remarks about her were set down in black ink for the world to read. Nevertheless, Savile did the office of a friend but to no purpose. Informed of his failure—the Duchess stayed adamant in her anger and the King did not want him on Bed Chamber duty— Rochester wrote another letter to Savile early in September. Still protesting ("I have never been guilty of an error that I know to her"), the letter was tinted with a misanthropic streak and more than a little self-pity at being "run down by a company of rogues":

> she has ne'er accused me of any crime but of being cunning; and I told her, somebody had been cunninger than I to persuade her so. I can as well support the hatred of the whole world as anybody, not being generally fond of it. Those whom I have obliged may use me with ingratitude and not afflict me much; but to be injured by those who have obliged me, and to whose service I am ever bound, is such a curse as I can only wish on them who wrong me to the Duchess.[52]

The immediate cause of Portsmouth's indignation is known: she was told a "false, idle story" by "rogues," in Rochester's interpretation. Savile gained more information by bribing two Pages of the King's Bed Chamber, but Rochester's letter of appreciation in mid-September used circumlocutions difficult to decipher. Edward Progers and Thomas Windham, Grooms of the Bed Chamber, were indicated as the rogues of the affair. Perhaps they told lies—or the truth—about Rochester's candid witticisms concerning the Duchess that came to her outraged ears and the Pages, Francis Rogers and Arundel Bull, overheard in the telling. Tom Windham was a classmate of Rochester's at Wadham, and his family in Somerset were familiars to the Warres and Mallets. What Windham may have said and why he said it remains a mystery. Baseless malice was a strong motivation in Whitehall, however, as Rochester emphasized in the "Satyr" on Man:

> *Man*, undoes *Man*, to do himself no good . . .
> But *Man*, with smiles, embraces, Friendships, praise,
> Unhumanely his Fellows life betrays;
> With voluntary pains, works his distress,
> Not through necessity, but wantonness.

Unkind as the malevolent cuts of Courtiers were, they were not the unkindest given to John Wilmot in the fall of 1675. Danby's inquiry about Woodstock in July was the warning of severe reversals in fortune and family relationships for Rochester in September. The rights he held were traditional prerogatives of the Lees; and Edward Henry Lee was the family heir in line. Lee's mother, Lady Lindsey, kept an eye on his future rights; she was indignant at illegal cutting of timber and slaying of deer by Lord Lovelace. She wanted Lovelace dismissed from his post, custodians for Woodstock and Wychwood appointed, and rights of reversion to the Lees guaranteed at Rochester's death. She took her demands to the Lord Treasurer, her brother-in-law Danby, who was naturally delighted to use this means of reminding Lord Rochester that his cooperation in political matters was expected.

On September 18, 1675, the King signed a Warrant for Woodstock, Wychwood, and other preserves over to Sir Ralph Verney, Sir Walter St. John, and John Cary Esq. in reversion of Rochester's estate to the Earl and Countess of Lichfield. Rochester's guardian, uncle, and long-time friend had combined against him and Charles, his son and heir—with the approval of Rochester's mother. Stung, he swung into action. He removed his *caveat* against Crockson (who may have been an agent for Lady Lindsey); and after conferring with Lovelace, he left for London when the Woodstock races were over. On September 27, he filed a petition that Lovelace not be replaced without formal notice to Rochester himself.[53] Not much more could be done until Parliament convened on October 13, when his bargaining position with Danby would be improved.

Rochester turned his attentions upon Mrs. Barry, giving her last-minute coaching for her first named part with the Duke's Players while worrying that public exposure on the stage could only produce other rivals for her favors. About September 22 Barry appeared as Draxilla in Otway's *Alcibiades*. The King, Queen, and Maids of Honor attended the opening performance of what has been compared with Lee's *Nero* as "another example of the couplet blood-bath."[54] Furbished with rape, poisonings, stabbings, scenic marvels (Elysium), and a ghost, *Alcibiades* even employed the surefire device of killing off all but two minor characters, then having the dead Queen of Sparta arise from the gore to speak the comic Epilogue, as Nelly had done at *Tyrannic Love* years earlier. Otway was eager to write a dramatic opus as popular as *Calisto* had been. Rochester, however, judged *Alcibiades* as lacking the dubious merit of pleasing both rabble and Court, a success which "puzling Otway, labours at in vaine."

We do not know whether Rochester encountered the King before the opening performance of *Alcibiades*, which both attended. But with the Queen and Maids of Honor present, the atmosphere at the Dorset Garden Theatre was considerably warmer. The very first speech of the play (I, 3–8), was something of an ice-breaker with an unmistakable allusion to Rochester's smashing the Sundial:

> When last Night the Youth of *Athens* late
> Rose up the *Orgia* to celebrate,
> The Bacchanals all hot and Drunk with Wine
> He led to the Almighty Thun'rers shrine,
> And there his Image seated on a Throne
> They violently took and tumbled down. . . .[55]

The theatrics of the Sun Dial episode appealed widely, even as far away as Croydon, where a young teacher, John Oldham, imagined an heroic persona, a "Hector" willing to destroy the Privy Garden monument.[56] By dramatizing the destruction, giving it classical and historical dimensions, Otway replaced reality with heroic myth, a technique pleasing to an age that believed itself "Augustan." He elevated Rochester's drunken defiance of the King to a charismatic Greek's defiance of Zeus. By apotheosizing real passions, he dehumanized them and briefly managed to render them innocuous. Perhaps Otway eased Rochester's way into royal acceptance if not good favor. The scapegrace again appeared a dramatic hero, as he had in 1669. Understandably, he championed the play, calling it to the attention of the Duke of York, who gave Otway his patronage. The grateful recipient acknowledged his indebtedness by dedicating his second play, *Don Carlos*, to Rochester. *Alcibiades* itself was tactfully dedicated to Buckhurst, who also rewarded Wilmot's latest protégé. Rochester had launched another dramatic career. And for a short time, a surface harmony was maintained among the noble patrons and playgoers, although discordant notes soon grew louder.

On October 9, the King signed another Warrant for grant of the Woodstock Rangership to Sir Walter St. John, after the determination of Rochester's estate, during the two lives of Lord and Lady Lichfield. When Rochester protested the Warrant would interfere with his own rights of use and pleasure, he was assured his rights were inviolate. Unsatisfied, Rochester made a joint petition with Lovelace that the King himself hear their case.[57]

Parliament opened on October 13, with Lord Rochester much in evidence among the peers, resuming his places in the Committees on Privileges and Petitions. The session went on until November 22 as a replay of the spring. In a *Letter* attacking Danby during the summer, Shaftesbury tried to reintroduce the stalemate.[58] The King and Danby organized an elaborate plan to influence the Members, with Danby keeping secret lists of how each of the Lords was likely to vote: "Rochester For me if present."[59] On October 19, however, the Lords began debate with Buckingham pressing for new elections. Shaftesbury also wanted to force a dissolution, a plan his usual ally, Lord Halifax, opposed. Another stalemate was the result.

From October 13 to October 27, Rochester was regularly present, carefully "trimming" in his own interests.[60] He was fully aware of the worth of his vote for Danby's money bills; the King had opened the session with a mea culpa:

> I find, by a late Accompt I have taken of My Expences, that I have not been altogether so good an Husband as I might have been, and as I resolve to be for the future; although, at the same Time, I have the Satisfaction to find, that I have been far from such an Extravagancy in My own Expence, as some would have the World believe.

But just in case the M.P.s proved stubborn about providing him funds, Charles had reached a secret agreement with Louis XIV that, should they not vote a money supply or should they prove hostile to France, he would dissolve Parliament and in return receive an annual subsidy of £100,000.[61]

On October 29 Rochester was directed to select a third party to overhear his case concerning Woodstock before the Lord Keeper Finch.[62] Claiming that Rochester concurred, Lady Lindsey had forced the dismissal of Lovelace and, with Rochester protesting he had agreed to no such dismissal, the case was to come before the King's Court. Lady Lindsey and Rochester, her step-brother by a former marriage, faced in combat with the strongest weapons in her hands. Amid all the double dealings, however, Rochester had a weapon of his own. Until the Woodstock matter was settled, he failed to appear in the Lords. The tactic seemed to work. On November 9, ten days after he stopped going to Parliament, the Treasury gave Rochester £250; and on November 20, two days before the King was forced to prorogue, another £750 was paid to him. But on November 22, with the Houses deadlocked, Danby and Charles had to admit defeat and Parliament was dismissed for fifteen months. Not coincidentally, the Treasury payment to Rochester on the 20th was the last he received for a very long time.[63]

His frustrations in political and property matters in November 1675 were major; but lesser annoyances did not help Rochester's mood. With the ostentatious patronage of Mulgrave, John Dryden was showing that he did not need Rochester's help to gain royal interest. Mulgrave had taken a new Dryden heroic tragedy in verse, *Aureng-Zebe*, and showed it to the King, who made suggestions for changes.[64] On November 17, *Aureng-Zebe* was acted for a receptive audience, with Kynaston highly praised in the role of Morat, a pivotal counselor in the tale of intrigue and incest among Indian royalty. Rochester could have seen the play before his prolonged country exile.

The relationship between Dryden and Rochester, already strained, grew acrimonious at the close of 1675. As Dryden's biographer suggests, his "attempt to court Rochester probably looked like an embarrassing episode" to the proud Dryden.[65] He knew about Rochester's opinion of him from "Timon," even before the full blast of "An Allusion to Horace" soon after the debut of *Aureng-Zebe*. And Rochester's overt contempt for Mulgrave, Dryden's "foolish patron," certainly rankled.[66] Dryden's mood was not improved when his mistress, the minor actress Anne Reeve, left the King's Company and the Laureate's arms, to the scoffing amusement of Shadwell.

Preparing his Indian heroics for the press, Dryden permitted himself the relief of attacking Rochester: but fearful of the beatings fellow playwrights suffered by satirizing the peerage too brazenly, Dryden was subtle in his castigation.[67] He made a veiled reference to the Mulgrave-Rochester duel in 1669: "And he who is too lightly reconcil'd after high Provocations, may recommend himself to the World for a Christian, but I should hardly trust him for a friend." He publicly applied to Mulgrave the praise he had privately bestowed on Wilmot earlier, quoting the passage from Lucretius that Rochester translated and Dryden had professed to admire in 1673: *Omnis enim per se Divum natura* ("*The Gods*, by right of Nature, must possess. . . .") Then to Mulgrave he offered the accolade he snatched back from Rochester: *Ipsa suis pollens opibus*, etc.[68]

When Rochester dispiritedly left London for the country in December 1675, the turnabout of his fortune from its apex in January was approaching its nadir. He was truly beginning the winter of his discontent.

LIVY AND SICKNESS (JANUARY–APRIL 1676)

> [H]e took occasion in the Intervals of those woful
> Extravangancies that consumed most of his time to read
> much . . . the Comical and witty Writings of the Ancients and
> Moderns, the *Roman* Authors, and Books of Physic. . . . In his
> later years, he read Books of History more.
> —Gilbert Burnet, *Some Passages*, 6–7, 26–27.

Rochester's winter exile of 1676 was made drearier by his recurrent ills, which grew increasingly serious as time passed. A letter to Savile dated February 29 (1676 was a leap year) mentions receiving "the unhappy News of my own Death and Burial," probably a reference to rumors in London that bad health threatened his life. A letter to Rochester from Sir Robert Howard on April 7 proves that a report of his death had been circulating. The nature of his sickness is shown by a letter to Lady Rochester. His blindness and pain in his bone joints suggests late secondary or early tertiary syphilis, while the bloody urine, a clear symptom of gonorrhea, added further discomfort—and danger—to his weakening system. As usual, the medical science of the time was of no help. Rochester reported that:

> my pissing of blood Doctor Wetherly say's [sic] is nothing My eyes are
> almost out but that hee says will nott doe mee much Harme, in short he
> make[s] mee eate flesh & drinke dyett-drink . . . my duty to my mother,
> thanke her for my cordialls.[1]

Hapless victims of disease had the option of trusting the Doctor Witherleys; however, as Rochester's mother candidly remarked, "there is noe trust in phisitions words they are but men and often deceived."[2] One could brew one's own cordials and concoct home remedies that were sometimes poisonous, more often harmless, and occasionally beneficial. Or one could turn to "Books of Physic." Burnet indicated that Rochester's reading of these prepared him for one of his most elaborate masquerades later in 1676.[3]

Figure 16. Lord Rochester. Portrait by Mary Beale. Ransom Collection, University of Texas, Austin. Reproduced by permission.

Medical treatises of the time were odd compilations of classical *dicta* from Hippocrates, Galen, Cato, and Pliny the Elder; spurious works by "Aristotle" or "Paracelsus"; weird jumbles of ignorance, folklore, superstition, and astrology; or horrifying records of experiments by "empiricks," trial-and-error quacks who seared lesions off with hot pokers. Joseph Wiseman's *Severall Chiurgicall Treatises*, a prominent medical book in 1676, prescribed purging, bleeding,

Figure 17. Lady Rochester. Portrait by Sir Peter Lely. Collection of Sir Harry Malet, Somerset County Council, Dillington House. Reproduced by permission.

vomits, clysters, opiates, and juleps for everything from fever and "putridity" to cancer. If Rochester was not enlightened by such gibberish, it nevertheless enabled him to parody it and its practitioners later in the year as Dr. Alexander Bendo, the Famous Pathologist.

While he suffered poor health and sought a cure, Rochester followed his country routines. His fourth and last child, the Lady Mallet Wilmot, was christened

Figure 18. Anne Wilmot. Pastel portrait by Willem Wissing. Private Collection. Reproduced by permission.

at Adderbury Church on January 6, 1676.[4] Given her mother's family name, Mallet appears to have been raised alongside her father's bastard child by Elizabeth Barry. As an adult she maintained a friendship and correspondence with the actress and former mistress, receiving family news from her in London after Mallet retired to her husband's estate in Wales as Lady Lisburne.[5]

Aside from Mallet's birth, family affairs brought little happiness to the ailing Rochester. On February 15, the Lichfields petitioned for reversion of

Figure 19. Charles Wilmot. Portrait by Willem Wissing and Jan Van der Vaart. Private Collection. Reproduced by permission.

Joseph Ash's *custos brevium* of the Common Pleas on their behalf, and Rochester was notified that judgment had been made in their favor in the Woodstock quarrel. The Wilmots had lost again to Lee interests. About the same time, the Earl directed the Treasury that £100 of his pension be paid to Agnes Curzon "after a long solicitation and attendance." This was a ploy to force Danby to release a token amount of Rochester's pension, but the Treasurer took no action.[6]

Figure 20. Lady Elizabeth and the Lady Mallet Wilmot. Painting by Willem Wissing and Jan Van der Vaart. Private Collection. Reproduced by permission.

Rochester's ire was increased by the steady rejection of his petitions, large or small. He told Savile on February 29:

> This day I receiv'd the unhappy News of my own Death and Burial. But hearing what Heirs and Successors were decreed me in my Place, and chiefly in my Lodgings [Woodstock], it was no small joy to me that those

Tidings prove untrue; my Passion for living is so encreas'd, That, I omit no Care of myself, which before I never thought Life worth the trouble of taking. The King, who knows me to be a very ill-natur'd Man, will not think it an easy matter for me to dye, now I live chiefly out of spight.[7]

His resolution to live and take care of himself for the sake of revenge explains the optimistic report to his wife at this period:

my Condition of health alters I hope for the better, though various accidents succeed, my paines are pritty well over, & my Rheumatisme begins to turne to an honest gout. . . .

Rochester's anger toward the King also suggests why "the D of B came hither to night & stay's two dayes, I must Lend him my Coach half way back therfore pray send itt mee."[8] Buckingham's trip to Woodstock was not simply a consolation visit to an ailing friend.

After the Parliamentary sessions ended in November 1675, activists in the Country Party continued their efforts to recruit allies in their plan to force the King to dissolve the sixteen-year-long Cavalier Parliament, elect new M.P.s more favorable to the Country Party, end Danby's rule, and secure power over the King. "In the spring of 1676, Shaftesbury stayed in London, and rumour coupled his name with that of Buckingham in 'populaires menées' appealing to Londoners."[9] Buckingham himself might be successful at appealing to Rochester. Rochester's disaffection with Danby and the King possibly could be used to seduce him into the ranks of the Opposition.

The moment seemed propitious. Rochester had voted against the King in the last Parliamentary session and revealed a willingness to defy royal anger by smashing the Sun Dial. He was allied in friendship with Henry Savile and he admired Savile's brother Halifax, an Opposition leader. He had shown his persuasive powers with the Duke of York, who could prove a useful ally. Rochester's crony Lovelace, furious at losing his Woodstock sinecure, was railing against that Northerner Danby to the Oxfordshire gentry. Rochester looked ripe for the plucking and Buckingham aimed to gather him into the Opposition basket.[10] He made a surreptitious visit to Woodstock in the first months of 1676, perhaps in early March.

Buckingham evidently had a measure of success even though Rochester resisted an open alliance with the Opposition. As J. R. Jones points out, in the Exclusion Crisis two years later, Halifax and Rochester could be classed as "country peers," willing to vote against Danby's policies, but "they were not consistent opponents of the Court."[11] Even so, Rochester belonged to the

Guinea Club in 1676 and he worked in subsequent Parliamentary sessions
to fend off reprisals on Buckingham for his rashness, interceding on his behalf
in 1677.[12] If the true extent of their political collusion is uncertain, their
personal friendship and literary collaboration after 1676 indicate considerable
intimacy.

In contemplating political changes, Rochester turned to Roman history,
Livy in particular. He told Savile in a Lenten letter of 1676, "Livy and Sickness
has a little inclined me to policy." In assuming that historical precedents might
illuminate the present, Rochester was not alone. Shaftesbury drew upon the
Catiline conspiracy in a pamphlet of 1676, and Halifax began his later tract,
The Character of a Trimmer (1683), with reference to Roman precedent, but not
in detail.[13] The founders of the Country Party were notably non-theoretical in
their political suppositions. Although somewhat educated in the classics, they
largely addressed themselves to "practical" issues: personal interest, alliances,
and strategy.[14]

Rochester's choice of Livy as an inspiration for "policy" is doubly interesting. Clearly, his model for using ancient history as a guide to understanding
political powers and prerogatives was Thomas Hobbes. Investigation of the
sources and exercise of power in a "Common-Wealth" constituted a major
part of the *Leviathan* and cited Roman precedents.[15] Hobbes, however, made little use of Livy as a source. Livy's account of the Roman republic, transformed
first into a dictatorship then monarchy, was useful to Milton and similar theoretical defenders of an English commonwealth; but Livy's republican sympathies and distrust of the Emperor Augustus made him suspect in an age that
styled Charles II a second Augustus.[16] Rochester, who saw similarities between
the King and Nero and was beginning to compare him with Valentinian III,
one of the last Roman Emperors, had no such reservations about Livy and policy.[17] If Livy was irreverent toward monarchs, so was John Wilmot.

The "spite" he felt toward the King was another version of the "malice" he
termed essential to writing satire. Feeling spite early in 1676, Rochester
reverted from "philosophical" satire to his earlier pasquinade mode, attacking
individuals. His irritation with the King and Lady Portsmouth was somewhat
mollified at the news that one of Charles Stuart's *amours* before his Restoration
had arrived on the scene and had seemingly displaced Portsmouth as reigning
royal mistress. The beautiful, nobly born Italian, Hortense Mancini, had fascinated young Prince Charles in the 1650s; but she thought it best not to cast
her lot with a vagabond king. She married the Duc Mazarin, who then developed a puritanical religious mania, began defacing nude statues, and forbade
his maids to milk cows lest they have impure thoughts. He finally cast Hortense
out to make her own way. After staying for a short time in a nunnery, haunting

various European courts, becoming adept in all the fashionable vices, and being snubbed at Versailles, she came in male disguise to England.

After all, she was the aunt of Mary D'Este, the Duchess of York. Once in England, she was taken up by Ralph Montagu (who rashly fell in love with her) and his sister, Lady Hervey, experts at petticoat strategy. Together with the Earl of Arlington, who hoped to revive his waning power, they plotted to use her to displace Portsmouth and Portsmouth's ally, Danby.[18] Mazarin's impact was immediate. Anne the Countess of Sussex became her benefactress, giving Hortense lodgings at Whitehall and thus easy access to Sussex's father, the King. The ever-chivalrous Charles immediately fell prey to her charms again and took Hortense into his harem early in 1676. Unable to compete with even greater continental beauty and sophistication than her own, Portsmouth miscarried in March and went into a prolonged decline, which Nell Gwyn mocked by dressing in mourning.[19] The jealous Duchess of Cleveland decamped for France, conducted by Gramont, who earlier had escorted Hortense across the Channel.

Buckingham's response to the new favorite went unrecorded, but his cohort Shaftesbury in a pamphlet compared her to Sempronia of the Catiline conspiracy. Savile wrote the news of Portsmouth's eclipse to Rochester, who replied with obvious satisfaction: "I am sorry for the declining D——ss and would have you generous to her at this time, for that is true pride and I delight in it." He also delighted in penning an obscene parody of a popular broadside ballad of the day.

> When first I bid my love goodmorrow
>   With tear in eye and hand on breast,
> My heart was even drowned in sorrow
>   And I, poor soul, was much oppressed.

In Rochester's version, this sentimental ballad became a verse "Dialogue."

> Nell: When to the King I bid good Morrow,
>   With Tongue in Mouth, and Hand on Tarse,
> Portsmouth may rend her Cunt for Sorrow,
>   And Mazarine may kisse myne Arse.

> Ports: When Englands Monarch's on my Belly
>   With Prick in Cunt, tho' double Cramm'd,
> Fart of mine Arse, for small whore Nelly
>   And Great Whore Mazarine be damn'd.

> King: When on Portsmouths Lapp I lay my Head
>   And Knight do's sing her Bawdy Song,
> I envy not George Porters Bed
>   Nor the Delights of Madam Long.

People: Now Heav'ns preserve our Faiths Defendor,
         From Paris Plotts, and Roman Cunt,
         From Mazarine, that new Pretendor.
         And from that Politic Gramount.[20]

Interestingly enough, regardless of its personal satire, this lampoon retained the political and historical dimensions of Rochester's mature thought.

Friends kept the ruralized Wilmot supplied with London gossip. He knew that, in his absence, Elizabeth Barry was open to the financial support of a more generous lover than he. Close with money, Rochester was lax in providing for his mistress's upkeep—and she was just as lax in providing him with regular epistolary assurances of her love. A letter to her in the spring of 1676 showed him in better health, well enough to be "restless," and eager to enthrall her with promises and fine speeches in lieu of cash. He wanted her to remain in escrow for his return to town.

> Madam,
> If there be yet alive within you the least memory of me . . . give me leave to assure you that I will meet [your kindness] very shortly with such a share on my side as will justify me to you from all ingratitude . . . If there can be any addition to one of the highest misfortunes, my absence from you has found the way to give it me, in not affording me the least occasion of doing you any service since I left you. It seems till I am capable of greater merit, you resolve to keep me from the vanity of pretending any at all. Pray consider, when you give another leave to serve you more than I, how much injustice you run the hazard of committing, when it will not be in your power to reward that more deserving man with half so much happiness as you have thrown away upon my worthless self.
>
> Your restless servant[21]

Mrs. Barry's reaction to this moving plea is unrecorded but it was certainly not one of tearful gratitude.

His friends also supplied the new publications. Rochester was quite aware that in his absence some theatrical adversaries dared to speak out against him. Dryden's sly assault in the Dedication to *Aureng-Zebe* was published in February 1676; and devious Johnny Crowne had begun his extended campaign against Rochester in his comedy, *The Country Wit*, acted in January.[22] This was the King's favorite comedy, probably because it was a pro-Royalist lampoon on his critics.

The Prologue jabbed at rash "judges" talking of wit when they were motivated by anger—or jealousy. "Then he, who has but little wit, wou'd know it, / And not presume to be a judge, or poet." So much for the author of "Timon" and "An Allusion to Horace"! A more pointed blow at Rochester came in

Sir Thomas Rash's railing in Act I of *The Country Wit*. (Rochester was known as a member of the Guinea or "Guiney" Club.)

> Go to the refin'd wits, go!—refin'd wits? with a pox; unrefin'd, lewed, debauch'd fops . . . that understand nothing but writing lampoons upon civil people, breaking of jests on all things, turning all things civil and sacred into ridicule, as they call it . . . To show you a broad . . . wit of the last age, is, I take it, of as much value, as a little Guiney wit of this.[23]

Although Crowne stopped short of depicting Rochester more specifically, Rash's bill of indictment came close.[24] In fact, it established some of the catalogue of sins that other satirists later used as identifying qualities of the Rochester persona.

Where thin-skinned Dryden and belligerent Crowne took injured offense at Rochester's jibes and tried to strike back, jovial Tom Shadwell took a different tack. Shadwell countered Rochester's satirical strategies with deployments of his own. After Rochester's criticism of him in "Timon," Shadwell wrote *The Libertine*, acted on June 12, 1675.[25] This "sober-faced burlesque" was the Don Juan story, exaggerated by rapes of nuns, butcherings, and plunder, with "Don John" meeting a "dreadful punishment," at the conclusion. The play began with a speech by Don John that sounded suspiciously like John Wilmot's "Satyr" on Man, which had widely circulated in manuscript. There were also echoes of Rochester's translation of Lucretius.

> Nature gave us our Senses, which we please . . .
> By Natures order, Sense should guide our Reason. . . .
> But Fools for shaddows lose substantial pleasures,
> For idle tales abandon true delight . . .
> Away, thou foolish thing, thou collick of the mind,
> In spight of thee, we'll surfeit in delights,
> And never think ought can be ill that's pleasant.[26]

The Libertine ended with "Don John" dragged off to Hell amid the showers of flame for which Rochester criticized Shadwell's *Tempest*. The Epilogue to Don John's tragic story offered a truce. Shadwell presented "Articles of Approval" to "men of wit": He would get rid of all theatrical "Machines" and allow the wits behind the scenes of the Duke's Theatre to make love to the actresses. Mrs. Barry was, of course, one of these.

Among the "*Roman* Authors" that Rochester read in his winter retreat was Horace, whose *Satire* 1.10 on some deceased Roman writers struck him with its contemporary possibilities.[27] He had written verse parody of poor dramatic criticism in "Timon." Why not write genuine critiques of playwrights of the day in the manner of Horace? The nature of Rochester's use of the Horatian original is indicated by the title given it in the earliest manuscript copies: "imitation" is used in very few, "allusion" in many more.[28] After 1665, to allude was "to refer by play of fancy" and an "allusion" was a "covert or implied reference."[29] Rochester apparently was less interested in drawing exact parallels between Roman and English writers than an imaginative contemplation of the principles of writing inherent in the practice of ancient and modern authors.

In 1665–66 Dryden had written an "Essay of Dramatick Poesie" in dialogue form, featuring *personae* representing himself, Sir Robert Howard, Sedley, and Buckhurst.[30] Rochester may have had this in mind when he wrote his own dialogue-parody, "Timon"; and by beginning his "Allusion" with a severe examination of Dryden the practicing playwright, Rochester implicitly alluded to Dryden the dramatic theorist as he alluded to Horace. The Horatian *Ars Poetica* was a *locus classicus* for theorists and it became a conceptual touchstone for neo-classical literary critics, Rochester being among the first. "An Allusion to Horace" not only assesses specific poets and playwrights; it also sets forth very particular principles of composition in lines 91–109. These resemble the "rules" of writing in the *Ars Poetica*; herein lies the real allusion to Horace.

The uncertainty of the compositional date of the "Allusion" makes separating the strands of literary influences difficult. The "satire" (if indeed it is such) was certainly written in the last weeks of 1675 or the first few weeks of 1676.[31] If it circulated before Dryden published *Aureng-Zebe* in February, Dryden's criticism of Rochester in the dedication to Mulgrave (provided Dryden saw the "Allusion") reflected his pique at Rochester's cavils. Dryden's biographer suggests that the play itself might have been more carefully prepared for the press because of Rochester's strictures.[32] According to Shadwell, however, Dryden's reaction to Rochester's epithet for him in "An Allusion" ("Poet Squab") was both loud and violent, as Savile told Rochester at the time.[33] His jabs at Rochester in the Mulgrave dedication were remarkably restrained if Dryden raged as much as everyone said; but Rochester's putative threat to have him beaten if he attacked "with the blunt" would have kept him quiet.[34]

It is apparent, however, that Rochester satirized both Dryden and Mulgrave, his patron, in "An Epistolary Essay from M.G. to O.B." This poem has always been one of the most controversial in Rochester's canon. Although his once questioned authorship is now acknowledged, the date of the poem, its narrator, and its point of view have been widely disputed.[35] His contemporaries titled it in a way that suggested the "I" narrator was Rochester himself and the verse epistle was addressed to Mulgrave. David Vieth has shown conclusively that the narrator (M.G.) is a satiric Mulgrave-persona and O.B. is Dryden his protégé-collaborator. Vieth posits the date of the poem as 1679 on grounds that others reject. Keith Walker places the "Essay" as the first of a sequence of satires on or by Rochester, Mulgrave, and Scroop.[36] Stylistically and thematically this placement is appropriate, locating the "Essay" in 1675–76.

Seen in literary contexts in the winter of 1675–76, and put beside Dryden's Dedication of *Aureng-Zebe* to Mulgrave, the "Essay" is the imagined reply of Mulgrave to Dryden's effusive Dedication. The "foolish patron" is writing a fatuous response to the praise of his fawning sycophant. As in "Timon," Rochester satirizes an inept, pompous writer by having a silly, myopic admirer laud him. "An Epistolary Essay" further refines the satiric technique Rochester employed in "An Allusion": to "attack those areas of vulnerability exposed by the gestures of modesty in Dryden's published criticism."[37] Rochester attacks the areas of Mulgrave's vulnerability exposed in the immodest response to Dryden's published criticism (i.e., Dedication). The opening lines of "An Allusion" play upon Dryden's implication that Mulgrave assisted in writing *Aureng-Zebe*, the nature of Mulgrave's patronage, and Mulgrave's own gestures of modesty:

> Deare Friend,
> I heare this Towne does soe abound,
> With Sawcy Censurers, that faults are found,
> With what of late wee (in Poetique Rage)
> Bestowing, threw away on the dull Age . . .
> Their thanks at least I merit since through me,
> They are Partakers of your Poetry;
> And this is all, I'll say in my defence,
> T'obtaine one Line, of your well worded Sense
> I'd be content t'have writ the Brittish Prince.
> I'm none of those who thinke themselves inspir'd,
> Nor write with the vaine hope to be admir'd. . . .

Edward Howard's ludicrous *The British Princes* was widely scorned by Buckingham and the other wits. Rochester's satiric method in these lines is clearly that of "Timon": to have the foolish "critic" damn himself by praising another foolish author and work.[38]

M.G. goes on to reveal himself impetuous, self-indulgent, narcissistic, boorish, and stupid. The ludicrous image of M.G.'s urge to write being "natural" like the need to fart expands into the scatological metaphor Rochester used later in "My Lord All-Pride," another satire on Mulgrave.

> What though the Excrement of my dull Braine,
> Runns in a harsh, insipid Straine,
> Whilst your rich Head, eases itself of Witt?
> Must none but Civet-Catts, have leave to shit?

M.G.'s concluding assertions that he writes only to please himself and
therefore disdains the poetical standards of others reflects the egotism of the
historical Mulgrave but also implies that Rochester has not entirely abandoned
his own goal of pleasing others (at his own expense). By imputing to M.G.
seriously held ideas of his own, Rochester implicates himself—as usual—in his
satire.

> For shou'd my Sense be nought, how cou'd I know,
> Whether another Man's, were good, or noe?

In generalizations such as this, Rochester implicates not only himself, Mulgrave,
and Dryden, but the reader:

> Yet most Men shew, or find great want of Witt,
> Writeing themselves, or Judging what is writ. . . .

In "An Epistolary Essay," M. G. is literally "writing [creating] himself"; but
as the creator of M.G., Rochester also is engaged in imaginative self-creation.
Before 1665, "allusion" meant, primarily, "illusion."[39] Rochester the master of
disguises and illusions is nowhere more at work than in the "Epistolary Essay"
except, perhaps, in "A Letter from Artemiza." Small wonder that readers in
the seventeenth century—and the twentieth—have been tricked when guessing
the illusory poetic identities of a Rochester-in-disguise.

The treatment of Dryden in the "Essay" is appropriately mild since
Mulgrave is the main satiric target. The Laureate's major weakness is shown
in his choice of a pompous jackass for a patron. Possibly Rochester thought his
criticism of Dryden as writer was severe enough earlier in "An Allusion to
Horace." The criticism of him there as a would-be "tearing blade" had proved
lacerating:

> For Songs, and Verses, Mannerly Obscene . . .
> Sidley, has that prevailing gentle Art . . .
> Dryden, in vaine, try'd this nice way of Witt,
> For he, to be a tearing Blade thought fit,
> But when he wou'd be sharp, he still was blunt,
> To friske his frollique fancy, hed cry Cunt;
> Wou'd give the Ladyes, a dry Bawdy bob,
> And thus he got the name of Poet Squab. . . .

In the usage of the times, "squab" meant "stuffy," "plump and squat," "heavy-
hanging," as well as "newly hatched," "fledgling," and "undeveloped."[40] Thus,
"Poet Squab" derided Dryden's person, appearance, and manner as well as
his intellect and poetry. For Dryden, a proud and sensitive man who did in

truth aspire to be a tearing blade, the blow was almost too much to bear. Shadwell described his reaction:

> So raging once 'twas thought himself he'd stab'd
> 'Cause Rochester Baptis'd him Poet Squab.[41]

In reply to a letter from Savile telling him of Dryden's response to "An Allusion," Rochester wrote a candid assessment of the disparity between Dryden's social gaucherie and literary genius that was not so unkind as it initially appears:

> You write me word that I'm out of favour with a certain poet whom I have ever admired for the disproportion of him and his attributes. He is a rarity which I cannot but be fond of, as one would be of a hog that could fiddle, or a singing owl. If he falls upon me at the blunt, which is his very good weapon in wit, I will forgive him if you please and leave the repartee to Black Will with a cudgel.[42]

How serious Rochester's intention was about leaving the quarrel to Black Will with a cudgel is obscured by the arch style he used with Savile—as is the sincerity of his statements about being fond of Dryden and forgiving him. No evidence exists that Rochester ever authorized cudgelings by bully-boys, whereas evidence abounds that his friends and associates did.

If "An Epistolary Essay" is a gloss on Mulgrave, a poetic exchange between "Ephelia" and "Bajazet" written by Etherege and Rochester during this period is a reiteration.[43] Etherege's mock verse-letter from abandoned, lovesick Ephelia was a parody of the Ovidian *Epistles* popular at the Court. Ephelia's plea to "Bajazet" identified him through Mulgravian details: the star of the Order of the Garter, the affair with Moll Kirke, the duel with her brother.[44] Etherege enjoyed such poetic exchanges with friends, which he had begun with verses to and from Buckhurst in 1663–64.

Rochester entered into the spirit of the thing with a reply, "A very Heroicall Epistle to Ephelia." "Bajazet," a bombastic Emperor of the Turks in Marlowe's drama, *Tamburlaine*, was a pseudonym for Mulgrave, as was "M.G." In his self-revealing epistle, Bajazet sums up his ethic in a sentence—"In my deare self, I center ev'ry thing"—but Mulgrave's vaunted expertise as a warrior-lover is satirically undercut by Bajazet's envy of the Sultan's (Charles II) harem and his fear of avenging Kinsmen (Percy Kirke) and Rivals (Monmouth). The "Heroicall Epistle" showed little satiric advancement beyond the "Essay," but it provided a new epithet for Mulgrave and stimulated Rochester's admirer, Francis Fane, to write a "tragedy," *The Sacrifice*, featuring Bajazet's humiliating imprisonment in a cage.[45]

While keeping Rochester in malicious good humor by exchanging these *jeux d'esprits*, Etherege was engaged in a more extended work, widely construed as a compliment to his banished friend. On March 11, 1676, the Duke's Players acted a new "wit comedy," *The Man of Mode*.[46] John Dennis later wrote:

> I remember very well that upon the first acting this Comedy, all the World was charm'd with Dorimant; and that it was it was unanimously agreed, that he had in him several qualities of *Wilmot* the Earl of *Rochester*, as, his Wit, his Spirit, his amorous Temper, the Charms he had for the fair Sex, his Falshood, and his Inconstancy; his agreeable Manner of chiding his Servants . . . and lastly, his repeating, on every Occasion, the verses of Waller, for whom that noble Lord had a very particular Esteem; witness his Imitation of the Tenth Satire of the First Book of *Horace*. . . .[47]

It might be added that in the opening acts, Dorimant was "the archetypal Don Juan," as Shadwell had previously implied Rochester to be.

As Dennis shrewdly indicated, Dorimant was charming but not entirely admirable—like Rochester himself. If Etherege did not consciously pattern his glamorous protagonist on John Wilmot, Thomas Betterton, who acted the part, knew the Earl well enough to incorporate his mannerisms in the role. And it was scarcely coincidence that the part of Mrs. Loveit, Dorimant's rejected mistress, was taken over in further performances by none other than Elizabeth Barry. Dorimant's self-serving, harsh treatment of Loveit reflected much in the relationship of Rochester and Barry.[48] Indeed, Rochester wrote a letter to her, perhaps as early as 1675, sounding the Dorimantian note:

> If you distrust me and all my professions upon the score of truth and honour, at least let 'em have credit on another, upon which my greatest enemies will not deny it me, and that is its being notorious that I mind nothing but my own satisfaction.[49]

Barry had been expertly coached by her keeper to act the exploited then neglected mistress, Loveit.

The Man of Mode is, of course, not a realistic depiction of the world that Rochester lived in. Critics justly doubt whether Etherege meant his characters to be recognizable portraits. As J. H. Wilson writes:

> Etherege seized upon and embodied in his play not the real, day by day life of Whitehall, but the life which Whitehall was pleased to imagine it led. Individual items may be factual, but the total picture is a comic illusion.[50]

Absorbed with play-acting and staging spectacular masques, Restoration Courtiers were accustomed to exaggerating themselves and their lives. Rochester and Barry played a game of pretense, as did Dorimant and Loveit. An audience viewing *The Man of Mode* could discern this and other similarities and decide the play was a *drame à clef.*

Certainly, *The Man of Mode* created a renewed interest in the man who had been rumored to be dying in the country. In mid-March, a verse-essay, *Faith and Reason, or The Grief of Astragon* began circulating. Sir Ralph Verney received a copy with the notation, "said to be by Rochester . . . much after the same manner of his satyr against man." This exercise in romantic *Weltschmertz*, the very antithesis of Rochester's characteristic poetry, indicates what a complex image he held in the popular imagination.[51] And the charm of Dorimant appears to have generated a desire in the Court to see Dorimant's supposed original. Not long after the première of the comedy, the King decided to recall Wilmot from disgrace and banishment.

Did Rochester himself see a resemblance between John Wilmot and Etherege's dissembling "hero," Dorimant? A year later, in October 1677, when he was in worse favor than ever, he told Henry Savile, "I ever thought you an extraordinary man and must now think you such a friend who, being a courtier as you are, can love a man whom it is *the great mode to hate* [my italics]."[52] For a consummate actor such as he was, assuming himself to be "The Man of Mode" or becoming a "real" Dorimant was an easy transformation for Rochester, as natural as becoming a beggar, porter, woman, or devoted lover to Elizabeth Barry. Indeed, whether he was the "I" voice of the satires or the amusing companion of King Charles II, Rochester was often himself "a comic illusion."[53]

While Etherege was preparing the way for yet another triumphant return from disgraced exile, Rochester was penning a somewhat doleful Lenten letter to Savile, who had forgotten to write. He was feeling well enough to complain about "the tediousness of doing nothing" and his frustration at not being summoned to Chamber duty: "'twere vain to hope there were any alterations. . . ." Only the reconvening of Parliament would be an excuse to come to town; reading Livy had inclined Rochester to policy a little.

> When I come to town I make no question but to change that folly for some less, whether wine or women I know not, according as my constitution serves me. Till when, dear Harry farewell! . . . This is a season of tribulation, and I piously beg of Almighty God that the strict severity shown to one scandalous sin [sodomy?] amongst us may expiate for all grievous calamities—so help them God whom it concerns![54]

The faithful Savile answered with an abundance of news. Rochester jokingly called his letter "almost a gazette": "Now, to me, who think the world as giddy as myself, I care not which way it turns and am fond of no news but the prosperity of my friends. . . ." But he scorned Mulgrave's "mean ambition"— Mulgrave had become a Catholic in an effort to win favor with the Duke of York—and those who attempted to be "great in our little government." He also disdained Dryden as a "rarity" and urged kindness to the declining Duchess of Portsmouth. In conclusion, he wrote:

> And now, dear Harry, if it may agree with your affairs to show yourself in the Country this summer, contrive such a crew together as may not be ashamed of passing by Woodstock. And if you can debauch Alderman G———y, we will make a shift to delight his gravity.

"Alderman Georgy" was George Villiers, the Duke of Buckingham. The King had given him this nickname in 1675 as a put-down for the high-spirited "great Duke," who was making the political rounds, behaving like a candidate for representative of a London ward or a co-opted member of a county council. Savile probably knew that "Georgy" had made a furtive visit to Woodstock earlier in the year. Rochester did not know just how soon dear Harry himself would appear at Woodstock to delight Rochester's own gravity.

His discontented winter had given John Wilmot the leisure to think. As a result, he had written several major poems as well as a revised version of *Sodom*. He had begun work on a scene for a play by Sir Robert Howard and, possibly, a revision of Fletcher's drama, *Valentinian*, to be acted by the Duke's Players. His letters show him reading widely and reflecting on personal and political matters. By the time he was released from his solitude, he had added to his interests in wine, women, song, friendship, money, and bawdry a few more: medicine, history, politics, government—and penitence. These were to dominate the remaining years of his life.

FLIGHTS AND DISGUISES
(MAY–DECEMBER 1676)

He that can rail at one he calls his *Friend*,
Or hear him absent wrong'd, and not defend;
Who for the sake of some ill natur'd Jest,
Tells what he shou'd conceal, Invents the rest;
To fatal *Mid-night* quarrels, can betray,
His brave *Companion*, and then run away;
Leaving him to be murder'd in the *Street*,
Then put it off, with some *Buffoone* Conceit;
This, this is he, you shou'd beware of all. . . .
   —Carr Scroop, "In Defence of Satyr"

In April 1676 the King made his semi-annual pilgrimage to the races at Newmarket, where in 1671 and 1674 he rode his own horse to victory.[1] One of his retinue was Henry Savile, who became the King's messenger to Woodstock after the races ended. Savile had the happy task of informing Rochester that he was at last readmitted to Court. Delighted at the news and their reunion, Rochester engaged in a joyous celebration with dear Harry, Lovelace, and another, unidentified companion. They began carousing and, as the drinking continued, they threw off both inhibitions and clothes. The evening climaxed with a naked dance around Rosamond's fountain, as Rochester reminded Savile a year later:

> [B]e pleased to call to mind the year 1676, when two large fat nudities led the coranto round Rosamund's fair fountain while the poor violated nymph wept to behold the strange decay of manly parts since the days of her dear Harry the Second. P[rick], 'tis confessed, you showed but little of, but for a[rse] and b[uttocks] (a filthier representation, God wot!) you exposed more of that nastiness in your two folio volumes than we altogether in our six quartos.[2]

The giddiness he suffered earlier in his illness was forgotten in giddy hilarity at being recalled to Whitehall.

He told Mrs. Barry in a letter he wanted to return to town as soon as possible "to be blessed again with seeing my dearest dear." After his cheerless exile, he also wanted to rejoin the merry rakes and resume his unending efforts to pry some money out of the Lord Treasurer. Parliament would not meet until October, but Rochester was back in May. From Chester, a fellow rake, Henry Bulkeley, wrote to him in London, a letter filled with clumsy affection in anticipation of an imminent reunion and ill-suppressed anger at mutual enemies including "ye Genius y^t Governs now" (Danby, presumably).[3]

Coming into town late at night, Rochester went to kiss the King's hand and be reconciled. Receiving him readily enough, Charles, informed by Nell Gwyn, told Rochester distressing news. Mrs. Barry had done something to disturb the "heaven of thought" he had been dreaming of. (Most likely, she had taken another "patron.") The anxious lover sent a hasty note to Barry: "I must beg that I may speak with you this morning at ten o'clock. I will not fail to be at your door. The affair is unhappy. . . ."

Later, he sent a more cheerful one to his wife about his enthusiastic reception in London and business matters:

> Since my coming to towne, my head has bin perpetually turn'd round, but I doe nott find itt makes me giddy; this is all the witt you shall receive in my first Letter, hereafter you may expect more, God willing; pray bid John Tredway purchase my Oates, as soone as possible, & what-ever Coale you order I shall returne money for upon notice; ready Cash I have but little, 'tis hard to come by, but when Mr. Cary comes downe hee shall furnish you wth as much as I can procure. . . .[4]

Although Barry was distant at first, most of the London world welcomed Rochester back with open arms. The King showed forgiveness by allowing him another small piece of the Privy Garden to construct a staircase for his added wing. And despite his straitened circumstances, Charles ordered Danby to give Rochester the sum of £302–6–9 "without account" as royal bounty in June.[5]

Fortunately, some detractors were not in town when Rochester returned. Sunk into a depression that even Dr. Goddard's Drops could not cure, Lady Portsmouth was in Bath, drinking the waters for her health.[6] A crisis in the management of the King's Company indicated a lean fall season to come, and John Dryden had no play in the offing; he was in semi-seclusion, perhaps working on *All for Love*.[7] For once the name of Mulgrave was not on everyone's tongue. After being wounded in a duel with Percy Kirke, he was recuperating at his Yorkshire estate.[8] Even little Johnny Crowne was silent. But friends were on hand: Buckhurst, Henry Guy, Baptist May the Keeper of the Privy Purse, Harry Killegrew and, for a while, Henry Savile.[9] Later in May,

Savile offended the Duke of York yet again. When York opined that Bishop Burnet was a better preacher than the others at Court, Savile sneered and said York was not competent to judge since he never came to Court to hear them preach. This slap at the Duke's Catholicism was compounded by Savile's rejoinder when York insisted a standing army was needed to prevent tumults. Such an army had turned out King Richard, Harry said, and he was afraid an army might turn out others.[10] Savile was dismissed from Court for his prophetic sauciness.

The reunited merrymakers often dined at Nell Gwyn's with the King; and although Nelly did not like Rochester's neglect of Mrs. Barry, she did like his bawdy wit, so like her own. Rochester worked hard to ingratiate himself with Barry, calling up reserves of charm and false sincerity. His *billets doux* swore his own fidelity (his wife notwithstanding) while warning her against giving her favors to any man but himself and using a female "neighbour" as a go-between.[11] This neighbour was "the lean lady" urging Barry to quit Rochester for a more generous patron. She came to Barry's rooms one evening when he was present and he saw in her "all the marks and behaviour of a spy." Rochester castigated the "spy" and all those who warned his mistress against him:

> I mean, all the fools of my own sex . . . with the other lean one of yours whose prudent advice is daily concerning you, how dangerous it is to be kind to the man who upon earth loves you. . . . This is writ between sleeping and waking, and I will not answer for its being sense; but I, dreaming you were at Mrs. N[elly]'s with five or six fools and the lean lady, waked in one of your horrors, and in amaze, fright, and confusion send this to beg a kind one from you. . . .[12]

Later on, her confidantes told Barry that he had another "Miss." Rochester denied it; he never heard of her. He hoped Barry would believe him and meet him at the Duke's Theatre in Dorset Garden—or at least permit him to visit her "after the play."

The play may have been Tom Shadwell's satire on The Royal Society, *The Virtuoso*, acted on May 25, 1676, and dedicated to Rochester's friend, Cavendish the Duke of Newcastle. References in *The Virtuoso* followed the earlier pattern of exchanges between Rochester and Shadwell but were updated in light of Dryden's compliments to Mulgrave in the dedication to *Aureng-Zebe*. Shadwell's dedication of *The Virtuoso* to Newcastle mocked Dryden, a member of The Royal Society though a negligent one.[13] The text of the play retrieved the Lucretian laurels Dryden gave first to Rochester then to Mulgrave; Shadwell ostentatiously bestowed them on Rochester and Newcastle.

The Virtuoso contrasted the foolish Sir Formal Trifle and Sir Nicholas Gimcrack, leaders of the Virtuosi, with two young men of wit, Bruce and Longvil. Bruce's opening speech echoed his Rochester prototype:

> Thou great Lucretius! Thou profound Oracle of Wit and Sence! . . . Thou reconcil'st Philosophy with Verse, and dost, almost alone, demonstrate that Poetry and Good Sence may go together.[14]

Bruce then quoted the passage of which Rochester's translation had been much praised—by John Dryden: *Omnis enim per se Divum Natura necesse est.* . . . Joined by Longvil, Bruce further extolled Lucretius, then Longvil echoed the closing lines of Rochester's *Tunbridge Wells*, noting that "the Race of Gentlemen is more degenerated than that of Horses." Bruce and Longvil were in part simulacra of Rochester and Newcastle.

As a favorite, Rochester may have used his influence with the Duke's Company to entice the reluctant Elizabeth Barry to reconcile with him. Her career as an actress had not flourished after her debut in *Alcibiades* the previous November. He may have secured a part for her in a new play, so she could enact her horrors, fright, and amaze before an appreciative audience. Her success as Leonora in Aphra Behn's *Abdelazar* at Dorset Garden in July 1676 opened the way for a string of triumphs in the next twelve months, starting her on a long, dazzling career.[15]

"Amazon" Aphra Behn, so named for her popular novel set in South America, had *Abdelazar: or, The Moors Revenge,* "a non-political example of the blood and villainy mode," ready for performance.[16] Her own career as a playwright had flagged after her first play in 1670, despite Rochester's efforts to promote it and (she intimated) his assistance in revising it. In a poem of 1684, "To Mrs. W[harton], on her Excellent Verses (Writ in Praise of Some I had made on the Earl of Rochester)," Behn described a dream:

> I saw the lovely Phantom . . .
> The Great, the God-like Rochester . . .
> To me Addrest, to worthless me it spoke:
> With the same wonted Grace my Muse it prais'd,
> With the same Goodness did my Faults Correct;
> And careful of the Fame himself first rais'd,
> Obligingly it School'd my loose Neglect.[17]

Notorious for "loose morals," Mrs. Behn's relationship with Rochester may have been something more than pupil to teacher. Late in 1676 a lampoon remarked on her "Conquests" and "her Black Ace." Her poems dedicated to Nan Wharton prompted Gilbert Burnet's reprimand that the female libertine was no proper associate for Rochester's niece.[18] Whatever the nature of their relationship, Mrs. Behn derived from Rochester's escapades some dramatic material in her later plays about *The Rover* and its hero "Wilmore" (1677).[19]

Rochester's most important theatrical friendship in the early summer of 1676 was "gentle" George Etherege, whose *Man of Mode* prepared for Rochester's return to London. The poet-rakes had become friends in 1665, soon after Rochester returned from the Grand Tour. Twelve years older, Etherege shared interests besides drinking with John Wilmot. Both admired Waller and Shadwell, scorned Settle and Mulgrave, adapted Petronius and imitated French lyrics. Their poetical exchange in 1675–76 between Bajazet and Ephelia was one of several actual or putative collaborations. The hedonistic creed they shared was expressed in a drinking song-poem widely believed to have been a joint effort by Etherege and Rochester:

> Since Death on all lays his impartial hand . . .
> Let's wisely manage this last span,
> The momentary life of man,
> And still in pleasure's circle move,
> Giving to our friends the day, and all our nights to love.
> Thus, thus, while we are here, let's perfectly live,
> And taste all the pleasures that nature can give;
> Fresh heat, when life's fading, our wine will inspire,
> And fill all our veins with a nobler fire.[20]

If the two did not share the writing, they shared the sentiments.

They also shared mistresses. Sarah Cooke had affairs with both; and after Mrs. Barry broke with Rochester in 1679, she began a liaison with Etherege and had a daughter by him. Their affair continued until Etherege left for Ratisbon in 1685. Off in Germany as an emissary, he reminisced in an associative train of thought about old friends in a letter to William Jephson on May 8, 1688:

> I am beholden to you for leading me behind the Scenes [of the theatres]. You put me in minde of the time I well employed there. Sarah Cooke was always fitter for a player than a Mistresse . . . Mrs. Barry bears up as well as I myself have done. My poor Lord Rochester cou'd not weather the Cape and live under the line fatal to puling constitutions.[21]

Perhaps Etherege was also put in mind of a night that he (and maybe Jephson) shared with Rochester at Epsom on Sunday, June 18, 1676.[22] This was one of Rochester's most disgraceful episodes, reported to his discredit, central to such lampoons as Scroop's "In Defence of Satyr," and causing great remorse in Rochester himself. When Rochester told Savile in March that he thought to change his reflections on politics for some other "folly" when he came to town, he could not have foreseen that folly would become criminal. With Parliament not sitting, Wilmot had too much time to fill with wenching, drinking, and gambling. Etherege was only too ready to help him fill it. The profligates decided to vary their amusements by going to Epsom for the races in mid-June. A letter from Christopher Hatton recounted what happened there.[23]

Late on Saturday night, June 17, drunkenly searching for entertainment, they and George Bridges, a Captain Downs, and possibly Jephson met some fiddlers, who refused to play for them. In retribution, the revelers began tossing the musicians in a blanket and when a barber, hearing the noise, came to see what was the matter, they seized him. To free himself, he offered to take them to the handsomest woman in Epsom. When they raucously agreed, the wily barber showed them to the house of the local constable. Behind his locked door, the constable met their shouts with a demand to know what they came for and the rakes told him, "A whore." When the constable refused to let them in, they broke down the door and beat him in the head and severely in the body. When he managed to escape, he called the armed watchmen, who soon appeared. At that, Etherege sobered himself enough to appease them with a "submissive oration," and the reassured constable dismissed the watch.

Once the watchmen were gone, however, Rochester drew his sword against the constable, moved probably by a burst of drunken irritation. The constable cried, "Murder!" and to prevent Rochester from striking, Downs siezed him. The watchmen, rushing back, misread the situation in the dark street; one of them struck Downs a violent blow on the head with a "sprittle staff" or thick pole, parting his skull. Unarmed, Downs snatched up a stick to defend himself but the watchmen ran a pike into his side, leaving his arm dangling and helpless. The unlucky Downs died a few days later "of his hurts received from the rustics," Jack Verney told his brother Mun.[24] As Downs skirmished fatally with the watchmen, to their discredit "Y^e Lord Rochester and ye rest run away."

Andrew Marvell put it even more bluntly:

> they told me the L: Rochester with Ettridge, Bridges and Downs had in a debauch at Epsome caused the Constable to defend himselfe. Rochester said to have first ingaged & first fled and abjectly hid himselfe when the rest were exposed. . . .[25]

When Downs died, his death officially became a murder occasioned by riot, with blame placed on the aggressors. Gossip placed most of the blame on Rochester, however. Correspondents told the Earl of Essex that Rochester would be tried for murder. No records indicate that he was indicted but he was ostracized by the King and forced into hiding for a while, giving out the report that he had left for France.[26]

Their widely differing responses to Downs's death by its perpetrators demonstrates how Rochester's passion and intellect set him apart from other Restoration wits. Etherege nonchalantly returned to his usual life of casual indolence. Bridges began a callous pursuit of Moll Kirke, now a married woman whose soldier-husband was fighting on the Continent. But Rochester's deep distress led to soul searching and a darkly sardonic self-indictment that detractors like Carr Scroop dismissed as a "buffoon conceit." It has been more accurately called "one of the strangest acts of contrition on record."[27]

Casting his poem in the form of a dramatic dialogue that resembled the sort of emblem literature used to teach children lessons of morality, Rochester wrote "To the Post Boy" not long after the Epsom disaster, again using the dialogue form.[28]

> Rochester
> Son of A whore God dam you can you tell
> A Peerless Peer the Readyest way to Hell?
> Ive out swilld Baccus sworn of my own make
> Oaths wod fright furies and make Pluto quake.
> Ive swived more whores more ways than Sodoms walls
> Ere knew or the College of Romes Cardinalls.
> Witness Heroick scars, look here nere go
> Sear cloaths and ulcers from the top to toe.
> Frighted at my own mischeifes I have fled
> And bravely left my lifes defender dead.
> Broke houses to break chastity and died [dyed]
> That floor with murder that my lust denyed.
> Pox on it why do I speak of these poor things?
> I have blasphemed my god and libelld Kings;
> The readyest way to Hell come quick—
> Boy   nere stirr
> The readyest way my Lords by Rochester.[29]

If letters in his own hand did not prove how savagely ironic Rochester could be about himself, it would be difficult to believe this poem his. Circulated in manuscript, it was never printed until 1926. In this condemnation of himself, Rochester uses all the traits of his satiric persona as they were utilized by his detractors.

> Almost every detail of the familiar mythic image is here, slightly exaggerated: Rochester depicts himself as blasphemer, drunkard, brawler, bully (even a murderer), coward, whoremaster, and sexual degenerate covered with sores from venereal disease. Rochester succeeds, however, in transcending the limitations inherent in the traditional image of himself. . . . [He] infuses his self-portrait with almost Satanic energy and grandeur. The result gives the electrifying impression of being in contact with both myth and reality.[30]

Small wonder that lesser beings saw him as larger than life or that Robert Parsons compared him to Lucifer.

Probably more than any other single poem, "To the Post Boy" shows the explosive creativity that came from Rochester's abrasive, divided selves. It demonstrates his despairing attempts to integrate his Christian upbringing with his classical education, to "explain" his fantastic behavior through a fusion of pagan and Christian myths of demonic possession and hell. Rochester's portrait of himself as a grotesque, a hellish gargoyle, stands before his other works that combine God and Pluto, the Christian and Bacchic, in a controlling image of punishment. Like John Bunyan or Richard Baxter, Rochester's seventeenth-century intellect saw damnation in terrible, personal dimensions, in spite of all his efforts at Stoic repudiation or Epicurean dismissal.

Self-condemnation like that in "To the Post Boy" cannot be endured for very long at a time. Typically, Rochester took refuge in disguise. His disguises, as one perceptive critic points out, were in fact other versions of the mythicized selves he created as poetic personae, nowhere more strikingly than the Post Boy poem.[31] The dual sexual disguise he assumed in the aftermath of the Epsom tragedy may have provided him temporary relief through concealment but it also became another myth embellished by his contemporaries. According to Gilbert Burnet, the books of medicine that Rochester had read

> qualifi'd him for an odd adventure. . . . Being under an unlucky Accident, which oblidged him to keep out of the way; He disguised himself, so that his nearest Friends could not have known him, and set up in *Tower-Street* for an *Italian Mountebank*, where he had a Stage, and practised Physick for some Weeks not without success.[32]

This most elaborate of masquerades attracted the admiration of Gramont, back in England in 1676. He made it a central episode in his *Memoirs* by displacing it ten years earlier in time, miscasting Rochester as a German doctor, and supplying erotic innuendoes.[33] However, a more authentic version of the Bendo episode was written by one of the participants. In December 1687, as a New Year's amusement for Rochester's oldest daughter, Anne Wilmot Baynton, Thomas Alcock wrote *The Famous Pathologist, or The Noble Mountebank*. He had been attached to the Wilmot family for at least fifteen years, probably as clerk or secretary to Rochester himself. Since Alcock witnessed an Indenture for the Rochesters in 1672, it seems likely that he began as a clerk-amanuensis.[34]

Alcock's version of events was determinedly jocose. He described Rochester's weeks enacting "our Pathological, and Immortal Dr. Bendo" as "his Pleasant, and Innocent, Diversion," filled with "Joys" and "Pleasures" for his servant conspirators. To the modern reader, on the other hand, Rochester's actions seem a joyless *danse macabre*, a genuinely pathological interlude. Even Alcock concluded his account thus: "And this is as much as I can remember, fit to be spoken, of this famous Pathologist Doctor Bendo."[35] Rochester himself, of course, was very aware of the perversity that led him to substitute torment for happiness or joy for punishment. His undated poem, "A Song" ("Absent from thee I languish still"), depicted perversity in love:

> *Dear*, from thine Arms then let me flie,
>   That my Fantastick mind may prove,
> The Torments it deserves to try,
>   That tears my fixt Heart from my Love.

In a letter to his wife, he declared, "I myself have a sence of what the Methods of my Life seeme soe utterly to contradict, I must not bee too wise about my owne follyes. . . ."[36] During a serious illness in 1678 he wrote a bawdy parody of a romance in a letter to Savile then said, "But it is a miraculous thing (as the wise have it) when a man half in the grave cannot leave off playing the fool and the buffoon. But so it falls out to my comfort. . . ."[37]

Rochester, in effect, mocked his former faith in the curative powers of physicians by becoming the mountebank, Dr. Alexander Bendo, in July 1676. He was close to abandoning hope for his own cure. His body covered with ulcers and cerecloth, he concealed himself with his green doctor's gown, adding a false "great Reverend Beard," fake "exotick furrs," and a massive ersatz medallion full of jewels "of the same Cognation."[38] He was hiding the real in the spectacularly false to cover his vulnerability with a cynical pretense of omniscience. He made elaborate preparations for the masquerade, which was in fact a theatrical production complete with posters and play bills. He hired carpenters to build a mountebank's stage for him to perform on and sent "sonorous Hawkers" into the City to cry his fame and disperse handbills he had written. Large banners were painted, showing the King of Cyprus's "darling Daughter, the Princess Aloephagina" cured by Dr. Bendo's medical wizardry. So ensconced, "Dr. Bendo" made diagnoses, weighed out medical potions, cast horoscopes, interpreted dreams, and gulled the credulous.[39]

He fooled them doubly by taking them behind the scenes to his laboratory, where they could see with their own eyes the "honest" ingredients that went into Dr. Bendo's cure-alls. He picked these up in the streets, which he said "was all Indies": "Ashes, Soote, Lime, Chalk, Clay, old Wall, Soap . . . anything that came to Hand." Using other substances to color and shape mixtures of these, he undersold the Apothcaries to "the Poor, who were crying him up for a conscionable good Doctor, & praying for his prosperity."[40] The climax of

Alcock's Gothic narrative comes in an Hieronymus Bosch description of Dr. Bendo presiding over "his damned Operators" as they labored:

> Some stirring an old boyling kettle, of Soote and Urine, tinged with a little Asafedita . . . some grinding Oyles, wth a Stone upon Marble, till they sweat again; whilst the drops from Face and Nose made ye Medicine the bigger and consequently more beneficial; other Labouring at the Pestill & Mortar, and all of them dress't like the old Witches in Mackbeth. . . . We of the Fraternity kept a perpetual Jangling to one anotherr . . . in a Jargon of damn'd unintelligible Gybberish all the while, & indeed we judged it not convenient, in our Circumstances, to do anything in plain English but Laugh. And all this to amuse the Gentle Spectators . . . that they might see, we took pains for what we had, and consequently were no Cheats. . . .[41]

In this passage the cynical cruelty of the "prank" is graphically shown.

But if Rochester/Bendo performed a double deception on his clients, he gave them warning in his handbill. Alcock sent a copy of this bill to Anne Baynton in 1687; Jacob Tonson reprinted it almost word for word in his edition of Rochester's *Poems* in 1691.[42] This parody of a quack's mendacious advertisement attempted to inform the gullible by showing the cheats of apothecaries, doctors, astrologers, fortune tellers, and other charlatans. Dr. Bendo's handbill gives insights into Rochester's state of mind in 1676. It is also a brilliant prose satire, the only one of its kind that he wrote. Yet, Dr. Bendo's advertisement has received little critical attention.[43]

Bendo's handbill shows Rochester growing nostalgic about his days as a student in France and Italy. In the fall of 1676, after he retired the green doctor's gown, he told Savile about his increasing desire to return to the continent to study and think.[44] More importantly, the handbill discloses Rochester's view of double or mirror identities and his scorn for the men in power at Whitehall. Disguised as Bendo, he could voice the true feelings of John Wilmot:

> The Politician . . . finding how the People are taken with Specious, Miraculous Impossibilities . . . protests, declares, promises I know not what things, which he's sure can ne'er be brought about; the people believe, are deluded, and pleas'd. The expectation of a future good, which shall never befall them, draws their Eyes off a present evil. Thus are *they* kept and establish'd in Subjection, Peace, and Obedience. *He* in Greatness, wealth, and Power: so you see the *Politician* is, and must be a *Mountebank* in State-Affairs, and the *Mountebank* (no doubt if he thrives) is an errant *Politician* in Physick.[45]

These sentiments smack of Machiavelli, who was a point of reference for Rochester and Savile between 1674 and 1676; but they are also a cynical commentary on Thomas Hobbes's description in the *Leviathan*: "A Publique

Minister, is he, that by the Soveraign, (whether a Monarch, or an Assembly,) is employed in any affaires, with Authority to represent in that employment, the Person of the Commonwealth." The satiric treatment of self-aggrandizing, dishonest "statesmen" in the "Satyr" on man (1675) is continued and explicated in Bendo's advertisement, which shows the growth of Rochester's public spirit.[46]

As a revelation of his private anxieties, no part of the medical charade was more telling than Rochester's repeated impersonations of "Mrs. Bendo." In disclosing her father's transvestism to Anne Baynton for the first time in 1687, Thomas Alcock tried to suggest Wilmot's amorous conquests, which the family apparently approved when *Valentinian* was acted four years earlier in 1683, however inconsistent they were with the Wilmots' promotion of Rochester's saintly legend.[47] Alcock wrote:

> Dr. Bendo, among other practices, made: Judgements upon Moles, Wenns, Warts and natural Marks, according to their severall Kinds, and accidental Positions, in various parts of the naked Body; And if the modest Lady had any such about her where without blushing she could not well declare them; why the Religious Doct^r Bendo would not, for all the world, so much as desire to see it . . . she was to leave a token with the Doctor and appoint an hour when his Wife was to bring it, as a Credential that she came on that Errand, upon which she was immediately to be admitted into the Bed Chamber, to View and report the matter.

Alcock was confident that Rochester's eighteen-year-old daughter would be inquisitive about Bendo's wife, whom she had not heard of, and that she would be "pleased to accept of this part of the diversion, as the only piece of News in the Story; For I believe that y^r Ladyship never heard that Man & Wife was one Flesh before without a Mistery."

> For we divested the Noble Doctor of his Magisterial Robes, and by the Assistance of a Tyre [attire] woman putt him into the habit of a grave matron; so away she trudged with the return of the expectant Lady's Token, by which Ticket, she soon found the admittance agreed on between the Lady and the Doctor, and did her business effectually.[48]

Alcock's—and Gramont's—erotic titillation at the idea of him as a transvestite seducer may have reflected Rochester's own sexual stimulation at his disguise. Heterosexual males can find such cross-dressing sexually exciting. Given his description of active symptoms of syphilis in the Post-Boy poem, however, it seems likely that Rochester was again feeling impotent and may have dressed as a phallic woman to reassure himself about his virility.[49] Rochester's ability to identify with a female perspective and his male anxiety at the threat of impotence fuse in a lyric poem perhaps written about this time.[50] "A Song of a Young Lady to Her Ancient Lover" had both classical and contemporary analogues, but Rochester's version rang changes that have caused commentators to vary widely in their readings. One sees it as a satire on "dirty old men," some as sweetly romantic, and others as evidence of Rochester's "own divided nature" or the perverse artistry that entraps his readers through irresolvable contradictions.[51]

Certainly, the "Song" presents interpretive difficulties in its opening lines:

> Ancient Person, for whom I,
> All the flattering Youth defy;
> Long be it e're thou grow Old,
> Aking, shaking, Crazy Cold.
> But still continue as thou art,
> *Ancient Person of my Heart.*

What is the present age of the man addressed as "Ancient Person"? The Lady says it will be a long time before he is old and manifesting the aches, pains, and "coldness" of advanced age. Is the fifth line a command that he stay unchanged in old age or a prediction that advanced age will find him in his present condition at a comparatively young age?

The crux is the meaning of "ancient," as Rochester uses it. After 1659 "ancient" was used as a synonym for "senior"; it also had associations of duration.[52] The "young" lady addresses her lover of some time, who is older than she but not yet aged. If, for example, the lady was eighteen years old and her lover of the past three years was almost thirty, she might well call him her "ancient" or senior. His present condition of "coldness" (or temporary impotence) might appear a portent of his future old age when his "Nobler part" would be "by Ages frozen grasp possest." If so, the lady hopes she can restore her lover's "youthful Heat" in his autumnal days, pouring kisses on his brow and recalling a "second Spring." She teasingly describes the future appearance he fears ("withered Lips and dry") and with arousingly false modesty tells him she will "soothe" that part "which but to name / In our Sex wou'd be counted shame." She will make it "In former Warmth and Vigor stand." She will anticipate his future wishes, become the sexual aggressor and provide him pleasure through her loving "Art" (amorous techniques) but her love will be genuine and "without Art" (guile, craftiness).

The "Song" is Rochester's imagined version of a young woman's loving, cajoling, playful mocking of a lover still young but momentarily impotent. It is the sort of provocative promise to restore his virility that could have been murmured by the nymph in "The Imperfect Enjoyment"

as her fair Hand, which might bid heat return
To frozen *Age*, and make cold *Hermits* burn,
Apply'd to my dead Cinder. . . .[53]

Or sung to the aging King by Lady Portsmouth as his head lay on her lap. Or by Nelly, laboring to raise his member. Or, most fancifully, by the eighteen-year-old Elizabeth Barry to Rochester, temporarily impotent, nearing thirty in 1676, and sensitive about both his potency and age.[54]

Rochester was not the only man to console himself for a lapse in potency or attempt a hoped-for arousal with masturbatory fantasies of a loving, exciting young mistress. The rapidly growing amount of sexually explicit writing in his day was full of such drybob day-dreams.[55] Whether the modern reader finds the sexual imagery in the "Song" funny, romantic, or disgusting, the response is irrelevant insofar as it relates to authorial intention. Rochester wrote the "Song of a Young Lady" for much the same reason he wrote "To the Post Boy": to relieve his psychic stress through fantasy. "To the Post Boy" envisioned the emotional torment of a Hell to atone for guilt at Downs's murder. The "Song of a Young Lady to Her Ancient Lover" envisioned a sexual heaven achieved through a woman's lasting devotion.

After enough time had passed for Dr. Bendo to cause a stir that reached as far as Whitehall, infuriate the apothecaries whose business was slackened by his practice, and permit Rochester to grow bored, Charles recalled him to Court. Alcock said "the noble Doctor" made

> the Quickest Voyage from France that ever Man did, which was the talk and admiration of the whole Town, for those that saw his Ostracism Cancelled this night at Whitehall, did the very next see him there in Splendor dancing in a Ball, in as great Favor as ever.

Dr. Bendo's sudden disappearance was reported by his baffled clients to be the effect of necromancy. Rochester's creditors suffered the usual fate of losing their money as though by magic. After his return to Whitehall in late July or early August, John Wilmot spent a few days among his friends, recounting his adventures to an appreciative Savile before returning to Adderbury. Harry joked about Rochester's medical expertise in a letter of August 15.[56] Medical concerns were great in the late summer of 1676, when hot weather was blamed for many illnesses. In July, Danby became seriously ill and upon his recovery in August, he went to Oxfordshire about the same time Rochester did. On August 16, Danby wrote a letter to his wife:

> I am here become as errand [arrant] a Nimrod [hunter] as ever you knew mee, and your brother Norris and I so in love with one another that wee

are both unwilling to thinke of parting. And I do assure you I find him
heartily to endeavour both the Kings interest and mine among the gentlemen in this country.[57]

Knowing how unpopular Danby was with such Oxfordshire gentry as Lord
Lovelace because of the Woodstock affair, Danby's brother-in-law Norris, the
husband of Rochester's niece, was trying to reconcile the opponents. Danby
realized the importance of the Oxonian gentry in the King's affairs, and pic-
turing both his and Rochester's efforts at renewing their friendship, however
hypocritical, requires little imagination. Despite his diatribe against statesmen
when he acted Dr. Bendo, Rochester was well aware of the importance of
Danby's good offices toward him. Hunting, drinking, and attending the
Woodstock races together presented ample opportunities to rebuild the sem-
blance of a mutual regard. Yet, Rochester longed to escape the life he had created for himself together with its burdens, hypocrisy, and guilt, as an exchange
with Savile in August and September 1676 showed.

Harry's letter of August 15 related some recent news. The hot weather had
caused "poor Harry Bayly" to sweat heavily, fall into a fever, and die. An old
suitor of Lady Rochester's was also dead in Paris.

> And tothers death spares noe place, nor g[reatness, it] has seized upon my
> Lord John Butler [himself], who was lately called Earle of Gowran, [and
> now being] dead is pittyed as a man of parts, I suppose as all who are
> hanged are called proper men, it is unimaginable how absence, a new
> name, and dyeing at last, will change a man's character. . . .

In recollection of their naked cavortings in April, Savile asked to be remembered to Lord Lovelace if he was in the country. He concluded by asking for
a prescription for the Court's faults, urging Rochester to produce more poems
to show "the world theire follyes" and to benefit from "a hansome mixture of
the sobriety of Adderbury and the debauchery of Woodstock."[58]

Savile's letter was a reminder of the tiresome rounds of his daily life and,
hearing that his friend was going on a diplomatic mission to France, Rochester
began wistfully imagining an escape from his psychic dilemmas. He thought of
his youth with nostalgia and regret and caught at the notion of returning to
places and times when his own follies had not yet been committed. He was
accustomed to visit Burford and Oxford, both near Ditchley and Woodstock.
When business took him there to consult with John Cary and others, he would
stop over to share a bottle with Robert Whitehall or discourse with Dr. John
Fell. On an Oxford jaunt early in September, be began to think of his years as
a student and his Grand Tour with Dr. Balfour, remembrance of which was
evoked in his pose as Dr. Bendo.

Savile was to accompany his one-time mistress, Lady Cleveland, and her escort, Gramont, to take up residence in France. Cleveland's promiscuity and that of her sluttish daughter, Lady Sussex, had become too great an embarrassment for the King to tolerate any longer. The two ladies were sent off to France to prevent further talk about their common nymphomania. Besides, Lady Cleveland could live more cheaply there on the funds given her by Charles. On September 5 from Oxford, Rochester penned a roguish but wistful note to Savile.

> Whether love or the politics have the greater interest in your journey to France, because it is argued among wiser men I will not conclude upon; but hoping so much from your friendship that without reserve you will trust me with the time of your stay in Paris, I have writ this to assure you, if it can continue a month I will not fail to wait on you there. My resolutions are to employ this winter for the improvement of my parts in foreign countries, and if the temptation of seeing you be added to the desires I have already, the sin is so sweet that I am resolved to embrace it and leave out of my prayers "Libera nos a malo"—for thine is my kingdom, power and glory, for ever and ever.[59]

John Wilmot did not make the journey he wished for, it seems, although Savile stayed in Paris for three months.[60] Escape from one's self and a life of habitual beliefs, desires, and needs is more easily talked about than accomplished. At twenty-nine, after ten years of marriage and four children, after fighting and pimping and amusing a royal "master," Rochester had forever ceased to be the naive youth fresh from a Grand Tour.

On October 6 he composed a letter to Mrs. Barry in all-too-familiar phrases: disclaiming any accusations of unfaithfulness, regretting his inability to "serve" her (i.e., send money), fretting that she had other admirers, scorning the "malice" of "wretches" she had mentioned in a letter brought to him by a messenger that very day. In conclusion, he told her,

> And now to let you know how soon I propose to be out of pain, two days hence I leave this place in order to my journey towards London, and may I then be but as happy as your kindness can make me. . . .[61]

Although Parliament was still in its fifteen-month-long prorogation, Rochester was back in London in early October, to all appearances the same as ever. His role was too fixed to throw it off, however much he would have liked to. The gang of jovial wits reassembled. The equilibrist affair with Barry resumed its perilous imbalances. The drinking and play-going and writing started over. As always, the luminous Lord Rochester was sought as "top *Fidler* of the *Town*."[62] Dorimant was back on stage.

During October and November, behind the public scene of political inactivity, Danby was busily working to implement his power. Shaftesbury and Buckingham, still distrustful of each other and vying for leadership of the Country Party, were trying to gather enough support to dissolve Parliament when it would convene in February 1677. Old Lord Wharton stood with them; but the Duke of York resisted Shaftesbury's efforts to get Catholic allies. Even Halifax, Shaftesbury's nephew, proved recalcitrant.[63] It appears that Buckingham intensified his own attempts to recruit Rochester into active participation. The friendship of the two men was certainly accelerating at this period; they drank together, went to plays, and perhaps joined in verses to reheat a war between the playwrights.

The weather in December 1676 was so cold that the Thames froze solid, but dramatic tempers flared. Both Thomas Otway and John Crowne were working on plays about the Roman Emperor Titus and his Jewish mistress, Berenice. Otway's twin bill of *Titus and Berenice*, an innovational three-act recension of Racine's tragedy, and *The Cheats of Scapin*, derived from Molière's farce, was acted first in December and dedicated to Lord Rochester.[64] Clearly, the Roman drama and French farce reflected John Wilmot's tastes. Even though it featured a brilliant new acting team, Thomas Betterton and Elizabeth Barry, the double bill was a limited success.[65] Crowne's *The Destruction of Jerusalem*, in January 1677, however, would be enormously popular. Crowne's success rankled Otway; and rumors that Rochester wrote the best parts of *Jerusalem* galled Crowne.

The *cause célèbre* in December 1676 was Wycherley's *The Plain-Dealer*, an anomalous play that troubled its audiences as much as it has baffled twentieth-century critics. Some spectators were shocked at its "savage, sardonic social commentary" and others were confused by the double nature of its hero, Manly, as both comic misanthropist and serious satiric spokesman. Less an example of the Etheregean wit-comedy than a continuation of the old sex-and-intrigue *cum* swordplay school, *The Plain-Dealer* left its first audiences baffled about whether to like or dislike it.[66] As John Dennis, Wycherley's latter-day champion, reported it:

> I must confess the Town was now and then in the wrong. Deluded by the enchanting performance of soe just and soe great an Actour, as Mr. Hart [who played Manly] or Mr. Mohun, or by the opinion They might have of a celebrated Author who had pleased them before. But then there were several extraordinary men at Court who wanted neither Zeal nor Capacity, nor Authority to sett them straight again. There was Villers Duke of Buckingham, Wilmot Earl of Rochester, the late Earl of Dorset [Buckhurst], the Earl of Mulgrave who was afterwards Duke of Buckinghamshire, Mr. Savil, Mr. Buckley [Henry Bulkeley], Sir John Denham, Mr. Waller &c. When these or the Majority of them Declard themselves upon any new

Dramatick performance, the Town fell Immediately in with them. . . . And when upon the first representations of the *Plain Dealer*, the Town, as the Author has often told me, appeard Doubtfull what Judgment to Form of it: the foremention'd gentlemen by their loud approbation of it, gave it both a sudden and a lasting reputation.[67]

Wycherley's play continued to be successful for many years to follow because of the unanimity of praise afforded it by Rochester and his friends; but the momentary harmony of their critical agreement soon turned into a cacophony of outrage when a theatrical squib written by some of those same "extraordinary men," exploded on the London scene about the same time.[68]

SESSIONS POETICAL AND POLITICAL (1677)

> Apollo thought fit, in soe weighty a Cause,
> T'Establish a Government, Leader, and Laws:
> The hopes of the Bayes, at this Summoning Call,
> Had drawne 'em together, the Devill and all. . . .
> —*A Session of the Poets*

> But [Nothing] why does Somthing still permit
> That Sacred Monarchs should at Councell sitt
> With persons highly thought of, at best for nothing fitt. . . .
> —Rochester, "Upon Nothing"

One of the collaborations attributed to Rochester and Buckingham was *A Session of the Poets*, written in late November or early December 1676. Evidence for authorship of this satiric assessment of contemporary playwrights is contradictory.[1] Nevertheless, two playwrights, Elkanah Settle and John Crowne, openly blamed Rochester for it. When the lampoon first appeared, Thomas Otway, then Rochester's protégé, believed that Settle wrote the *Session*. Otway reportedly challenged Settle to a duel and, when he refused to fight, forced him to acknowledge his authorship and call his mother a whore in writing. This episode provided a comic scene in a play, *Wits Led by the Nose*, ca. July 1677.[2]

In *The Poet's Complaint of his Muse* (January 1680), Otway used Rochester's "blundering" epithet from *An Allusion to Horace* to indicate Settle again as author of the *Session*. In *A Supplement to the Narrative* in 1683, however, Settle denied writing *A Session*, asserting the common belief that Rochester was its "father." Likewise, John Crowne flatly asserted in the Preface to *Caligula* (1698) that Rochester was the author.[3] If Rochester was not responsible for *A Session*, some of its target-victims nonetheless believed he was; and in fact the satire anticipates *ad hominem* pasquinades he and Buckingham penned later in 1677.

Henry Savile hinted at a possible joint authorship by Rochester and Buckingham. In a November 1677 letter, Savile archly suggested that group compositions by the wits had been made on earlier occasions with Rochester as the *primus inter pares*.[4] J. H. Wilson has theorized that *A Session* was composed jointly by the same circle of wits (including Buckingham) who wrote *Advice to Apollo* at Woodstock in October 1677. Wilson's hypothesis explains the rugged meter, assessments of Shadwell, and others unlike those by Rochester in *An Allusion*, as well as the interposed cry of Dick Newport in line 49 concerning Settle: "Ballocks . . . I hate that dull Rogue."[5]

A Session satirically depicts the condition of Restoration drama at its mid-point. John Dryden ("That Antient grave Witt, soe long lov'd and fear'd") is gently mocked for rumors that he will "turne Priest."[6] Next, "gentle George" Etherege is praised for his "fancy, Sense, Judgment and Witt" but unpardoned for "his long Seav'n yeares silence." "Brawney Witcherley" is deemed "too Good for the Place" of Bayes, being a "Gentleman-Writer," not a "trader in Witt."

Tom Shadwell, with "his Gutts, his Paunch, and his Tallow," vows he is a main support of the Stage. Apollo says he wishes Tom had half the sense he claims but bids "soe Joviall a Witt," to keep drinking, "Railing at Poets, and shewing his Prick." Ruby-faced from wine, Nat Lee has succeeded once in three plays but Apollo makes him an Ovid in Augustus's Court. Elkanah Settle "humbly" desires to give "noe offence" but Apollo refuses the bays to "soe modest a Foole, / And bid[s] the great Boy should be sent back to Schoole"— the same judgment made in Rochester's *Allusion to Horace*.

Tom Otway claims superiority in "Heroicks," having killed his lice with the profits from *Don Carlos* (which had been dedicated to Rochester). Apollo rejects the failed actor: "The Scumm of a Play-House." "Little Starcht-Johnny Crowne" grasps at the laurel for "shiteing of Plays." Apollo ironically praises Crowne's best "Tallent"—"to be past Sense of Shame"—and bids him keep on being dull.

Aphra Behn pleads her Plays and the Conquests of "her black Ace" as title to the bays; but Apollo says that claim should have been pleaded twelve years earlier. Edward Ravenscroft, Tom Rawlin, Tom Durfey, and other, unnamed pretenders to the honor appear. Tiring of them all, Apollo sees the actor Thomas Betterton in the mob and gives him the laurel:

> His Witt had most worth, and most Modesty in't,
> For he had writ Plays yet ne'er came in Print.

A Session offended the "present generation of unwitty poets" as Rochester termed them in November 1677; they resented the disdainful peer already for his slurs in *An Allusion to Horace*. Their antagonism was unanimous after 1676: Dryden, Lee, Settle, Otway, Crowne, Ravenscroft, and Durfey, all of whom earlier sought Rochester's favor, wrote attacks on him. Once the *Session* squib exploded on the London scene, the playwrights' war intensified. Edward Ravenscroft took revenge by satirizing Rochester and his dramatic enthusiasms in *Scaramouch* (1677). John Crowne mocked Otway and his patron Rochester in the preface to *The Destruction of Jerusalem*, sneering at Otway's *Titus and Berenice*. His abortive duel with Settle forced Otway into army exile in the Lowlands; subsequently, Otway's disgruntlement with Rochester grew when his patron proved characteristically tight-fisted with money. Estranged from Rochester, Nat Lee soon drifted into Dryden's orbit.

Dryden was angry with almost everyone. When Shadwell condescended toward him in the Dedication to *The Virtuoso* in July 1676, Dryden drafted *Macfleckno*, the lampoon that demolished "mountain belly" Shadwell's reputation for centuries. His anger at Rochester also mounted during 1676. Stung by *An Allusion* and frustrated by gossip that he was denied a sinecure at his alma mater Cambridge because his old enemy Buckingham was Chancellor, Dryden could not have been pleased by the reference in *A Session* to malicious reports of efforts by him to secure a post at Oxford by turning priest.[7] Furthermore, Sedley was writing a play about a subject that Dryden wanted for his own. Although *Anthony and Cleopatra*, staged in February 1677, failed miserably— "awful is the word for it"[8]—Dryden kept having problems getting his own *All for Love* produced. He was still complaining about it in June 1677 to Viscount Latimer, Danby's son.

In the first months of 1677, the playwrights' renewed combat was aided by political divisions between their patrons. Shadwell's Lord Newcastle aligned himself with the Country Party led by Shaftesbury and Buckingham. Halifax, Rochester, and Buckhurst gravitated toward it as well. Contrariwise, Dryden and his officious patron, Mulgrave, were allied with Danby and his party. Both political sides had busily laid the groundwork to resume their battle for power when Parliament reassembled after its fifteen months' prorogation. Throughout January and early February 1677, they were poised and waiting.[9]

In the interim, Rochester found a new disciple. Son of a clergyman, graduate of St Edmund Hall, Oxford, now a teacher at the Croydon free school, Whitgift, John Oldham had developed a crush on "our witty, bawdy peer" by hearing tales of his outrageous exploits and reading his shocking verse. Repressed and bored, Oldham eased the tedium of marking student papers by copying Rochester's poems and writing imitations of them, to wit, "A Satyr against Vertue . . . Suppos'd to be spoken by a Court Hector."[10] (The "Court Hector" smashed the Privy Garden Sun Dial.) According to a contemporary account, Sir Nicholas Carew saw Oldham's verse and passed it on to Buckingham. Several wits, including Rochester, then rode to Croydon to meet the twenty-one-year-old poet and release him from his "Grammar-Bridewel."

When the befuddled headmaster, John Shepherd, a "tottering pedagogue" thought the visitors came to see him, Rochester encouraged his mistake with "laughing gravity." Error explained, they met Oldham.[11]

Pleased with him, they introduced him to the delights of libertine London, which encouraged him to write "A Dithyrambique on Drinking . . . Suppos'd to be Spoken by Rochester at ye Guinny Club" in August 1677.[12] Oldham went on to write other verses similar to Rochester's (Anacreontics and imitations of Horace); and despite a sodomitic verse-attack on *Sodom*, he wrote his own erotic fantasy: the obscene, mock-epic *Sardanapalus*.[13] When Rochester died in 1680, Oldham eulogized him in a lengthy elegy, "Bion, a Pastoral, in Imitation of the Greek of Moschus," declaring the wish to die in his stead. On his own deathbed in 1683, he again imitated Rochester in agonized penitence, decrying the "gay monsters" who had "inveigled" him into the service of vice.

On February 6, 1677, the formal wedding of the Lady Charlotte Fitzroy and Edward Henry Lee, Earl of Lichfield, took place. Young Lichfield showed affection for his Uncle Rochester, who professed to return it.[14] The wedding was lavish. The bride's mother, Lady Castlemain, returned from her exile in Paris to spend £1,200 on the festivities. Edward Henry received a dowry of £18,000 along with his bride and an annual income of £2,000 payable to his mother, Lady Lindsey. Thus the Lichfields began a marriage euphemistically described on their epitaph thirty-odd years later:

> It was Justly Observed
> That at their Marriage, They were
> The most Grace-full Bride=
> groom, + most Beautyfull Bride.
> And that till Death They remaind
> The most Constant Husband + Wife
> Their Conjugal Affection was blest
> By their Numerous Offspring
> Thirteen Sons and Five Daughters. . . .[15]

With the young Lichfields wedded, bedded, and breeding, the wedding guests turned again to the business of money and power.

When Parliament convened at last on February 15, an expectant majority of members were present, including Rochester. The King began the joint session with a blast against enemies who urged the dissolution of Parliament and new elections, then he appealed for money. When the Members of the House of Commons left for their own chambers, the Duke of Buckingham, resplendent in "liveries of blue," rose and cited an archaic statute of Edward III that no Parliament legally existed because of the fifteen-month prorogation. He argued "That ancient statutes were not like women, the worse for being old."[16]

The crisis had come. Danby's allies were ready but Shaftesbury's were weakened by their distrust of the capricious Buckingham.[17] Lord Frecheville, Danby's cousin, moved that Buckingham be "called to the bar" for his temerity; Lord Arundel of Trerice seconded. Intimidated, only Shaftesbury, Lord Wharton, and Lord Salisbury supported Buckingham, although Halifax argued that Buckingham was in order by giving his opinion. Lord Holles, a nominal Country Party man, had dithered earlier and was silent when the hour came. Meanwhile, in the Commons, a similar move to find the Parliament dissolved was forwarded by Sir John Mallet, Lord Newcastle, and two more; but other members of the Country Party were too fearful to confront Danby. Such moderates as Edmund Waller and Sir Robert Howard also failed to support the move.[18]

Rochester too was unwilling to defy the King and Danby openly. Back again on the Committees for Privileges and Petitions, he voted with the majority to continue the session. Their revolt defeated, the dissidents were given the chance to recant; and, one after the other, Wharton and Salisbury refused to kneel and beg pardon of the King and Lords. Shaftesbury gave a lengthy, "humble" speech but refused to change his opinion. Sentenced to the Tower, Shaftesbury insinuated that Danby's men were not above using poison, requesting he be permitted his own cook during his imprisonment. Amid laughter and shouts, the Lords approved his request. In the tumult, Buckingham sneaked away but was hauled back by the Gentleman Usher of the Black Rod the next day to be given the same sentence.[19]

In the Tower, Buckingham and his allies were given double guards. Their wives, at first refused permission to see them, were "very troublesome" to the Lieutenant of the Tower; other would-be visitors were turned away.[20] Any efforts by Rochester to help Buckingham soon after his confinement in the Tower on February 16 are not documented; but it is clear Rochester worked with their mutual friend, Sackville Lord Middlesex, to get Buckingham released as soon as possible.[21] Harry Savile wrote to his brother Halifax, "My Ld Middlesex is the most earnest man alive for the Duke of Buckingham."[22]

Rochester worked within the House of Lords to earn credits with the King that he used eventually to help release Buckingham. On February 16, he was put in commission "to enquire who was the Author and Contriver and Printer" of a recent book that supported the rebels' cause: *Some Considerations upon the Question, Whether the Parliament Is Dissolved by Prorogation for Fifteen Months*. The Commission reported on March 1 that silent Lord Holles was the author and, on March 5, that Samuel Smith was the printer. On March 8, the Lords voted to prosecute the two offenders and burn their "libels" at Westminster, the Royal Exchange, and Tower Hill as a warning to others.[23]

Meanwhile, Rochester was placed on another commission to draft an "Act for Prevention of Frauds and Perjuries." He worked conscientiously on the two special, as well as his standing, committees. The Frauds Commission reported promptly on March 6 and the Committee on Privileges gave its report on March 20 with Rochester present and speaking. His attendance record throughout the session from February 15 to May 28, 1677, was exemplary. As Robert Wolseley wrote later:

> a considerable time before his last Sickness, his Wit began to take a more serious Bent, and to frame and fashion it self to publick Business; he begun to inform himself of the Wisdom of our Laws and the excellent Constitution of the *English* Government, and to speak in the House of Peers with general approbation . . . and set himself to read the Journals of Parliament Proceedings.[24]

Rochester's active involvement owed as much to his private concerns as public business. Penalties for practicing Catholics were proposed and hotly debated.[25] Since Lady Rochester persisted in her Catholicism, Rochester was well aware that his family could be seriously affected by new anti-Catholic laws. He may have secretly worked for the proposal on March 19 that Popish Recusants could avoid all penalty by taking communion in the Church of England. One of the final acts of his life was persuading his wife to take Anglican communion and making sure the word was widely spread that she had done so.

The first week in April brought Rochester's crony Lovelace before the Lords to petition for his wife's jointure: Lovelace lost his case. Louis XIV was back in the Netherlands, so Parliament was willing to vote ship money on April 11. On April 13, Rochester was present to vote for an Act to Suppress Unlicensed Books. The following day, pleased with the votes of the session, especially new excise taxes, the King adjourned Parliament for a month until May 21.[26]

All business, Rochester used the time to catch up on other matters, including the cause of Buckingham, still locked in the Tower. But first he needed to placate Nell Gwyn, who was annoyed with him for several reasons including his treatment of Elizabeth Barry, and this meant placating Barry, who had become pregnant by Rochester in March and whose temper was not improved by her condition. Soon after his return to London in October 1676, the lovers resumed their bickering. Mutually jealous, with good cause, they found themselves being manipulated by her servants and interested friends: "wretches," to Rochester.[27] Bribes, tale-telling, and spying took on added importance as Rochester resorted to excuses for absences from his mistress coupled with protestations of his undying passion.

Lady Rochester may have joined her husband in town for the season, thereby limiting somewhat his freedom to come and go. He had, nevertheless, found occasion to impregnate Mrs. Barry. A letter in the Spring of 1677 shows the state of their relationship.

> Madam, I found you in a chiding humour today, and so I left you. Tomorrow I hope for better luck, till when neither you nor any you can employ shall know whether I am under or above ground. Therefore lie still and satisfy yourself that you are not, nor can be, half so kind to Mrs. [Nelly?] as I am.
>
> Good night.[28]

This letter, like some to his wife, shows Rochester walking out when a woman tried to criticize him, threatening to remain away from her for as long as she persisted, then cajoling her with indirect promises to make amends. He would be kind to Barry's friends, no one of whom was closer than her champion, Mrs. Gwyn.

During the previous year after Lady Cleveland's departure for France, Nelly had been vying with the Duchess of Portsmouth for the position of the King's chief mistress. Lodged in her own house in Pall Mall, given a place in the Queen's Privy Chamber, and paid a pension far less than Portsmouth's, Nelly longed to secure the future of her sons fathered by the King with titles for herself and them.[29] Having gotten her older son provisionally made the Earl of Burford, she approached Danby early in 1677 about being made a countess and was stiffly rebuked. Consequently, her ties with his enemies in the Country Party grew stronger.[30]

In April 1677, Rochester provided financial services for Nelly. Ireland was "a happy hunting ground for courtesans" since "as the result of war, rebellion, and Cromwell's colonizing, there were many estates with clouded titles."[31] Charles gave Nelly a warrant for one such property, reversion of the estate of a Mr. Holywood, a forty-year-old man with no heirs. On April 13, Rochester petitioned in Nelly's name for a 900-year reversion with a *caveat* by "Gwynne." Lest the Irish Claims Court act against her, he wrote an urbane letter to Arthur Capel, the Earl of Essex and Lord Lieutenant of Ireland, on April 22, soliciting his interference and hinting at a bribe. Nelly was granted her claim in November 1677.[32] For a few months at least, Rochester, back in her good graces, worked harmoniously with Nelly to effect Buckingham's release from the Tower.

Pleading that the "dirty, stinking air" of the Tower affected their health, the four Country peers petitioned for respite.[33] The elderly Wharton was given leave until Parliament reconvened on May 21. Working with Sackville, Buckingham drew up a petition and sent a signed copy of it to Rochester with

The Sculpters part is done the featuires hitt
P.Lely Pinxit. *of Ma:am Gwin No Arte can shew her Will,* *g Valck Sculp dex*

Figure 21. Nell Gwyn. Engraving by George Valck after portrait by Sir Peter Lely. National Portrait Gallery, London. Reproduced by permission.

a covering letter begging him to "loose noe time in making use of the Kings good nature and kindness."[34] Even though Sackville Lord Middlesex (and perhaps Rochester) presented it in person, the King refused Buckingham's petition in May because it was not capitulative enough by the "rules" for pardon established by Danby and the Lords. A letter of June 14 from Thomas Sprat to Middlesex shows that they and Buckingham's secretary, Matt Clifford, steadily continued their efforts for the Duke.[35] Then, on June 21, Buckingham's revised plea for a "change of air" because of a "growing distemper prevailing every day more and more" gained him two days to visit Cliveden through the intercession of Nell Gwyn. Later, the Duke was freed for a month. In July he wrote a letter to Rochester from Cliveden, sending him a present of two large carp, reporting that he was "very busy drinking your Lordships health," awaiting "your Lordships and Mrs. Nellis Commands," and vowing he was "more than any man living" Rochester's most humble and faithful servant.[36]

The confederacy of Nelly, Rochester, and Middlesex succeeded through a strategy of appeasement by cooperation and amusing the King. A letter from Andrew Marvell dated August 7, 1677, provides details.

> The D: of Buckingham petitioned only that he had layd so long, had contracted severall indispositions and desired a moneths aire. This was by Nelly, Midlesex, Rochester, and the merry gang easily procured with presumption to make it an intire liberty. Hereupon he layd constantly in Whitehall at my L: Rochester's lodgings leading the usual life. The D: of Yorke, the Treasurer [Danby] and, they tell me too, the D: of Munmouth, remonstrated to the King that this was . . . to suffer his authority to be trampled on but if he had a fauor for [Buckingham] he might do it in a regular way &c. Neverthelesse it was for some days a moot point betwixt the Ministers of State and the Ministers of Pleasure who should carry it. At last Buck. was advertised [*sic*] that he should retire out of Whitehall. He obeyd and since presented they say a more acknowledging Petition . . . whereupon I heare that he was yesterday by the same Rule dismissed.[37]

When Buckingham withdrew from Rochester's lodgings at Whitehall, he simply moved into Nelly's house at Pall Mall, where the King visited every day and was vastly amused by the Duke mimicking Danby and Nelly impersonating Lady Danby.[38]

His exertions on Buckingham's behalf did not co-opt Rochester's other interests. On May 12, 1677, young Charles Davenant, the nominal co-manager of the Duke's Theatre, saw his musical oleo, *Circe*, performed. This "peculiar redaction of the Iphigenia in Taurus story," ostensibly an opera, boasted an Epilogue by Rochester.[39] Although he had scorned similar fare, Rochester did a favor for the son of an old friend by writing an amusingly sophistical epilogue damning "impotent" "dull" critics rather than praising the play itself. Equating critics ("these Enemies of Wit") with the enemies of ladies, whom *Circe* pleased, Rochester concluded smoothly:

> Our Poet the Dull herd no longer fears.
> What e'er his fate may prove, 'twill be his pride
> To stand or fall, with Beauty on his side.

On May 21, Parliament reconvened and the peers adjudged a dispute between the Earl of Rutland and a man of whom Rochester's coterie were growing increasingly contemptuous: the unfortunate Sir Carr Scroop.[40] Short, homely, squinting Sir Carr affected to be a *beau garçon* with most lamentable results. Scroop not only had foolish affairs with Lady Castlemain and the wanton Carey Frazier but was Nelly's sometime lover in 1677, helping stir up trouble between Gwyn, Rochester, and Mrs. Barry.[41] Inevitably, Rochester despised his fellow alumnus of Wadham College. In 1676, Scroop had contributed the Prologue and a "Song" to Etherege's portrait of Dorimant, the *faux* Rochester in *The Man of Mode*, even as Rochester was describing Scroop as a silly, "purblind knight" in *An Allusion to Horace*.[42] Scroop celebrated his wooing of Carey Frazier later in 1676 with a love song, "I cannot change as others do":

> I cannot change as others do
>   Though you unjustly scorn
> Since that poor *Swayne* that sighs for you
>   For you alone is born.
>
> No *Phillis*, no, your heart to move,
>   A surer way I'll try
> And to revenge my slighted love
>   Will still love on, will still love on, and dye.

Rochester parodied it mercilessly.

> I swive as well as others do,
>   I'm young, not yet deform'd,
> My tender heart, sincere and true,
>   Deserves not to be scorn'd.
>
> Why *Phillis* then, why will you swive
>   With *Forty Lovers* more?
> Can I (said she) with *Nature* strive,
>   Alas I am, alas I am a Whore.[43]

After such an attack, Scroop could not doubt that the "silly purblind knight" was a reference to him. He retaliated with *In Defence of Satire*, giving a rationale for satire that resembled Rochester's own:

> Nothing helps more than *Satyr*, to amend
> *Ill Manners*, or is trulier *Virtue's Friend*.

In an imitation of Horace's Fourth Satire, he castigated a series of character-types (the Fop, the Buffoon, the Cuckold) and two specific targets: Grandio

(Mulgrave) and the "top *Fidler* of the *Town*" (Rochester).[44] So began a series of vitriolic exchanges that peaked in the summer of 1677.

When Parliament adjourned on May 28, it was due to reconvene on July 16, and Rochester remained in town. On June 6, he was dining in the Mall, not far from Nelly's house, when a quarrel erupted and a French cook was stabbed. The violent Lord Lumley was on the scene, but rumor accused Rochester of the stabbing. Concerned at his blackening reputation, he asked Harry Savile to write to his brother Halifax for help in quelling the rumor in Yorkshire.[45] To add to his uneasiness, the pregnant Mrs. Barry asserted her independence by acting in Thomas Porter's *The French Conjurer* in June.

Rochester vented his frustrations with a lampoon on Scroop, *On the Suppos'd Authour of a Late Poem in Defence of Satyr.* Beginning with the familiar paradox that Scroop was a satire on himself and his person was God's own satire on man, Rochester compared his victim to an ape, "Fram'd for meer sport," then an ass, "A lump deform'd, and shapeless wert thou born."[46] A catalogue of oxymorons follows:

> Curse on that silly hour, that first inspir'd
> Thy madness, to pretend to be admir'd;
> To paint thy grizly *Face*, to dance, to dress,
> And all those Awkward *Follies* that express,
> Thy loathsome Love, and filthy daintiness.
> Who needs will be an Ugly *Beau-Garcon*,
> Spit at, and shun'd by ev'ry *Girl* in *Town.* . . .

After jibes that all women, including prostitutes, are repelled by Scroop, the satire concludes:

> Half-witty, and half-mad, and scarce half-brave,
> Half-honest (which is very much a *Knave*.)
> Made up of all these Halfs, thou can'st not pass
> For anything intirely, but an *Asse.*

The hapless Scroop unwisely composed a retort:

> Raile on poor feeble Scribbler, speake of me,
> In as bad Terms as the World speakes of thee . . .
> Thou canst blast noe Mans Fame with thy ill word,
> Thy Pen is full as harmlesse as thy Sword.

And received another blast from Rochester for his trouble.

As he had before, Rochester found a satiric context and a pseudonym for his victim in Shadwell's *The Sullen Lovers*, in which the comedian James Noakes had acted the role of Ninny, "A conceited Poet, always troubling men with impertinent Discourses of Poetry, and the repetition of his own Verses."[47] "On Poet Ninny" took up Scroop's charges that the world scorned Rochester and that Rochester's satire was innocuous, turning the screw on Scroop himself as a poetic simpleton and fool:

> Crusht by that just contempt his Follys bring
> On his Crazd Head, the Vermin faine would sting;
> But never Satyr did soe softly bite,
> Or gentle George, himself, more gently write.

Rochester renewed his charges of Scroop's ugliness and dual, ambiguous nature.

> Thou canst not e'en offend, but with thy face:
> And dost at once, a sad Example prove,
> Of harmlesse Malice, and of hoplesse Love.
> All Pride, and Uglinesse! Oh how wee loath,
> A nauseous Creature soe compos'd of both! . . .
> For of all Folly, sure the very topp,
> Is a conceited Ninny, and a Fopp . . .
> The worst that I cou'd write, wou'd be noe more,
> Then what thy very Friends have said before.

Whether this silenced homely Sir Carr for good is not clear; no rejoinders from him are known. But hints about his "hopeless Love" and "very Friends" using the terms of "Poet Ninny" to describe him were confirmed some months later. Scroop began to importune Mrs. Nelly, saying "he could not live always at this rate." Nelly found him "a little uncivil" for an "Ugly *Beau-Garçon*" and turned him away, later telling Laurence Hyde she had "utterly lost Sir Carr Scroop, never to be recovered again."[48] Pall Mall was a rather dismal place without his amusing presence, but Nelly was never one to pine for long.

Rochester was in London more or less steadily in June and July 1677, trying to release Buckingham and placate Mrs. Barry. He was more successful at the former. After Buckingham's two-day reprieve at Cliveden ca. June 21–23, he probably spent the first days in July with Rochester at Whitehall. This was an appropriate time for Buckingham to join in the satiric assaults on Scroop with "A Familiar Epistle to Mr. Julian Secretary of the Muses," which dubbed Scroop "Knight o'th' wither'd Face" and jeered at his cowardice:

> His Brother Murder'd, & his Mother Whor'd
> His Mistresse lost, & yet his Pen's his Sword.[49]

By mid-July, Buckingham had returned to Cliveden, leaving Rochester and Nelly in the city. By August 1 or so, when the result of his final petition was

still unknown, he wrote to Rochester again, voicing his concern with the growing strength of the King's cabinet-ministers. By August 11, Rochester was at
Woodstock and Buckingham, pardoned, was back in London. Shaftesbury,
however, remained in the Tower for a year.[50]

Before leaving the city, Rochester tried repeatedly to cajole his pregnant
mistress. Her habitual jealousy and fear were increased by her forced retirement from the stage and thus her greater dependence on him. His every action,
he assured her in a letter, was intended to provide her "the strongest security
our frail and daily changing frame can give."[51] But Mrs. Barry suspected him
of seeing other women, dining in the company of several at once, and she
found fault with his love letters. When they met, neither was able, or willing,
to confront the other directly, a pattern Rochester also followed with his wife.
He resorted as usual to inked charm:

> I fear staying at home so much gives you the spleen, for I am loathe to
> believe 'tis I. I have therefore sent you the two plays that are acted this
> afternoon—if that diversion could put you into so good a humour as to
> make you endure me again, I should be very much obliged to the stage.
> However, if your anger continue, show yourself at the play that I may look
> upon you and go mad. Your revenge is in your own eyes and if I must suf-
> fer, I would choose that way.[52]

Barry remained truculent, and when Rochester left for the country in August
1677 to be gone for the last four months of her pregnancy and delivery, it was
a deadening blow to their four-year liaison. Rochester's prolonged stay in
Oxfordshire owed to many circumstances, among them family duties, convivial
reunions at Woodstock, and relapses in health. After his tempestuous relations
with a mistress, the domestic scene at Adderbury was a welcome change. His
marriage was serene for the time being; Elizabeth Rochester was "my deare
Wife" instead of an ironic "Y^r L^{sp}" and her husband's mood returned to loving if teasing fondness.

Rochester resumed his fatherly duties. His son Charles was almost seven
years old: a fair-haired, brilliant boy praised by his father's associates. The
Duke of Monmouth, struck by his beauty during a visit to Woodstock, reportedly
gave him the present of a fine horse.[53] And Robert Whitehall, possibly hoping
to become his governor, gave Charles a copy of his *Exasticon* (1677), illustrated
Biblical events taken from Dutch drawings, to which Whitehall added ostensibly
"pious" verses of his own making. There were only twelve copies of the *Exasticon*.
Anthony Wood dipped his pen in acid and wrote of them:

> [Whitehall] caused each to be richly bound, and afterwards presented a
> very fair copy to the King, and the rest mostly to persons of quality: of

which number was *Charles* son and heir of *Joh. Wilmot* Earl of Rochester, for whom he pretended 'twas chiefly compos'd.[54]

We may wonder what young Charles (and his father!) made of such pieties as this beneath a picture of Lot chatting with two visiting angels in Sodom:

> *Lot* entertains two Angels, and next morn
> *Unnatural Sodom* and *Gomorrah* burn,
> As soon as he (in hast) was got to *Zoar*
> They are calcin'd that burnt in lust before:
> The Law denouncing sentence *let him die*
> *Hell* falls from *Heaven* to punish *Sodomie.*[55]

Not trusting to Whitehall's rhymes to educate Charles, Rochester engaged a tutor—probably Thomas Smith, B.A. Oxon—whom he sent to Adderbury, provided with a letter admonishing Charles to study hard, obey his parents and tutor, and to love and serve God.[56] Only four years later in 1681, little Charles, frail in health due to Rochester's diseased legacy, fulfilled his father's reported prayer that his son might not live to become a debauched man like himself. He died, "although scarce ten years old [but] of parts beyond twenty."[57]

Rochester spent most of the time from August 1677 to January 1678 at Woodstock, with intermittent trips to Adderbury. On August 11, Buckingham wrote, urging him to return to Whitehall before "the King comes to Towne" from a sea cruise. Enemies seizing on their recent activities as satirists were trying to foist "a new Treasonable lampoone" on Rochester as its author.[58] Buckingham proposed that he and "Mr. Sheapheard" visit Woodstock to provide details too compromising to trust to paper. Sir Fleetwood Shepherd, "a debauchee and atheist, a grand companion with Charles Lord Buckhurst, Sedley, Buckingham, Rochester, Henry Savile and others," had become tutor to Nell Gwyn's younger son, Lord Beauclerc, in 1676 and was much involved with the political as well as poetical concerns of Rochester's clique.[59]

In reply, Rochester sent a "kinde letter" inviting Buckingham to Woodstock, which prompted the Duke to express his affectionate gratitude somewhat fulsomely on August 19:

> I doe assure your Lordship that I hartily love you, and shall doe soe till the last minute of my life; and nothing is truer then what is elegantly expressed in a frensh song: Le plaisir est extresme, daymer et destre aymé, quand on ayme.

A visitor to Cliveden, Mr. Pome, had provided some silly advice on breeding carp. Buckingham mocked him commenting:

> I wish with my all my hart that hee and our grand Politicians were always to goe together in couples; for it is a very great pitty that persons of such extraordinary parts showld euer bee parted. Hee is as angry against Lampoons as they, and as much affrayed of them, though he does not deserue them soe well, for hee is a foole that only makes one laugh; the others make one cry too, which, that it may come to bee theyre turnes to doe in Gods propper time is the harty wish of
>
> . . . Buckingham.[60]

He would get in touch with Fleetwood Shepherd and Sackville and let Rochester know when to expect them.

Rochester's correspondence with Mrs. Barry was more limited. In an undated letter he expressed uneasiness at not hearing from her. He was "unsatisfied yet why that inconsiderable service you gave me leave to do you, and which I left positive orders for when I came away, was left unperformed." He thought at times it might be best (he said, posturing) if she should quite forget him, but it troubled him vastly that she might think ill of him or remember him only to hate him. "Command some real service and my obedience will prove the best reward my hopes can aim at."[61] If Barry did request his service, it was not given; and Nelly Gwyn resumed her indignant stance as champion of the abused mistress, criticizing Barry's lover to the King.

After waiting some days for Shepherd and Sackville to join him, Buckingham wrote on October 8 to say they had failed him. After a mock-pretentious, nonsensical opening, the Duke said he would "imediatly wayte upon [Rochester], with the best pack of Hownds that euer ran upon English soil" with his leave. However, not knowing how long the Earl's "occasions" would keep him at Woodstock, Buckingham requested that he inform the letter-bearer "whither it would not bee inconuenient at this time to receiue a visit."[62]

Evidently it was. A week later on October 16, Harry Savile returned to London to hear "the scurvy report of [Rochester] being very ill." Reports said he had run naked with some companions on a Sunday at Woodstock, appalling churchgoers. Feigning shock, Savile wrote to ask after his health. Had Rochester really shed his prudence with his breeches? A reply came speedily.

> Though I am almost blind, utterly lame, and scarce within the reasonable hopes of ever seeing London again, I am not yet so wholly mortified . . . not to be extremely revived at the receipt of a kind letter from an old friend who . . . can love a man whom it is the great mode to hate. Catch . . . Sir Carr [Scroop] at such an ill-bred proceeding and I am mistaken. For the hideous deportment which you have heard of concerning

running naked . . . we went into the river somewhat late in the year and
had a frisk for forty yards to dry ourselves.

He reminded Savile of their own naked romp around Rosamond's fountain
the previous year and concluded with *double entendres* about buggery, William of
Orange, and himself. The message was carried by James Paisable, Rochester's
musician-Ganymede, who had diverted the invalid with his tunes. Rochester
recommended him and his airs to Savile and the King.[63]

His nude escapade was less the cause of the convalescent's blindness and
lameness than the fact that he was well into the tertiary stage of syphilis.[64]
When both he and Savile were venereally afflicted later, their letters in 1678
sustained the tone of ironic, self-mocking complaint sounded in this letter.
Rochester's note to Elizabeth Barry in the fall of 1677 was more calculatingly
pathetic:

Madam,
This is the first service my hand has done me since my being a cripple,
and I would not employ it in a lie so soon; therefore, pray believe me sincere when I assure you that you are very dear to me; and as long as I live,
I will be kind to you.
P.S. This is all my hand would write, but my heart thinks a great deal
more.[65]

Rochester may have exaggerated the severe state of his health to both Savile
and Barry. Savile remarked in his next letter: "I was mighty glad to find a man
both lame and blind could bee soe merry."[66] In any case, Rochester was sufficiently recovered by late October to host a jovial crew. The delayed visit by
Buckingham, his pack of hounds and others began about October 20 and
lasted two weeks. On November 5, a letter-writer reported: "The D. of
Buck . . . has been at Woodstock with the E. of R., and other nobles, this fortnight." After the group dispersed, Buckingham went to Oxford in his role of
Alderman Georgy, hoping to gain support for the Country Party in another
effort to dislodge Danby.[67]

Word of the Woodstock gathering spread in London; and when a new "libell"
began to circulate, Harry Savile suspected it a product of the Wilmot/Villiers
reunion. On November 1 he wrote a veritable gazette of news.[68] Will Fanshaw's
hemi-demi-semi-royal wife had given birth to a daughter, and the question of
who would be godfather provided much sport for Savile. The Duke of
Monmouth did not admit his connection to Mrs. Fanshaw, refusing to hold his
"niece" up to the font. And Nell Gwyn told Will not to spend all his money on
the christening but to use some to replace his odorous shoes and wig. William
of Orange had married the Princess Mary, but only the Queen knew "how

many times the first night."[69] Harry Killegrew had been a widower for two days and regretted only that fortune made it possible for him to play the fool again. Old Edmund Waller had celebrated the royal wedding with verse tributes, copies of which Savile meant to enclose so Rochester could "judge whether the old Gentleman stinke in the sockett, or blaze a little yett." More Court gossip followed; then Savile concluded, saying the atmosphere was ripe for Wilmot's return, "though upon croutches," to Court; Harry urged him to do so.

Rochester wrote in response to Savile's news. Why should Rochester be sad because of his "lean arms, small legs, red eyes and nose," particularly when he received a fine letter from Mr. Savile full of wit and good nature, "two qualities able to transport my heart with joy. . . ." He asked for a copy of the verses on "the present poets . . . He cannot want wit utterly that has a spleen to those rogues, though never so dully expressed."[70]

On November 6, Savile sent the promised verses. Lines urging that he come quickly to town to "make amends" were cut out of the preserved letter by someone. Probably they gave details about Rochester's enemies at Court who had begun to prevail again. Chit-chat about various peers concluded with these telling words:

> Pray, my deare Lord, let's heare some good newes of your recovery which would bee welcome to many good people, though it may bee some dull ones had rather heare of your funeral. . . .[71]

Reports in London claimed Rochester would be in town almost any day, but continuing bad health kept him in the country. On December 17, 1677, Savile wrote to ask about him, "your health beeing what I am most concerned for when I have not your company." The latest news followed. Fleetwood Shepherd was run under the eye with a sword, trying to part Henry Bulkeley and George Etherege "squabbling in a Taverne," then broke his head when his coach overturned at Matt Clifford's funeral. War talk against France dominated at Court while Barillon, the French ambassador, stood neglected. Savile then imparted a bit of information in a most blasé way:

> The greatest newes I can send you from hence is what the King told mee last night, that your LP has a daughter borne by the body of Mrs. Barry of which I give your honour joy. I doubt shee dos not lye in much state, for a friend and protectrice of hers in the Mall was much lamenting her poverty very lately not without some gentle reflexions on your LPs want either of generosity or bowells toward a lady who had not refused you the full enjoyment of all her charmes.

He then smoothly went on to report other recent developments. The Duchess of Portsmouth had been seriously ill but recovered. Rumor said she had promised the Virgin Mary to become a nun if she grew well again. She was leaving for France on March 10, and the Court was buzzing with tales she would never return to England. A troop of seaborne French comedians had been blown off course to England and were acting at Whitehall temporarily. Among them was Françoise Pitel:

> a young wench of fifteen who has more beauty and sweetnesse then ever was seen upon the stage since a friend of ours [Barry] left it. In good earnest you would bee delighted above all things with her, and it were a shame to the nation shee should carry away a maydenhead shee pretends to have brought. . . .

The King yearned to have her but said that only the wealthy Sir George Downing or Lord Ranelagh could afford her. Sir Robert Shirley, without bribing anyone, had actually been appointed to Parliament (which would meet next month); Savile closed with compliments and flourishes.[72]

In the last days of 1677, Rochester languished at Woodstock; but he managed letters to his mistress, nephew, and wife in styles wooing, avuncular, and uxorial. He sent a box of "trifles" for Barry to use in her lying in: "Sick and in bed as I am, I could come at no more of 'em; but if you find 'em, or whatever is in my power, of use to your service, let me know."

> Your safe delivery has delivered me too from fears for your sake, which were, I'll promise you, as burthensome to me as your great-belly was to you. Everything has fallen out to my wish, for you are out of danger and the child is of the soft sex I love.[73]

Apparently he sent no money.

Lord Lichfield had invited his uncle for the Christmas holidays to make peace over the family dispute about Woodstock the previous year. Rochester offered a gracious excuse: The change of weather made it dangerous for a man in his poor health to travel:

> If I am ever soe happy to live wher my inclinations to you may shew themselves, bee assur'd you shall not want very good proofes, how much the memory of y^r father [Frank Lee], the favours of my Lady Lyndsey, (how Long-soever past) y^r own merritt, can oblidge a very gratefull man to bee faithfully sincerely & eternally deare Nephew
>
> Y^r most humble[74]

At his most affectionate, Rochester could not avoid a note of irony in his reference to Lady Lindsey. A message to his wife joked at her perpetual rivalry with the dowager countess.

I have my deare wife sent you some Lamb about an ounce I have sent to my Mother one Westphalia Ham, one joule of Sturgeon & on Christmas day I will send her a very fatt Doe. I feare I must see London shortly, & begin to repent I did not bring you wth mee for since these rake Hells are nott here to disturb us you might have past y^r devotions this Holy season as well in this place as Adderbury. . . .[75]

Rochester's sympathy with his wife's Catholic devotions seems surprising; but it may have been a ploy to soften his imminent departure for London—and Mrs. Barry.

The close of 1677 found Rochester suspended once more between Adderbury and London, wife and mistress, physically degenerating and spiritually disoriented. He could not know that the next thirty months, the remainder of his life, were to prove the most vexing and fearsome of all.

SCURVY ALARUMS (1678)

> But it is a miraculous thing (as the wise have it) when a man
> half in the grave cannot leave off playing the fool and the buf-
> foon. But so it falls out to my comfort. . . .
> —Rochester to Savile (1678)

On January 15, 1678, Parliament convened. Rochester was in his place but not for long; the session was postponed until January 28. He was absent that day and thereafter, sending his proxy on February 16. A letter to Mrs. Barry suggests that he was traveling during those weeks. On February 25 he was present but then he disappeared until April 4. Given his awakened interest in Parliament, its proceedings, and its powers, his steady absence in March could have been due only to a relapse in health, exacerbated by his stormy relations with Elizabeth Barry.[1]

The new father's hopes of seeing his mistress "with all her beauty about her" were rudely dashed.[2] Infuriated by his box of trifles, she told him in no uncertain terms that she regretted their affair, and otherwise poured out her "torment of repentance." Rochester tried to appease her with words. She had taken away the quiet of his life with an "extraordinary" expression of emotions that troubled him greatly to witness. Could not these feelings, "equally cruel and unjust to us both," be allowed to die? They could not—at least so quickly. Barry's continuing refusal made him experience "Anger, spleen, revenge and shame."

> But I thank God I can . . . see very woman in you, and from yourself am
> convinced I have never been in the wrong in my opinion of women. . . .
> You need but continue to make it fit for me not to love you and you can
> never want something to upbraid me with.[3]

The estrangement continued for some time. Although Barry sullenly reaccepted his addresses (probably in February) and Rochester grew fond of his bastard-daughter, also named Elizabeth, mutual anger had become greater than sexual

Figure 22. Elizabeth Barry. D. Knight after portrait by Sir Godfrey Kneller. National Portrait Gallery, London. Reproduced by permission.

attraction or financial expectations. The note of *odi et amo* in this letter was prophetic.

His determination to regain Mrs. Barry's sexual favors made Rochester jeopardize his wife's good graces and the mutual harmony they had enjoyed for so long. His paternal fondness—or guilt—aroused, he sent gifts to his two old-est legitimate children, Anne and Charles, but he unwisely used the services of one of Barry's counselors (the "lean lady," perhaps) to deliver them. She carried a letter to Lady Rochester, together with one of King Charles's water spaniels for young Charles Wilmot and an elegant French doll for his older sister:

> Madam,
> This illustrious personage is my ambassador to my son and daughter. The presents she brings are great and glorious and I hope will gain her an equal reception. To my son she will deliver a dog of the last litter of lap-dogs so much reverenced at Indostan for the honour they have to lie on cushions of cloth of gold at the feet of the Great Mogul. The dog's name is Omrah. To my daughter I have sent the very person of the Duchess la Vallière, late mistress to the King of France, dried up and pined away to a very small proportion by fasting.[4]

The children duly received their presents—later in 1678 Charles was painted with Omrah—and Lady Rochester received the emissary with a cordiality that encouraged the visitor to divulge some salient details about the Earl, his kept woman, and their love child. Rochester reported the results to Mrs. Barry.

> My omitting to write to you all this while were an unpardonable error. . . . But I have never been two days in a place since Mrs._____ went away, which I ought to have given you notice of and have let you know that her crime was making her court to [Lady Rochester] with stories of you, entertaining her continually with the shame she underwent to be seen in the company of so horrid a body as yourself in order to be obtaining of her [Ladyship's] employment, and lastly that my [legitimate] daughter Betty was ten times prettier than that nasty B[astard] I was so fond of at London, which I had by you. This was the grateful acknowledgments she made you for all your favours, and this recompense for all the little services which upon your account she received from
> Your humble servant, etc.[5]

This letter failed to ingratiate the writer with its recipient. Its barely concealed hostility provoked Mrs. Barry into greater anger toward the father of her child, who then became the focus of a vengeful competition.

Her long-dormant jealousy flared up again in Lady Rochester. (In typical duality, Rochester had a wife, mistress, and legitimate and bastard daughters all named Elizabeth.) She resolved to confront him with her displeasure at his infidelities. She so informed him, to which he replied with paradoxical wit, irony, and the same misogyny he displayed to his mistress. He had never been transported with great admiration for "Heroick resolutions in woemen," he told her, and he had "noe very greate estime for a high spirited Lady." The oppositions of heat and cold were like virtue ("that sparke of primitive grace") and vice ("that seede of originall sin"), which were mixed in men and women, who otherwise would be "perfect angells, or absolut divills." People were called good or bad by the "preheminence" of their qualities:

> [B]ut yett as contrarietyes though they reside in one body, must they ever bee opposite in place, thence I inferr that as heate in the feete makes cold in the head, soe may it bee wth probabilyty expected too, that greatenes & meaness should bee as oppositely seated, & then a Heroick head is liker to bee ballanc't wth an humble taile; besides reason, Experience has furnish'd mee with many Examples of this kinde: my Lady Morton, nell [Gwyn], Villers [Duchess of Cleveland] & twenty others, whose honour was ever soe exessive in theire heads that they suffered a want of it in every other part. . . .[6]

He would be sorry if any of his "friends" adorned their other perfections with "that most transcendent Accomplishment." With a parting, ironic dismissal of the "waiting gentlewoman" whose "gentil convers" had incited Lady Rochester to her show of high spiritness, her husband assured her of "all the dotage in the world." Then, "downe att the bottom wth a greate space betweene" his reprimand and the postscript, he told her he had too much respect to come near her "whilst I am in disgrace, but when I am a favorite againe I will waite on you."

His long-suffering wife had little choice but to accept John Wilmot as he was. She allowed his bastard daughter to be raised on their estate at Enmore when he took the nineteen-month-old away from his former mistress; and the life income he bequeathed to her in his will was assured by his wife's properties. Lady Rochester may even have permitted her own children to associate with their half-sister: Mallet Wilmot maintained a cordial friendship as an adult with her father's one-time mistress.[7]

While personal affairs occupied Rochester, public events and private plots were readying the major crises of 1678–80. On February 18, 1678, Parliament voted one million pounds to support a war. A pamphlet by Andrew Marvell, *An Account of the Growth of Popery*, attacked Danby, arguing that he conspired to bring in Popery and arbitrary government. The army raised for the war against France would further these aims. Several days later, Shaftesbury was finally released from the Tower.[8]

At court, Henry Coventry resigning the lucrative post of Secretary of State led to a scramble. Ralph Montagu, Ambassador to France, wanted it; but Nelly, Buckingham, Harry Savile, and Lawrence Hyde formed a plan of their own. Coventry would sell the post to Hyde for £10,000 and Hyde would sell his post as Master of the Robes to Savile (Coventry's nephew), but Savile first needed to sell his place as Groom of the Bedchamber to get the money. He appealed to his former (and Montagu's recent) mistress, the Duchess of

Cleveland, to persuade the king to let him do so. In the thick of all this was Nelly, who allied herself with Hyde, the "Country" cause, and Buckingham, who aimed for reinstatement as a Groom of the Bedchamber.[9]

As these plots went on, the brawls of Philip Herbert the Earl of Pembroke were attracting ever greater attention. In January, Pembroke was committed to the Tower "for uttering such horrid and blasphemous Words, and other Actions proved upon Oath, as are not fit to be repeated in any Christian Assembly."[10] After petitioning both the Lords and the King, he was freed but soon after, on February 2, without any provocation, Pembroke viciously beat up a complete stranger in the Strand. Hauled before the Lords, he was reproved then released.

The next day, Sunday, Pembroke went drinking in a Haymarket tavern, where he compelled an acquaintance, Nathaniel Cony, and Cony's companion, Henry Goring, to join him. After several hours of steady drinking, Pembroke quarreled with Goring and threw a glass of wine in his face. Goring drew his sword but was hustled out by a burly drawer (bartender) and some helpers. Then, without provocation, Pembroke struck Cony, knocking him to the floor; and as Cony lay stupified, the Earl repeatedly kicked him in the head, stomach, and back. Rescued at last, Cony lingered for six days then died on February 10. The following day, Pembroke was indicted for felony and murder. Tried by a Middlesex court headed by Justice Edmund Berry Godfrey, he was found guilty and sent to prison to await judgment by his peers in the House of Lords.[11]

Dryden, meanwhile, took revenge on his aristocratic critics. His long-suppressed anger was vented in the Dedication to *All for Love*, published in February. Inscribing the Roman tragedy to the Lord Treasurer Danby, Dryden again exercised his propagandistic talents in the cause of His Sacred Majesty and his cabinet.[12] Perhaps hoping for Danby's support, Dryden unleashed an assault on Danby's Parliamentary opponents: those who would subvert the government (Buckingham, Shaftesbury), those who confused Treasury procedures (Sir Robert Howard), and the friend of these traitors (Rochester). Given its contexts, Dryden's attack on Rochester had political as well as personal and literary dimensions. He wanted to demolish Wilmot's public credibility as well as his literary reputation.

Commencing with a reference to Shakespeare's version of the Anthony-Cleopatra story, the polemic glanced at other "wits" who had "treated" the classical lovers (Sedley) and asserted Dryden's own historical accuracy and superiority:

> I . . . have drawn the character of *Anthony* as favourably as *Plutarch*, *Appian*, and *Dion Cassius* would give me leave; the like I have observed in Cleopatra. . . .

The polemicist then narrowed his attention to "those allowed for witty men," especially those who set themselves up falsely as critics and composers of tragedy. After some general asperities, he aimed at the author of *An Allusion to Horace* and *Valentinian*.

> Men of pleasant Conversation (at least esteemed so) and indued with a tri-fling kind of Fancy, perhaps helped out with some smattering of Latin, are ambitious to distinguish themselves from the Herd of Gentlemen, by their Poetry. . . . And is not this a wretched affectation, not to be contented with what Fortune has done for them, and sit quietly with their Estates, but they must call their Wits in question, and needlessly expose their nakedness to public view? . . . If a little in discourse has passed them on us for witty men, where was the necessity of undeceiving the World? . . . Nero had the same longings, but with all [his] power [he] could never bring [his] busi-ness well about . . . Maecenas took another course. . . . But they who should be our patrons are for no such expensive ways to fame. . . . Some of their little Zanies yet go farther; for they are Persecutors of Horace him-self, as far as they are able, by their ignorant and vile imitations of him. . . .

With a parting shot at "this legitimate Son of Sternhold"—Sternhold's prose translation of the Psalms of David had been scorned by Rochester himself—and at "hasty" Drudges who write (Shadwell), the Poet Laureate concluded with some lofty assertions.[13] He had imitated the divine style of Shakespeare by abandoning rhyme and writing blank verse in *All for Love*, but had not "servilely followed his Elizabethan predecessor." He concluded, "Yet, I hope I may affirm and without vanity, that by imitating him, I have excelled myself throughout the Play. . . ." Needled out of his usual disdain, and aware that Dryden was denigrating him at the behest of Mulgrave and Danby's syco-phants, Rochester began a contemptuous lampoon:

> —To forme a Plott,
> The blustring Bard whose rough unruly Rhyme
> Gives Plutarch's lives the lye in ev'ry Lyne
> Who rapture before nature does preferr
> And now himself turn'd his own Imager
> Defaceth god's in ev'ry Character.[14]

This fragment was all Rochester put on paper before he suffered a serious relapse in health.

Still furious at the Earl's parsimony and lampoons of him, Dryden contin-ued his attack. He provided some Rochesterian details in the "hero" of his "roaring, dirty farce," *The Kind-Keeper; or Mr. Limberham*, acted by the Duke's Players on March 11, 1678.[15] Woodall, a rake newly returned from France (where he learned to act Scaramuchio, and became a devotee of Jean-Baptiste

Lully's music), takes lodgings in a brothel under an assumed identity in order to take "a Ramble in the Town." He masquerades as an Italian merchant in one scene, speaking a pidgin Italian. In another, he is hailed as the "Genius of Whoring" and "worshipped" by male prostitutes in a clearly homosexual context: "the midst of Sodom." Though the play was banned from the stage for its "particular Satyre," Dryden denied he meant anyone specifically but revised the text before printing it. Woodall nonetheless retains many characteristics of the Rochester-persona employed by other satirists.

All the bustle took its toll. Nelly had an "illness" lasting three months. Lady Portsmouth, who vigorously opposed Montagu as Secretary of State, was convalescent until April. Having exerted himself on Buckingham's behalf, Sackville, now Earl of Dorset, avoided the fray by drinking ale all day at the Duke's Playhouse with Fleetwood Shepherd and Tom Shadwell—to the detriment of his health. Harry Savile drank mercury for the pox. And in March 1678, Lord Rochester collapsed onto what he feared was his deathbed.

He lay there until mid-April while the spectres of mortality raised unspeakable terrors. He recalled the deaths of Ned Montagu and George Windham at Bergen and the death pact he made with Windham. Perhaps he envisioned the catacombs of Rome. A strange episode at his mother-in-law Lady Warre's (in 1673?) returned to haunt him. One Saturday night at dinner, a family chaplain who dreamed of his own death was teasingly reminded of it by a young lady, who noticed thirteen were at the table, an omen that one would die soon. The frightened chaplain predicted he would die before long although he was in good health. The family refused to take him seriously, and Lady Warre reproved him for un-Christian superstition. But the chaplain was found dead in bed the next morning, the candle burned down to the socket beside the notes for the sermon he was to give that day.[16] The episode had revived Rochester's childhood fears. In his renewed sickness in March 1678, it was another reminder of the horrors of death.

Gilbert Burnet later described the "agony in his Mind" during "the Sickness which brought [Rochester] so near death before I first knew him, when his Spirits were so low and spent, that he could not move nor stir, and he did not think to live an hour."

> He said, His Reason and Judgment were so clear and strong, that from thence he was fully perswaded that Death was not the spending or dissolution of the Soul; but only the separation of it from matter. He had in that Sickness great Remorses for his past Life . . . general and dark Horrours. . . .[17]

Clergymen came to pray beside him, which he allowed but he did not join in their prayers himself.

His friends gave him support in their own ways. Francis Fane, himself off recovering from syphilis in the country, wrote a flattering Horatian ode: "To the Earl of Rochester, upon the Report of his Sickness in Town."[18] Jack Verney visited him and reported to his father, Sir Ralph, on April 25: "Lord Rochester has been very ill and very penitent, but is now bettering."[19] Harry Savile hovered about and reported on his friend's condition. Young Charles Wilmot wrote a letter to his father and Rochester forced his trembling hand to reply:

> Charles I take itt very kindly that you write to mee (though seldome). . . . Obedience to y^r grandmother & those who instruct you in good things, is the way to make you happy here & for ever, avoyde Idleness, scorne Lying, & god will Bless you, for wch I pray
>
> Rochester[20]

Considering how weak and demoralized he was, Rochester's leaving his bed to vote in Pembroke's trial by the House of Lords on April 4 becomes all the more significant. There was little if anything about Pembroke that could endear him to Rochester: not his coarse stupidity, his unpredictable violence, his ties with Lady Portsmouth, nor his part in previous real estate dealings.[21] In November 1678, he would bodily assault Rochester's dear friend Buckhurst. Rochester must have left his sickbed to vote Pembroke guilty of the charges against him.

When he was conducted into the Lords and the accusation of murder read, Pembroke pled "Not Guilty." A series of witnesses, probably threatened or bought off, then testified that they either failed to see Pembroke strike Cony or saw him only strike but not kick him. When the evidence concluded, the Lords withdrew *in camera* for two hours' debate. By a sizeable majority, they found Pembroke guilty of manslaughter—not murder. He pled the privilege of a statute that declared a peer found guilty might go free for one offense. (A commoner would be burned in the hand and released.) Thus Pembroke got off with paying minor fees and was released to continue his insane mayhem.[22]

Forty peers (probably including Rochester) voted Pembroke guilty of murder, not manslaughter, for reasons suggested by an elliptical account in Latin by the *Journal of the House of Lords*. Although details of the Pembroke case are given in *State Trials*, no mention is made of a deposition by Justice Edmund Berry Godfrey, who presided over Pembroke's conviction by the Middlesex jury in February. The Lords' *Journal*, however, notes the Godfrey deposition, implying it was given *in camera*. (The debate there is not detailed.) Since the evidence in open session would not have warranted a "guilty of murder" verdict, Godfrey's deposition was obviously responsible for persuading forty Lords to find Pembroke guilty of murder. But Pembroke went free; and six months later, on October 17, Sir Edmund Berry Godfrey was found murdered in a ditch near Primrose Hill. His killer has never been identified.[23]

His duty done, Rochester dragged himself back to his bed and several more weeks of suffering and despair. In contrast to those solicitous about him were some who used his illness to exert their spite, including Danby the Treasurer. Rochester told his wife:

> I recover soe slowly, and relaps soe continually that I am allmost weary of myself; if I had the Least strength I would come to Adderbury, but in the condition I am in, Kensington and back is a voyage I can hardly support. I hope you excuse my sending you noe money, for till I am well enough to fetch itt my self they will not give mee a farthing, & if I had not pawn'd my Plate I believe I must have starv'd in my sickness, well god Bless you & the Children whate[ver] becomes of Y[r] humble servant
>
> Rochester[24]

Being forced to pawn his silver or starve may have been an added incentive when Rochester voted to impeach Danby in the year following; but his sickness apparently left him disinclined to waste energy on scribbler-commoners. His answer to Dryden's castigation was left unfinished; and Tom Otway's harsh portrait of him as the vicious Malagene in the "bitter" *Friendship in Fashion* (April 1678) went unnoticed.[25]

For a time, Rochester took a pose of Christian forgiveness. His mood change was noted by Lady Chaworth in late April. She told Lord Roos: "Lord Rochester hath bin att the gates of death, and so penitent that he is upon an amendment, and says he will be an example of penitence to the whole world, and I hope he will be so."[26] When further recovery diminished his pious resolution, restoring his asperity and verbal wit, Rochester's former bursts of savage indignation subsided into resigned, steady cynicism.

As soon as his health allowed, Rochester left London. In early May 1678, Nell Gwyn informed Lawrence Hyde, in Holland as England's ambassador, "My Lord Rochester is gon in the cuntrei." He may have gone first to Somerset to see to business there, but he was at Adderbury by early June. Savile, meanwhile, was recovering from the pox and had plans to marry an heiress. Nelly wickedly told Hyde the bride "wont have too hard a time on't if he holds up his thumb."[27]

On June 2, Savile wrote to Rochester, directing the letter to be held at Banbury until called for. There had been "some scurvy alarums" concerning Rochester's health since leaving town, but Lord Cornwallis had told Savile he was "upon the improving hand." Harry himself had double misfortune, His "venereall paines" had thrown him back to "dry mutton & dyett drinke"; he was in the surgical hands of Dr. Barton. And the King had dismissed him from royal favor for voting in the Commons to censure the Duke of Lauderdale.[28]

Lauderdale was blamed when the English Army delayed going to the Lowlands, as the new Anglo-Dutch Treaty against France required. When Savile came to the Bedchamber to perform his duties after voting against Lauderdale, the King dismissed him in a pale fury. Savile told Rochester, "I have been sacrificed to that filthy dogg Lauderdale." As usual, Charles II was double-dealing: allying England with Holland in wake of the marriage of William and Mary but secretly treating with Louis XIV. His refusal either to declare war or disband the troops led Parliament to vote money on June 4 to disperse what it feared was a standing army and a yacht was sent to bring Hyde back from Holland.

On June 4, Savile wrote again. Will Fanshaw reported that Rochester had recovered beyond any hazard of a relapse, but because of the "many returnes of your disease . . . till you are growne to a considerable strength, wee shall all-wayes thinke you in some danger."[29] Savile engaged in some sallies about Fanshaw, who was suffering from the same malady as Savile and Rochester. A trip to take the waters had done him little good: Fanshaw was still lame, "slen-derer than [Jack] Churchill," and had a mouth twisted by the mercury he had drunk as a curative. Savile was abashed at rallying the hapless Fanshaw, but in his own misery he looked for "something to trihumph over" and "in this case poor Fanshaw is the onely trophy I have in this world."

After some jaunty bits of news about Parliament, Savile wrote: "Your Cosen her Grace of Cleaveland having (as shee thinks) broak the match of her sonn Grafton & gott her sonn Northumberland made Duke prepares for her returne into France on Monday next." With Arlington out of power, Cousin Barbara wanted to end the engagement of young Grafton to "Tata" Bennet. Savile then came to the central purpose of his letter.

In plotting to become Secretary of State, Ralph Montagu had run afoul of both Portsmouth and Gwyn; and he was trying to render them both ineffec-tual. In Nelly's case, through his sister, Lady Hervey, Montagu was promoting sixteen-year-old Jenny Middleton (reputed to be Montagu's natural daughter) as the King's new mistress.[30] The good-hearted but imperceptive Gwyn ("one who is allways your friend and sometimes [especially now] mine") had been wheedled by Lady Hervey into dining with her in the chambers of William Chiffinch, the royal procurer for "Charlemagne." Worried that Nelly was "too giddy to mistrust a false friend" and thus would "pimp against herself," Savile wanted Rochester to intervene in some way to preserve their friend and her power but "I doe not see in y^r present condition how you can make her sen-sible of this, for to write to her were vain." Prudence would dictate silence in this matter, but Savile trusted Rochester "alone of all men living," with this information through "zeale for your service and my trust in your secrecy."

Rochester responded promptly and concisely to the letters of June 2 and 4. Only being very ill would make him lose the opportunity of writing to such a friend as Harry, whom he congratulated on his "glorious disgrace" while wishing for his "happy restoration" to royal favor.

> I would say something to the serious part, as you were pleased to call it, of your former letter. . . . But to confess the truth, my advice to the lady you wot of has ever been this: take your measures just contrary to your rivals . . . you may judge whether I was a good pimp or no. But some thought otherwise and so, truly, I have renounced business; let abler men try it. More a great deal I would say, but upon this subject and for this time I beg this may suffice. . . .[31]

Rochester kept his promise to say a great deal more. When he died, among his papers was a *History of the Intrigues of the court of Charles II,* which his mother and Uncle Walter hastily burned. Probably begun as a series of secret letters to Savile when he was off in France, the *History* certainly was sexual in nature, but it must have been much more.[32] Written during the crucial events of 1678–79, Rochester's eye-witness account of the schemings and plottings behind them would have been of inestimable value as a primary source from the Restoration era. Biographers and historians alike must rue the Dowager Countess's destruction of papers that the Penitent himself spared from his general orders to burn his writings.[33]

On June 15 the affable Savile agreed with Rochester's advice to Nelly:

> I doe very much approve it, and have myselfe been of late soe battered in Politicks that if there bee a man alive who ought to retire from businesse and have noe more civil plotts it is myselfe. . . .

His tone grew sharper when he spoke of Lauderdale, a "dungboate" he hoped would transform into Charon's ferry to Hell. Details followed about doings in Parliament where two of Rochester's kin were entering:

> doubtlesse there may some prudent embers lye hiddenin y^r L^{sp} if you would racke them up which in time might bee of use to your King and Country. . . .[34]

Warmed by the masculine intimacy of their correspondence, Rochester promptly replied to Harry, starting with a reference to Sir John Falstaff in Shakespeare's *Henry IV, Part II*:

> Now, dear Mr Savile, forgive me if I confess that upon several occasions you put me in mind of this fat person. . . . For my own part, I'm taking

> pains not to die without knowing how to live on when I have brought it
> about. But most human affairs are carried on at the same nonsensical rate,
> which makes me (who am now grown superstitious) think it a fault to laugh
> at the monkey we have here when I compare his condition with mankind.[35]

This letter resonates of ambiguous feelings and beliefs voiced three years earlier in the "Satyr" on Man, to which Rochester alludes here. Hedonistic enthusiasm for wine and women is undercut by the appeal to God's mercy and
confession of religious superstition reborn in the fear and remorse of his recent
sickness. The desire to learn how to live after dying led Rochester in coming
months to appeal to such classical free-thinkers as Charles Blount and such
orthodox spokesmen as Gilbert Burnet.

Poor health intensified the urgency of his search. In the portrait painted
later in 1678 by Jacob Huysman, neither his elegant clothes nor supercilious
pose of crowning the monkey with poetic laurels could conceal the phthisic
quality of Rochester's lean arms, watery eyes, and red nose. Even with one
foot in the grave, however, he could not stop being a man of wit or acting the
role of Harlequin, the pathetic clown.[36]

On June 25, Savile wrote another clever letter despite suffering from
"spleentick vapours that make me dislike the world." Nothing pleased his eye
or ears but "a moment's titillation" at French "new Aires" brought over by
Nicholas Staggins, Master of the King's Music. With witty gloom, Savile said:

> I will not say how good a time this is to bee in the country, how good a
> time to be sick, nay how good a time to dye in for fear you should either
> think mee neer my end or beleeve I thaught you soe; and were therefore
> gathering some philosophicall comfort out of Solomon or Seneca or any
> other who has treated de vanitate mundi. . . .

Savile's dual reference to the Biblical Ecclesiastes and Roman Stoic perfectly reflects Rochester's own admixture of Christian and classical thought
and suggests the bond of sympathy between the two friends. Savile concluded
with a denunciation of diseased womankind.[37]

Ten days later, a letter dated July 2 from Leather Lane in Hatton Garden
arrived. The place would inform Rochester why Savile had not written. There
he had "chosen a neate privacy to sweat in" and finish the last act of "a long
teddious course of Physick which has entertained mee ever since December
last." Had he known then what he had learned from "that masse of Mercury
that has gone downe my throat in seven monthes" and been given the choice,
he might have "turnd Turke, [i.e., pederast] notwithstanding all my Zeale for
the true Protestant faith." Wonder of wonders, Rochester's old mistress, Jane
Roberts, was worse off than Savile.

I will not spoyle her story [by] making it worser, or by making your hayre stand on end & hinder anything else from doeing soe for a month after soe tragicall a relation. The other day Mr Fanshaw came and made a third with us. . . .[38]

Rochester must have burst out laughing when he read this. He sketched a romantic parody with the sun gilding "the tops of the palaces in Leather Lane," as the "vile enchanters," the Doctors Barton and Ginman, led "forth their illustrious captives in chains of quicksilver [mercury]" and confined them by charms "to the loathsome banks of a dead lake of diet-drink." Savile would break the silence with a speech, "the most passionate fine things that ever heroic lover uttered." Mrs. Roberts would reply, "softly and sweetly," but be "interrupted by the envious F[anshaw]."

Thus would I lead the mournful tale along, till the gentle reader bathed with the tribute of his eyes the names of such unfortunate lovers—and this, I take it, would be a most excellent way of celebrating the memories of my most pocky friends, companions and mistresses.

Rochester rounded off this sally with a sardonic notation that he was "half in the grave."

I am in a damned relapse brought by a fever, the stone and some ten diseases more which have deprived me of the power of crawling, which I happily enjoyed some days ago. And now I fear I must fall, that it may be ful-filled which was long since written for our instruction in a good old ballad,

But he who lives not wise and sober
Falls with the leaf still in October.

About which time, in all probabilty, there may be a period added to the ridiculous being of

Your humble servant,
Rochester.[39]

On July 13, back at Whitehall and revived in spirits, Savile informed Rochester that he was on his way to Paris in the company of Robert Spencer the Lord Sunderland, Savile's brother-in-law and the new Ambassador Extraordinary to France. Sunderland was replacing Ralph Montagu because of the "terrible doeings att Paris betwixt my Lady Cleaveland and her daughter Sussex" that Savile had recounted in his letter of July 2:

as I am a friend to the family till the story bee more compleate I will not venture at sending you the whole relation, but whilst y[e] Mother was in

England the daughter was debauched by our Embass^dr Mr Montaigue who has lived with her in a most open scandall to the wonder of the French court and the high displeasure of this, the K. being very angry with the Emb^dr and his friends & ennemyes now struggling att Court to support or ruine him, the latter is I thinke the likelyest in every Court.[40]

The struggle at Court and in Parliament was just beginning. Montagu had brought back documents from France that incriminated the King and Danby in their secret negotiations with Louis XIV. Not only was the very future of the House of Stuart at stake; so were the futures of the royal ministers, mistresses, and their foes and friends. But Rochester would not hear of this from Harry. Savile planned to be in France for three weeks. He stayed much longer than that, in time replacing Sunderland as the envoy to France. In his last letter to Rochester in the summer of 1678, he kept their private style of writing:

> Your LP is soe well read, that you can not but have heard of an old Romane Generall, who was recalled from banishment to command at the army. . . . I shall desire y^r LP to let that old Gentleman putt you in mind of mee . . . my stay need not bee long and shall not bee above three weekes, unlesse I can heare that y^r LP will take the advice which all y^r friends would give you, viz. to goe into France, & then I would stay your coming. . . .[41]

Whatever his wishes, Rochester's health kept him in Oxfordshire during August.[42] Beneath the calm of the English summer in 1678, political chaos was brewing; and the nation verged on the worst of storms. A warning of its coming destruction was reported to Sir Ralph Verney on September 12.

> I hear Lord Norrice and Lord Rochester or Lord Lovelace had a quarrel, but it was taken up by my Lord Treasurer.[43]

The perilous balance between Danby the Treasurer and his brother-in-law Norris on the one side, and Lovelace and the Country Party sympathizers on the other, which had been made at the Woodstock Races two years earlier in 1676, was overturned. The opponents were angrily confronting each other. Rochester, predictably, was caught in the middle, his political as well as physical survival at stake.

EXTREMITY ON ALL SIDES (1678–1679)

Is or Is Not, the two great ends of ffate
And True or False the Subject of debate
That perfect or destroy the vast designes of state. . . .
—Rochester, "Upon Nothing"

When he intervened in the quarrel at Woodstock in September, 1678, Danby was deep into political intrigues that trapped and left him powerless.[1] Anti-Catholic feelings, fed by Marvell's pamphlet against him in February 1678, grew in the weeks following as the King wavered between his open treaty with the Dutch and his secret monetary ties to Louis XIV. When the army raised to assist the Dutch left for the Lowlands too late to prevent the French from capturing Ghent and Ypres, Parliament voted funds for its disbandment on June 30. An armistice on May 23 had led Charles and Danby to maintain the standing army while they pressed Louis to accept terms of the Treaty of Nijmegen.[2] As a result, Danby was believed to be working to submit England through military force to absolute monarchism and Popery, one and the same to the Protestant mind.

At the same time, through his fervent Catholic secretary, Edward Coleman, the Duke of York continued a surreptitious correspondence with the French King, intent upon getting funds to bribe members of Parliament who wanted to exclude Catholic heirs from the English throne. These double-dealings began to be hopelessly snarled on August 14, when the King, leaving for Windsor with Nelly Gwyn, sent a Gentleman of the Bed Chamber around to Danby with a packet of papers. These were the forty-three articles concocted by Titus Oates to "prove" that the Society of Jesuits had a plot to murder Charles II. Without knowing it, Danby had been handed the means for his own overthrow.[3]

Titus Oates, co-inventor of "The Popish Plot," was born in 1649, the son of an Anabaptist ex-weaver who took orders in the Anglican church and, in 1660, was given the living of All Saints' in Hastings by Sir Richard Barker, a City physician. As a boy, Titus went to Westminster School, then to Merchant Taylors', but was expelled. In 1667 he was expelled again from Gonville and

The most Noble and Mighty Prince
THOMAS, DUKE OF LEEDS, MARQUIS OF CARMARTHEN, EARLE OF DANBY,
Viscount Latimer, Baron Osborne of Kiveton. L.ᵈ President of His Ma.ᵗⁱᵉˢ most Hon.ᵇˡᵉ Privy Council
L.ᵈ Leiutenant of the three Ridings of Yorkshire, Govern.ʳ of the Town & Fort of Kingston upon Hull
And Knight of the most Noble Order of the Garter.

Figure 23. Thomas Osborne, Earl of Danby, First Duke of Leeds. Engraving by Robert White after portrait by Sir Peter Lely. National Portrait Gallery, London. Reproduced by permission.

Caius College, Cambridge, where he failed to master Latin; despite his phenomenal memory, his tutor called him "a great dunce." He took orders and was given a curacy by Henry Howard, Lord Norwich, and then a living in Kent, but he was ousted for drunkenness, Anabaptist ravings, and "indecent expression" about the Christian mysteries.

Joining his father in Hastings, Titus Oates foolishly accused the son of the prominent Parker family of sodomy and the father of treason. Both were cleared of the charges, whereupon young Parker brought action against him for £1,000 damages and Oates was bound over to Quarter Sessions for perjury. He immediately signed up as chaplain on the frigate *Adventure* in May 1675, leaving for Tangier. On its return, however, he was dismissed and his secret was out: Titus Oates was a practicing homosexual. In 1676 he continued his erratic career in London, where he met the crack-brained Protestant fanatic, Israel Tonge.[4]

Israel Tonge had gone to Oxford as a Puritan; Anthony Wood called him "cynical and hirsute, shiftless in the world." He then attended a new college at Durham, which collapsed in 1659, leaving him adrift to find a clerical living among renewed Anglicanism. In June 1666 he managed to get a parish in London, but his church and living were destroyed three months later in the Great Fire. Cracked and crazed, Tonge began blaming all his ills on the Jesuits, who he was sure had set the fire. After a two-year interval in Algiers, he returned to England and gained for a patron Sir Richard Barker, who had gotten rid of Oates the Elder after a passionate dispute.

Israel Tonge and Titus Oates found much in common; but after a brief stint as chaplain in the family of the Catholic Lord Norwich, Oates converted to Catholicism on March 3, 1677. First, he went to study in Valladolid, Spain, and then St. Omers in northern France. Swiftly ejected at both, he came back to England in June 1678, full of resentment at the Jesuits, and joined up with Tonge, who continued a quixotic campaign to convince Parliament of a Jesuit plot. Oates was able to provide specific details about the Jesuits that could be construed to prove the truth of Tonge's claims; thus an unholy alliance was forged. In due course, Oates wrote out an indictment of the Jesuits, which Tonge managed to present to the King by waylaying him on his morning walk in St. James's Park on August 12, 1678.

Confronted with Tonge's copy of forty-three articles invented under pressure by Oates, the King asked for a summary of its points and Tonge embellished Oates's fantasies: after Charles's death, the Duke of York would come to the throne only to face an uprising of the three kingdoms (orchestrated by the Jesuits) while the country was taken over, piece by piece, by Louis XIV. Charles greatly distrusted this tale but thought it needed investigating and turned the business over to Danby, who began considering how to use it to manipulate Parliament when it met on October 21.

Oates provided further help on August 21 in the form of five forged letters, purportedly written by members of the Plot to Thomas Bedingfield, the Duke of York's Jesuit confessor. These were meant to be intercepted by Danby's agents in the London post office but by mistake were delivered to Bedingfield at Windsor. Upset and apprehensive, he showed them to the Duke of York, who promptly entered the melee.

Danby visited Windsor sporadically in August to report his findings to Charles and he was growing aware of their ominous implications when he went to the Woodstock races on September 12. There he found gathered Norris (his dedicated, Royalist brother-in-law), Lovelace (turned intemperate Whig), and Rochester, still angry from the Lord Treasurer's treatment of him in his late sickness.[5] Suppressed tensions promptly surfaced. The precise nature of the quarrel between Lovelace and Norris is not clear, although it was certainly an extension of the Woodstock dispute; but its consequences were certain: Lovelace lost all his prerogatives in January 1679 and he began criticizing Danby openly in Parliament.[6] It also deeply affected Rochester, as well as his relatives by marriage.

Like Lovelace, Tom Wharton (Norris's brother-in-law, the husband of Rochester's niece Nan) favored Monmouth rather than York as successor to Charles. This and other differences between the husbands of Rochester's two nieces led to a family fight with the Dowager Countess of Rochester, who refused to treat with Norris for three years or more, distressing the gentle Ellen. The Countess' antipathy toward Wharton fed a growing hostility that embittered Nan Wharton in her last years and climaxed when "that vyle man" would not return a miniature portrait of Rochester to his mother.[7]

From the very beginning, the so-called "Popish Plot" affected Rochester's life directly. Any Catholic witch hunt was a threat to Lady Rochester and thus to him. Her persistence in remaining a Catholic troubled Rochester greatly. A glancing reference in a letter to her hints at this:

> If you heare not from mee it is not that I either want time or will to write to you, I am sufficiently at leasure & thinke very often of you, but you would expect an account of w^{ht} has befall'n mee, wch is not yett fitt for you to know, only thus much I will tell you, it was all in vindication of you. . . .
>
> For the Countess of Rochester. . . . wth care[8]

To make matters worse, Stephen College, who had played a part in her conversion in 1667 and then worked on the estate at Enmore, was angry at Rochester. After Rochester fired him there, College roamed around the countryside, drinking and "vilifying" his former master. One Thomas Harris testified that in September 1677, he had talked with College in Glastonbury about Lady Rochester being a papist.[9] Then in 1678 College came to Oxfordshire and resumed his trade of carpentering. He became close friends with Stephen

Dugdale, who was working for Lord Lovelace after being dismissed as Lord Aston's steward for gambling with Aston's money. College and Dugdale often spent the night at Lovelace's country house, Lady Place, sleeping in the same room.[10]

College, "a rash but harmless man . . . with some native wit, spiced with obscenity," was never one to hold his tongue.[11] He was heard to refer to the King as "Old Rowley" (the name of Charles's pet stallion).[12] He fashioned a lashing type of weapon, the "Protestant flail," useful for beating and slashing in mobs. In 1679 he wrote an omnium-gatherum verse, "Truth Brought to Light, or Murder Will Out," which accused the Catholic Howard, Lord Norwich, of complicity in the murder of Sir Edmund Berry Godfrey, together with "dukes, earls, lords, and queens of royal bands" whom College then specifically named: Danby ("treach'rous Tom . . . That Osborne villain"); the Duchess of Portsmouth, Lord Belayse, et al. He also wrote an imprudent satire on Lord Chief Justice William Scroggs, who sustained a "paranoic fear of Catholicism" that led to unrelenting prosecution of any and every one accused of involvement in the Popish Plot.[13]

The danger of loose-tongued College's association with Dugdale became apparent in mid-November 1678, when Dugdale joined Titus Oates in making accusations against aristocratic papists. In December, himself accused of papism, Dugdale testified against his former employer, Aston.[14] Eventually, in 1681, Dugdale testified against Stephen College when, among other charges, College was accused of helping to convert Lady Rochester to Catholicism.[15] There is little doubt that Rochester was fully aware of the threat posed by Stephen Dugdale. His first appearance in the House of Lords was on November 15, 1678, the day of Dugdale's first testimony.

By that time, the "Popish Plot" had caused mass hysteria. On September 6, Titus Oates gave sworn testimony before Justice Edmund Berry Godfrey. After Godfrey disappeared on October 12, he was mysteriously missing until October 17, when his corpse was found in a ditch near Primrose Hill with his own sword run through his body.[16] Rumors spread that Godfrey was murdered by the Jesuits because he had told Edward Coleman, York's Catholic secretary, the content of Oates's deposition. Immediately a host of Protestant zealots, opportunists, and madmen came forth with wild tales of seeing Godfrey murdered at Somerset House (Queen Catherine's residence), helping to murder him, knowing the Queen's Jesuit confessor had planned it all, and so on. From October 1678 until May 1679, London was in a constant panic.[17]

From November 15 to December 9, 1678, Rochester regularly attended the Lords' sessions. On November 18 there was a furor over Godfrey's unsolved murder. On the 19th, Titus Oates was voted a money supply, which Danby

paid immediately. On the 20th, the Catholic Lady Dunbar, the daughter of
Lord Belayse and wife of Rochester's fiery duelist, was forbidden to enter
London save for medical reasons. From November 22 to 27, a series of spiteful domestic servants trooped in to testify that their masters were Catholics and
probably a part of the invidious Plot. This could hardly have been reassuring
to Rochester. On November 20, a day-long debate over the credibility of Titus
Oates took place. (Rochester's stance is not known, although his private opposition to Oates is quite certain.) After more Oates testimony on November 29,
the Lords decided to go through an orgy of oath-swearing to the king and
Protestantism. On December 4, Rochester publicly took the oath.[18]

Reassured that for the time being Oates and his cronies would not accuse
peers other than the relatively feeble Five Catholic Lords of planning to lead
an armed insurrection, Rochester left London after attending his last session on
December 9.[19] His whereabouts from then until March 6, 1679, are unknown;
but he probably divided his time as usual between Adderbury, Woodstock, and
Enmore. He certainly renewed his skeptical examination of Christian beliefs
about the soul and its condition after death. At this period he may have written the anti-Catholic verses titled *"On* Rome's *Pardons"*:

> If *Rome* can pardon Sins, as *Romans* hold. . . .
> Whence came this knack, or when did it begin?
> What *Author* have they, or who brought it in?
> Did *Christ* e'er keep a *Custom-house* for Sin?
> Some subtle *Devil*, without more ado,
> Did certainly this sly invention brew,
> To gull 'em of their *Souls*, and *Money* too.[20]

As the remorse from his relapse in April 1678 had ebbed, he engaged in
conversations with twenty-four-year-old Charles Blount, a self-professed *libertin*,
or free-thinker.[21] Blount's knowledge of Roman history and the classics and his
enthusiasm for the ideas of Thomas Hobbes appealed to Rochester. They met
and talked about Livy, among other topics. Rochester's "candour" encouraged
Blount to expatiate on his own daring views of religion and, in December
1678, to send the Earl a holograph of his tract, *Of the Subversion of Judaism*, and
to write a lengthy letter expanding his views.[22] On February 8, 1679, he sent
a supplementary tract in Latin: an "undigested heap of my father's thoughts
concerning the soul's acting, as it were, in a state of matrimony with the
body."[23] This was a collection of the Ancients' wisdom on the soul after death,
a topic Blount was exploring in his forthcoming *Anima Mundi* or *Soul of the Earth*.

As Rochester and Blount began their correspondence in the winter of
1678–79, the Exclusion crisis continued. The question of who would succeed

Charles II as King had begun to loom on October 31, 1678, when evidence was found in the papers of Edward Coleman, York's secretary,

> that there hath been and still is a damnable and hellish plot contrived and carried on by the popish recusants for the assassinating and murdering the King, and for subverting the government, and rooting out and destroying the Protestant religion.[24]

So declared the House of Commons. Inevitably, suspicion about York's role in all this revived efforts to pass an Act of Exclusion that would remove him as heir to the throne. Alarmed by the threat of a plot, Arthur Capel the Earl of Essex came forward more boldly in the Lords in opposition to the Court; and Halifax, moved by hatred of Danby and by Oates's inflammatory accusations, voted to banish the Queen from Whitehall. Shaftesbury and the Country peers attempted to oust the Duke from the Council at once but were successfully out-maneuvered by Danby and the King in the fall session.[25]

Since Charles II had no legitimate heirs by Queen Catherine, Exclusionists faced the problem of his successor if James was eliminated. James's Protestant daughter Mary and her husband, William of Orange, were possible heirs; however Mary of Modena, James's twenty-year-old wife, might yet produce a Catholic male heir, who would then precede Mary. A better candidate was Charles's oldest bastard son, the Protestant Duke of Monmouth, popular with the rank and file and the King's favorite of all his bar-sinister offspring. Rumors that Monmouth might be legitimized because Charles had secretly married his mother, Lucy Walters, had been around since 1667 and were renewed in 1678, with Shaftesbury acting Achitophel, the false counselor, to Monmouth's Absalom, the ambitious dupe.[26] However, the King stayed loyal to his brother, resisting all efforts to persuade him to declare Monmouth his legal heir. To appease the Opposition, however, Charles agreed to command York to leave the country for a while. James and his wife accordingly left for Holland; on March 3, 1679, Charles declared he had never married anyone but the Queen.[27]

On March 6, Rochester was back in the Lords. His exact views on Exclusion are not documented but those of his nearest relatives are. His mother naturally sided with James, as did the Lichfields. Lady Rochester's stepbrother, Francis Warre, resigned his commission from Monmouth's regiment in 1682 to declare his loyalty to James. Norris, newly made the Earl of Abingdon, led a regiment against Monmouth in the 1685 rebellion. Most tellingly, Rochester's favorite daughter, Elizabeth, worked tirelessly after 1688 to put James II's son on the throne. Her letters to the Stuart Pretender, stating her loyalty, still exist.[28] We may safely infer that Rochester sided with the King and James on the Exclusion issue.

In 1679 he had a vast deal of "business" to occupy his time and energy, aside from the future of the Stuarts. His first day back in the Lords, the peers were informed the King had excluded the Five Popish Lords from the House, and Rochester once more swore his allegiance to the King and the Protestant faith. On March 8, a warning of things to come was given when the King and Danby spoke in turn and the sections of their speeches dealing with popery were "echoed with great hums of applause."[29] Between March 6 and May 27, 1679, Rochester attended fifty-five sessions of the Lords, many lasting all day or well into the evening. Given the perilous nature of the times, he was wise to do so. The furor over the Popish Plot resumed, all the greater because it had claimed the lives of some victims, including Edward Coleman, who thus became a martyr to the Roman Catholic Church. Rochester drolly told his wife:

> I have noe news for you but that London growes very tiresome and I long to see you, but things are now reduc'd to that extremity on all sides that a man dares nott turne his back for feare of being hang'd, an ill accident to bee avoyded by all prudent persons & therefore by
>
> > Y^r humble servant
> > Rochester[30]

Fortunately for him, although he was far from robust, his diseases underwent remission. Burnet said of him:

> He was in the Milk-Diet, and apt to fall into Hectical Fits; any accident weakened him. . . . Yet during his being in Town he was so well, that he went often abroad, and had great Vivacity of Spirit.[31]

The Lords' *Journal* for 1679, together with his letters to Savile, show Rochester at his most politically energetic. On March 11, he resumed his place on the Committees for Privileges and Petitions. And he was caught up in a move to impeach Danby that had begun on December 23 in the Commons after he left for the country.

Following his return in disgrace from France, Ralph Montagu had continued a brazen attempt to get the post of Secretary of State but was fought down by Danby. Danby tried to turn the Popish Plot to his own advantage by adopting anti-Catholic tactics that angered the Duke of York and caused many to suspect that Danby himself was a secret Catholic. In mid-December, 1678, he accused Montagu of secret meetings with a Papal nuncio in Paris. Montagu retaliated by disclosing to Parliament Danby's letters to the French negotiating sizeable subsidies to Charles II. He held back the most damning of these, one bearing Charles's signature of approval; but with becoming modesty and reluctance,

Montagu supplied the others to the members of the Commons. After a stunned pause, they began a raging debate that resulted in a vote to impeach Danby for high treason.[32]

When the bill of impeachment came to the Lords on December 23, the King's and Danby's supporters were able to stave off the Lord Treasurer's doom despite the adversarial efforts of Shaftesbury and Essex. Fearful of the consequences to himself, the King prorogued Parliament on December 30 until February 4, declaring himself "ill-used" by its proceedings. Hopeful that a new Commons might be more manageable, he dissolved it on January 24, 1679. So ended the so-called "Cavalier" Parliament after eighteen years, to the regret of no one. But the new Parliament that convened on March 6 did not strengthen the royal hand. Contrariwise, Danby's impeachment was taken up and vigorously pushed toward an end.[33]

On March 22, Titus Oates made a deposition against Danby, who went into hiding on March 24. On March 26, a bill to disable the Lord Treasurer was brought before the Lords. On April 10, Rochester was placed on a Commission to frame a bill that would prevent Danby and other officials "from taking undue Advantages of their Places." After Danby emerged from hiding and entered the Tower, Rochester was at his hearing before the Lords on April 25, and again on April 28 when York was accused of encouraging the plot, Danby was summoned to the bar, and Titus Oates gave further "evidence" against him.

On May 10 those anxious to get on with the impeachment proposed a conference with the Commons about the trial of peers. The Lords voted "NO," and Rochester signed the Dissent to that vote. He wanted the impeachment to proceed, obviously. He did the same on May 23. The King continued to keep the vote pending, fearful of what Danby might reveal under pressure. The sinister Stephen Dugdale appeared to testify against the Five Popish Lords, then from May 24–27 during the Danby debates, Rochester continued his stand for impeachment: a third "No" vote on trial proceedings found him again dissenting.

Meanwhile, Danby was keeping private lists. The earliest named the Lords "Against mee" ("Shaftesbury . . . Hallifax . . . Wharton . . . Lovelace"). Rochester was "For mee if present in the House." The Treasurer's supporters were to solicit the Lords on this list; the King himself spoke to Rochester on Danby's behalf but to no purpose. Danby's later lists placed an "x" (doubtful) beside Rochester's name; and Rochester's final vote was recorded in Danby's own hand: "Against."[34] Youthful, ambitious John Wilmot may have been the King's creature in the Clarendon impeachment of 1667, but eleven years later the mature Lord Rochester stood his ground.

By 1679 Rochester's relationship with his quondam "father" had reached
the ultimate stage described by Gilbert Burnet:

> He [Charles] loved to talk over all the stories of his life to every new man
> that came about him. . . . He went over these in a very graceful manner,
> but so often, and so copiously, that all those who had been long accus-
> tomed to them grew very weary of them . . . which drew a severe censure
> from Wilmot, earl of Rochester. He said he wondered to see a man have
> so good a memory as to repeat the same story without losing the least cir-
> cumstance, and yet not remember that he had told it to the same persons
> the day before.
>
> The king loved [Rochester's] company for the diversion it afforded, better
> than his person; and there was no love lost between them.[35]

Another of Rochester's relationships had reached the point where no love
was lost. In spite of his threats and cajoling, Mrs. Barry had refused to give in
to Rochester's despotic misogyny. She returned to the stage in April 1678 and
appeared successfully in a series of roles that won her increasing fame and
independence. "Her talent for noble wretchedness" was developing.[36] Indeed,
she was becoming the leading lady of the Duke's Company, with plays written especially for her by the persistent Thomas Otway, among other admirers.
Her liaison with Rochester ended, other would-be "kind keepers" (including
George Etherege) hovered about her; and John Wilmot found himself increasingly annoyed with the lack of prudence shown by the mother of his love child.

When Mrs. Barry ignored his warnings, Rochester reacted typically. As he
had before with his wife and son Charles, he abducted the child. Barry was
acting at Dorset Garden in March, 1679 and therefore not always with her
nineteen-month-old infant. In the afternoon of March 26, after the bill dis-
abling Danby that morning, William Clark, Rochester's steward at Enmore,
appeared before the House of Lords to accuse Luke Hemmings, a constable, of
arresting him "within the Time of Privilege" at the instigation of Elizabeth
Cross, probably the child's wet nurse. Clark had pled the rights of a nobleman's servant to diplomatic immunity, which Hemmings had ignored. At
Rochester's demand, both Hemmings and Cross were arrested. On March 29,
Elizabeth Cross was released with his consent but Hemmings was kept in custody by the Gentleman Usher.[37]

William Clark was one of Rochester's most trusted agents. He had
co-signed the property indenture in 1672 that was the basis for Rochester's
Will; and in 1681 he would give evidence in the College Trial before Sir
Leoline Jenkins that Lady Rochester had spoken often of College's role in her
conversion to Catholicism. His loyalty was unquestionable. All evidence points

to him as the man who abducted Rochester's bastard daughter and gave her his own name: she is designated in Rochester's Will as "Elizabeth Clerke."[38] After the infant was taken to Enmore, Rochester wrote to his former mistress:

> Madam,
> I am far from delighting in the grief I have given you by taking away the child; and you, who made it so absolutely necessary for me to do so, must take that excuse from me for all the ill nature of it. On the other side, pray be assured I love Betty so well that you need not apprehend any neglect from those I employ, and I hope very shortly to restore her to you a finer girl than ever. In the meantime you would do well to think of the advice I gave you, for how little show soever my prudence makes in my own affairs, in yours it will prove very successful if you please to follow it. And since discretion is the thing alone you are like to want, pray study to get it.[39]

Despite the harshness of this letter, Rochester seems to have genuinely cared for Betty, who lived until 1689 or after. But she never was returned to her mother, who acquired "a scandalous reputation as a mercenary whore."[40] Barry's growth as a tragic actress was marked after Betty's loss. In February 1680, as Monimia in Otway's *The Orphan*, she "forc'd Tears from the Eyes of her Auditory, especially those who have any Sense of Pity for the Distress't."[41] We can only wonder whether her former lover saw her in *The Orphan* and how he reacted when the mother of his bastard daughter lamented the fate of a love child born of a doomed and illicit union.[42]

In April and May 1679, fear and suspicion ran rampant in Whitehall and Parliament as the Plot and Danby's impeachment became a series of chess moves and counter-moves between the King, Justice Scroggs, Shaftesbury, the Whigs, Danby, the Tories, and the Oates gang. On April 7, the first official notification to the Lords of the "Popish Lords' Plot" was given. Rochester was scrutinizing events carefully; he read and corrected the account in the Lords' *Journal* of that day's proceedings. On April 8, the Danby impeachment began in earnest, and the next day the Catholic Lords Petre, Stafford, and Arundell of Wardour were impeached and sent to the Tower.

So engrossed was Rochester in these affairs that he neglected writing to his wife and friends. When he did write, he adopted the practice of the Duke of Ormande and other cautious correspondents: not naming his correspondent or signing his letters. He sent messages only by the safest couriers, instructing his recipients to destroy after reading. Lady Rochester was told in one preserved letter, "I would [not] have you lose my letter it is not fitt for every body to find." Central parts of the letter are cut out.[43]

If all letters were risky, conveying information about current affairs was a daredevil undertaking. When Savile wrote to him from Paris on April 6,

Rochester delayed answering him. One of Ralph Montagu's "servants" was belatedly returning to England; by him Savile sent Rochester some medicinal items—an acid lemon drink and a syrup, "both great coolers"—along with instructions on how to use them. There was a dollop of ribaldry, as usual. Savile sent some wig powder and a bottle of myrtle water "to keep the ladyes heades sweet, and . . . theire tailes streight." Some raillery followed about "two Caledonian Countesses who are most in your favour. . . ."

The letter referred to Savile meeting him in Boulogne soon when Rochester came to France "upon that errand which I hope is allready secured for you, for I have sett my heart soe much upon meeting you there that I shall runn madd if anybody else should come in your place." Perhaps the doting Scottish Countesses might lure him to Paris afterward. "I cannot but thinke a long vacation as well past att Paris as at Woodstock." Savile closed by assuring Rochester of his affection and faithfulness in those suspicious times.[44]

Rochester did not answer this letter for two months; when he did, he made no reference to any errand to France. What might have been its purpose is unknown. Probably it had to do with some delicate financial matters. By 1679 Rochester was acting as a trustee to both Nell Gwyn and Lucy Fanshaw. Another letter from Savile on June 30 mentions a letter in Savile's diplomatic pouch to Rochester from a former mistress of the King—probably "Cousin Barbara," the Duchess of Cleveland. In his reply late in June, Rochester said, "if I can prove so unexpectedly happy to succeed in my endeavours for that [starving] fair unfortunate, she shall have a speedy account."[45] These clues suggest fiscal tasks. It is unlikely that any proposed errand to France was related to Danby's impeachment, James's Exclusion or the Popish Plot.

Nevertheless, Rochester continued to follow events in the Plot closely, staying in London after Parliament was prorogued on May 30 to see the outcome of the trials of Sir George Wakeman, the Queen's physician, and Richard Langhorn, a prominent Catholic barrister of Lincoln's Inn. Langhorn, as the Jesuits' lawyer, was said to know of vast wealth held secretly by his clients. During his trial in early June, he tried to discredit Titus Oates's perjured testimony by producing a series of witnesses from St. Omer's, who contradicted Oates's claims of being in London in April 1678. During the trial, Roger Palmer the Earl of Castlemain, who had gone to France and recruited some of the witnesses, interrupted, complaining to Justice Scroggs that spectators were manhandling them as they left the hall.[46]

Palmer, a pugnacious and testy Irish Catholic, had been married to Cousin Barbara when she became the King's whore in 1660. Given an Earldom as recompense for his wife's favors, Palmer was compelled to pose as father of Barbara's bastards but he finally escaped into a long self-exile on the

Continent.[47] He was in Venice when Rochester and Dr. Balfour came there in 1664; and if the young lord indeed formed an attachment to the Roman church during his Grand Tour, Palmer was in a unique position to know about it.[48] He was, after all, related by marriage to the St. Johns and Wilmots. His rash interventions in the Popish trials got him put into the Tower more than once in 1679–80; he was tried himself on June 23, 1680.[49] With such irascible associates as Palmer and Stephen College privy to his secrets and involved in the Popish affair, Rochester had good reason to feel uneasy.

He also showed a deep interest in Langhorn, who volunteered to reveal Jesuit assets after he was found guilty on June 14, 1679.[50] On May 30, in Whitehall, Rochester began a letter that he finished there on June 25, thanking Savile for his gifts and explaining his delay in writing by idleness and "not knowing what to say."

> Changes in this place are so frequent that F[anshaw] himself can now no longer give an account why this was done today and what will ensue tomorrow, and accidents are so extravagant that my Lord W[inchester?], intending to lie, has with a prophetic spirit once told truth.

Danby fallen for good, speculation was rife about who would succeed him as Minister. Old Mr. Waller predicted (correctly) that Robert Spencer, the Earl of Sunderland, would. The Scottish Covenanters had rebelled; Lauderdale was perversely trying to use this to his own advantage; and Monmouth was leading a force against them. Rochester then made a curiously oblique reference to Richard Langhorn:

> The most profound politicians have weighty brows and careful aspects at present, upon a report crept abroad that Mr. Langhorn, to save his life, offers a discovery of priests' and Jesuits' lands to the value of fourscore-and-ten thousand pounds a year, which upon being accepted, it is feared, partisans and undertakers will be found out to advance a considerable sum of money upon this fund, to the utter interruption of parliament's—and the destruction of many hopeful—designs. This, I must call God to witness, was never hinted in the least by Mr. P_____, to whom I beg you will give me your hearty recommendations.[51]

The "partisans and undertakers" may well have been a reference to Shaftesbury and Essex. Shaftesbury visited Langhorn in prison and secured the Lords' permission for Langhorn's friends to have access to him. On June 18, both Shaftesbury and Essex visited him. Langhorn's (attributed) posthumous memoirs said that Shaftesbury's agents had proposed "something to me in charity, for the saving of my life" and that later Shaftesbury himself visited and offered Langhorn "as good a post, both as to honour and estate, as my own

heart could wish" in return for "a full discovery of the plot." Langhorn resisted
the offer, however, thereby shielding the King and York. His reward was execution for treason.[52]

The reference to "Mr. P_____" has long baffled attempts to identify him.
Rochester's syntax is confusing, but it is clear that Mr. P_____ was privy to
information about Langhorn that he never "hinted" to Rochester. P_____, it
seems, was an informant to Rochester. Rochester's letter also suggests that
P_____ was in Paris in June 1679 and that Savile knew and communicated
with him. In April 1680, Rochester wrote to Savile:

> I met your packet, and truly was not more surprised at the indirectness of
> Mr. P's proceeding than overjoyed at the kindness and care of yours.
> Misery makes all men less or more dishonest and I am not astonished to
> see villainy industrious for bread, especially living in a place [i.e., France]
> where it is often so *de gaieté de coeur*. I believe the fellow thought of this
> device to get some money, or else he is put upon it by somebody who has
> given it him already. But I give him leave to prove what he can against
> me. However, I will search into the matter and give you a further account
> within a post or two.[53]

P_____, then, knew secret details about actors in the Popish Plot tragedy-
farce and had informed Rochester about them, withholding some details
through strategy (or ignorance). He had gone to Paris by June 1679 and established contact with Savile and thus through him, Rochester. Then in April
1680, he disclosed—or threatened to disclose—information about Rochester
that would in some way injure him. Savile found out about this and dealt with
P_____ in a way to silence him for the time being, then informed Rochester
of P_____'s potential threat. Whoever he was, P_____ tried to blackmail
Rochester by linking him to the Popish Plot just weeks before Rochester had
his final relapse. Rochester's deathbed urging that his wife renounce her ties
to Catholicism thus becomes more understandable, in light of William Clark's
testimony at the College trial in 1681 after Lady Rochester died suddenly.
There can be little doubt that Rochester felt seriously and constantly at risk
during the Popish Plot scare.[54]

At the end of June 1679, Rochester retired to Oxfordshire for the month of
July. He may have done some final writing there. The follies in glaring evidence
during the Popish Plot episode incited his ironic scorn and the satirist again took
up his pen. In 1679 a notable number of his satiric pieces came into print.
Etherege's lampoon on Mulgrave, "Ephelia to Bajazet," and Rochester's "A
Very Heroicall Epistle in Answer to Ephelia" were first printed then, as were
another three major satires composed earlier: "Upon Nothing," the "Satyr" on
Man and "A Letter from Artemiza to Chloe." Contrary to the truism that

English noblemen wrote only for the eyes of their peers, many of Rochester's poems found their way to the public during his lifetime. The broadside versions of 1679 were obviously aimed at a wide reading public by their printers, and Rochester may have leaked some of the lampoons deliberately.

Among the broadsides of 1679 was a new, scatological lampoon on Mulgrave, "My Lord All-Pride."

> Bursting with Pride, the loath'd Impostume swells,[55]
> Prick him, he sheds his Venom strait, and smells;
> But tis soe Lewd a Scribler, that he writes,
> With as much force to Nature, as he fights . . .
> And with his Arme, and Head, his Brain's soe weake
> That his starv'd Fancy, is compell'd to rake,
> Among the Excrements of others Witt,
> To make a stinking Meale of what they Shitt.

The causes for Rochester's revived barrage against him are not immediately perceivable. Mulgrave's name is conspicuously absent in records of the times, despite the fact that he converted to Catholicism in 1675 or 1676 to win York's favor. He was, to be sure, engaged in his military career and more often away from Court than not. In 1679, however, he became Lord Lieutenant of East Ryding in Yorkshire and Governor of Hull, posts taken away from Monmouth. Despite his initial reluctance to assume titles stripped from his longstanding opponent, the honors would surely puff up a man as egotistical as Mulgrave. Apparently he was at Whitehall in late Spring, attending to affairs political and amorous. In the letter composed during May 30–June 25, Rochester slily mentioned "a great goggle-eye to business," an allusion to Lord All-Pride as a "Coxcomb . . . With a Red Nose, Splay Foot, and Goggle Eye."

> Goe where he will, he never finds a Friend,
> Shame and derision all his Steps attend:
> Alike abroad, at home, i'th' Camp, and Court,
> This Knight o'th' Burning Pestle makes us sport.[56]

Rochester's reference to Mulgrave's venomous but feeble attempts to write and his dependence on others' wit suggests Mulgrave's "Essay on Satire," which widely circulated in November 1679 and was first thought to be by Dryden and later to be a joint effort by Dryden and Mulgrave. Mulgrave eventually declared the piece to be entirely his; and it is tempting to suppose that acting the peacock at Whitehall in May–June, Mulgrave may have tried his hand at an early version of this—he later claimed to have written it as early as 1675—and Rochester caught wind of it. Uncertain chronology of composition, however, leaves in doubt whether Mulgrave's "Essay" provoked Rochester's "All-Pride" or vice-versa.[57] Possibly, the broadside appearance of earlier satires against him in 1679 stimulated Mulgrave to reply in the updated "Essay"; but more evidence is needed to resolve the problem.

On August 13, 1679, Rochester went on Bed Chamber duty at Windsor, together with his old friend, Sackville Lord Dorset, and Danby's brother-in-law, Robert Bertie, Lord Lindsey, in whose house Danby probably hid during his March exile.[58] This combination of political opponents may have been the King's way to remind his servants of his central place in their lives. An even stronger reminder came on August 21, when after a hard game of tennis Charles walked by the river and caught a chill. His condition became so serious that the nation feared he would die and civil war would break out with a coup by Monmouth. In Paris, Harry Savile wrote: "Good God, what a change would such an accident make! The very thought of it frights me out of my wits."[59] The royal doctors did their worst; the royal ministers were in a panic; and the Duke of York was secretly summoned back from Brussels. Congregations prayed for the King in the churches of London, and in Oxford Robert Whitehall penned Latin verses to assist his recovery. Something worked. By the time James arrived at Windsor on September 2 for "a touching reunion," Charles was sitting up and dining on mutton and partridges. But James's presence in England provoked threats to reopen the issue of Exclusion; and Charles was compelled to respond to them. He stripped Monmouth of his rank as Commander-in-Chief of the army, exiled him to the Netherlands on September 24, and sent James back to Brussels on September 25.[60] This done, the King left for Newmarket.

Dorset had departed from Windsor when his wife (Mary Bagot) died in childbirth on September 12. His own Chamber duty over, Rochester returned to Woodstock, where his prized grey won the races. This victory and a renewed, loving intimacy with his wife provided solacing contrast to the troubles a year ago at Woodstock when Norris and Lovelace came to blows.[61] Even so, in the turbulent uncertainty of the year's events, the fate of the Stuarts—and the aristocrats allied with them—was uncertain at best. On what, or whom, could a clever, skeptical peer rely? In "Upon Nothing," Rochester had posed as a cynic without beliefs or illusions:

> Ere Time and Place were, Time and Place were not
> When Primitive Nothing, somthing straight begott
> Then all proceeded from the great united what—
>
> Somthing, the Generall Attribute of all
> Severed from thee [Nothing], its sole Originall,
> Into thy boundless selfe must undistinguisht fall. . . .

Yet this of thee the wise may truly say:
Thou from the virtuous, Nothing does delay
And to be part of thee the wicked wisely pray.

The Great mans Gratitude to his best friend
Kings promises, Whors vowes towards thee they bend
fflow Swiftly into thee, and in thee ever end.

Despite its witty nihilism, "Upon Nothing" shows that its author unwittingly still clung to one long-embedded belief. If the wicked pray that after death nothing is, to whom—or to what—do they pray? Lord Rochester was destined soon to find out.

AN END OF COMMUNION (1679–1680)

> I was not long in his Company, when he told me . . . That he
> was not so engaged to his old Maxims, as to resolve not to
> change, but that if he could be convinc'd, he would choose
> rather to be of another Mind.
>
> Gilbert Burnet, *Passages*, 30–31

Concerned with how much his future—and his family's—depended on shifting judicial and political conditions, Rochester returned to London in October 1679, to sit in yet another reconstituted Parliament. Displeased with the March assemblage, in which Whigs replaced a substantial number of "Cavalier" loyalists, the King had dissolved it on July 12, and a second election took place. The results decreased the number of his Tory supporters even more.

Counting on continued financial aid from Louis XIV, Charles decided to try to rule without Parliament and thus render impotent the power it exerted by holding the purse-strings. To this end, he replaced Danby with a triumvirate of advisers—Sunderland, Godolphin, and Hyde—whose relative youth and inexperience led their opponents to dub them "the Chits."[1] When the new Parliament met on October 17, Charles immediately prorogued it to January 26, 1680, to the Whigs' frustration and Shaftesbury's fury. Partisan emotions over stalemated issues mounted rather than diminished in the months following, and, threatened by growing dissatisfaction, the King prorogued Parliament six times in succession from January to October, 1680.[2]

Of course, John Wilmot could not know that the Parliament in March 1679 was the last full session he would ever attend. Alert to potential dangers, he remained in London during the winter of 1679–80, except for the Christmas interval. Returning in late January 1680, he stayed on until his final departure in April. To his mind, Parliament might be called into session at any time. Even if it was not, too many troublesome situations kept occurring in town for him to turn his back and risk being hanged. The specter raised by the King's

possible death in September led, in October 1679, to a new uproar: the revelation of a "Meal Tub Plot."[3]

Encouraged by Monmouth's exile, Shaftesbury's dismissal as Minister, and
Sir George Wakeman's acquittal on charges of plotting to poison the King,
some rash supporters of York worked to turn the tables on the Whigs and
Shaftesbury. An idea of how to do this came initially from Elizabeth Cellier, a
somewhat disreputable Catholic midwife who housed the witnesses over from
St. Omers. Employed by York in his dealings with Shaftesbury, she published
the lurid account of a hackney-coachman, who revealed Shaftesbury's alleged
manipulations of witnesses in the Popish trials.[4] The coachman's later confession that he lied failed to dampen Cellier's ardor for York's cause. With Lady
Powis as her intemperate patroness—Lord Powis stayed in the Tower—she
looked for a way to get revenge on those who persecuted good Catholic
Royalists. In this cause, she recruited Thomas Dangerfield, a former inmate at
Newgate Prison, as her ally.

A ruffian-adventurer with masculine good looks and persuasive charm, he
had masqueraded as "Captain Willoughby." Between them, Cellier and
Dangerfield contrived a plan to prove that Protestants, not Catholics, were
plotting to kill the King. Dangerfield fabricated the necessary evidence and
planted it in a meal tub, where he later "discovered" it. Tories were jubilant
but the Whigs were further enraged and set out to prove Cellier and
Dangerfield were papist liars. When the Meal Tub Plot was disclosed to be a
fraud, Dangerfield hastily turned informant against Cellier and her cohorts. He
even charged other prominent Catholics, including the Lords Arundell and
Castlemain, of joining in Cellier's schemes. With another set of witches to
hunt, anti-papism resurged.[5]

On November 1, 1679, Rochester told Savile about this and other developments in a message carried to Paris by the "pretty fool" Belle Fasse, his valet.
He was careful to let Savile know he was using their "familiar style" of treating important matters archly. Veiled by irony, paradox, innuendo, and cryptic
references to sodomy, Jesuits, and the Popish Plot, the letter dealt with very
serious matters.

> Harry,
> I am in a great strait what to write to you. . . . We are in such a settled
> happiness and such merry security in this place [Whitehall] that if it were
> not for sickness I could pass my time very well between my own ill-
> nature . . . and the policies of the times. . . . The news I have to send, and
> the sort alone which could be so to you are things "Gyaris et carcere
> digna" which I dare not trust to this pretty fool the bearer . . . news that
> Mr. Grimes [James Graham], with one gentle man more [Monmouth],
> had invaded England, Mr. S[hepard]'s apology for making songs on the

Duke of M[onmouth], with his oration-consolatory on my Lady D[orset]'s death, and a politic dissertation between my Lady P[owis] and Captain Dangerfield, with many other worthy treatises of the like nature are things worthy your perusal, but I durst not send 'em to you without leave, not knowing what consequence it might draw upon your circumstances and character.[6]

In this circumspect way, Rochester informed Savile, newly made Ambassador to France as Sunderland's replacement, that Monmouth had returned from his banishment contrary to Royal decree; that the investigation into the Meal Tub Plot had turned up some incriminating evidence; that Sunderland was having problems with the King and his fellow ministers over James's Exclusion; and that Titus Oates's homosexuality was known and about to become an issue in the Popish Plot.[7]

The Latin *gyaris et carcere digna* ("worth exile and chains") was adapted from Juvenal's First Satire, a fierce denunciation of a wealthy but corrupt Rome peopled by forgers, bribers, seducers, liars, fanatics, and swindlers. The analogy with England was clear:

> Dare nobly, man, if greatness be thy aim,
> And practice what may chains and exile claim.
> On guilt's broad base thy towering fortunes raise,
> For virtue starves on universal praise.
> While crimes, in scorn of niggard Fate, afford
> The ivory couches and the citron board.

Concluding, Rochester promised to keep Savile informed of all matters "of that kind, in which alone I dare presume to think myself capable." Only one such letter is preserved but Rochester may have supplied others that Savile was careful to destroy. In any event, the two friends maintained mutual loyalty and affection until Rochester's death. Although they did not meet again, each kept the other informed and looked out for his interests.

On November 17, 1679, a massive Pope-Burning procession took place, not on Guy Fawkes Day as in the past but Accession Day of the Protestant Elizabeth I. Whigs of the Green Ribbon Club were believed responsible for organizing it, complete with an effigy of the murdered Edmund Berry Godfrey, an array of marchers dressed as Jesuits with bloody daggers, richly costumed "Cardinals," and at last the "Pope" himself, an effigy seated on a scarlet chair with banners showing bloody knives. The "Pope" was duly burned before the Green Ribbon Club at the Temple Bar, toasts of "No Popery" drunk, and with the militia watching, the crowds dispersed without incident and went home to bed. Rochester would have been drawn to such a carnivalesque spectacle and was certainly there if his health allowed it. Everybody else was.[8]

A combination of circumstances made Rochester's last season in London very unlike previous ones. Declining health was one factor; political uncertainty, another. Because of health, his career as a promiscuous Lothario was on the wane. Mrs. Barry, totally estranged, had become the mistress of Sir George Etherege. Rochester's amorous propensities suffered an additional check when Jane Roberts, his former mistress, died in November 1679 of the very diseases that were wasting him. Aside from Savile's banter about Caledonian Countesses and their partiality for him, Rochester was linked in 1679–80 with only one other woman, Jane Clark, about whom nothing is known. A lurid but suspect eighteenth-century source reported that Rochester kidnapped her in 1679, kept her at Woodstock and, with her grandmother's help, raped her while quoting lines from Sophocles' *Oedipus*.[9] Rochester's poor health and brief stay in the country in 1679 do not support this prurient canard.

His luminous career as a patron of playwrights and the theater was also diminished by conditions at the start of "The Political Eighties." The theaters themselves were having severe problems:

> The King's Company was already in dire straits at the start of the Popish Plot, and matters rapidly worsened. In the 1679–80 season they produced but two new plays, only one successful; part of the company defected temporarily to Scotland, and reconciliation proved difficult; quarrels over alleged theft of scenes, costumes, and properties by company members divided the remaining actors. . . . The Duke's Company, meanwhile, was doing passably well. And in these last years of competition, a surprising number of new plays got produced. . . .[10]

Partisan playwrights developed three broad sorts of topical plays: Tory-oriented, Whig-oriented, and generalized Warnings. At first, Whig and Tory writer-partisans thrived on the anti-Catholic hysteria and made priests the butt of their humor; but opposing political sentiments in play dialogue soon led to shouting matches and fights among spectators or even riots by an audience-at-large. These scarcely enhanced the allure of theater-going for a weakened Rochester.

The most popular plays of the day were horror tragedies like *Caesar Borgia* (late 1679?) and *Thyestes* (March 1680), unrhymed heroic tragedies (*Theodosius*, spring 1680), or pathetic tragedies (Otway's *The Orphan* in February 1680). None of the types was apt to appeal to a man of Rochester's known tastes in drama. Moreover, the authors of these plays had been scorned by him earlier: John Crowne, Nat Lee, Elkanah Settle, Tom Otway, Edward Ravenscroft. Given their spiteful counter-attacks, neither they nor their later works were likely to get Rochester's enthusiastic approval. Dryden recorded Rochester's

instant response to the claim of one of them—probably Ravenscroft—that he had
written a (very bad) tragedy in three weeks. Said Rochester, "How the devil
could he be so long about it?"[11] Other playwrights in 1679–80, some new-
comers, were a motley crew: Tom Durfey, Thomas Southerne, Nahum Tate,
William Whitaker. Anxious, sick and jaded, Rochester could only find their
efforts equally unworthy.

If no playwright attracted his sponsorship, a few would-be poets did. John
Oldham remained his protégé, as did Francis Fane. John Grubham (Jack)
Howe, a "young amorous spark of the Court," was reported to have been
encouraged by Rochester to write verse. Related to the Scroops, Earl Rivers,
and Charles Pawlet the Lord Winchester, young Jack Howe gained some reputation as a minor satirist on the order of Will Fanshaw, Anthony Carey the
Viscount Falkland, Fleetwood Shepherd, and other of Rochester's would-be
imitators.[12] Howe's "envenomed pen" would have amused Rochester, whom
Howe aped by having his sisters spy on other Courtiers to get material for him
to lampoon. He acquired some sobriquets—"peevish Jack," "Libelling Jack"—
and himself became the later target of some half-dozen satires; e.g., "Satires on
Both Whigs and Tories" (1683):

> How oft has Howe (by Rochester undone,
> Who soothed him first into opinion
> Of being a wit) been told that he was none?

This satire goes on to say that Rochester flattered young Howe in order to
sodomize him, comparing Howe's "bum" with that of George Porter Jr.
("Nobs"), who was widely accused of catamite activities.[13]

Such libelous assertions cannot be taken at face value; however, there is evidence that both Howe and Rochester shared sexual adventures with a well-
known bawd of the time. From 1675 to 1683, "Madam" Sue Willis kept a
brothel near Whetstone Park famous for its gateposts with twin balls. In
November 1679, Howe, together with Nobs Porter and William Wharton (Tom
Wharton's younger brother), "on a Saturday night . . . came and broke down
Mrs. Willis's balls and called her all to naught, upon which she sent for the
constable, but he was so civil as not to secure them."[14] Howe's actions mimicked the legendary feats of the young Rochester. Rochester wrote a lampoon
"On Mistress Willis" that was printed in the *Poems on Several Occasions* after his
death in 1680. The composition date is not established but it may have been
among his last verses and Howe—or another late protégé—could have supplied
it to the printer. The scatological and misogynistic qualities of the satire are so
graphic as to suggest it was vented during one of Rochester's diseased relapses,
possibly his last.

> Against the Charms our *Ballox* have
>   How weak all human skill is
> Since they can make a man a slave
>   To such a Bitch as *Willis.* . . .

Whether he shared their carnal adventures or not, Rochester was the admired center of a group of young rake-poetasters in his last year. Two of these, Jack Howe and Robert (Bob) Wolseley, made panegyrics to "Strephon" (or his niece-image, Nan Wharton) when Rochester died in 1680.[15] Bob Wolseley even joined with her in reviving and pubishing *Valentinian* in 1685, with Wolseley's defense of Rochester against Mulgrave. The same year, Wolseley killed Nan's brother-in-law, Will Wharton, in a duel, "the result of a poetomachia between the two whiffling poets."[16] Rochester's demonic legacy assumed some grotesque forms in his disciples. Bob Wolseley attested to the shift in Rochester's interests and concerns during the last years of his life.

> [A] considerable time before his last Sickness, his Wit began to take a more serious Bent. . . . In effect, he seem'd to study nothing more, than which way to make that great Understanding [*sic*] God had given him, more useful to his Countrey, and I am confident, had he liv'd, his riper Age wou'd have serv'd it, as much as his Youth had diverted it.[17]

This was the beginning of a detailed panegyric that concluded with a quotation from his "loved Lucretius," extolling Rochester as divinely created and "adorned with excellence in everything for all time." Significantly, however, late in 1679 John Wilmot was reexamining the peculiar system of religion he had concocted earlier out of Lucretius (and Hobbes). He began a series of conversations with the man who would convert him into a Christian icon.

Gilbert Burnet (1643–1715), a canny Scotsman not unlike Rochester's former governor, Dr. Andrew Balfour, was educated at Aberdeen, after which he became a probationer for the Scottish ministry in 1661. After a six-months visit to Oxford and Cambridge (where he was greatly influenced by the Cambridge Platonists), he traveled in Holland and France, learning Hebrew in the process. Returning to Britain, he became friends with Robert Maitland, a fellow Scot who later became the powerful Duke of Lauderdale. From 1669 to 1673, as a Professor of Divinity at Glasgow, Burnet began to differ with Lauderdale's policies and was branded by him as a center of Scottish discontent. Accordingly, Burnet chose to settle in England in 1673, preparing his biography of the Dukes of Hamilton for publication while serving as preacher at the Rolls chapel and lecturer at St. Clements. The King viewed him with suspicion, thanks to Lauderdale; then in 1675, Burnet lost the favor of York because of his evidence against Lauderdale before the House of Commons. In the meantime, he was writing the first volume of his *History of the Reformation of the Church of England*, published in 1679.[18]

Rochester's spiritual quest led him to Burnet's *History*, which struck him forcefully with its sophistication and logic. Burnet had a subtle intelligence when it came to religious persuasion. Early in the *History* he remarked that it was not unusual for God's providence to employ men with gross mixtures of faults to do signal things for His service. He castigated Pope Leo X for prostituting the pardon of sin in that foul trade of indulgences. He urbanely noted that Pope Paul III "not only kept his whore, but gloried in it, and raised one of his bastards to high dignity . . . and himself is said to have lived in incest with others of them." Nevertheless, "God's ways are a great deep, who has often showed his power and wisdom in raising up unlikely and promising instruments to do great services in the world." The emotional appeal of Burnet's thesis drew Rochester magnetically. Within two years, Burnet's *Passages* would transform him into just such an instrument.

Burnet offered hope that nominal heretics might be saved and religious bigots be damned in his section on the Inquisition:

> Burning was the death they made choice of, because witches, wizards, and sodomites had been so executed. Therefore to make heresy appear a terrible thing, this was thought the most proper punishment of it. It also had a resemblance of everlasting burning, to which they adjudged [the heretics'] souls as well as their bodies were condemned to the fire; but with this signal difference, that [the Inquisitors] could find no way to oblidge God to execute their sentence, as they contrived against the civil magistrate. (19)

Burnet's survey of the rise of the Church of Rome was as skeptical about ecclesiastical institutions as Charles Blount and the libertines, but Burnet managed to retain the thesis of divine truths administered by fallible men. In summarizing John Frith's rebuttal of Thomas More, Burnet dispensed with Purgatory and the doctrine of punishment:

> He showed the difference between the punishments we may suffer in this life, and those in purgatory; the one are either medicinal corrections for reforming us more and more or for giving warning to others: the [purgatorial] others are terrible punishments with out any of these ends in them: therefore the one might well consist with the free pardon of sin, the other could not. (122)

Burnet further demonstrated his worldly, if anti-papist, realism by referring to various sexual corruptions in monasteries and nunneries, "abominations . . . equal to any that were in Sodom." He even jeered at the naïveté and "junior sophistry" that purported to "prove" God's omnipotence. Rochester was duly impressed, and said so to the King—or so he later informed Burnet:

> He told me he said to King Charles after the 1st Volume of my History of the Reformation came out, he wondered why he [Charles] would use a writer of History ill, for such people can revenge themselves, the King answered I [Burnet] durst say nothing while he was alive; when he was dead he should not be the worse for what I said.[19]

Having seen the urbane prelate only twice before, Rochester waited a while to engage with the author of the *History*; but when Burnet counseled his former "pocky mistress," Jane Roberts, as she lay dying in October–November 1679, the reputation Burnet had gained from the *History* grew even more lustrous. In Burnet's modestly self-congratulatory words:

> I was called on to assist manny who lay a dying particularly one with whom Wilmot E of Rochester had an ill concern. He heard that in a long attendance on her I treated her neither with a slack indulgence nor an affrighting severity, upon that he sent for me and in manny discourses with him I saw into the depths of Satan, and by a winter's conversation generally once a week I went thro much ground with him, and as he owned to me I subdued his understanding but touching his heart was that which God reserved to himselfe and which followed some time after that. [Wilmot] had been a malicious observer of the applications the Clergy made at Court for preferment, and fortified himselfe and others with prejudices against religion by the observations he made on their behaviour, and this made him so partiall to me because he observed nothing of aspiring to preferment in me.[20]

Rochester's admiration for the *History* and Burnet's seeming lack of ambition was shored by their similar views about the present state of politics. Both disdained Lauderdale, sought compromise in the Exclusion crisis, were friends to Halifax, scorned Papist doctrines, and inclined to Whiggism. Thus was the usually cynical Earl totally unprepared to contest a man who proved more than his match.

Many observers testified to Burnet's rhetorical brilliance. John Evelyn heard him preach many times, remarking on the initial occasion (October 15, 1674), "The *Anniversary* of my *Baptisme* I first heard that famous & Excellent Preacher Dr. *Burnet* (Author of the *Historie of the Reformation*) . . . with such a floud of eloquence, & fullnesse of matter as shew'd him to be a person of extraordinary parts."[21] And he was physically magnetic, as John Dryden noted:

> A portly prince and goodly to the sight,
> He seemed a son of Anach for his height,
> Like those whom stature to crowns prefer;

> Black-browed and bluff, like Homer's Jupiter,
> Broad-backed and brawny, built for love's delight,
> A prophet formed to make a female proselyte.[22]

Not only was Burnet mentally brilliant and physically, even erotically, attractive like Rochester himself; he was only slightly older—by four years—and therefore a suitable alter ego as well as mentor.

As the series of theological conversations started, Rochester continued his involvement with Court affairs and his correspondence with Savile. Mulgrave's *Essay Upon Satire*, with its sneers at Rochester among others and its self-congratulation, began circulating in manuscript in mid-November. The forty lines dealing with Rochester only repeated earlier satiric charges of impotent malice, treacherous flattery, cowardice, and poetic obscenity.

> *Roches[te]r* I despise for his meer want of wit,
> Though thought to have a Tail and Cloven Feet . . .
> Mean in each Action, lewd in every Limb,
> Manners themselves are mischievous in him . . .
> Of fighting sparks some may her pleasures say,
> But ' tis a bolder thing to run away . . .
> I'd like to have left out his Poetry . . .
> 'Tis under so much nasty rubbish laid,
> To find it out's the Cinder-woman's trade. . . .[23]

This vapid stuff appears to have roused in Rochester little more than indifferent amusement but others reacted more emotionally. In a letter to the Duke of Ormonde on November 22, Colonel Edward Cooke recounted its reception by some members of the Court, as he had been informed. Cooke's "play at small game" for the Duke of Ormande's amusement was quite similar to Rochester's own eyewitness version written to Savile a day earlier and sent together with a copy of Mulgrave's lampoon.[24]

> I have sent you herewith a libel in which my own share is not the least. . . . The author is apparently Mr. [Dryden], his patron my [Lord Mulgrave], having a panegyric in the midst, upon which happened a handsome quarrel between his L[ordship], and Mrs. B[ulkeley] at the Duchess of [Portsmouth's]. She called him the hero of the libel and complimented him upon having made more cuckolds than any man alive, to which he answered she very well knew one he never made nor never cared to be employed in making. "Rogue!" and "Bitch!" ensued, till the King, taking his grandfather's character upon him, became the peace-maker.[25]

Although Rochester's "share" of the satire was not the least in line count, many other Courtiers were lampooned also: the King himself, Sir Thomas

Armstrong, Colonel Edmund Ashton, Monmouth, Dunbar, Carr Scroop, Danby, Buckingham, Shaftesbury, Halifax, Heneage Finch, Sackville, Pembroke, Sedley, and Sir George Hewitt. Though not named, the "royal mistresses" were also abused, with easily deciphered references to Nelly Gwyn and Lady Portsmouth.[26]

On December 1, Rochester was officially designated a trustee for financial matters concerning Lucy Fanshaw, the wife of his friend Will and perpetual aspirant to the status of the King's bastard. Lord Anglesey was to be co-trustee for thirty-one years.[27] Confused Treasury records of the time refer to Lord Rochester as a Treasury Commissioner in 1680, but this was probably Laurence Hyde who assumed the title late in 1681. Whether he held an official post or not, John Wilmot was certainly enacting a significant role in the King's monetary affairs in the last months of his life.

The death of Thomas Hobbes on December 4, 1679, provoked the retelling of anecdotes that reminded Rochester of the appeal exerted by that stalwart iconoclast:

> When Mr. T. Hobbes was sick in France, the Divines came to him, and tormented him (both Roman Catholic, Church of England, and Geneva). Sayd he to them Let me alone, or els I will detect all your Cheates from Aaron to yourselves.[28]

The views of Thomas Hobbes and those of Gilbert Burnet were antithetical; the eloquent appeal of both kept Rochester unsure in his own maxims.[29] Even as he engaged with Burnet, in February 1680 he resumed his exchange with Hobbes's pupil, Charles Blount, whose *Anima Mundi* had provided him with ideas for Burnet to refute. The arguments that Rochester advanced to Burnet (as Burnet recorded in the *Passages*) and those in Blount's *Anima* have many, obvious similarities. Torn between "the Evil Genius of Malmesbury" and "that famous & Excellent Preacher," Rochester's conflicted selves continued to battle in the winter of 1679–80.

Some thought his evil angel triumphed. Barely a month after Rochester sent a copy of Mulgrave's *Essay upon Satire* to Savile, John Dryden, widely thought to be its author, was waylaid by three men in Rose Alley on December 18 and badly beaten.[30] On December 23 the *Domestick Intelligence* reported that the Poet was so severely injured "'Tis thought he will hardly recover it." On the 26th, the same paper offered £50 and immunity to any informant who could identify the assailants. They never were identified but Rochester, among several others, was rumored to have instigated the assault.[31] The rumor was recorded twelve years later by Anthony Wood in the *Athenae Oxoniensis* (1691–92) as an incidental aside in the biography of Buckingham, where Rochester was linked as a co-conspirator with the Duchess of Portsmouth. In another place, Wood garbled the supposed cause of the beating by substituting *Absalom and Achitophel* (1681) for *An Essay on Satire.* Obviously, as in many other instances, Wood's decade-old hearsay about Rochester is far from conclusive.[32] On the other hand, three contemporary accounts, including one by the usually reliable Narcissus Luttrell, laid the blame squarely on the Duchess of Portsmouth.[33]

Although it is impossible to prove him innocent of Dryden's beating unless someone else can be proved guilty beyond a doubt, the existing evidence indicates that Rochester was not responsible for the Rose Alley attack. In the first place, no records show that he ever used bullies for revenge, whereas several named in the *Essay* did (e.g., Sedley and Monmouth). Nor did he initiate physical assaults in person in the manner of Monmouth, Armstrong, Pembroke, Ashton, and Dunbar. The tone of Rochester's account to Savile of his share in the satire and the contretemps between Mulgrave and Mrs. Bulkeley is detached and amused.[34] If he were truly outraged at his portrait in the *Essay*, would he have sent a copy to anybody, even Savile? And was he certain that Dryden was truly the author of the *Essay*? A month before the Rose Alley episode, Rochester showed doubt: the author was "apparently" Dryden. Even if Dryden was its father, would Rochester take a violent physical revenge when Dryden's earlier thrusts had not provoked one? The castigation in the Preface to *All for Love*, known to be Dryden's, was far more personal and vicious than the feeble mewing of the *Essay on Satire.* It had caused Wilmot only to begin writing a satire, not arrange a beating.

More than nineteen months had elapsed since Dryden attacked him "with the blunt" in the "Preface." In the interim, Rochester had resolved to provide an example of penitence to the world. Soon after the attack took place, Rochester confessed his many transgressions in detail to Gilbert Burnet but Burnet makes no mention of hiring bullies or wanton physical attacks among Rochester's sins.[35] Wilmot was in poor health late in 1679, as he informed Savile, a condition that always provoked fear and penitence. The death of Jane Roberts at the same period was not likely to encourage him to further transgressions. Finally, if Dryden suspected Rochester of persecuting him, would he not have sought some kind of revenge—possibly with a pseudonymous character in *Absalom and Achitophel*? He did not. Indeed, Dryden's later references to Rochester and his wit were admiring, notably in 1700.[36] All in all, the evidence argues against Rochester's involvement in the Rose Alley ambush.

He was probably off in the country when the beating took place. It was his custom, when relieved of Chamber duty, to go to Adderbury or Woodstock from early or mid-December until Parliament reconvened toward the end of January. But given the uncertainty of affairs in the winter of 1679–80, he may not have ventured so far from London. He may have been with his uncle, Sir Walter St. John, in Battersea some of this time, scheming to assure that Parliament would really convene. The letter sent to his wife "with care," saying he had acted for her "vindication," was written there.[37]

During Rochester's absence from Whitehall, Etherege and Sedley were injured when the roof of the Clare-market Tennis Court fell on January 14.[38] On January 22, Rochester's uncle, Sir Walter St. John, Thomas Thynne, and other property owners in Wiltshire petitioned the King, requesting that Parliament be called. (Rochester himself owned property there.) Charles angrily rejected this petition, saying it came from "loose, disaffected people," and commanded Sir Walter and the rest not to meddle in royal business.[39] When Parliament met four days later on January 26, Charles quickly prorogued it, thus effectively ending John Wilmot's last public chance to become the disinterested patriot he had aspired to be. When the Lords met briefly before prorogation, Rochester was one of the few peers present.

He stayed in London for the aftermath of the prorogation. On February 6 or 7, several drunken supporters of Monmouth caused a brawl in the Duke's Theatre, throwing things at the actors, cursing the Duchess of Portsmouth, and calling Sunderland a traitor. So the Dowager Countess of Sunderland reported to her son. Among those drunkenly yelling "God bless his Highness, the Duke of Monmouth. We will be for him Against the world" was Tom Wharton. Again on February 19, she wrote:

> The players have been disturbed again by drunken people's jokes. They called my Lord Arran a rogue; and one Fitzpatrick pointed at Mr. Thinne, and called him that petitioning fool, and swore an hundred oaths; he said that he deserved £20,000 a-year, but that fool deserved nothing.[40]

On February 26, Narcissus Luttrell recorded that Nell Gwyn was at the Duke's Theatre when a man came into the pit and called her a whore; Pembroke's brother "vindicating, there were many swords drawn, and a great hubbub in the house." Only a few weeks earlier, Nelly's mother had drowned in a ditch while drunk.[41]

Even as these public brawls took place, Rochester was getting involved in the sticky, private business of the young Earl of Arran, James Douglas, the eldest son of the Scottish Duke of Hamilton.[42] Arran became a Gentleman of the Bed Chamber on Jan. 14, 1679; subsequently the twenty-one-year-old came into Rochester's sphere. The youth's impetuous wooing of Miss Pawlet (or Paulet), a relative of Charles Pawlet the sixth Marquis of Winchester, led him into marital rivalry with Edward the Earl of Conway. Miss Pawlet was also related to Sir Edward Seymour the Speaker of the House of Commons and

Captain Edward Cooke.[43] Rochester's contempt for Winchester and Seymour apparently led him to give young Arran advice that drew the ailing Wilmot into yet another duel in the last months of his life.

In November 1679, Lord Conway, resident in Ireland, began a proxy search for a wife. He was interested in Miss Pawlet for her connections but also for her wealth. Colonel Cooke, her uncle, wrote some details to the Duke of Ormonde in December, mentioning that she had £10,000 with prospects for more.[44] Since he was away from London, Lord Conway left the details of matchmaking to his relatives: Seymour and Mr. Francis Gwyn. These gentlemen espoused the suit of Conway, who was a great friend of the eclipsed Lord Treasurer Danby. When Seymour sought the King's approval, Charles readily gave it, as Seymour told Conway on December 2, 1679: the King "set you forth with a good deal of willingness." Conway's cause seemed assured.[45] Mistress Pawlet's father had other ideas, however. At Christmas, for reasons of his own, he proposed his daughter as wife to impetuous young Arran. The King disapproved and excuses were made to save Arran's face. A delay of four months was proposed while Seymour worked to ingratiate Conway with Miss Pawlet, "who has no affection" for Arran, one of Conway's agents asssured him. The Pawlet father and daughter left London after the Christmas season to spend some time in Somerset, but they were followed by both Seymour and Arran. The surrogate and real suitors clashed at Wells but the matter was hushed up.

Back in London, Rochester carried on his conversations with Gilbert Burnet, possibly taking the time to attend a lavish dinner on March 6, given by Sackville, now Earl of Middlesex and Dorset, at Copt Hall, his Middlesex estate. The guests included the King, York, Monmouth, and other "persons of the Greatest quality," who were feted "at a splendid dinner and returned the same evening to Whitehall."[46] Three days later, on March 9, Rochester's name was on everyone's lips, together with those of Seymour and Arran.[47]

As the months dragged on, young Arran had grown impatient. When he complained to Rochester, who loved to foment quarrels, John Wilmot lapsed into his non-Christian ways. Or so it was reported to Lord Conway. Arran angrily confronted Seymour as he was leaving the House of Commons; and when the Speaker nervously tried to disengage himself, Arran scornfully spat at Seymour's feet and stalked away. Thus entrapped and exposed, Seymour summoned his Cousin Gwyn and they worked out a strategy to save *his* face. Gwyn wrote this account on March 9 to Lord Conway:

> Mr. Seymour sent for me in the morning and commanded me to go to my Ld. Rochester, it having been publicly said at my Ld. Sunderland's table that my Ld. Rochester had used expression to encourage my Ld. Arrain in

this piece of insolency towards him before it was done and had spoke something of it since reflecting on Mr. Seymour.

I went immediately and my Ld. Rochester appointed to meet the next morning on horseback with his sword and pistol. His reason for it was as he told me because he had a weakness in his limbs but he thought he could do very well on horseback, though I believe the true reason was he thought it impossible horses and equippage should be provided for us all in so short a time. . . .

But at ten o'clock on Thursday night comes Mr. Collingwood . . . and told [Seymour] the King had commanded him not to stir out of his house. . . . Mr. Collingwood likewise told us he had already been with the Ld. Rochester with the same message. . . . And my Ld. Rochester laid hold of it, and goes out the next morning, pretending the King's commands to him was only not to concern himself with any quarrel relating to the L. Arrain; where not finding anybody, which he very well knew he should not do, he came back, and at first reported that he had been in the field and Mr. Seymour did not appear. . . .

After reading Gwyn's letter, Lord Conway endorsed it thus: "Giving an account of Sir Edward Seymour's heroic courage, a pack of the greatest lies that ever was told, for he durst not fight Lord Arran, but was the jest of the Court on that occasion. . . ."

All this to-do had consequences. On March 9, 1680, *The London Gazette* (no. 1493) printed a proclamation from Whitehall that since duels were "now too frequent among persons of quality . . . no pardon shall be granted to any that shall fight." A warrant was issued for the arrest of Arran, who took off for Scotland while friends spread the report he had gone to the Hague. They also insisted that he was sure of his suit with Miss Pawlet. Away from the furor she had caused, the lady grew bored at Wells awaiting the issue of the tangled courtship, and her father refused to say that Arran's suit was absolutely off. Seymour's kin hopefully speculated that Arran would lose his pension from the Bed-Chamber post but the King, having taken matters in hand for the nonce, departed for the Newmarket races, accompanied by Lord Rochester.

Charles planned to remain there until April 3; but reports of a new Irish plot summoned him and his party back to London in late March. On his return from Newmarket, Rochester met Savile's packet, informing him of the treachery of Mr. P_____. Alerted and disturbed, Rochester told Burnet in the last of their discussions, "He believed he should never come to Town more."[48] He left London for the last time early in April. On April 5, he wrote to Savile from Bishop Stafford.[49] His exact whereabouts from then until mid-May, when he set out from Adderbury on the fatal journey to Enmore, are unknown. Apparently he was variously at Woodstock, Adderbury, and Windsor. On May 6, a boy was born to Edward Henry Lee and Charlotte Fitzroy: little Charles, the King's namesake. His christening at Windsor was an important occasion with the King himself and Prince Rupert acting as godfathers. Presumably, Lord Rochester helped to celebrate the birth of his nephew Lichfield's first son and heir.[50]

His health seemingly improved, Rochester's spirits (and his religious doubts) revived. In mid-May, he made a fatal decision. Burnet's version was this:

> He had not been long in the Country when he thought he was so well, that being to go to his Estate in *Somerset-shire* he rode thither Post. This heat and violent motion did so inflame an Ulcer, that was in his Bladder, that it raised a very great pain in those parts: Yet he with much difficulty came back by Coach to the Lodge at *Woodstock-park.*[51]

At Woodstock, he was laid in a huge Elizabethan bed of carved black oak with high posters and a canopy. It was the scene of the legendary, deathbed drama played out over the next nine weeks.

SAPIENCE ANGELICAL (MAY–JULY 1680)

All my past life is mine no more
   The flying Houres are gone
Like transitory Dreames. . . .
            —Rochester, *Poems*

The great Idea's of his far-strech'd fame
And Sapience Angelical proclaime.
            Anonymous, "An Elegie upon . . . Rochester"

News of the dying man's condition spread quickly and an ever-enlarging group began to gather at Woodstock Lodge. Among the first at Rochester's side were his wife and mother. There was no staving them off this time from bringing domestic sobriety in to replace the debauchery of Woodstock. The old countess removed the obscene drawings from the walls in readiness for the arrival of the Wilmot children while Lady Rochester took up her anxious vigil beside the invalid's bed. They were joined by the family doctor, Dr. Alexander Radcliffe.[1]

Radcliffe saw at once the seriousness of his patient's condition just as Rochester himself did: the broken ulcer discharged large amounts of purulent matter.[2] His diagnosis was confirmed at the arrival of the King's own physician, Dr. Thomas Short, sent expressly by Charles II to see to John Wilmot's state of health, physical and mental, and report on it. Short was a Catholic and Rochester's mother, for one, looked on him with suspicion. Dr. Radcliffe made it a point later to inquire into Short's background.[3] Meanwhile the two men of medicine agreed that they could do very little for the dying man but dose him with laudanum. Simultaneously, the Dowager Countess fell back on an old, favorite remedy—asses' milk—and wrote to Sir Ralph Verney for assistance in locating an ass.[4]

Surrounded with this ineffectual bustle, Rochester tried desperately to deal with the problems of his disrupted life and reconcile himself to a rapid dissolution.

> He was then wounded both in Body and Mind: He understood Physick
> and his own Constitution and Distemper so well, that he concluded he
> could hardly recover. . . .[5]

During his earlier talks with Gilbert Burnet, he had virtually predicted the terror he was feeling.[6] Lying on his death bed at Woodstock, a terrified John
Wilmot resurrected the beliefs and emotions of his Christian upbringing. His
fear was magnified by Burnet's recent admonitions and his own later efforts to
reject them. According to Robert Parsons,

> Upon his journey he had been arguing with greater vigor against God and
> Religion than ever he had done in his life before, and he was resolved to
> run 'em down with all the argument and spite in the world, but, like the
> great Convert St. Paul, he found it hard to kick against the pricks.[7]

His resistance had been undermined by the very man Rochester hoped
could help him prove that the soul was not immortal. After reading Charles
Blount's *Anima Mundi*, he had sent Blount his translation of Seneca's stoic doctrine: "After Death Nothing Is." Blount wrote the following day on February 7,
1680:

> I cannot but esteem the Translation to be, in some Measure, a confutation
> of the Original; since what less than a divine and immortal Mind could
> have produced what you have there written? Indeed, the Hand that wrote
> it may become *Lumber*, but sure, the Spirit that dictated it, can never be so:
> No, my Lord, your mighty Genius is a most sufficient Argument of its own
> Immortality. . . .[8]

If he feared himself tied to a sinful, dying animal, Rochester could find no
solace in this flattering assurance from Blount, the rational classicist and free-
thinker, that he was also possessed of an immortal soul.

When Rochester had turned for elucidation to Gilbert Burnet, he found
himself caught in a dogmatic web firmly attached to two suspension points:
God and immortality of the soul. With these as givens, Burnet responded to
Rochester's questions simply by begging them. In their conversations over the
winter of 1679–80, usually private but occasionally witnessed by observers
including his wife, Rochester opened his mind to the clever churchman, who
used every available device to convert the roué. Burnet's *Passages* show plainly
how encumbered Rochester was by the preconceptions of his education.[9]

He was firmly resolved to change the course of his bestial life, Rochester told
Burnet, by studying philosophy. Burnet replied that philosophy was a matter of
speculation that few people had the time or capacity to inquire into. Having
subtly reminded Wilmot that his days were numbered, the cleric demolished

The Right Reverend Father in God
Gilbert Lord Bishop of Sarum &
Chancellor of ye most Noble Order of ye Garter.

Figure 24. Gilbert Burnet. Engraving by John Smith. National Portrait Gallery, London. Reproduced by permission.

philosophy as a guide to morality and, for a grace note, razed Seneca as both thinker and model. When Rochester defended his cravings for wine and women as "Natural Appetites," Burnet put them on the level of the beasts Rochester wanted to dissociate himself from. Rochester then proposed intellectual pursuits such as solving a problem in Euclid or writing a poem. Burnet dismissed all such, reminding him of the existence of a Supreme Being who preferred men to spend their time in prayer. When Wilmot, a self-professed latter-day pagan, admitted his belief in this Being, he became vulnerable to the same pressures on the earliest pagan convert to Christianity, of whom Gibbon said:

> His [pagan] fears might assist the progress of his faith and reason; and, if he could once persuade himself to suspect that the Christian religion might possibly be true, it became an easy task to convince him that it was the safest and most prudent party that he could embrace.[10]

Upon Wilmot's admission of God's existence, Burnet intensified his efforts. He shrewdly described God as the wise and loving Father that little John Wilmot never had. Denial of Him resulted in "Punishments": "a total exclusion from Him, with all the horrour and darkness that follows that." Having touched his pupil's psychic tender spot, Burnet spun the rest of his schema: "there was no reason to think [the soul] passed into a State of utter Oblivion"; its memory of past human actions "must raise joy or horrour in it" for all eternity. Eternal joy (Heaven) would come through union with a just, wise, holy, good Father. But, said Rochester, the immortal soul might transmigrate. Burnet called that notion "at best a conjecture, raised by fancy." He continued:

> We know so little of the Nature of our Souls, that it is a vain thing for us to raise an *Hypothesis* out of conjectures we have about it, or to reject one, because of some difficulties that occur to us; since it is as hard to understand how we remember things now, as how We shall do it in another State; only we are sure we do it now, and so we shall then, when we do it.

Burnet's sophistry convinced Rochester less by its logic than its affinity with the sort of experiential reasoning that Rochester had employed in the "Satyr" on man.

Burnet astutely dealt with Rochester's criticism of corrupt priests, another theme in the "Satyr," by agreeing with him.

> However, If some Men, have at several times, found out Inventions to corrupt [Religion], and cheat the World; it is nothing but what occurs in every sort of Employment, to which men betake themselves. *Mountebanks* Corrupt *Physick: Petty-Foggers* have entangled the matters of Property, and all Professions have been vitiated by the Knaveries of a Number of their Calling.

This alliance of sympathies with "Dr. Bendo" the Mountebank and the aristocratic owner of property did much to sway Rochester. However, he still clung to a wistful doubt about an eternity of torment. Burnet had an argument by analogy ready.

> I asked if when by the ill course of his life he had brought so many Diseases
> on his Body, he could blame God for it; or expect that he should deliver
> him from them by a Miracle. [Rochester] confessed there was no reason
> for that: I then urged that if sin should cast the Mind by a natural Effect,
> into endless Horrours and Agonies, which being seated in a Being [the
> soul] not subject to Death, must last forever, unless some Miraculous Power
> interposed, could he accuse God for that which was the effect of his own
> choice and ill life. He said they were happy that believed: for it was not in
> every man's power.

Yet he wished to believe, Rochester admitted, since those confident in God
and a life of eternal blessedness seemed "the happiest Men in the World."
Even so, Burnet's urgings, emotional appeals, and superiority in theological
argumentation still left his opponent unwilling to yield completely to clerical
reasoning. Rochester did, however, arrive one more time at some penitential
resolutions:

> He told me, He saw Vice and Impiety were as contrary to Humane
> Society, as Wild Beasts let loose would be; and therefore he firmly resolved
> to change the whole method of his Life: to become strictly just and true, to
> be Chast and Temperate, to forbear Swearing and Irreligious Discourse, to
> Worship and Pray to his Maker. And that though he was not arrived at a
> full perswasion of Christianity, he would never employ his Wit more to run
> it down, or to corrupt others. . . . At this pass he was when he went from
> London, about the beginning of April.

As usual, when his health improved, Rochester's doubts grew stronger as
well. As he set out from Adderbury in mid-May, he was arguing with renewed
vigor and spite against Burnet's dogma, more determined than ever to reject
the beliefs he had been taught as a child. Then he found himself struck down
on his Road to Damascus.

Rochester was brought to Woodstock about May 20 or 21. After the initial
flurry of activity, his mother summoned from Enmore the Wilmots' chaplain,
Dr. Robert Parsons, who was the same age as his patron and who was "a long
while a sad Spectator and a secret Mourner for his sins."[11] The Dowager
Countess also wrote the first of a series of letters to her sister-in-law in
Battersea, the Lady Johanna St. John, about June 1. Between them, Parsons
and the Countess left a record of the invalid's fright at impending death and
his concern at leaving his wife to face the threats of Stephen Dugdale, Stephen
College, and Titus Oates.

When he arrived on May 26, Parsons found Rochester "labouring under
strange trouble and conflicts of mind, his spirit wounded and his conscience full
of terrors." Wilmot received his chaplain gladly, thanking God for His mercy

in sending someone whose prayers and counsel he needed so much. He confessed that he had been questioning God but with strange new feelings generated by his talks with Burnet. "For God at that time had so struck his heart by
his immediate hand, that presently he argued as strongly for God and Virtue,
as he had before against it." The Wit who had once championed the cause of
atheism at a Person of Quality's house, now rejected his "odd Scheme of
Religion" out of Lucretius and Hobbes. Parsons began reading aloud to him
from the Scriptures, and after a few days he came to a passage that revealed
to Rochester a loving friend who would temper the judgment of a wrathful
God and Father. The miraculous text was Isaiah 53, "a lively description of the
Sufferings of our Saviour, and the benefits thereof":

> a man of sorrows, and acquainted with grief and we turned *our* faces from
> him, and we esteemed him not. Surely he hath borne our griefs, and car-
> ried our sorrows . . . he *was* wounded for our transgressions, he *was* bruised
> for our iniquities: the chastisement of our peace *was* upon him; and with
> his stripes we are healed. . . .

According to Parsons, God wrought upon Rochester's heart so that the
Penitent declared the Mysteries of the Passion were as clear to him as glass. He
expressed the joy and admiration in his soul when he heard these words and
delighted so much in his testimony that when Parsons was not there, Rochester
begged his wife and mother to read the same passage to him until he got it by
heart.

The effects of her husband's long-hoped-for change in character were great
on "his truly loving Consort," as Burnet called her. The long-suffering Elizabeth
Wilmot was rewarded at last by his penitence, his expressed affection for her
and their children, and his anxiety at what lay ahead for them if she persisted
in Catholicism. Although she had endured his absences and infidelities, anger
and sarcasm, and the fatal disease he passed to her, Lady Rochester loved her
husband, especially in his altered state. She had yielded before to his wish in
religious matters. Now he urged her to renounce the Catholic faith, which she
could do by taking communion in the Anglican Church and thus escape from
the threat of the Popish Plot. She had sat in on some of Rochester's talks with
Gilbert Burnet, and the "dark mists" of papist error had started to dissipate.
Again, she acceeded to Rochester's urgings. Several members of the Wilmot
circle made sure her re-conversion was widely known. Parsons's funeral sermon
emphasized the Earl's:

> great joy at his Ladies conversion from Popery to the Church of *England*
> (being as he term'd it, *A faction supported only by Fraud and Cruelty,*) which was
> by her done with deliberation and mature judgment; the dark mists . . . now

cleared, by her receiving the blessed Sacrament with her dying husband, at the receiving of which no man could express more joy and devotion than he did. . . .

The Dowager Countess wrote to Lady St. John, who could spread the news in Whitehall and London:

> Sweet Sister,
> It has pleased God to lay his afflictive hand upon my poor son, in visiting him with a sore sickness, and whether for life or death we cannot guess, but he is reduc'd to great weakness in the outer man. . . . I can only say this, that tho' he lies under as much misery almost as human man can bear, yet he bears his sufferings with so much patience and resignation to God's will, that I confess I take more comfort in him under this visitation, than ever I did in all his life before. . . . He has, I must tell you too, converted his wife to be a protestant again. Pray, pray for his perseverance, dear sister. . . .[12]

Honest John Cary told the Verneys (and Buckinghamshire at large):

> [My Lord Rochester] certainly would make a most worthy brave man, if it would please God to spare his life, but I feare the worst, at present he is very weake & ill. But what gives us much comfort is we hope he will be happy in another world, if it please God to take him hence. And further what is much comfort to my Lady Dowager & us all in the midst of this sorrow is, his Lady is returned to her first love the protestant religion, And on Sunday last received the Sacrament with her lord & hath bin at prayer with us, so as if it might please God to spare & restore him, It would altogether make upp a very great joy to my lady his mother & all us that love him.[13]

Into this atmosphere of Christian joy and pious hope at Woodstock there came, about June 8 or 9, Rochester's malodorous friend, Will Fanshaw. His reasons for coming to the sickbed were mixed; but the results of his visit were the same for all the Wilmots: distress and anger. Fanshaw had already been the propagator of rumors before he ventured to Oxfordshire. On June 5, Gilbert Burnet wrote to Lord Halifax:

> Will Fanshaw just now tells me, Letters are come from the Earl of Rochester, by which it seems he must be dead by this time. Dr. Lower is sent for, but they think he cannot live till he comes to him, an ulcer in his bladder is broken and he pisses matter, he is in extreme pain: he has express'd great remorse for his past ill Life, and has perswaded his Lady to receive the Sacrament with him, and hereafter to go to Church, and declare herself a Protestant, and dies a serious Penitent, and professes himself a Christian. Since Mr. Fanshaw told me this, I hear he is dead.[14]

Burnet's letter further proves that the Wilmots widely reported Lady Rochester's change of faith. It also shows that Fanshaw had advance knowledge of an alteration in Rochester, whether he chose to accept it or not.

Fanshaw was present to witness the Earl's Will when it was drawn and signed about June 10. So were Robert Parsons and Dr. Thomas Witherly, another of the Royal Physicians, who may have substituted for Dr. Lower at the last minute.[15] When Fanshaw was exhorted by the saint-in-the-making to repent his ways, Parsons was in the household to hear about the episode. He included a version of the Earl's speech to a "Gentleman of some character" in the funeral sermon. The fullest account of the Fanshaw-Rochester encounter was given some twenty-two years later, on June 16, 1702, by Dr. Alexander Radcliffe. His story fills in events between June 10 and 12. William Thomas recorded it thus:

> When Wilmot Lord Rochester lay on his Death bed Mr. Fanshaw came to visit him with an intention to stay about a week with him. Mr. Fanshaw sitting by the Bedside perceived his LordP. praying to God through Jesus Christ, and acquainted Dr Radcliff (who attended My Lord R. in his illness and was then in the House) with what he had heard, and told him that My Lord was certainly delirious for to his knowledge (he said) he believed neither in God nor Jesus Christ. The D^r (who had often heard him pray in the same manner) proposed to Mr F. to go up to his Ld^{s}P to be further satisfyed touching this affair. When they came to his Room, the D^r told My Lord what Mr F. had said. Upon which his L^{s}P. addressed himself to Mr F. to this effect: S^{ir} It is true you and I have been very lewd & profane together, and then I was of the opinion you mention; but now I am quite of another mind, & happy am I that I am so. Sr You may assure yourself that there is a Judge & a Future State, & so entred into a very handsom Discourse concerning the last Judgment, Future States, & concluded with a serious & pathetick Exhortation to Mr F. to enter into another Course of Life, adding that he (Mr F.) knew him to be his friend, that he was never more so than at this time. And I (said he) to use a Scripture Expression, I am not mad but speak the words of Truth to Soberness. Upon this, Mr F. trembled & went immediately afoot to Woodstock, & there hired a Horse to Oxford and thence took Coach to London.[16]

Once in London, Fanshaw told everyone that Rochester had gone mad. Back at Woodstock Lodge, the invalid's doctors were conversing before Dr. Short's departure.

> At the same time Dr Shorter [*sic*] (who also attended My Lord in this illness) walking together in the Park, and discoursing touching his Ldp's condition which they agreed to be past remedy, Dr Shorter fetching a very deep sigh, said, Well, I can do him no good, but he has done me a great

deal. When Dr Radcliffe came to reside in London he made enquiry about
Dr Shorter & understood he was before that time a Libertine in Principles,
but after that professed the Roman Catholick Religion.[17]

After both Fanshaw and Dr. Short left Woodstock, the penitent's health still
encouraged those who loved him to sustain hope. On June 15, John Cary
wrote:

> My lord we hope is on the mending hand, but many changes he meets
> withall, pretty good days succeed ill nights, which help to keep up his spir-
> its, but he is very weake, and expresses himself very good, I hope God will
> spare him for his own service for the future.

Robert Parsons suggested the cause of the invalid's "ill nights": "His continual
crying out, one night especially, *how terribly the Temter did assault him, by casting
upon him lewd and wicked imaginations, but I thank God* (said he) *I abhor them all.*"

Toward the end of June, some of the gossip in London began to waft back
to Woodstock Lodge. The Dowager Countess had been away from Adderbury
for five weeks and felt compelled to make a day's journey over to see to matters there; but before going she wrote a long letter to Lady St. John, first detailing her son's condition.

> [He] continues weak, but is sometimes better than he is others. The great-
> est comfort he enjoys is his sleep, and that he does much. He has a kind
> of hectick fever upon him, as the doctors call it, which is not at all times;
> for some times his temper is good outwardly, but the doctor says he is hot
> inwardly; yet I cannot think it, because he is seldom dry. He drinks asses
> milk, and it digests well with him, and some other spoon meats, but he
> takes no broaths made with meat for fear of heat. He spits mightily within
> these two days, which some say is good for him, but I find all evacuations
> weaken him. I confess I can not discern amendment in him yet, but as
> long as life is we have hope.[18]

If her son's physical state was variable, his spiritual amendment, happily,
remained constant. He continued pious and repentant of "his former ill life"
and "with great humility he lays himself low before the throne of grace, begging favour . . . upon account of the merits of Christ alone," while acknowl-
edging himself "the greatest of sinners." On the subject of religion he had not
said "an unsensible word"; but one night a fortnight earlier,

> he was disordered in his head; but then he said no hurt, only some little
> *ribble-rabble*, which had no hurt in it. But it was observed by his wife and
> I particularly, that, whenever he spoke of God, that night, he spoke well &
> with great sense, which we wondered at.[19]

Having reasserted her son's spiritual clarity, the countess went on to censure those who denied it. She was particularly incensed at a manuscript lampoon passing about the Court at Windsor, "Rochester's Farewell"; and she believed Dr. Short to be responsible for rumors about Rochester's mental state.

> But let the wicked of the world say what they please of him . . . I take comfort that the devil rages against my son; it shows his power over him is subdued in him, and that he has no share in him. Many messages and compliments his old acquaintance sent him; but he is so far from receiving of them, that still his answer is "let me see none of them, and I would to God I had never convers'd with some of them." One of his physicians, thinking to please him, told him the K[ing] drank his health the other day. He look'd earnestly upon him, and said never a word, but turn'd his face from him. . . .[20]

As proof of his God-taught wisdom and the penitent's total rejection of the world, the Countess told Lady St. John that in his prayers the previous night, he had asked God for "that unspeakable bliss, of a place in heaven (tho' he were but a door-keeper), to sing to the Lord with the heavenly host."

On June 19, Rochester's mother gave her version of the convert's reproof of Fanshaw. As "his great friend" stood beside the bed, Rochester

> looked earnestly upon him and said, "Fanshaw, think of a God. . . . Believe what I say to you: there is a God, and a powerful God, and he is a terrible God to unrepenting sinners. . . . The time draws near that he will come to judgment with great terror to the wicked, therefore delay not your repentance. His displeasure will thunder against you if you do. . . ." Fanshaw stood and said never a word to him, but stole away out of the room. "Is a gone?" says he, "poor wretch, I fear his heart is hardened."

Told that Fanshaw was saying he should be kept from such melancholy fancies, Rochester tried to dismiss him, saying, "I gave him my advice, but I could say no less to him than I did, let him take it as he pleases." Nevertheless, the callousness of Fanshaw (and others) rankled him and raised self-doubts. "This day has not been so good a day with him as yesterday. He has had some faint fits."[21]

Rochester's anguish was fed by the thought that those who had encouraged him to sin now mocked his professions of faith and called him mad. On the same day as the Countess's letter, June 19 he signed a Remonstrance witnessed by his mother and Robert Parsons. This document, written by an amanuensis (perhaps Lady Rochester), was signed in the unmistakable hand of his mother and the trembling script of the dying Wilmot. There is no reason to suspect a conspiracy between the old Countess and her chaplain to coerce Rochester into signing such a document. His whole life had been lived in terror of death and Hell; in his last days he almost seemed to feel that salvation depended on his ability to convince all the Doubting Thomases of his spiritual rebirth. His widely published Remonstrance read in part:

> For the benefit of all those whom I may have drawn into sin by my example and encouragement, I leave to the world this my last Declaration. . . . That from the bottom of my soul I detest and abhor the whole course of my wicked life. . . . And that the greatest Testimony of my Charity to such is, to warn 'em in the Name of God, and as they regard the welfare of their Immortal Souls, no more to deny his being . . . no more to make a Mock of Sin, or contemn the pure and excellent Religion of my ever Blessed Redeemer, thro whose Merits alone, I one of the Greatest of Sinners, do yet hope for Mercy and Forgiveness.   Amen.[22]

Some of those to whom the Remonstrance was clearly directed, notably Will Fanshaw, failed to respond in the way Rochester and his mother had hoped. On June 26, the Countess told Lady St. John:

> I hear Mr. Fanshaw reports my son is mad, but I thank God he is far from that. . . . I wish that wretch Fanshaw had so great a sense of sin as my poor child has, that so he might be brought to repentance before it is too late; but he is an ungrateful man to such a friend.

Her "poor weak son . . . gives us little hopes of his life, the weakness increasing so much."[23]

As his strength ebbed, Rochester's desperation to prove himself worthy of salvation led him to expend it in increasingly dramatic outbursts. No doubt his agony was sincere, but his long cultivated genius for role-playing aided his determination to prove his sincerity by acting the Greatest of Penitential Sinners to the fullest. In Parsons's words:

> He was . . . more ready to accuse himself than I or anyone else can be; publicly crying out, *O Blessed God, can such a horred creature as I be accepted by thee? Can there be mercy and pardon for me? Will God own such a wretch as I?* . . . Indeed he had a true and lively sense of God's great mercy in striking his hard heart . . . crying out, *that he was the vilest Wretch and Dog that the sun shined upon, or the earth bore*; that now he . . . wish'd he *had been a starving Leper crawling in a ditch*, that he *had been a Linkboy* or a Beggar for his whole life time confin'd to *a dungeon, rather than thus to have sinn'd against his God*.[24]

The Penitent's compulsion to berate himself publicly led him to summon the lowliest swineherd and cattle driver on the estate to his bedroom, where he humiliated himself before those he had formerly scorned and begged the pardon of his servants.[25] His new-found humility, alternating with extreme agitation and fear, made his last month a series of histrionic speeches and actions to which he goaded himself only to sink back into an ever-increasing weakness and lethargy.

On June 22, following the proper ritual set forth in *ars moriendi* literature, the Earl drew together still another set of supporting actors in the drama of codicil-signing. They were an oddly assorted but colorful group: Dr. Witherley, Honest John Cary, the valet Belle-Fasse, and Thomas Smith the children's tutor.[26] On June 25, he wrote a moving plea to Gilbert Burnet, begging for a visit and his prayers; a copy of the letter immediately appeared in a broadside sheet.[27]

> I hope in your Conversation to bee exalted to that degree of Piety, that the World may See how much I abhorr what I Soe long loued, & how much I Glory in repentance in Gods Service. bestow your prayers upon mee that . . . if the Lord Pleaseth to put an end to my Worldly being now, that hee would mercifully except of my death bed repentance, & performe that promise hee hath binn pleased to make, that att what time soever a sinner doth repent hee would receiue him. . . .

Burnet delayed going to Woodstock, however. After the death of Jane Roberts, he had indiscreetly written a reproving letter on January 29, 1680, to the King, who was greatly offended; and the churchman was apprehensive of antagonizing Charles further.[28]

On July 2, the Dowager Countess informed Lady St. John that her poor sick son was yet alive, but only God knew whether he would be restored out of his bed of sickness. She continued:

> I cannot tell you, that there is much sign of a recovery of my son, tho' his fever has left him; little heats he has still, which we imagine proceeds from his ulcer. But that, as I like worst in him, is, he gathers no strength at all, but his flesh wasts so much, and we fear a consumption, tho' his lungs are very good. He sleeps much. His head for the most part is very well. He was this day taken up, and set up in a chair for an hour, and was not very faint when he went to bed. He does not care to talk much. . . . I told my son what Mr. Fanshaw said, that he hoped, he would recover, and leave those principles he now profess'd. He answered,—wretch, I wish I had convers'd all my life time with link boys, rather than with him and that crew, such I mean as Fanshaw is. Indeed I would not live to return to what I was for all world. . . .[29]

Considering his condition on July 2, Rochester's sporadic outbursts of passion for the last three weeks of his life are all the more remarkable and revealing of his mental agony. Distraught that Gilbert Burnet had not responded, Wilmot sent another hyperbolic appeal to Dr. Thomas Pierce of Magdalene Oxford in July.

HOLY MAN! to you I owe w^t consolation I enjoy, in urging God's mer-
cyes agst despair, and holding me up under ye weight of those high and
mountainous sins my wicked and ungovernable life hath heaped upon
me. . . . Pray for me, dear Doctor; and all you y^t forget not God pray for
me fervently. Take Heaven by force, & lett me enter wth you, as it were
in disguise; for I dare not appear before the dread Majesty of that Holy
One I have so often offended.[30]

Rochester's reference to his habitual use of "disguise" is striking. Did he fear
that God discerned his deathbed repentance as mere role-playing, a sinner's
effort to trick Him?

Another "holy" man of Oxford, Bishop John Fell, paid regular visits to the
sick bed. The nature of his Christian consolation may be gauged from the
numerous letters of commiseration he sent to the Hatton family. On July 18,
1680, he was stressing the theme of Ecclesiastes, "All is Vanity," and referring
to Job as a model of resignation to God's will.[31] Burnet said, "[Rochester] was
visited every Week of his sickness by his *Diocesan*, that truly Primitive Prelate,
the Lord Bishop of Oxford who . . . treated him with that decent plainness and
freedom which is so natural to him; and took care also that he [Rochester]
might not on terms more easy than safe, be at peace with himself." The extensive collection of Fell's largely undated letters in June and July 1680 are severe
enough in tone to explain Rochester's viewing Dr. Thomas Pierce as his best
consolation.

When he was not sleeping or pouring out his fears to men of the cloth, the
Earl was making restitution to persons he had injured, paying off his debts,
"which, before, he confessed he had not so fairly and effectually done," forgiving injuries done to him, and showing a tender concern for his servants,
"pittying their troubles in watching with him, and attending him, treating them
with candour and kindness, as if they had been his intimates." The dying
father also on occasion summoned his children to his side for Dickensian
tableaux of pathos and regret.

He called often for his Children, his Son the now Earl of Rochester, and
his three Daughters, and spake to them with a sense and feeling that cannot be expressed in Writing.

Toward little Charles particularly, Rochester directed his parental concern,
"wishing that his *Son might never be a Wit* . . . *but that he might become an Honest and
a Religious Man, which could only be the support and blessing of his Family.*" He
deplored the "vitious" world he had brought his children into, insisted on a
"pious Education" for them, and in God's name "blessed them, pray'd for
'em, and committed them to his Protection."[32]

In mid-July, Rochester's strength improved slightly; and Gilbert Burnet at last resolved his doubts about the wisdom of a trip to Woodstock. On July 17, he told Halifax: "I am to go next week to the Earl of Rochesters who is a little better but not so that there seems great hopes of his recovery."[33] John Cary wrote a similar appraisal on July 18 to Sir Ralph Verney: "My lord Rochester continues very weake, he is sometimes a little lively & gives good hope of his recovery, but anon downe againe, which makes us much to feare the worst."[34] The drama was nearing its denouement. On July 20, Gilbert Burnet arrived at Woodstock Lodge. With the actors assembled and the stage set, the death scene was ready to be played.

If the events of the week had taken place earlier, on April 5–10, 1680, the details for Rochester's canonization would have been complete. Even without Passion Week, the conditions of July 20–26 were strikingly canonical. John Wilmot was 33 years old. He had set out on his final journey home at the start of Passion Week in April, and he had gone through a Gethsemane of isolation and doubt. The Passion of Christ, as related in Isaiah 53, made him see through a glass clearly, to the wonder of his mother, who thought him inspired by God and viewed her son as the conqueror of the Devil and a blessed saint. The doubting physician had been converted, and his disciples had gathered about the sacrificial victim in his final agony. Will Fanshaw had betrayed him, Judas-like. When Burnet arrived, he would witness Wilmot's suffering until Friday and then abandon him on Saturday. On Sunday, John Wilmot would commune with his God in silence, and finally die at 2:00 a.m. on Monday morning. He would be laid to rest in an unmarked tomb. There were all the elements for Burnet and other myth-makers to seize upon.

But Rochester was merely human and his life persisted in jumbling the trivial and absurd with the details from which legends spring. When Burnet arrived at the Lodge, the French valet Belle-Fasse misundertood his name. Wrongly informed, the dying man thought his visitor someone he had no wish to see and refused him. The eminent divine was kept waiting in the lower hall for quite a long time. Then the invalid had convulsions and was dosed with opium. Not until the following morning was Burnet admitted to the sick room. When Rochester awoke and found his mentor beside him, Burnet recounted, he "broke out in the tenderest Expressions concerning my kindness" in traveling so far to visit "such a *One*" as he.

The Penitent's strength was gone, however, and he was lethargic most of the time. Only when he contemplated not being admitted in heaven did

he spake once, not without some extraordinary Emotion. It was indeed the only time he spake with any great warmth to me: For his Spirits were then

low, and so far spent, that, though those about him told me, He had
expressed formerly great fervor in his Devotions; Yet Nature was so much
sunk, that these were in a great measure fallen off.[35]

Even so, Rochester managed to restage the essentials of his dying performance.

He anxiously asked Burnet's opinion of deathbed conversions; as of yore,
the clergyman catechized the Earl, who then recounted his delight in Isaiah 53
and glossed the individual verses from memory. Astonished, Burnet was so
"transported" that afterward he could not recall more than two of Rochester's
textual applications—to his chagrin. Rochester repeated the details of his lady's
reconversion to Protestantism, admitting that he had promoted her seduction
into Catholicism. Burnet later found himself all admiration for Rochester's
husbandly concern and the Wilmots' uxorial devotion. (Burnet himself was not
happy in his three marriages.)

> [D]uring his whole sickness, he expressed so much tenderness and true kind-
> ness to his Lady, that as it had been in fault formerly, so it drew from her
> the most passionate care and concern for him that was possible: which indeed
> deserves a higher Character than is decent to give of a Person yet alive. . . .

John Wilmot also demonstrated once again his paternal fondness. Gathering
his children about him,

> He called me once to look in on them all, and said, *See how Good God has
> been to me, in giving me so many Blessings, and I have carried myself to Him like an
> ungracious and unthankful Dog.*

Once, lapsing into his old ways, he called a servant, "That damned Fellow."
Then he agonized about the oath and asked Burnet to call the man back so the
Earl could beg forgiveness. Burnet said that would not be necessary.[36] Briefly, the
invalid recalled his aspirations to true patriotism. One morning after a good sleep
induced by laudanum, he felt he just might recover after all and spoke of his
friends in government, most favorably of Halifax, as Burnet told Halifax later.

Halifax's brother, Harry Savile, also seems to have been on the dying
man's mind. Harry returned to England from France early in July to transact
some business. His political career was flourishing at last: he had been given
the important post of Vice-Chamberlain so he made a quick trip across the
Channel to kiss the King's hand and sell his post as Groom of the Chamber.
By July 15, he was back at Dunkirk. He apparently made no journey to
Woodstock, and Rochester was worried about him. Burnet said:

> [He] gave it to me in charge, to tell it to one for whom he was much con-
> cerned, that though there were nothing to come after this life, Yet all the

Pleasures he had ever known in Sin, were not worth that Torture he had
felt in his Mind. . . .[37]

If Rochester had Savile in mind, his old friend did take the lesson to heart.
Nan Wharton went to France in 1681; on March 29, she wrote:

> I was at Charenton on Easter day & was heare sheverly cencured to be a
> presbiterian for forsaking M[r] Savile's Scongevigation . . . the Duches of
> Monmouth M[rs] Lafter My Lady Lucy y[e] Duke of Somersett & my Lord
> Lansdown, I hear wear there that day & M[r] Savile himself very
> devout. . . .[38]

Some of Rochester's old friends, like Savile, were moved by his death to mend
their ways: Sedley and Francis Fane among them. Others, however—Dorset,
Etherege, Harry Killegrew, Charles Blount, Elizabeth Barry, Nelly, and Will
Fanshaw—were not.

It was just as well that those friends who loved him were not on hand to
witness his last days. As the week came to a close, John Wilmot grew percep-
tibly worse. Gilbert Burnet was there to see most of it and he left a description
of Rochester's death that cannot be equaled for its bare realism.

> In this disposition of Mind did he continue all the time I was with him,
> four days together; He was then brought so low that all hope of Recovery
> was gone. Much purulent matter came from him with his Urine, which he
> passed always with some pain; But one day with unexpressible torment: yet
> he bore it decently, without breaking out into Repinings or impatient
> Complaints. He imagined he had a Stone in his Passage; but it being
> searched, none was found. The whole substance of his Body was drained
> by the Ulcer, and nothing was left but Skin and Bone: and by lying much
> on his Back, the parts there began to mortifie; But he had been formerly
> so low, that he seemed as much past all hopes of life as now: which made
> him one Morning after a full and sweet Night's rest procured by
> Laudanum, given him without his knowledge, to fancy it was an effort of
> Nature, and to begin to entertain some hopes of Recovery: For he said, He
> felt himself perfectly well, and that he had nothing ailing him, but an
> extreme weakness, which might go off in time: and then he entertained me
> with the Scheme he had laid down for the rest of his life, how retired, how
> strict, how studious he intended to be: But this was soon over, for he
> quickly felt that it was only the effects of a good sleep, and that he was still
> in a very desperate state. I thought to have left him on *Friday*, but, not
> without some Passion, he desired me to stay that day: there appeared no
> symptome of present death; and a Worthy Physitian then with him, told
> me, That though he was so low that an accident might carry him away on
> a suddain; Yet without that, he thought he might live yet some Weeks. So
> on *Saturday*, at Four of the Clock in the Morning I left him, being the 24th
> of *July*. But I durst not take leave of him; for he had expressed so great an

unwillingness to part with me the day before, that, if I had not presently yielded to one day's stay, it was like to have given him some trouble, therefore I thought it better to leave him without any Formality. Some hours after he asked for me, and when it was told him I had gone, he seem'd to be troubled, and said, *Has my Friend left me, then I shall die shortly.* After that he spake but once or twice till he died. He lay much silent: Once they heard him praying very devoutly. And on *Monday* about Two of the Clock in the Morning, he died without any *Convulsion*, or so much as a groan.

At last John Wilmot had found repose.

AFTERWARDS

The day after Rochester's death, his Will was read in the presence of his widow, his mother, John Cary, Francis Warre, and two serving women. His son Charles was to receive his "hereditaments" and Lady Rochester kept the estates legally hers by jointure. The Wilmot daughters were to share £12,000: Anne to be paid £4,000 when she became eighteen and Elizabeth and Mallet the same when they reached sixteen. All this money was guaranteed by the Indenture of 1672. The Earl's debts were to be paid, with charges against £5,000 "due to mee upon two severall grants or patents out of his Majesties Court of Exchequer." Even in death, John Wilmot demanded every farthing owed him by Charles II. Belle-Fasse got his master's clothes and linen; Robert Parsons got the living at Charlence; and "an infant child by the name of Elizabeth Clerke" got "fourty pounds annuitie . . . to contynue during her life."

Finally, the widow and her mother-in-law were joint executrixes of the estate—so long as the widow remained single and lived in harmony with the Dowager Countess. If she did not, the estate fell entirely to the management of Anne Wilmot or, in the event of her death, to Rochester's "verie good uncle," Sir Walter St. John. Sir Allen Apsley was also an executor, along with "John Cary of Woodstocke esquire." Thus the dying penitent reconciled with his opponents in the Woodstock controversy. Since Rochester's Woodstock patents expired when he died, his effects had to be removed from the Lodge in readiness for the Lichfields. The Dowager Countess had already followed her son's instructions to burn the "filthy pictures" adorning the walls. She and Sir Walter then proceeded to destroy his remaining papers, including whatever might prove politically embarrassing.

On August 9, two weeks after he died, Rochester's body was carried to the hamlet of Spelsbury, where the Lee family vault was located. All of the immediate family were present but no record exists of others who gathered to weep and rejoice for the man hailed as Strephon in broadsheets being hawked in London on the same day. However, it is clear that many of those nearest to Rochester in life were absent. Parsons used the two-week interval between Rochester's death and funeral to compose a sermon. Praised in time by Dr. Samuel Johnson, the sermon was Parsons's masterpiece, assurance of earthly reputation, and passport to an ecclesiatical career of decent obscurity.

John Wilmot's survivors then turned to their own affairs. His widow devoted herself to her children and reaffirmed her Protestantism by speaking out against papists and her "perversion" by them. On July 27, 1681, a year to the day after Rochester's death, she too died. On August 2, one of the Hattons wrote: "The young La: Rochester is dead suddenly of an apoplexie." Again, the family journeyed to Spelsbury Church to lay the wife beside the husband. The Dowager Countess, at the age of sixty-seven, resumed her role as guardian to another set of young heirs.

Ten-year-old Charles Wilmot declined swiftly after his mother's death, however. On Nov. 12, 1681, Captain Edward Cooke hurried to London on business, "particularly young Lord Rochester's . . . of whose life Dr. Radcliffe is hopeless." About the same time, Charles Bertie informed his sister, "I am told the young Earl of Rochester is given over by the doctors." Even as the letters posted across the country, Charles lay dead at Adderbury. In nearby Oxford, Anthony Wood recorded in his journal that Charles Wilmot died on Saturday, Nov. 12, and was "Buried at Spillsbury by his father and mother, W. Dec. 7." With only three female Wilmots left, Wood wrote, "So is that family extinct." With no more to build on in the way of male issue, the Dowager Countess never got around to erecting a monument to the fallen Wilmots.

Instead, she worked to further the interests of Rochester's daughters through the favor of her Lee grandson, the Earl of Lichfield. She appended reminding postscripts in her letters to the Lichfields, off at Court: "Your tow littel cosens are your sarvants"; "Bette Wilmot and Mallet are your sarvants." In 1685 she solicited Lady Lichfield's sponsorship of Anne Wilmot, her oldest granddaughter, who married Henry Baynton, a "contry gentellman but truly I think an honest man and one she will have in her power to bee hapy in if she pleases":

> I am glad my daughter Bainton has gave your La:^SP a satesfaction too your desires I am sure she will ever bee ambitious too keep your La:^SP good opinion, and favor as the greatest hapiness she has. . . .[1]

The Lees themselves, as always, required a good deal of direction from their grandmother. She supplied a constant stream of advice to Edward Henry, as did Lady Lindsey, his dictatorial mother. Young Lichfield's marriage brought him many problems. His wife, truly the daughter of Barbara Villiers and Charles Stuart, was wantonly extravagant. Family finances, complicated by greed, caused quarrels with the husbands of his two cousins. Lichfield's royal father-in-law and uncle kept him in endless disputes and political difficulties. So long as the Stuarts remained on the throne, the indecisive Earl underwent perpetual squabbles. When William of Orange replaced them in 1688, the Lichfields went into permanent banishment from court. And the constant meddling of old Lady Rochester and Lady Lindsey only made matters worse.

Her Lee granddaughters were also a vexation to the Dowager Countess. Soon after Rochester's death, Ellen (Lee) Bertie's husband was created the Earl of Abingdon. His support of Danby had produced severe family strains in 1679–80. Money and estate disagreements brought Abingdon and his wife's grandmother to a rupture unhealed for four years. Distressed by the death of Uncle Rochester and the animosity between her husband and grandmother, gentle Ellen underwent a long depression that elicited worried letters from her relatives. In time she found solace in her domestic duties, religion, and charitable works.

Of all the Lees, Nan was the most troublesome. When Uncle Rochester died, Nan was deeply grieved. She kept a miniature portrait of him in a velvet case and began writing a series of poems venting her sorrow and remorse. Early in 1681, she left for France, apparently for reasons of health. Letters to her rakish husband, Tom Wharton, in March and April show her back in cheerful spirits, but her health was impaired as her witty letter of April 1 showed. Nan's infatuation with her unfaithful husband balanced uneasily against her realization of his indifference to her and his feeling that a wife was an inconvenience. After her return to England in July 1681, a series of letters between Nan and Gilbert Burnet charted her growing disillusionment and despair.

On July 14, 1681, Burnet discerned Nan's Christian faith was flagging; he urged her to read theology to improve her "temper" and assured her of his great affection. On December 5, 1682, an un-Christian (and Rochesterian) mention of the soul being dissolved in death's dark night in one of Nan's poems elicited Burnet's censure. Another shocking piece of news produced an even sharper reprimand on December 8:

> I heard you were upon parting with Mr. Wharton. . . . I look upon all such things as both the wickedest and the maddest things possible; it is a downright rejecting the yoke of God, and rebelling against his providence . . . in the moment one takes up such a resolution, unless they are really in danger of their lives, which I am sure is not your case. . . .[2]

Burnet was mistaken; Nan's life was in danger. But Wharton appealed to him to intervene with her; the Dowager Countess came to London in December 1682 to exert her own views; and between them all, Nan stayed with her debauched husband until her death three years later. The old Countess told her Grandson Lichfield in a letter of 1685 what had ensued.

> I am vex that ill man [Wharton] should carry that forteine of my unfor-
> tunate daughter whom hee used soe Barbarous . . . for hee gave her the
> pox a great many yeares agoe and never told her of it, hee kept another
> woman whom hee had children by, in three year's almost before she dyed,
> hee never went in bed with her, and though she had bin an howre together
> upon her knees to know his reason why hee was angry with her hee would
> never tell her for the last of her life. . . .

Nan was angered by Burnet's reproof at the report of her wishing to leave Wharton. She was also resentful of his literary obtuseness when he admired Mulgrave's *Essay on Satire*, as she was by those who continued to attack her beloved uncle: Nat Lee, who simultaneously attacked and venerated him in *The Princess of Cleves* (September 1680); John Crowne, who satirized him in *The City Politiques* (January 1683); Thomas Otway, who mocked the genuineness of his conversion in the person of Daredevill in *The Atheist* (May 1683). She welcomed the aid of Rochester's disciples—Aphra Behn, Jack Howe, Bob Wolseley, Francis Fane—who deflected the blows of his enemies, answered his critics, praised his genius and person, and kept his fame alive with the staging and printing of *Valentinian* (1685, 1686). Such comfort as she got from guarding Rochester's reputation was sustained in the last year of her life by a greater closeness with Ellen, who "maid it her business too bee oftenor with her sister," as the old Countess sharply observed. In the summer of 1685, Ellen Bertie spent time at Adderbury with Nan, and the sisters helped with wedding preparations for Rochester's eldest daughter, Anne, "a tall handsome body," to Henry Baynton.

Soon after the wedding took place at Adderbury Church on September 1, 1685, Nan Wharton was on her deathbed at Adderbury Manor. Robert Parsons came up from Wiltshire to comfort her, as he had her Uncle Rochester, but her comfort was cold indeed. Her vicious husband sent his agents to make sure no one tampered with her Will that left everything to him. Her own family badgered her. And poor, unhappy Nan's death was made worse for seeing that nobody cared about anything but her money.

The disruption of John Wilmot's public world came in 1685. King Charles died, reportedly with the final words, "Don't let poor Nelly starve." York mounted the throne as James II, soon dispersing the royal mistresses. He packed Lady Portsmouth back to France with the plunder from her days as chief mistress, first stripping her son of his title. Mrs. Nelly was retired to obscurity in Windsor with a small pension, and Hortense Mancini was banished to spend the remainder of her life soaked in brandy. In July 1685, Robert Whitehall died in Oxford after being a "hanger-on" at Merton for thirty-five years, as Anthony Wood acidly remarked. Tom Otway emerged from a life of poverty to die horribly by choking on a piece of begged bread, rumor said.

John Oldham's deathbed repentance was published, asking God for forgiveness at being "inveigled" by "gay Monsters" into writing works that were "Pimps and Panders to Vice."

A series of letters from the old Countess to her "dearest sonne," Lichfield, in 1685–86, chronicled the parallel disintegration of John Wilmot's family. After Nan Wharton's death on October 29, 1685, at the age of 25, the Countess wrote to Lichfield on November 13:

> [She] has gave all her estate too that vyle husband of hers both present and future, without clodging of it with any legecys but to Sarvants and Little peopell . . . she has not gave mee as much as an inameld ring too ware for her sake. I sent to that unworthy husband of hers for a picture of my sonne Rochesters which she had but in a shagering case and hee refused it mee soe base a man was never borne to refuse soe small a thing when I had, had the trobell of them and there family in my house for nothing. . . .[3]

Apparently this was the miniature portrait of Rochester that Anne Lee had given to Gilbert Burnet in 1682.

At the close of January 1686 the old Countess reported that Dr. Radcliffe was tending her in a vague illness, but she maintained sufficient strength to scold Lichfield for his usual dilatoriness at "business" and to be suprised when John Cary proved not to be of sterner stuff. "Poore Cary is soe strangly afflicted for the death of his wife. . . . hee takes' excessively one for her. . . ."

In July 1686, Lichfield's younger brother Frank, lodging in London above a confectioner's shop, became acquainted with a sergeant's daughter, who ensnared the gullible youth into wedlock. Jack Verney passed the news on to Sir Ralph: "she is not a beauty, but her portion is £1,000." The family turned cold faces against the wayward son and his lowly bride. Sternest of all was old Lady Rochester, whose last preserved letter to Lichfield on August 11, 1686, unmistakeably reveals the woman who was mother to John Wilmot.

> My Deare Sonne . . .
> Your unfortunate brother Frank Lee was heare to see mee yesterday and brought his wife which in my opinion is a very plane woman not such a won as tow make a man run the hazard of his ruine by her. I confes they were a malencholy sight too mee and I beleive they decerned it for I never invited them too mee as much as one night with mee . . . I askt him wether hee had a great portion with his wife hee said noe hee had a very littell one but a 1000 Pd. . . . I told him hee was undone. hee said nothing too that nether but I descerned the teares was in his eyes, soe I said noe more . . . beefore hee went away I saw him frowne . . . but sayd not as much as too ask mee blessing and soe wee parted. . . .

In the letters to Lichfield, Rochester's mother showed her constant self.

She told him that her granddaughter urged her to visit, despite her "infir-mityes." Anne Baynton probably was less concerned with the old lady's presence than her refusal to yield up Anne's dowry before her eighteenth birthday. The Bayntons tried repeatedly to persuade the Countess to pay the money left to her in Rochester's Will and at last filed legal claims against her, but not until 1688, when she was nineteen, did Anne Baynton pry her dowry out of her grandmother's custody.

In August 1686, the aging Countess mentioned "the littell busines yet, I would faine doe before I dye": there were still two Wilmot girls to marry off. Elizabeth was matched with the son of the Second Earl of Sandwich, "Ned" Montagu, whose tepid courtship of Elizabeth Mallet had lost her to Lord Rochester. In time-honored fashion, negotiations between the Wilmots and Montagues dragged on at length; finally, after his father's death in 1688, the Third Earl made Elizabeth Wilmot his Countess in 1689. She brought a fortune of £22,000, which her grandmother (in time-honored fashion) delayed paying until the Montagues, like the Bayntons, took to the law; but not until 1692 did the Earl sign a legal discharge of claims against his wife's grandmother.

Mallet Wilmot, Rochester's youngest daughter, was paired off with the son of an old friend of her father's, the Welsh Lord Edward Vaughan. On August 18, 1692, at St. Giles in the Fields, Mallet and John Vaughan were married. John Vaughan was made Viscount Lisburne of Antrim; and from 1694 until 1698, the Lisburnes divided their time between Trawscoed, Wales, and London, where Lisburne was the M.P. for Cardiganshire. After settling down in Wales, Mallet was kept informed of family and theatrical events by Elizabeth Barry, her father's former mistress. Her quiet life interrupted on occasion by the lawsuits to which the old Countess obligated her descendents, Lady Lisburne died at last on 13 January 1709.

The Countess's last Lee granddaughter, Ellen Bertie, Lady Abingdon, died suddenly on May 31, 1691, in Wiltshire, leaving her husband to commission John Dryden to write the commemorative elegy, "Eleonora." With all three Wilmot granddaughters safely married and both Lee granddaughters dead, old Lady Rochester had completed her "littell busines." She left Oxfordshire for London and settled in the parish of St. Anne's Soho on Carlisle Street. There she died in 1696 at the age of eighty-two.

For some time to come, the legacy of John Wilmot lived on in his vivacious daughter Elizabeth, the Countess of Sandwich. In 1697, after her grandmother's death, Lady Sandwich left for Paris, ostensibly for her health but also to work for the Stuarts' restoration to the throne. Matthew Prior, on a diplomatic mission to Paris, reported her "dangerously ill." But the aged Ninon de l'Enclos declared that Lady Sandwich had more spirit and true merit than all the women of France. Back in England after 1700, Elizabeth Montague and her dimwitted husband received visitors and compliments on their estate at Broughton. When the succession of the Hanovers dampened her hopes for a Jacobite return, she left England for residence in France. She continued to support the Pretender, writing him of her "faithful zeal for your service" and declaring her pleasure at his marriage to the Princess Clementina Sobieska of Poland. Like her grandfather, Henry Wilmot, Elizabeth Wilmot followed a banished Stuart to the Continent, spent her life working for his restoration, and died at last in a self-imposed exile—at the age of eighty-three. Her death meant the end of the Wilmots, though the bloodline continued through the Earls of Warwick, Sandwich, and Lisburne.

Long before that, a final confrontation between the Wilmots and the Lees took place.[4] On February 25, 1701, the House of Lords heard the suit filed against Edward Henry Lee the Earl of Lichfield by the Earl of Sandwich and the Lady Elizabeth, John Viscount Lisburne and the Lady Mallett, and the Honorable Francis Greville, Esq. and the Lady Anne. (Greville, Anne Wilmot's second husband, was ancestor to the Earls of Warwick.) The case concerned the Wilmot estate at Adderbury. The plaintiffs asserted that Adderbury Manor had been held by the Wilmot family since the tenth year of the reign of James I and that Henry Wilmot had inherited it part freehold and part on lease from the Bishop of Winchester.

> His widow Lady Anne, as mother and guardian to John, Earl of Rochester, sold Wilmot House, in Scotland Yard, and got Dr. Duppa, then Bish. of Winchester to renew the lease on favorable terms.

Then, in 1682, after the death of Charles Wilmot, the Third Earl of Rochester, she named the Earl of Lichfield her heir.

The daughters of John Wilmot and their husbands asserted that this action was illegal and prejudicial to their interests. As usual, the old Countess had robbed the Wilmots to enrich the Lees. A Deposition filed by Sir Walter St. John supported the Wilmot claim. Nevertheless, the Lords found in favor of Lichfield; and the ancestral manor of the Wilmots became another spoil for the progeny of Francis Henry Lee, the first love of Anne St. John.

Banished from Court life, the Earl and Countess of Lichfield reportedly did good works and acts of charity. They felt, however, that charity begins at home. Once possessed of Adderbury Manor, they had it pulled down and a new, suitably stylish Palladian manor built to replace it. Likewise, they built a new Ditchley manor house designed by James Gibbs with elegant wood carvings and plaster work by Henry Flitcroft and William Kent. When it was completed, they had the old, half-timbered Tudor mansion torn down. The new

Ditchley Manor became a major attraction for tourists in the eighteenth century.[5] A guidebook, *A Tour from Stow to Blenheim and Ditchley*, published in 1760, shows how totally the physical world of John Wilmot had changed since John Evelyn described it in 1664. The Royal Preserves at Woodstock, given by Queen Anne to the Duke of Marlborough for services rendered, was no longer a hunting preserve but the site of Blenheim Palace, Vanbrugh's gigantic pile of masonry, and the sculpted grounds of "Capability" Brown.

Ditchley Park had become an elegant shrine to the ancestry of the Earl and Countess of Lichfield. A visitor could see Lely portraits of the old Countess of Rochester and Lady Lindsey and a Van Dyck portrait of Francis Henry Lee in the Tapestry Drawing Room, then view a Lely painting of Charles II and the Duchess of Cleveland, together with a portrait of the Lady Charlotte Fitzroy in the White Drawing Room. There were numerous Lee portraits in the Hall and a Lely portrait of the Duke and Duchess of York with their daughters, the Princesses Mary and Anne, in the Tapestry Room.

Nowhere was there anything to suggest that the Earls of Rochester had once been intimately connected with Ditchley or Adderbury. At Woodstock, the bed in which John Wilmot died was on view, as it is today. Everything else had vanished. His lodgings at Whitehall were consumed by fire in April 1691. Within thirty years of his death in 1680, the world of that profane wit had been razed, totally altered, or transformed.

> Dead, wee become the Lumber of the World,
> And to that Masse of matter shall be swept.
> Where things destroy'd, with things unborne, are kept.
> Devouring tyme, swallows us whole
> Impartiall Death confounds Body, and Soule.

APPENDIX: GENEALOGICAL CHARTS

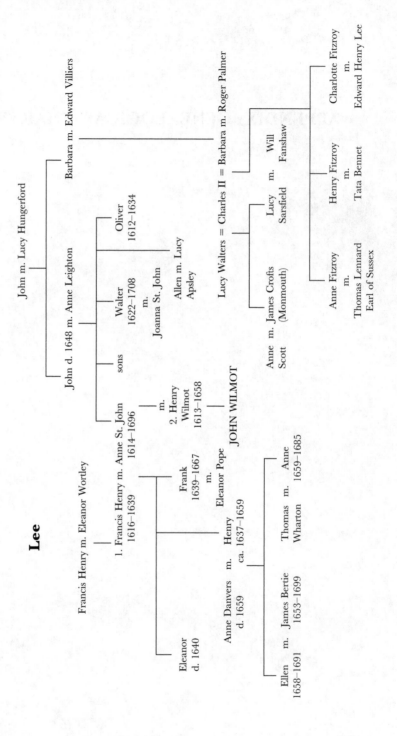

St. John

John m. Lucy Hungerford

Barbara m. Edward Villiers

John d. 1648 m. Anne Leighton

sons

Walter
1622–1708
m.
Joanna St. John

Oliver
1612–1634

Allen m. Lucy
Apsley

Lucy Walters = Charles II = Barbara m. Roger Palmer

Anne m. James Crofts
Scott   (Monmouth)

Lucy m. Will
Sarsfield   Fanshaw

Anne Fitzroy
m.
Thomas Lennard
Earl of Sussex

Henry Fitzroy
m.
Tata Bennet

Charlotte Fitzroy
m.
Edward Henry Lee

Lee

Francis Henry m. Eleanor Wortley

1. Francis Henry m. Anne St. John
1616–1639   1614–1696

m.

2. Henry
Wilmot
1613–1658

JOHN WILMOT

Eleanor
d. 1640

Frank
1639–1667
m.
Eleanor Pope

Anne Danvers m. Henry
d. 1659   ca. 1637–1659

Thomas m. Anne
Wharton   1659–1685

Ellen m. James Bertie
1658–1691   1653–1699

Wilmot

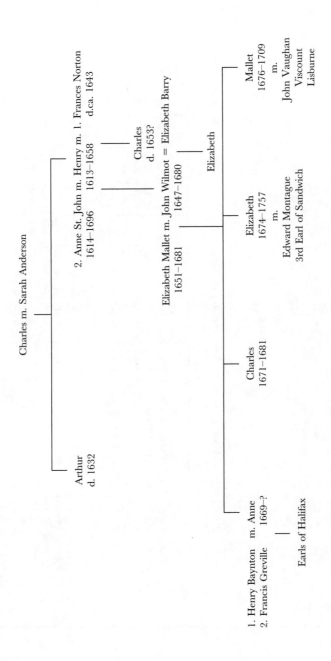

Charles m. Sarah Anderson

Arthur
d. 1632

2. Anne St. John m. Henry m. 1. Frances Norton
1614–1696   1613–1658   d.ca. 1643

Charles
d. 1653?

Elizabeth Mallet m. John Wilmot = Elizabeth Barry
1651–1681   1647–1680

Elizabeth

Charles
1671–1681

Elizabeth
1674–1757
m.
Edward Montague
3rd Earl of Sandwich

Mallet
1676–1709
m.
John Vaughan
Viscount
Lisburne

m. Anne
1669–?

1. Henry Baynton
2. Francis Greville

Earls of Halifax

Bertie

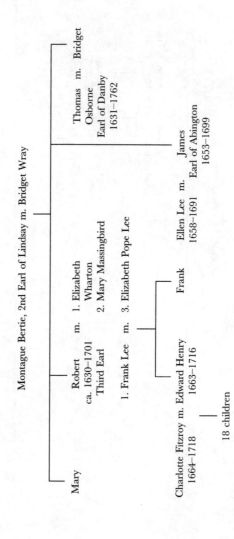

Montague Bertie, 2nd Earl of Lindsay m. Bridget Wray

Mary

Robert m. 1. Elizabeth
ca. 1630–1701   Wharton
Third Earl   2. Mary Massingbird
3. Elizabeth Pope Lee

1. Frank Lee m.

Frank

Ellen Lee m. James
1658–1691   Earl of Abington
1653–1699

Thomas m. Bridget
Osborne
Earl of Danby
1631–1762

Charlotte Fitzroy m. Edward Henry
1664–1718   1663–1716

18 children

Stuart

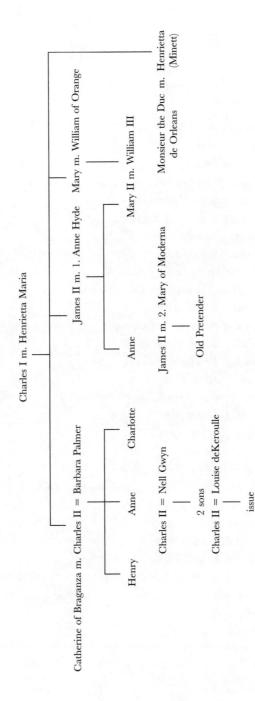

Charles I m. Henrietta Maria

Catherine of Braganza m. Charles II = Barbara Palmer

James II m. 1. Anne Hyde   Mary m. William of Orange

Henry   Anne   Charlotte

Charles II = Nell Gwyn

2 sons

Charles II = Louise deKeroulle

issue

Anne   Mary II m. William III

James II m. 2. Mary of Moderna

Old Pretender

Monsieur the Duc m. Henrietta
de Orleans   (Minett)

ABBREVIATIONS

ARP	*Attribution in Restoration Poetry* (Vieth)
BL	British Library
BodL	Bodleian Library
CC	*Calendar of the Clarendon State Papers Preserved in the Bodleian Library*
CSPD	*Calendar of State Papers. Domestic*
DNB	*Dictionary of National Biography.*
DUJ	*Durham University Journal*
ECL	*Eighteenth-Century Life*
EL	*Essays in Literature*
HMC	Historical Manuscripts Commission
JH	*Journal of Homosexuality*
JHC	*Journal of the House of Commons*
JHI	*Journal of the History of Ideas*
JHL	*Journal of the House of Lords*
JSH	*Journal of Social History*
LSB	Library of Shakespeare's Birthplace
MLN	*Modern Language Notes*
MLR	*Modern Language Review*
N&Q	*Notes and Queries*
PBA	*Proceedings of the British Academy*
PBSA	*Publications of the Bibliographical Society of America*
PLL	*Papers on Language and Literature*
POAS	*Poems on Affairs of State*
PRO	Public Records Office
RES	*Review of English Studies*
R-SL	*The Rochester-Savile Letters*
SEL	*Studies in English Literature*
SP	*Studies in Philology*
ST	*State Trials* (Howell)

NOTES

Introduction

1. Farley-Hills, *Critical Heritage*, 86.
2. Ibid., 116, 128.
3. Ibid., 87.
4. Ibid., 46.
5. Ibid., 204.
6. Foucault, *Uses of Pleasure*, passim.
7. Laqueur, *Making Sex*, 13, 22.
8. Sedgwick, *Epistemology*, 1.
9. Rochester, *Letters* (Treglown), 99.

Chapter 1

1. Prinz, *John Wilmot, Earl of Rochester*, 22; Hearne, *Remarks and Collections of Thomas Hearne*, 3:104.

2. *A History of Wiltshire*, 9:78–80; *Wiltshire Visitation Pedigrees, 1623*, 105–6:167–70.

3. Bodleian Library, Clarendon Mss., Sept. 1640–Jan. 1641, f. 1459; BL, Add. Mss. 23682. Information about the Lees, not all of it accurate, can be found in G. E. C., *The Complete Peerage*, ed. V. Gibbs, (1910–1914); Sir John Burke, *A genealogic and heraldic history*, 304. (Harry) Lee is pictured in Margaret Verney, *Memoirs of the Verney Family*, vol. 4. In the early seventeenth century, the average age for male heirs at a first marriage was approximately 21–22. Stone, *Family*, 46.

4. Verney, *Memoirs*, passim.

5. He was nursed by Honest John Cary. Smallpox was the second deadliest disease in England in the seventeenth century, killing about 16 percent of its victims and leaving many of the rest blind and scarred. Stone, *Family*, 76–77.

6. Near the west entrance of Spelsbury Church, a plaque erected by her mother reads in part: "In hanc capsula sunt quoque recondita, instar gemmarum, Ossa Ellenorae Lee . . ., pulchritudinis forma praestantissimae . . ., Augusti MDCXL."

7. BodL, Clarendon Mss., Sept. 1640–Jan. 1641, f. 1491.

8. Writing from near Oxford in October 1642, Cary Gardiner told Sir Ralph Verney: "My lady Lee on Thursday came to Oxford to speak with my lord Saye concerning the armes she had sent to the Kinge. If she could she would have made peace with him. But he not being a courtier would not listen to her, so she returned away with a great blame the contry laid upon her; her being a widow made her to be a little pittied, twas that her fearfulness." [*sic*]Cf. Anthony Wood, 1640–45 in Wood, *Life*; Beesley, *History of Banbury*, 294–337; Varley, *The Siege of Oxford*; Clarendon, *Selections*, 214–16.

9. BodL, Clarendon Mss., Sept. 1640–Jan. 1641, f. 1457.

10. Pickering's funeral plaque (in English) says he was 81 years old when he died on March 13, 1645, having served "the hon:ble familie of the Lees of Ditchley" for "XXX yeares." Rochester's mother used the term "friends" to refer to members of the family but she also used it to refer to people "joined to one another in mutual benevolence." Cf. *Shorter Oxford English Dictionary*, 3rd ed., 1:752.

11. Details about Charles Wilmot's chequered career in Ireland are given in the *Irish State Papers, 1611–1614*, and *1615–1625*; and *Privy Council Acts, June 1623–March 1625*.

12. The ancestry of the Wilmot family appears in Trinity College Dublin Ms., vol. F.4.18. Biographical information about Henry Wilmot is found in Burke, *Peerage* (1883), 588–89; *Collins's Peerage of England* (1812), 2:559; 3:783; 9:401; and Clarendon's *Selections*, 276–79. The life of Wilmot in Lloyd's *Memoires* gives specifics that are often suspect. For an account of the rebellion of the Seven Provinces of the Netherlands against Spain and the role of English troops, see Pieter Geyl, *The Netherlands in the Seventeenth Century*.

13. Cf. Oxford, *Alumni Oxoniensis, 1500–1714*, Early Series, vol. 4.

14. Clarendon, *The History of the Rebellion*, 2:11–12, 3:224–26; 5:441; 6:82–85, 115–19; 8:64. For Charles I and the Civil Wars, see Kenyon, *The Stuarts*, 73–111. Cf. Thomas, "Two Cultures?" 168–93.

15. BodL, Clarendon Mss, March–July 1654, f. 311.

16. Clarendon, *History*, 8:94, 269, 275. Lloyd quotes the Queen Mother as writing, "his good carriage here hath merited his good entertainment," on April 7, 1645. *Memoires*, 466.

17. Verney dates the wedding in 1644. Henry Wilmot appears to have been in Oxfordshire steadily from April through June. In a letter dated April 2, 1644, he reported to Prince Rupert from Oxford about the condition of local troops. BL, Add. Mss. 18981, f. 125.

18. Verney, *Verney Papers* (1925), 1:149.

19. On July 4, 1680, when John Wilmot was dying, Anthony Wood wrote in his diary, "I have been credibly enformed by knowing men that this John earl of Roff. was begotten by Sir Alan Apsley, kt." Apsley, who had been raised by Sir John St. John, was the husband of Lady Rochester's younger sister. Wood, *Life*, 2:492.

20. On July 12, 1646, Edward Hyde, whose business it was to keep track of both the Wilmots, wrote that he had sent them a joint letter the week before. BodL, Clarendon Mss., May 1646–Dec. 1646, f. 147.

21. Wilmot's key role in the King's escape after Worcester is clear not only from Charles's account to Pepys but other sources as well. See Pepys, *Charles II's Escape from Worcester*, 38–77, 88, 106.

22. BodL, Clarendon Mss., Nov. 1652–Feb. 1654, f. 383; March–July 1654, ff. 188, 311. Ratisbon was the ancient name of the modern Regensburg in Bavaria.

23. BodL, *Calendar of the Clarendon State Papers Preserved in the Bodleian Library*, 3:336; 4:503. Future references are to *CC*. Rochester's financial plight was due to the notorious extravagance of Charles Stuart. The Clarendon Mss. contain letters from the future King to Wilmot begging for additional money and promising "he will be a very good husband of it." CC, 2:40, 411. See also BL Add. Mss. 32093, ff. 296, 336–37. Cf. *Shorter O.E.D*, 2:1451: "Pawn: A thing (or person) given, deposited, or left in another's keeping, as a security for a debt." Brussels, Ghent, and Dunkirk as the death place of Henry Wilmot seem incapable of resolution.

24. Cf. Stone, *Family*, 68.

25. "Spellsbury. In the north isle of this church is a great vault . . . In the said vault lyeth buried Henry Lord Wilmot, with this inscription on his coffyn graven on a brass

plate: Henricus Wilmot, baro de Adderbury, vicomes Athlone, comes Rossensis, serenissimo regi Carolo 2do e conciliis sanctoribus. . . . obiit 19 Febr. an. dom. 1657 [O.S.] aetatis 45." Wood, *Life*, 2:492.

26. *Committee for Compounding Cases, 1647–June 1650*, 2235–36; *Interregnum Acts and Ordinances, 1642–1660*, 2:521; *Compounding Proceedings, 1643–1660*, 674, 684, 690, 696, 705, 728; Verney, *Verney Papers* (1899), 3:277. Thomas Appletree, Cary's predecessor, recommended him for the job and was seconded by Edward Ashe (who reportedly bought Adderbury Manor).

27. Parsons, *Sermon*, 1–9; cf. Burnet, *Passages*, 15.

28. Verney, *Verney Papers* (1899), 2:228; 4:119. Verney, *Verney Papers* (1925), 2:60–61. *CC*, 4:166–67; Stone, *Family*, 183–84.

29. *CC*, 2:240.

30. The Lees' governor was probably the Henry Godfrey listed in the *Alumni Cantabrigiensis*, Part I, 2:227. He entered Cambridge at 15 and studied at Caius from 1642 to 1648, when he took the M.A. He would have gone to Ditchley in 1648, stayed there until 1653, when he left for Paris, and died there at the age of 27.

31. Clarendon Mss., Nov. 1653–Feb. 1654, ff. 123, 282, 383; March–July 1654, ff. 188, 311; *CC*, 2:357.

32. *Spelsbury Church Warden's Book*. Cf. Verney, *Verney Papers* (1925), 1:149.

33. Verney, *Verney Papers* (1925), 2:9.

34. *Spelsbury Church Warden's Book*.

35. *CC*, 4:619; G. E. C., "Lees," in *Complete Baronetage*; BL, Harleian Ms. 7003. f. 254; Prinz, *John Wilmot*, 273; Verney, *Verney Papers* (1925), 1:149.

36. Stone gives an illuminating account of child-rearing from swaddling and breast-feeding to tutorial supervision, *Family*, 424 ff.

37. A detailed account of Francis Giffard's career is given in *Alumni Cantabrigiensis*, Vol. I, Pt. 2. The gap between 1654 and 1660 is explained by his stay with the Wilmots. Hearne, *Collections*, 3:273. Giffard displayed the maturation of his monarchism and learning in a sermon preached before the Northants Assizes on March 1, 1681: *The Wicked Petition*. Anthony Wood said of this sermon (which has interesting similarities to Dryden's *Absalom and Achitophel*), that it was "seasonably delivered, the King being then tired out by factitious people with Petitions relating to Parliaments." Wood, *Athenae Oxoniensis*, 2:808.

38. BL, Harleian MS 7003, f. 249. Cf. Rochester, *Letters* (ed. Treglown), 143. Hereafter referred to as *Letters*. My citations are to the original sources of Rochester's letters: manuscripts (e.g. Harleian) and early editions (*The Rochester-Savile Correspondence*). Treglown's edition (Chicago, 1980) is available to contemporary readers and its texts are reliable. Its dates, however, are not in some instances.

39. See Vincent, *Grammar Schools*; Mulder, *Temple of the Mind*, 13–31. Educational tracts composed during Rochester's lifetime included those of John Eachard, Henry Wotton, and Obadiah Walker. The educational tracts of Jan Amos Comenius (1592–1670) were also widely read in England.

40. See John Miller, "The Development of the Anti-Catholic Tradition," 67–90.

41. Clifton, "Fear of Popery," 144–67.

42. Ibid., 146.

43. Ibid.

44. Lloyd, *Memoires*, 464–68; Clarendon, *History*, 7:30, 94, 169; *CC*, 2:260.

45. Parsons, *Sermon*, 5–6, 31, 36. Anne Wilmot's letters can be found in the Bodleian and University of Rochester (N.Y.) libraries.

46. On October 22, 1664, when John Wilmot was off on the Grand Tour, John Evelyn visited Ditchley and viewed "a Picture of a Pope & our Saviour's head." James Ussher or Usher (1581–1656) was the Bishop of Armagh, best known for establishing the date of the world's creation as 4,004 B.C. Caught in England by the outbreak of the Civil War, he devoted himself to writing on theological matters. Ussher's efforts to define and enunciate the principles of Christianity anticipated the Act of Uniformity in 1661. Cf. Beddard, "The Restoration Church," 155–66; Tyacke, "Puritanism, Arminianism and Counter-Revolution," and Jacob, "Restoration, Reformation and the Origins of the Royal Society," in *Seventeenth Century England: A Changing Culture*, ed. Owens, 139, 144, 245.

47. Burnet, *Passages*, 32.

48. See, for example, *Letters*, 73, 75, 91, 138.

49. Hearne, *Collections*, 3:263.

50. Ibid., 3:236, 263.

51. Stone, *Family*, 517.

52. "Sexual identity is the awareness of belonging to either the male or female sex. It is the first stepping-stone in the formation of gender identity . . . which reflects a person's erotic and sexual self-image, and is therefore part and parcel of the imagination." Wolff, *Bisexuality*, 52.

53. Cf. Wolff, *Bisexuality*, 4–5; Limentani, "Object Choice and Bisexuality," in *Between Freud and Klein*, 88–101; Socarides, "The Disturbance of Gender Role Formation," in *Homosexuality*, 170–75; Socarides and Volkan, *The Homosexualities*. Recent psychoanalytic theories suggest that polymorphous sexuality is neither unique nor "perverse" in the way Freud and other proponents of bi-polar sexuality claim. Laqueur, *Making Sex*, 5. Robert Stoller states flatly, "we—psychoanalysts and everyone else, professional or otherwise—do not understand homosexuality. Our ignorance includes not knowing what is to be called homosexuality . . .," *Observing the Erotic Imagination*, 167. Likewise, in "Bisexuality Reconsidered: An Idea in Pursuit of a Definition," Charles E. Hansen and Anne Evans argue that "genitality is not sexuality" and the perceived opposition between homo- and hetero-sexuality has led to an erroneous category of bisexuality; see Fritz Klein et al., eds., *Bisexualities*. Given the uncertain state of contemporary views toward sexuality, their use to "explain" Rochester must remain cautious.

54. Hearne, *Collections*, 3:263. Ronald Paulson has seen Rochester's attraction to travesty as connected with his boyhood constipation.

55. Burnet, *Passages*, 14.

56. Cf. Wood, *Athen. Oxon.*, 3:1228–32. The "Notes on Play," in Winnicott, *Psycho-Analytic Explorations*, 59–63, gives some possible insights into Rochester's "imaginative elaboration" and "creativity" as a child.

57. Rochester eventually entrusted Charles, his only son and heir, to the supervision of his mother. Cf. *Letters*, 229; Prinz, *John Wilmot*, 300.

Chapter 2

1. Parsons, *Sermon*, 7.

2. Wood, *Athen. Oxon.*, 2:488.

3. Burnet, *Passages*, 3.

4. Hearne, *Collections*, 3:263.

5. Rochester gave the living at Charlench to Parsons in his Will. Cf. Prinz, *John Wilmot*, 298–302. After Rochester's death, Parsons became chaplain to his mother the Countess and Curate of Adderbury to Dr. Beau, Bishop of Llandaff, who gave him a prebend at Adderbury.

6. Burnet, *Passages*, 6.

7. Hearne, *Collections*, 3:263.

8. Cf. Winn, *Dryden and His World*, 552n33; James A. Sutherland, *English Literature of the Late Seventeenth Century*, 25–26. Matthew Arnold called the Restoration upper class "Barbarians," in recall of their classical deficiency. For changing attitudes toward classical learning during Rochester's lifetime, see J. W. Johnson, "The Classics and John Bull."

9. Cf. Rochester, "To His Sacred Majesty," ll. 13–18. "The Lord Wilmot . . . was so *Great a Scholar*, that he could give the best advice. . . ." Lloyd, *Memoires*, 464. Wilmot's Latin report to Charles from Ratisbon is preserved in BL, Add. Mss. 32093, ff. 297–99v. Written in a beautiful scribal hand with a notation that the text was *dicitur* by Henry Wilmot, the Ratisbon Address exists in several ms. versions. It was printed after 1660. The letters that still exist in Wilmot's own script do not testify to his superior literacy, employing colloquialisms and treating pressing military matters in a hasty scrawl; BL, Add. Mss. 21506, ff. 77, 78; Add. Mss. 28980, ff. 76, 139, 167.

10. See chapter 1, note 10.

11. Cf. Farley-Hills, *Critical Heritage*, 145–46, 149, 151, 167.

12. E.g., Robinson, "Rochester and Semonides," 522–23.

13. Griffin, *Satires against Man*, 62–63, 159, 161–62, 168–71, 176, 272.

14. Cf. Quaintance, "French Sources," 190–99.

15. Cf. Selden, "Oldham's Versions of the Classics."

16. Rochester's episode in which Valentinian and his eunuch Lycias are murdered does not appear in Fletcher's play. Only Evagrius's *History of the Church*, VII, gives this version of Valentinian III's death. Rochester may have read Evagrius in translation. English versions had appeared in 1650 and 1663.

17. Giffard alludes to all three in *The Wicked Petition*, 1–20.

18. See "The Role of Historiography" and "Rome" in Johnson, *The Formation of English Neo-Classical Thought*, 31–68, 91–105.

19. James Winn gives an illuminating portrait of Busby, *Dryden and His World*, 37–42. See also Westminster School, *Commemoration of the Bicentenary of the Death of Richard Busby*; Barker, *Memoir of Richard Busby*.

20. Raman Selden argues that this passage is endebted to Juvenal's description of Hannibal in the Tenth Satire: "Rochester, Lee, and Juvenal."

21. Fraser, *Cromwell the Lord Protector*, 516–17. For another study of Cromwell's character, see Christopher Hill, *God's Englishman: Oliver Cromwell and the English Revolution*.

22. If Parliamentary agents had decided to interrogate nine-year-old John Wilmot in the manner shown in the painting "When Did You Last See Your Father?" the consequences for Henry Wilmot, who visited England and Ditchley in disguise, might have been fatal.

23. Wood, *Athen. Oxon.*, 2:487. It is possible to fix, more or less, the date of Rochester's entry at Burford because his master was John Martin, who held the post from 1656 to 1687.

24. Gretton, *Burford Past and Present*, and *Burford Grammar School, 1571–1971*, a quadricentennial commemorative.

25. In May, 1649, Cromwell crushed the last resistance by the Levellers with a night-time raid on Burford. Hill, *God's Englishman*, 108–10. He imprisoned three hundred of the mutineers in the Church, haranguing them from the pulpit after executing three of their leaders. *The Church of Saint John Baptist Burford*, 14–15. See also Hill, *The World Turned Upside Down*, 87 ff.

26. Sylvia Free of the Burford School kindly provided me with a copy of the *Constitucions* as well as the *Commemorative*.

27. Cf. Burford Grammar School, 13–14.

28. Simon Wysdome, *Constitucions*, Fifte Item.

29. Burnet, *Passages*, 3.

30. For other English grammar schools, their curricula, and practice, see W. A. L. Vincent, *Grammar Schools*, and John Mulder, *Temple of the Mind*. For Westminster, see Winn, *Dryden and His World*, 36–57.

31. Both the *Amores* and *Ars Amatoria* of Ovid were too sexually explicit to be used as grammar school texts; however, Rochester's mastery of Latin enabled him at a later stage of sophistication to read and utilize them. For analogues and parallels to the *Amores*, see "To Love" (*Amores* 2.9), "The Imperfect Enjoyment" (*Amores* 3.7), "Song: Absent from Thee" (*Amores* 2.10), "The Disabled Debauchee" (*Amores* 1.9). Similarly, those works by Tibullus suitable for classroom study left no traces in poems by Rochester while Tibullan themes and attitudes of more erotic cast left their mark. Such sentiments as "Now let gay love be my pursuit while it is no shame to break a door down and a joy to have plunged into a brawl" (Tibullus, I.i) are very Rochesterian. So are parts of a dialogue, "To Priapus" (II.iv), lines dealing with love between old men and young women (I.ix.73–74), and "An Apology" (IV.viii).

32. Cf. Weinbrot, "The 'Allusion to Horace'; Moskovit, "Pope and the Tradition of the Neoclassical Imitation."

33. Burnet, *Passages*, 31, 68.

Chapter 3

1. *Wadham College Registers*, Part I, 30–31.

2. *CC*, 4:166–67, 190, 209. Ann Danvers died on July 31 and was buried on August 11, 1659, according to the Spelsbury Church Warden's records.

3. Blandford's compliance with the Parliamentary Visitors compares interestingly with the response of John Fell; cf. Fell, *The Privilege of Oxford*. After Blandford left the University, Fell succeeded him as Vice-Chancellor. The index to Anthony Wood's *The Life and Times of Anthony Wood*, vol. 5, gives a short chronology for Blandford.

4. Wood said that Blandford "reformed the madness of the University contracted by the kings comming in," in 1660; Wood, *Life*, 1:455. His orthodoxy led him to be among the Anglican clergy who argued in vain with Anne Hyde, the Duchess of York, when she proposed converting to Catholicism in 1670; *CC*, 2:633.

5. *Wadham Registers*, 230–42 passim. There was George Penruddock, whose father had been in league with Henry Wilmot in the 1655 uprising and was executed for it; Wadham Strangewayes, who eventually died fighting in support of James II against Monmouth in 1685; and Thomas Windham, whose brother George was killed before Rochester's eyes aboard the HMS *Revenge* in the naval battle of Bergen in 1665.

6. Wood, *Life*, 2:34, 195, 444. "Coffee-berry" was one of several Oxonians with nicknames, Wood notes. One, a "little dark man," was "Black-berry," and "Goose-berry" had foolishly tried to stab himself.

7. For the history of Wadham College, see *The Foundation of the Universitie of Oxford*; Davies and Garnett, eds., *Wadham College*; and Fulman, *Academiae Oxoniensis Notitia*, 10. Fulman's account of Oxford and its colleges was written to honor King Charles II and Queen Catherine when the Court moved to Oxford in 1665 to escape the plague.

8. The origins of the Royal Society are given in Hunter, *Science*, 32 ff. For John Wilkins, cf. Aubrey, *Brief Lives*, 319–20.

9. Cf. *A Short Catalogue of Books in the Library of Wadham College*. This catalogue includes only books published before 1645. Most were the bequests of Philip Bisse (d. 1612) and Gilbert Drake (1600–1629); they were thus at Wadham when Rochester was enrolled there.

10. The Bodleian acquired John Selden's books in 1659, and Edward Hyde, Earl of Clarendon, was about to become its benefactor. When he came to the Convocation of 1661 as Chancellor, Robert Whitehall addressed him with characteristic lack of subtlety: "Live our Mecaenus, pile on Books to th'height / Until Sir Thomas Bodley groan with weight. . . ." Wood, *Life*, 1:411, 414.

11. Hutton, *Restoration*, 85–123. Cf. Fraser, *Cromwell*, 179 ff.; Ashley, *General Monck*, 180 ff.; Jones, "The Concept of Restoration," 8 ff.

12. Burnet, *Passages*, 3–4: "When he went to the *University* the general Joy which overran the whole Nation upon his Majesties Restauration but was not regulated with that Sobriety and Temperance, that became a serious gratitude to God for so great a Blessing, produced some of it's [sic] ill effects on him: He began to love these disorders too much."

13. Verney, *Verney Papers* (1925), 2:161–62; *CSPD, 1660–61*, 30, 70; *CSPD, 1670*, 663–64; *CC*, 5:345; *CSPD, 1661–62*, 119. Historical Manuscripts Commission, *Seventh Report* Appendix, 120–21.

14. There are three chief sources of information about Whitehall: Wood's *Athen. Oxon.*, 2:595–96, Wood's *Life*, passim, and the *Dictionary of National Biography* account. Whitehall's poems in print form and a few mss. in his hand are in the British Library.

15. Wood, *Life*, 1:144; Wood, Athen. Oxon., II, 595. The Act of Forfeiture was passed on July 16, 1651. Cf. R.W., *ΤΕΧΝΗΠΟΛΑΙΜΟΥΑΜΑ: or, The Marriage of Armes and Arts, July 12, 1651. Being an Accompt of the Act at Oxon. to a Friend.*

16. Wood, *Life*, 1:510.

17. Wood, *Athen. Oxon.*, 2:595. When Richard Cromwell became Chancellor of Oxford in 1657, Whitehall penned a companion-piece to his earlier verse-reconciliation with Oliver, his father.

18. Wood, *Life*, 1:59.

19. Wood, *Athen. Oxon.*, 2:488.

20. Cf. Stone, *Family*, 517. "Castilian calenture" or "Spanish fever." Phrygian Ganymede's abduction by an enamored Zeus in the form of an eagle is told by Ovid, *Metamorphoses*, X.155–61.

21. Stone, *Family*, 517. Cf. *A Faithful Narrative*. Further details about Thistlethwayte are given in Davies and Garnett, eds., *Wadham College*, 39–40. The episode prompted a limerick:

> There once was a Warden of Wadham
> Who approved of the folkways of Sodom,
> For a man might, he said,
> Have a very poor head
> But be a fine Fellow, at bottom.

22. Whitehall, *The Woman's Right Proved False* (1674); reprinted in Margaret Ezell, *The Patriarch's Wife*, 205–25.

23. E.g., "Song: Love a Woman? You're an Ass!" (ll. 13–16), "The Disabled Debauchee" (ll. 36–40), "The Imperfect Enjoyment" (ll. 41–42), *Sodom* (IV, 161–205), *Valentinian* (V.v.1–14). Cf. Gilmore, *Manhood in the Making*, 151, 154–55: "sexual inversion per se is not universally linked to a lack of masculinity in all the major Western traditions, nor is pederasty always a sign of effeminacy. . . . So long as this homosexuality conformed to current images of the "male" (active) role in sex play, it was entirely compatible with, in fact supportive of, a fully masculine image in the society at large." See also Trumbach, "The majority of boys who were seduced by sodomites had just reached the age of puberty. . . . Aristocratic boys were often taken away from school at fifteen or sixteen because puberty had begun . . . lawyers declared the age of sexual consent for boys to be fourteen, after which a boy's sexual passivity in sodomy made him as equally guilty as his active partner"; "Sodomitical Assaults," 409–10.

24. "A Ramble in Saint James's Parke," ll. 143–44. Rochester shows in *Sodom* a fourteen-year-old youth masturbated by two girls (III, 90–109). A song celebrating female self-masturbation appears in the same Act (ll. 84–87). Cf. "Fair Chloris in a Pig Sty Lay" (ll. 36–40). For masturbation in Restoration pornography, see Thompson, *Unfit for Modest Ears*, 24 ff. See also Laqueur, *Solitary Sexuality*, for an exhaustive survey.

25. Wood, *Life*, 1:414. Thompson gives an account of prostitutes in Oxford and elsewhere after the Restoration, *Unfit for Modest Ears*, 57 ff. Also, see Samuel Pepys, *Diary*, 11:240. The continuing tradition of undergraduate licentiousness during the reign of Charles II is evidenced by a letter from Dr. Humphrey Prideaux to John Aubrey on January 24, 1675. Dr. John Fell had happened upon a group of students from All Souls who were using the Oxford Press to print the *Postures* of Aretino for their personal use.

26. In January 1667, about the time of Rochester's marriage, Whitehall sent the Earl a miniature portrait of himself as a Christmas present with an accompanying verse that read in part: "Tis not in vest, but in that gowne / Your Lordship daggled through this towne / To keepe vp discipline, and tell vs / Next morning where you found goodfellows." Whitehall also professed himself, "My Dearest Lord. Y^r hon^rs most entirely devoted." Needham, ed., *Welbeck Miscellany* No. 2, 44–45.

27. For theories of play, masturbation in adolescence, and adolescent development, see Winnicott, *Psycho-Analytic Explorations*, 61–62. For its role in compartmentalizing aspects of the self, see Laing, "Masturbation," 153–55.

28. *Burford Parish Church*, 23.

29. Burnet, *Passages*, 23–24, 68.

30. Cf. Righter, "John Wilmot, Earl of Rochester"; Treglown, "Satirical Inversion, 42–48; Vieth, "Divided Consciousness," 46–62. N.B. Vieth, *Attribution in Restoration Poetry*, xxxvi: "Rochester's discovery of the way to link *discontinuous modes of experience* in a poem may have been his great gift to the new literary sensibility as it developed from 1670 to 1675" (italics mine).

31. Wood, *Athen. Oxon.*, 2:488. Cf. *Alum. Oxon.*, 4:1619.

32. Rochester's epigrams and impromptus include: "Under King Charles II's Picture," "Rhyme to Lisbon," "On Louis XIV," "And after singing Psalm the Twelfth," "To a Country Clerk after Having Heard Him Sing Psalms," "To My More Than Meritorious Wife," "On Charles II," "On the English Court," and "On Cary Frazier." The recording and preservation of these by others indicates how highly

regarded they were as examples of Rochester's extemporaneous wit. Analogous themes and attitudes for Rochester's impromptus can be found in Martial's *Epigrams*, I.xxxii; I.lviii; I.xc; I.xcvii; I.cxii; II.li. For a comparison of Martial and Rochester, see Porter, "The Professional Amateur," 61–62. It is tempting to think that Robert Whitehall (or John Wilmot) was responsible for the Latin epigram on Dr. John Fell, an adaptation of Martial which reads in one loose translation: "I do not love thee, Dr. Fell. / The reason why I cannot tell, / But this I know and know full well: / I do not love thee, Dr. Fell."

33. Blandford's imitation of the opening of Virgil's *Aeneid* was hyperbolic in its estimate of King Charles II: "I sing of arms and a man whom no Trojan hero could equal. . . ."

34. Whitehall's Latin poem also exploited the Virgilian myth, together with numerous other literary allusions and some Whitehallian tropes:

> CAROLE, magne, redi; nil suspiria tangent Crebra togatorum?
> CAROLE, magne redi. Occidit infelix Academia; stridula
> Athenis Vixit ab egressu Noctua, Phoebe, Tuo.
> Nos suimus Troes, cujus peregrinus & exul Non poteris,
> Caesar, non meminisse loci. . . .

His English poem was more rollicking:

> Now, most Illustrious PRINCE, since *Dover*-peere
> Mount's higher to behold its Soveraigne neare,
> And every wave t'wixt it and *Callis* sands
> Speak's and reiterat's, He Land's, He Land's . . .
> Since all the Roaring-Meggs the river scour,
> And bring the newes to *London* in an hower;
> *London* that with her shouts so rend's the sky
> That Birds drop down astonish't as they fly. . . .

35. In his *Memoires*, 467, David Lloyd called Henry Wilmot, "Caroli *Secundi* fidus Achates." Cf. Virgil, *Aeneid*, I.174 ff.

36. Wood, *Athen. Oxon.*, 2:488.

37. *The Poems of John Wilmot, Earl of Rochester*, ed. Keith Walker, 3.

38. Whitehall's poem on the Coronation of Charles II in 1661 read in part:

> *Divisum Imperium cum Jove Caesar habet*
> Give me an Eagles quill that dropt at Noon,
> While she was gazing on the mounted Sun;
> That I may write Great *Charles* his Name, & tell
> The rescued Royalist that things go Well . . .
> With indignation then the Valiant *Monk*
> Took this same *Hydra Elephant* by th' truck,
> And made him yawn; still holding by the Nose
> The late triumphant huge Rinoceros. . . .

For the standard use of the hydra to symbolize the Rebellion, see Ogilby, *Entertainment*, 17. Later in 1661, when Lord Clarendon came to Oxford, Whitehall's Muse produced an acrostic Latin poem, *Viro . . . Honoratissimo . . . Amplissimoque Domino, Edvardo Hide* with an English verse translation.

39. Those who deny Rochester's authorship of *Sodom* usually resort to assertions that the Earl was incapable of writing badly. A leading scholar has told me, despite all evidence to the contrary, "Rochester couldn't write couplets that bad if he tried."

40. *Treasury Books*, 1660–1667.

41. Wood, *Life*, 1:411–14. The scarlet doctor's gown was yet another deception or disguise since Rochester hardly earned it.

42. Cf. the Countess of Rochester's letters to Clarendon on April 23, 1662; BodL, Clarendon Mss., Jan.–June 1662, ff. 172, 174. On his deathbed, Rochester repented his habit of not paying his debts to tradesmen; Parsons, *Sermon*, 29.

Chapter 4

1. After his sallies between 1661 and 1665, Whitehall settled into the academic routine without pressing his poetic and political luck. Apparently he had been involved in Sir George Booth's uprising in Cheshire in 1659. As a consequence, he claimed, he had lost £1,000 plus "spirituals" worth £250 a year; "to prescribe to you how to lick myself whole were to call Oedipus an ignoramus," he told Joseph Williamson. In 1671, he became Sub-Warden of Merton. After becoming Bursar in 1672, he engaged in university affairs while he secretly used paper from supplies granted Merton by Dr. Fell to record erotic satires. In 1677 he produced his literary masterpiece, the *EXASTICON IERON, Sive Iconum*. On a trip to Holland, Whitehall acquired a series of woodcuts illustrating the Scriptures; he reproduced these, fixing one to a page and printing beneath it his versified explanation. In 1679, Whitehall published *Gratulamini mecum*, a poem celebrating the King's recovery at Windsor from a putative attack of ague suffered during the Popish Plot. In 1680 he developed a serious ear infection and was forced to seek a diagnosis (BL *Sloane* 810. f. 603): "The advice I had from London." The physician told him "That claret & sack are both my enimy, but sider my freind, so I drink freely of, (wch I am the more unwilling to doe for Mother Eros sake.)" His illness led him to write *The English Recabite* (1681). Whitehall died on July 8, 1685, and was buried in the church of Merton College.

2. For English Protestant views on permitting young men to travel to Italy, see *Sodom Fair*.

3. Robert Sibbald gives an account of Balfour's life and career in *Memoria Balfouriana*, including his acting as governor to Rochester, 53–54. Cf. Sibbald, *Auctarius Musaei Balfouriana*, 208–16; *Memoria*, 54 ff.

4. *Letters . . . by Sir Andrew Balfour*, M.D., ii. This edition duplicates pagination; future references indicate duplication by placing d after the page number, e.g., 103–4d.

5. Balfour, *Letters*, 6.

6. Burnet, *Passages*, 6–7. Cf. Thomas Alcock, *Famous Pathologist*, 29.

7. Balfour, *Letters*, 6–9.

8. Ibid., 19–20, 76–77.

9. Ibid., 10–11.

10. Ibid., 11.

11. Ibid., 11–12. In 1675, Rochester smashed a similar astronomical apparatus, the Sun-Dial in the Privy Garden at Whitehall.

12. Ibid., 13–14. Cf. *The Gospel According to John*, 2.1–11.

13. Balfour, *Letters*, 12–16.

14. Hartmann, *Charles II and Madame*, 135–36.

15. Cf. "Dialogue," in *Poems*, 102–3; *Letters*, 56–58, 85. Gramont (or Grammont) was in France until the spring of 1662, when his imprudent attentions to Mlle. de la Mothe Houdancourt, one of Louis XIV's mistresses, served to get him banished to England.

Cf. Anthony Hamilton, *Memoirs of the Comte de Gramont*, 370 ff. Hereafter cited as Hamilton, *Memoirs*.

16. Griffin, *Satires against Man*, 173–82.

17. Abraham, *Corneille*, 9–11; Hume, *Development of English Drama*, 172; Yarrow, *Racine*, 60.

18. Cf. Gaines, *Molière Encyclopedia*.

19. For French music and the operas of Giovanni Battista Lulli or Jean-Baptiste Lully (1632–87), see Headington et al., *Opera*, 40–43 ff. For Rochester's songs, see Rochester, *Poems* (Walker), 140–41. In Dryden's *Kind Keeper*, IV.i, Woodall, who suspiciously resembles Rochester, engages in an effusive conversation about the "dear Battist" and "his new Compositions in the last *Opera*." See also Fisher, "Love in the Ayre."

20. Balfour, *Letters*, 20–23.

21. Ibid., 24–26.

22. Ibid., 27–30.

23. Ibid., 33–34. Calculated on the heliacal rising and duration of either Sirius or Procyon, Dog-Days vary but generally are connected with the date of August 11.

24. Ibid., 34–37.

25. Ibid., 39–42.

26. Ibid., 43–45. For Rochester and Petrarch, see Rochester, *Complete Poems* (Vieth), xxxvi.

27. Balfour, *Letters*, 55 ff., 76–77.

28. Ibid., 57–62. Cf. Alcock, *Famous Pathologist*, 29. In July, 1678, Henry Savile urged Rochester to winter at Montpellier for his health.

29. Balfour, *Letters*, 63–65, 67, 71.

30. Ibid., 71–83.

31. Ibid., 46–49d. Pagination begins to duplicate here.

32. Ibid., 52–54d. We may wonder whether young Rochester was learning here the ritual of penitence he later practiced when he was dying.

33. Ibid., 84d. By "wardrobe," Balfour probably meant "closet": another term for a monarch's private collection of valuables or curiosities.

34. Ibid., 85–86. It is apparent from the *Letters* that Balfour's description of Italy closely reflects his trip with Rochester. Balfour was there only once, he says; and the letters make frequent reference to "we" and "us."

35. Ibid., 87. Sibbald wrote in his *Memoria Balfouriana*, 54: "Gradu *Doctoratus* assumpto, mox in *Angliam* reversus est, ibique parum moratus est, tum enim a Serenissimo Rege *Carolo* II, optimae Memoriae, *Gubernator* datus est Comiti *Rossensi*, egregiae Spei Juveni, qui *Studia & Mores* ejus regeret; Quo Munere functus est quadriennium, partim in *Gallia*, partim in Italia . . . Cum illustrissimo *Comite* circulum *Galliae & Italiae* perfecit; in Italiae autem circulo peragendo, varia etiam ad *Historiam Naturalem* spectantia, observavit."

36. Balfour, *Letters*, 88–90.

37. Ibid., 92–96. Pagination after page 92 returns to 90 and duplicates pagination 90–96.

38. Ibid., 94–97 (second series).

39. Ibid., 97–99. Evidently they did not bother to see Dante's house. Balfour does not mention it.

40. Ibid., 99–109.

41. Ibid., 111. See note 35 above.

42. Ibid., 113–14, 122. The pagination for pages 115 through 121 is erroneously omitted in this edition.

43. Ibid., 123. Sibbald said of Fr. Lesly: "Amicissimum quoque sensit conterraneum suum, D. *Gulielmum Lesleum*, qui tunc quidem Cardinali *Barberino* a Sacris erat. Is idem fuit postea Conventui de *propaganda fide*, a *Secretis* erat qui conterraneis suis aliisque Curiosis, Rariora *Artis* et Naturae Opera, *Missionariis* per *Orbem* sparsis detecta, libere communicare solebat, hujus *Viri* Memoriam *Balfourius* semper cum *Laude* recolebat, multum etiam debebat. . . ." Sibbald, *Memoria*, 57. Fr. Lesly's commitment to proselytizing is clear, as is Balfour's very close friendship with him.

44. Balfour, *letters*, 124, 130, 201. For Francesco Barberino, see Miller, *Popery*, 30, 129.

45. Sibbald, *Memoria*, 51.

46. Balfour, *Letters*, 127–28.

47. The vexing question of when Charles Stuart became a Catholic has no definite answer. As Fraser points out, all that is known for certain is that he was christened an Anglican Protestant and died a self-professed Catholic; *Royal Charles*, 149–52. While noting Charles's admiration for the Roman Church, J. P. Kenyon asserts that "he postponed his conversion until his deathbed," and underplays the role of religion on his life; *The Stuarts*, 122–23, 131–32. Miller finds evidence of Charles's "leanings toward Catholicism" throughout his life. *Popery and Politics*, 18, 22, 25, 110–11, 119–20, 208. In "A Character of King Charles II," based on his long, personal observations, Lord Halifax wrote: "I conclude that when he came into *England* [in 1660] he was as certainly a *Roman Catholick*, as that he was a Man of Pleasure; both very consistent by visible Experience"; Halifax, *Works*, 189.

48. For Catholicism at the Restoration court and its background, see Miller, *Popery*, 21–27. Also, see Pepys, "Roman Catholicism," *Diary*, 12:244–45.

49. For terms of the Restoration Settlement, see Miller, *Popery*, 91–107; Kenyon, *Stuart Constitution*, 411 ff. Since Charles II's affiliation with the Roman Church was still a secret, it is small wonder that information about Rochester remains elusive. In view of Balfour's obvious ties to Catholic officials and his interest in the sites and relics of Catholicism, Sibbald's summary of his religious position seems suggestively ambiguous: "Constans in Sincera *Fide, Amoreque in Deum* fuit, Sublime de tanta *Majestate* sentiens, ac summe de ejus *Bonitate* sperans." Sibbald, *Memoria*, 87.

50. Balfour, *Letters*, 129–31. In 1663, "gusto" meant "particular relish or fondness" (1647) or "artistic style" (1662). The later meaning also at times signified "fashionable style in matters of taste," which was probably Balfour's meaning.

51. Ibid., 121–44.

52. Ibid., 145.

53. Stone, *Family*, 518. Stone quotes the tutor of the seventeen-year-old Lord Herbert urging the youth's mother to postpone his trip to Italy until later: "I would not for the world have his passions first awakened there. . . . In Italy they scout every idea of decency and morality, and will give him too little trouble."

54. Cf. *Dr. Bendo's Advertisement*: "I have seen Physician Bills as Bawdy as Aretine's Dialogues. . . ." For Aretino's influence during the Restoration period and on Rochester in particular, see Turner, *Schooling Sex*, 267–84.

55. Balfour, *Letters*, 138. Aretino was known in England during the reign of Henry VIII, one of his royal patrons and a hearty consumer of Aretino's erotic works. See Frantz, *Festum Voluptatis*, 43–90. He was praised by Thomas Nashe as one of the wittiest knaves God ever made and castigated by John Milton as a notorious ribald. In Venice, the pious John Evelyn visited "St. Lukes famous for the Tomb of Peter Aretine" in July 1645; by 1668, Pepys was describing the Pseudo-Aretinian *Putana errante* as lewd and bawdy. If they visited Aretino's tomb in Venice themselves, Balfour is silent

about it. For Aretino's imitators, see "The Aretines," in Frantz, *Festum Voluptatis*, 91–117.

56. Aretino prided himself on the "delicacy" of his language, however, whereas Rochester deliberately used the bluntly demotic and obscene. Cf. Aretino, *Selected Letters*, 227.

57. Cf. "My Lord All-Pride," ll. 18–22. Otway used the Scaramuchio figure to satirize Rochester in *Friendship in Fashion* 3:78–91, as did Edward Ravenscroft (purportedly) in *Scaramouch a Philosopher*; cf. Langbaine, *Lives and Characters*, 422. Ravenscroft's play was "an experiment in *commedia del'arte*"; Hume, *Development of English Drama*, 302.

58. Balfour, *Letters*, 145–51, 188. While in Rome, the two met Obadiah Walker, who converted to Catholicism and later published *Of Education* in 1673. Chapter 14, "Of Travelling into Foreign Countries," with a tutor, may reflect his observations of Rochester and Balfour. Sibbald, *Memoria*, 57. Cf. Miller, *Popery*, 208, 256.

59. Balfour, *Letters*, 154–60.

60. Ibid., 161–62, 165.

61. Ibid., 166–70.

62. Ibid., 178–79, 187 (misnumbered 167).

63. Ibid., 176. Cf. Sibbald, *Memoria*, 58–60. Sibbald was fascinated by the episode; he recounts it in detail.

64. Balfour, *Letters*, 182–90. Cf. Sibbald, *Memoria*, 61.

65. Balfour, *Letters*, 187 (misnumbered 167). See Lee's Dedication to *The Tragedy of Nero*, Oldham's linking of Rochester to Nero in "A Satyr on Vertue," and Dryden's thinly-veiled attack on Rochester as Nero in the Preface to *All for Love*. Cf. Winn, *Dryden and His World*, 590; Hume, *Development of Drama*, 200, 289; Vieth, *ARP*, 187.

66. Balfour, *Letters*, 191–93. Cf. *Sodom and Gomorah*, Act V. At the time of their visit, Pompeii had not been excavated.

67. Balfour, *Letters*, 195–96.

68. Ibid., 198–99.

69. Ibid., 202–5.

70. Ibid., 207–8, 213. He commissioned Lord Murray later to purchase Aldrovandus's works for him.

71. Ibid., 214–15.

72. Ibid., 216, 218–24.

73. Balfour, 225. For "Gusto," see note 50 above. In 1675, Rochester's protégé, Francis Fane, dedicated *Love in the Dark*, a romantic comedy of intrigue set in Venice during Carnival time, to Rochester, who was sufficiently pleased to write an Epilogue for it. Cf. Hume, *Development of Drama*, 302. The summer celebration that Balfour refers to was probably a form of the Festival of the Redentore (Redeemer) during the third week of July in commemoration of the Venetians' deliverance from the Plague in 1576 and 1630.

74. See note 37 above. For Claudio Monteverdi (1567–1643) and Venetian opera, see Headington et al., *Opera*, 23–29; Harewood, ed., *Definitive Kobbe's Opera Book*, 13–18. For Busenello (1598–1659), see Warrack and West, *The Concise Oxford Dictionary of Opera*, 103. I am endebted to Professor Ellen Rosand of Yale for information about Busenello's text and its ties with libertinism. Rochester's interest in Seneca and the stoic attitude toward death apparent in *Poppea* also was manifested in the 1670s.

75. For a full account of the courtesans and the *Postures* of Aretino, see Lawner, *I Modi*, 2–56. Lawner says of the "sodomy" (anal intercourse) fashionable in Venice in Aretino's time: ". . . the interchangeability of the locus of pleasure provided a playful

way of making a girl into a boy, something many a Renaissance lover enjoyed doing" (45). Cf. the concluding line of Aretino's first sonnet: "E chi non fotte in cul, Dio gliel perdoni." See, too, Vignale, *La Cazzaria*, 82–83.

Despite Lawner's assertion that the drawings had vanished by the early seventeenth century, Rochester's ownership of the *Postures* was attested to by John Aubrey, Robert Parsons, and Henry St. John; and a letter from Dr. Humphrey Prideaux to John Aubrey in January, 1675, proves that Oxford students were still printing copies of them. A printed copy from the sixteenth century exists today in private hands. A photocopy of it is kept in the Fine Arts Library at Harvard; cf. Frantz, *Festum Voluptatis*, 47. Cf. Olivieri, "Eroticism, 95–102.

76. Balfour, *Letters*, 230; Isaacs, "Grand Tour," 75–76. A facsimile of Rochester's signature appears in Fisher, ed., *Second Bottle*, xv.

77. Balfour, *Letters*, 236.

78. Ibid., 239 (misnumbered 139), 240–45.

79. Cf. Hutton, *Restoration*, 225–26, 356nn28–33.

80. Balfour, *Letters*, 247–51.

81. Ibid., 255–56. Compare Thomas Gray's impressions of the same route in his letter to Richard West (Nov. 16, N.S., 1739).

82. Balfour, *Letters*, 251–53.

83. Ibid., 257–64.

84. Yarrow, *Racine*, 60.

85. Hartmann, *Charles II and Madame*, 135–36.

86. Sibbald, *Memoria*, 54.

87. Samuel Pepys recorded his sighting of the comet on Christmas Eve 1664. Also, see Pepys, *Diary*, 5:346, 348, 354–57 passim. For astronomy and the role of Edmond Halley in Restoration science, see Hunter, *Science and Society*, 132–33, 173–74, 212–19.

Chapter 5

1. Sir Walter St. John had joined the Parliamentarians to the extent of fighting on their side in the Battle of Worcester. *CC*, 4:166–67, 209; 5:2, 28. Sir Walter was in a hopeless dilemma. When his Puritan father-in-law went to The Hague on a mission in 1651, a Royalist brother-in-law of Sir Walter's tried to stab him.

2. *CC*, 4:619; 5:21, 345. Verney, *Verney Papers* (1925), 2:155–57. See also *CSPD 1660–61*, 70; *1661–62*, 30. For the 1659 and 1660 versions of the Act of Indemnity, see *Statutes at Large*, 7:419–35; Burnet, *History*, 1:289. Cf. Hutton, *Restoration*, 132–36, 162–66; Jones, *Court*, 82. The Act of 1660 exempted witches, Jesuits, and sodomites from indemnity. Charles's desire to heal the nation's wounds caused him to extend general pardon to all but the regicides and led his disappointed supporters to say he had given indemnity to his enemies and oblivion to his friends. Colonel John Hutchinson, a regicide, was granted indemnity when the Countess of Rochester and her relatives signed affadavits on June 26, 1660, that he had assisted Henry Wilmot to escape after Worcester. HMC *Seventh Report Appendix*, 120–21.

3. Articles XXXVII and XXXVIII of the Act exempted Danvers from the general pardon because of the enormity of his crimes; *Statutes*, 8:431. *CSPD 1661–62*, 119. The aristocracy in general took advantage of the privilege of swearing to business transactions for which no documentary evidence existed. On Dec. 6, 1670, because of flagrant

abuses of this privilege, a bill was introduced in the House of Lords "That henceforth no Estates shall be transferred from Person to Person but such Conveyances shall be enrolled." JHL, 12:381. See London County Council, *Survey of London*, vol. 4: *The Parish of Chelsea*, Pt. 2, 9–10. HMC *Portland*, 10:84.

4. Cf. Robinson, "Rochester's Income," 46–50. The honorary M.A. degree from Oxford was probably another benefit.

5. For illustrations of the route, cavalcade, and coronation processional see Ogilby, *Entertainment*. Ogilby does not name the thirty-one Earls who participated, but even in the unlikely event that Rochester, being underage, was not among the Earls, he would have been among the Earls' eldest sons, who were also present.

6. BodL, Clarendon Mss., Jan.–June 1662, f. 103.

7. Ibid., f. 172. I have altered the Countess's punctuation to make her syntax more clear for modern readers.

8. f. 174.

9. The Countess used her money to satisfy her own expensive tastes. A catalogue of the Lee Papers includes her certification of personal debts amounting to £19,230 in 1664.

10. HMC *House of Lords*, N.S., 4:172–73. Pugh, *History of Oxfordshire*, 9:7. Adderbury Manor had been greatly damaged by successive occupying forces during the Civil Wars. It was shelled by the Parliamentarians in 1645 while being used as headquarters by Prince Rupert.

11. Burnet, *Passages*, 2.

12. *CC*, 5:205; BodL, Clarendon Mss., Jan.–June 1662, f. 103. Edward Chamberlayne's *Angliae Notitia* for 1669 lists the Countess at an annual salary of £400. As Groom of the Stole (or Stool), she was in charge of the royal chamber pot.

13. Lady Denham (Margaret Brooke) was eighteen and Denham was fifty and already subject to fits of madness when they married. The Duke of York's pursuit of her provided matter for the Court gossips; when she died in January 1667, claiming she had been poisoned by chocolate, it was widely rumored the Duchess had engineered the poisoning. Pepys and Gramont both thought Denham himself had done it; John Aubrey was the only one to accuse Lady Rochester. See O'Hehir, *Sir John Denham*, 203–8. O'Hehir dismisses all notions that Lady Rochester was involved and suggests, plausibly, that Lady Denham died of a ruptured appendix. J. H. Wilson has asserted that Aubrey's reference was not to Anne Wilmot but to Henrietta Hyde, wife of Laurence Hyde and sister-in-law to the Duchess of York. Henrietta Hyde became Countess of Rochester in 1682. Aubrey's editor, O. L. Dick, identifies the Countess as Anne Wilmot.

14. University of Rochester, Mss. D.26, ff. 14–32.

15. Cf. *The Dictionary of National Biography*, 58:312–17. *Wiltshire Visitation Principles 1623*, 36–37, explains the relationship between Lady Rochester and Barbara Villiers, who were first cousins. See Appendix B.

16. BL, Add. Mss. 19253, "Number 12," f. 12. Cf. Winn, *Dryden*, 125; Kenyon, *Stuarts*, 127–28.

17. It was the fate of common scolds to be tied into a ducking stool and plunged in the village pond. When the Court fled to Oxford to avoid the Plague and Lady Castlemain arrived at Merton College on January 27, 1666, an academic wit (Robert Whitehall?) tacked a "libell" (lampoon) on her door. It read:

> *hanc Caesare pressem a fluctu defendit onus.* The reason why she is not duckd
> ' Cause by Caesar she is fucked. (Wood, *Life*, II, p. 67)

18. A diagram of Whitehall Palace appears in *The Shorter Pepys*, 1036–37.

19. Collinson, *History and Antiquities of Somerset*, 1:89, 92; 3:262, 430. *CSDP 1661–62*, 435–36. BL, Add. Mss. 32093, ff. 93–94, 318; Burke, *Peerage*, 251, 553; G. E. C. *Baronetage*, 6:418. *The Victoria History of Somerset*, 2:231 ff. The pertinent records for Elizabeth Mallet's birth were destroyed during World War II. A source on the Internet gives the date as 1651. See Mallett Family History Home Page (www.ott.igs.net/rhmal-lett/). For Hawley's intentions, cf. Greene, *Monkey*, 56–57. Cf. Pepys, 6:110, for her fortune.

20. Fitzhardinge was not the only one eager to impugn Anne Hyde's chastity. Henry Killegrew ("Lying Killegrew") declared he had enjoyed her in a jakes built over the water and "three or four swans had been witness to his happiness." Kenyon, *Stuarts*, 121. Cf. Wilson, ed., *A Rake and His Times*, 37.

21. Hartmann, *The King's Friend*, 89, 100. Pepys said of Berkeley Lord Fitzhardinge of Berlhaven (1630–1665), "A witty man . . . in every respect, but of no good nature." Clarendon's estimate was understandably jaundiced: "A fellow of great wickednesss . . . He was young and of an insatiable ambition, and a little more experience might have taught him all things which his weak parts were capable of." Berkeley never got the experience. He was killed by an exploding shell aboard the *Royal Charles* in the sea battle of June 1665, and his blood reportedly splashed the Duke of York. G. E. C., 5:407–8.

22. Lord John Butler (1643–1676) as a younger son had few prospects from the rewards given his father for service to Charles II in exile. He entered Gray's Inn to study law in November 1660, and he was the M.P. for Dublin in 1662–66 when he was proposed for Elizabeth Mallet. His fortunes were always precarious. In 1672, the Ormonde Mss. show he had due from his estate the sum of £668–0–0 whereas he owed £2,135–19–6 1/2. In January 1676, he married Anne, daughter of the Earl of Donegal, and in April 1676, he was created Earl of Gowran. In August 1676, he died of consumption in Paris at the age of thirty-four, without heirs; G. E. C., 6:38–39. William Fielding (1640–1685), a first cousin to Lord John Butler, succeeded to the Earldom in 1666 and was further created the Earl of Denbigh in 1675. He died in 1685 at the age of forty-four. William Herbert became the sixth Earl of Pembroke in 1669. He never married. He died in 1674 and was buried in Salisbury Cathedral; G. E. C., 10:421. Lord Hinchingbrooke's tepid courtship of Elizabeth Mallet has been chronicled somewhat inaccurately in F. R. Harris, *The Life of Edward Montagu, K.G., First Earl of Sandwich*, 2:175–77. Cf. Pepys, 6:110, 119, 193; Tomalin, *Samuel Pepys*, passim.

23. *CSPD 1664–65*, 116. For the "veto" power of children over their parents' choice of a spouse after 1660, see Stone, *Family*, 272.

24. Greene, *Monkey*, 35.

25. Cf. ibid., 56–57.

26. *Savile Correspondence*, 7.

27. Aubrey, *Lives*, 321; Burnet, *Passages*, 6–7.

28. For the similarities, and differences, between the two poet-aristocrats, see Holton, "Sexuality and Social Hierarchy."

29. Griffin, *Satires*, 3; Aubrey, *Lives*, 90–93; O'Hehir, *Sir John Denham*, passim.

30. Aubrey, *Lives*, 308–10; Griffin, *Satires*, 28–30, 49, 65, 239n, 240n, 254.; Richmond, "The Fate of Edmund Waller."

31. *Savile Correspondence*, 5.

32. Burnet, *Passages*, 23–24.

33. Cf. Wilders, "Rochester and the Metaphysicals," 50–54; and Porter, "The Professional Amateur," 66–69.

34. One source for "A Pastoral Dialogue" says it was written by Rochester at Bath in 1674; but its tone and character suggest an earlier date. Cf. Rochester, *Poems* (Vieth), 171–72.

35. Rochester's choice of the name "Alexis" for his misogynist has a subtle, satiric resonance. Like Ganymede, Alexis was a beautiful youth who symbolized pederastic love; cf. Virgil, *Eclogues* II; Propertius, *Elegies*, II.xxxiv.ll.73–74.

36. Jeremy Treglown has found a similar use of "the language of courtly adoration . . . to disguise an aggressive assertion of male superiority" in "The Advice" to Celia ("All things submit themselves to your command"); *RES*, n.s. 24 (February 1973): 42–48. Cf. *Poems*, 232n36. See Anthony Easthope's comment on a twentieth-century song: "This song . . . shows clearly, perhaps in an extreme form, the basic structure of being in love. It is at root a masculine idea, a position offered for masculinity in the dominant culture. Although elsewhere being in love may presuppose more balance between the partners, it nevertheless repeats the version of masculine mastery concealed inside the male lover's seeming subservience"; *What a Man's Gotta Do*, 145.

37. Corinna was actually a Greek woman-poet; but the cognomen was used by Ovid (*Amores* I.5) for a prostitute. Its Greek analogues would suggest a change from a susceptible maiden (Gk. *Kor*) to a prostitute (woman of Corinth). "Strephon" was a latter-day coinage, which may have been derived from the Greek word for "change" or "turn." Certainly Rochester's Strephon is always changeable.

38. Cf. Stone, *Family*, 180–82, 270–274, 282–87. Burnet, *Passages*, 23–24. Cf. Burnet, 100–101: "The restraining a man from the use of Women, Except one in the way of Marriage, and denying the remedy of Divorce, he thought unreasonable Impositions on the Freedom of Mankind." See also Rochester's "Against Constancy."

39. Cf. Stone, *Family*, 637; Thomas, "The Double Standard." Cf. Rochester, "A Letter from Artemiza," ll.240–52.

40. Charles Stuart's letters to Henry Wilmot in exile state his lasting gratitude to the man who came to aid the twenty-year-old heir to the throne in time of great need. (BL, Add. Mss. 32093. f. 310) Charles was thirty-four when John Wilmot at seventeen returned to Court. Just as he had seen Henry Wilmot at thirty-one as something of a surrogate-father, so he saw himself as a substitute father to John Wilmot.

41. Cf. Vieth, *ARP*, 209–12.

42. Among those who kept actress-mistresses were King Charles, Prince Rupert, Sackville Earl of Middlesex, and Sir Robert Howard.

43. Burnet, *Passages*, 27–28; Hamilton, *Memoirs*, 238–42, 338; Highfill et al., *A Biographical Dictionary of Actors*, 3:473–75; Etherege, *Letters*, 185–86.

44. Burnet, *Passages*, 11.

45. The original of this version exists in Rochester's holograph in Nottingham, Portland PwV. 31, ff. 1a–1b. Since this collection contains the poetic exchange between the Rochesters, it is tempting to conjecture that the verse was originally meant for Mrs. Mallet in this least carnal and cynical version. But the double meaning of "purse" (scrotum) and the sporting proposition that Chloris take the juice of lusty men is at odds with other addresses to Elizabeth Mallet as a divine Celia. Possibly "Chloris" was Miss Sarah.

46. "Could I but make my wishes insolent." The statement that he had preserved a love "soe many yeares" need not be taken literally. Time stretches infinitely for unhappy and thwarted lovers.

47. *Savile Correspondence*, 5.

48. Pepys, 6:110. Pepys continues: "Hereupon, my Lady did confess to me, as a great secret, her being concerned in this story—for if this match breaks between my Lord Rochester and her, then, by the consent of all her friends, my Lord Hinchingbrooke stands fair, and is invited for her. She is worth, and will be at her mother's death (who keeps but a little from her) 2500 l. per annum."

49. Plate #12 of Ogilby's *Brittania Vol. I* is a pictorial strip map of the Uxbridge-Banbury road. The distance from London to Banbury is about 72 miles.

50. For Hawley's financial interactions with the Stuarts, see *CSPD 1660–61*, 50, 214; *CC*, 5:163; *CSPD 1661–62*, 589; *CSPD 1663–64*, 31, 264, 271–72, 516, 586; *CSPD 1664–65*, 33.

51. *CSPD 1664–65*, 389, 435.

52. Aubrey, *Lives*, 321.

53. PRO, Ms. SP 29, f. 122. "Inadvertency" was not being properly attentive.

54. BL, Sloane Ms. 1519, f. 192. Cf. Greene, *Monkey*, 45.

55. For the Court during the Plague, see Clarendon, *Life*, 2:31–89. For life at Oxford during the same period, cf. Wood, *Life*. For a modern account, see Hutton, *Restoration*, 225–33.

56. Pepys, 6:19.

57. Sir John Warre was put in charge of recruiting colonists to settle Tangiers, which Queen Catherine had brought as part of her dowery. Sir Francis Hawley went to York in August with a horse-troop. On his return to Somerset, he joined Warre in his efforts, going from Taunton and Bridgewater as far as Land's End, appealing to the natives' "personal affection" to volunteer for "the plantations" but "with very little confidence" and very little success. *CSPD 1664–65*, 523; *CSPD 1665–66*, 68–70, 74, 389.

58. For the background of Anglo-Dutch relations and the three wars from several perspectives, see Geyl, *Netherlands*, 53–106; Jones, *Britain and Europe*, 38–66; Rogers, *The Dutch in the Medway*; Haley, *The Dutch in the Seventeenth Century*; Gordon Jackson, "Trade and Shipping," in Jones, *Britain and Europe*, 136–54.

59. Jones, *Britain and Europe*, 58; Geyl, *Netherlands*, 84–85.

60. Burnet, *Passages*, 11.

61. *Savile Correspondence*, 5.

62. *CSPD 1664–65*, 478; Greene, *Monkey*, 47–49.

63. As a consequence of the English raid, Denmark declared war on England in January 1666. Rogers, *The Dutch in the Medway*, 44.

64. BL, Harl. Ms. 7003, f. 193.

65. Burnet, *Passages*, 16–18. Cf. Thomas, *Religion*, 591 ff.

66. For the Battle from Clifford's viewpoint, see Hartmann, *Clifford*, 46–81.

67. Cf. Pepys's account: *Diary*, 6:195 ff.

68. Burnet, *Passages*, 16–18.

69. Ibid., 9.

70. *CSPD 1664–65*, 562.

71. For a facsimile of the bill, cf. Greene, *Monkey*, 55.

72. *CSPD 1665–66*, 35, 310.

73. Ronald Paulson has identified the war imagery in "Timon," "The Disabled Debauchee," and the "Scepter-Prick" satire in "Rochester: The Body Politic and the Body Private." See also "Upon His Drinking a Bowl," "The Imperfect Enjoyment," "The Advice," "To Love," "Grecian Kindness," et al.

Chapter 6

1. Harris, *Sackville*, 17–20.

2. Ibid., 21–23, 27–29.

3. Ibid., 26, 31.

4. Etherege, *Poems*, 38–45, 109–11.

5. Harris, *Sackville*, 33–34.

6. Cf. Pinto, *Sedley*; Sedley, *Poetical and Dramatic Works*.

7. Hume, *Development of Drama*, 255–56, 314, 369.

8. Pepys, *Diary*, 8:71–72. Cf. also 5:288.

9. *R-SL*, 2–11; Lives of Savile, Buckhurst, and Sedley appear in the *DNB*.

10. For Savile's alleged affair with the Duchess, see Pepys, *Diary*, 6:302.

11. *Savile Correspondence*, 13. Cf. Vieth, *ARP*, 107, 337; Winn, *Dryden*, 330–31.

12. After Hinchingbrooke returned to England from France in August 1665, a bout with smallpox prevented his meeting Mrs. Mallet and delayed his courtship; Pepys, *Diary*, 6:193. On May 30, 1666, Sir George Carteret recorded that the Duke of Ormonde and Lord John Butler had withdrawn from negotiations, whereupon Lord Sandwich and Hinchingbrooke made their final attempt with Hawley and Warre. After Hinchingbrooke and Mrs. Mallet agreed they did not share the same "genius," Hinchingbrooke married Lady Anne Burlington in 1667.

13. Quoted in Greene, *Monkey*, 57.

14. Pepys, *Diary*, 7:56. Hamilton, *Memoirs*, 323.

15. *CSPD 1665–1666*, 35, 310; cf. Greene, *Monkey*, 55.

16. *R-SL*, 102; Kenyon, *The Stuarts*, 127–28; *Treasury Books 1660–67*, 566. Cf. Hamilton, *Memoirs*, 337. David Ogg summed up the unsavory Chiffinch, saying that he performed a great and honorable service to the Stuarts by *not* writing his memoirs. For more on the duties of the Gentlemen of the Bedchamber, cf. Wilson, *Rake*, 56–58.

17. Wilson, *Rake*, 29–48; Hutton, *Restoration*, 253. Biographical information about Buckingham also can be found in the *DNB* and in Chapman, *Great Villiers*.

18. A detailed description of these maneuverings appears in later chapters.

19. Hutton, *Restoration*, 252. Cf. Wilson, *Rake*, 6–10; Kenyon, *The Stuarts*, 67–69.

20. Cf. Chapman, *Great Villiers*, 14, 21, 24–25, 65, 142, 184 passim; Aubrey, *Lives*, 45, 76, 87; Griffin, *Satires*, 311–12, 316.

21. Wilson, *Rake*, 25.

22. Chapman, *Great Villiers*, 109–10; Wilson, *Rake*, 164. See also chapter 4.

23. Wilson, *Rake*, 20–21.

24. For their mutual like of French songs, cf. Rochester, *Letters* (Treglown), 152. Henry Savile shared this enthusiasm; cf. *Letters*, 26, 160, 165. Wilson, *Rake*, 24, 26. Rochester, *Letters* (Treglown), 51–52; cf. Wilson, *Rake*, 20–25, 55, 80, 99, 113, 153, 214, 233, 255.

25. BL, Harl. Ms. 7003, f. 276.

26. Pepys, *Diary*, 8:302, 349; 11:298. See Dryden's portrait of Zimri in "Absalom and Achitophel," ll. 543–68, and Butler's "Character" of "A Duke of Bucks."

27. See Hamilton, *Memoirs*, 188.

28. *CSPD 1665–66*, 426, 428–31; Pepys, *Diary*, 7:221 ff.

29. For Gramont on Rochester and Miss Price, see Hamilton, *Memoirs*, 220. Price sent a copy of the verses to Chesterfield, perhaps in the hope of inciting him to seek revenge on Rochester. For her accompanying note, see Rochester, *Poems* (Vieth), 24.

30. Cf. Rogers, *Medway*, 44–46; Ogg, *England in the Reign of Charles II*, 1:297 ff.; Hutton, *Restoration*, 241–45; Geyl, *Netherlands*, 2:89–90. Of Rochester's second venture,

Burnet said: "Nor did the Rigours of the Season, the hardness of the Voyage, and the extream danger he had been in, deter him from running the like on the very next Occasion; For the Summer following he went to Sea again, without communicating his design to his nearest Relations." Burnet, *Passages*, 10–11.

31. Burnet, *Passages*, 10–11. For more on the St. James's Fight, see Pepys, *Diary*, 7:221–30; Hutton, *Restoration*, 244; Rogers, *Medway*, 46, 78.

32. Pepys, *Diary*, 5:298. Carte Mss. 223, ff. 113, 132, in Greene, *Monkey*, 57; Harris, *Sackville*, 177.

33. Hutton, *Restoration*, 247 ff.

34. Pepys, *Diary*, 7:267 ff.; Evelyn, *Diary*, 494–500.

35. Hutton, *Restoration*, 248.

36. Ibid., 249.

37. Cf. "To Love" (ll. 31–32), "Chorus from *Troas*" (ll. 13–14), "Epilogue to *Love in the Dark*" (l. 12), "The Disabled Debauchee" (ll. 5–12, 43), Rochester, *Letters* (Treglown), 48.

38. Greene, *Monkey*, 58. For the Pophams and their long-term relationship with the Mallets, see BL, Add. Mss. 5496.

39. Hume, *Development of Drama*, 245–46, 284.

40. The play fragment has been reprinted by John Hayward, V. DeS. Pinto, and Harold Love, among others.

41. Hamilton, *Memoirs*, 239. Gramont, who was in London in 1675–76, may have simply appropriated Wycherley's *ficelle* to enliven his later anecdotes about Rochester, of course. But Rochester's identification with the stage remains plain in any case.

42. Hamilton, *Memoirs*, 224–25.

43. "Olinda" may be a feminine version of "Olindo," a hero of Tasso's *Jerusalem Delivered* and a potential martyr. Cf. Gramont, "He was careful never to flatter her on the charms of her appearance, declaring that, if heaven had wished to captivate him by her beauty, he would have had no chance of escaping . . . It was after some open-hearted avowal of this kind, that he would show her some new copy of verses or lately composed song . . . It was pathetic to behold how such insinuations turned her little head"; Hamilton, *Memoirs*, 228–29. One wonders whether Miss Temple discerned in this passage Rochester's rather frank statement that he had only to fantasize intercourse with her to have an orgasm.

44. See Hamilton, *Memoirs*, 222, for a description of "Miss Hobart," whose qualities (aside from her imputed sexual preference) match those given of Dorothy Howard. In the first English editions of Gramont's *Memoirs*, the Maids in Waiting were elliptically designated: Miss B____t (Mary Bagot), Miss Bl____e (Margaret Blagge), Miss Pr____e (Henrietta Maria Price), and Miss H____t. In the 1719 edition now in the British Library, an eighteenth-century script fills these blanks and Miss H____t becomes "Miss Hobart" (for "Miss Howart"). Contemporary sources are void of references to Miss Hobart, whereas Dorothy Howard is listed by Chamberlayne as a Maid in Waiting to the Duchess and Evelyn constantly refers to her in that role before 1671, when the Duchess died and she became a Maid to the Queen. Cf. Evelyn, *Diary*, 530, 587, 599, 606 ff.; Pepys, *Diary*, 9:468.

45. Cf. Hamilton, *Memoirs*, 222 ff. Gramont accused Howard of showing Temple a Rochester lampoon on Henrietta Maria Price in which Howard had substituted Temple's name for Price's.

46. Pepys, *Diary*, 7:371–73; cf. ibid., 4:366.

47. One way he did this was by employing spies to watch chamber doors at night and report to him on who was slipping into whose bedroom. Burnet, *History*, 476–77.

48. Pepys, *Diary*, 7:385.

49. The possible endebtedness of the "Prayer-Book" verse to Malherbe and/or Plato's *Symposium* has been noted. The verse was not printed until 1697 and its date of composition is unknown. The attitude toward love is positive, however, which argues for a relatively early date of composition.

50. "Nothing adds to your fond fire," ll. 17–20. Thomas Coysh recruited Joseph Haynes at about the same time to join his company in Cambridge.

51. Burnet, *Passages*, 10–11: "He had so entirely laid down the Intemperance that was growing on him before his Travels, that at his Return he hated nothing more."

Chapter 7

1. In 1665, Edmund Waller's "Advice to a Painter" celebrated the victory at Lowestoft. The anonymous Second and Third Advices, berating York, Sandwich, the King, and Albemarle for the sea disasters of 1666, appeared in December 1666 and January 1667. Cf. Pepys, *Diary*, 7:407–8; 8:21.

2. Pepys, *Diary*, 8:1–2.

3. Ibid., 8:4. See chapter three, note 26.

4. Ibid., 8:14, 27; Wilson, *Nell Gwyn*, 59–60. Cf. Winn, *Dryden*, 178.

5. Pepys, *Diary*, 8:8, 15, 16, 38, 40.

6. HMC *Le Fleming Ms.*, 44. He was nineteen and she was fifteen.

7. Pepys, *Diary*, 8:44.

8. *CSPD 1666–67*, 310, 504. On May 9, 1671, when fire broke out in Dublin Castle and threatened a powder magazine, Lord John and Anthony Hamilton (Gramont's amanuensis and brother-in-law) rushed in and carried the powder barrels out. *CSPD 1671*, 256.

9. Verney, *Papers* (1925), 2:335.

10. HMC *Ninth Report*, Part II, 25a. Cf. HMC *Le Fleming Ms.*, 100. See also *JHL*, 12:524 ff., 563–64.

11. BL, Harl. Ms. 7003, f. 262. See also Rochester, *Letters* (Treglown), 49n. Treglown's argument that this letter was to his wife is persuasive.

12. BL, Harl. Ms. 7003, f. 209.

13. In May 1668, he told his wife that Lady Warre was planning a visit; "in the meantime pray behave y^r selfe well, & let me hear of noe miscarriages, if I doe, my partiallyty to you will make mee apt to lay them to y^r maide Joane, as I have before, rather than to you." BL Harl. Ms. 7003, f. 216.

14. Ibid., f. 258.

15. Rogers, *Medway*, 70 ff.; Hutton, *Restoration*, 268 ff.

16. Pepys, *Diary*, 8:254 ff.; Library of Shakespeare's Birthplace, Fane Ms., f. 318. "Swive" meant "fuck." The *OED* cites its first usage in 1440. Cf. Suetonius, "Nero," XXXVIII.

17. *CSPD 1667*, 179, 183; Hutton, *Restoration*, 269.

18. Fane Ms., f. 324, records "A Song upon ye disbandinge ye horse in 1667":

> Quoth ye King to his new raysed Troope of Horse
> I've don wth you come kiss myne Arse myne Arse
> Good Sir wee are at yo:^{r} command,
> & when you please wee disband
> T'is not fit y^t any thing in this land,
> But yo:^{r} Royall Tar[se] should stand should stand.

"Tarse" was slang for penis. One of the issues of the day was whether a standing army should be maintained. See Schwoerer, *No Standing Armies!*.

19. Cf. Collinson, 1:92; 3:430. Plate #33 of Ogilby's *Britannia* (1675) is a strip-map of the London-Barnstable Road showing "Ld Rochesters Park" at Enmore. The estate was located beside the main road where it intersected with the road to Cannington. Cf. Burnet, *Passages*, 143.

20. Evelyn, *Diary*, 3:373–74, 382–83.

21. *State Trials*, 3:718–23. Details of College (and his relations with the Rochesters) are given in *CSPD 1681*, 406, 415–16, 420; *JHL*, March 1679; HMC *Rutland II*, 56; Luttrell, *A Brief Historical Relation of State Affairs*, 1:120–21. See also Burnet, *History*, 281 ff.; Kenyon, *Popish Plot*, 241–42; Pollock, *Popish Plot*. For College's lampoons on Justice Scroggs, see *POAS* 2:280–91.

22. Cf. Hobbes, *Leviathan* (1651), Chapter 37 ("Of Miracles and Their Use") and Chapter 45 ("Of Daemonology, and Other Reliques of the Religion of the Gentiles").

23. Simons, an English Jesuit who wrote plays, also taught the humanities, literature, sacred scripture, and theology; he was rector of the English College in Rome and the Anglo-Bavarian College in Liège. See Oldani and Fischer, *Jesuit Theater Englished*. Cf. Kenyon, "James II," in *The Stuarts*, 123, 132 ff., 158–171. Lauderdale said of James, "he is as very papist as the Pope himself. . . ." See chapter 3, note 4.

24. Burnet, *Passages*, 19–20.

25. BL, Harl. Ms. 7003, f. 258; Burnet, *Passages*, 144.

26. Burnet, *History*, 2:450–53.

27. Cf. Pepys, *Diary*, 11:275, for the gossip about her. Also see HMC *Various Collections*, 8:65; *DNB*, 58:314; Hartmann, *La Belle Stuart*, 35.

28. Pepys, *Diary*, 4:230.

29. Castlemain had betrayed the King sexually with Sir Charles Berkeley, Sir Henry Jermyn, and the actor, Charles Hart. When she became pregnant in 1667, Charles II denied his paternity and Castlemain, insisting he was the father, threatened to dash the infant's brains out before his face unless he relented. This was one of a series of explosions until Charles sent her away "permanently" in 1676. Cf. Pepys, *Diary*, 8:355.

30. Burnet, *History*, 452–53; Rochester, *Poems* (Walker), 122.

31. Hutton, *Restoration*, 270.

32. Ibid., 271–72. Hutton suspects Buckingham to have been behind many of these attacks. Cf. *POAS*, 2:64–65.

33. Wilson, *Court Satires*, 11.

34. BL, Add. Mss. 21,505, f. 237, is a long account in French of remarks allegedly made before Clarendon and members of the Commons; the remarks were "scandaleux, seditioux, et contenant des reproches a la justice du Roy." Accused and stripped of his places, Buckingham went into hiding. He surrendered to Arlington in June and went to the Tower. On July 1, he appeared before the Privy Council and was acquitted; HMC *Le Fleming*, 51. Cf. Pepys, *Diary*, 8:330, 348; Evelyn, *Diary* (1955), 3:454, 457; Hutton, *Restoration*, 252–55, 280–85. Clarendon's version of the events leading up to his trial is given in Clarendon, *Life*, 2:416 ff.

35. Pepys, *Diary*, 8:360.

36. "The Downfall of the Chancellor," in *POAS*, 2:65.

37. Clarendon, *Life*, 2:419–69. Cf. Burnet, *History*, 1:444–62; *POAS*, 2:64.

38. Haley, *First Earl of Shaftesbury*, 192–201; Hutton, *Restoration*, 276–78. Haley says, "In these circumstances one obvious line of escape for the government was by making the unpopular Clarendon the scapegoat for all. The Lord Chancellor had clearly outlived

his usefulness; perhaps the prorogation of 29 July had saved him even then from an impeachment planned for that very morning, and an impeachment could certainly be expected in the next session," 195–96. Hutton agrees: "One general conclusion subsumes all: the Earl had become an increasing political liability with ever diminishing assets as a servant and a decreasing claim upon his master's affections. All that is extraordinary about the matter is that Charles still felt enough for him to hesitate five days over his dismissal," 278.

39. *JHL*, 12:114; *CSPD 1667*, 450.

40. Hutton, *Restoration*, 280. The Earl of Lindsey wrote, " 'Tis well if a single sacrifice can make a perfect atonement, and that the punishment of one can purge the guilt of all the rest." For Lindsey's account of Clarendon, Buckingham, and the events of the summer in 1667, see HMC *Fourteenth Report*, Part IX, 367–71.

41. Hutton gives a succinct account of proceedings during the weeks following, *Restoration*, 281–84. Although Buckingham had earlier scoffed at Sir Robert Howard and made him the "hero" of a version of *The Rehearsal*, he with Howard in the Commons worked in league to impeach Clarendon—Howard was angry at Clarendon's part in his recent divorce—and common cause had produced a new friendship. See Oliver, *Sir Robert Howard*, 131–36. Cf. Chapman, *Great Villiers*, 168, 172.

42. For Apsley, see Pepys, *Diary*, 7:416. A contemporary lampoon in BL, Sloane Ms. 1709, f. 22, described Buckingham thusly, in a liturgical parody:

> From a sensual proud Atheisticall life
> From arming of Laquey's wth Pistoll and Knife
> From murth'ring the Husband & kissing the wife
> *Libera nos Domine.*

43. *JHL*, 12:114–15, 117–18, 119, 121, 122–32, 133, 135–40. Rochester was absent on November 19, when a report was given on a conference between the Lords and Commons that opened the way for an impeachment vote. Mulgrave did not attend any sessions between October 10 and December 19, 1667. At the roll call on February 17, 1668, he was absent, listed as *infra aetatem. JHL*, 12:186.

44. *JHL*, 12:142. Arlington, its deviser, also signed the Demurrer.

45. Ibid., 12:142–50, 154–56, 162–65. Edward Hyde's second son, Laurence, had no doubts of Rochester's part in his father's disgrace. Cf. BL, Add. Mss. 15, 892, ff. 1–5: "Meditations on the Anniversary day of Ld Clarendon's death (qth of Dec̲m̲ 1675) Wrote by his son Laur̲ce̲ Hyde." Hyde wrote: "When all the checks of conscience being removed, as they will quickly be from those are onely eyeservers & pleasers, there appeared a total defection in all sorts of men Ecclesiasticall & Secular—from their known duty to God, their Country, & their friend—& such a friend, who had been so instrumentall under God, & by Gods blessing, in restoring them to all their livings, dignitys, honours, Estates, pleasures, & profitts which they have enjoyed since the K: happy restoration. . . ." Placed significantly after the "Meditations" was a copy of Rochester's repentant letter to Dr. Burnet in 1680. Ironically, after the death of Rochester's son Charles Wilmot in November 1681, Laurence Hyde was given the title Earl of Rochester.

46. The death was recorded in the *Spelsbury Church Wardens' Book*; cf. G. E. C., *Baronetage*, 7:644.

47. *Treasury Books 1660–1667*, 116, 121.

48. BL, Harl. Ms. 7003, f. 196. Treglown places this letter in ?1673–74 and identifies the place as Adderbury, but biographically it seems clear that the place is Ditchley and the date is soon after Frank Lee's death.

Chapter 8

1. Burnet, *Passages*, 11–12.
2. Clarendon, *History*, 8:30, 94, 169.
3. Cf. "Dutch Prowess" in Rochester's poem "Upon Nothing." The *Dictionary of American Slang* identifies the term as British slang originating during Anglo-Dutch warfare in the seventeenth century.
4. Burnet, *Passages*, 11–12.
5. Clarendon, *Life*, 2:260 ff.
6. See Wilson, *Rake*, 102–12, for Buckingham's part in the Clarendon impeachment. Buckingham sometimes mimicked Arlington by wearing a black plaster on his nose and swaggering about with a cane of the sort Bennet carried. In his farce, *The Rehearsal*, Buckingham had Mr. Bayes injure his nose while trying to dance so that he could return in the next act wearing a black patch on it.
7. The material on Bennet is based on Barbour, *Henry Bennet*, and the *DNB*.
8. See Chapter Five above.
9. Cf. Hutton, *Restoration*, 200–204. The Fane Ms., f. 172, lists the members of the Cabal thus: C: Clifford A: Arlington B: Buckingham A: Ashley L: Lautherdale. This verse is appended:

> Our State affaires are like to thrive
> Whilst they are govern'd by these five
> A formall Ass, a surly Dog,
> A Mole, a Divell, & a Hog.

10. Haley, *Shaftesbury*, 279–80; Harris, *Sackville*, 35–40.
11. Wilson, *Nell Gwyn*, 75–95.
12. Harris, *Sackville*, 37–39.
13. Cf. Pepys, *Diary*, 9:27; Wilson, *Rake*, 113–14. In fact, Anna Maria was off in France at the time of the duel.
14. Pepys, *Diary*, IX, 54; Harris, *Sackville*, 37.
15. *JHL* 12:186–245. Cf. Pepys, *Diary*, 9:173.
16. *JHL*, 12:232, 245–57. Cf. Pepys, *Diary*, 9:27n2.
17. A letter to his wife about that time said he had "a poore living to gett"; he was paid for Bedchamber duties in May 1668. BL, Harl. Ms. 7003, f. 201. *Treasury Books 1660–1667*, 320, 566.
18. Burnet, *Passages*, 11–12.
19. BL, Harl. Ms, f. 296.
20. Pepys, *Diary*, 9:218–19. The dildo or *olisbos* had been used by the ancient Greeks and the Chinese, who referred to it in their writings; cf. Tannahill, *Sex in History*, 98–99, 158, 178–79.
21. Hamilton, *Memoirs*, 235–39; Rochester, *Letters* (Treglown), 175. Cf. Lawner, *I Modi*, 2–56.
22. Burnet, *History*, 1:74–75. Cf. Rochester, *Letters* (Treglown), 34, 198, 202. Burnet dates the advent of Jane Roberts after Clarendon's fall. Ashley Lord Shaftesbury has been credited with managing Roberts, but see Haley, *Shaftesbury*, 280.
23. Cf. Prinz, *Rochesteriana*.
24. Burnet, *History*, 2:299–300.
25. Ibid., 1:473.

26. In Chapter XVI of the *Leviathan*, Hobbes wrote: "The word person is Latine: instead whereof the Greeks have *prosopon*, which signifies the *Face*, as *persona* in latine signifies the *disguise*, or *outward appearance* of a man, counterfeited on the Stage; and somtimes more particularly that part of it, which disguiseth the face, as a Mask or Visard. . . ."

27. Burnet, *Passages*, 27–28. The precedent for monarchs and aristocrats disguising themselves as the low born to carry on sexual affairs had been set by the Romans. Janus and Janus, *Sexual Behavior*, 53–55: "Everyone needs some form of escape into fantasy if his daily life does not allow for it. The difference between politicians and other people is that [he] who has acquired power in the first place by acting out fantasies of dominance in a permissable form, can use that power to convert his most baroque sexual dreams into reality."

28. Castle, *Masquerade*, 6, 55.

29. Kay Dick, quoted in Pepper, *A Man's Tale*, 94–95.

30. Burnet, *Passages*, 27–28.

31. Gepp, *Adderbury*, 58–60; Beesley, *History of Banbury*, 488.

32. Kott, *Shakespeare's Bitter Arcadia*. The passage continues: "Male attire was to protect a girl when on a journey, but the disguise made her even more attractive, and that in three ways: for men who are fond of women and who were able to discern female shape under the disguise; for men who are fond of youths and who saw in the disguised girl the girlish youth they desired; and for women, deceived by the garments and roused to violent affection by the smooth and charming youth. . . ." Cf. Lawner, *I Modi*, 45; Olivieri, in Ariès and Béjin, *Western Sexuality*, 95–102.

33. Wilson, *Nell Gwyn*, 66–69; Pepys, *Diary*, 1:224; 2:7.

34. See note 42 below. [Milton]

35. Cf. Trumbach, "Sodomy Transformed," 105; Trumbach, "London's Sodomites," 1–33.

36. Trumbach, "Sodomy Transformed."

37. In a letter to Savile (1677), Rochester calls himself "un bougré." Letters in 1678 refer to his French valet, Belle-Fasse, whose "beauties have been tasted by both sexes."

38. BL, Harl. Ms. 7003, f. 216.

39. BL, Harl. Ms. 7003, f. 225. Blancourt was an agent of the Rochesters in Somerset as John Cary was in Oxfordshire. He witnessed their Indenture in 1672, and Rochester had him made an official designee to receive payments in his stead from the Treasury.

40. BL, Harl. Ms., f. 201.

41. Harris, *Sackville*, 38–39. *Paradise Lost* was published in 1667.

42. Cf. John Milton, *Paradise Lost*, Book IV, 288–330, 689–715, 736–47; Book VIII, 491–522, 595–605. Barbara Everett sees within Rochester's stanzas metaphysical eroticism. "It is as if, in order to undress his fallen couple, to get them back towards whatever innocence once meant, *he* has to take off their very bodies, which in this poem are dissolving towards the Platonic condition of shadowy Idea, under trees so abstract as to have grown mere generic 'Shades'. . . ." In Treglown, ed., *Spirit of Wit*, 17–18.

43. Cf. Hobbes, *Leviathan*, 159.

44. Ibid., 488 ff.; cf. xxv ff. Also cf. Aubrey, *Lives*, 156.

45. Aubrey, *Lives*, 152. See Pearson, *Stags and Serpents*, 59–79, for the life of William Cavendish the First Duke (1640–1707). Cavendish was among the earliest Whig lords, and his political leanings, along with those of Halifax and Dorset, may have helped to influence Rochester in the late 1670s. See Burnet, *History*, 2:91–92.

46. Cf. Albert S. Borgman, *Shadwell*, 17–19; Hume, *Development of Drama*, 258–59; Winn, *Dryden*, 193, 197, 200, 222.

47. Borgman, *Shadwell*, 49, 72, 94, 96, 97, 107. See also Seldan, "Rochester and Shadwell," 177–190.

48. Pepys, *Diary*, 9:335–36. Cf. Harris, *Sackville*, 38.

49. Pepys, *Diary*, 9:382.

50. Barbour, *Bennet*, 7, 133 ff.

51. Pepys, *Diary*, 9:451–52.

52. Fane Ms., ff. 326, 330, 356. According to Lord Sandwich, Killegrew's jibe concerned Rochester's marriage.

53. Pepys, *Diary*, 9:451–52.

54. HMC *Seventh Report Appendix*, 531A.

55. Barbour, *Bennet*, 7, 130 ff.

56. Cf. Hume, *Development of Drama*, 259; Oliver, *Howard*, 109, 119.

57. The parody referred to the Ballers and the vermin they acquired from Lady Bennett. A ms. version of the poem was titled "A Duell Between two Monsters upon my Lady B—ts C—t." Oliver, 161–65; Harris, *Sackville*, 48, 238. The parody is printed in Sackville, *Poems*, 118–23.

58. On July 4, 1668, Pepys was proudly shown this desk by Sir William Coventry, who as a Naval Commissioner and Treasury Commissioner figures prominently in Pepys's *Diary*. Cf. Tomalin, *Pepys*, 134–35.

59. For a detailed account of the "lost" play and its circumstances, see the Introduction by Scouten and Hume to Howard and George Villiers, *The Country Gentleman*, 1–44.

60. HMC *Le Fleming Ms.*, 61–62; Pepys, *Diary*, 9:462, 466–67, 469, 473.

61. BL, Harl. Ms. 7003, f. 226. Rochester had declared his intense love for his pregnant wife in Harl. Ms. 7003, f. 224.

62. Hartmann, *Charles II and Madame*, 240; *The Royal Letter Book*, 178–79. The King's letter to Madame dated March 12 indicates that he was not displeased with Rochester:

> This bearer my Ld Rochester has a minde to make a little iorny to paris and would not kisse your hands without a letter from me, pray use him as one I have a very good opinion of. You will find him not to want witt, and did behave himself in all the duch warr as well as any body as a volontire. I have no more to add but that I am intierly Yours C.

63. Fane Ms., f. 696.

64. See Rochester, *Poems* (Vieth), 21.

65. Ibid., xxiv–xxv.

66. Cf. Pearson, *Stags and Serpents*, 60.

67. Rochester's flight may have been the teaching of Thomas Hobbes that the avoidance of violent death is the end of all reason. In Epistle Dedicatory to *De Cive* (1651), Hobbes said that reason "teaches every man to fly a contranatural dissolution (*mortem violentam*) as the greatest mischief that can arrive to nature." Satirists who castigated Rochester for "cowardice," as did Thomas Lessey, associated him with Hobbesian theory.

68. HMC *Buccleugh and Queensbury Mss.*, 1:429–30. HMC *Sixth Report*, Part One, 366; *Calendar of State Papers . . . in the Archives and Collections of Venice*, 36:71–72.

69. The *Mémoires* of the Abbé de Choisy gives details about Monsieur; but also see Bulliet, *Venus Castina*, 185–87. For more on Monsieur's regency and the sexual tastes of his son, see "The Scandalous Regent," in Watson, *Wisdom and Strength*, 183 ff.

70. Choisy, *Mémoires*; Bulliet, *Venus*, 187–96. For an extended discussion of Choisy and the Chevalier D'Éon, as well as the psychodynamics of transvestitism, see Garber, *Vested Interests*, 256–66.

71. Pepys, *Diary*, 2:7; Bulliet, *Venus*, 169–70. Colley Cibber verified the story of Kynaston's offstage appearances as a woman by asking the actor himself as an old man. Kynaston testified to them. Garber, *Vested Interests*, 39, 52–53.

72. Alcock, *Famous Pathologist*, 26–27; Prinz, *Rochesteriana*, 200–201; Hamilton, *Memoirs*, 257–59. Gramont's account of Rochester as Dr. Bendo had him recognizing Miss Temple's maid and, through her, warning Temple to "beware of a man dressed up in woman's clothes." This presumably was a mocking reference to Dorothy Howard, but Alcock said that Rochester dressed as "Mrs. Bendo" to inspect unwitting female patients. Cf. Rochester's uncompleted poem beginning "What vain unnecessary things are men," ll. 27–28: "But whils't th'insulting wife the Breeches wore / The Husband tooke her cloathes to give his [o're]." His transvestite episodes allegedly took place between 1675 and 1677, a period when Rochester's sexual potency was considerably diminished by venereal disease. A modern explanation for this type of cross-dressing has been given. "Transvestism is in great part a defensive structure raised to protect a threatened but desired sense of masculinity and maleness, and the corollary, to preserve a badly threatened sense of potency." Stoller, *Presentations of Gender*, 1:180.

73. The "Regime d'viver" possibly dates ca. 1671–73, given the nature of its subject matter and tone, which find parallels in Rochester's life as well as works at that period.

74. Hamilton, *Memoirs*, 222.

75. A lampoon in the BL Sloane Ms. 1709, f. 122, describes Buckingham as a lover of boys and men:

> From transposing Nature upon ye bon Garse
> With Kinaston acting both Venus and Mars
> And owning of seventie other mens tarce
> *Libera nos Domine*

(A "bon garse" was a *beau garcon*, a "pretty boy" or "beau.") Hester Chapman believed that Buckingham had an affair with Kynaston in 1675 when he was forty-eight, a "climacteric" age; *Great Villiers*, 224. Kynaston would have been in in his early thirties. Cf. Fane Ms., f. 134; Wilcoxon, "Mirrors of Men's Fears," 45–51.

76. Cf. Fane Ms., f. 320: "A young noble man of France cominge on[e] morning to visite ye old Prince of Conde found him in his bed he made him sitt upon ye bed by him, his business was about religion, of wch when they had discoursed half an hour ye Prince putt his hand into ye noblemans codpise saying lett us have un peu de reinissance; but ye nobleman, wondering, tooke his leave & retyred." *Reinissance*, a pun on *renaissance*, is untranslatable; *rein* meant the loins.

77. Lewisohn, *A History of Sexual Customs*, 202 ff. "Pisanus Fraxi" (Henry Spencer Ashbee) included information about the Order in his surveys of forbidden books, the *Index* and *Centuria*. The Marquis de Sade based his *120 Days of Sodom* loosely on the Order of Sodomites.

78. Cf. "The Imperfect Enjoyment," ll. 41–43. The narrator's verbal abuse at his impotent penis includes this triplet: "Stiffly resolv'd, twou'd carelessly invade, / *Woman* or *Man*, or ought its fury staid, / Where e'er it pierc'd, a *Cunt* it found or made."

79. For studies of Rochester's possible homosexuality, see Hammond, "Rochester's Homoeroticism," 47–62. This essay is reprinted as the final chapter in Hammond's *Figuring Sex*.

Chapter 9

1. BL, Harl. MS 7003, f. 199. In 1582 France had adopted the New Style Gregorian calendar, which compensated for the mis-measurements of the Old Style Julian calendar. In the seventeenth century, Englishmen began designating dates as OS or NS; and the first three months of the year were double dated by some; e.g., Rochester's son Charles was christened in January 1670/71 or NS 1671.

2. Adderbury Church *Parish Registers.*

3. BL, Harl. MS. 7003, ff. 189, 192, 220.

4. HMC *Buccleugh and Queensbury Mss.*, 1:430.

5. See Treglown's Introduction in Rochester, *Letters*, 34.

6. BL, Harl. Ms 7003, f. 189. Treglown dates this letter as ?1672; but the reference to Ann as sole daughter and heir, Mulgrave's testimony about Rochester's health in November 1669, and the cheerful tone of the letter all argue for October 1669.

7. *JHL*, 12:251–52, 255–59. On October 26, when the roll was called, Rochester was not listed among either the present or absent, 263.

8. HMC *Seventh Report Appendix*, 488B.

9. Cf. Rochester, *Poems* (Walker), 116.

10. Carr Scroop, "In Defense of Satire," in *Poems on Several Occasions by the Right Honourable E. of R*—(1680), 48. Cf. Vieth, *ARP*, 139–56. A short biography of Scroop appears in the *DNB*, 17:1071–72.

11. "The True Englishman," in BL, Sloane Ms. 655, f. 46. The comparison of Mulgrave to one of the King's water spaniels was no doubt deliberate.

12. Mulgrave's family came from Yorkshire, where they owned the alum works at Whitby. Like Rochester, his father died when he was ten and he was supervised by his widowed mother and a baronet guardian. Mulgrave "was put in the hands of a tutor with whom he was so little satisfied, that he got rid of him in a short time, and at an age not exceeding twelve years resolved to educate himself." Consequently, he never went to university or had the Grand Tour. At seventeen, he volunteered for naval duty with the results noted above. In 1670–71, Sheffield was conspicuously attending Parliament, ingratiating himself with the King and York. He gained fame in the Third Anglo-Dutch War, when he served on the *Prince Rupert* in May 1672 under Lord Hawley, and he fought in the disastrous Battle of Solebay, when Lord Sandwich was killed. In January 1673, when the Duke of Richmond died, he became Gentleman of the Bedchamber. From 1669 to 1673, his contacts with Rochester apparently were few but civil. Cf. *DNB*, 18:13–15. See Wilson, *Court Satires*, 269–70 for a later chronology.

13. J. Sheffield, *Works*, 2:8–10. David Vieth has constructed an informative account of Ashton's life, works, and place in Restoration writing in *ARP*, 249–70. In Vieth's words, "he was a nobody who knew everybody who was anybody," 254.

14. Details of this account are given in Sheffield's *Memoirs* in the *Works* and in *JHL*, 12:272–74, 276–77, 278 ff.

15. Gramont would have Rochester impotent from his "debauches and all the trollopes of London" as early as 1666; Hamilton, *Memoirs*, 239.

16. Cf. Rochester, *Letters* (Treglown), 198. Other husbands silently infected their wives by not admitting their disease, wittingly or otherwise, and thereby preventing them from getting such treatment as existed. The wife then died, as did Rochester's niece, Anne Wharton. Cf. Stone, *Family Sex*, 487.

17. For contemporary medical writings, see Hodge, *Medical Commonplace Book*, ff. 331–338, 572v–576; Wiseman, *Severall Chirurgical Treatuses*. Treatise 8, "Of Lues

Venerea," defines syphilis as "a venemous contagious Disease gotten either Immediately or Mediately from an impure Coition." It could also be passed on through inheritance or suckling. Wiseman describes the mercury cure and diet in detail, 8–15, and remarks that some men thought difficulty in urinating was due to "the stone" and so failed to get proper treatment, 24.

18. Cf. Rochester, *Letters* (Treglown), 68, 80–81, 82, 88, 106, 114, 115, 139, 155–56, 158, 171, 172, 176–77, 181–82, 201–03, 104. Treglown's tentative dating of some of these removes them from their proper sequence which shows the progression of Rochester's disease and his response to it. For his death as due to his dealing with women, see Hearne, *Remarks*, 9:78–79.

19. In "Rochester and Davenant," Treglown locates lines in "The Imperfect Enjoyment" that apparently refer to Dryden's *The Conquest of Granada*, which was acted in two parts, December 1670 and January 1671. Cf. Rochester, *Poems* (Walker), 241–42; Hume, *Development of Drama*, 272. Winn believes Dryden may have begun work on the play as early as the winter of 1668–69, however; and he dates Dryden's theatrical collaboration with Rochester on *Marriage-A-La-Mode* as beginning in June 1671. Winn, *Dryden*, 200, 225. Rochester might have seen parts of *Conquest* in draft as early as 1670. A terminal date for "Enjoyment" is ca. 1672, after which Rochester abandoned the eroticism found in the opening parts of the lyric and began treating sex (and women) with overt disgust and obscenity. Cf. Griffin, *Satires*, 91–100.

20. See Farley-Hills, *The Benevolence of Laughter*, 132–83; Paulson, "Rochester: The Body Politic and the Body Private"; O'Neill, "Rochester's 'Imperfect Enjoyment' "; Wilcoxon, "Pornography, Obscenity, and Rochester's 'Imperfect Enjoyment' "; Braudy, "Remembering Masculinity"; Ober, "The Earl of Rochester and Ejaculatio Praecox." Ober, who sees the poem as autobiographical in its intensely personal use of a first-person narrator and its reference to premature ejaculation rather than impotence, says, "Caught in a conflict between female and male object-choice, Rochester's psyche demanded retreat to infantile behavior in the form of premature ejaculation."

21. Burnet, *Passages*, 25–27. Ovid, *Heroides and Amores*, 506–08. The translations do not include III.vii: "The translator has felt obliged to omit one poem entire . . . where, in spite of the poet's exquisite art, a faithful rendering might offend the sensibilities of the reader, if not the literary taste." This in 1963! Cf. Griffin, *Satires*, 91–92 for precedents in Petronius and Ovid. In 1680, Jacob Tonson published *Ovid's Epistles* with an important Preface by Dryden, two translations by him, and one by Dryden and Mulgrave jointly. The translator of Ovid III.vii is unknown; but similarities between it (Griffin, *Satires*, 91–92) and Rochester's version (published in *Poems on Several Occasions* in the same year) are strikingly similar. See Rochester, *Poems* (Walker), 241–42.

22. Cf. Rochester's fragment, "Sab: Lost":

> Shee yeilds, she yeilds,
> Pale Envy said Amen
> The first of woemen to the Last of men.
> Just soe those frailer beings Angells fell
> Ther's noe mid way (it seemes) twix't heav'n and hell,
> [Gods!] Was it your end in making her to show
> Things must bee rais'd soe high to fall soe low?

For an extended discussion of the "Enjoyment" poem, see Turner, *Schooling Sex*, 273–82.

23. *CSPD 1670*, 49. Some sources give 1669 as the date of death, probably because of confusion between Old and New Style dating. See Burke, *Peerage*, 251, 553.

24. *JHL*, 12:524 ff.; HMC *Ninth Report, Part II*, 25a: *JHL*, 12:563–64; HMC *Le Fleming*, 100.

25. HMC *Fifth Report Appendix*, 324.

26. HMC *Portland*, 3:357; Andrew Marvell, *Poems and Letters*, 2:331.

27. Verney, *Verney Papers* (1925), 1:149–50.

28. Cf. Rochester, *Letters* (Treglown), 176–77.

29. Cf. ibid., 97–101; Prinz, *Rochester*, 301. Francis Warre (ca. 1659–1718) was created a baronet on June 2, 1673, and he matriculated at Oriel College in 1674, age 15. He was a Captain in Monmouth's regiment until the Exclusion Crisis, when his fierce royalism caused him to retire. The M.P. from Bridgewater four times and from Taunton eight times, he supported James II; after the Bloody Assizes in 1687, he was a leader in an uprising against the cause of William III. His first wife was Anne Cuffe, whom he married ca. 1675; she died in 1690. In 1715, he was barred from returning to the House of Commons by a franchise issue. He died in Ghent in 1718. See Burke, *Peerage*, 553; G. E. C., *Complete Baronetage*, 4:56; *The Victoria History of Somerset*, 2:231.

30. Hearne, *Remarks*, 9:78–79; Huntington Library, Huntington Ms. HA 12525, quoted in Hook "Something More about Rochester."

31. Harris, *Sackville*, 40–43; Chapman, *Villiers*, 156–61.

32. Cf. Burnet, *History* 1:536 ff.; Jones, *Restored Monarchy*, 11, 15, 35, 128: Haley, *Shaftesbury*, 280; Kenyon, *The Stuarts*, 131–34. Kenyon asserts that Charles's willingness to declare himself a Catholic was totally out of character and attributes it to the bewitching influence of his sister, Minette.

33. Jones, *Country and Court*, 104–5, 167–73.

34. Downes, *Roscius Anglicanus*, 29. Cf. Hume, *Development of Drama*, 258, 263. "The king's sister, the duchess of Orleans, was thought the wittiest woman in France, but had no sort of virtue, and scarce retained common decency. The king of France had made love to her and was highly incensed when she saw this was only a pretence to cover his addresses to mademoiselle la Vallière, one of her maids of honour, whom he afterwards declared openly to be his mistress. Yet she had reconciled herself to the king, and was now so entirely trusted by him that he ordered her to propose an interview with her brother at Dover. The king [Charles] went thither, and was so charmed with his sister that it did not pass without censure; every thing she proposed, and every favour she asked, was granted: the king could deny her nothing." Burnet, *History*, 1:538–39. Charles himself told Madame in a letter that he could deny her nothing. Kenyon, *The Stuarts*, 131–32. Cf. Hartmann, *The King My Brother*.

35. Treglown gives Montagu's report verbatim; Rochester, *Letters* (Treglown), 57.

36. Other letters of unspecific dates suggest that estrangement between the Rochesters was due to her inability (or unwillingness) to tell him directly of her grievances against him. Since these were probably due to his sexual liaisons with other women, and since Rochester reacted to quarrels with sarcastic contempt, walking out of the house, his wife's reluctance to confront him is understandable. Cf. Rochester, *Letters* (Treglown), 77, 170.

37. BL, Harl. Ms. 7003, f. 202. Madame had been ill before her trip to Dover, and historians agree that she probably died from a duodenal ulcer that perforated. On July 1, 1670, Henry Savile told his brother Halifax that "every body is convinced that Madame's death was very natural."

38. Treglown puzzles about "Nan" as Rochester's daughter, too young at thirteen months to be a godmother. The other "Nan," his Lee niece, however, is the obvious person.

39. Cf. Rochester, *Letters* (Treglown), 58.

40. Hume, *Development of Drama*, 280; cf. Mary Edmond, *Rare Sir William Davenent.*

41. Highfill et al., *Biographical Dictionary*, 1:313–25.

42. Cf. Rochester, *Letters* (Treglown), 142.

43. Several of Rochester's letters state his intention not to "wait" on his mother when she was in a dictatorial mood. For her joining the Lees at the expense of the Wilmots, see the account of the Woodstock dispute with Lady Lindsey in chapters following.

44. For Sir Thomas Cobb, see Pugh, *Victoria History of Oxfordshire*, 9:9–10.

45. *The Museum* 31 (May 23, 1747): 158.

46. Cf. Rochester, *Letters* (Treglown), 70–71.

47. Cf. Rochester, *Poems* (Walker), 64–68.

48. *JHL*, 12:352–53. See the entry for November 21, 1670. It was typical of Rochester's Parliamentary attendance from 1667 until ca. 1675 to go to sessions only when royal or family business was about to be affected by legislation under consideration.

49. BL, Harl. Ms. 7003, f. 235.

50. Ibid., f. 245.

51. Burnet, *Passages*, 12–13.

52. Evelyn, *Diary*, 547.

Chapter 10

1. Cf. Dering, *Parliament Diary 1670–73*, 43–45; Marvell, *Letters*, 2:307–8; BL, Additional Mss. 36, 916, f. 202; Whitcombe, *Charles II*, 115–19.

2. *Journal of the House of Commons*, 9:180–89.

3. BL, Harl. Ms. 7003, f. 268.

4. Ibid., f. 270. The danger was that of being damned so long as an infant remained unchristened. The ecclesiatical position of the Roman Catholic Church at the time was that "a child before he is baptized is not a child of God but a child of the Devil." Stone, *Family*, 68.

5. *Adderbury Church Parish Register*. For an explanation of the date of 1670 instead of 1671, see Chapter Nine, note 1.

6. HMC *Rutland II*, 22. Rochester's lack of compunction about having his son christened in the Anglican Church indicates that whatever attractions Catholicism formerly held for him were ended by 1671.

7. For Rochester's reliance on his mother to act as guardian to his son, see Rochester, *Letters* (Treglown), 229; Prinz, *Rochester*, 300. He was even willing to tease his wife about the preference for his mother in some instances. See *Letters* (Treglown), 177.

8. For information about James Bertie, future Earl of Abdingdon, see *Collins's Peerage of England* (1812), 3:628–30.

9. Cf. Verney, *Verney Papers* (1925), 1:149; 2:334–35, 338.

10. HMC *Rutland II*, 22. *Granada* Part I was acted in late December, 1670; Part II was acted on January 3 or 10, 1671. Dryden, *Plays*, 11:411.

11. For details about Dryden at this period and a close account of *Conquest*, see Winn, *Dryden*, 208–24. Cf. Hume, *Development of Drama*, 272–73 ff.

12. Maximillian Novak gives the full background of *Tyrannic Love* in the California Edition of his *Works*, 10:380–432. For the fox, see Winn, *Dryden*, 204.

13. See Smith, "St. Catharine." Sébastien Tillemont (1637–98), the French ecclesiastical historian is the authority for Catharine's reputation in the seventeenth century.

14. See Barber, *Pepys*, 8, 23. Mrs. Pepys was painted by John Hales. For Castlemain, see Figure 4.

15. Wilson, *Nell Gwyn*, 107 ff.

16. Cf. Winn, *Dryden*, 200–207. Hume calls the play an experiment and finds much to admire in Dryden's execution of "epic magnitude and near-exemplary characters," *Development of Drama*, 272.

17. Hume, *Development of Drama*, 167.

18. Ibid., 272–73, 290–91.

19. Chapman gives an account of *The Rehearsal* in *Great Villiers*, 167–80, and repeats the story that Buckingham himself coached Lacy in Dryden's mannerisms and that he and Rochester invited Dryden to sit with them at the première of the play, the better to witness his reactions. Since *The Rehearsal* was staged by Dryden's own company, the King's, he must have known about it beforehand. Cf. Winn, *Dryden*, 229. Winn notes that as a sharer at the King's, Dryden had every reason to hope the play would be a success.

20. BL, Harl. Ms. 7003, f. 296.

21. Dryden, *Plays*, XI, 411.

22. HMC *Ninth Report, Part II*, 448a.

23. Rochester's reason for taking a dildo into the country with him in December 1670 is moot. Possibly it contributed to debauchery at Woodstock in January with such local misses as the comely but dirty Nell Browne. Hearne, *Remarks*, 9:79.

24. Lady Mary's letters can be found in HMC *Rutland II*, 22–23.

25. For a general account and some broadside ballads on Vernell's death, see *POAS*, 1:172–76. Information about Robert Constable is given in the *Peerages* of G. E. C. and Collins.

26. BL, Add. Mss. 27,962T, f. 149. Cf. *Calendar of Venetian State Papers*, 37:40. The HMC *Eleventh Report Appendix* cites the Venetian *Calendar* as the source for placing Rochester among Vernell's murderers.

27. *CSPD 1671*, 142, 183.

28. *JHL*, 12:352–458.

29. See Miller, *Popery*, 112–16.

30. Among the miscellaneous pamphlets in the British Library is *A Copie of a Paper Written by the Late Dutches of York*, dated "St. James's Aug. 20th. 1670." (The Duchess died in early summer, 1671). The unknown author writes in the first person as the Duchess, saying she was so impressed by observing French Catholic practice and piety that she was moved to convert. The piece refers to the efforts of Bishop Blandford to keep her a Protestant and ends with "My only Prayer is, That the poor Catholicks of this Nation, may not suffer for my Being of their Religion . . .," 7.

31. *JHL*, 12:450–51, 454.

32. Miller, *Popery*, 106–7; Jones, *Country and Court*, 170–72; Wilson, *Rake*, 182–85; Haley, *Shaftesbury*, 287 ff.; Kenyon, *The Stuarts*, 132–33.

33. Brown, ed. *Familiar Letters etc.*, 1:4; BL, Harl. Ms. 7003, f. 252; Henry Guy (1631–1710) was Savile's friend and both the friend and, after 1679, Groom of the Bed Chamber to the King. He advised Henry St. John, Rochester's first cousin, to be modest in applying for favors for friends but to be very greedy on his own behalf.

34. HMC *Rutland II*, 23.

35. Cf. Rochester, *Letters* (Treglown), 73–74. Treglown dates this letter as early 1672, probably because James Bertie married Ellen Lee on February 1, 1672, but Lady Mary's letters detail the courtship in the first months of 1671 and other circumstances indicate this letter was written in late March or early April of that year.

36. The fullest life study of Wycherley (1641–1716) is B. Eugene McCarthy's *Wycherley*.

37. See Hume, *Development of Drama*, 278–79; Loftus, *Spanish Plays*, 121–25. For other influences, see Turner, *Schooling Sex*, 240–59.

38. Wycherley, *Plays*. Charles II had made improvements to St. James's Park in 1660–61 and Edmund Waller had written a poetic tribute to the pastoral setting; cf. Griffin, *Satires*, 28–29. Subsequently it became the scene for numerous illicit *al fresco* pairings, losing its elegance and panache. For Wycherley and Rochester, see Turner, *Schooling Sex*, 240–59.

39. This was John Dennis's version; Alexander Pope quoted the remark to Joseph Spence as "Sir, you're a rascal! You're a villain!" Spence, *Observations*, 1:34; Dennis, *Works*, 2:409. Wycherley, *Plays*, 10.

40. Wilson, *Rake*, 180–81.

41. Dennis, *Works*, 2:410.

42. BL, Harl. Ms. 7003, f. 192. Treglown notes that Rochester parodies the burial service and the Easter Day Epistle.

43. Preface to *Juliana*, in Crowne, *Dramatic Works*, 1:16. Cf. Van Lennep, *The London Stage 1660–1700*, 182–82; Hume, *Development of Drama*, 286–87.

44. Winn, *Dryden*, 221, et seq.

45. The salient facts about Etherege's life are given in the *Letters*, xvi–xvii, 3–5.

46. Thomas Shadwell, *The Medal of John Bays*, in *The Complete Works*, 3. Cf. Winn, *Dryden*, 225.

47. Cf. Rochester, *Poems* (Walker), 99, 101 and Rochester, *Letters* (Treglown), 119–20.

48. Winn, *Dryden*, 222–23.

49. Dryden openly jeered at Rochester for his lack of monetary patronage in the published Dedication to *All for Love* in 1678. Cf. Winn, *Dryden*, 307–9.

50. BL, Harl. Ms. 7003, f. 293.

51. Pinto, "Rochester and Dryden."

52. Colbert de Croissy, quoted in Hartmann, *Clifford*, 209.

53. Cf. Turner, *Schooling Sex*, 267–73.

54. Rochester, *Letters* (Treglown), 70–71, and *Poems* (Walker), 64–68.

55. Hartmann, *Clifford*, 25.

56. Cf. Rochester, *Letters* (Treglown), 68.

Chapter 11

1. See Marshall, *Woodstock Manor*, for its history and some anecdotes about Rochester. Cf. Pugh, *The History of Oxfordshire*, vols. 9 and 10.

2. BL, Harl. Ms. 7003, f. 195. Cornbury is three miles from Woodstock. It was the home of Henry Hyde, Clarendon's son, after the Lord Chancellor's fall in 1667. The Hydes were, of course, relatives by marriage to Rochester's mother.

3. Cf. Rochester, *Letters* (Treglown), 68–72.

4. The terms were used more or less interchangeably in the 1670s. For a twentieth-century attempt to distinguish them, see Fowler, *Dictionary of Modern English Usage*, 314. The *OED* dates the first uses of the terms as follows: lampoon, "a virulent or scurrilous satire upon an individual" (1645); pasquinade, "a lampoon affixed to some public place" (1658); satire, "the employment, in speaking or writing, of sarcasm, irony, ridicule

etc. in denouncing, exposing, or deriding vice, folly, abuses or evils of any kind" (1675); squib, "to assail or attack (a person) with squibs or witty sarcasm; to lampoon or satirize smartly" (1631); travesty, "a grotesque or debased image or likeness" (1674).

5. Larry D. Carver sees the poem as a juxtaposition of Christian idealism represented by Waller with the pagan materialism of Catullus. Several critic-contemporaries remarked on Rochester's use of sources. Cf. Rymer, "Preface" to *Poems on Several Occasions*, in *Critical Heritage*, ed. Farley-Hills, 169. "Whatsoever he imitated or Translated, was Loss to him. He had a Treasure of his own; a Mine not to be exhausted. His own Oar [Ore] and Thoughts were rich and fine; his own Stamp and Expression more neat and beautiful than any he cou'd borrow or fetch from abroad."

6. Burnet, *Passages*, 14.

7. Ibid., 25–26. Robert Wolseley confirmed Rochester's view of himself as reformer: "he was a continual Curb to Impertinence and the publick Censor of Folly . . . never did he stab into the Wounds of fallen Virtue, with a base and cowardly Insult, or smooth the face of prosperous Villany, with the Paint and Washes of a mercenary Wit; never did he spare a Fop for being rich, or flatter a Knave for being great. . . . Never was his Pen drawn but on the side of good Sence. . . . Thus was Vanity kept within some tolerable bounds, while my *Lord Rochester* liv'd, by the general Dread of a Pen so severe and impartial." Farley-Hills, 139–45. This, in brief, was the neo-classical credo for satire in the next century. See Elkin, *The Augustan Defence of Satire*.

8. Hodgart, *Satire*, 111. Hodgart writes, "[Wit] rests on the ability to discover and reveal the power hidden in language"; its essential features are "ingenious compression, a sudden revelation of hidden implications, and the linking together of two incongruous ideas," in what Arthur Koestler called "bi-sociation." In Koestlerian terms, wit "is the effect of perceiving an idea or event simultaneously or in quick alternation, in two habitually incompatible frames of reference." Vieth points out that "Rochester's distinctive technique as a poet involves the simultaneous manipulation of several conflicting levels or planes of experience." Rochester, *Complete Poems* (Vieth), xxxv.

9. Quoted by Hodgart in *Satire*, 109.

10. Cf. Chapter 6 of Farley-Hills, *Benevolence*, which treats "A Ramble" and the other poems as Rochester's triumph over chaos by means of laughter. Edmund Waller, one of Rochester's targets, declared, "That men write ill things well, and good things ill; that Satyricall writing was downe-hill, most easy and naturall; that at Billingsgate one might hear great heights of such witt. . . ." Aubrey, *Lives*, 310.

11. Hodgart, *Satire*, 118. See also Turner, *Schooling Sex*, 267–73. Cf. Rochester's "The Fall."

12. Cf. Rochester, *Letters* (Treglown), 157, 159.

13. Freud quoted in Hodgart, *Satire*, 110.

14. "A Ramble," ll. 105–28.

15. This device of sophisticated self-denigration was widely used by later authors; e.g., Swift's "Verses on His Death," Pope ("Epistle to Arbuthnot"), and Boswell's self-portrait in *The Life of Johnson*.

16. Pasch, "Concentricity, Christian Myth."

17. Wolseley, quoted in Farley-Hills, ed., *Critical Heritage*, 156–57. He specifically compares Rochester to Juvenal, Martial, Petronius, Catullus, Tibullus, Ovid, and even Horace, 151. For modern critics on his serious use of obscenity as a basic term of moral argument, see Sitter, "Rochester's Reader"; Wilcoxon, "The Rhetoric of Sex."

18. Cf. Radcliffe, *Works*.

19. Orrell, "A New Witness," 90.

20. *Adderbury Parish Register, CSPD 1671–72; Treasury Books 1675*, 784.

21. Oliver, *Howard*, 180 ff.

22. BL, Harl. Ms. 7003, f. 261. It is possible that this letter was never sent, that even as she wrote it, Rochester had repented of his first message and sent his carriage and a second letter (see next note) to her. Rochester appears not to have kept his wife's letters, as she did his; the existence of the two cryptic letters suggests either that they were not sent or that she reclaimed them.

23. BL, Harl. Ms. 7003, f. 206. The reference to his mother suggests that Lady Rochester was with her at either Adderbury or Ditchley.

24. Ibid., f. 264.

25. Jones, *Country and Court*, 166–76; Price, "Restoration England and Europe," 127 ff.

26. Harris, *Sackville*, 49–50; Wilson, *Rake*, 204 ff.; Chapman, *Great Villiers*, 196. The British Library has several copies of Savile's Account.

27. BL, Harl. Ms. 7003, f. 241. The reference to the unusual solicitation of Court finances could refer to the Exchequer Stop in 1672 or the panic after the Test Act in 1673, but Lady Rochester was in London at the later date, and this letter was sent to her at Adderbury. The probable year of the letter is 1672.

28. "Indenture (1671). A deed between two or more parties with mutual covenants, executed in two or more copies, all having their tops or edges correspondingly indented for identification or security. Hence any deed or sealed agreement between two or more parties." *Concise Oxford Dictionary* (1965), 1:989. The Rochester Indenture is now in the manuscript collection of the Princeton University Library.

29. Pugh, *The History of Oxfordshire*, 9:9.

30. HMC *Rutland II*, 26.

31. *CSPD 1672–73*, 101.

32. Cf. Rochester, *Letters* (Treglown), 87–88; Behn, "On the Death of the Late Earl of Rochester"; Wolseley, Second Prologue to *Valentinian*. Dryden told Rochester in April or May 1673, "You are that Rerum Natura of your own Lucretius." Behn and Barry verified a life-long interest, and Wolseley described him as Lucretius's ideal man. Rochester was familiar with Thomas Hobbes's ideas in conversation, but it seems clear that he also read those works which increased his cynicism about theology, religion, miracles, and the morality of the clergy, Catholic and Protestant. See Parsons, *Sermon*, 26; and Burnet, *Passages*, 73 ff. for details of Rochester's doubts about inspiration, Biblical authority, the morals of the clergy, miracles, etc. in Hobbesian terms. It was said he blamed his religious doubts on "Mr. Hobbs and the [pagan] philosophers."

33. "A Ramble," ll. 21–24. See Turner, *Schooling Sex*, 268–69. Copies of "A Ramble" were circulating by March 1673.

34. Rochester, *Complete Poems* (Vieth), xxxvi–xxxvii. For the date of the "Song," see 188. For women as objects of Restoration sexual satire, see O'Neill, "Sexuality, Deviance, and Moral Character." Sarah Wintle and Raman Selden have commented on class aspects of the "Song," in Treglown, ed., *Spirit of Wit*, 164, 186–87.

35. "German" was Henry Jermyn. He was Castlemain's lover in 1667. John Churchill succeeded Wycherley as her paramour in the summer of 1671, and Castlemain was made Duchess of Cleveland in August 1671. Her daughter by Churchill was born on July 16, 1672. The King disclaimed the bastard and Churchill exploited Cleveland without qualms for all the money he could get from her. Cf. Andrews, *The Royal Whore*, 228 ff.

36. The acting date of the play is uncertain; cf. Hume, *Development of Drama*, 276.

37. BL, Harl. Ms. 7003, f. 289. Oliver dates the letter in May, 181.

38. Ibid., f. 302.

39. Ibid., f. 189.

40. Cf. Wiseman, *Treatises*; Browne, *Adenochoiradelogia*. Louis XIV also touched for the Evil, making the sign of the cross and saying, "God healeth thee, the King toucheth thee." Fane Ms., f. 180.

41. Browne, *Adenochoiradelogia*, 44–49, 68–71.

42. Wiseman, *Treatises*, 266–69.

43. Cf. Rochester, *Letters* (Treglown), 79n.

44. BL, Harl. Ms. 7003, f. 220.

Chapter 12

1. The evidence for Rochester's authorship is given in my article "Did Lord Rochester Write *Sodom?*" in *PBSA* 81, Second Quarter (June, 1987): 119–53. In a subsequent issue, Harold Love disputes it. However, he includes *Sodom and Gomorah* in his edition of Rochester's works. Traditionally, British scholars, with a few exceptions, accept *Sodom* as Rochester's work whereas Americans, with some exceptions, do not.

2. The fragment of a sexual farce titled *Actus Primus Scena Prima* ("For standing *Tarses* we kind Nature thank") was included in the 1680 *Poems on Several Occasions*. It is a dialogue between "Tarsander" and "Swiveanthe," then between her and "Celia," and thus follows the tradition of Nicolas Chorier's *Satyra Sotadica*. See Turner, *Schooling Sex*, 166–220. The author is unknown and its relationship to *Sodom* is uncertain, although both are efforts at the same species of composition and may suggest that Rochester's circle agreed to try disparate efforts at composing obscene parodies of heroic drama. The *Actus* corresponds roughly to Act IV of the five-act *Sodom*. David Vieth attributes the piece to Buckhurst (*ARP*, 82–97, 437–38), but Brice Harris, Buckhurst's biographer, does not include it among the works (Dorset, *Poems*, 185) and he told me before his death he was quite sure Buckhurst did not write it.

3. For further information about *Sodom*, see the section in Vieth, *Rochester Studies, 1925–1882*, 118–21.

4. Cf. *Advice-to-a-Painter Poems*, 26–39. The author of several of these, "Mr. Andrew Marvell (who was a good Judge of Witt) was wont to say that [Rochester] was the best English Satyrist and had the right veine," Aubrey, *Lives*, 321.

5. For the heroic genre, see Hume, *Development of Drama*, 192–99, 269–80. The latter section discusses the heroic drama and "the crisis around 1670."

6. See Bailey, *Homosexuality and the Western Christian Tradition*, 21–27, 149–50. Boswell, *Christianity, Social Tolerance, and Homosexuality*, traces the history of homosexual and anti-homosexual literature and thought.

7. Cf. Harbage, *Annals of English Drama*, 161; Rosten, *Biblical Drama*, 67–68. A play by Andreas Saurius, *Conflagratio Sodomae*, acted by students at Strasbourg and printed in 1607, is preserved in the British Library. Another play, Cornelius à Marca's *Bustum Sodomae Tragoedia sacra* (1615) was known as late as 1740 but is now presumably lost. Prinz, *Rochester*, 399.

8. Rochester told Burnet the first three chapters of *Genesis* "could not be true, unless they were Parables," *Passages*, 73. The Sodom story appears in *Genesis* 19.

9. For Hobbes on Sodom, see *Leviathan*, Part 3, chap. 38.

10. Cf. Richard Elias, "Political Satire in *Sodom*."

11. Monmouth's sobriquet stuck; he became "Prince Pricket" in several underground lampoons.

12. Cf. Andrews, *Royal Whore*, 229.

13. See Lindsay, *Charles II and Madame Carwell*, for a full scale study of the lady and the royal relationship. J. H. Wilson gives a succinct chronology for Kéroualle in *Court Satires*, 276–77.

14. See Chapter Eight, "The King's Pimp." For Colbert's reports to Louis, see Lindsay, *Charles II*, 42, 43–44, 48–49, 52 ff.

15. Evelyn, *Diary* (1959), 559–60.

16. Ibid., 547. Evelyn saw Rochester soon after on November 24; we can safely assume Rochester and Louise were moving in the same circles soon after she arrived in England.

17. Lines 86–91. This is a modernized version of the P1 Ms. in Princeton, Ms. AM 14401.

18. Act III, ll. 23–24, 55–60.

19. The Prologue has been the basis of unfounded assertions that *Sodom* was actually staged before the King. Cf. Jeffreys, *The Libertine*, 53–55. Considering its overt assault on him, Charles II was doubtless unaware that the travesty existed. As to it being acted before the Ballers, I doubt it. Much of the sexual activity might be simulated, as it is in Kenneth Tynan's *Oh! Calcutta!*—or the Ballers might have required that sex acts really take place, as Suetonius reported one Emperor decreed for the Roman stage. Staging *Sodom* would be possible, but I doubt that it ever was.

20. Cf. "A Ramble," ll. 115–21, 133–34. The false hair was a "merkin," a sort of wig for the *Mons Veneris* when it had been depilatated by disease or friction.

21. On January 27, 1666, after the Court's departure, Wood wrote: "To give a further character of the court, they, though they were neat and gay in their apparell, yet they were very nasty and beastly, leaving at their departure their excrements in every corner, in chimneys, studies, colehouses, cellars. Rude, rough, whoremongers; vaine, empty, carelesse"; *Life* (Abridged), 154.

22. Stone, *Family*, 405–6.

23. The "Song" begins:

> By all *Loves* soft, yet mighty *Pow'rs,*
> It is a thing unfit,
> That *Men* shou'd Fuck in time of *Flow'rs,*
> Or when the *Smock's* beshit.
> Fair nasty *Nymph,* be clean and kind,
> And all my joys restore;
> By using Paper still behind,
> And Spunges for before. . . .

"Flowers" was the name for menstrual blood.

24. Stone comments: ". . . contemporary complaints about the dirtiness of women, and the use of the bagnio as a place of sexual assignation, both suggest that men in the seventeenth and eighteenth centuries found cleanliness a positive asset to sexuality," *Family*, 406.

25. Cf. Rochester, *Complete Poems* (Vieth), xxxviii.

26. Farley-Hills, *Benevolence*, 132 ff.

27. Lahr, "Introduction," in *The Orton Diaries*, 14.

28. BL, Harl. Ms. 7003, f. 218.

29. Huntington Library, Huntington Ms. HA 12525, quoted in Hook, "Something More about Rochester," 478–85. The nature of the "coffin" is not clear. In 1677 the

word was used in the sense of a chest or box, as well as a burial case. Perhaps the Hatton Garden "coffin" was some kind of steam-box used in the sweating treatment. *Concise OED*, 1:337.

30. University of Rochester, MS D.26, f. 22.

31. In his discussions with Burnet, the paradox of the innocent suffering was over-whelmed by the Bishop's insistence that the guilty brought suffering upon themselves. *Passages*, 71. Hobbes also was uninterested in the problem, which he considered archaic: "The Book of *Job* . . . seemeth not to be a History, but a Treatise concerning a question in ancient time much disputed, *why wicked men have often prospered in this world, and good men have been afflicted. . . .*" *Leviathan*, Part 3, chap. 33.

32. Parsons, *Sermon*, 23.

33. Paul Hammond has suggested that "Upon Nothing," which Vieth describes as "an ironic eulogy of an Uncreation opposite to God's original act," may have been written before 1673. "The Dating of Three Poems by Rochester," 52–59. Vieth, *ARP*, 106. If so, it is further testimony of Rochester's "atheism" in that year.

34. The Parliamentary session stimulated Rochester to write a "Lampoone" ("On the Women about Town") sometime before March 20 that combined current debates about the King's Money Bills and the incipient Test Act ("Money, and Conscience those Trifles of State") with references to earlier Irish Cattle Bills regulating importation, religious ritual, sexual intercourse, the theology of damnation and a misogynistic attack on "Irish whore[s]."

> The Cootes (blacke, and white) Clenbrazel, and Fox
> Invade us with Impudence, beauty and pox.
> They carry a Fate, which noe man can oppose;
> The losse of his heart, and the fall of his nose . . .
> Is it juste, that with death cruell Love should conspire
> And our Tarses be burnt by our hearts taking fire?
> There's an end of Communion, if humble Beleavers
> Must bee damn'd in the Cup, like unworthy Receavers.

35. *JHL*, 12:564, 568–69. Marvell, *Poems and Letters*, 2:318. Miscellaneous Letter #21 is undated but it obviously refers to Bradford Bridge. Marvell's editor, H. M. Margoliouth, perhaps remembering the syphilitic disfigurement of Sir William Davenant, rhetorically asks, "Of his nose?" Obviously not. William Wissing's portrait of Rochester ca. 1678 shows his nose intact; and Rochester himself told Savile in a letter of November 1677 that he had "red eyes and nose." Rochester, *Letters* (Treglown), 166.

36. Robert Constable (1651–1712), the third Viscount Dunbar, married Bellasis' daughter Mary, ca. 1672. I have not found any relevant information about his duel with Rochester in the Bellasis/Belasyse papers in the BL. Cf. Geoffrey Ridsill Smith, *In Well Beware*. In 1670, Lady Newton reported:

> "Poor Henry Savill and the Lord Dunbar, both foule drunk, quarreled and cuff'd, then drew, Henry could not stand, but fell, then Dunbar run him through but 'tis hoped not through the body, though he hath a terrible wound." Wilson, *Court Satires*, 234–35.

37. *JHL*, 12:562–63.

38. Rochester, *Letters* (Treglown), 91–92. Cf. Etherege, *Letters*, 118.

39. Hume, *Development of Drama*, 282, 288–89.

40. Rochester's goggle-eyed counterpart, Mulgrave, provided the First Prologue. Cf. Winn, *Dryden*, 245.

41. Vivian de Sola Pinto was among those who noticed early on Rochester's special sympathy for the woman's point of view: "John Wilmot, Earl of Rochester."

42. Cf. Wilson, *Rake*, 238–39; Rochester, *Poems* (Walker), 75; Rochester, *Complete Poems* (Vieth), 149.

43. For an account of Buckingham's role and motives in the Lords, cf. Wilson, *Rake*, 216–18.

44. *JHL*, 12:524–25, 539–40, 542 ff. Cf. Miller, *Popery*, 124 ff.

45. For the history of anti-Catholic statutes, their contents, and enforcement (or lack thereof), see Miller, *Popery*, 52 ff.

46. *JHL*, 12:567–69. It is conceivable that Dunbar's averted duel with him in the midst of all this activity was related somehow to Rochester's position on the anti-Catholic legislation, which he had to support despite Lady Rochester's Catholicism. After the Test Act passed, Dunbar's father-in-law, Lord Bellasis, resigned as Lord Lieutenant of West Riding, Yorkshire, and Governor of Hull, posts he had held since 1661 for his loyalty to Charles I. (Miller, *Popery*, 65. For more on Bellasis, see pp. 15, 18, 33n, 65–66, 112, 149, 209, 221–24.) In the wake of the Act, Papists were forbidden to live in London, and Lady Dunbar had to be given special Parliamentary permission to enter the city for medical treatment, being allowed to remain only as long as she was ill. See the *JHL* entry for November 20, 1678.

47. Quoted in Farley-Hills, *Heritage*, 107.

48. For the Arundells and Charles II, see Haley, *Shaftesbury*, 209, 269, 401, 413–14, 417, 440 and ff.; Miller, *Popery*, 15, 17, 19n, 96–98, and ff.

49. Verney, *Verney Papers* (1925), 2:334–35.

50. Cf. Jones, *First Whigs*, 9–19, 45–47, 99–103. Tom Wharton was allied to the Shaftesbury group who urged the Exclusion Bill in 1678 and were sent to the Tower; (Haley, *Shaftesbury*, 420, 425n, 500, 580) He was assisted in reelection to office by Sir Ralph Verney in 1679. (Jones, *First Whigs*, 45–47; Verney, *Verney Papers*, 2:388–91). After the accession of James II as king, he composed the song, "Lilliburlero," which was said to "sing James II out of three kingdoms." Queen Anne made him the Marquess of Wharton in 1714. As Lord Lieutenant of Ireland, he incurred the hatred of Jonathan Swift, who attacked him as "Verres" and defamed him in a "Character." Pope described him with reference to Rochester in the "Epistle to Cobham":

> Wharton, the scorn and wonder of our days,
> Whose ruling Passion was the Lust of Praise . . .
> Shall parts so various aim at nothing new?
> He'll shine a Tully and a Wilmot too.

51. Wharton, *Memoirs*, 18–19.

52. G. E. C., *Peerage*, 12:Part 2, 608; *Adderbury Parish Registers*; HMC *Rutland II*, 26.

53. Details appear in "Afterwards," the final chapter of this book.

54. Verney, *Verney Papers* (1925), 2:334. For the treasonous fortune the King gave to Nan and the Countess's part in securing it, see Chapter Five above.

55. Hartmann, *Clifford*, 257–300.

56. See Jones, *Country*, 179–81; Miller, *Popery*, 124 ff. Lee, *Cabal*, 202–54.

57. *JHL*, 12:588–94.

58. Possible sources for this lyric have been located in Anacreon, Ronsard, and English translations of the *Anakreonta*. Cf. Rochester, *Poems* (Walker), 246–48. In *Spirit of Wit*, 26, however, Barbara Everett writes: "[Rochester] has given this exquisite but shocking small poem a wholly original structure, necessitating two opposed poles: the

one creating in fantasy an extremity of imagining; the other with one casually dropped word shattering everything that has gone before."

59. Cf. Highfill et al., *Biographical Dictionary*, 1:313–25.

60. Brown, ed., *Familiar Letters*, 2:9, 10, 29. Barry may have been naive, but the fact that Rochester did not sign or date his notes to her must have made her wonder at times about the depth of his commitment. His reputation for seduction surely was known to her. In any case, she had the wit to keep his letters and sell them for publication in the 1690's after his death.

61. Cf. Rochester, *Poems* (Walker), 271.

62. Miller gives a full account in *Popery*, 128–31.

63. Wilson, *Court Satires*, 3–9.

64. The techniques for pleasing the King in 1673 that Rochester describes Nelly engaged in here are the same he advised her to continue in 1678; cf. Rochester, *Letters* (Treglown), 189.

65. These meanings are dated by the *OED* as "hector" (1655) and "cully" (1664).

66. A letter dated January 20, 1674, reported that "my Lord Rochester fled from Court some time since for delivering (by mistake) into the King's hands a terrible lampoon of his own making against the King, instead of another the King asked him for." Haley, *Shaftesbury*, 60–61, 172.

67. Cf. *Genesis*, 19:12–24. When Abraham Cowley left London in 1665 for retirement in Barnes, he wrote to John Evelyn, saying he had left Sodom but was not yet come to Little Zoar.

Chapter 13

1. Cf. Gramont's account: "As long as he had been at Court, Rochester had scarcely ever omitted to get himself banished once a year, at the very least; for, as often as he had some sally quivering on the tip of his tongue or on the nib of his pen, he let it fly . . . without the smallest regard for consequences. Ministers, mistresses, and often even the Master himself, were involved; and, if he had not had to do with one of the most kindly monarchs who has ever lived, his first disgrace would also have been his last." Hamilton, *Memoirs* (1930), 248. We recall that Gramont had been exiled by Louis XIV for looking sideways at a royal mistress.

2. Cf. Burnet, *Life*, 1:476.

3. *JHL*, 12:603.

4. Cf. Miller, *Popery*, 55–56, 163, 173, 214.

5. The prohibition against the King's entry into London without permission of the Lord Mayor had been revoked just a few weeks earlier.

6. Cf. Hamilton, *Memoirs* (1930), 256–57.

7. Jones, *Country*, 180–96, follows Danby's career from 1673 to 1678. See also Andrew Browning's three-volume biography of Danby for a fuller account of his life (*Thomas Osborne, Earl of Danby and Duke of Leeds*).

8. Violet Barbour provides details in her biography of Henry Bennet (*Henry Bennet, Earl of Arlington*). The second wedding took place in November 1679 despite the efforts of the groom's mother to prevent it. John Evelyn, who adored Tata, was very distressed at the marriage; *Diary*, 577, 641, 674.

9. Verney, *Verney Papers*, 1:150.

10. Cf. Burnet, *Passages*, 70 ff., 120 ff. According to Parsons, *Sermon*, 23, Rochester had felt misgivings at times: "One day at an Atheistical Meeting, at a person of Qualitie's, I undertook to manage the Cause, and was the principle Disputant against God and Piety, and for my performances received the applause of the whole company; upon which my mind was terribly struck, and I immediately reply'd thus to myself. Good God! that a Man, that walks upright, that sees the wonderful works of God, and has the uses of his senses and reason, should use them to the defying of his Creator!" Francis Giffard had worked his ways. After the Test Act passed, a pasquinade was placed on the gates of Whitehall: "Heare may Enter, / Turk, Jew, or Atheist, / But not a Papist." Fane Ms., f. 177.

11. *JHL*, 12:603 ff.

12. See Verney, *Verney Papers* (1899), 4:225; Verney, *Verney Papers* (1925), 1:150; *CSPD 1673–75*, 182; G. E. C. *Peerage*, 7:644; Pugh, *History of Oxfordshire*, 9:15; Rochester, *Letters* (Treglown), 94–95, 137; Greene, *Monkey*, 87.

13. John Lovelace (1638–1693) matriculated at Oxford on July 25, 1655, but did not receive the M.A. degree until September 1661, at the same time Rochester did. He seems to have learned very little in the six year period. Ca. 1660, he wrote to his father: "[My mother] askt me if shee shoulde find owt a neibors daughter with 8 or 10 thowsand pounds, whether or no I would tell your Lords^p that I was in love with hur. I answered hur that I could be in love with nothing but conveniency"; BL, Add. Mss. 22186, ff. 5, 195. From 1661 until 1670 Lovelace was the M.P. for Berkshire. He married Martha Pye in 1662; and in 1669, he became Steward and Lieutenant of Woodstock Manor. That same year, he fell from his horse and broke his neck, "riding home from Oxford, after a good large dose of the University Helicon." Fortunately (or otherwise) someone jerked his neck back into place and he recovered; HMC *Seventh Report*, 531. On April 4, 1677, a bill was read in Parliament to enable him to get his wife's jointure and provide £15,000 for his daughters' portions but was not proceeded with. In 1681 he attended Stephen College's trial in Oxford and gave testimony. He was a violent Whig who took arms for the Prince of Orange in 1688. On November 11 of that year, he got into a fight with Jacobite Royalists, killed two men, and was arrested, but Captain Bertie rescued him on November 28. On December 5, he captured Oxford for William III, who gave him many posts in reward. He was acting Chief Justice of Eyre, near Trent, when he deliberately killed a deer in St. James's Park, offending Queen Mary, who later gave him all the privileges he once held under Charles I and II. He died in 1693 after disinheriting his only child. After his death the contents of his manor, Lady Place, had to be sold to pay off his debts: seventeen damask chairs and twenty pictures fetched a total of £45. Lovelace's widow, Lady Wentworth, accused Sir Walter St. John of cheating her out of her inheritance, and Henry St. John wrote a protesting letter to her son Lovelace. (BL Add. Mss. 31,141, ff. 35–36) See G. E. C. *Peerage*, 8:232–34.

14. If the poem was addressed to Barry, it dates after her debut in 1675.

15. Hume, *Development of Drama*, 205–6.

16. "Clouts" were cloth-pieces, as in "breech clouts."

17. Hume, *Development of Drama*, 200–201, 220, 289.

18. Facts about Lee are given in Armistead, *Nathaniel Lee*.

19. Spence, *Observations*, 1:180. None of Buckingham's biographers link him with Lee, however. Wilson, *Rake*, 185–87, gives a detailed account of his gaining the position and his inaugural ceremony on June 7, 1671.

20. See Cibber, *Apology*, 1:113–14.

21. *POAS*, 1:36–37. Cf. Armistead, *Lee*, 41–42. For Rochester on Marvell as satirist, see "Tunbridge Wells," ll. 70–74.

22. Hume, *Development of Drama*, 200.

23. Lee, *Works*, 1:22. Cf. Thomas Lessey's "Were I a Sp'rt" in BL, Sloane Ms. 1458, f. 43r; Vieth *ARP*, 179–80.

24. The belief that Rochester's translation of Seneca's *Troas* was not made until 1680 has been questioned by Paul Hammond, who sees evidence in the arrangement of Bodleian MS Don. b.8. that the translation was made in 1674 ("The Dating of Three Poems," *Bodleian Library Record*, 11 [1982]: 58–59.) This dating lends further credence to Rochester's involvement with *Nero*.

25. For instance, after Rochester's death, Lee's *The Princess of Cleves* ostensibly complimented Rochester as Count Rosidore; but the villainous Nemours has been seen as a "profoundly hostile depiction of that noble rake." Hume, *Development of Drama*, 256–57.

26. See Novak, ed., *The Empress of Morocco*. James Winn suggests a number of motives for Dryden's joining in the *Notes* but believes him responsible for only the Preface and Postscript. Crowne claimed to have written three of four parts. He also said that Shadwell wrote the criticism of Act IV. Cf. Winn, *Dryden*, 255–61, 582–83; Borgman, *Shadwell*, 44–45; Hume, *Development of Drama*, 288–89.

27. For the dating of "Timon," see Harold Brooks, "The Date of Rochester's 'Timon,' " *N&Q* 174 (28 May 1938): 384–85; Vieth, *ARP*, 274–75.

28. Critical treatments of "Timon" include Griffin, *Satires*, 35–42; Brooks, "The 'Imitation' in English Poetry," 124–40; Love, "Rochester and the Traditions of Satire"; Treglown, *Spirit of Wit*, 75–91.

29. See "Song: *Phillis*, be gentler I advice," in Rochester, *Poems* (Walker), 36. For Shadwell and Sedley, see *Poems*, 274–75. For *Epsom Wells*, see Hume, *Development of Drama*, 295–96. The hearty English meal in lines 69–90 of "Timon" may allude to Clodpate's gustatory preferences in *Epsom Wells*. See Shadwell, *Works*, 2:112, 151.

30. See Harvey, *Oxford Companion to Classical Literature*, 431. The eighteenth-century work, Lemprière's *Classical Dictionary of Proper Names in Ancient Authors*, 634, says Timon of Athens was partial to Alcibiades because he would ruin his country one day. For another view, cf. Griffin, *Satires*, 40.

31. Kernan, *Cankered Muse*, 102, 116–17. Cf. Preston, *Not in Timon's Manner*.

32. For a rather imaginative etymological tracing of satire to acts of eating (*gula*, throat) and drinking (lampoon), see Kernan, *Cankered Muse*, 1.

33. Treglown, *Spirit of Wit*, 77.

34. "An Allusion to Horace," ll. 121–22. Interestingly enough, Rochester includes Shadwell here but does not name Savile.

35. See Hume, *Development of Drama*, 195–96; "Allusion to Horace," line 96; Chapman, *Great Villiers*, 171; Vieth, *ARP*, 437, cites the All Souls College, Oxford, MS. Codrington 174, with a notation to Actus Primus ("For standing tarses. . . ."): "Tarsander, in imitation of the L^{d}: Orreryes Poetry."

36. Crowne had dedicated his first play, *Juliana*, to Orrery, a fact that hardly offset the impertinence of his dedication of *Charles the Eighth* to "the Right Honourable Gentleman of His Majesty's Bed-Chamber" [Rochester]: "Perhaps your lordship may admire to see your name fixed before this trifle; but it is the fate of persons of your obliging temper to receive persecutions of this nature, in return of candour and indulgence. . . . And this I am bold to affirm though I have not the Honour of much Acquaintance with your Lordship; for it is sufficient that I have seen in some little

sketches of your Pens, excellent Masteries and a Spirit inimitable; and that I have been entertained by others with the wit, which your Lordship . . . sprinkles in your Converse"; Crowne, *Dramatic Works*, 1:127–28.

37. Marshall, *Woodstock*, 234–35.

38. See Vieth, *ARP*, 174–77. No evidence exists about the possible author, although Alexander Radcliffe is the guess of Prinz and Thorpe. Prinz, *Rochester*, 149. Thorpe, ed., *Poems on Several Occasions*, 35–40.

39. *DNB*, 18:13; Winn, *Dryden*, 154–55. Mulgrave had been made a Gentleman of the Bed Chamber in February 1673, volunteered for naval duty at Solebay, took command of *The Captain*, the best second-rate ship in the navy, then on Dec. 23, 1673, was appointed colonel of the Old Holland foot-regiment. Until 1674, Rochester saw relatively little of him.

40. Cf. Rochester, *Complete Poems* (Vieth), 172.

41. One hypothesis might be that whoever dated the Alexis/Strephon "Dialogue" in 1674 was confusing it with the "Song." See Thorpe, *Poems*, 55–56, 176; Vieth, *ARP*, 172–74, 404–5.

42. See Rochester, *Poems* (Walker), 266–67; Vieth *ARP*, 274–78. The terminal composition date as 1675 has been established by Jordan, "The First Printing of Rochester's 'Tunbridge Wells.' " Harold Love traces the development of the popular couplet lampoon in the 1670s, treating "Timon" as a relatively loose lampoon but seeing "Tunbridge Wells" as already venturing beyond the lampoon in its vivid scenes and characters, replacement of invective with moral argument, and generalized rather than particular satire. Love also sees the identification of the speaker with the author. Love, "Rochester and the Traditions of Satire."

43. Hamilton, *Memoirs* (1930), 270–71.

44. For Rochester's mimickry of colloquial speech and the movement of the persona's mind, see Rothstein, *Restoration and Eighteenth Century Poetry*, 31–42. For the treatment of sexuality, see Wilcoxon, "Rochester's Sexual Politics"; Fabricant, "Rochester's World of Imperfect Enjoyment." For echoes of *Epsom Wells* see articles in *N&Q* 221 (May–June 1976): 242–43; 226 (June 1981): 210–11; and 227 (December 1982): 46–49. Cf. Selden, in *Spirit of Wit*, 184–86.

45. Griffin, *Satires*, 43; Vieth, *Rochester Studies*, 74.

46. Rochester repeats phrases directly from Marvell, who had quoted Parker's letter to him as part of *The Rehearsal transpos'd*. Cf. Legouis, "Three Notes on Rochester's 'Poems.' "; Vieth, *ARP*, 277–78.

47. Cuff, Kick, and Fribble are all taken from *Epsom Wells*.

48. Cf. Trotter, "Wanton Expressions," 126. Trotter links Rochester's theriophily to contemporary Latitudinarian attacks on such praise of animals, citing sermons by Edward Stillingfleet and Joseph Glanville, 126–28. Treglown finds a satirical inversion of Thomas Sternhold's version of Psalms 8:4 in the poem's conclusion. *RES*, n.s. 24 (February 1973).

49. Weinbrot, "Rochester's 'Fribble' Revisited," 523–24. Paul Hammond sees the resemblance to Dryden's translation of Virgil's *Georgics*, 3.155 ff.:

> For when his Blood no Youthful Spirits move,
> He languishes and labors in his Love.
> And when the sprightly Seed shou'd swiftly come,
> Dribling he drudges, and defrauds the Womb.

The similarity of "dribble" to "fribble" is obvious.

50. Cf. *Sodom*, V.114–119:

> To love and nature all their rights restore;
> Fuck women and let buggery be no more.
> It does that propagable end destroy
> Which nature gave with pleasure to enjoy.
> Please her and she'll be kind; if you displease,
> She turns into corruption and disease.

This speech does not appear in the 1672–73 version.

51. For Epicurus and Epicureanism in the Restoration era, see my *The Formation of English Neo-Classical Thought*, 81–84, 274–75. For Rochester and Epicureanism, cf. Griffin, *Satires*, 62–63, 168–71 et passim. See also Bailey, *Greek Atomists*; Mayo, *Epicurus in England*; Zeller, *Stoics, Epicureans, and Sceptics*; Hicks, *Stoic and Epicurean*. Rochester's "lov'd Lucretius" was his agent to Epicureanism. The teachings of Epicurus were interwoven with those of Lucretius. For a table of correlations, see Epicurus, *Letters, Principle Doctrines, and Vatican Sayings*, 91–92. Cf. Charleton, *Epicurus' Morals*; Sir William Temple, "Upon the Gardens of Epicurus."

52. Cf. Wilson's Introduction to *R-SL*, 9–12.

53. Cf. Wilson, *R-SL*, 12; Fraser, *Royal Charles*, 223–26. Arlington once remarked that twenty leagues at sea pleased the King more than two on land.

54. Brown, *Familiar Letters*, 1:1.

55. Treglown dates these two letters some years apart; but viewed biographically they belong together as a sequence.

Chapter 14

1. *Adderbury Parish Register.*

2. Rochester, *Letters* (Treglown), 140. This letter was written when Mallet was an infant and Betty was less than two years old.

3. Cf. Bernard Falk, *Way of the Montagues*, 288–304.

4. Johnson, "John Sheffield, the Duke of Buckinghamshire," in *Lives of the Poets*, 453–54: "He had a quarrel with the Earl of Rochester, which he has perhaps too ostentatiously related, as Rochester's surviving daughter, the Lady Sandwich, is said to have told him with very sharp reproaches."

5. John Montagu, the Fourth Earl of Sandwich (1718–92), was a founder of the Mad Monks of Medmenham and the Hellfire Club, sexual and atheistic private societies. Unwilling to interrupt a gambling session, he was said to have originated the sandwich: meat between two slices of bread. As First Lord of the Admiralty, 1771–82, his administration was among the most corrupt in British naval history; however, Captain James Cook named the Sandwich Islands of the Pacific for him.

6. BL, Harl. Ms. 7003, f. 252. Treglown questions J. H. Wilson's date of this letter because of a mistake about the duration of Dog Days. The letter obviously was written on August 8 and the other possible years, 1673 and 1675, are eliminated by Rochester's reflective tone here (unlike his agitation in August 1673) and his illness in 1675, as well as his estrangement from both the Duchess of Portsmouth and the Lord Treasurer then.

7. Cf. Lindsey, *Charles II*, 86 ff.

8. For Gwyn and Kéroualle, see Wilson, *Nell Gwyn*, 140 ff.

9. Fane Ms., f. 182.

10. Lindsey, *Charles II*, 92–95. For Pembroke's brawls and other altercations, cf. Verney, *Verney Papers* (1925), 2:314–15; Harris, *Sackville*, 77; *State Trials*, 6:1310–50; Lever, *The Herberts*, 121 ff.

11. Harris, *Sackville*, 51.

12. Ibid., 77–78; *Treasury Books 1676–79*, 2:1356. Dorset got the Weybridge and Byfleet manors after Kéroualle's temporary rout by Hortense Mancini in 1676.

13. Danby inherited a floating debt of £1,036,000; cf. Jones, *Country*, 61–63.

14. William Doble's commonplace book (BodL, MS. Don. f. 29) contains two separate versions of the satire, the first set down before Rochester finished writing the poem. See Maccubbin, "Unique Scribleriana Transferred 1973." Cf. Vieth, *ARP*, 293–95, 370–75.

15. See Griffin, *Satires*, 156–96; Treglown, "Satiric Inversion"; Farley-Hills, chapter 5 of *Rochester's Poetry*. Many of the key ideas in the "Satyr" have equivalents in chapters 46–47 of Hobbes's *Leviathan*.

16. Bishop Burnet and John Evelyn voiced such fears.

17. For the satire on mankind as a distinct sub-type of the genre, see Tierney, "Satire on Mankind."

18. Main, "The Right Vein of Rochester's *Satyr*."

19. R. Johnson, "Rhetoric and Drama in Rochester's ' Satyr against Reason and Mankind' "; White, " 'So Great a Disproportion' "; Knight, "The Paradox of Reason." These critiques stem from the "New Criticism" edict that the reader must approach the poem as a self-contained entity and study the "poem *qua* poem." To find the poem revelatory of its creator is to commit "the biographical fallacy." Cf. K. Paulson, "A Subject of Debate: A Re-evaluation of the Major Satires of John Wilmot, Second Earl of Rochester."

20. Robinson, "Rochester's Dilemma"; Selden, *English Verse Satire*, 92–100; Wilcoxon, "Rochester's Philosophical Premises."

21. Clark, *Boileau and the French Classical Critics in England*, 7–8, 114–15; Whitley, "Rochester: A Cosmological Pessimist."

22. In 1674, "maxim" meant a proposition expressing some general truth of science or experience; Rochester seems to have anticipated the later (1692) meaning of a self-evident proposition assumed as a premise for further philosophical thinking; *Shorter OED*, 1220.

23. This intimate mode of exchange is very obvious in their letters between 1674 and 1679, Cf. *Letters* (Treglown), 106–227 passim. After a lapse in their correspondence, Rochester began a letter on November 1, 1679, thus: "Harry, I am in a great strait what to write to you. The style of business I am not versed in, and you may have forgot the familiar one we used heretofore."

24. Fujimura, "Rochester's 'Satyr against Mankind' "; Robinson, "Rochester's Dilemma"; Knight, "The Paradox of Reason"; Cope, "The Infinite Perimeter"; Vieth, "Divided Consciousness." One critic has argued for the unity of the "Satyr"; cf. Gill, "Mind against Itself." See Vieth's refutation in *Rochester Studies*, 70–71.

25. Vieth, "Toward an Anti-Aristotelian Poetic."

26. "Satyr," ll. 191–204 passim.

27. "[Rochester] told me plainly, There was nothing that gave him, and many others, a more secret encouragement in their ill ways, than that those who pretended to believe, lived so that they could not be thought to be in earnest, when they said it. . . ." Burnet, *Passages*, 20.

28. Cf. Ibid., 72: "He could not apprehend how there should be any corruption in the Nature of Man, or a Lapse derived from *Adam*. Gods communicating his mind to one Man, was the putting it in his power to cheat the World."

29. Cf. Rochester, *Poems* (Walker), 25.

30. Epicurus, *Letters*, 63, 139. Cf. Lucretius, *De Rerum Natura*, I.44–49.

31. Epicurus, *Letters*, 139. Cf. Seneca, Chorus of *Troas*, Act 2.

32. Epicurus, *Letters*, 60–63 passim.

33. Kristoffer Paulson has suggested Walter Charleton as the *adversarius*, forgetting his own spurning of the biographical fallacy; see note 19 above. Charleton had attempted a reconciliation of Epicureanism with Christianity and had included a witty section on Epicurus in his adaptation of Petronius's tale of the Widow of Ephesus. Cf. Sutherland, *English Literature*, 217–18; Miner, *Dryden's Poetry*, 243–46.

34. I agree with Reba Wilcoxon that, philosophically speaking, Rochester was a skeptic who consistently rejected Christian eschatology and metaphysical speculation and affirmed the evidence of the senses. I think, however, that he started as an "ethical hedonist" but changed to the more moderate Epicureanism set forth in the "Satyr." Cf. Wilcoxon, "Rochester's Philosophical Premises." Vieth criticizes Wilcoxon for relying on Rochester's translations and adaptations, saying the Satyr "not only is adapted from Boileau but is spoken by a persona." He then criticizes a "major weakness," in James Gill's discussion of the "Satyr": "his treatment of the speaker is a version of the old persona theory, now out of date for almost twenty years." *Rochester Studies*, 51, 71. Rochester obviously translated sources congenial to his thinking and adapted them to better conform to his own views.

35. Cf. Griffin, *Satires*, 164–68, 173–75; Sutherland, *English Literature*, 193, 218.

36. Treglown implicitly recognizes the "Satyr" as a transitional work when he identifies it as a burlesque journey of the metaphorical pilgrimage in Simon Patrick's *The Parable of the Pilgrim* and Nathaniel Ingelo's *Bentivolio and Urania*; "The Satiric Inversion." Cf. Griffin, *Satires*, 188–96.

37. Burnet, *Passages*, 71.

38. Boswell, *Restoration Court Stage*, 130–31.

39. Winn, *Dryden*, 271.

40. Borgmann, *Shadwell*, 27–28; Hume, *Development of Drama*, 299–300.

41. The short life of Crowne supplied by him to John Dennis is accurate in facts but biased in their interpretation, especially concerning Rochester. Crowne's resentment of Rochester began in 1674 and lasted for the rest of his life. Dennis, *Works*, 2:406–8. Cf. Boswell, *Restoration Court Stage*, 179.

42. Boswell conjectures that the command was either Princess Mary's or, following Langbaine, Mary of Modena the Duchess of York; *Shadwell*, 186. But Dennis and Crowne state plainly that the King gave the command.

43. Crowne, *Dramatic Works*, 1:236 ff.

44. Dryden may have written the anonymous epilogue which was published in *Miscellany Poems* (1684) and titled "*EPILOGUE* intended to have been spoken by the Lady Henr[ietta] Mar[ia] Wentworth when *Calisto* was acted at Court." Dryden, *Poems and Fables*, 318–19. Boswell treats the Epilogue as part of an "unauthenticated tradition that Dryden wrote an epilogue that was rejected," *Shadwell*, 188. Kinsley argues that the poem is Dryden's; and after viewing the pros and cons for his authorship, James Winn says, "Although the evidence is inconclusive, I believe Dryden wrote these lines," *Dryden*, 585, 271–72. If he did write the epilogue and Crowne chose not to use it, Crowne's effusive praise of Dryden in the Epistle to the Reader could have been an attempt to smooth the ruffled feathers of Poet Squab. John Wilmot would have relished any falling out between the two.

45. A spurious "Life" of Rochester by "St. Evremond" was published first in 1707; cf. Vieth, *ARP*, 502–4. The author was an anonymous hack writer for Edmund Curll

(possibly Abel Boyer), who proclaimed Rochester's jealousy of Crowne's dramatic superiority. A similar charge by Mulgrave appeared in Joseph Spence's *Observations*, 201. Crowne ingratiated himself with Mulgrave by a dedication to *The Married Beau: or, The Curious Impertinent* (1694) and the two made common cause thereafter in vilifying Rochester. In an Epistle to the Reader published with *Caligula, a Tragedy* (1698), Crowne said:

> I have in my Jerusalems, made too beautiful an Image of an Atheist. . . . Some endeavor to clear me of the guilt, and wou'd perswade the World they were written by a Noble and Excellent Wit, the late E. of R—— But they were printed long before my Lord died; his Lordship in his Poem, call'd *The Session of Poets*, charges me not with theft, but my Scenes with dulness and want of Wit and Poetry, which he wou'd not have done, if they had been his own.

Crowne revised the facts to suit his thesis that Rochester envied him the success of the Jerusalem plays. The charges of dullness and want of wit were leveled in "An Allusion to Horace," written before the summer of 1676, a full seven months before *The Destruction of Jerusalem* was acted in January 1677; Rochester, *Poems* (Walker), 99; Vieth, *ARP*, 156–60; Hume, *Development of Drama*, 312–13. The Epistle proves that as late as 1698, Crowne still smarted from Rochester's criticism, still believed that Rochester wrote the "Session" poem with its sneers at little starched Johnny Crowne who shitted plays, still felt irked at rumors Rochester had written the best parts of his plays, and still blamed the dead Earl for a beating Crowne got after satirizing him viciously in *The City Politiques* in 1683. Cf. Hume, *Development of Drama*, 366–67.

46. Ovid, *Metamorphoses*, II.401–535. Cf. Wall, *The Callisto Myth*.

47. Boswell, *Restoration Court Stage*, 197–202.

48. Mrs. Blagge managed somehow to marry Sidney Godolphin between performances in January 1675.

49. Wilson, *Court Satires*, 147 ff.; Wilson, *Nell Gwyn*, 147–55; Wilson, *Rake*, 242 ff.; Harris, *Sackville*, 57–62.

50. When Moll delivered a stillborn child nine months later, her brother Percy accused Mulgrave of being the father, fought with, "worsted and wounded him." Wilson, *Court Satires*, 269–70.

51. Jones, *Country*, 183–85; Wilson, *Rake*, 230–53.

52. See Haley, chapter 17, "The Country Party (1674–75)" in *Shaftesbury*, 348–71; Miller, *Popery*, 134–37; Cf. Jones, *Country*, 188; *JHL*, entry for Nov. 10, 1674.

53. *Treasury Books 1674*, passim.

54. Lindsey, *Charles II*, 88.

55. HMC *Hodgkin*, 39:315.

56. BL, Harl. Ms. 7003, f. 228. Lady Rochester's "pictures" may have been copies of a portrait by Sir Peter Lely now in the Courtauld Institute. Rochester's description applies to it. The date and circumstances of this letter are conjectural. The reference to Lady Warre implies that Lady Rochester was at Enmore. Treglown posits that the "Babyes" are Anne, Charles and Betty, dating the time between Summer 1674 and Autumn 1675. "My brother" is Lady Rochester's step-brother, Francis Warre; and "my Sister" would be his wife Anne Cuffe. The Warres were married ca. 1675. Rochester's letter of attorney on December 9, 1674, clearly shows his intention to be out of London. He was back by December 20 and his presence there in January 1675 is documented. If he wrote to his wife about the same time he gave Blancourt the power of attorney, that date would support Lady Rochester's pictures as a Christmas gift. On a quick trip to Enmore between December 9 and 20, 1674, Rochester could have

brought his wife back to London. A scarcity of letters between them in 1675 indicates that they were together much of the time.

57. Cf. *Essex Papers*, quoted in Marvell, *Letters*, vol. 2.

58. *CSPD 1673–75*, 474.

Chapter 15

1. Evelyn, *Diary*, 936. As an architect, John Evelyn noted various additions to Whitehall as he designed others. On October 10, 1675, "I was Casualy shewed the *Dutchess* of *Portsmouth's* splendid Appartment at *Whitehall*, luxuriously furnished, & with ten times the richnesse & Glory beyond the *Queenes*," 618. In January 1682, he dined "at the Dut: of *Portsmouth's* glorious Appartment at W.hall."

2. *Shorter Pepys*, 1036–37; Lindsay, *Charles II*, 82; Boswell, *Restoration Court Stage*, 24.

3. Ibid., 1038–39.

4. Fraser, *Royal Charles*, 50, 183, 193–94, 214, 225, 296, 382, 441.

5. London County Council, *Survey of London*, vol. 13: The Parish of St. Margaret, Pt. 2, 87–88.

6. On April 10, 1691. Evelyn, *Diary*, 936.

7. For a comparison of Wycherley and Shadwell, see Hume, *Development of Drama*, 65. For one of Rochester and Wycherley, see Rogers, *William Wycherley*, 49. "Slow" Wycherley needed five years (1670–75) to write two plays; "hasty" Shadwell wrote nine plays in seven years (1668–75). See also Turner, *Schooling Sex*, 340–59.

8. Boswell, *Restoration Court Stage*, 181.

9. Ibid., 193–96.

10. Hume, *Development of Drama*, 205, 207.

11. Boswell, *Restoration Court Stage*, 201.

12. *Familiar Letters* (1697), 2:39. Treglown suggests a homosexual tie between Rochester and Paisable. Even more evidence exists for such between him and his valet, Jean-Baptiste de Belle Fasse, another young Frenchman. Cf. Hammond, "Rochester's Homoeroticism."

13. Boswell, *Restoration Court Stage*, 197, 201.

14. Wilson, *Court Satires*, 236–37.

15. Cf. Stone, *Family*, 485–86.

16. Cf. *Letters* (Treglown), 161.

17. In a letter of 1685, the Dowager-Countess called Fanshaw "pitifull" in a contemptuous way. University of Rochester, Ms. D.26, ff. 5–6.

18. *Familiar Letters*, 2:39.

19. Ibid, 2:1.

20. BL, Add. Mss. 23722, ff. 52a–52b.

21. Their fourth child Mallet was born early in January 1676.

22. See *JHL*, XII. Haley, *Shaftesbury*, 372–84. Cf. Jones, *Country*, 86–90; Miller, *Popery*, 140–42.

23. Haley gives a detailed account of the maneuverings.

24. The fullest account of Francis Fane (1640?–1691) is that in the *DNB*. Cf. Verney, *Verney Papers* (1925), 2:265; *Alumni Cantabrigiensis*; Love, *Penguin Book of Restoration Verse*, 202–3; Fane, Dedication to *Love in the Dark*; Vieth, *ARP*, 303; Walker, *Poems*, 258–59.

25. Love includes Fane's masque in his edition of Rochester's works.

26. For Fane's play, cf. Hume, *Development of Drama*, 302–3; Langbain, *Lives*, 54. For subsequent plays about Venice, the Carnival and the Venetian influence on 18th century masquerades, see Castle, "Culture of Travesty" (15).

27. For data about Otway's life, see his *Works*, 1:1–38.

28. Cf. Rochester, *Letters* (Treglown), 111–13. In November 1675, Rochester was in no position to help anybody get royal favor, including himself.

29. Hume, *Development of Drama*, 214, 284; Wood, *Alumni Oxoniensis*; Cibber, *Apology*, 1:114n; Dennis, *Works*, 1:184; Langbain, *Lives*, 107.

30. Cf. Rochester, *Poems* (Walker), 134.

31. Otway, *Works*, 2:408 ff.

32. *JHL.*

33. See Browning, *Osborne*, 1:126–45; *State Trials*, 6:1026–62; Wilson, *Rake*, 221–49: Whitcombe, *Charles II*, 150 *ff.*

34. *Familiar Letters*, 1:22.

35. *CSPD 1675–76*, 87; Greene, *Monkey*, 87.

36. Treasury Books 1676–79, 2:1356.

37. See the epigraph to this chapter. Thomas Lennard, the Earl of Sussex, seems to have been bought for Charles's promiscuous, bar-sinister daughter Anne Fitzroy. When the two married at Woodstock in June 1674, Sussex received an annual pension of £2,000 with another £600 "for dyet." Browning, *Osborne*, 3:47–48. In exchange, when he was not behaving insanely, Sussex earned his money by supporting the King's bills in the Lords and providing a name for his wife's offspring. In 1679, after Anne Fitzroy had joined her mother, Cleveland, in exile and had a scandalous affair in Paris with Ralph Montagu, Sussex voted against the ensuing impeachment of Danby. Not long afterwards, he blew out his brains with a pistol.

38. Hearne, *Reliquiae* (1869), 1:119–20, cited in Rochester, *Poems* (Walker), 304.

39. This improptu was widely repeated in contemporary manuscripts; cf. Love, *Works*, 292–94, for ten variants.

40. One text dates this lampoon in 1676. Hearne says the verse toast was made at the King's request; however; since Rochester was in royal disgrace all of 1676 except late May, June, and brief parts of the autumn, Charles was not likely to have invited a drunken, potentially treasonous libel on the occasions he did see Wilmot. I think 1675 the likelier date.

41. Aubrey lists Fleetwood Shepherd with Rochester and Buckhurst; Fane names Sussex and Savile. Fane's closeness to Rochester in 1675 at the time of the incident makes him the more credible source. London County Council, *Survey of London*, 13:88–95, gives a history of the sundial, including its destruction.

42. Dutton, *Sir Christopher Wren*, 10. The King appointed John Flamested the Astronomer Royal at Greenwich in October 1676; Evelyn, *Diary*, 629. Cf. Chambers, *Christopher Wren*.

43. John Aubrey called the shape a "candlestick" and left a dash in words attributed to Rochester, "doest thou stand heer to _____ time?" Aubrey's ostensible evidence has led modern scholars to talk about phallic symbolism. In Aubrey's day, however, a "candlestick" was the stalk of a candelabrum or chandelier; *Shorter OED*, 256. Aubrey left blanks until he could fill them in with the proper words, which he did with the quote in question. The omitted word was "marke."

44. Hall, *Explication of the Diall*.

45. Oliver Lawson Dick, "Introduction" to *Aubrey's Brief Lives*, xci; Fane Ms., f. 358.

46. HMC *Laing*, 405.

47. Lindsay, *Charles II*, 95.

48. *CSPD 1675*, 784.

49. *CSPD 1675–76*, 244, 477.

50. *Familiar Letters*, 2:7. The Rochester-Barry correspondence during the spring and early summer of 1675 indicates her increasing friendship with Nell Gwyn, a fellow actress. One of Barry's requests was for Rochester to accompany her to Windsor, where Nell had a house; cf. Rochester, *Letters* (Treglown), 103–4.

51. *Familiar Letters*, 1:43.

52. *Familiar Letters*, 1:33.

53. *Treasury Books, 1670–75*, 818; *CSPD 1675–76*, 244 ff., 473, 477. Perhaps Joseph Crockson was an agent of Lady Lindsay's who caught the Woodstock bailiff, the subordinate of Lovelace, illegally cutting timber and killed him in an ensuing dispute.

54. Hume, *Development of Drama*, 200–201.

55. Otway, *Works*, 1:101. An undated "Song" by Rochester was first published in 1691 and entitled "Grecian Kindness." A possible dating of "Grecian Kindness" from biographical evidence is 1675–76. Could Rochester have written it in conjunction with Otway's *Alcibiades*—perhaps as a song that was not included?

56. Vieth says of the "Satire Against Vertue," "Oldham succeeds, however, at one point where all other satirists failed; he endows the mythic image of Rochester with some of the stature which the man possessed in real life"; *ARP*, 185–86.

57. *CSPD 1675–76*, 473.

58. *JHL*, XII; Haley, *Shaftesbury*, 393 ff.; Jones, *Country*, 188–92; Miller, *Popery*, 140–43.

59. Browning, *Osborne*, III, passim.

60. Cf. Halifax, "The Character of a Trimmer," in *Works*, 47–103. Rochester concluded his letter to Henry Savile in mid-September 1675: "I wish my Lord Halifax joy of everything, and of his daughter to boot," *Letters*, 108n, 109n. Elizabeth Savile was born on August 28, 1675. Burnet told Halifax that Rochester, on his dying bed, had praised him.

61. Jones, *Country*, 188.

62. *CSPD 1675–76*, 367.

63. Browning, *Osborne*, 2:185 ff.; *JHL*, XII.

64. Winn, *Dryden*, 273.

65. Ibid., 260.

66. Ibid., 281–82. Cf. Shadwell, *The Tory-Poets, a Satyre* (1682).

67. In 1673, Dryden told Rochester openly of his apprehension of a "worse mischief than I designed my Enemy" from lampoon writing.

68. Dryden, "Dedication" to *Aureng-Zebe*.

Chapter 16

1. BL, Harl. Ms. 7003, f. 211.

2. University of Rochester, Ms. D.26, f. 42.

3. Burnet, *Passages*, 27.

4. *Adderbury Parish Register*.

5. Cf. *Morrice Letter Book*, quoted in Van Lennep, *The London Stage*, 507.

6. *CSPD 1675–76*, 559; *Treasury Books, 1676–79*, 2:1371. Agnes Curzon was a mercer, or cloth merchant, near Lincoln's Inn Fields.

7. *Familiar Letters*, 1:7.

8. BL, Harl. Ms. 7003, f. 211.

9. Haley, *Shaftesbury*, 406.

10. For the formation and constituents of the Opposition party, see Jones, *First Whigs*, 4–19.

11. Ibid., 72.

12. See note 23 below.

13. Halifax, *Works*, 15–16.

14. Cf. Wilson, *Rake*, 253 ff.; J. W. Johnson, "The Classics and John Bull."

15. Cf. Hobbes, *Leviathan*, Part 2, chapters 18–20 ff.

16. See Weinbrot, *Augustus Caesar*, 110–11, 19, 132–33, 231.

17. Cf. Wilson, "Satiric Elements," 41–48. Wilson's citations of works later shown not to be Rochester's do not invalidate his basic thesis. See also Hume, *Development of Drama*, 364–65.

18. See Wilson, *Nell Gwyn*, 184–89 ff.

19. Hartmann, *Vagabond Duchess*. Cf. *Letters* (Treglown), 120n. Cf. Gilmour, *Great Lady*, 317–18; Harris, *Sackville*, 210–11; Andrews, *Royal Whore*, 233 ff.; Haley, *Shaftesbury*, 613–13; According to J. P. Kenyon, Hortense managed to infatuate Charles for little more than three months, after which she settled down in Chelsea and, subsidized by three kings in succession, stayed until her death in 1699; *The Stuarts*, 156–57.

20. George Porter, a friend of Rochester's, was so enamoured of the actress Jane Long that after 1673 he neglected his duties as a Groom of the Bed Chamber. Cf. Rochester, *Letters* (Treglown), 172 ff.; Wilson, *Court Satires*, 275–76. A "politique" was a worldly-wise temporizer, indifferent to religion.

21. *Familiar Letters*, 2:3.

22. Crowne, *Works*, 3:12, 13–14, 24–25.

23. Cf. Oldham, "A Dithyrambick on Drinking." The Guinea Club was apparently a combination political/drinking society. Naval clashes off the West African coast of Guinea had sped the outbreak of the Second Anglo-Dutch War in 1664. An expedition to Guinea under Prince Rupert was planned in that year; and Gramont recorded that "Persons, who had some practical experience, told marvellous stories of the perils of the expedition—that they would not only have to fight against the inhabitants of Guinea, a race of Devils whose arrows were poisoned, but they must also bear insufferable heat and downpours, of which every drop turned into a serpent. . . ." The expedition never took place; but the "Guinea Trade" in gums, ivory, and wood later became economically important to England. Shaftesbury's family were prominently involved in this trade. (Haley, *Shaftesbury*, 64, 172, 230) Given these data, we may hypothesize that the Guinea Club was a group of men loosely connected with the Opposition in 1676–77. When the Opposition party became the Whigs, the raffish, informal Guinea Club would have transformed into the more formal Green Ribbon Club. See Jones, "Green Ribbon Club"; Jones, "Parties and Parliament"; Miller, *Popery*, 182.

24. Hume, *Development of Drama*, 312.

25. Shadwell, *Works*, 3:26.

26. Ibid., 3:92–93.

27. Horace, *Satires, Epistles, and Ars Poetica*, 112–23. For comparisons between the satires of Horace and Rochester, see Weinbrot, " 'Allusion to Horace' "; Pat Rogers, "An Allusion to Horace," in *Spirit of Wit*, pp. 166–76; Rochester, *Poems* (Walker), 287. Rochester's reawakened interest in Horace could have owed in part to Francis Fane, whose own writings are mostly Horatian translations and adaptations. For Buckhurst and Horace, see Sackville, *Poems*, xvi, xix.

28. Vieth, *ARP*, 386–90.

29. *Shorter OED*, 1:47.

30. Cf. Winn, *Dryden*, 159–65.

31. Vieth, *ARP*, 158.

32. Winn, *Dryden*, 286–89, looks closely at the "Allusion" and its possible effects on Dryden.

33. Shadwell, *Tory-Poets*; cf. Rochester, *Letters* (Treglown), 119–20.

34. Winn, *Dryden*, 289–93, 307–9. Dryden's slashing attack on Rochester in the Preface to *All for Love* (1678), which was dedicated to Danby, had a more powerful protector from Rochester's retribution than Mulgrave could be.

35. Vieth, *ARP*, 129–36, 369–70.

36. Both Walker and Love place the poem among the cluster of satires.

37. Winn, *Dryden*, 286.

38. Cf. Rochester, *Poems* (Walker), 107; Winn, *Dryden*, 226.

39. *Shorter OED*, 1:47.

40. Ibid., 2:1986.

41. Shadwell, *ToryPoets*. Charles Ward describes Dryden's physique in his *Life of John Dryden* as "Rather short in stature and inclined to plumpness," and comments, "he was not without reason to be called 'Poet Squab,' " 30.

42. *Familiar Letters*, 1:4. Critics have taxed their ingenuity to identify Black Will. A "Will" appears on a list of presumable servants in Rochester's handwriting in the Nottingham Mss. PwV 31; and a William Clark, who served the Rochesters at Enmore, was employed in abducting Rochester's daughter by Elizabeth Barry in March 1679. Clark's complexion is not known. No evidence connects him with Dryden, however.

43. Vieth, *ARP*, 337–39; James Thorpe in Etherege, *Poems*, 79–82.

44. Thorpe in Etherege, *Poems*, 109 ff.; Cf. Rochester, *Poems* (Walker), 111–14. "Ephelia" may—or may not—be Etherege's pseudonym for Moll Kirke. Etherege's poem was sometimes titled "Ephelia's Lamentation" in manuscripts. The name itself does not appear in classical literature. As a latter-day coinage, it could have derived from the Greek *euphilos* (well-beloved), the Latin *ephelis* (freckles), or both. I have not been able to learn whether Moll had freckles—or red hair. In 1679, a collection included this poem: *Female Poems on Several Occasions. Written by Ephelia*. See Greer, "How to Invent a Poet." Cf. Wilson, *Court Satires*, 258–59; Thorpe in *Poems*, 81–83.

45. Cf. Langbain, *Lives*, 54. Both Aphra Behn and Nahum Tate contributed puffs when *The Sacrifice*, never acted, was printed. Cf. Aphra Behn, *Works* (ed. Summers), 6:343–45. Summers gives a short biography and critical evaluation of Fane, 4:429.

46. See Hume, *Development of Drama*, 86–97, for this term, its applicability to *The Man of Mode*, and various critical interpretations of the play.

47. Dennis, *Works*, 2:248–49; Van Lennep, *London Stage*, 243; Hume, *Development of Drama*, 95. Hume calls Dorimant "glamorous but reprehensible." For the argument that Dorimant was a composite of Rochester and Buckhurst, see Harris, *Sackville*, 67–68.

48. Hume notes that other critics often remark on Dorimant's "brutality" toward his mistresses but also on Loveit's "transports of rage" and "contemptible lack of self-control," 86–97. For Barry's fits of rage, see *Letters* (Treglown), 105, 121, 139, 140–41, 148, and ff.

49. *Familiar Letters*, 2:29.

50. Wilson, *Court Wits*, 164. Cf. Hume, *Development of Drama*, 91.

51. HMC *Seventh Report Appendix*, 467a. The poem has been assigned to Sir William Davenant. The letter is dated March 23, 1676. The poem read in part:

> Thus studious Thanour speaks and Astragon,
> Of death's cold company now hasty grew,
> Grieved that so little in this life is known,
> And that this little is confined to few.

52. *Familiar Letters*, 2:39.

53. Probably, Rochester is better described as an impersonator or performer rather than an actor. Cf. Holden, *Olivier*, 1–5. "All his life he . . . needed this escape from himself, this assumption of alien features and gestures. . . . Acting is not imitation but revelation of the inner self. This is not what he does or sets out to do. He is a performer." I would argue, of course, that Rochester inadvertently revealed a great deal about his inner self through the disguises he chose.

54. *Familiar Letters*, 1:22. Passion Week in 1676 was March 20–25. Following Wilson, Treglown suggests that the "strict severity" was venereal disease, following a "scandalous sin," i.e., fornication. I suggest that the reference is a continuation of the arch mentions of homosexuality in the Rochester-Savile correspondence. The strict legal penalty for sodomy was death.

Chapter 17

1. Kenyon, *The Stuarts*, 135–36.

2. *Familiar Letters*, 2:39.

3. BL, Harl. Ms. 7003, f. 287. Henry Bulkeley (1638–98), a Welshman, was notoriously irascible; he engaged in frequent duels. In 1668 he had killed a man, been found guilty of manslaughter and sentenced to be burned in the hand but received a royal pardon. In July 1673, he was involved with his friend Buckhurst in a brawl outside the Theatre Royal and wounded in the neck. In December 1673, he married Sophia Stuart (ca. 1648–1715), one of the Queen's Maids of Honor, who was equally notorious for promiscuity. In 1675 Henry went to the Tower for challenging the Earl of Ossory, Sophia's latest swain. Among others who enjoyed her favors was King Charles, according to Secret Service accounts. She received an annual pension of £400. Cf. Wilson, *Court Wits*, 230–31; Lindsey, *Charles II*, 146.

4. BL Harl. Ms. 7003, f. 198.

5. London County Council, *Survey of London*, 8: 87–88; *Treasury Books 1676–79*, 1:232.

6. Wilson, *Nell Gwyn*, 188–89.

7. Winn, *Dryden*, 294.

8. *DNB*, 18:13.

9. Harris, *Sackville*, 69–70.

10. *R-SL*, 15.

11. Cf. Rochester, *Letters* (Treglown), 122–24.

12. *Familiar Letters*, 2:5.

13. Winn, *Dryden*, 129, 285, 289.

14. Shadwell, *Works*, 3:105. Dryden took revenge by making Bruce and Longvil the agents of Shadwell's crowning as King of the Dunces when they sprung the trap door that plunged Fleckno to his end; "MacFlecknoe," ll. 211–17. Cf. ll. 149–50: "Let *Virtuoso's* in five years be Writ, / Yet not one thought accuse thy toyle of wit."

15. Cf. Hume, *Development of Drama*, 201. For Behn's life and writings, see Link, *Aphra Behn*; Duffy, *Passionate Shepherdess*; Cameron, *New Light on Aphra Behn*; Goreau, *Reconstructing Aphra*. Goreau's study is not trustworthy for its statements about Lord Rochester, indexed as Thomas Wilmot.

16. Hume, *Development of Drama*, 201.

17. Farley-Hills, *Critical Heritage*, 105–6.

18. Duffy, *Passionate Shepherdess*, 197. Apparently Behn knew of Burnet's censure. Cf. "A PINDARIC POEM to the Reverand Doctor Burnet, on the Honour he did me of Enquiring after me and my MUSE," in Behn, *Works*, 6:407–10.

19. Cf. Hume, *Development of Drama*, 284, 305. See Duffy, *Passionate Shepherdess*, 189–201 and passim. In 1682, Behn seized on the publication of Thomas Creech's translation of Lucretius to laud Wadham College, Rochester's alma mater, and "*Strephon* the Great . . . Who writ, and Lov'd, and Lookt like any God. . . ." Behn, *Works*, 6:169.

20. Etherege, *Poems*, 59. Charles Blount was also credited with this poem. Rochester apparently had no hand in it.

21. See Etherege, *Letters*, 185–86; Mann, *Sir George Etherege*, 20–21; William Oldys, *Biographica Britannica*, vol. 3.

22. Not much is known about William Jephson, who is named in only one of several Epsom accounts. At the time of his death in June 1697, he was Secretary to the Lords of the Treasury. Luttrell, *Historical Relation*, 2:242. Earlier, he may have been secretary to the Prince of Orange; Burnet, *Supplement to the History*, 532, 558. He apparently had no formal ties with the London stage but he was a friend to Etherege and Shadwell, who left him a mourning ring in 1690. He was a fringe member of the Rochester-Buckhurst-Sedley circle after 1675, it seems. Borgman, *Shadwell*, 89. Cf. Wilson's index to *R-SL*. Wilson also gives biographical data on Bridges, p. 90.

23. Hatton Family, *Correspondence*, 1:133–34. Cf. Vieth, *ARP*, 142–43.

24. HMC *Seventh Report Appendix*, 467b. See also Selections from the Capel *Correspondence*, 59, 61.

25. Marvell, *Letters*, 2:322.

26. Alcock, *Famous Pathologist*, 26.

27. Vieth, *ARP*, 199–203. See Wilson, "Rochester's 'Buffoon Conceit,' " 372–73. In calling "To the Post Boy" a "conceit," Scroop appears to have implied its self-glorification. After 1605, "conceit" was the short version of "self-conceit": "favorable opinion, esteem." *Shorter OED*, 1:360.

28. Cf. John Bunyan's Meditation XXVII, "On the Post Boy":

> Behold the Post-Boy, with what haste and speed
> He travels on the road: and there is need
> That he so does, big business calls for haste
> For should he in his journey now be cast,
> His life for that default might hap to go:
> Yea, and the kingdom come to ruin too.
> Stays are for him fixed, his hour is set,
> He has a horn to sound, that none may let
> Him in his haste, or give him stop or stay.
> Then, Post-Boy, blow thy horn and go thy way.
>   Comparison:
> The Post-boy in his haste an emblem is,
> Of those that are set out for lasting bliss.
> Not posts that glide the road from day to day,

> Has so much business, nor concerns as they.
> Make clear the road then, Post-boy, sound thy horn.
> Miscarry here, and better ne'er be born.

One critic sees in Rochester's poem the paradox that Christian logic finds redemption for the perfect crime in the perfect act of love. Carver, "Rascal before the Lord," 155–69.

29. Dustin Griffin finds Rochester's defiant departure for Hell similar to that of Don Juan (Don John) in Shadwell's *The Libertine*. Cf. Griffin, *Satires*, 55–56.

30. Vieth, *ARP*, 202–3.

31. Righter, "John Wilmot," 47–69.

32. Burnet, *Passages*, 27.

33. Cf. Hamilton, *Memoirs*, 257 ff., 375.

34. Alcock, *Famous Pathologist*, 8–10.

35. Ibid., 25, 29–30.

36. BL Harl. Ms. 7003, *f.* 212.

37. *Familiar Letters*, 1:12.

38. Alcock, *Famous Pathologist*, 29.

39. Rochester's name for the "Princess of Cyprus," the birthplace of Aphrodite, goddess of Love, resembled the nomenclature in *Sodom and Gomorah* and reiterated his misogyny. "Aloephagina" was a phonic pun: "bitter-tasting vagina." Cf. "aloe" in *Shorter OED*, 1:48.

40. Alcock, *Famous Pathologist*, 28.

41. Ibid., 28–29.

42. Pinto in ibid., 10–12; Vieth, *ARP*, 11, 13.

43. The handbill in different versions was printed by Jacob Tonson (1691), Edmund Curll (1707), John Hayward (1926), Prinz (1926), V. de S. Pinto (1961), and Love (1999). An original of the bill is among John Hayward's papers and books at King's College, Cambridge. Cf. Vieth, *Rochester Studies*, 110. In 1891, G. S. Street called the Bendo paper "excellent reading"; Farley-Hills, *Heritage*, 254. Dustin Griffin did not mention it in 1973 nor did any of the contributors to Treglown's *Spirit of Wit* in 1982. Anne Righter is one of a few who find the Bendo episode especially significant. See note 31 above. Vieth sees ties between "Rochester's speaker" in the *Handbill* and Erasmus's *Stultitia* in *The Praise of Folly*; see his "The Moriae Encomium."

44. Cf. Rochester, *Letters* (Treglown), 138.

45. Alcock, *Famous Pathologist*, 25–26.

46. Hobbes, *Leviathan*, Chapter XXIII. For Machiavelli, see Rochester, *Letters* (Treglown), 92, 135. Savile referred to Etherege and Machiavelli in a pair of contrasts on August 15, 1676.

47. Cf. the Third Prologue to *Valentinian*, lines 35–39:

> He charmed the tenderest virgins to delight . . .
> Some beauties here I see
> Though now demure, have felt his pow'rful charms
> And languished in the circle of his arms.

48. Alcock, *Famous Pathologist*, 26–27.

49. See Stoller, *Sex and Gender*, 1:176–83. Dustin Griffin connects Rochester's impotence to Don Juanism.

50. Cf. Griffin, *Satires*, 130. Griffin gives no reason for suggesting that the period of the poem was ca. 1674–76. It was first printed in 1691, as both Vieth and Walker state.

51. Clark, "Satiric Singing"; Wilcoxon, "Rochester's Sexual Politics"; Carol Fabricant, "Rochester's World of Imperfect Enjoyment"; Vieth, " 'Pleased with Contradiction and the Sin.' "

52. *Shorter OED*, 1:64.

53. Compare this poem with Catullus XXXII ("Amabo, mea dulcis Ipsithilla"). Rochester's technique of imagining a woman's sexual feelings to be the same as a man's and then speaking *in propria feminae* originated with Aretino and was widely copied by male "pornographers." J. G. Turner, in *Schooling Sex*, treats this *ficelle* as a technique for "sexual schooling." For medical comparisons between female and male anatomy before the eighteenth century, cf. Laqueur, "New Science, One Flesh," in *Making Sex*, 63–113.

54. Savile indicated Rochester's concern about aging in a letter of 1677, when he said the "Old Bard" Waller (then seventy-one) was nearing fourscore and urged Rochester "to shew us that five and twenty is a much better age for Poetry. . . ." Rochester was in fact over thirty when Savile flattered him by saying his age was twenty-five.

55. See Thompson, *Unfit for Modest Ears*.

56. Cf. Rochester, *Letters* (Treglown), 137.

57. Browning, *Osborne*, 2:38 (Letters).

58. BL, Harl. Ms. 7003, f. 300.

59. *Familiar Letters*, 1:29.

60. Halifax, *Savile Correspondence*, 41–43.

61. *Familiar Letters*, 2:19.

62. Scroop, "In Defence of Satyr." line 59.

63. Haley, *Shaftesbury*, 410–16; Jones, *Country*, 192 ff.; Miller, *Popery*, 143 ff.; Verney, *Verney Papers* (1925), 2:314 ff.; Burnet, *Life*, 2:96 ff.; Winn, *Dryden*, 294 ff.

64. Hume, *Development of Drama*, 312–13.

65. Downes, in the *Roscius Anglicanus*, said of *Titus and Berenice*: "This Play, with the Farce, being perfectly well Acted; had good success." In the published Preface, however, Otway said it was damned by a critical clique (by implication Crowne and Dryden).

66. Hume, *Development of Drama*, 303–4.

67. Dennis, *Works*, 2:277.

68. For the dispute about the authorship of "A Session of the Poets" ("Since the Sons of the Muses, grow num'rous and lowd"), see Vieth, *Rochester Studies*, Items 20, 26, 60, 257–61, 289, 295, 297; Rochester, *Poems* (Walker), 133, 312. I agree with J. H. Wilson and Keith Walker that, although the evidence is not conclusive, the satire can be plausibly ascribed to the circle of wits around Rochester and Buckingham.

Chapter 18

1. Vieth, *ARP*, 296–321.

2. Cf. Ibid., 319.

3. Crowne, Preface to *Caligula*.

4. Cf. Rochester, *Letters* (Treglown), 163–64, 167.

5. Cf. Macdonald, *Journal from Parnassus*. Treglown rejects Wilson's guess to make his own that the "libell" referred to by Savile was Mulgrave's *In Defence of Satyr*. Wilson's theory seems to me the surer one. Cf. Keith Walker in Rochester, *Poems* (Walker), 312.

6. See Winn, *Dryden*, 536–38.

7. For "An Allusion," Rochester, Dryden, Shadwell, and *Macfleckno*, see ibid., 286–94. For the university post, see ibid., 270–71.

8. The judgment is Robert Hume's. Cf. ibid., 302–03.

9. See Jones, *Country*, 189 ff.; Haley, *Shaftesbury*, 411 ff.

10. Vieth, *ARP*, 151, 185.

11. Vieth, "John Oldham"; Harris, *Sackville*, 76.

12. Vieth, *ARP*, 188.

13. Cf. Griffin, *Satires*, 247, 250–51. Turner discusses at length Oldham's relationship with Rochester and their mutual participation in the art of writing "Heroic Pornography." *Schooling Sex*, 260–305.

14. G. E. C. *Baronetage*, 7:644; *DNB*, 58:316; Marshall, *Woodstock*, 234–38; cf. Rochester, *Letters* (Treglown), 176–77.

15. This inscription appears on a marble tablet in Spelsbury Church on the south side of the altar and choir. Transcription is mine. The Lichfields' conjugal affection notwithstanding, their numerous offspring proved to be decadent wastrels and roués, and the Ditchley Lee family line died off in the next century.

16. Cf. Burnet, *History*, 2:115–20.

17. Cf. Wilson, *Rake*, 253–55.

18. See *JHL*, XIII; BL, Sloane Ms. 3087, ff. 1–7; Whitcombe, *Charles II*; Halifax, *Works*.

19. Haley, *Shaftesbury*, 416 ff.

20. Ibid., 420.

21. Marvell, *Works*, 2:329 (Letters).

22. Harris, *Sackville*, 71.

23. *JHL*, XIII.

24. Robert Wolseley, Preface to *Valentinian* (1685), in Spingarn, *Critical Essays*.

25. Cf. Miller, *Popery*, 143–48.

26. *JHL*, XIII.

27. *Familiar Letters*, 2:14.

28. *Familiar Letters*, 2:11, 20.

29. Wilson, *Nell Gwyn*, 87–94. Between June 3 and Dec. 20, 1676, Portsmouth received £8,773 while Gwyn got £2,862. In 1677 Gwyn got only £5,250 to Portsmouth's £27,300. Lindsey, *Charles II*, 145.

30. Wilson, *Rake*, 200.

31. Ibid., 199. BL, Stowe Ms. 211. Cf. Rochester, *Letters* (Treglown), 143–44.

32. Cf. Haley, *Shaftesbury*, 427 ff.

33. BL, Harleian Ms. 7003, f. 280. Cf. Rochester, *Letters* (Treglown), 145–46.

34. BL, Harl. Ms. 7003, f. 280. Haley, *Shaftesbury*, 428; Wilson, *Nell Gwyn*, 104.

35. Harris, *Sackville*, 71.

36. BL, Harl. Ms. 7003, f. 282.

37. Marvell, *Works*, 2:329. On Aug. 2, a letter to Sir Ralph Verney reported: "The great discourse of the town is that the Duke of Bucks shall be restored to favour, and be Lord Steward of the Household in place of the Duke of Ormonde; but of this they are very silent at Court, only his sacred Majesty and his Grace (I hear) were very merry one night at Lord Rochester's lodgings, which, I conceive, created this discourse." HMC *Seventh Report Appendix*, 469b.

38. See Wilson, *Nell Gwyn*, 201–4, for a fuller account.

39. Hume, *Development of Drama*, 314. Cf. Downes, *Roscius Anglicanus*, 36–37.

40. See "Scrope or Scroop, Sir Carr," *DNB*, 17:1071–72.

41. Cf. Wilson, *Nell Gwyn*, 205.

42. Sir Carr's mother, the sharp-tongued Lady Mary Scroop, a Dresser to Queen Catherine, became the mistress of Henry Savile about the same time.

43. Rochester's new minion, John Oldham, also parodied Scroop's "Song" in "A Dithyrambick," spoken by his own Rochester *manque* (August 1677).

44. The passage on Rochester is quoted in the epigraph to Chapter Seventeen above. Vieth posits that "In Defence of Satyr" was "probably in circulation soon after the Epsom brawl in June 1676" and that "On the Suppos'd Author" came soon after (Vieth, *ARP*, 349). I place the two poems some six months or so later because the known relationships between Carey Frazier, Scroop, Nell Gwyn, Mrs. Barry, and Rochester from late 1676 until the summer of 1677 provide additional motivations for the Scroop-Rochester exchanges.

45. Halifax, *Savile Correspondence*, 58. A biography of Richard Lord Lumley is given in *Collins' Peerage of England*, 3:712–15.

46. Dryden appropriated this image to describe Shaftesbury in *Absalom and Achitophel*, l. 172 (1681).

47. The date of Rochester's "Poet Ninny" is uncertain. Vieth thinks it was "his verses on Sir Car. Scroope at large" sent by Jack Verney to Sir Ralph on April 25, 1678 (*ARP*, 49). If "Poet Ninny" was written in the summer of 1677, it may very well have taken until April 1678 to come into Verney's hands. In wake of the smashing setback to the Country Party in 1677, the prudent Verneys lay low in the country for the rest of the year. Cf. Verney, *Verney Papers* (1925), 2:360 ff.

48. Wilson, *Nell Gwyn*, 210.

49. Cf. Vieth, *ARP*, 159–63, 331–36, 351–52. In 1684 an anonymous "Letter to Julian" berated Mulgrave for his bad verse and "basely railing at the dead" (i.e., Rochester). Wilson, *Court Satires*, 133.

50. Cf. Rochester, *Letters* (Treglown), 146–49. For Shaftesbury, see Haley, 403 ff. The intimacy between Rochester and Buckingham at this time probably gave rise to an eighteenth-century canard. Reportedly out of royal favor at the same time, the two friends went into the country and disguised themselves as tavern-keepers. Seeing an attractive but closely guarded wife living across the way, Rochester dressed as a woman and pretended to faint on her doorstep. Taken indoors and "revived," he revealed his true sex and then seduced the fair recluse. After enjoying then tiring of her, he took her to London and turned her over to his roué friends. Rochester, *Memoirs*. Prinz reprints the story in *Rochesteriana*. The chronology of events from February to December 1677 makes the story improbable if not impossible.

51. *Familiar Letters*, 2:16.

52. Ibid., 2:25.

53. See Prinz, *Rochesteriana*, 15.

54. Wood, "Whitehall," in *Athen. Oxen.*

55. Whitehall, *EXASTICON*, Icon. 22.

56. See Chapter One above. The Thomas Smith who witnessed Rochester's Will in 1680 (Prinz, 301) may have been the Smith listed in the *Alumni Oxoniensis*, 4:1382. The son of Thomas Smith of Betson, Cheshire, he matriculated as a *paup.* at Christ Church on June 14, 1672, at the age of sixteen. He received the B.A. in 1676, and the M.A. in March 1681. The dates, college, and chronology make him a probable tutor for Charles. The Editor's Preface to Rochester's letters in *The Museum* on May 23, 1747, says that Charles, "while a Child of eight Years old [was] at *Eaton*"; Rochester, *Letters* (Treglown), 263. However, the registers of Eton do not show that Charles Wilmot ever went there. See ibid., 229.

57. Colonel Cooke to the Duke of Ormonde on Nov. 12, 1681. HMC *Rutland*, 59.

58. BL, Harl. Ms. 7003, f. 283.

59. J. H. Wilson gives a short account of Fleetwood Shepherd (1634–1698) in *Court Wits*, 285. See also Wilson, *Nell Gwyn*, 136, 215, 243, 277. About 1673, Shepherd, a life-long bachelor, became Steward to Sackville Lord Buckhurst and thereafter lived most of his life in that nobleman's sphere. In the 1690s, when Sackville became Lord Chamberlain, Shepherd achieved wealth (and a scandalous reputation) for selling royal posts.

60. BL, Harl. Ms. 7003, f. 272. Mr. Pome (Prinz's transcription of the name) or Mr. Povey (Treglown's). The former could have been a pseudonym for Dryden, the Poet Laureate, which explains the visitor's association with politicians and his fear of lampoons; but would Dryden visit the home of his longtime Nemesis since 1671? Cf. Winn, *Dryden*, 304–9. On the other hand, Thomas Povey, a Master of Requests and "a nice contriver of all Elegancies," had little cause to fear lampoons since he does not appear in those preserved. Cf. Wilson, *Court Wits*; *POAS*.

61. *Familiar Letters*, 2:24.

62. BL, Harl. Ms. 7003, f. 274.

63. *Familiar Letters*, 2:39.

64. Although progressive lengths and stages of syphilis vary, Rochester's symptoms described here and those detailed in Burnet's *Passages* indicate the third and final stage. The description in "To the Postboy" shows a very advanced state of deterioration in mid-1676; recurrences in the last months of 1677, February–April 1678, and the winter of 1678–79 were followed by a latent period, April 1679 to May 1680, as Gilbert Burnet noted.

65. *Familiar Letters*, 2:10.

66. Cf. Rochester *Letters* (Treglown), 161.

67. Ibid., 21, 154n. An account of Buckingham at Oxford is given in *POAS*, 1:429–37; Marvell, *Works*, 2:331.

68. *R-SL*, 48.

69. The Prince of Orange, later William III, was reputed to have homosexual interests, in part because of his chilling behavior toward his wife, Mary II. His odd behavior on their wedding night was widely gossiped about in the royal families of Europe; cf. the account by Liselotte, Monsieur's second wife, in a letter to her aunt, Sophie of Hanover, on January 11, 1678: "There is a great deal of talk about the Prince of Orange's wedding, and among other things it is said that he went to bed in wollen drawers on his wedding night. When the King of England suggested that he might care to take them off, he replied that . . . he was accustomed to wearing his woolens, and had no intention of changing now. And instead of having supper with the English royal family he went to eat in the town, and kept the King and the bride, who had been put to bed in the bridal chamber, waiting until after midnight." Charlotte Elizabeth, *Letters from Liselotte*, 32. For a full study of William's propensities, see Hammond, "William III," in *Figuring Sex*, 172–85.

70. *Familiar Letters*, 1:36.

71. *R-SL*, 51. On Nov. 17, Rochester became alderman of the town of Taunton, Somerset, but he was too ill to be there for the ceremonies. HMC *Portland*, 3:357; Marvell, *Works*, 2:331.

72. *R-SL*, 52–53.

73. *Familiar Letters*, 2:9.

74. BL, Harl. Ms. 7003, f. 254.

75. Ibid., f. 237.

Chapter 19

1. *JHL*, XIII; *Familiar Letters*, 2:35. These events probably took place in late February or early March 1678. Rochester was sick in London between mid-March and late April. Nell Gwyn reported that he went to the country in early May, and Lord Anglesey's diary noted that he spent the rest of 1678 with his wife.

2. Ibid., 2:9.

3. Ibid., 2:36.

4. *The Museum* 31 (May 23, 1747): 157. Treglown places this letter in 1671–74 on the grounds that only two children (Anne and Charles) are mentioned. Charles was painted with Omrah by William Wissing in 1678; the boy looks about eight and the dog was still a puppy. I place the letter in that year. Betty and Mallet were only four and two in 1678 and thus not eligible for gifts of this quality.

Louise Françoise de la Baume le Blanc, Duchesse de La Vallière (1644–1710), a Maid of Honor to Madame, Charles's sister, became the mistress of Louis XIV in 1661. When he took Madame de Montespan as his second mistress in 1667, the humiliated Louise tried to escape to a nunnery. She was compelled to remain at Court until 1674, when she entered the Carmelite convent in the rue d'Enfer in Paris. She spent the rest of her life fasting and doing self-imposed penance for her sins; but she could hardly have fasted and shrunk so rapidly in one year, as Rochester jested. This is another reason to date the letter later than 1674.

5. *Familiar Letters*, 2:35.

6. BL, Harl. Ms 7003, f. 233. The phonetic spelling evident in this letter suggests that "my Lady Morton" was almost certainly "Lady Mordaunt," Rochester's long-time scapegoat, Carey Frazier, who in 1678 married Charles Mordaunt after being his mistress for some time. He became the second Viscount Mordaunt in June 1675. Wilson, *Court Satires*, 267.

7. Cf. Prinz, *Rochester*, 300.

8. Miller, *Popery*, 148 ff.; Haley, *Shaftesbury*, 438–40. See Schwoerer, "Principle and Propaganda in the 1670s," in *No Standing Army*, 95–136.

9. Wilson, *Nell Gwyn*, 208.

10. *JHL*, XIII.

11. Howells, *State Trials*, 6:1310–50. Cf. Lever, *Herberts*, 131–35.

12. Winn gives a full account of the political/ideological background, *Dryden*, 305–9, and explicates the assault on Sackville in the pages following.

13. For Rochester on Sternhold, see Rochester, *Poems* (Walker), 122, 305. "Hasty" was Rochester's own epithet for Shadwell in *An Allusion*.

14. Vieth thinks this fragment was intended as a retort to Otway's *The Poet's Complaint of his Muse* (January 22, 1680); but Otway had insulted Rochester in print several times before then without any rebuttal from the Earl. It is not likely that Rochester would take so belated a revenge on so insignificant a foe at the time he had vowed to mend his ways to Gilbert Burnet. See Vieth, *ARP*, 214–19. While Rochester could hardly refute Dryden's charges of drunkenness, public nakedness, and so on, he could prove his knowledge of more than a smattering of Latin by criticizing Dryden's misuse of Plutarch—as he had once criticized Lee's historical inaccuracy. He could also sneer at Dryden's blank verse by describing it ironically as rough, unruly rhyme. Dryden had become his own "imager" in self-tributes to his Shakespearean grandeur. Cf. Dryden's command to Titus Oates, "Erect thyself, thou monumental brass."

15. Hume, *Development of Drama*, 329–31. Hume finds the play "great fun" and "cheerfully indecent." Cf. Winn, *Dryden*, 309 ff.

16. Burnet, *Passages*, 17–20.

17. Ibid., 20–21.

18. Francis Fane, in Nahum Tate, *Poems by Several Hands* (London, 1685), 11.

19. HMC *Seventh Report Appendix*, 470a.

20. BL, Harl. Ms. 7003, f. 251. Rochester's wavering script in this letter is the same in one to his wife. Both were written during his sickness of 1678. See note 24 below.

21. Lever, *Herberts*, 135.

22. *JHL*, XIII: April 4, 1678. See note 12 above.

23. Lever makes a strong circumstantial case for Pembroke as Godfrey's murderer, *Herberts*, 136–39. Ogg and Pinto also subscribe to the Pembrokean theory, as do I.

24. BL, Harl. Ms. 7003, f. 214.

25. Malagene is accused of malice, stinginess, betraying friends, cowardice, and tripping a lame man, among other vices. He acts Scaramouche and has other qualities of the satiric Rochester-persona. Otway also meant *Friendship in Fashion* to satirize Sackville and his wife, Mary Bagot; but fearing Sackville's anger, Otway dedicated the play to him as a not very ingenious disclaimer. See Hume, *Development of Drama*, 331–32, 369.

26. HMC *Rutland II*, 50.

27. Wilson, *Nell Gwyn*, 210.

28. *R-SL*, 54. Cf. Rochester, *Letters* (Treglown), 181–83. Treglown's edition of the letters, based on the Portland Mss., rings minor variations on earlier editions by the Camden Society and J. H. Wilson.

29. Ibid., 55.

30. Falk, *Montagus*: "A Cultured Knave" (Ralph Montagu), 71–151; "A Born Intriguer" (Elizabeth Montagu Hervey), 152–67.

31. *Familiar Letters*, 1:20.

32. Cf. Walpole, *Royal and Noble Authors*, 2:37–39.

33. Prinz, *Rochester*, 235.

34. *R-SL*, 58–59.

35. *Familiar Letters*, 1:24.

36. The portrait of Rochester attributed to Jacob Huysman is now in the National Portrait Gallery. The putative date (ca. 1675) was probably assigned because of the reference to a monkey in the 1675 "Satyr" on Man; but Rochester's wan appearance and his reference to "the monkey we have here" in 1678 make that the more reasonable date.

37. *R-SL*, 61–62. Cf. Rochester, *Letters* (Treglown), 196–97 for the conclusion to the letter, which Wilson omitted: "I can send you noe newes of Ladyes, it is none, that Ladyes are weomen, and that weomen are bitches whom God confound & let every cripple say Amen."

38. *R-SL*, 63–64.

39. *Familiar Letters*, 1:12. Rochester is inverting lines from a cheerful drinking song in John Fletcher's *Rollo, Duke of Normandy*:

> And he that will to bed goe sober,
> Falls with the leafe still in October.

40. *R-SL*, 64.

41. Ibid., 66.

42. Rochester's whereabouts from July 13 to September 12 are not documented. Savile stayed in Paris until the late autumn, but no letters to Rochester from there are extant. Savile's letters to Halifax from Paris make no mention of Rochester, however, so we may assume he remained in England. Cf. Halifax, *Savile Correspondence*, 78–119.

43. HMC *Seventh Report Appendix*, 494b.

Chapter 20

1. For background of the Popish Plot, see Miller, *Popery*, 48–53; Haley, *Shaftesbury*, 443–52; Kenyon, *Plot*, 1–44. For Burnet's version of events, see *History*, 2:156–201.

2. Kenyon, *Plot*, 41–43.

3. Ibid., 52–54.

4. Ibid., 46–47. All of this account is based on Ibid., 45–58. Cf. Hammond, "Titus Oates," in *Figuring Sex*, 155–72.

5. Jones, *First Whigs*, 46, 103, 164; HMC *Seventh Report Appendix*, 494b. The designations of "Whig" and "Tory" for opposing factions developed at this time.

6. See G. E. C., *Peerage*, 8:232–34. On April 8, 1679, Colonel Edward Cooke reported to the Duke of Ormonde: "As yesterday my Lord Lovelace began in the Lords with a complaint of one Robert Hicks, a farrier and gamekeeper at Woodstock, having a vindictive woman's deposition (who had threatened to do him a mischief) that he said he hoped my Lord Treasurer would yet show as honest a face as those that stickled against him." HMC *Ormonde*, N.S. 5:36.

7. Letters written by the Countess in 1685–86 now at the University of Rochester give some details about these (and other) family quarrels. Cf. J. W. Johnson " 'My dearest sonne' " See also HMC *Rutland II*.

8. BL, Harl Ms. 7003, f. 239.

9. *CSPD 1678–79*, 420.

10. Howell, *State Trials*, 8:595, 598, 600. Lovelace verified this information at College's trial in 1681.

11. Ogg, *Charles II*, 2:626.

12. *POAS*, 201–4, 227–30.

13. Kenyon, *Plot*, 4.

14. Ibid., 138 ff.

15. Howell, *State Trials*, 8:595 ff.

16. Kenyon, *Plot*, 77–78, 264–69. Kenyon examines the various theories of who killed Godfrey, including Pembroke, and suggests that the murderer may have been a common footpad.

17. Miller, *Popery*, 182; Kenyon, *Plot*, 177 ff.

18. *JHL*, XIII.

19. I.e., Powis, Petre, Stafford, Belayse, and Arundell of Wardour. Kenyon, *Plot*, 31.

20. Walker notes that this verse is an expansion of Francis Quarles's *Divine fancies* (1632).

21. Charles Blount (1654–93), the son of Sir Henry Blount and the younger brother of Sir Thomas Pope Blount, was an eager advocate of Thomas Hobbes. In 1673 he defended Dryden when others criticized *The Conquest of Granada*, and he may have met Rochester about that time. In 1678 he sent a copy of his *Anima Mundi* to Hobbes.

Blount's *Subversion of Judaism* (1678) faulted many postulates of the Old Testament and questioned priestcraft. *Great Is Diana of the Ephesians: or, The Original of Idolatry* (1680) examined comparative religions and skeptically questioned religious superstitions. Unlike Rochester, he maintained his skepticism until death. In 1693 he shot (or stabbed) himself and died a lingering, reflective death. He was much maligned for his suicide and "cowardice" in taking the Stoic's way out. In 1695 his *Miscellaneous Works* was edited by Charles Gildon. Cf. *DNB*, 5:243–45.

22. Cf. Rochester, *Letters* (Treglown), 206–13; Harth, *Contexts of Dryden's Thought*, 62, 73–77, 81–83, 91–94, 98.

23. Blount, *Works* (1695), 158–68. Cf. Rochester, *Letters* (Treglown), 214–16, 256–57.

24. Quoted in Kenyon, *Plot*, 84–85.

25. Cf. Jones, *First Whigs*, 20–33.

26. Cf. Haley, *Shaftesbury*, 459–67. Dryden's *Absalom and Achitophel* exploited the analogy with Absalom's rebellion against King David in 2 Samuel:15–19.

27. Jones, *Whigs*, 80 ff.; Ogg, *Charles II*, 2:584 ff.

28. G. E. C., *Peerage* 1:46; BL, Additional Mss. 15,892, ff. 216–24; HMC *Stuart*, 6:234; 7:416; University of Rochester, Ms. D.26, ff. 2–3 ff.

29. Cooke to Ormonde, HMC *Ormonde*, N.S. 4, 345–47. Colonel Edward Cooke of Chesterton was the long-time friend and financial agent of Rochester as well as of James Butler the Duke of Ormonde. (HMC *Ormonde*, N.S. 3:268–69, 273; N.S. 4:345–47, 356–57, 359–60, 368–71; N.S. 5:2, 6–11, 30–33, 39–40, 102 and passim.) As early as 1667, he was managing the deer and plantings at Moor Park for Ormonde; and he supplied a steady stream of reports about Parliamentary matters to Ormonde in Dublin in 1679. At Ormonde's suggestion, when these became too delicate, they left off "the formalities of titles in the beginning and subscriptions at the end of our letters." An intelligent man and lucid writer, Cooke could also be wryly witty. On May 14, 1679, he told of a madcap race at Banstead: "Tom Wharton's [horse] threw him and he was taken up for dead, yet is alive again but much battered, and this they call sport." He kept very high company; in January, 1684, John Evelyn met him when dining at Lambeth Palace with the Archbishop of Canterbury, several lords, and other divines. Evelyn, *Diary*, 764. He may even have been the author of a play, *Love's Triumph, or The Royal Union*, listed in the term catalogues for May 1678. Cf. DNB, 4:1003; Van Lennep, *London Stage 1660–1700*, 263.

30. BL, Harl. Ms. 7003, f. 230; Cf. Kenyon, *Plot*, 118–25.

31. Burnet, *Some Passages*, in Farley-Hills, *Heritage*, 56.

32. Haley, *Shaftesbury*, 489–91; Miller, *Popery*, 169–88.

33. Jones, *Whigs*, 27–30; Kenyon, *Plot*, 31; Haley, *Shaftesbury*, 504 ff.

34. Browning, *Osborne*, 3:141. Cf. Colonel Cooke's report to the Duke of Ormonde on April 15, 1679: "but the Court party did not befriend [Danby] as the Duke Mon[mouth], the Lords Roch[ester], Mul[grave]" etc. HMC *Ormonde*, N.S. 5:48.

35. Burnet, *History* 1:476.

36. Hume, *Development of Drama*, 220.

37. All dated references to the Lords appear in *JHL*, XIII.

38. Prinz, *Rochester*, 299, 300; Howells, *State Trials*, 8:595 ff.

39. *Familiar Letters*, 2:22.

40. Cf. Wilson, *Court Satires*, 220, 224.

41. Downes, *Roscius Anglicanus*, 38.

42. See Otway, *The Orphan*, Act IV, ll. 440–46. Hume finds it "an exciting play, and even a moving one," *Development of Drama*, 218–19.

43. BL, Harl. Ms.7003, f. 191. The Duke of Ormonde had instructed Captain Cooke not to use the names of either recipient or sender in his letters. See note 29 above.

44. *R-SL*, 67. The Caledonian (i.e., Scottish) Countesses have been identified as Katherine, Countess of Kinnoul, who was widowed in 1677 and went to live in France, and Elizabeth Hamilton, the Comtesse de Gramont, the sister-in-law of the Gramont who dictated his Memoirs to her husband.

45. *Familiar Letters*, 1:16.

46. See Kenyon, *Plot*, 164.

47. Andrews, *Royal Whore*, 15–17, 20–22, 30 ff.

48. Isaacs, "Rochester's Grand Tour." A photograph of Rochester's signature on the University of Padua register is given in Fisher, *Bottle*, xv.

49. Kenyon, *Plot*, 199–200: Andrews, *Royal Whore*, 257.

50. Langhorn did disclose a small number of pounds but he was executed on July 14, leaving behind a long letter of self-justification. Howells, *State Trials*, 7:418–591. This volume also contains the trials of Pickering, Grove, Coleman, Wakeman, and the Five Popish Lords.

51. *Familiar Letters*, 1:16.

52. Haley, *Shaftesbury*, 491, 541–42. Cf. Luttrell, *Brief Relation*, 1:17: "Mr. Langhorn, who was lately executed on account of the plott, stood on his innocence to the last; but when he was cutt down and stripp'd, 'twas found he had been disciplin'd or whipt ('tis thought) the reason was he had discovered the settlements of estates to popish uses."

53. *Familiar Letters*, 1:14.

54. *R-SL*, 70, 74. John Hayward suggested that Mr. P_____ was Miles Prance, a Catholic silversmith in Covent Garden, who testified against Queen Catherine's confessor and Lord Stafford to save his own neck. Treglown suggests that Mr. P_____ was an error for Mr. B_____, Rochester's French valet, Mr. Baptist, who went to Paris in November 1679 on an errand for Rochester. However, Baptist was at Rochester's deathbed in 1680 and received his master's linen as a bequest. There is another candidate for Mr. P_____. One Pierce Powell, "A man of ill fame," was a minor informer in the Plot. He was an intimate of Stephen Dugdale's and joined with him in October 1681 after Dugdale had sent College to his death by testifying about his part in Lady Rochester's conversion. Powell, Dugdale, and Titus Oates all swore evidence against Sir Thomas Preston on November 21, 1681. By that time both Rochester and his wife were dead. During their lifetimes, Powell stayed out of the limelight; and he was in France in 1679–80. On December 26, 1678, a pass to France was issued to Pierce Powell. *CSPD 1674–1679, Addenda*, 620; *CSPD 1680–81*, 52, 574.

55. An impostume is a purulent swelling or abcess.

56. Wilson, *Court Satires*, 270; cf. Rochester, *Letters* (Treglown), 226; Rochester, *Poems* (Walker), 116–17. Carr Scroop seems to have originated the opprobrious "goggle-eyed" to describe Mulgrave, *In Defence of Satyr* (1677). His portrait suggests that Mulgrave was hyperthyroid.

57. See Vieth, *ARP*, 134–36; Winn, *Dryden*, 325–26.

58. *Treasury Books 1679–80*, 180. Cf. Chamberlayne, *Angliae Notitia*, 172.

59. Savile, *Correspondence*, 119n; Falkus, *Charles II*, 181; Haley, *Shaftesbury*, 545.

60. Haley, *Shaftesbury*, 546.

61. HMC *Anglesey*, quoted in Greene, *Monkey*, 146; cf. Rochester, *Letters* (Treglown), 228.

Chapter 21

1. "Chit . . . *contemptuous*, a girl or young woman 1624." *Shorter OED*, 1:304.

2. *JHL*, XIII; Haley, *Shaftesbury*, 529–83; Ogg, *Charles II*, 2:584 ff.; Browning, *Osborne*, 2:314–52.

3. Kenyon, *Plot*, 189 ff.

4. Haley, 475–76, 554–55 ff.

5. Jones, *Whigs*, 109–14; *State Trials*, 7:1045–66.

6. *Familiar Letters*, 1:9.

7. Cf. Jones, *Whigs*, 115–26. For a 1679 Tory lampoon on Monmouth, see "A Ballad Called Perkin's Figary," Lord, *Anthology*, 222–26. For Rochester's report of Oates's trial for sodomy, see *R-SL*, 73; cf. Rochester, *Letters* (Treglown), 232.

8. Kenyon, *Plot*, 187–88.

9. Smith, *School of Venus*, 142–51.

10. The statement is Robert Hume's. My account of the theater in 1679–80 draws from his chapter of that title; *Development of Drama*, 340–79.

11. Dryden, *Essays*. "Ravenscroft endeavored to shew himself Master of the Art of Swift-Writing; and would perswade the World, that what he writes is ex tempore Wit. . . ." Langbaine, *Lives*, 417–18.

12. For a brief biography of Jack Howe (1657–1722) and the satires upon him, see Wilson, *Court Satires*, xiv–xv, 24–254 passim.

13. Ibid., 124.

14. HMC *Seventh Report*, 477B. Cf. Wilson, *Court Satires*, 293–95.

15. See Farley-Hills, *Heritage*, 108–9.

16. Wilson, *Court Satires*, 293.

17. Wolseley, in Farley-Hills, 141–42.

18. Cf. *DNB* and *Encyclopedia Britannica* (1965), 4:448–49. For the background of the *History*, see Sutherland, *English Literature*, 280–82.

19. Burnet, *Supplement*, 486.

20. Ibid.

21. Evelyn, *Diary*, 604.

22. Anach, or Anak, was a giant of a man whose descendents were renowned for their enormous size. They lived in the hills near Hebron and were absorbed by the Philistines. Cf. Numbers 13:22–23, Deuteronomy 9:12, Joshua 15:13–15, Judges 1:20. Wilson conjectures that Burnet was satirically called "Young Rowley" in "The Lovers' Session" (June, 1687). Since Rowley was Charles's stallion, the allusion suggests Burnet's virility, as do the lines from Dryden's *The Hind and the Panther: Part Two*. His muscular calves, revealed by his clergyman's knee-breeches, were often cited as an attraction to female converts.

23. Cf. Vieth, *ARP*, 189–91.

24. HMC *Ormonde* n.s. 5:242. Rochester may well have been Cooke's informant. The two men had a longtime, close friendship. Cooke witnessed the Rochesters' Indenture in 1672 and he was named in Rochester's Will as the chief financial agent to the Wilmot heirs, a duty he took very seriously. Cf. Prinz, *Rochester*, 299; HMC *Rutland*, 59.

25. *Familiar Letters*, 1:47.

26. Lord, *Anthology*, 184–96.

27. *Treasury Books 1679–80*, 284.

28. Aubrey, *Brief Lives*, 156. Aubrey planned a memorial volume of poetic tributes to Hobbes. Aubrey told Anthony Wood in a letter of March 27, 1680: "I have engaged the Earle of Dorset, my Ld John Vaughan to write verses, and they will engage my L^d

Mulgrave, & the Earl of Rochester. I first engaged Mr. Dreyden & Mr. Waller, who will try he tells me for they were old acquaintances, but he's something afrayed of the Ecclesiastiques." Bodleian Library, *Ballard Ms. 14*, f.131, quoted in Harris, *Sackville*, 80.

29. Cf. Luttrell, *Brief History*, 1:30: "Mr. Hobbs of Malmsbury died the middle of this month being 92-years old: he was a very learned man, but broacht severall pernicious principles destructive to religion and government."

30. Winn, *Dryden*, 326–27. Cf. Jack Verney's letter to Sir Ralph: "there is a satyr come out against the men of the town, wherein two of your friends, Rochester and the Chancellor, are paid off, but 'tis very long and thought to be by Dryden." HMC *Seventh Report Appendix*, 1:477b. Cf. Ward, *Dryden*, 144; Lord, *Anthology*, 184–85. Lord cites Mulgrave and Dryden as co-authors; Winn puts the *Essay* under Mulgrave in his Index but entertains the possibility in the text that Dryden may have written some passages.

31. Lord sums up the evidence pro and con in *POAS*, 396–401, and decides: "At any rate the available evidence still leaves Rochester very much in the running as instigator of the famous Rose Alley ambuscade." Dryden's biographers are not so sure. Charles Ward gives a cautious account of the event and concludes: "But in the absence of any evidence, it is best to label the Rose Alley affair 'unsolved,' " 143–44. James Winn reviews all the data, considers the cases against Lady Portsmouth, Pembroke, Rochester, and anonymous Whig enemies (i.e., Shaftesbury) and finds that against Portsmouth the strongest but says that Dryden's later career does not suggest that he placed the blame on any of them. Winn, Dryden, 325–29, 593–94.

32. Wood's account is also wrong about the date and place of the beating.

33. Luttrell, *Historical Relation*, 1:30.

34. Cf. Winn, *Dryden*, 594. Sophia Bulkeley's fury was genuine, however. One might reasonably add the name of her husband Henry Bulkeley, always prone to violence, to the list of possible perpetrators.

35. Rochester confessed to "giving lip-service to morality for selfish gain, professing friendship to those he hated, lying to seduce women, defaming innocent persons, spreading false reports out of revenge or ill-will, causing quarrels, and deceiving just creditors." Burnet, in Farley-Hills, *Heritage*, 56.

36. Cf. Winn, *Dryden*, 328.

37. BL, Harl. Ms. 7003, f. 239: "I am now at Battersy & have binn this weeke here, wounder not if you receive few letters from mee, & bee satisfied wth this that I thinke continually of you. . . ."

38. Hatton Family, *Correspondence*, 1:216.

39. Luttrell, *Historical Relation*, 1:32. Cf. Elias Mengel, *POAS*, 2:312; *JHL*, XIII.

40. Van Lennep, *London Stage*, 284.

41. Luttrell, *Historical Relation*, 1:35.

42. Ibid., 1:5. A lampoon in 1681, "An Heroic Poem," called Douglas "Whig Arran" and a Scottish Fool and referred to his "notorious face." Mengel, *POAS*, 2:230–31.

43. *CSPD 1679–80*, 422–23.

44. HMC *Ormonde*, n.s. 4:261–62

45. The troubled career of Sir Edward Seymour (1633–1708) has been chronicled by Witcombe, Ogg, and Browning. From November 1680 until January 1681, Seymour was threatened with impeachment by Parliament but was saved when Charles prorogued in his customary manner.

46. *CSPD 1679–80*, 409; Harris, *Sackville*, 215. In time, a portrait of his "dear Lord Rochester" at Knole, Sackville's estate in Kent, acquired a label, "Died repentant after a profligate life." Sackville-West, *Knole*, 149.

47. Details of the Conway-Pawlet-Arran business and Rochester's part in it are recorded in HMC *Hastings II*, 389–90; *CSPD 1679–80*, 409–10, 419–20, 422–23.

48. Burnet, in Farley-Hills, 56.

49. *Familiar Letters*, 1:14.

50. G. E. C., *Baronetage*, 7:644. The infant died after 22 weeks and was buried at Battersea.

51. Burnet, *Passages*, 79.

Chapter 22

1. According to Verney, *Verney Papers* (1925), 3:195–96, Radcliffe earned fees of £4,000 p.a. and represented Buckinghamshire in Parliament. Thomas Hearne recorded his death in 1714. Radcliffe left an estate of £140,000. Hearne wrote: "He was a Yorkshire Man and his Father a Plebian. He had little or no Learning, but had a strange Sagacity, and was so wonderfully successful in his Practise of Physick, that he never had his equal, by which means he got such a vast sum of Money." He left £40,000 to Oxford to build the Radcliffe Camera. Hearne, *Remains*, 154–55.

2. Parsons, *Sermon*, 22–24.

3. Dr. Thomas Short (1635–1685) was "the most approved & famous Physitian of all his Majesties Doctors." Evelyn, *Diary*, 420. Short was honored by his fellow physicians with a volume of poems, puns, and epigrams in 1665, *In Lauream*. In 1675 he became a Fellow in the College of Physicians by Royal Mandate. About the same time, he converted to Catholicism. *DNB*, 52:154. See *On the Universally Lamented Death of the Incomparable Dr. Short*.

4. Verney, *Verney Papers* (1925), 2:336. Asses' milk was a form of yogurt.

5. Burnet, *Passages*, 79.

6. Ibid., 64.

7. Parsons, *Sermon*, 22–24.

8. Blount, *Works*, 117–27.

9. Burnet, *Passages*, 56–57, 59–65, 78–79.

10. Gibbon, *The Decline and Fall*, 1:366.

11. Parsons, *Sermon*, 22 ff.

12. BL, Additional Mss. 6269, f. 33.

13. Verney, *Verney Papers* (1925), 2:336 ff.

14. Burnet, *Some Unpublished Letters*, 32.

15. Prinz, *Rochester*, 300.

16. BL, Harl. Ms. 7003, ff. 81–82.

17. The pious distortion of Rochester's final days is evident here. In fact, Dr. Short converted to Catholicism five years before he attended Rochester.

18. BL, Additional Mss. 6269, f. 33v.

19. Ribble-rabble: (1602) "Confused, meaningless language; rigmarole," *Shorter OED*, 2:1734.

20. Rochester's remorse for his choice of court life came from his realization that it had involved "the *service of sin* and *the lusts of the flesh, of th* [sic] *eye, and the pride of life*." Parsons, *Sermon*, 24, 27.

21. BL, Additional Mss. 6269, f. 35.

22. Prinz, *Rochester*, 297–98.

23. BL, Additional Mss. 6269, f. 36.

24. Parsons, *Sermon*, 2, 25–26.

25. Aubrey, *Lives*, 321.

26. Prinz, *Rochester*, 301.

27. The original letter is in the Houghton Library, Harvard MS. pf. Eng. 1063, catalogued under Burnet. Treglown glosses the phrase "att that time etc." as "an interesting example of the hold the Prayer Book liturgy had on Rochester's memory." Since 1604 this version of Ezekiel 18:27 had been read in the first sentence before the Morning Prayer. Rochester would have recited this phrase daily at Burford Free School. Treglown says the letter was signed by Rochester but written by his mother. The Old Countess's inimitable writing never changed between 1641 and 1686; the hand in the Remonstrance is decidedly *not* hers. It appears rather to be Lady Rochester's hasty penmanship.

28. "nor was the King pleased with my being sent for by Wilmot, Earl of Rochester, when he died. He fancied that he [Wilmot] had told me many things, of which I might make an ill use; yet he had read the book that I wrote concerning him [the *Passages*], and spoke well of it." Burnet, *History*, 333–35.

29. BL, Additional Mss. 6269, f. 36v.

30. Bodleian Library, Ms. Ballard 10. Cf. Prinz, *Rochester*, 298; Rochester, *Letters* (Treglown), 245–46. Dr. Thomas Pierce (1622–1691) had been a Calvinist in his younger days, then an Anglican tutor to Robert Spencer, the future Earl of Sunderland. He was a Chaplain to Charles II after 1660 and, from 1661 to 1672, President of Magdalene College.

31. BL, Additional Mss 29, 583, f. 237.

32. Burnet, *Passages*, 65. Cf. Parsons, *Sermon*, 29–31: His "Kindness to his good Lady, beyond expression . . . and to his Children, obliging them with all the endearments that a good Husband or a tender Father could bestow."

33. Burnet, *Unpublished Letters*, 41.

34. Verney, *Verney Papers* (1925), 2:336.

35. Parsons's sermon extolled Rochester's "extraordinary fervent Devotions" and "frequent Prayers of his own": for the King, the Church and Nation, "some particular relations," and then all mankind. "towards the end of his sickness [he] would heartily desire *God to pardon his informities, if he should not be so wakeful* and *intent through the whole duty as he wished to be. . . .*" Parsons, *Sermon*, 27.

36. Burnet expounded at length on Rochester's "ill Habit of *Swearing*" before his conversion.

37. Burnet seems not to have detected the unorthodox sophistry in this logic.

38. BL, Additional Mss 4262, f. 232.

Afterwards

1. This and further passages from the Countess' letters are taken from the University of Rochester MS D.26.

2. This and further passages from Burnet's letters come from Burnet, "Letters," 224–30.

3. Wharton may not have had the miniature of Rochester in a "shagreen" case. (Shagreen was untanned leather with a granular surface.) On September 2, 1682, Gilbert Burnet wrote to Anne Wharton:

> I have had brought me this morning the most acceptable present that was ever made me in my whole life, from the hand in the whole world I value most: I suppose you guess that I mean the Earl of Rochester's picture. . . . I shall

> never weary of looking on it, both to preserve the memory of one whose ashes
> I shall always honor and to offer up the highest acknowledgments possible to
> her in whom the best part of him lives to advantage.

The miniature, presumably, is that in the Victoria and Albert Museum collection, reportedly missing since 1989.

4. The series of events is given in *JHL* for 1701.

5. Ditchley Park served as the center for British counter-intelligence during World War II and is now an Anglo-American conference center.

BIBLIOGRAPHY

Primary Sources

Adderbury Church Parish Register.

Alcock, Thomas. *The Famous Pathologist or The Noble Mountebank.* Nottingham University Miscellany no 1. Nottingham, 1961.

Alumni Cantabrigiensis. Part I: To 1751. Edited by J. A. Venn. Birmingham (U.K.) Central Library.

Aretino, Pietro. *Selected Letters.* Translated by George Bull. Penguin, 1976.

Aubrey, John. *Aubrey's Brief Lives.* Edited by Oliver Lawson Dick. Ann Arbor, Mich., 1957.

Balfour, Andrew. *Letters Write to a Friend, By the Learned and Judicious Sir Andrew Balfour, M.D. Containing Excellent Directions and for Travelling thro' FRANCE AND ITALY. With Many and Judicious Remarks and Observations Made by, in His Voyages thro' These Countreys.* Edinburgh, 1700.

Behn, Aphra. "On the Death of the Late Earl of Rochester." In *Critical Heritage,* edited by David Farley-Hills, 103.

———. *The Works of Aphra Behn.* Edited by Montague Summers. London, 1915.

Blandford, Walter. *Articles of Visitation and Inquiry.* Oxford, 1674.

Blount, Charles. *Miscellaneous Works.* Edited by Charles Gildon. London, 1695.

Borgman, Albert S. *Thomas Shadwell: His Life and Comedies.* New York, 1928.

Britannia Rediviva. Oxford, 1660.

British Library. Additional Manuscripts.

———. Harleian Manuscripts.

———. Sloane Manuscripts.

Browne, Dr. John. *Adenochoiradelogia.* London, 1676.

Bunyan, John. "Meditation XXVII, On the Post Boy," from *Divine Emblems or Temporal Things Spiritualized.* Reprinted by Edna Johnson et al. in *Anthology of Children's Literature.* 4th ed. New York, 1970.

Burke, Sir John Bernard. *A Genealogic and Heraldic History of the Extinct and Dormant Baronetcies of England, Ireland, and Scotland.* Baltimore, 1977.

Burnet, Gilbert. *History of His Own Times.* Oxford, 1897.

———. "Letters to Anne Wharton." In *Letters between the Rev. James Grainger . . .,* edited by James Grainger, 224–30. London, 1805.

———. *Some Passages in the Life and Death of John Earl of Rochester: Written by His Own Direction on His Deathbed.* Oxford, 1680. Reprinted in *Critical Heritage,* edited by David Farley-Hills, 56.

———. *Some Unpublished Letters.* London, 1907.

———. *A Supplement to the History.*

Butler, Samuel. *Characters.* Edited by Charles Daves. Princeton, N.J., 1970.

Capel, Arthur Earl of Essex. *Selections from the Correspondence.* . . . Camden Third Series, 24. London, 1913.

Chamberlayne, Edward. *Angliae Notitia, or The Present State of England.* 5th ed. London, 1671.

Charleton, Walter. *Epicurus' Morals.* London, 1656.

Choisy, abbé de. *Memoirs.* New York, 1930.

———. *Mémoires de l'abbé de Choisy habillé en femme.* Paris, 1927.

Cibber, Colley. *An Apology for the Life of Mr. Colley Cibber, Comedian, and Late Patentee of the Theatre-Royal.* 2 vols. Edited by Robert W. Lowe. London, 1889.

Clarendon, Edward Hyde Earl of. *The History of the Rebellion and Civil Wars in England, Begun in the Year 1641.* Oxford, 1888.

———. *The Life of Clarendon by Himself.* Oxford, 1956.

———. *Selections.* The World's Classics, 544. London, 1968.

Collins's Peerage of England. Edited by E. Bridger. 1812.

Collinson, John. *History and Antiquities of Somerset.* 3 vols. Bath, 1791.

Committee for Compounding Cases, 1647–June 1650.

Compounding Proceedings, 1643–1660.

A Copie of a Paper Written by the Late Dutches of York, St. James's Aug. 20th. 1670. BL, Miscellaneous Pamphlets.

Crowne, John. *The Dramatic Works of John Crowne.* Edited by James Maidment and W. H. Logan. London, 1873.

———. *The History of Charles the Eighth of France, or The Invasion of Naples by the French.* London, 1672.

G. E. C. *Complete Baronetage.* London, 1904.

———. *The Complete Peerage.* Edited by V. Gibbs, 1910–1949.

Dennis, John. *The Critical Works of John Dennis.* Edited by Edward N. Hooker. Baltimore, 1939–1943.

Dering, Sir Edward. *Parliament Diary, 1670–73.* London, 1940.

Downes, John. *Roscius Anglicanus.* London, 1708.

Dryden, John. *The Conquest of Granada by the Spaniards. In Two Parts. Acted at the Theatre-Royall.* London, 1672.

———. *Essays.* Edited by W. P. Ker. 2 vols. Oxford, 1900.

———. *The Kind Keeper, or Mr. Limberham.* London, 1678.

———. *The Plays of John Dryden.* Edited by John Loftus et al. California, 1978.

———. *The Poems and Fables of John Dryden.* Edited by James Kinsley. London, 1962.

———. *The Works of John Dryden.* Edited by H. T. Swedenberg et al. 20 vols. Berkeley, Calif., 1956–2000.

Eacherd, John. *The Grounds and Occasions of the Contempt of Clergy.* London, 1670.

Elizabeth Charlotte, Princess Palatine and Duchess of Orleans. *Letters from Liselotte.* Translated and edited by Maria Kroll. London, 1970.

"Ephelia." *Female Poems on Several Occasions. Written by Ephelia.* London, 1679. Facsimile edition, 1993.

Epicurus. *Letters, Principle Doctrines, and Vatican Sayings.* The Library of Liberal Arts. New York, 1964.

Etherege, George. *The Letters of Sir George Etherege.* Edited by Frederick Bracher. California, 1974.

Etherege, George. *Poems.* Edited by James Thorpe. Princeton, N.J., 1963.

Evagrius. *History of the Church.* London, 1663.

Evelyn, John. *Diary.* Edited by E. S. de Beer. 6 vols. Oxford, 1955.

Evelyn, John. *A Devotionarie Book of John Evelyn of Wotton, 1620–1706*. Introduction by Walter Frere. London, 1936.

———. *Diary*. Oxford Standard Authors Edition. Oxford, 1959.

A Faithful Narrative of the Proceedings in a Late Affair between the Rev. Mr. John Swinton, and Mr. George Baker, both of Wadham College, Oxford . . . to Which is Prefix'd, a Particular Account of the Proceedings against Robert Thistlethwayte for a Sodomitical Attempt upon Mr. W. French, Commoner of the Same College. London, 1739.

Fane, Francis. *Love in the Dark*. London, 1675.

Fell, John. *The Privilege of Oxford*. Oxford, 1647.

The Foundation of the Universitie of Oxford. London, 1651.

Fulman, W. *Academiae Oxoniensis Notitia*. Oxford, 1665.

A Genuine Letter from the Earl of Rochester to Nell Gwyn. Undated pamphlet.

Gepp, Francis J. *Adderbury*. Adderbury, n.d.

Giffard, Francis. *The Wicked Petition, or Israel's Sinfulness in Asking a King, Explained in a Sermon*. London, 1681.

Gramont, Philippe, Comte de. See Hamilton, Anthony.

Halifax, George Savile First Marquis of. *The Complete Works*. Edited by Walter Raleigh. Oxford, 1912.

———. *Savile Correspondence: Letters to and from Henry Savile, Esq.* Edited by W. D. Cooper. London, 1858; reprint New York, 1968.

Hall, Rev. Francis (Franciscus Linus). *Explication of the Diall, etc. 1669*. London, 1673.

Hamilton, Anthony. *Memoirs of Count Gramont*. Edited and with notes by Sir Walter Scott. New York, n.d.

———. *Memoirs of the Comte de Gramont*. Edited and translated by Peter Quennell. New York, 1930.

Harris, Brice. *Charles Sackville, Sixth Earl of Dorset: Patron and Poet of the Restoration*. Urbana, Ill., 1940.

Hatton Family. *Correspondence of the Hatton Family*. Edited by E. M. Thompson. 1878.

Hearne, Thomas. *Reliquiae*. 1869.

———. *The Remains of Thomas Hearne*. Edited and with an Introduction by John Buchanan-Brown. Centaur Classics. 1966.

———. *Remarks and Collections of Thomas Hearne*. Edited by C. E. Doble. 11 vols. Oxford, 1884–1918.

A History of Wiltshire. See Pugh, Ralph Bernard.

Hobbes, Thomas. *De Cive*. London, 1651.

———. *Hobbes's Leviathan, with an Essay by the Late W. G. P. Smith*. Oxford, 1909.

———. *Leviathan*. London, 1651.

Hodge, N. *Medical Commonplace Book*. In BL, Sloane Ms. 810.

Horace. *Satires, Epistles, and Ars Poetica*. Translated by H. Rushton Fairclough. London, 1970.

Howell, T. B., ed. *State Trials*. London and Middlesex Archeological Society, 1935.

Hutchinson, Lucy. *Memoirs of the Life of Colonel Hutchinson*. London, 1995.

Interregnum Acts and Ordinances, 1642–1660.

Irish State Papers, 1611–1614, 1615–1625.

Kenyon, John P. *The Stuart Constitution 1603–1688: Documents and Commentary*. Cambridge, 1966.

Langbain, Gerard. *The Lives and Characters of the English Dramatick Poets: Continued Down to This Time by Charles Gildon*. London, 1699.

Lee, Nathaniel. *The Works of Nathaniel Lee*. Edited by T. B. Stroup and A. L. Cooke. 2 vols. New Brunswick, N.J., 1955.

Lesly, George. *Sodom's Flames*. London, 1676.

Lessey, Thomas. "Were I a Sp'rt, to chuse for my own share." BL, Sloane Ms. 1458, f. 43r.

Library of Shakespeare's Birthplace. Fane Manuscript.

Lloyd, David. *Memoires*. London, 1668.

London County Council. *Survey of London*. Vol. 4: *The Parish of Chelsea*.

———. *Survey of London*. Vol. 13: *The Parish of St. Margaret*.

Luttrell, Narcissus. *A Brief Historical Relation of State Affairs from September 1678 to April 1714*. Oxford, 1857.

Marshall, Edward. *The Early History of Woodstock Manor*. London, 1873.

Marvell, Andrew. *The Poems and Letters of Andrew Marvell*. Edited by H. M. Margoliouth. 2 vols. Oxford, 1952.

The Memoirs of the Earl of Rochester. London, 1739.

Motteux, Peter (?). *The Rape of Europa by Jupiter*. Augustan Reprint Society, 208. Los Angeles: Clark Memorial Library, 1981.

Needham, Francis, ed. *Welbeck Miscellany*, No. 2 (1934).

Nottingham University Library. Portland MS. PwV 31.

Ogilby, John. *Brittania Vol. I or an Illustration of ye Kingdom of England and dominion of Wales*. ____, 1675.

———. *The Entertainment of His Most Excellent Majestie Charles II in His Passage through the City of London to His Coronation*. London, 1662.

Oldham, John. *Collected Works*. London, 1684–85.

———. *Poems and Translations*. London, 1683.

———. *Some New Pieces*. London, 1684.

Oldys, William. *Biographica Britannica*. 3 vols. London, 1750.

On the Universally Lamented Death of the Incomparable Dr. Short, a Pindaric. London, 1685.

Otway, Thomas. *Friendship in Fashion*. London, 1676.

———. *The Works of Thomas Otway: Plays, Poems, and Love-Letters*. Edited by J. C. Ghosh. 2 vols. Oxford, 1932.

Ovid. *Ovid's Epistles, Translated by Several Hands*. London, 1680.

———. *Heroides and Amores*. Edited and translated by Grant Showerman. Loeb Classical Library. London, 1963.

———. *Metamorphoses*. Translated by Frank Justus Miller. Loeb Classical Library. 2 vols. Cambridge, Mass., 1966.

Oxford. *Alumni Oxoniensis, 1500–1714*, Early Series, 4.

Oxford University Bodleian Library. *Calendar of the Clarendon State Papers Preserved in the Bodleian Library*. Oxford, 1876.

Oxford University Bodleian Library. Clarendon Manuscripts.

Parsons, Robert. *A Sermon Preached at the Funeral of John Earl of Rochester*. Oxford, 1680.

Pepys, Samuel. *Charles II's Escape from Worcester: A Collection of Narratives Assembled by Samuel Pepys*. Edited by William Matthews. Berkeley, Calif., 1966.

Pepys, Samuel. *The Diary of Samuel Pepys*. Edited by Robert Latham and William Matthews. 11 vols. London, 1970–83.

———. *The Shorter Pepys*. Selected and edited by Robert Latham. Berkeley and Los Angeles, 1985.

Poems on Affairs of State: Augustan Satirical Verse, 1660–1714. 7 vols. Edited by George de F. Lord et al. New Haven, Conn., 1963–75.

Pope, Alexander. *Poetical Works.* London, 1966.

Prinz, Johannes. *John Wilmot, Earl of Rochester: His Life and Writings.* Leipzig, 1927.

———. *Rochesteriana, Being Some Anecdotes Concerning John Wilmot Earl of Rochester.* Leipzig, 1926.

Privy Council Acts, June 1623–March 1625.

Pugh, Ralph Bernard. *History of Oxfordshire.* Victoria History of the Counties of England. Oxford, 1970.

———. *History of Wiltshire.* Victoria History of the Counties of England. London, 1953.

Radcliffe, Alexander, *The Ramble, Antiheroick Poem, Together with Some Terrestial Hymns and Carnal Ejaculations.* London, 1682.

———. *The Works of Alexander Radcliffe.* 1696. Scholars' Facsimiles, 1981.

Ravenscroft, Edward. *Scaramouch a Philosopher, Harlequin a School-Boy, Bravo, Merchant, and Magician: A Comedy after the Italian Manner.* London, 1677.

Rochester, John Wilmot Earl of. *The Collected Works of John Wilmot, Earl of Rochester.* Edited by John Hayward. London, 1926.

———. *The Complete Poems of John Wilmot, Earl of Rochester.* Edited by David M. Vieth. New Haven, Conn., 1968.

———. *Familiar Letters: Written by the Right Honourable John Late Earl of Rochester and Several Other Persons of Honour and Quality.* Edited by Tom Brown. 2 vols. London, 1697.

———. *John Wilmot, Earl of Rochester: The Complete Works.* Edited by Frank Ellis. Harmondsworth, 1994.

———. *The Letters of John Wilmot Earl of Rochester.* Edited by Jeremy Treglown. Chicago, 1980.

———. *Poems by John Wilmot, Earl of Rochester.* Edited by V. de Sola Pinto. London, 1953.

———. *The Poems of John Wilmot, Earl of Rochester.* Edited by Keith Walker. Oxford, 1984.

———. *Poems on Several Occasions by the Right Honourable E. of R—.* "Antwerp," 1680.

———. *Poems on Several Occasions. Written by a Late Person of Honour.* London, 1685.

———. *Poems on Several Occasions.* Facsimile, edited by James Thorpe. Princeton, N.J., 1950.

———. *Poems etc. on Several Occasions: With Valentinian, a Tragedy.* London, 1691.

———. *Valentinian, a Tragedy.* As 'tis Alter'd by the Late Earl of Rochester. London, 1685.

———. *The Works of John Wilmot Earl of Rochester.* Edited by Harold Love. Oxford, 1999.

Rochester-Savile. *The Rochester-Savile Letters, 1671–1680.* Edited by J. H. Wilson. Columbus, Ohio, 1941.

The Royal Letter Book. Edited by Herbert Van Thal. London, 1937.

Rymer, Thomas. "Preface" to Rochester, *Poems on Several Occasions.* In *Critical Heritage,* edited by David Farley-Hills, 169.

Sackville, Charles, Earl of Dorset. *The Poems of Charles Sackville, Sixth Earl of Dorset.* Edited by Brice Harris. New York, 1979.

Saurius, Andreas. *Conflagratio Sodomae: Novum tragicum.* Strasbourg, 1602.

Sedley, Sir Charles. *The Poetical and Dramatic Works of Sir Charles Sedley*. Edited by V. de Sola Pinto. 2 vols. New York, London, 1928.

Seward, William. *Biographiana*. London, 1699.

Shadwell, Thomas. *The Complete Works of Thomas Shadwell*. Edited by Montague Summers. 5 vols. London, 1927.

———. *The Medal of John Bays*. London, 1682.

———. *The Tory-Poets, a Satyre*. London, 1682.

Sheffield, John, Earl of Mulgrave. *Works*. 2 vols. London, 1722.

Short, Thomas (subject). *In Lauream*. London, 1665.

———. *On the Universally Lamented Death of the Incomparable Dr. Short: A Pindaric*. London, 1685.

A Short Catalogue of Books in the Library of Wadham College. London, 1929.

Sibbald, Robert. *Auctarius Musaei Balfouriana. . . .* Edinburgh, 1697.

———. *Memoria Balfouriana*. Edinburgh, 1699.

Smith, Alexander. *The School of Venus*. London, 1716.

Sodom Fair: or, The Market of the Man of Sin, a Treatise Very Useful and Necessary for All Young English Papists Who Intend to Take Holy Orders, or Travel through Italy. . . . London, 1688.

Spelsbury *Church Warden's Book*.

Spence, Joseph. *Observations, Anecdotes, and Characters*. Oxford, 1966.

Spingarn, J. E. *Critical Essays of the Seventeenth Century*. 3 vols. Oxford, 1908.

United Kingdom Official Publications.

  Calendar of State Papers. Domestic Series.

  Calendar of State Papers. Venetian Series.

  Historical Manuscripts Commission Publications.

  Irish State Papers.

  Journal of the House of Commons.

  Journal of the House of Lords.

  Proceedings of the Committee for Compounding State Trials.

  Statutes at Large.

University of Rochester Library. Manuscripts D.26.

Van Lennep, William, ed. *The London Stage 1660–1800*. Pt. I: 1600–1700. Introduction by E. L. Avery and A. H. Scouten. Carbondale, Ill., 1965.

Verney, Frances, and Parthenope Verney. *The Verney Papers*. 1892 and 1925.

The Victoria History of the Counties of England: Somerset. Ed. William Page. London, 1911.

Vieth, David M. *Rochester Studies, 1925–1982: An Annotated Bibliography*. New York & London, 1984.

Wadham College Registers. Pt. I. Oxford, 1889.

Walker, Obadiah. *Of Education, Especially of Young Gentlemen. In Two Parts*. Oxford, 1673.

Walpole, Horace. *A Catalogue of the Royal and Noble Authors of England, with Lists of Their Works*. Strawberry Hill, 1758.

Westminster School. *Commemoration of the Bicentenary of the Death of Richard Busby, Nov. 18th 1895*. London, 1895.

Wharton, Anne. *The Surviving Works of Anne Wharton*. Edited by G. Greer and S. Hastings. Stump Cross, 1997.

Wharton, Thomas. *Memoirs of the Life of the Most Noble Thomas Wharton late Marquess of Wharton . . . To Which Is Added His Lordship's Character by Sir Richard Steele*. London, 1715.

Whitcombe, Dennis Trevor. *Charles II and the Cavalier House of Commons 1663–1674*. New York, 1966.

Whitehall, Robert. *Carmen gratulatorium Olivero Cromwell in Protectorem inaugurato*. London, 1653.

————. *Carmen Onomasticon Gratulatorium Ricardo Cromwell*. London, 1657.

————. *The English Recabite: Or, a defyance to Bacchus and all his Works*. Oxford, 1681.

————. *Exasticon Ieron, Sive Iconum . . . Being an Epigrammatical Explanation of the Most Remarkable Stories throughout the Old and New Testament after Each Sculpture or Cut*. Oxford, 1677.

————. *Technepoligama: or, The Marriage of Armes and Arts, July 12, 1651. Being an Accompt of the Act at Oxon. to a Friend*. London, 1651.

————. *Viro, Favore Regio, et Meritis suis Honoratissimo, Amplissimoque Domino, Edvardo Hide . . . Carmen Congratulatorium*. Oxford, 1661.

————. *The Woman's Right Proved False*. 1674. Reprinted in Margaret Ezell, *The Patriarch's Wife*, Chapel Hill, N.C., 1987, 205–25.

Wiltshire Visitation Pedigrees 1623. Vols. 105–6.

Wiseman, Robert. *Severall Chirurgical Treatises*. London, 1676.

Wood, Anthony. *Athenae Oxoniensis*. Oxford, 1691–92.

————. *The Life and Times of Anthony Wood, Antiquary of Oxford, 1632–1695, as Described by Himself*. Edited by Andrew Clark. Oxford, 1981–1900. (5 vols.)

Woodford, Samuel. "Ode to the Memory of Rochester 1680." In *Critical Heritage*, edited by David Farley-Hills, 116.

Wotton, Henry. *An Essay on the Education of Children, in the First Rudiments of Learning*. London, 1670.

Wycherley, William. *The Plays of William Wycherley*. Edited by Arthur Friedman. Oxford, 1979.

Wysdome, Simon. *Constitucions of the Burford Grammar School*. n.d.

Secondary Sources: Books and Selected Articles

Abraham, Claude. *Pierre Corneille*. New York, 1972.

Advice-to-a-Painter Poems 1633–1856: An Annotated Finding List. Introduction by Mary Tom Osborne. Austin, Texas, 1949.

Andrews, Allen. *The Royal Whore: Barbara Villiers, Countess of Castlemaine*. Philadelphia, 1970.

Armisted, J. M. *Nathaniel Lee*. New York, 1979.

Artaud, Antonin. *The Theater and Its Double*. Translated by Mary Caroline Richards. New York, 1958.

Ashbee, Henry Spencer (Pisanus Fraxi). *Centuria Librorum Absconditorum*. London, 1879.

————. *Index Librorum Prohibitorium*. London, 1878.

Ashley, Maurice. *General Monck*. Totowa, N.J., 1977.

Bailey, Cyril. *The Greek Atomists and Epicurus*. Oxford, 1928.

Bailey, D. S. *Homosexuality and the Western Christian Tradition*. London, 1955.

Barber, Richard. *Samuel Pepys Esquire*. London, 1970.

Barbour, Violet. *Henry Bennet, Earl of Arlington*. London, 1914.

Barker, George. *Memoir of Richard Busby*. London, 1895.

Beddard, R. A. "The Restoration Church." In *The Restored Monarchy, 1660–1688*, edited by J. R. Jones, 155–66. London, Macmillan, 1979.

Beesley, Alfred. *History of Banbury.* London, 1841.

Boswell, Eleanore. *The Restoration Court Stage, 1660–1702, with a Particular Account of the Production of Calisto.* New York, 1966.

Boswell, John. *Christianity, Social Tolerance, and Homosexuality.* Chicago, 1980.

Braudy, Leo. "Remembering Masculinity: Premature Ejaculation Poetry of the Seventeenth Century." *Modern Language Quarterly* 33, no. 11 (1994): 177–201.

Brooks, Harold F. "The Date of Rochester's 'Timon.' " *N&Q* 174 (28 May 1938): 384–85.

———. "The 'Imitation' in English Poetry." *RES* 25 (April 1949): 124–40.

Brown, F. C. *Elkanah Settle: His Life and Works.* Chicago, 1910.

Browning, Andrew. *Thomas Osborne, Earl of Danby and Duke of Leeds.* Glasgow, 1944–1951.

Bulliet, C. J. *Venus Castina: Famous Female Impersonators Celestial and Human.* New York, 1928, 1956.

Burford Grammar School, 1571–1971. Burford, 1971.

Burke's *Peerage* (1883). London, 1826–2001.

Cameron, W. J. *New Light on Aphra Behn.* Auckland, 1979.

Carver, Larry D. "Rascal before the Lord: Rochester's Religious Rhetoric." *SEL* 9 (Fall 1982): 155–69.

Castle, Terry. "The Culture of Travesty, Sexuality and Masquerade in Eighteenth-Century England." In *Sexual Underworlds of the Enlightenment,* edited by George S. Rousseau and Roy Porter. Chapel Hill, N.C., 1988.

———. *Masquerade and Civilization: The Carnivalesque in Eighteenth-Century English Culture and Fiction.* Stanford, Calif., 1986.

Chambers, James. *Christopher Wren.* Phoenix Hills, U.K., 1998.

Chapman, Hester. *Great Villiers: A Study of George Villiers, Second Duke of Buckingham, 1628–1687.* London, 1949.

The Church of Saint John Baptist Burford. Gloucester, 1968.

Clark, A. F. B. *Boileau and the French Classical Critics in England (1660–1830).* Paris, 1925.

Clark, John R. "Satiric Singing: An Example from Rochester." *The English Record* 24 (Fall 1973): 16–20.

Clarke, Walter H. *The Story of Adderbury Parish Church.* Adderbury, 1965.

Clifton, Robin. "Fear of Popery." In *Origins of the English Civil War,* edited by Conrad Russell, 144–67. London, 1983.

Cope, Kevin. "The Infinite Perimeter: Human Nature and Ethical Mediation in Six Restoration Writers." *Restoration* 5, no. 2 (Fall 1981): 58–75.

Davies, C. S. L., and Jane Garnett, eds. *Wadham College.* Oxford, 1944.

Dictionary of National Biography. Edited by Sir Leslie Stephen and Sir Edward Lee.

Dover, K. J. *Greek Homosexuality.* Cambridge, Mass., 1978.

Duffy, Maureen. *The Passionate Shepherdess.* London, 1977.

Dutton, Ralph. *Sir Christopher Wren.* London, 1969.

Easthope, Antony. *What a Man's Gotta Do: The Masculine Myth in Popular Culture.* Boston, 1990.

Edmond, Mary. *Rare Sir William Davenant.* Manchester, 1987.

Elias, Richard. "Political Satire in *Sodom.*" *SEL* 18 (Summer 1978): 423–38.

Elkin, P. K. *The Augustan Defence of Satire.* Oxford, 1973.

Everett, Barbara. "The Sense of Nothing." In *Spirit of Wit,* edited by Jeremy Treglown.

Ezell, Margaret J. M. *The Patriarch's Wife.* Chapel Hill, 1987.

Fabricant, Carole. "Rochester's World of Imperfect Enjoyment." *JEGP* 73 (July 1974): 338–50.

Falk, Bernard. *The Way of the Montagus.* London and New York, 1947.

Falkus, Christopher. *The Life and Times of Charles II.* Garden City, N.Y., 1972.

Farley-Hills, David. *The Bevolence of Laughter: Comic Poetry of the Commonwealth and Restoration.* Totowa, N.J., 1974.

———. *Rochester's Poetry.* Totowa, N.J., 1978.

Farley-Hills, David, ed. *Rochester: The Critical Heritage.* London, 1972.

Fisher, Nicholas. "Love in the Ayre: Rochester's Songs and Their Music," in Fisher, ed., *That Second Bottle*, ed. Nicholas Fisher. Manchester, 2000.

Fisher, Nicholas, ed. *That Second Bottle: Essays on John Wilmot, Earl of Rochester.* Manchester, 2000.

Foucault, Michel. *The Uses of Pleasure.* New York, 1985.

Fowler, H. W. *A Dictionary of Modern English Usage.* Oxford, 1952.

Frantz, David O. *Festum Voluptatis: A Study of Renaissance Erotica.* Ohio State, 1989.

Fraser, Antonia. *Cromwell the Lord Protector.* New York, 1974.

———. *Royal Charles.* New York, 1979.

Fujimura, Thomas H. "Rochester's 'Satyr against Mankind': An Analysis." *Studies in Philology* 55 (October 1958): 576–90.

Gaines, James F. *The Moliere Encyclopedia.* Westport, Conn., 2002.

Garber, Marjorie. *Vested Interests: Cross-Dressing & Cultural Anxiety.* New York and London, 1992.

Geyl, Pieter. *The Netherlands in the Seventeenth Century, Part One: 1609–1648.* London, 1961.

Gibbon, Edward. *The Decline and Fall of the Roman Empire.* 3 vols. New York, 1946.

Gill, James E. "Mind against Itself: Theme and Structure in Rochester's *Satyr against Reason and Mankind*," in *Texas Studies in Language and Literature* 23 (Winter 1981): 555–76.

Gilmore, David D. *Manhood in the Making: Cultural Concepts of Masculinity.* New Haven, Conn., 1990.

Goreau, Angeline. *Reconstructing Aphra: A Social Biography.* New York, 1980.

Greene, Graham. *Lord Rochester's Monkey: Being the Life of John Wilmot, Second Earl of Rochester.* New York, 1974.

Greer, Germaine. "How to Invent a Poet," *Times Literary Supplement* (June 25, 1993), 7–8.

Gretton, M. Sturge. *Burford Grammar School, 1571–1971.* Burford, 1971.

———. *Burford Past and Present.* Oxford, 1920.

Griffin, Dustin H. *Satires against Man: The Poems of Rochester.* Berkeley, Calif., 1973.

Haley, K. D. H. *The Dutch in the Seventeenth Century.* New York, 1972.

———. *The First Earl of Shaftesbury.* Oxford, 1968.

———. *William of Orange and the English Opposition, 1672–4.* Oxford, 1953.

Hammond, Paul. "The Dating of Three Poems by Rochester from the Evidence of Bodleian MS. Don. b. 8." *Bodleian Library Record* (1982): 52–59.

———. *Figuring Sex between Men from Shakespeare to Rochester.* Oxford, 2002.

———. "The Robinson Manuscript Miscellany of Restoration Verse in the Brotherton Collection, Leeds." *Proceedings of the Leeds Philosophical and Literary Society, Literary and Historical Section* 18, Pt. 3 (December, 1982): 275–324.

———. "Rochester's Homoeroticism." in *Second Bottle*, edited by Nicholas Fisher, 47–62. Manchester, 2000.

Hansen, Charles E., and Anne Evans. "Bisexuality Reconsidered: An Idea in Pursuit of a Definition." In Fritz Klein et al., *Bisexualities: Theory and Research*, edited by Fritz Klein et al. New York, 1985.

Harbage, Alfred. *Annals of English Drama*. Philadelphia, 1940.

Harewood, Earl of, ed. *The Definitive Kobbe's Opera Book*. Revised ed. New York, 1987.

Harris, F. R. *The Life of Edward Montagu, K.G., First Earl of Sandwich*. 2 vols. London, 1912.

Harth, Philip. *Contexts of Dryden's Thought*. Chicago, 1968.

Hartmann, Cyril Hughes. *La Belle Stuart, Memoirs of Court and Society in the Times of Frances Teresa Stuart Duchess of Richmond and Lennox*. London and New York, 1924.

———. *Charles II and Madame*. London, 1934.

———. *Clifford of the Cabal: A Life of Thomas First Lord Clifford of Chudleigh*. . . . London, 1937.

———. *The King My Brother*. 1954.

———. *The King's Friend: A Life of Charles Berkeley, Viscount Fitzhardinge, Earl of Falmouth (1630–1665)*. London, 1951.

———. *The Vagabond Duchess: The Life of Hortense Mancini Duchesse Mazarin*. London and New York, 1927.

Harvey, Paul. *The Oxford Companion to Classical Literature*. Oxford, 1962.

Hatton. *Correspondence of the Family of Hatton*. 1878.

Headington, Christopher, et al. *Opera: A History*. New York, 1987.

Hicks, R. D. *Stoic and Epicurean*. New York 1962.

Highfill, Philip H. Jr., et al. *A Biographical Dictionary of Actors, Actresses, Musicians, Dancers, Managers and Other Stage Personnel in London, 1660–1800*. 16 vols. Carbondale, Ill., 1973–93.

Hill, Christopher. *God's Englishman: Oliver Cromwell and the English Revolution*. London, 1970.

———. *The World Turned Upside Down: Radical Ideas during the English Revolution*. London, 1972.

Hodgart, Matthew. *Satire*. New York, 1969.

Holden, Anthony. *Olivier*. London, 1989.

Holland, Samuel. "Elegy on Rochester 1680." In *Critical Heritage*, edited by Farley-Hills.

Holton, S. "Sexuality and Social Hierarchy in Sidney and Rochester." In *Spirit of Wit*, edited by Jeremy Treglown, 47–65.

Hook, Lucyle. "Something More about Rochester." *MLN* 73 (June 1960): 478–85.

Hume, Robert. *The Development of English Drama in the Late Seventeenth Century*. Oxford, 1976.

Hunter, Michael. *Science and Society in Restoration England*. Cambridge, 1981.

Hutton, Ronald. *Charles II*. Oxford, 1989.

———. *The Restoration: A Political and Religious History . . ., 1658–1667*. Oxford, 1985.

Isaacs, J. "The Earl of Rochester's Grand Tour." *RES* 3 (January 1927): 75–76.

Jackson, Gordon. "Trade and Shipping." In *Britain and Europe*, edited by Jones, 136–54.

Jacob, J. R. "Restoration, Reformation and the Origins of the Royal Society." In *Seventeenth Century England: A Changing Culture*, edited by W. R. Owens, 245.

Janus, Samuel, and Cynthia L. Janus. *Janus Report on Sexual Behavior*. New York, 1993.

Jeffreys, Stephen. *The Libertine*. London, 1995.

Johnson, J. W. "Anthony Wood and John Wilmot: The Antiquary as Autobiographer and Biographer." *Restoration* 12, no. 2 (Fall, 1988): 69–79.

———. "The Classics and John Bull." In *England in the Restoration and Eighteenth Century*, edited by H. T. Swedenberg. Berkeley and Los Angeles, 1972.

———. "Did Lord Rochester Write *Sodom?*" *PBSA* 81 (1987), 1–26.

———. *The Formation of English Neo-Classical Thought*. Princeton, N.J., 1967.

———. " 'My dearest sonne': Letters from the Countess of Rochester to the Earl of Lichfield." *University of Rochester Library Bulletin* 28, no. 1 (Summer 1974): 24–32.

Johnson, Ronald W. "Rhetoric and Drama in Rochester's 'Satyr against Reason and Mankind.' " *SEL* 15 (Summer 1975): 365–73.

Johnson, Samuel. *The Lives of the Poets*. Garden City, N.Y., n.d.

Jones, J. R. "The Concept of Restoration." In *Restored Monarchy*.

———. *Country and Court: England 1658–1714*. 1978.

———. *The First Whigs: The Politics of the Exclusion Crisis, 1678–1683*. London, 1961.

———. "The Green Ribbon Club." *DUJ* 18 (1956): 17–20.

———. "Parties and Parliament." In *Restored Monarchy*, 58 ff.

Jones, J. R., ed. *Britain and Europe in the Seventeenth Century*. New York, 1967.

———, ed. *The Restored Monarchy, 1660–1688*. London, 1979.

Jordan, Robert. "The First Printing of Rochester's 'Tunbridge Wells.' " *English Language Notes* 10 (June 1973): 267–70.

Kenyon, John P. *The Popish Plot*. London, 1972.

———. *The Stuarts*. London, 1958.

Kernan, Alvin. *The Cankered Muse: English Satires of the Renaissance*. New Haven, Conn., 1959.

Klein, Fritz, et al., eds. *Bisexualities: Theory and Research*. New York, 1985.

Knight, Charles A. "The Paradox of Reason: Argument in Rochester's 'Satyr against Mankind,' " *MLR* 65 (April 1970): 254–60.

Kott, Jan. *Shakespeare's Bitter Arcadia*. Translated by Boleslaw Taborski. New York: 1968.

Lahr, John. "Introduction." In *The Orton Diaries*. London, 1986.

Laing, R. D. "Masturbation." In *Sexual Self-Stimulation*, edited by R. E. L. Masters, 153–55. Los Angeles, 1967.

Laqueur, Thomas. *Making Sex: Body and Gender from the Greeks to Freud*. Cambridge, Mass, 1990.

———. *Solitary Sex: A Cultural History of Masturbation*. New York, 2003.

Lawner, Lynne. *I Modi: The Sixteen Pleasures*. Evanston, Ill., 1989.

Lee, Maurice, Jr. *The Cabal*. Urbana, Ill., 1965.

Lee, Sidney. "John Wilmot, Lord Rochester." In *DNB*.

Legouis, Pierre. "Three Notes on Rochester's 'Poems,' " *MLN* 69 (November 1954): 502.

Lemprière, John. *Lemprière's Classical Dictionary of Proper Names in Ancient Authors*. London, 1963.

Lever, Sir Tresham. *The Herberts of Wilton*. London, 1967.

Lewis, Kenneth. *The Psychoanalytic Theory of Male Sexuality*. New York, 1988.

Lewisohn, Richard, M.D. *A History of Sexual Customs*. New York, 1964.

Limentani, Adam. *Between Freud and Klein*. London, 1989.

Lindsey, John. *Charles II and Madame Carwell*. London, 1937.

Link, Frederick M. *Aphra Behn*. New York, 1968.

Loftus, John. *The Spanish Plays of Neoclassical England*. New Haven, Conn., 1973.

Lord, George de F., et al. *Anthology of Poems on Affairs of State*. New Haven, Conn., 1975.

Love, Harold. *The Penguin Book of Restoration Verse*. Baltimore, 1968.

———. "Rochester and the Traditions of Satire." In *Restoration Literature: Critical Approaches*, 145–75. London, 1972.

MacCubbin, Robert P. "Unique Scribleriana Transferred 1973." *The Scriblerian* 7, no. 1 (Autumn 1974): 53–54.

MacCubbin, Robert P., ed. *'Tis Nature's Fault: Unauthorized Sexuality during the Enlightenment*. Cambridge, 1988.

Macdonald, Hugh. *A Journal from Parnassus*. London, 1937.

Main, C. F. "The Right Vein of Rochester's *Satyr*." In *Essays in Literary History Presented to J. Milton French*, edited by Rudolph Kirk and C. F. Main, 93–112. Rutgers, N.J., 1960.

Mallett, Robert H. *Mallett Family History*. Internet: http://www.ott.igs.net/rhmallett/.

Mann, David D. *Sir George Etherege: A Reference Guide*. Boston, 1981.

Mayo, Thomas F. *Epicurus in England, 1650–1725*. Austin, Texas, 1934.

McCarthy, B. Eugene. *William Wycherley: A Biography.*, 1979.

Miller, John. "The Development of the Anti-Catholic Tradition." In *Origins of the English Civil War*, edited by Russell, 67–90.

———. *Popery and Politics in England 1660–1688*. Cambridge, 1973.

Miner, Earl. *Dryden's Poetry*. Bloomington and London, 1967.

Moskovit, Leonard A. "Pope and the Tradition of the Neoclassical Imitation." *SEL* 8 (Summer 1968): 445–62.

Mulder, John. *The Temple of the Mind: Education and Literary Taste in Seventeenth Century England*. Pegasus, 1969.

The Museum 31 (May, 23, 1747): 158.

Norton, Rictor. *Homosexuality in 18th-Century England*. Internet: http://www.infopt.demon.co.uk/eighteen.htm.

Novak, Maximillian, ed. *The Empress of Morocco and Its Critics*. Los Angeles, 1968.

Ober, William B. "The Earl of Rochester and Ejaculatio Praecox." In *Boswell's Clap and Other Essays: Medical Analyses of Literary Men's Afflictions*, 233–52. London, 1979.

Ogg, David. *England in the Reign of Charles II*. 2 vols. Oxford, 1955.

O'Hehir, Brendan. *Harmony from Discords: A life of Sir John Denham*. Berkeley, Calif., 1968.

Oldani, Jouis J., and P. C. Fischer. *Jesuit Theater Englished: 5 Tragedies of Joseph Simons*. (Ser. 1, No. 7) Institute of Jesuit Sources, 1989.

Oldham, John. "A Dithyrambick on Drinking. Suppos'd to be Spoken by Rochester at yᵉ Guinny Club in 1676." In Vieth, *ARP*, 188.

Oliver, H. J. *Sir Robert Howard (1626–1698): A Critical Biography*. Durham, N.C., 1963.

Olivieri, Achillo. "Eroticism and Social Groups in Sixteenth-Century Venice: The Courtesan." In *Western Sexuality Practice and Precept in Past and Present Times*, edited by Philippe Ariés and Andre Béjin, 95–102. Oxford, 1986.

O'Neill, John. "Rochester's 'Imperfect Enjoyment': 'The True Veyne of Satyre' in Sexual Poetry," *Texas Studies in Language and Literature* 25 (1980): 57–71.

———. "Sexuality, Deviance, and Moral Character in the Personal Satire of the Restoration." *Eighteenth Century Life* 2 (September 1975): 16–19.

Orrell, John. "A New Witness of the Restoration Stage, 1670–1680." *Theatre Research International* 2 (1977): 86–97.

Owens, W. R. *Seventeenth Century England: A Changing Culture*. 1981.

Pasch, Thomas K. "Concentricity, Christian Myth, and the Self-Incriminating Narrator in Rochester's *A Ramble in St. James's Park.*" *Essays in Literature* 6 (Spring 1979): 21–28.

Patterson, John D. "The Restoration Ramble." *N&Q* 226 (June 1981): 209–10.

Paulson, Kristoffer. "The Reverend Edward Stillingfleet and the 'Epilogue' to Rochester's *A Satyr against Reason and Mankind.*" *PQ* 50 (October 1971): 657–63.

———. "A Subject of Debate: A Re-evaluation of the Major Satires of John Wilmot, Second Earl of Rochester." (Ph.D. diss., University of California Davis, 1968).

Paulson, Ronald. "Rochester: The Body Politic and the Body Private." In *The Author in His Work: Essays on a Problem in Criticism*, ed. Louis Martz and Aubrey Williams, 103–21. New Haven, Conn., 1978.

Pearson, John. *Stags and Serpents: The Story of the House of Cavendish and the Dukes of Devonshire.* London, 1983.

Pepper, John. *A Man's Tale.* London, 1982.

Pinto, Vivian de Sola. *Enthusiast in Wit: A Portrait of John Wilmot Earl of Rochester 1647–1680.* rev. ed. London, 1962.

———. "John Wilmot, Earl of Rochester, and the Right Veine of Satire," *Essays and Studies* The English Association, n.s. 6 (1953): 56–70.

———. "Rochester and Dryden." *Renaissance and Modern Studies* 5 (1961): 29–48.

———. *Sir Charles Sedley, 1639–1701.* London, 1927.

Pollock, Sir John. *The Popish Plot.* Cambridge, 1944.

Porter, Peter. "The Professional Amateur." In *Spirit of Wit*, edited by Jeremy Treglown.

Preston, Thomas R. *Not in Timon's Manner: Feeling, Misanthropy, and Satire in Eighteenth Century England.* Tuscaloosa, 1975.

Price, J. L. "Restoration England and Europe," in *Restored Monarchy*, edited by Jones.

Quaintance, Richard. "French Sources of the Restoration 'Imperfect Enjoyment' Poem." *PQ* 42 (April 1963): 190–99.

Richmond, H. M. "The Fate of Edmund Waller." In *Seventeenth-Century English Poetry*, edited by W. R. Keast, 291–99. New York, 1962.

Righter, Anne. "John Wilmot, Earl of Rochester." *PBA* 53 (1967): 47–69.

Robinson, Ken. "A New Verse Portrait of Rochester." *Restoration* 3, no. 1 (Spring 1981): 2–5.

———. "Rochester and Semonides." *N&Q* 224 (December 1979): 521–22.

———. "Rochester's Dilemma." *Durham University Journal*, n.s. 40 (June 1979): 223–31.

———. "Rochester's Income from the Crown," *N&Q* 227 (February, 1982): 46–50.

Rogers, Katharine M. *William Wycherley.* New York, 1972.

Rogers, Philip G. "An Allusion to Horace." In *Spirit of Wit*, edited by Jeremy Treglown, 166–76.

———. *The Dutch in the Medway.* Oxford, 1970.

Rosten, Murray. *Biblical Drama in England from the Middle Ages to the Present Day.* London, 1968.

Rothstein, Eric. *Restoration and Eighteenth Century Poetry.* London, 1981.

Rousseau, G. S., and Roy Porter. *Sexual Underworlds of the Enlightenment.* Chapel Hill, N.C., 1988.

Runte, Rosann, ed. *Studies in Eighteenth Century Culture.* Madison, Wis., 1979.

Russell, Conrad, ed. *The Origins of the English Civil War.* London, 1983.

Rymer, Thomas. "Preface to *Rochester's Poems on Several Occasions.*" In *Critical Heritage*, edited by Farley-Hills, 169.

Sackville-West, Vita. *Knole and the Sackvilles*. London, 1969.

Schwoerer, Lois G. *No Standing Armies! The Antimilitary Ideology in Seventeenth-Century England.* Baltimore, 1974.

Scouten, A. H., and R. D. Hume. "Introduction." In Sir Howard and George Villiers, Duke of Buckingham, *The Country Gentleman.* London, 1976.

Sedgwick, Eve K. *Between Men: English Literature and Male Homo-social Desire.* New York, 1985.

——. *Epistemology of the Closet.* Berkeley and Los Angeles, 1990.

Selden, Raman. *English Verse Satire.* London, 1978.

——. "Oldham's Versions of the Classics." In *Poetry and Drama 1570–1700*, edited by Antony Coleman and Antony Hammond, 110–35.

——. "Rochester and Shadwell." In *Spirit of Wit*, edited by Jeremy Treglown, 177–90.

——. "Rochester, Lee, and Juvenal." *N&Q* 217 (January 1972): 27.

The Shorter Oxford English Dictionary on Historical Principles. Revised and edited by C. T. Onions. 3rd edition. 2 vols. Oxford, 1963.

Sitter, John E. "Rochester's Reader and the Problem of Satiric Audience." *Papers on Language and Literature* 12 (Summer 1976): 285–98.

Smith, Geoffrey Ridsill. *In Well Beware: The Story of Newburgh Priory and the Belasyse Family, 1145–1977.* Kineton, 1978.

Socarides, Charles W. *Homosexuality.* New York, 1978.

——, and Vamik Volkan. *The Homosexualities: Reality, Fantasy, and the Arts.* Madison, Wis., 1990.

Stoller, Robert J. *Observing the Erotic Imagination.* New Haven, Conn., 1985.

——. *Presentations of Gender.* New Haven, Conn., 1985.

——. *Sex and Gender.* 2 vols. London, 1975.

Stone, Lawrence. *The Family, Sex, and Marriage in England, 1500–1800.* New York, 1977.

Sutherland, James. *English Literature of the Late Seventeenth Century.* New York and Oxford, 1969.

Swedenberg, H. T., ed. *England in the Restoration and Eighteenth Century: Essays on Culture and Society.* Berkeley, 1972.

Tannahill, Reay. *Sex in History,* New York, 1980.

Temple, Sir William. "Upon the Gardens of Epicurus . . . in the Year 1685." In *Five Miscellaneous Essays*, edited by S. H. Monk. Ann Arbor, Mich., 1963.

Thomas, Keith. "The Double Standard." *JHI* 20, no. 2 (April 1959): 195–216.

——. *Religion and the Decline of Magic.* New York, 1971.

Thomas, P. W. "Two Cultures? Court and Country under Charles I." In *Origins of the English Civil War*, edited by Russell, 168–93.

Thompson, Roger. *Unfit for Modest Ears: A Study of Pornographic, Obscene and Bawdy Works Written or Published in England in the Second Half of the Seventeenth Century.* Totowa, N.J., 1979.

Tierney, Thomas Patrick. "Satire on Mankind: The Nature of the Beast." Ph.D. diss., Loyola University of Chicago, 1982.

Tomalin, Claire. *Samuel Pepys, The Unequalled Self.* New York, 2002.

Treglown, Jeremy. "Rochester and Davenant." *N&Q,* 221 (December 1976): 554–59.

——. "The Satiric Inversion of Some English Sources in Rochester's Poetry." *RES* n.s. 24 (February 1973): 42–48.

Treglown, Jeremy, ed. *Spirit of Wit: Reconsiderations of Rochester.* Oxford, 1982.

Trotter, David. "Wanton Expressions." In *Spirit of Wit,* edited by Jeremy Treglown, 126.

Trumbach, Randolph. "London's Sodomites: Homosexual Behavior and Western Culture in the Eighteenth Century." *JH* 2 (1977–78), 1–33.

———. "Sodomitical Assaults, Gender Roles, and Sexual Development in Eighteenth-Century London," *JH* 16 (1988): 407–29.

———. "Sodomy Transformed: Aristocratic Libertinage, Public Reputation, and the Gender Revolution of the Eighteenth-Century." *ECL* 9 (1985): 109–21.

Turner, James Grantham. *Schooling Sex: Libertine Literature and Erotic Education in Italy, France, and England 1534–1685.* Oxford, 2003.

Tyacke, Nicholas. "Puritanism, Arminianism and Counter-Revolution." In *Seventeenth Century England: A Changing Culture,* edited by W. R. Owens, 139–44.

Varley, F. J. *The Siege of Oxford.* Oxford, 1932.

Vieth, David. *Attribution in Restoration Poetry.* New Haven, Conn., 1963.

———. "Divided Consciousness: The Trauma and Triumph of Restoration Culture." *Tennessee Studies in Literature* 22 (1977): 46–62.

———. "John Oldham, the Wits, and *A Satyr against Vertue.*" *PQ* 32 (January 1953): 90–93.

———. "The *Moriae Encomium* as a Model for Satire in Restoration Court Literature: Rochester and Others." In *Rochester and Court Poetry* (Los Angeles, 1988), 9–12.

———. " 'Pleased with Contradiction and the Sin': The Perverse Artistry of Rochester's Lyrics," *TSL* 25 (1980): 35 ff.

———. "Toward an Anti-Aristotelian Poetic: Rochester's Satyr against Mankind. . . ." *Language and Style* 5 (Spring 1972): 123–45.

Vignali, Antonio. *La Cazzaria: The Book of the Prick.* Translated by Ian F. Moulton., 2003.

Vincent, W. A. L. *The Grammar Schools, Their Continuing Tradition, 1660–1714.* London, 1969.

Walker, Robert G. "Rochester and the Issue of Deathbed Repentence in Restoration and Eighteenth Century England." *South Atlantic Review* 47 (January 1982): 27–37.

Wall, Kathleen. *The Callisto Myth from Ovid to Atwood: Initiation and Rape in Literature.* Montreal, 1988.

Walsh, Elizabeth, and Richard Jeffree. *The Excellent Mrs. Mary Beale.* London, 1975.

Ward, Charles. *The Life of John Dryden.* Chapel Hill, N.C., 1961.

Warrack, John, and Ewan West. *The Concise Oxford Dictionary of Opera.* Oxford, 1992.

Watson, Peter. "The Scandalous Regent." In *Wisdom and Strength.* New York, 1989.

Weinbrot, Howard D. "The 'Allusion to Horace': Rochester's Imitative Mode." *SP* 69 (1972): 348–68.

———. *Augustus Caesar in "Augustan" England.* Princeton, N.J., 1978.

———. "Rochester's 'Fribble' Revisited." *N&Q* 227 (December 1982): 523–24.

Wentworth, Harold, and Stuart Flexner, comps. and eds. *Dictionary of American Slang.* New York, 1960.

Whitcombe, Dennis Trevor. *Charles II and the Cavalier House of Commons, 1663–1674.* New York, 1966.

White, Isabelle. " 'So Great a Disproportion': Paradox and Structure in Rochester's *A Satyr against Reason and Mankind.*" *Kentucky Philological Association Bulletin* (1976): 15–23.

Whitley, Raymond K. "Rochester: A Cosmological Pessimist." *English Studies in Canada* 4 (Summer 1978): 179–92.

Wilcoxon, Reba. "Mirrors of Men's Fears: The Court Satires on Women." *Restoration* 3, no. 2 (Fall 1979): 45–51.

———. "Pornography, Obscenity, and Rochester's 'Imperfect Enjoyment.' " *SEL* 15 (Summer 1975): 375–90.

———. "The Rhetoric of Sex in Rochester's Burlesque." *PLL* 12 (Summer 1976): 273–84.

———. "Rochester's Philosophical Premises: A Case for Consistency." *Eighteenth Century Studies* 8 (Winter 1974/75): 183–201.

———. "Rochester's Sexual Politics." In *Studies in Eighteenth-Century Culture* 8, ed. Rosann Runte, 137–49. Madison, Wis., 1979.

Wilders, John. "Rochester and the Metaphysicals." In *Spirit of Wit*, edited by Jeremy Treglown.

Wilson, John Harold. *The Court Wits of the Restoration*. Princeton, N.J., 1948.

———. *Nell Gwyn, Royal Mistress*. New York, 1952.

———. *A Rake and His Times, A Biography*. New York, 1954.

———. "Rochester's *A Session of the Poets*." *RES* 22 (1946): 109–16.

———. "Rochester's 'Buffoon Conceit.' " *MLN* 56 (May 1941): 372–73.

———. "Satiric Elements in Rochester's Valentinian." *Philological Quarterly* 16 (January 1937): 41–48.

Wilson, John Harold, ed. *Court Satires of the Restoration*. Columbus, Ohio, 1976.

Winn, James A. *Dryden and His World*. New Haven, Conn., 1987.

Winnicott, Donald W. *Psycho-Analytic Explorations*. Cambridge, Mass., 1989.

Wolff, Charlotte, M.D. *Bisexuality, A Study*. London, 1979.

Yarrow, P. J. *Racine*. Oxford, 1978.

Zeller, Edward. *Stoics, Epicureans, and Sceptics*. Edited and translated by O. J. Reichel. New York, 1962.

INDEX OF PROPER NAMES

SUBJECT INDEX FOR JOHN WILMOT

WILMOT, JOHN, Baron of Adderbury, Viscount Athlone, Third Earl of Rochester (1647–1680)

Act of Exclusion, attitude toward, 301, 314; Adderbury Manor, mother controls, 94, 159; lawsuit over, 350; pulled down, 350
Alcock, Thomas (secretary), 252, 254
alcoholism, 68–69, 103ff, 181, 379n51, 418n14
appearance, 62–63, 278, 292, 396n35; portraits: frontispiece, 63, 75, 228, 419n36, 424n46, 426n3
Apsley, Sir Allen (uncle), 40, 58, 219, 344, 360n19, 381n42
Aretino, Pietro, influence of, 50, 108, 109, 160, 370n54, 371n56, 414n53; Postures, 107, 145, 371n75
Ariosto, 52, 64
Ashton, Colonel Edmund, 124–25
astronomy, knowledge of, 42, 54, 368n11, 372n87
atheism, professes, 18, 399n10
Aubrey, John, reports on, 220, 407n41, 407n43, 423n28

Balfour, Dr. Andrew (governor), guides, 40ff, 64, 369n35, 370n49
Ballers Club, founds and takes part in, 106–7, 140, 146, 179, 384n57, 395n19
Barry, Elizabeth (mistress), 132, 410n48; becomes mistress, 178, 185, 216; differences with, 246, 247; and Nell Gwyn, 247, 267–68, 278, 408n50, 416n44; pregnancy, 267; quarrels, 267, 274, 281; daughter taken, 304; growth as actress, 305; mistress to Etherege, 315; letters to, 215–16, 221, 246, 259, 276, 277, 279, 281, 283, 305, 398n60; portrait, 282

Behn, Aphra, sponsors, 248–49
Belle-Fasse, Jean-Baptiste (valet), 313, 340, 344, 383n37, 406n12, 422n54
Bendo, Dr. Alexander. *See* disguises
Bennet, Henry, Earl of Arlington, 62, 84; relationship with Wilmots, 104–5; angry at R, 113; appeased, 120; daughter wed, 184; in "Tunbridge Wells," 194
Berry (Bury), Phineas (Oxford tutor), 29
Bertie, Eleanor Pope Lee, Lady Lindsey (sister-in-law), kindness to R., 16; remarries, 129, 138, 184, 279; Woodstock controversy, 185, 223ff
Bertie, James, Earl of Abingdon (niece's husband), 138, 156
Betterton, Thomas, imitates R, 132
birth, 6, 14; gossip about, 360n19
Blancourt, Richard (Somerset agent), 110–11, 131, 210, 383n39
Blount, Charles, correspondence with, 300, 321, 420n21
botany, interest in, 41, 44
Boyle, Roger Lord Orrery, contempt for, 191
brawls, 114, 115, 156, 210–11, 249–50, 272
Browne, Nell (mistress), 171, 390n23
Burford School, attendance at, 25–26, 28
Bulkeley, Henry, letter from, 246, 411n3, 424n34
Burnet, Gilbert (mentor), 317–18, 426n3; *History of the Reformation*, 318, 319, 321, 328–31, 423n22; Rochester's final days, 340–42, 424n35, 426nn27–28; letters from, 333, 346; letters to, 338; portrait, 329
Busby, Dr. Richard, refers to, 24

Price, Henrietta Maria, satirizes, 84, 377n29

proteges. *See* Fane, Francis; Howe, John Grubham (Jack); Oldham, John; Wolseley, Robert (Bob)

Radcliffe, Captain Alexander, 192

Radcliffe, Dr. Alexander (physician), 327ff, 425n1

Ravenscroft, Edward, scorns, 316, 423n11; *Scaramouch*, 264

religion, 18, 35, 73, 171–72, 184, 391n42

Remonstrance, 336–37

Restoration, effects on R, 32

riches, desire for, 98–99, 135, 144

Roberts, Jane (mistress), 107, 292–93; death, 315, 319, 382n22

Rome, visits, 24, 47–50, 51

Rose Alley attack, part in, 321–22, 424n31

Sackville, Charles Lord Buckhurst, Earl of Middlesex and Dorset(friend), 76–78, 410n47, 419n25, 423n28, 424n46; godfather to R's son, 136–37; sun dial episode, 212, 407n41; dinner of, 324; letters, to R, 137

satire, theory of, 152–53, 154, 155, 392n7, 392n10, 394n4

Savile, George Earl of Halifax, respect for, 217, 341, 408n60

Savile, Sir Henry (best friend), 69, 79–80; correspondence with, 103; brawls in Tower, 114; private language, 202, 313; sun dial, 212, 407n41, 403n22; visits Woodstock, 245; Rochester's death, 341–42; letters to, 197–98, 199–200, 232, 245, 259, 276, 291–92, 307, 308, 313–14, 320, 403n23; letters from, 278, 289, 290, 291, 292, 294, 305–6; portrait, *80*

Scaramouch, fondness for, 50, 115, 264, 419n25

Scripture, 50, 292, 332, 394n8, 396n31, 403n28, 426n27

Scroop, Sir Carr (satiric brunt), 121, 271–73, 416n44, 422n56; contempt for, 271, attacks R, 272; satires on, 272–73

Sedley, Sir Charles, (friend), 76–79; godfather to R's son, 136–37; portrait, *79*

Seneca, translates, 188, 329

sexuality, 34–35, 49, 53, 109, 375n38. *See also* homosexuality; impotence; masturbation; pederasty; transvestism

Shadwell, Thomas, 112, 418n13; *The Sullen Lovers, or The Impertinents*, 112–13, 272–73; *Epsom Wells*, 189, 401n47; *The Libertine*, 237; *The Virtuoso*, 247–48 "The Tory Poets," 410n41

Sheffield, John Earl of Mulgrave (enemy), 121–25, 166, 192, 194, 225–26, 238, 386n12, 402n4, 423n28 "Essay on Satire," 320–21; portrait, *122*, 422n56

Shepherd, Fleetwood (companion), 275, 407n41, 417n59

Smith, Thomas (son's tutor), 416n56

Sodomites, Order of, 45, 117, 385n77

St. John family. *See* Appendix

St. John, Anne. *See* Wilmot, Anne

St. John, Lady Joanna (aunt), 14, 184; letters to, 333, 335–36, 337, 338

St. John, Sir Walter (uncle), 14, 184, 223, 224, 323, 344, 350, 399n10

Somerset, Deputy Lieutenant of, 129

Stuart family. *See* Appendix

Stuart, Charles. *See* Charles II

Stuart, Frances (court beauty), 70, 88

Stuart, Henrietta Duchess of Orleans (Minette), 42, 54, 83, 114, R's account of death, 130–31; R carries letter to, 384n62

Stuart, James. *See* James II

Sun Dial, 220, 264, 407n41, 407n43

Taunton, alderman of, 129, 417n71

Temple, Anne, flirtation with, 87, 89, 378n43, 378n45, 385n72

Test Act, takes oath, 175, 183, 184, 197

theriophily, use of, 205, 401n48

Tibullus, knowledge of, 364n31, 392n17

Tower of London, sent to, 70–71

transvestism, 108–9, 116, 255, 362n54, 385n72

Tunbridge Wells, 193

WORKS